THE ILIAD OF HOMER

OTHER TITLES IN

THE CLASSICS OF GREECE AND ROME SERIES

Dudley Fitts, *General Editor*

THE AENEID OF VIRGIL

Translated by John Dryden. Edited, with an Introduction and Notes, by Robert Fitzgerald.

OVID'S METAMORPHOSES

The Arthur Golding translation (1567). Edited, with an Introduction and Notes, by John Frederick Nims.

THE

ILIAD

OF

HOMER

TRANSLATED BY ALEXANDER POPE

EDITED, WITH AN INTRODUCTION AND TEXTUAL NOTES

BY REUBEN A. BROWER AND W. H. BOND

THE MACMILLAN COMPANY, NEW YORK

Collier-Macmillan Limited, London

Library of Congress Catalog Card Number: 65-16934

First Printing
The Macmillan Company, New York
Collier-Macmillan Canada, Ltd., Toronto, Ontario

Printed in the United States of America

CONTENTS

INTRODUCTION

᠄᠄᠄

On Translations and the Ancient Past

FOR READERS OF LITERATURE the ancient world is not any one thing.
Certainly it is not the carefully reconstructed past of a scientific his-
torian; for the meaning of antiquity, Greek, Roman, or Biblical, is
more than any historical "reality". Our commerce with all of these
early worlds has been enriched—a purist may say, distorted—by the
writers and artists, particularly of the Renaissance, who have interpreted them in powerful and unforgettable expressions. Whatever Julius
Caesar or Brutus may have been in fact, their significance for most of
us has been permanently affected by Shakespeare's play. We accept
Shakespeare's interpretation as clearly among the valid ones—unless,
of course, we are provincial enough to suppose that the true meaning
of the Roman past has been settled by the reigning school of ancient
historians. The characters of the Bible have been similarly shaped
for us by great versions in art and in literature. Who can think of
Moses or David without a flitting image of Michaelangelo's sculp-
tures coming between him and his reading of the Old Testament?
The tough and canny Israelite of the biblical story can hardly have
been much like the Graeco-Roman heroic youth that we see in
Florence. Nor can the biblical hero have been exactly like the young
man in Nicolas Poussin's *Triumph of David* (1630), who strides
through a crowd of matrons and elders gathered before the portico of
a great Roman temple.

The King James translation of the Bible is a prime example of a
work of literature that has imposed its vision of antiquity as the true
and only one on readers of many generations. It is also an example
of the fact that an earlier version of a great text may have values not
to be replaced by a later one, though the later version may be lin-
guistically and historically more accurate. The reader of the *New*

9

English Bible will undoubtedly find fewer obscurities than in the older version, but he may feel that he is no longer reading a sacred book. In this up-to-date translation the divinely inspired writers of the Gospels seem at times to have turned over the job—and "job" is the proper term—to a committee of tone-deaf sociological historians. Although the King James version is from one point of view so obviously dated, from another it is dateless. Like all true works of literature it is irreplaceable, and like Shakespeare's plays it is at once Elizabethan-Jacobean and contemporary with anyone who makes the effort to learn its language. Who would care to read *Antony and Cleopatra* in a translation produced by the authors of the new New Testament? Both the Jacobean Bible and Shakespeare's great Jacobean play point to the paradoxical conclusion that if a translation is to live, it must be thoroughly contemporary, a literary success in the style of its time and in a distinct style of its own.

Alexander Pope's *Iliad* is a triumph of exactly this sort. Since its appearance in the early eighteenth century (1715-20), scholars have kept saying with Richard Bentley that it is "not Homer," but readers have happily gone on reading. Despite the Romantic prejudice against Pope, his *Iliad* has continued to be reprinted, and to judge from the sheer number of editions published throughout a period of nearly two hundred and fifty years, it has been the most readable and most read of all English translations of Homer. We live in an age of excellent translations from Greek, many of them more accurate than Pope's in relation to the original language and to historical fact, but only a rash prophet would assert that they will have a longer literary life than Pope's *Iliad*. Like George Chapman's *Homer* and John Dryden's *Virgil*, Pope's *Iliad* goes to prove that the way for a writer to ensure a long life for his translations is to be a poet of a high, if not the highest, order.

The way for a twentieth century reader to enjoy the works of these great translators is to give them the hearing they demand, not to complain that they are not Keats or Yeats, but to be alert to their special style and vision. Because of a considerable change in taste during the past forty years, we are today better prepared to read Pope's version than at any time since the Romantic revival. T. S. Eliot and Ezra Pound, who did a great deal to effect a change in attitude toward Dryden and Pope and other poets of wit, also did much to encourage the present generation of translators. The public for the new poetry has also been the public for the new versions of Homer and the Greek dramatists.

What sort of a hearing does Pope expect? He offers one important hint as he concludes his comparison of Homer and Virgil in his admirable *Preface* to the *Iliad*: "Homer makes us Hearers, and Virgil leaves us Readers." Though Pope is talking here of Homer's power of engaging us in the action—as if "we were there"—he has just been praising the speeches of the Iliad, saying that "It is hardly credible in a Work of such length, how small a Number of Lines are employ'd in Narration." As his translation will show, Pope is looking for readers who have an appetite for speeches in the oratorical sense, for resounding declamations. He also expects his reader to have a painter's eye for effects of light and shade, color and movement, for over-all pictorial design. (In Jane Austen's *Northanger Abbey*, the heroine finds that she can not see the views admired by her sophisticated friends, because she has not had lessons in drawing.)

One might offer the heretical advice that the best way to begin reading Pope's *Homer* is to go to the nearest museum or art library and look long and hard at mythological paintings and "Historical Pieces" by masters of the seventeenth and eighteenth centuries. Here we can find analogues to the visual world of the antique evoked by Pope's translation: grand figures of heroes, gods, and goddesses, caught in sculptural poses of dramatic gesture and swift motion, the heroes and gods of magnificent physique, the goddesses voluptuously charming. We see these supernatural beings resting on billowy clouds, or moving in earthly paradises of dark and rich foliage, or posed against backgrounds of threatening rocks and seas or of pompous Roman architecture. The presiding genius of these paintings, from Flemish Rubens to the Venetian Giambattista Tiepolo, is Roman-Virgilian and Ovidian, not Greek and Homeric. When on rare occasions a subject is taken from Homer, the settings, costumes, and poses are usually more Roman than Greek.

In one of his greatest frescoes, *Achilles on the Seashore* (about 1757), Tiepolo paints a scene that might well be used to illustrate Pope. "Under the shadow of towering rocks," a critic writes, "Thetis and her Nereid companion gaze mournfully at the brooding hero; and the note of pagan sadness looks back to early Renaissance treatment of classical story. . . ." Here are the first few verses on the scene as it is described in Pope's translation:

> Not so his Loss the fierce Achilles bore;
> But sad retiring to the sounding Shore,
> O'er the wild Margin of the Deep he hung,
> That kindred Deep, from whence his Mother sprung.
> There, bath'd in Tears of Anger and Disdain,
> Thus loud lamented to the stormy Main.
>
> I, 454-59

The "sad retiring" hero, "the sounding Shore," and the "wild Margin of the Deep" are in feeling and pictorial effect closely related to Tiepolo's painting. The image a few lines later of the goddess rising as "the Waves divide" and her tender "exploring" of Achilles' sorrow are also matched in Tiepolo's fresco, where Thetis looks out from the hollow of a wave, gazing sadly toward her son.

But as Pope continues, he moves into a style that is neither elegiac nor pictorial:

> O Parent Goddess! since in early Bloom
> Thy son must fall, by too severe a Doom,
> Sure, to so short a Race of Glory born,
> Great Jove in Justice should this Span adorn:
> Honour and Fame at least the Thund'rer ow'd,
> And ill he pays the Promise of a God;
> If yon proud Monarch thus thy Son defies,
> Obscures my Glories, and resumes my Prize.
> Far in the deep Recesses of the Main,
> Where aged Ocean holds his wat'ry Reign,
> The Goddess-Mother heard.
>
> 460-70

Achilles' address to his mother is in Pope's high oratorical manner, marked as usual with him by distinctly Roman touches in diction. "O Parent Goddess" reminds us of the way Virgil's Aeneas speaks to his mother (O dea certe), and "proud Monarch" together with "Jove" and the Latinate verbs "obscures" and "resumes" recall the imperial ruler of the Aeneid. Pope's original audience would have been reminded too of the Virgil they perhaps knew best, of Dryden's great translation. Two phrases in the last line and a half, "Goddess-Mother" and "wat'ry Reign," are in fact both used by Dryden in his Aeneis. Although eighteenth century readers might not have remembered exactly where they had seen these expressions before, they would have felt, either from knowing Dryden or Milton or other narrative poets of the seventeenth century, that Pope was writing in the "truly heroick" way.

Pope would expect then some familiarity with this heroic style in poetry and in art, and he could also count on a considerable agreement as to what an epic, or "heroic poem," should properly be—assumptions very generally shared by Pope's literary public, though most unfamiliar today. What is meant by "heroic poetry" and by "Homer" has changed a good deal since 1715, and most decidedly during the past thirty or forty years. To understand better what Pope was trying to do, how his view of Homer helped and hindered him, we shall need at least a rough notion as to how we ourselves regard Homer and his world. We may discover that in some respects Pope was in a better position to translate the *Iliad* than even the most knowledgeable of recent translators. Because of his easy familiarity with the heroic tradition in classical and in English poetry, and because of attitudes then prevailing toward traditional poetic styles, he was able to create certain poetic equivalents for Homer's art that have not been surpassed in any English version.

Pope's Heroic Poetry: Some First Impressions

Before turning to eighteenth and twentieth century views of the Homeric and the heroic, let us look briefly at a number of passages where Pope's heroic poetry is at its best. First hear Agamemnon, leader of all the Greeks, as he calls his soldiers to battle:

> Ye Greeks be Men! the Charge of Battel bear;
> Your brave Associates, and Your-selves revere!
> Let glorious Acts more glorious Acts inspire,
> And catch from Breast to Breast the noble Fire!
> On Valor's side the Odds of Combate lie,
> The Brave live glorious, or lamented die;
> The Wretch who trembles in the field of Fame,
> Meets Death, and worse than Death, Eternal Shame.
>
> V, 651-58

By any view, this is the language of heroes, noble and eloquent speech with a confidence of accent matched only in the best of Shakespeare's history plays. Hear next the equally certain and convincing voice of a great god, Jove himself, as he threatens the Olympians and asserts his unshakeable will:

> But know, whoe'er Almighty Pow'r withstand!
> Unmatch'd our Force, unconquer'd is our Hand:
> Who shall the Sov'reign of the Skies controul?
> Not all the Gods that crown the starry Pole.
> Your Hearts shall tremble, if our Arms we take,
> And each immortal Nerve with Horror shake.
> For thus I speak, and what I speak shall stand;
> What pow'r soe'er provokes our lifted Hand,
> On this our Hill no more shall hold his Place,
> Cut off, and exil'd from th' Æthereal Race.
>
> VIII, 560-69

We may recall the militant God of *Paradise Lost*, or perhaps rather Satan, especially because of the tough strength in

> For thus I speak, and what I speak shall stand . . .

Or see the field of battle glorified by the act of a god:

> He [Nestor] spoke, and round him breath'd heroic Fires;
> Minerva seconds what the Sage inspires.
> The Mist of Darkness Jove around them threw,
> She clear'd, restoring all the war to view;
> A sudden Ray shot beaming o'er the Plain,
> And shew'd the Shores, the Navy, and the Main:
> Hector they saw, and all who fly, or fight,
> The Scene wide-opening to the Blaze of Light.
> First of the field, great Ajax strikes their Eyes,
> His port Majestick, and his ample Size:
> A pond'rous Mace, with Studs of Iron crown'd,
> Full twenty Cubits long, he swings around.
> Nor fights like others, fix'd to certain Stands,
> But looks a moving Tow'r above the Bands;
> High on the Decks, with vast gigantic Stride,
> The godlike Hero stalks from side to side.
>
> XV, 806-821

For a contrast in scene and in feeling consider how Pope announces the coming death of Patroclus: (The Greeks are trying to carry off the body of Cebriones, whom Patroclus has just killed.)

> Now flaming from the Zenith, Sol had driv'n
> His fervid Orb thro' half the Vault of Heav'n;
> While on each Host with equal Tempest fell
> The show'ring Darts, and Numbers sunk to Hell.

But when his Ev'ning Wheels o'erhung the Main,
Glad Conquest rested on the Grecian Train.
Then from amidst the Tumult and Alarms,
They draw the conquer'd Corpse, and radiant Arms.
Then rash Patroclus with new Fury glows,
And breathing Slaughter, pours amid the Foes.
Thrice on the Press like Mars himself he flew,
And thrice three Heroes at each Onset slew.
There ends thy Glory! there the Fates untwine
The last, black Remnant of so bright a Line.

XVI, 938-51

In the final couplet Pope characteristically marks this prophetic moment by a beautiful and memorable image (his own invention, not Homer's). A little later he will bring out the historic sense of the actual death by rhythmic "pointing" and a portentous reflection:

The Lance arrests him with a mortal Wound;
He falls, Earth thunders, and his Arms resound.
With him all Greece was sunk; that Moment all
Her yet-surviving Heroes seem'd to fall.

989-92

In Achilles' prayer before he sends Patroclus out to meet this end we hear the voice of absolute heroic joy:

Oh! would to all th' immortal Pow'rs above,
Apollo, Pallas, and almighty Jove!
That not one Trojan might be left alive,
And not a Greek of all the Race survive;
Might only we the vast Destruction shun,
And only we destroy th' accursed Town!

XVI, 122-27

Finally, consider Pope's description of Achilles in one of the most splendid moments in the *Iliad*, when he strikes terror among the Trojans by his tremendous shout from the trench:

The Hero rose;
Her Aegis, Pallas o'er his Shoulders throws;
Around his Brows a golden Cloud she spread;
A Stream of Glory flam'd above his Head.
As when from some beleaguer'd Town arise
The Smokes high-curling to the shaded Skies;

(Seen from some Island, o'er the Main afar,
When Men distrest hang out the Sign of War)
Soon as the Sun in Ocean hides his Rays,
Thick on the Hills the flaming Beacons Blaze;
With long-projected Beams the Seas are bright,
And Heav'ns high Arch reflects the ruddy Light;
So from Achilles' Head the Splendours rise,
Reflecting Blaze on Blaze, against the Skies.
Forth march'd the Chief, and distant from the Croud,
High on the Rampart rais'd his Voice aloud;
With her own Shout Minerva swells the Sound;
Troy starts astonish'd, and the Shores rebound.
As the loud Trumpet's brazen Mouth from far
With shrilling Clangor sounds th' Alarm of War;
Struck from the Walls, the Echoes float on high,
And the round Bulwarks, and thick Tow'rs reply:
So high his Brazen Voice the Hero rear'd:
Hosts dropp'd their Arms, and trembled as they heard;
And back the Chariots roll, and Coursers bound,
And Steeds and Men lye mingled on the Ground.
Aghast they see the living Light'nings play,
And turn their Eye-balls from the flashing Ray.
Thrice from the Trench his dreadful Voice he rais'd;
And thrice they fled, confounded and amaz'd.

XVIII, 241-70

A Twentieth Century View of Homer

"Splendid, certainly," the reader is saying, "but is it Homer?" A question to be asked, but not easily answered, since what Homer *is* "really" is still being debated, and since the views held by scholars and critics have been changing so rapidly of late. It was only in the mid-twenties and early thirties of this century that the oral composition of Homer's poems was clearly proved and accurately described. Only toward the end of World War II were the Achaeans, the Greeks of the Iliad, surely (more or less surely!) shown to be a Greek-speaking people. To speak more generally, our understanding of the world in which Homer's heroes lived and in which the *Iliad* was composed is continually being altered by the work of archaeologists, linguists, and literary critics. We can sketch here only a rough outline of the view of Homeric poetry that seems to be most commonly held today.

First, a word about the *Iliad* and history. The war of Troy—or something like it—did take place; the bare story of the expedition goes back to the destruction of a small city, the Seventh Troy on the same site, at a date somewhere around 1200 B.C. Archaeological finds indicate that this city was connected by trade with the Mycenaean civilization of the Greek mainland, the home of the Achaeans. Their leader, Agamemnon, lived in Mycenae, one of the great centers of this civilization; the sage, Nestor, lived in another, the city of Pylos. The Bronze-Age culture of these and other mainland cities—which was related to the older culture of Crete—had its last and greatest age in the two centuries preceding the fall of Troy (1400-1200 B.C.). The massive stone work of palaces and tombs, the royal ornaments of gold and silver that have been found at Mycenae, and the written records discovered there and elsewhere show that these cities were fairly impressive centers of military and commercial power. We must not think of the last great period of Mycenaean civilization as a golden age of peace and plenty, but rather as an era of warlike chieftains and their followers, who made frequent raids on one another and on the territories of various Mediterranean peoples, including the Hittites and the Egyptians. This period, the Heroic Age of the Greek world, is recalled, much altered by the deceptions of memory and imagination, in Homer's *Iliad*. There are only a few details in the poem that can be surely identified as Mycenaean, such as the body-covering shield of "great Ajax" and the boar's tusk helmet of the Cretan hero, Meriones.

Other archaeological features of the poem—casual references to iron weapons, the round shield, fighting in close "hoplite" formation—belong to the centuries that follow the downfall of Mycenae, anywhere from the eleventh to the eighth century B.C., a very dark period indeed. It is during this period that the geometric style of vase-painting, the first distinctly Greek style in art, emerges. The *Iliad* as we know it must have been composed in Ionia, on the coast of Asia Minor, toward the end of the eighth century; this is the time when Homer lived and sung.

Although the language of the *Iliad* is primarily Greek of the Ionic dialect, it shows a mixture of dialects of three other regions, and some touches of the much earlier Mycenaean Greek. The diction is enriched further by many archaisms and by obscure terms peculiar to Homer, some of them totally incomprehensible to the Greeks themselves. The language of the Homeric poems is thus a special poetic one, never spoken on land or sea. Perhaps the diction of Spenser in *The Shepherd's Calendar* or *The Fairy Queen* might give an English reader some sense of the peculiar character of Homeric Greek. The verse form, the dactyllic hexameter (six dactyls— ᴗ ᴗ or equivalent spondees — —) is governed by complex and strict conventions, to which there are a dazzling number of exceptions, which are in turn governed by rules of exception. The style is also marked by the repeated use of a great number of identical phrases and lines; a third of the lines in the *Iliad* recur elsewhere in the poem, some of them many times.

During the nineteenth century, studies of Homer's style and language made it increasingly clear that so special a style, with its set phrases, blended dialects, and elaborate metrics, could hardly have been the creation of one poet or even one generation of poets. From the mid eighteenth century on, various critics had been saying or assuming that the poems or the separate lays from which they grew must have been orally composed by "folk" bards or singers. It was in the nineteen twenties of this century that a young American scholar, Milman Parry, following hints of German and French critics, proved conclusively that the Homeric poems were composed in a traditional oral style. Parry showed that the Homeric technique of "oral verse-making" was completely different from that of any written style and that, in the future, literary criticism of Homer must always bear this fact in mind. Although readers must always have noticed the many fixed phrases or formulas in Homer, no one had defined exactly their character and use. Parry pointed out that (1) each formula expressed some given essential idea (e.g., a man's name or an act of warfare), and (2) that it filled one and only one metrical position in the verse (i.e., the last part, after one of the regular pauses or caesuras). Moreover, for any one idea and position there was ordinarily only one or at the most two formulas available for the singer to use. For example, if in the first half of the line up to the caesura the singer had described some act of Hector, he had only one phrase with which to complete the line: "great Hector of the flashing helmet." There were an immense number of such phrases for various characters and actions, all ready-made for the singer to use—an obvious advantage to a poet who was making up his poem orally. It seems quite certain that only poets composing aloud would have invented such a style and have continued to use it, and to use it so extensively in a single poem. Most of the diction of the Homeric poems, if not all, is formulaic. In thinking of Homer, we have then to adjust ourselves to a way of making verse quite unlike that of a writer who constantly varies his idiom, adjusting each adjective and verb to fit a special context. The oral poet is working much of the time not with single words, but with the larger units of phrase, line, and theme.

But what sets traditional oral poetry apart especially is the attitude toward language and style that it imposes on the singer and his listeners. The singer uses the fixed phrase because it is convenient, and also because it is the true epic way of saying that particular thing. The listener too feels the special character of the singer's rhythm and diction, that it has been consecrated to the expression of the heroic way of life. So when he hears "cloud-gathering Zeus," he will hardly see a very precise image, since he has heard the phrase so often. But the formula is not without meaning, because it does name something peculiar to Zeus; no one else is described by this same epithet. As the phrase becomes familiar to the listener, he is left with some transient "great-cloudy-sky-god" impression, generalized, though not utterly without sensuous value. We do not meet this and similar epithets in isolation, but in context with many other epithets and action phrases: Zeus is also "of crooked counsels," and he is the god "who turns his shining eyes toward the scene of battle." These expressions, and many others for the qualities and actions of other gods and heroes, build up our "Zeus-sense," our "Achilles sense," our impressions of all sorts of persons, events, and relations. Together they excite and define our living awareness of the character of the Homeric world. For a comparison, we might think of our response to an impressionistic painting: we do not consciously see the individual splotch or dot of color, but the total visual form, the glowing haystack or the sunlit field of grass and flowers.

What is the total configuration that the Homeric style composes? Something too complex to reduce to the formulas of literary criticism, although the large outlines are clear and distinct. The traditional language gives us above all a picture of the hero, of his characterizing acts and loyalties. Seen in his purest form, he is the man who fights

skillfully in the front ranks, who faces death while clearly acknowl-
edging its terrors, who lives for the moment of action, whether "he
wins glory or gives it to others." He has the highest sense (*aidòs*) of
his obligation to live heroically, and the clearest awareness that his
lot and the lot or fate of all men (*Moira*) cannot be changed and
will be fulfilled. The hero fights for glory while he lives and for honor
in the praises of men after he is dead. But his glory also includes
substantial rewards here and now of wine, food, sheep, and farmland.
The Homeric hero is an aristocrat enjoying his social and material
prerogatives, not the knight of an other-worldly ideal seeking his true
reward in heaven.

But the *Iliad* is not a poem about a hero without a face, or about a
set of merely typical heroes; nor does it give the impression of having
been composed by an archetypal poet-computer. There are few persons in literature that we remember more distinctly than Achilles and
Hector or Helen and Paris, and though like all of Homer's characters
they speak in the formulaic style, all have their personal dramatic
voices. We are "Hearers" of men acting and suffering in a tragic
drama that ranks with the greatest plays of Sophocles and Shakespeare. But no critic with an understanding of the traditional oral
style has been very successful in describing this extraordinary literary
achievement. By contrast, critics have pointed out considerable differences in conversational idiom, imagery, and psychological notation
in the language of individual characters and scenes in plays by Shakespeare and the Greek tragedians. Yet it is here that Homer—whoever
he was—comes in: a great dramatic poet and a master of the traditional style, who not unlike Shakespeare reworked the poems of earlier poets, who yet made something so new and so commanding that
the *Iliad* as a whole could not be forgotten or lost. While singing
the deeds of many heroes and working in traditional themes and
episodes, Homer skillfully focused his poem on the wrath of Achilles:
its rise in the opening episode and its fierce renewal in the embassy
scene (Book IX); its slackening as Achilles sends Patroclus to fight
in his place (XVI), the transformation after Patroclus' death of
anger into violent grief and more violent revenge, and finally, in the
meeting with Priam, the recognition of the tragic mystery of all heroic
violence. Achilles has asserted the heroic values more fully than any
other hero in the *Iliad*, he has fought more nearly alone, and by
killing Hector, he has surely won the highest glory. But the irony of

his success is underlined by the death of Patroclus, by the joylessness of his own triumph, and by the ever-present sense of his coming death: ("What he lives by, he dies by.") Achilles does not actually die in the *Iliad*, but he is dying from the very beginning of the poem:

> Sing the wrath—oh goddess—of Peleus' son Achilles
> The destroying [wrath] which brought the Achaeans
> ten thousand sufferings. . .

The second half of the first line, and in the second line both the first two words and the final phrase, are all formulaic. Very characteristic too is the grammatical and rhythmic pattern of this second line, with the enjambement or run-over of the participle followed by a relative clause. But to point out these conventional features is not to diminish the effect on ear and mind of having wrath-and-death struck as the keynote of the career of Achilles and of the thousands who suffered with him. These two opening lines, in their seemingly casual but formulaic and subtly balanced pattern, again illustrate the stylized character of Homeric poetry. Still other qualities of Homer's art and imagination will come out more clearly when we come to review the *Iliad* in Pope's version.

The Eighteenth Century Heroic Poem

But first we need to have a notion of what Pope and his audience expected a heroic poem to be, what they regarded as Homeric. Two characteristics strike us as we read late seventeenth and eighteenth century critics of the epic and the poems they regarded as "heroick": their relative lack of the historical sense, and their willing acceptance of the ideal of a traditional style reserved exclusively for heroic poetry. The first separates them from most twentieth century readers and critics; while the second brings them nearer to the Homeric singer and his original audience. Both characteristics are better understood in relation to the Renaissance theory of the heroic poem and the literary situation in which poets attempted to write one. The notion of "the true heroick poem"—to us one of the curiosities of literature—seemed to the literary public of the seventeenth and eighteenth centuries exactly as valid as the theory of traditional oral composition seems to present-day writers on the epic. Its authority rested on the testimony of a long series of writers, mostly Italian and French, including some of the best poets and critics of the sixteenth and seventeenth centuries. From the sixteenth to the late eighteenth century, translators of Homer and Virgil like Chapman, Dryden, and Pope, and poets like Milton who undertook to write modern epics, were all more or less influenced by this fashionable and imposing critical theory.

By Pope's time the theory had very nearly become, in Swift's mocking phrase, "a receipt for an Heroick Poem." Contemporary critics tell us, for example, that the heroic poem must have an explicit moral purpose and unity of action, a perfect hero, a subject taken from the history of Christian times, and supernatural agents or machinery. The poet must not, however, take as his subject the central mysteries of the faith. As the requirements suggest, the model is more often the *Aeneid* than the *Iliad*, but the *Aeneid* Christianized and allegorically interpreted. The style considered appropriate to heroic themes was also more Virgilian than Homeric: the diction tends to be grand and Latinate, the tone and ordering of sentences, rhetorical in the Roman sense of the term.

Because of the lack of a strict historical sense, critics could easily regard Homer and Virgil and Renaissance poets as contemporaries, or rather as almost outside time. But because of this deficiency by our standards and because of the common habit of imitating the ancients in school exercises and in original compositions, a poet of the early eighteenth century felt quite naturally that to write heroically was to write as other poets before him had written. Among writers and readers generally there was an assured acceptance of traditional styles that has not been possible in English poetry since the Romantic revolt. But this was a cheerful and loving acceptance, as the acceptance of the oral style must have been for the Homeric singer. As Parry once pointed out, the traditional diction of Homer represented something more than a fixed code in vocabulary and phrasing, it was "the work of a way of life which we may call the heroic. . . a term that can only be understood in the measure that one can think and feel as they did, for the heroic was to them no more or less than the statement of all that they would be or would do if they could." The traditional oral style was their way of epitomizing the whole outlook on life—the love of glory and clear-eyed facing of death, the paradoxical sense of absolute mastery combined with the acknowledgement of fated limits—that Hector, Achilles, and other heroes in the *Iliad* constantly express. They express it, because they are expressed in a language that keeps reminding us of the heroic values and vision.

When Pope and his contemporaries use a fixed metaphor such as "the flames of fight" or "the fields of fame," they are not merely satisfying a neo-classical standard of correctness in style. For them, as for the Homeric singer and his listeners, to use these and similar phrases was to pay homage to a noble manner of life. Although English society in the eighteenth century was hardly heroic, the ancient aristocratic tradition was not quite dead. The noble lords knew, if with irony, what high manners and high virtues were, and on occasion they could exhibit them in speech and in action. There is the classic story recounted by Arnold of Lord Granville, who though near death insisted on tending to affairs of state, and who supported his resolve by reciting an appropriate speech from Homer. "I quote this story . . ." Arnold explains, "because it is interesting as exhibiting the English aristocracy at its very height of culture, lofty spirit, and greatness, towards the middle of the last century."

For Pope as for Granville, it was altogether natural to find in the language of an earlier poet the best expression of a modern attitude. In his original poems Pope often concentrates his richest and most precise meanings in a word or phrase echoed from Virgil or Homer, or from Dryden or Milton, or from any other writer who comes to mind. In the early eighteenth century the language of old authors did not belong to a dead historical past, in part because the boundaries were so uncertain between what we call the periods of Greek, Roman, Renaissance, and modern history. The boundaries between translation and original composition were correspondingly less precise. When Pope was translating Homer, he often found what Homer meant by consulting the English poets who had prolonged and renewed the heroic tradition in English poetry. For Pope and his generation there *was* a heroic language and style that they could accept and use. But since the style had been built up by writers who were thoroughly soaked in current theories of the heroic poem, their diction carried with it a Virgilian and late-Renaissance vision of Homer's world and Homeric attitudes. As the story of Granville also reminds us, this vision had a reality that was more than merely literary. The literary vision of antiquity was based on a living cultural

tradition, in particular on a knowledge of the ancient languages that
the modern reader may well envy: Lord Granville quoted his lines
from Homer in Greek.

A Further View of Pope's Version

We can hardly expect Pope to have a twentieth century scholar's
knowledge of Mycenaean and other early Greek cultures. (It is well
to remember that Homer and the Greeks of later centuries didn't
have it either.) But the few relics of historical fact surviving in
Homer are as discoverable in Pope's version as in the original. The
learned commentator can point out the same references to Mycenaean shields and helmets, or to Greek hoplite formations, though
the hints of the latter are much broader in Pope, thanks to his happy
unawareness that this mode of fighting belongs to a much later
period. But both the Preface and the Observations (or notes) show
that he and his editorial assistants are reasonably alert to differences
between the world of Homer and the modern period. Pope like Swift
sides with the Ancients against the Moderns, but where he defends
the simplicity and roughness of manners in the *Iliad* as an "authentick
Picture of that ancient World," he is approaching the viewpoint of
nineteenth and twentieth century historians. It is however one thing
to see the differences and another to translate them into poetry, and
it is easy enough to demonstrate that Pope's style is often more polite
than Homer's, particularly in scenes of court life and gallantry. But
on occasion, as in the comic scene of Book I where Vulcan serves the
feasting gods, Pope renders Homer's beauty of impression and familiarity of fact more perfectly than a prosily exact scholar can:

> He [Vulcan] said, and to her Hands the Goblet heav'd,
> Which, with a Smile, the white-arm'd Queen receiv'd.
> Then to the rest he fill'd; and, in his Turn,
> Each to his Lips apply'd the nectar'd Urn.
> Vulcan with awkward Grace his Office plies,
> And unextinguish'd Laughter shakes the Skies.
> Thus the blest Gods the Genial Day prolong,
> In Feasts Ambrosial, and Celestial Song.
> Apollo tun'd the Lyre; the Muses round
> With Voice alternate aid the silver Sound.

Meantime the radiant Sun, to mortal Sight
Descending swift, roll'd down the rapid Light.
Then to their starry Domes the Gods depart,
The shining Monuments of Vulcan's Art:
Jove on his Couch reclin'd his awful Head,
And Juno slumber'd on the golden Bed.

I, 766-81

The two couplets beginning "Vulcan with awkward Grace. . ."
indicate how Pope—quite consciously, we know—tries to find an
equivalent for Homer's curiously mixed diction. Like some later translators, Pope thinks it right to use some words "of a venerable *Antique
Cast*," both biblical and more or less archaic, but he nicely diminishes
their pious associations by introducing Latinate or classical expressions, so adding at the same time another strand of antiquity and re-
moteness from common use. "Unextinguish'd," for example, is rigidly
literal, but almost comically Latin. "Blest" might sound sufficiently
sacred or biblical, if it weren't countered by the pagan "Genial," and
"Celestial" is Christian "heavenly," but with a Latin resonance. The
level is not too polite: "Laughter shakes the Skies" is vigorous enough
for Dryden, though not clownish, like "rude skinker" in Dryden's
own translation of the passage. Pope's "dialect" is not Homer's, but
it does give an appropriate impression of a language artfully created
for its special purpose. Everyone who reads a modern plain translation should read Pope once, if only to be reminded that Homer's
style is, as Pope might say, a "designed" style. Homer's music is closer
to Mozart than to a tune of a popular ballad.

Pope like Homer is not the untutored genius of the Folk. He is
master of an art very remote from that of a traditional oral poet; like
Virgil he is a self-conscious craftsman, selecting language to give his
verse an aura of the antique and the heroic. But the conventions of
his period favored the effort to achieve modes of expression and
effects that were as he once said "parallel" to Homer's, "tho' not the
same." Although he does not translate every single Homeric formula,
nor attempt to use the same English words for each recurrence, his
habitual poetic use of epithets is often more Homeric than that of
any later poet-translator in English. Fixed phrases recur—as they do
in Virgil or Milton, though much more frequently—and they tend
to recur in the same part of the verse, usually at the close. Looking
back at passages quoted earlier (pp. 12-16) we have for example: "the

sounding Shore," "the stormy Main," the "wat'ry Reign," "the Field of Fame," and "th' Æthereal Race." (Hundreds of others can easily be found elsewhere in the translation.) Their convenience in rhyming couplets may seem painfully obvious, but it is a convenience very nearly in the full Homeric sense. Phrases of this sort are essential to heroic poetry as Pope understands it, they suit the characteristic rhythmic pattern of the couplet with its strong mid-line pauses, and they fit the balancing patterns of phrasing and thought that the rhythm all but demands.

Because these fixed phrases are used so often by Pope, we read them in a quite Homeric way as action-image units and as ornamentally heroic. As Parry says of Homer's epithets, they adorn not the local contest, but the whole poem. "This," the reader of both Pope and Homer feels, "is how the heroic line and the heroic world are made." In many of the phrases Pope's eighteenth century audience would also have recognized a Homeric or Virgilian or Miltonic parallel. As one critic has noted, Pope often uses these expressions with a bardlike lack of regard for the special context. "The stormy Main" does not mean that a storm is going on; nor is "the sounding Shore" any more noisy than usual. In the unchanging nature of Homer—and of the eighteenth century epic—the Main is always sounding. Pope must have seen that the fixity of Homer's epithets implied a fixity in the scheme of things, an order that he naturally interpreted as the Great Show of Nature of seventeenth and eighteenth century philosophers. In comparison with later translators Pope thus has a further advantage in the eternal return of his rhymes. As in his original poems they lend added assurance that all is ordered for the best in the best of imagined worlds. They do this simply by being heard, and by recurring so often in company with familiar words and orders of words, and with familiar kinds of meaning. Pope also had like Homer the advantage of working in a recognized style, one whose norms were accepted without question by his contemporaries. They are more easily recoverable for readers of this century than for those of the nineteenth century—recoverable, that is, for anyone who has made the rediscovery of the poetry of Dryden, Samuel Johnson, and Pope himself.

But Pope was first a poet, and only secondarily a translator, and in his treatment of many epithets he deftly and beautifully adapts the original phrase to its new setting or rejects it because it does not tone in well with the local dramatic and emotional context. In translating many episodes of the *Iliad* Pope can be seen practicing his favorite pictorial type of composition, working up harmonious groupings of characters in action, or depicting scenes as fitting backgrounds for action. When he speaks of "the sounding Shore" in the scene where Thetis comes to Achilles (p. 12), he is using a phrase based on Homer's "much-resounding sea," but he introduces it into a passage where Homer had not used the corresponding phrase in Greek. As the whole passage in Pope's version makes clear, something quite new and un-Homeric is being presented: the impression as in Tiepolo's fresco of a lonely and wild seascape, of a melancholy atmosphere appropriate to Achilles' "loud lament."

But in judging these Homeric paintings, we must see what Pope— and contemporary artists—were doing, what they were intentionally bringing out in Homer. No one, however well indoctrinated in the technique of oral verse-making, can fail to feel that the *Iliad* is a poem of vividly heard and seen events, both human and natural. We hear the roar and slap of waves, the crash of trees cut down in the forest, the brazen shout of Achilles. We see the wine-dark sea, the blaze of forest fires and city beacons, the clouds swept from the starry sky, the old men and Helen on the wall of Troy, Hector bouncing his son in the air, and Priam putting his hand to the face of Achilles. In Homer these images are entangled in human actions—of heroes and men of state, of woodcutters and shepherds, of besieged inhabitants of cities.

But with Pope we begin to approach the image as art: we are being asked to contemplate it and enjoy it for the sensuous excitement it arouses or for the emotion it symbolizes. It is one thing for a Homeric shepherd to see a stormy mist coming over the sea and to turn away in terror; another, to enjoy the picturesque melancholy of the scene. The visual and aural excitement is often there in Homer; but Pope and seventeenth century painters of the heroic world were responding to it overenthusiastically and overpictorially. In the battle scene quoted earlier (p. 14), Homer too tells how a divine light dispells the "Mist of Darkness," but Pope's "sudden Ray shot beaming o'er the Plain" and his "scene wide-opening to the Blaze of Light" is by comparison with the Homeric narrative a baroque *coup de théâtre*. The illustrations of divine interventions in Pope's text are in much the same dazzling style (e.g., Books V, VIII), but in spite of some

excesses both Pope and his illustrator strike us as true to our remembered impressions of sudden shifts of dark and light in many episodes
of the *Iliad*. The "heroic Fires" that Pope adds to the figure of Nestor
in the "Mist of Darkness" scene are again quite Homeric. As a recent
critic has shown, images of fire have a metaphorical value throughout
the *Iliad*, particularly in association with Achilles. In his Preface
"fire" is Pope's prime metaphor for Homer's genius, and in the translation he may have unconsciously been trying to underline this quality
by lavish use of words like "glittering," "refulgent," "radiant," and
"blaze."

In his bravura version of Achilles at the trench (p. 15-16)—a real
epiphany—Pope gives us all the brilliance and terror of heroic glory
and destructiveness. A brief comparison with the Greek original will
show that the Homeric singer is not always simple and economical.
In twenty-two lines, he heaps up in addition to many images of sound
all sorts of details suggesting "murky fire and brightness:"

> . . . with a cloud his head was wreathed by the glorious goddess;
> —a golden cloud it was—and from it she kindled a flame far-shining,
> as when smoke rising from a burning city strikes the upper air . . .
>   and with the sun's setting,
> torches flame out in masses, and high above, the radiance
> darts up for neighbors round about to see . . .
>   so from Achilles' head the flame strikes the upper air . . .
>   when they saw the invincible fire
> —frightful, above the head of great-hearted Peleus' son—
> blazing up, set aflame by the goddess, grey-eyed Athena. . .

In place of Homer's enrichment by adding one narrative detail after
another, Pope gives us brilliant visual effects arranged in the dynamic
oppositions of the couplet. But different as his style is from Homer's,
he has kept Homer's emphasis on the splendor and terror of fire,
both of the burning city and of Achilles.

The original of this passage shows that Homer too has his rhetoric
and devices of sound that enhance rhetorical emphasis. Note here the
"as when . . ." and "so . . ." of the simile and the matching repeti-
tions of formulas, types of symmetry that are brought out further
by alliteration and assonance (especially of endings) and by striking
enjambements. We have for example in the last two lines translated:
Deinon/Daiomenon/Daie. Pope has the same or equivalent resources in English, plus rhyme: "Rays/ Beacons blaze/ Reflecting

Blaze on Blaze." Homer also offered Pope the model for the climac-
tic punch of "*Thrice* from the Trench . . . *thrice*": Tris men hyper
Taphou/Tris de . . .

The Roman-English rhetoric of Pope's version of Agamemnon's
appeal to his men (p. 13) is certainly coarser and more pompous
than Homer's austere and quiet eloquence. But

> "Ye Greeks be Men! and yourselves revere"
> could hardly be bettered,

and in Homer's repetition of the *aidòs* root there is a cue for Pope's

> "Let glorious Acts more glorious Acts inspire" . . .

Again Pope has an advantage over later translators in having a style
of eloquence, and a known historic style derived from the Roman.
Pope's hero is much more self-conscious than Homer's in proclaiming his valor, and he is more given to expressing himself in maxims
of the Roman sententious type. But Homer too has his grave moral
sentences, as in the concluding line of Agamemnon's appeal:

> When men fall back, there's neither glory, nor any battle-might.

The beautiful couplet in which the death of Patroclus is fore-
shadowed (p. 14-15) also has a solemn Roman tone:

> There ends thy glory! there the Fates untwine
> The last, black Remnant of so bright a Line.

But in the original, the formulaic "end of life," *biotoio teleuté*, also
has fairly solemn associations, since it is related in form and meaning
to the tremendous word used elsewhere by Zeus: "What I speak *shall
stand*" ("shall be brought to its appointed end"), *tetelesmenon*. In
the somewhat obscure and very human theology of the *Iliad*, the
question is at times raised as to whether the will of Zeus may not
alter fate, but the event always shows that what must be, must be,
that even Zeus must accept what Moira has alloted. In Pope's translation, as Gibbon and others have observed, the use of Hebraic and
Miltonic terms often brings his Jove fairly close to the supreme deity
of the Old Testament. In the passage quoted earlier (p. 14) Jove is
called an "Almighty Pow'r" and "the Sov'reign of the Skies," and
in many other contexts Pope, like Milton and the translators of the
King James version, invests his Jove-Jehovah with the attributes of

modern majesty. But—and here we may again cite the plain translators of the *New Oxford Bible*—Pope's Jove is indisputably a god, tremendous and awful as was Zeus to the gods and heroes of the *Iliad*. Like the heroes, he is more consistently grand in Pope than in Homer, although the translation brings out very well the toughness and social sophistication of Zeus and his "Senate of the Skies."

But the Homeric blend of grandeur, domestic comedy, and personal tragedy in the scene where Zeus foresees the death of his son Sarpedon—one of the great scenes in Homer and a favorite of Pope's —is beyond Pope, and indeed beyond translation. Pope can convey in his Roman-biblical style the majesty of Jove's speech and gestures, and he can describe with elegiac charm how Apollo

> from the War the breathless Hero bore,
> Veil'd in a Cloud, to silver Simois' Shore:
> There bath'd his honourable Wounds, and drest
> His manly Members in th' immortal Vest;
> And with Perfumes of sweet Ambrosial Dews,
> Restores his Freshness, and his Form renews.
> Then Sleep and Death, two Twins of winged Race,
> Of matchless Swiftness, but of silent Pace,
> Receiv'd Sarpedon, at the God's Command,
> And in a Moment reach'd the Lycian Land;
> The Corpse amidst his weeping Friends they laid,
> Where endless Honours wait the sacred Shade.
>   XVI, 825-36

In his version of the scene Pope is high heroic *and* pathetic, but not quite tragic. What we miss is the note of human bewilderment that we cannot fail to recognize in Antigone and Othello, and in Hector and Achilles. In high tragedy the hero discovers that heroic resolve is not enough; and he comes to question the very value that he has asserted more completely than most other men. "Who can control his fate?" Othello asks at the end of the play. To face and express doubt of this kind requires the moral courage and humility that we see in Hector when he is tempted to avoid Achilles and hide in the city, and in Achilles when with Priam before him he has a vision of the inevitability both of heroic action and suffering. Pope's notes on Hector's terror show that he had some understanding of the tragic quality of the scene, though like contemporary critics of the epic he felt bound to justify terror in a perfect hero.

Only the greatest dramatic poets, working easily in their native language, have been able to make their heroes speak so simply and humanly as to convince us that fatal courage is "fortitude to highest victory." For a translator of Homer, the difficulty of striking the right tone in such crucial moments is almost overwhelming. A twentieth century translator can often command the simple and the human, but the heroic of the unquestioning yet noble kind is alien to him and his world. To put it too plainly: he and his contemporaries no longer quite believe in the heroic ideal, just as they no longer believe in the older unquestioning patriotism. Pope was just able to—because the idea of the patriot-hero was still alive in eighteenth century England, very nearly the last period when "decent" patriotic verse could be written by an English poet. In Pope's version, Hector becomes a hero of this eighteenth century patriot-type. Pope is certainly the last English poet to use the Roman patriotic-heroic style in a serious narrative poem. His later poetry, where he rarely uses the style without irony, shows how rapidly the corrosion of the ideal was progressing in his own lifetime. (The same change was also taking place in painting and sculpture.)

We must therefore praise Pope's *Iliad* for what he could do in a style that so easily invited parody. He could and triumphantly did express the noblesse and splendor of the eighteenth century aristocratic ideal, the closest equivalent he knew for Homer's heroic code. His poem, like Lord Granville's famous gesture, exhibits "the English aristocracy at its very height of culture, lofty spirit, and greatness. . ." Nor is this expression of the aristocratic code a mere distortion of Homer; it represents one level of meaning in the total Homeric vision, one very important aspect of Homer's style. Pope was also fortunate in finding some equivalents for other, if not for all the qualities of Greek epic style. In poems written in the Renaissance heroic tradition, he had at hand an idiom rich in associations going back to Virgil and ultimately to Homer. Thanks to the continuity of this tradition, Pope could use certain kinds of language for convenience and ornament in a way not wholly alien to the ancient Homeric mode of composition. In the heroic couplet he had a strict rhythmical convention that like the hexameter favored the use of fixed phrases and frequently recurring rhetorical patterns. Most important of all, Pope and his contemporaries had a confident belief in a high, *formed*, poetic style, a belief typical of the classic, Mediterranean literary mind. To read Pope's *Iliad* is to have some experience in English of the nature and resources of this mind and of the kinds of expression it has fostered in Greece, Rome, and France. It is a mind and an art that is anti-Gothic, anti-Romantic.

But Pope was decidedly an English poet, and less correct, less classic than he sometimes liked to suppose. The Renaissance tradition in poetry and in art, within which he was writing, was also not quite classic. Since Spenser, "Hobgoblin had always been running away with the garland from Apollo." Nowhere does Pope show the modern and northern temper more clearly than in translating Homer's accurate visual reporting into exciting pictorial effects. The reader whose taste is sufficiently impure to enjoy seventeenth and eighteenth century mythological and historical painting can also enjoy Pope's *Iliad*. While he reads, as when he is looking at Rubens or Tiepolo, he will not be able to question; he will surely know that he is experiencing one of the compelling visions of the Greek world of gods and of men like gods.

R. A. B.

THE TRANSLATION
AND ITS PUBLICATION

"Homer will at last do me justice; he was the first author that made me catch the itch of poetry, when I read him in my childhood." So Pope wrote to William Broome in 1715, just after the first volume of his *Iliad* made its appearance; and he added wryly, "and he will now cure me of it entirely." The task was indeed formidable, and it was to occupy Pope for most of the next five years, whenever he was not distracted by bad health, family problems, and other personal or literary affairs.

The translation of Homer was a labor worthy of the poet, and one he had long contemplated, but his motives for undertaking it were not purely literary. The family fortunes were at a low ebb. As Roman Catholics, Pope and his parents had a limited range of investments open to them. Their annuities in French *rentes* were paying badly and even threatened to default, just when the needs and expenses of old age began to make ever larger demands, and punitive measures against their religion threatened them with further problems. The publication of such a large work, in the illustrious tradition of Dryden's *Virgil*, promised a good financial return without exposing Pope to the charge of pot-boiling. He began work on the translation in the spring of 1714, but he did not plunge wholeheartedly into it until he was sure that the subscription would succeed.

In October 1713, proposals were issued and subscriptions invited for the edition. No copy of the subscription leaflet is known to survive, but its text is probably embodied in an advertisement printed at the end of the third edition of *The Rape of the Lock* (1714):

Proposals for printing, by Subscription, a Translation of *Homer's* Iliad into Verse and Rhime. By Mr. *Pope*. To which will be added, explanatory and critical Notes; wherein the most curious and useful Observations, either of the Ancients or Moderns, in relation to this Author in

33

general, or to any Passages in particular, shall be collected and placed under their proper Heads.

This Work shall be printed in six Volumes in Quarto, on the finest Paper, and on a Letter new Cast on purpose; with Ornaments and initial Letters engraven on Copper. Each Volume containing four Books of the Iliad; with Notes to each Book.

It is proposed at the rate of one Guinea for each Volume: The first Volume to the deliver'd in Quires within the space of a Year from the Date of this Proposal, and the rest in like manner annually: Only the Subscribers are to pay two Guineas in hand, advancing one in regard of the Expence the Undertaker must be at in collecting the several Editions, Criticks and Commentators, which are very numerous upon this Author.

A third Guinea to be given upon delivery of the second Volume; and so on to the sixth, for which nothing will be required, on consideration of the Guinea advanced at first. Subscriptions are taken in by *Bernard Lintott.*

Subscriptions were also taken by Pope's friends and supporters, not least among them Jonathan Swift. By the second week of January 1714, Pope reported to John Caryll, "I now think it pretty certain, that I shall be warmly supported on all sides in this undertaking." The text of the proposals, with a list of the subscribers to date, was republished in May, according to an advertisement in the *Evening Post,* May 15, 1714. Eventually the names of 574 subscribers were printed at the beginning of the first volume, and they took up 652 sets; at least one receipt survives made out to a name not appearing in the printed list. Very few subscribers failed to claim the later volumes, and the edition soon became uncommon. By February 1729, Pope complained to Caryll, "The *Iliad* in 4° is not to be procured but by great accident. I have wanted a set these two years, and the only one I could hear of, Lintot had the conscience to ask 10 l. for."

The enthusiasm that greeted his project enabled Pope to secure very favorable terms from Bernard Lintot, his publisher, who was in competition with Jacob Tonson for it. Pope received two hundred guineas for each of the six volumes upon delivery of the text, and was to be supplied free of charge with 660 copies of each volume for transmission to the subscribers, who paid their fees to him. Long afterwards, when he was exercised over evidence of some other chicanery on Lintot's part, Pope claimed that he should have received 750 copies, but this may have been a confused recollection of the later contract for translating the *Odyssey,* which called for 750 subscription copies. The whole proceeds of the subscription accrued to the translator, amounting with Lintot's payments to between £5,000 and £6,000, or perhaps even more. Pope's goal of recouping his fortune was thus brilliantly achieved.

For his part, Lintot received the right to future editions and a royal patent of copyright for fourteen years, with the proviso that he would not compete with the subscription by publishing the work in quarto or with the engraved headpieces and initials that ornamented Pope's edition. One week after the issue of each quarto volume, Lintot brought out his own edition in folio at half the price, 10s. 6d. the volume. He had 1,750 copies of the first volume printed in this format, which was evidently a gross overestimate of the demand, for he reduced the order to 1,000 copies for the subsequent volumes. He also had 250 copies of each volume printed on large paper for sale at two guineas the volume, a venture that does not appear to have prospered, for later his son found himself with a remainder to sell off. Curiously enough, the large paper folio includes the printed list of subscribers, which has no legitimate reason for appearing in it. Was Lintot trying to cheat on the contract by pretending to customers that he was actually selling the author's subscription edition, or was he merely adding a little snob appeal?

The printing was done by William Bowyer, perhaps the best printer in England at that time. The quarto text is set in a good font of double pica type (about 24 point by modern measure), leaded to space the lines further apart; the notes are set in a smaller size. The block of type measures about 7⅝ by 5½ inches, exclusive of headlines and catchwords, on a page about 10¾ by 8½ inches: a bold black area framed with well-proportioned margins. The title pages are in red and black, much in the style of Dryden's *Virgil*; Pope had already seen his own work introduced in such a manner, though on a smaller scale, in the first edition of *The Rape of the Lock* (1714). There are large copper engravings by some of the leading practitioners of the day: John Senex (a map, "Græcia Homerica"), John Harris (another map, in bird's eye style, "Troja cum locis pertingentibus"), Simon Gribelin (the shield of Achilles), and George Vertue (the frontispiece portrait of Homer). Vertue was probably also the anonymous engraver of the excellent and delicate headpieces, tailpieces, and ornamental initials in each book. The first volume has an extremely complicated bibliographical structure, with five fragmentary and irregular sequences of signatures and two inserted single leaves, together with considerable irregularities in pagination. These are mute evidence of changes of plan in content and design in launching the edition, and show the pains taken to determine a proper typographic style. The last five volumes are relatively regular in structure; the trials of Volume I had established the format. In no case do the structural irregularities mar the general effect of the books. Paper, composition, and presswork were all of the best, and neither Pope nor his subscribers can have found reason to complain.

Set in its large, bold type, the quarto contains twenty lines of text to the page, except where a triplet occurs; then it drops to nineteen lines. This prevents the division of a couplet or triplet between two pages, a rule perhaps laid down by the poet, and strictly observed throughout. (The same rule was also observed in the folio and subsequent 12mo editions.) Of course the smaller type of the notes permits more text to the page. The result of this careful layout is a splendid example of the great tradition of book design. Verbal description can hardly do it justice. The modern reader desiring to understand its importance and influence cannot do so without at least a glimpse of the original edition.

The thrifty Lintot did not have the text reset for his folio edition. Instead, Bowyer reimposed the standing type to make up pages of twenty-two lines, thus adapting the type-mass to the taller oblong of the folio page, and incidentally effecting a ten percent saving in length. The pages were equipped with new headlines, pagination, and catchwords, and only a few lines at the beginning of each book were reset, where the absence of the large ornamental initial forced a change. The printer did not even trouble to correct the errata that are noted in print in the quarto: the same errata-list appears (and is needed) at the end of Volume VI of the folio, with two additional entries arising from the mixing up of lines in the process of rearrangement. The quarto and the folio are superficially so much alike that Dr. Johnson believed them to have identical type-pages; and cutdown copies of the folio, reduced to a squarer shape, were offered by the unscrupulous as quartos when these became scarce and commanded a premium.

One volume was supposed to come out each year, with the first originally scheduled for May 1715. The date was later advanced to

March, but an extraordinary spell of wet weather prevented the printed sheets from drying, and publication had to be delayed until June 6, greatly to the distress of Lintot, who unlike Pope could not sell his edition in advance. There is no need to rehearse here the complicated literary, political, and personal squabbles that preceded and accompanied the debut of Pope's *Iliad*. They have been lucidly discussed by George Sherburn in *The Early Career of Alexander Pope*, especially in chapter V, "Addison, the Little Senate, *et al.*" It is enough to say that Pope's translation carried the day against Thomas Tickell's rival translation of Book I. Thereafter, although attacks and slurs did not cease, Pope held the field triumphantly against all enemies and detractors.

The second volume appeared on March 22, 1716; the third, probably on June 3, 1717; and the fourth, June 28, 1718. At this point the regular schedule of publication was interrupted, and the last two volumes were published together on May 12, 1720. Various complication's in Pope's life may have contributed to the delay, but R. H. Griffith is probably right in believing that the principal reason for it was a desire to circumvent a cheap foreign piracy of the work.

T. Johnson, a printer in The Hague, and possibly the most active literary pirate of his day, announced in his *Journal littéraire* for 1718 the publication in 8vo of Pope's *Works* and of the *Iliad* at a price one-sixth that of the English edition. The *Works* and three volumes of the *Iliad* appeared in 1718, and the fourth volume in 1719. All pretended to a spurious legitimacy by a false imprint giving London as the place of publication, and using Lintot's initials. T. Johnson also began to issue a more condensed version of the translation, consisting of the text only without the notes.

Importation of these unauthorized editions would violate Lintot's patent, but it no doubt took place, and Lintot had to meet the competition. This would be easier if Johnson could not have access to the text of the last two volumes until after Lintot had published his own complete text in smaller and cheaper format. William Bowyer's records show that by October 1719, he had already printed for Lintot 2500 copies each of the first three volumes of the *Iliad* in 12mo, and the remaining three by June 5, 1720. All title pages were dated 1720. Thus he was able to put them on the market one month after the subscribers' quarto edition and only three weeks after the folio. Pope took advantage of the opportunity to make a few revisions in the text, most noteworthy among them a line and a half (I.452-3) borrowed from Tickell's translation without acknowledgement.

Since T. Johnson's last two volumes are dated 1721, Lintot scored a clear beat with his edition. In fact, he soon had to bring out a second 12mo edition, this time of 5000 copies. Although piracy had threatened their patent, Lintot and his son did not suffer in the long run from the bargain with Pope. So many editions were sold in the next thirty years that it was clearly a profitable venture.

Pope had begun the long task of translation at least partly from mercenary motives. He ended it with both a financial success and a literary triumph. By 1718 he could afford to lease the celebrated villa at Twickenham that was his home for the rest of his life. And, as George Sherburn says, Pope's *Iliad* was an achievement that "opened all doors, and increased the circle of his acquaintance as well as his fame."

W. H. B.

A NOTE ON THIS EDITION

Although both editors share the responsibility for all aspects of the present edition, the notes and the index have been the particular care of R. A. Brower, the text and its bibliographical analysis that of W. H. Bond.

The notes, which have been kept to a minimum, are limited to: (1) identifying persons where the reference in the text is obscure; (2) Latinate words used with some frequency in Pope's heroic style.

The index is limited mainly to the names of more important characters and places. References are given to some of the more famous passages in which the names occur. For the most part Pope uses the Roman names for Greek divinities. (His more frequent variations in spelling are also listed.)

The aim of the text is to reproduce that of the first quarto edition as faithfully as possible. We have not taken account of the manuscripts (British Museum Add. Mss. 4807-4809), and we have consulted later editions only where corrections of the first edition text seemed to be called for. We vary from this text in the following respects. We have eliminated long s (ſ) and the use of italics for proper names, as typographical features of no textual significance which only distract the modern reader. Only once does Pope employ italics for emphasis (I.731), and these have been retained. We have corrected the errata listed at the end of the sixth volume of the first edition, together with further errata noted by the present editors. These are listed in the back. We have eliminated the infrequent side-notes, incorporating their substance in footnotes wherever this seemed useful.

Pope often preferred slightly archaic spellings, which we have retained. The most frequent is *battel* for *battle*, except in its rare occurrences as a verb; less frequent are others such as *carrier* (*career*) V.732, *deterrs* (*deters*) V.1008, *hoast* (*host*) IX.565, *trophee* (*trophy*) X.621, and the like. We have made no attempt to regularize one eccentricity, the apparently interchangeable use of the diphthongs *æ* and *œ* in certain names such as *Phænix* (*Phœnix*).

39

Pope, or his compositors, or both, seemed quite indifferent to this varying usage. We have followed Pope's punctuation except where it seems clearly at fault.

The editors are grateful for advice and criticism, particularly in the bibliographical side of this work, generously given by Professor R. W. Rogers, Mr. David Fleeman, Mr. David F. Foxon, and Mr. Daniel E. Whitten. They also wish to thank the Grolier Club for permission to make use of information from the manuscript ledgers of William Bowyer, preserved in the Club's library.

R. A. B. and W. H. B.

THE

ILIAD

OF

HOMER,

Tranſlated by Mr. *POPE.*

Te ſequor, O Graiæ gentis Decus! inque tuis nunc
Fixa pedum pono preſſis veſtigia ſignis:
Non ita certandi cupidus, quàm propter Amorem,
Quòd Te imitari aveo ————

LUCRET.

L O N D O N:

Printed by W. BOWYER, for BERNARD LINTOTT between the *Temple-Gates.* 1715.

Title page of the first edition (1715)
of *The Iliad of Homer*

꒭꒭꒭

THE FIRST BOOK
OF THE ILIAD

THE ARGUMENT

The Contention of Achilles and Agamemnon

IN THE WAR OF TROY, the Greeks having sack'd some of the neighbouring Towns, and taken from thence two beautiful Captives, Chruseïs and Briseïs, allotted the first to Agamemnon, and the last to Achilles. Chryses, the Father of Chruseïs and Priest of Apollo, comes to the Grecian camp to ransome her; with which the Action of the Poem opens, in the Tenth Year of the Siege. The Priest being refus'd and insolently dismiss'd by Agamemnon, intreats for Vengeance from his God, who inflicts a Pestilence on the Greeks. Achilles calls a Council, and encourages Chalcas to declare the Cause of it, who attributes it to the Refusal of Chruseïs. The King being obliged to send back his Captive, enters into a furious Contest with Achilles, which Nestor pacifies; however as he had the absolute Command of the Army, he seizes on Briseïs in revenge. Achilles in discontent withdraws himself and his Forces from the rest of the Greeks; and complaining to Thetis, she supplicates Jupiter to render them sensible of the Wrong done to her Son, by giving Victory to the Trojans. Jupiter granting her Suit incenses Juno, between whom the Debate runs high, 'till they are reconciled by the Address of Vulcan.

The Time of two and twenty Days is taken up in this Book; nine during the Plague, one in the Council and Quarrel of the Princes, and twelve for Jupiter's Stay with the Æthiopians, at whose Return Thetis prefers her Petition. The Scene lies in the Grecian Camp, then changes to Chrysa, and lastly to the Gods on Olympus.

The Wrath of Peleus' Son, the direful Spring
Of all the Grecian Woes, O Goddess, sing!

43

That Wrath which hurl'd to Pluto's gloomy Reign
The Souls of mighty Chiefs untimely slain;
Whose Limbs unbury'd on the naked Shore
Devouring Dogs and hungry Vultures tore.
Since Great Achilles and Atrides strove,
Such was the Sov'reign Doom, and such the Will of Jove.
   Declare, O Muse! in what ill-fated Hour
Sprung the fierce Strife, from what offended Pow'r?   10
Latona's Son a dire Contagion spread,
And heap'd the Camp with Mountains of the Dead;
The King of Men his Rev'rend Priest defy'd,
And, for the King's Offence, the People dy'd.
   For Chryses sought with costly Gifts to gain
His Captive Daughter from the Victor's Chain.
Suppliant the Venerable Father stands,
Apollo's awful Ensigns grace his Hands:
By these he begs; and lowly bending down,
Extends the Sceptre and the Laurel Crown.   20
He su'd to All, but chief implor'd for Grace
The Brother-Kings, of Atreus' Royal Race.
   Ye Kings and Warriors! may your Vows be crown'd,
And Troy's proud Walls lie level with the Ground.
May Jove restore you, when your Toils are o'er,
Safe to the Pleasures of your native Shore.
But oh! relieve a wretched Parent's Pain,
And give Chruseïs to these Arms again;
If Mercy fail, yet let my Presents move,
And dread avenging Phœbus, Son of Jove.   30
   The Greeks in Shouts their joint Assent declare
The Priest to rev'rence, and release the Fair.
Not so Atrides: He, with Kingly Pride,
Repuls'd the sacred Sire, and thus reply'd.
Hence on thy Life, and fly these hostile Plains,
Nor ask, Presumptuous, what the King detains;
Hence, with thy Laurel Crown, and Golden Rod,
Nor trust too far those Ensigns of thy God.
Mine is thy Daughter, Priest, and shall remain;
And Pray'rs, and Tears, and Bribes shall plead in vain;   40

'Till Time shall rifle ev'ry youthful Grace,
And Age dismiss her from my cold Embrace,
In daily Labours of the Loom employ'd,
Or doom'd to deck the Bed she once enjoy'd.
Hence then: to Argos shall the Maid retire;
Far from her native Soil, and weeping Sire.
   The trembling Priest along the Shore return'd,
And in the Anguish of a Father mourn'd.
Disconsolate, nor daring to complain,
Silent he wander'd by the sounding Main: 50
'Till, safe at distance, to his God he prays,
The God who darts around the World his Rays.
   O Smintheus![1] sprung from fair Latona's Line,
Thou Guardian Pow'r of Cilla the Divine,
Thou Source of Light! whom Tenedos adores,
And whose bright Presence gilds thy Chrysa's Shores.
If e'er with Wreaths I hung thy sacred Fane,
Or fed the Flames with Fat of Oxen slain;
God of the Silver Bow! thy Shafts employ,
Avenge thy Servant, and the Greeks destroy.   60
   Thus Chryses pray'd: the fav'ring Pow'r attends,
And from Olympus' lofty Tops descends.
Bent was his Bow, the Grecian Hearts to wound;
Fierce as he mov'd, his Silver Shafts resound.
Breathing Revenge, a sudden Night he spread,
And gloomy Darkness roll'd around his Head.
The Fleet in View, he twang'd his deadly Bow,
And hissing fly the feather'd Fates below.
On Mules and Dogs th' Infection first began,
And last, the vengeful Arrows fix'd in Man.   70
For nine long Nights, thro' all the dusky Air
The Fires thick-flaming shot a dismal Glare.
But ere the tenth revolving Day was run,
Inspir'd by Juno, Thetis' God-like Son
Conven'd to Council all the Grecian Train;
For much the Goddess mourn'd her Heroes slain.
   Th' assembly seated, rising o'er the rest,
Achilles thus the King of Men addrest.

[1] Apollo

Why leave we not the fatal Trojan Shore,
And measure back the Seas we crost before?   80
The Plague destroying whom the Sword would spare,
'Tis time to save the few Remains of War.
But let some Prophet, or some sacred Sage,
Explore the Cause of great Apollo's Rage;
Or learn the wastful Vengeance to remove,
By mystic Dreams, for Dreams descend from Jove.
If broken Vows this heavy Curse have laid,
Let Altars smoke, and Hecatombs be paid.
So Heav'n aton'd shall dying Greece restore,
And Phœbus dart his burning Shafts no more.   90

He said and sate: when Chalcas thus reply'd,
Chalcas the wise, the Grecian Priest and Guide,
That sacred Seer whose comprehensive View
The past, the present, and the future knew.
Uprising slow, the venerable Sage
Thus spoke the Prudence and the Fears of Age.

Belov'd of Jove, Achilles! wou'dst thou know
Why angry Phœbus bends his fatal Bow?
First give thy Faith, and plight a Prince's Word
Of sure Protection by thy Pow'r and Sword.   100
For I must speak what Wisdom would conceal,
And Truths invidious to the Great reveal.
Bold is the Task, when Subjects grown too wise
Instruct a Monarch where his Error lies;
For tho' we deem the short-liv'd Fury past,
'Tis sure, the Mighty will revenge at last.

To whom Pelides. From thy inmost Soul
Speak what thou know'st, and speak without controul.
Ev'n by that God I swear, who rules the Day;
To whom thy Hands the Vows of Greece convey,   110
And whose blest Oracles thy Lips declare;
Long as Achilles breathes this vital Air,
No daring Greek of all the num'rous Band,
Against his Priest shall lift an impious Hand:
Not ev'n the Chief by whom our Hosts are led,
The King of Kings, shall touch that sacred Head.

Encourag'd thus, the blameless Priest replies:
Nor Vows unpaid, nor slighted Sacrifice,
But He, our Chief, provok'd the raging Pest,
Apollo's Vengeance for his injur'd Priest. 120
Nor will the God's awaken'd Fury cease,
But Plagues shall spread, and Fun'ral Fires increase,
'Till the great King, without a Ransom paid,
To her own Chrysa send the black-ey'd Maid.
Perhaps, with added Sacrifice and Pray'r,
The Priest may pardon, and the God may spare.
The Prophet spoke; when with a gloomy Frown,
The Monarch started from his shining Throne;
Black Choler fill'd his Breast that boil'd with Ire,
And from his Eyeballs flash'd the living Fire. 130
Augur accurst! denouncing Mischief still,
Prophet of Plagues, for ever boding Ill!
Still must that Tongue some wounding Message bring,
And still thy Priestly Pride provoke thy King?
For this are Phœbus' Oracles explor'd,
To teach the Greeks to murmur at their Lord?
For this with Falshoods is my Honour stain'd;
Is Heav'n offended, and a Priest profan'd,
Because my Prize, my beauteous Maid I hold,
And heav'nly Charms prefer to proffer'd Gold? 140
A Maid, unmatch'd in Manners as in Face,
Skill'd in each art, and crown'd with ev'ry Grace.
Not half so dear were Clytemnestra's Charms,
When first her blooming Beauties blest my Arms.
Yet if the Gods demand her, let her sail;
Our Cares are only for the Publick Weal:
Let me be deem'd the hateful Cause of all,
And suffer, rather than my People fall.
The Prize, the beauteous Prize I will resign,
So dearly valu'd, and so justly mine. 150
But since for common Good I yield the Fair,
My private Loss let grateful Greece repair;
Nor unrewarded let your Prince complain,
That He alone has fought and bled in vain.

Insatiate King (Achilles thus replies)
Fond of the Pow'r, but fonder of the Prize!
Would'st thou the Greeks their lawful Prey shou'd yield,
The due Reward of many a well-fought Field?
The Spoils of Cities raz'd, and Warriors slain,
We share with Justice, as with Toil we gain: 160
But to resume whate'er thy Av'rice craves,
(That Trick of Tyrants) may be born by Slaves.
Yet if our Chief for Plunder only fight,
The Spoils of Ilion shall thy Loss requite,
Whene'er, by Jove's Decree, our conqu'ring Pow'rs
Shall humble to the Dust her lofty Tow'rs.
    Then thus the King. Shall I my Prize resign
With tame Content, and Thou possest of thine?
Great as thou art, and like a God in Fight,
Think not to rob me of a Soldier's Right.   170
At thy Demand shall I restore the Maid?
First let the just Equivalent be paid;
Such as a King might ask; and let it be
A Treasure worthy Her, and worthy Me.
Or grant me this, or with a Monarch's Claim
This Hand shall seize some other Captive Dame.
The mighty Ajax shall his Prize resign,
Ulysses' Spoils, or ev'n thy own be mine.
The Man who suffers, loudly may complain;
And rage he may, but he shall rage in vain.   180
But this when Time requires—It now remains
We launch a Bark to plow the watry Plains,
And waft the Sacrifice to Chrysa's Shores,
With chosen Pilots, and with lab'ring Oars.
Soon shall the Fair the sable Ship ascend,
And some deputed Prince the Charge attend;
This Creta's King, or Ajax shall fulfill,
Or wise Ulysses see perform'd our Will,
Or, if our Royal Pleasure shall ordain,
Achilles self conduct her o'er the Main;   190
Let fierce Achilles, dreadful in his Rage,
The God propitiate, and the Pest asswage.

At this, Pelides frowning stern, reply'd:
O Tyrant, arm'd with insolence and Pride!
Inglorious Slave to Int'rest, ever join'd
With Fraud, unworthy of a Royal Mind.
What gen'rous Greek obedient to thy Word,
Shall form an Ambush, or shall lift the Sword?
What Cause have I to war at thy Decree?
The distant Trojans never injur'd me.   200
To Pthia's Realms no hostile Troops they led;
Safe in her Vales my warlike Coursers fed:
Far hence remov'd, the hoarse-resounding Main
And Walls of Rocks, secure my native Reign,
Whose fruitful Soil luxuriant Harvests grace,
Rich in her Fruits, and in her martial Race.
Hither we sail'd, a voluntary Throng,
T' avenge a private, not a publick Wrong:
What else to Troy th' assembled Nations draws,
But thine, Ungrateful, and thy Brother's Cause?   210
Is this the Pay our Blood and Toils deserve,
Disgrac'd and injur'd by the Man we serve?
And dar'st thou threat to snatch my Prize away,
Due to the Deeds of many a dreadful Day?
A Prize as small, O Tyrant! match'd with thine,
As thy own Actions if compar'd to mine.
Thine in each Conquest is the wealthy Prey,
Tho' mine the Sweat and Danger of the Day.
Some trivial Present to my Ships I bear,
Or barren Praises pay the Wounds of War.   220
But know, proud Monarch, I'm thy Slave no more;
My fleet shall waft me to Thessalia's Shore.
Left by Achilles on the Trojan Plain,
What Spoils, what Conquests shall Atrides gain?
  To this the King: Fly, mighty Warriour! fly,
Thy Aid we need not, and thy Threats defy.
There want not Chiefs in such a Cause to fight,
And Jove himself shall guard a Monarch's Right.
Of all the Kings (the Gods distinguish'd Care)
To Pow'r superior none such Hatred bear: 230

Strife and Debate thy restless Soul employ,
And Wars and Horrors are thy savage Joy.
If thou hast Strength, 'twas Heav'n that Strength bestow'd,
For know, vain Man! thy Valour is from God.
Haste, launch thy Vessels, fly with Speed away,
Rule thy own Realms with arbitrary Sway:
I heed thee not, but prize at equal rate
Thy short-liv'd Friendship, and thy groundless Hate.
Go, threat thy Earth-born Myrmidons; but here
'Tis mine to threaten, Prince, and thine to fear.   240
Know, if the God the beauteous Dame demand,
My Bark shall waft her to her native Land;
But then prepare, Imperious Prince! prepare,
Fierce as thou art, to yield thy captive Fair:
Ev'n in thy Tent I'll seize the blooming Prize,
Thy lov'd Briseïs with the radiant Eyes.
Hence shalt thou prove my Might, and curse the Hour,
Thou stood'st a Rival of Imperial Pow'r;
And hence to all our Host it shall be known,
That Kings are subject to the Gods alone.   250
    Achilles heard, with Grief and Rage opprest,
His Heart swell'd high, and labour'd in his Breast.
Distracting Thoughts by turns his Bosom rul'd,
Now fir'd by Wrath, and now by Reason cool'd:
That prompts his Hand to draw the deadly Sword,
Force thro' the Greeks, and pierce their haughty Lord;
This whispers soft his Vengeance to controul,
And calm the rising Tempest of his Soul.
Just as in Anguish of Suspence he stay'd,
While half unsheath'd appear'd the glitt'ring Blade,   260
Minerva swift descended from above,
Sent by the Sister[2] and the Wife of Jove;
(For both the Princes claim'd her equal Care)
Behind she stood, and by the Golden Hair
Achilles seiz'd; to him alone confest,[3]
A sable Cloud conceal'd her from the rest.

[2] Juno
[3] Revealed (Latin sense)

He saw, and sudden to the Goddess cries,
Known by the Flames that sparkled from her Eyes.
   Descends Minerva, in her guardian Care,
A heav'nly Witness of the Wrongs I bear   270
From Atreus' Son? Then let those Eyes that view
The daring Crime, behold the Vengeance too.
   Forbear! (the Progeny of Jove replies)
To calm thy Fury I forsook the Skies:
Let great Achilles, to the Gods resign'd,
To Reason yield the Empire o'er his Mind.
By awful Juno this Command is giv'n;
The King and You are both the Care of Heav'n.
The Force of keen Reproaches let him feel,
But sheath, Obedient, thy revenging Steel.   280
For I pronounce (and trust a heav'nly Pow'r)
Thy injur'd Honour has its fated Hour,
When the proud Monarch shall thy Arms implore,
And bribe thy Friendship with a boundless Store.
Then let Revenge no longer bear the Sway,
Command thy Passions, and the Gods obey.
   To her Pelides. With regardful Ear
'Tis just, O Goddess! I thy Dictates hear.
Hard as it is, my Vengeance I suppress:
Those who revere the Gods, the Gods will bless.   290
He said, observant of the blue-ey'd Maid;
Then in the Sheath return'd the shining Blade.
The Goddess swift to high Olympus flies,
And joins the sacred Senate of the Skies.
   Nor yet the Rage his boiling Breast forsook,
Which thus redoubling on the Monarch broke.
O Monster, mix'd of Insolence and Fear,
Thou Dog in Forehead, but in Heart a Deer!
When wert thou known in ambush'd Fights to dare,
Or nobly face the horrid Front of War?   300
'Tis ours, the Chance of fighting Fields to try,
Thine to look on, and bid the Valiant dye.
So much 'tis safer thro' the Camp to go,
And rob a Subject, than despoil a Foe.

Scourge of thy People, violent and base!
Sent in Jove's Anger on a slavish Race,
Who lost to Sense of gen'rous Freedom past
Are tam'd to Wrongs, or this had been thy last.
Now by this sacred Sceptre, hear me swear,
Which never more shall Leaves or Blossoms bear,   310
Which sever'd from the Trunk (as I from thee)
On the bare Mountains left its Parent Tree;
This Sceptre, form'd by temper'd Steel to prove
An Ensign of the Delegates of Jove,
From whom the Pow'r of Laws and Justice springs:
(Tremendous Oath! inviolate to Kings)
By this I swear, when bleeding Greece again
Shall call Achilles, she shall call in vain.
When flush'd with Slaughter, Hector comes, to spread
The purpled Shore with Mountains of the Dead,   320
Then shalt thou mourn th' Affront thy Madness gave,
Forc'd to deplore, when impotent to save:
Then rage in Bitterness of Soul, to know
This Act has made the bravest Greek thy Foe.
    He spoke; and furious, hurl'd against the Ground
His Sceptre starr'd with golden Studs around.
Then sternly silent sate: With like Disdain,
The raging King return'd his Frowns again.
    To calm their Passion with the Words of Age,
Slow from his Seat arose the Pylian Sage;   330
Th' experienc'd Nestor, in Persuasion skill'd,
Words, sweet as Honey, from his Lips distill'd:
Two Generations now had past away,
Wise by his Rules, and happy by his Sway;
Two Ages o'er his native Realm he reign'd,
And now th' Example of the third remain'd.
All view'd with Awe the Venerable Man;
Who thus, with mild Benevolence, began;
    What Shame, what Woe is this to Greece! what Joy
To Troy's proud Monarch, and the Friends of Troy!   340
That adverse Gods commit to stern Debate
The best, the bravest of the Grecian State.

Young as you are, this youthful Heat restrain,
Nor think your Nestor's Years and Wisdom vain.
A Godlike Race of Heroes once I knew,
Such, as no more these aged Eyes shall view!
Lives there a Chief to match Pirithous'[4] Fame,
Dryas the bold, or Ceneus' deathless Name;
Theseus, endu'd with more than mortal Might,
Or Polyphemus, like the Gods in Fight?   350
With these of old to Toils of Battel bred,
In early Youth my hardy Days I led;
Fir'd with the Thirst which Virtuous Envy breeds,
And smit with Love of Honourable Deeds.
Strongest of Men, they pierc'd the Mountain Boar,
Rang'd the wild Desarts red with Monsters Gore,
And from their Hills the shaggy Centaurs tore.
Yet these with soft, persuasive Arts I sway'd,
When Nestor spoke, they listen'd and obey'd.
If, in my Youth, ev'n these esteem'd me wise,   360
Do you, young Warriors, hear my Age advise.
Atrides, seize not on the beauteous Slave;
That Prize the Greeks by common Suffrage gave:
Nor thou, Achilles, treat our Prince with Pride;
Let Kings be just, and Sov'reign Pow'r preside.
Thee, the first Honours of the War adorn,
Like Gods in Strength, and of a Goddess born;
Him awful Majesty exalts above
The Pow'rs of Earth, and sceptred Sons of Jove.
Let both unite with well-consenting Mind,   370
So shall Authority with Strength be join'd.
Leave me, O King! to calm Achilles' Rage;
Rule thou thy self, as more advanc'd in Age.
Forbid it Gods! Achilles should be lost,
The Pride of Greece, and Bulwark of our Host.
    This said, he ceas'd: The King of Men replies;
Thy Years are awful, and thy Words are wise.

---

[4] King of the Lapiths, who with other heroes named here made war on the
Centaurs (357).

But that imperious, that unconquer'd Soul,
No Laws can limit, no Respect controul.
Before his Pride must his Superiors fall,   380
His Word the Law, and He the Lord of all?
Him must our Hosts, our Chiefs, our Self obey?
What King can bear a Rival in his Sway?
Grant that the Gods his matchless Force have giv'n;
Has foul Reproach a Privilege from Heav'n?

Here on the Monarch's Speech Achilles broke,
And furious, thus, and interrupting spoke.
Tyrant, I well deserv'd thy galling Chain,
To live thy Slave, and still to serve in vain,
Should I submit to each unjust Decree: 390
Command thy Vassals, but command not Me.
Seize on Briseïs, whom the Grecians doom'd
My Prize of War, yet tamely see resum'd;
And seize secure; No more Achilles draws
His conqu'ring Sword in any Woman's Cause.
The Gods command me to forgive the past;
But let this first Invasion be the last:
For know, thy Blood, when next thou dar'st invade,[5]
Shall stream in Vengeance on my reeking Blade.

At this, they ceas'd; the stern Debate expir'd: 400
The Chiefs in sullen Majesty retir'd.

Achilles with Patroclus took his Way,
Where near his Tents his hollow Vessels lay.
Mean time Atrides launch'd with num'rous Oars
A well-rigg'd Ship for Chrysa's sacred Shores:
High on the Deck was fair Chruseïs plac'd,
And sage Ulysses with the Conduct grac'd:
Safe in her Sides the Hecatomb they stow'd,
Then swiftly sailing, cut the liquid Road.

The Host to expiate next the King prepares,   410
With pure Lustrations, and with solemn Pray'rs.
Wash'd by the briny Wave, the pious Train
Are cleans'd, and cast th' Ablutions in the Main.
Along the Shore whole Hecatombs were laid,
And Bulls and Goats to Phœbus' Altars paid.

[5] Attack

The sable Fumes in curling Spires arise,
And waft their grateful Odours to the Skies.
   The Army thus in sacred Rites engag'd,
Atrides still with deep Resentment rag'd.
To wait his Will two sacred Heralds stood,   420
Talthybius and Eurybates the good.
Haste to the fierce Achilles' Tent (he cries)
Thence bear Briseïs as our Royal Prize:
Submit he must; or if they will not part,
Ourself in Arms shall tear her from his Heart.
   Th' unwilling Heralds act their Lord's Commands;
Pensive they walk along the barren Sands:
Arriv'd, the Heroe in his Tent they find,
With gloomy Aspect, on his Arm reclin'd.
At awful Distance long they silent stand,   430
Loth to advance, or speak their hard Command;
Decent[6] Confusion! This the Godlike Man
Perceiv'd, and thus with Accent mild began.
   With Leave and Honour enter our Abodes,
Ye sacred Ministers of Men and Gods!
I know your Message; by Constraint you came;
Not you, but your Imperious Lord I blame.
Patroclus haste, the fair Briseïs bring;
Conduct my Captive to the haughty King.
But witness, Heralds, and proclaim my Vow,   440
Witness to Gods above, and Men below!
But first, and loudest, to your Prince declare,
That lawless Tyrant whose Commands you bear;
Unmov'd as Death Achilles shall remain,
Tho' prostrate Greece should bleed at ev'ry Vein:
The raging Chief in frantick Passion lost,
Blind to himself, and useless to his Host,
Unskill'd to judge the Future by the Past,
In Blood and Slaughter shall repent at last.
   Patroclus now th' unwilling Beauty brought;   450
She, in soft Sorrows, and in pensive Thought,

---

[6] Becoming, decorous (Latin)

Supported by the Chiefs on either Hand,[7]
In Silence past along the winding Strand.
  Not so his Loss the fierce Achilles bore;
But sad retiring to the sounding Shore,
O'er the wild Margin of the Deep he hung,
That kindred Deep, from whence his Mother sprung.
There, bath'd in Tears of Anger and Disdain,
Thus loud lamented to the stormy Main.
  O Parent Goddess! since in early Bloom   460
Thy Son must fall, by too severe a Doom,
Sure, to so short a Race of Glory born,
Great Jove in Justice should this Span adorn:
Honour and Fame at least the Thund'rer ow'd,
And ill he pays the Promise of a God;
If yon proud Monarch thus thy Son defies,
Obscures my Glories, and resumes my Prize.
  Far in the deep Recesses of the Main,
Where aged Ocean holds his wat'ry Reign,
The Goddess-Mother heard. The Waves divide;   470
And like a Mist she rose above the Tide;
Beheld him mourning on the naked Shores,
And thus the Sorrows of his Soul explores.
Why grieves my Son? Thy Anguish let me share,
Reveal the Cause, and trust a Parent's Care.
  He deeply sighing said: To tell my Woe,
Is but to mention what too well you know.
From Thebè[8] sacred to Apollo's Name,
(Aetion's Realm) our conqu'ring Army came,
With Treasure loaded and triumphant Spoils,   480
Whose just Division crown'd the Soldier's Toils;
But bright Chruseïs, heav'nly Prize! was led
By Vote selected, to the Gen'ral's Bed.

[7] In 1720 Pope revised this passage to read,
    Past silent, as the heralds held her hand,
      And oft look'd back, slow-moving o'er the strand.
This revision is a virtual quotation of Tickell's version,
    Sore sigh'd she, as the Heralds took her Hand,
      And oft look'd back slow-moving o'er the Strand.
Both translators were "improving" Homer: neither couplet has any basis in the
original Greek.
[8] City near Troy

The Priest of Phœbus sought by Gifts to gain
His beauteous Daughter from the Victor's Chain;
The Fleet he reach'd, and lowly bending down,
Held forth the Sceptre and the Laurel Crown,
Entreating All: but chief implor'd for Grace
The Brother Kings of Atreus' Royal Race:
The gen'rous Greeks their joint Consent declare,   490
The Priest to rev'rence, and release the Fair;
Not so Atrides: He, with wonted Pride,
The Sire insulted, and his Gifts deny'd:
Th' insulted Sire (his God's peculiar Care)
To Phœbus pray'd, and Phœbus heard the Pray'r:
A dreadful Plague ensues; Th' avenging Darts
Incessant fly, and pierce the Grecian Hearts:
A Prophet then, inspir'd by Heav'n arose,
And points the Crime, and thence derives the Woes:
My self the first th' assembl'd Chiefs incline   500
T' avert the Vengeance of the Pow'r Divine;
Then rising in his Wrath, the Monarch storm'd;
Incens'd he threaten'd, and his Threats perform'd:
The fair Chruseïs to her Sire was sent,
With offer'd Gifts to make the God relent;
But now He seiz'd Briseïs' heav'nly Charms,
And of my Valour's Prize defrauds my Arms,
Defrauds the Votes of all the Grecian Train;
And Service, Faith, and Justice plead in vain.
But Goddess! thou, thy suppliant Son attend,   510
To high Olympus' shining Court ascend,
Urge all the Ties to former Service ow'd,
And sue for Vengeance to the Thund'ring God.
Oft hast thou triumph'd in the glorious Boast,
That thou stood'st forth, of all th' Æthereal Host,
When bold Rebellion shook the Realms above,
Th' undaunted Guard of Cloud-compelling Jove.
When the bright Partner of his awful Reign,
The Warlike Maid, and Monarch of the Main,
The Traytor-Gods, by mad Ambition driv'n,   520
Durst threat with Chains th' Omnipotence of Heav'n.

Then call'd by thee: the Monster Titan came,
(Whom Gods Briareus, Men Ægeon name)
Thro' wondring Skies enormous stalk'd along;
Not He[9] that shakes the solid Earth so strong:
With Giant-Pride at Jove's high Throne he stands,
And brandish'd round him all his Hundred Hands;
Th' affrighted Gods confess'd their awful Lord,
They dropt the Fetters, trembled and ador'd.
This, Goddess, this to his Remembrance call,   530
Embrace his Knees, at his Tribunal fall;
Conjure him far to drive the Grecian Train,
To hurl them headlong to their Fleet and Main,
To heap the Shores with copious Death, and bring
The Greeks to know the Curse of such a King:
Let Agamemnon lift his haughty Head
O'er all his wide Dominion of the Dead,
And mourn in Blood, that e'er he durst disgrace
The boldest Warrior of the Grecian Race.

    Unhappy Son! (fair Thetis thus replies,   540
While Tears Celestial trickled from her Eyes)
Why have I born thee with a Mother's Throes,
To Fates averse, and nurs'd for future Woes?
So short a Space the Light of Heav'n to view!
So short a Space, and fill'd with Sorrow too!
Oh might a Parent's careful Wish prevail,
Far, far from Ilion should thy Vessels sail,
And thou, from Camps remote, the Danger shun,
Which now, alas! too nearly threats my Son.
Yet (what I can) to move thy Suit I'll go,   550
To great Olympus crown'd with fleecy Snow.
Mean time, secure within thy Ships from far
Behold the Field; nor mingle in the War.
The Sire of Gods, and all th' Etherial Train,
On the warm Limits of the farthest Main,
Now mix with Mortals, nor disdain to grace
The Feasts of Æthiopia's blameless Race[10]:

[9] Neptune
[10] A fabulous people, beloved of the gods, living on the borders of Ocean

Twelve Days the Pow'rs indulge the Genial[11] Rite,
Returning with the twelfth revolving Light.
Then will I mount the Brazen Dome, and move   560
The high Tribunal of Immortal Jove.
 The Goddess spoke: The rowling Waves unclose;
Then down the Deep she plung'd from whence she rose,
And left him sorrowing on the lonely Coast,
In wild Resentment for the Fair he lost.
 In Chrysa's Port now sage Ulysses rode;
Beneath the Deck the destin'd Victims stow'd:
The Sails they furl'd, they lash'd the Mast aside,
And dropt their Anchors, and the Pinnace ty'd.
Next on the Shore their Hecatomb they land,   570
Chruseïs last descending on the Strand.
Her, thus returning from the furrow'd Main,
Ulysses led to Phœbus sacred Fane;
Where at his solemn Altar, as the Maid
He gave to Chryses, thus the Heroe said.
 Hail Rev'rend Priest! to Phœbus' awful Dome
A Suppliant I from great Atrides come:
Unransom'd here receive the spotless Fair;
Accept the Hecatomb the Greeks prepare;
And may thy God who scatters Darts around,   580
Aton'd by Sacrifice, desist to wound.
 At this, the Sire embrac'd the Maid again,
So sadly lost, so lately sought in vain.
Then near the Altar of the darting King,
Dispos'd in Rank their Hecatomb they bring:
With Water purify their Hands, and take
The sacred Off'ring of the salted Cake;
While thus with Arms devoutly rais'd in Air,
And solemn Voice, the Priest directs his Pray'r.
 God of the Silver Bow, thy Ear incline,   590
Whose Power encircles Cilla the Divine,
Whose sacred Eye thy Tenedos surveys,
And gilds fair Chrysa with distinguish'd Rays!
If, fir'd to Vengeance at thy Priests request,
Thy direful Darts inflict the raging Pest;

[11] Festive

Once more attend! avert the wastful Woe,
And smile propitious, and unbend thy Bow.
  So Chryses pray'd, Apollo heard his Pray'r:
And now the Greeks their Hecatomb prepare;
Between their Horns the salted Barley threw,   600
And with their Heads to Heav'n the Victims slew:
The Limbs they sever from th' inclosing Hide;
The Thighs, selected to the Gods, divide:
On these, in double Cawls involv'd[12] with Art,
The choicest Morsels lay from ev'ry Part.
The Priest himself before his Altar stands,
And burns the Victims with his holy Hands,
Pours the black Wine, and sees the Flames aspire;
The Youth with Instruments surround the Fire:
The Thighs thus sacrific'd, and Entrails drest,   610
Th' Assistants part, transfix, and roast the rest:
Then spread the Tables, the Repast prepare,
Each takes his Seat, and each receives his Share.
When now the Rage of Hunger was represt,
With pure Libations they conclude the Feast;
The Youths with Wine the copious Goblets crown'd,[13]
And pleas'd, dispense the flowing Bowls around.
With Hymns Divine the joyous Banquet ends,
The Pæans lengthen'd 'till the Sun descends:
The Greeks restor'd the grateful Notes prolong;   620
Apollo listens, and approves the Song.
  'Twas Night: the Chiefs beside their Vessel lie,
'Till rosie Morn had purpled o'er the Sky:
Then launch, and hoise the Mast; Indulgent Gales
Supply'd by Phœbus, fill the swelling Sails;
The milk-white Canvas bellying as they blow;
The parted Ocean foams and roars below:
Above the bounding Billows swift they flew,
'Till now the Grecian Camp appear'd in view.
Far on the Beach they haul their Bark to Land,   630
(The crooked Keel divides the yellow Sand)

[12] Enwrapped
[13] Filled

Then part, where stretch'd along the winding Bay
The Ships and Tents in mingled Prospect lay.
　But raging still amidst his Navy sate
The stern Achilles, stedfast in his Hate;
Nor mix'd in Combate, nor in Council join'd,
But wasting Cares lay heavy on his Mind:
In his black Thoughts Revenge and Slaughter roll,
And Scenes of Blood rise dreadful in his Soul.
　Twelve Days were past, and now the dawning Light   640
The Gods had summon'd to th' Olympian Height.
Jove first ascending from the Wat'ry Bow'rs,
Leads the Long Order of Ætherial Pow'rs.
When like a Morning Mist, in early Day,
Rose from the Flood the Daughter of the Sea;
And to the Seats Divine her Flight addrest.
There, far apart, and high above the rest,
The Thund'rer sate; where old Olympus shrouds
His hundred Heads in Heav'n, and props the Clouds.
Suppliant the Goddess stood: One Hand she plac'd   650
Beneath his Beard, and one his Knees embrac'd.
If e'er, O Father of the Gods! she said,
My Words cou'd please thee, or my Actions aid;
Some Marks of Honour on my Son bestow,
And pay in Glory what in Life you owe.
Fame is at least by Heav'nly Promise due
To Life so short, and now dishonour'd too.
Avenge this Wrong, oh ever just and wise!
Let Greece be humbled, and the Trojans rise;
'Till the proud King, and all th' Achaian Race   660
Shall heap with Honours him they now disgrace.
　Thus Thetis spoke, but Jove in Silence held
The sacred Counsels of his Breast conceal'd.
Not so repuls'd, the Goddess closer prest,
Still grasp'd his Knees, and urg'd the dear Request.
O Sire of Gods and Men! thy Suppliant hear,
Refuse, or grant; for what has Jove to fear?
Or oh declare, of all the Pow'rs above
Is wretched Thetis least the Care of Jove?

She said, and sighing thus the God replies   670
Who rolls the Thunder o'er the vaulted Skies.
What hast thou ask'd? Ah why should Jove engage
In foreign Contests, and domestic Rage,
The Gods Complaints, and Juno's fierce Alarms,
While I, too partial, aid the Trojan Arms?
Go, lest the haughty Partner of my Sway
With jealous Eyes thy close Access survey;
But part in Peace, secure thy Pray'r is sped:
Witness the sacred Honours[14] of our Head,
The Nod that ratifies the Will Divine,   680
The faithful, fix'd, irrevocable Sign;
This seals thy Suit, and this fulfills thy Vows—
He spoke, and awful, bends his sable Brows;
Shakes his Ambrosial Curls, and gives the Nod;
The Stamp of Fate, and Sanction of the God:
High Heav'n with trembling the dread Signal took,
And all Olympus to the Centre shook.
   Swift to the Seas profound the Goddess flies,
Jove to his starry Mansion in the Skies.
The shining Synod of th' Immortals wait   690
The coming God, and from their Thrones of State
Arising silent, wrapt in Holy Fear,
Before the Majesty of Heav'n appear.
Trembling they stand, while Jove assumes the Throne,
All, but the God's Imperious Queen alone:
Late had she view'd the Silver-footed Dame,
And all her Passions kindled into Flame.
Say, artful Manager of Heav'n (she cries)
Who now partakes the Secrets of the Skies?
Thy Juno knows not the Decrees of Fate,   700
In vain the Partner of Imperial State.
What fav'rite Goddess then those Cares divides,
Which Jove in Prudence from his Consort hides?
   To this the Thund'rer: Seek not thou to find
The sacred Counsels of Almighty Mind:
Involv'd in Darkness lies the great Decree,
Nor can the Depths of Fate be pierc'd by thee.

[14] Adornment; here, *Curls* (684)

What fits thy Knowledge, thou the first shalt know;
The first of Gods above and Men below:
But thou, nor they, shall search the Thoughts that roll   710
Deep in the close Recesses of my Soul.
   Full on the Sire the Goddess of the Skies
Roll'd the large Orbs of her majestic Eyes,
And thus return'd. Austere Saturnius, say,
From whence this Wrath, or who controuls thy Sway?
Thy boundless Will, for me, remains in Force,
And all thy Counsels take the destin'd Course.
But 'tis for Greece I fear: For late was seen
In close Consult, the Silver-footed Queen.
Jove to his Thetis nothing could deny,   720
Nor was the Signal vain that shook the Sky.
What fatal Favour has the Goddess won,
To grace her fierce, inexorable Son?
Perhaps in Grecian Blood to drench the Plain,
And glut his Vengeance with my People slain.
   Then thus the God: Oh restless Fate of Pride,
That strives to learn what Heav'n resolves to hide;
Vain is the Search, presumptuous and abhorr'd,
Anxious to thee, and odious to thy Lord.
Let this suffice; th' immutable Decree   730
No Force can shake: What *is*, that *ought* to be.
Goddess submit, nor dare our Will withstand,
But dread the Pow'r of this avenging Hand;
Th' united Strength of all the Gods above
In vain resists th' Omnipotence of Jove.
   The Thund'rer spoke, nor durst the Queen reply;
A rev'rend Horror silenc'd all the Sky.
The feast disturb'd with Sorrow Vulcan saw,
His Mother menac'd, and the Gods in Awe;
Peace at his Heart, and Pleasure his Design,   740
Thus interpos'd the Architect Divine.
The wretched Quarrels of the mortal State
Are far unworthy, Gods! of your Debate:
Let Men their Days in senseless Strife employ,
We, in eternal Peace and constant Joy.

Thou, Goddess-Mother, with our Sire comply,
Nor break the sacred Union of the Sky:
Lest, rouz'd to Rage, he shake the blest Abodes,
Launch the red Lightning, and dethrone the Gods.
If you submit, the Thund'rer stands appeas'd;   750
The gracious Pow'r is willing to be pleas'd.
    Thus Vulcan spoke; and rising with a Bound,
The double Bowl with sparkling Nectar crown'd,
Which held to Juno in a chearful way,
Goddess (he cry'd) be patient and obey.
Dear as you are, if Jove his Arm extend,
I can but grieve, unable to defend.
What God so daring in your Aid to move,
Or lift his Hand against the Force of Jove?
Once in your Cause I felt his matchless Might,   760
Hurl'd headlong downward from th' Etherial Height;
Tost all the Day in rapid Circles round;
Nor 'till the Sun descended, touch'd the Ground:
Breathless I fell, in giddy Motion lost;
The Sinthians rais'd me on the Lemnian Coast.
    He said, and to her Hands the Goblet heav'd,
Which, with a Smile, the white-arm'd Queen receiv'd.
Then to the rest he fill'd; and, in his Turn,
Each to his Lips apply'd the nectar'd Urn.
Vulcan with awkward Grace his Office plies,   770
And unextinguish'd Laughter shakes the Skies.
    Thus the blest Gods the Genial Day prolong,
In Feasts Ambrosial, and Celestial Song.
Apollo tun'd the Lyre; the Muses round
With Voice alternate aid the silver Sound.
Meantime the radiant Sun, to mortal Sight
Descending swift, roll'd down the rapid Light.
Then to their starry Domes the Gods depart,
The shining Monuments of Vulcan's Art:
Jove on his Couch reclin'd his awful Head,   780
And Juno slumber'd on the golden Bed.

⌐⌐⌐⌐

THE SECOND BOOK
OF THE ILIAD

THE ARGUMENT

The Tryal of the Army and Catalogue of the Forces

JUPITER IN PURSUANCE of the Request of Thetis, sends a deceitful Vision
to Agamemnon, persuading him to lead the Army to Battel; in order to
make the Greeks sensible of their want of Achilles. The General, who is
deluded with the hopes of taking Troy without his Assistance, but fears
the Army was discourag'd by his Absence and the late Plague, as well
as by length of Time, contrives to make trial of their Disposition by a
Stratagem. He first communicates his Design to the Princes in Council,
that he would propose a Return to the Soldiers, and that they should put
a stop to them if the Proposal was embrac'd. Then he assembles the
whole Host, and upon moving for a Return to Greece, they unanimously
agree to it and run to prepare the Ships. They are detain'd by the Manage-
ment of Ulysses, who chastises the Insolence of Thersites. The Assembly
is recall'd, several Speeches made on the occasion, and at length the Advice of Nestor follow'd, which was to make a general Muster of the
Troops, and to divide them into their several Nations, before they proceeded to Battel. This gives occasion to the Poet to ennumerate all the
Forces of the Greeks and Trojans, in a large Catalogue.

The Time employ'd in this Book consists not intirely of one Day. The
Scene lies in the Græcian-Camp and upon the Sea-Shore; toward the end
it removes to Troy.

Now pleasing Sleep had seal'd each mortal Eye,
Stretch'd in the Tents the Grecian Leaders lie,
Th' Immortals slumber'd on their Thrones above;
All, but the ever-wakeful Eyes of Jove.

To honour Thetis' Son he bends his Care,
And plunge the Greeks in all the Woes of War:
Then bids an empty Phantome rise to sight,
And thus commands the Vision of the Night.
   Fly hence, deluding Dream! and light as Air,
To Agamemnon's ample Tent repair.   10
Bid him in Arms draw forth th' embattel'd Train,
Lead all his Grecians to the dusty Plain.
Declare, ev'n now 'tis giv'n him to destroy
The lofty Tow'rs of wide-extended Troy.
For now no more the Gods with Fate contend,
At Juno's Suit the Heav'nly Factions end.
Destruction hangs o'er yon' devoted Wall,
And nodding Ilion waits th' impending Fall.
   Swift as the Word the vain Illusion fled,
Descends and hovers o'er Atrides' Head;   20
Cloath'd in the Figure of the Pylian Sage,
Renown'd for Wisdom, and rever'd for Age;
Around his Temples spreads his golden Wing,
And thus the flatt'ring Dream deceives the King.
   Canst thou, with all a Monarch's Cares opprest,
Oh Atreus' Son! canst thou indulge thy Rest?
Ill fits a Chief who mighty Nations guides,
Directs in Council, and in War presides,
To whom its Safety a whole People owes,
To waste long Nights in indolent Repose?   30
Monarch awake! 'tis Jove's Command I bear,
Thou, and thy Glory, claim his heav'nly Care.
In just Array draw forth th' embattel'd Train,
Lead all thy Grecians to the dusty Plain;
Ev'n now, O King! 'tis giv'n thee to destroy
The lofty Tow'rs of wide-extended Troy.
For now no more the Gods with Fate contend,
At Juno's Suit the Heav'nly Factions end.
Destruction hangs o'er yon' devoted Wall,
And nodding Ilion waits th' impending Fall.   40
Awake, but waking this Advice approve,
And trust the Vision that descends from Jove.
   The Phantome said; then, vanish'd from his sight,
Resolves to Air, and mixes with the Night.

A thousand Schemes the Monarch's Mind employ;
Elate in Thought, he sacks untaken Troy:
Vain as he was, and to the Future blind;
Nor saw what Jove and secret Fate design'd,
What mighty Toils to either Host remain,
What Scenes of Grief and Mountains of the Slain!　　50
Eager he rises, and in Fancy hears
The Voice Celestial murm'ring in his Ears.
First on his Limbs a slender Vest he drew,
Around him next the Regal Mantle threw,
Th' embroider'd Sandals on his Feet were ty'd,
The starry Faulchion glitter'd at his side;
And last his Arm the massy Sceptre loads,
Unstain'd, immortal, and the Gift of Gods.
　　Now rosie Morn ascends the Court of Jove,
Lifts up her Light, and opens Day above.　　60
The King dispatch'd his Heralds with Commands
To range the Camp, and summon all the Bands:
The gath'ring Hosts the Monarch's Word obey;
While to the Fleet Atrides bends his way.
In his black Ship the Pylian Prince he found,
There calls a Senate of the Peers around.
Th' Assembly plac'd, the King of Men exprest
The Counsels lab'ring in his artful Breast.
　　Friends and Confed'rates! with attentive Ear
Receive my Words, and credit what you hear.　　70
Late as I slumber'd in the Shades of Night,
A Dream Divine appear'd before my Sight;
Whose Visionary Form like Nestor came,
The same in Habit, and in Mien the same.
The heav'nly Phantome hover'd o'er my Head,
And, Dost thou sleep, Oh Atreus' Son? (he said)
Ill suits a Chief who mighty Nations guides,
Directs in Council and in War presides,
To whom its Safety a whole People owes;
To waste long Nights in indolent Repose.　　80
Monarch awake! 'tis Jove's Command I bear,
Thou and thy Glory claim his heav'nly Care;
In just Array draw forth th' embattel'd Train,
And lead the Grecians to the dusty Plain;

Ev'n now, O King! 'tis giv'n thee to destroy
The lofty Tow'rs of wide-extended Troy.
For now no more the Gods with Fate contend,
At Juno's Suit the Heav'nly Factions end.
Destruction hangs o'er yon' devoted Wall,
And nodding Ilion waits th' impending Fall.   90
This hear observant, and the Gods obey!
The Vision spoke, and past in Air away.
Now, valiant Chiefs! since Heav'n itself alarms,
Unite, and rouze the Sons of Greece to Arms.
But first, with Caution, try what yet they dare,
Worn with nine Years of unsuccessful War?
To move the Troops to measure back the Main,
Be mine; and yours the Province to detain.
    He spoke, and sate; when Nestor rising said,
(Nestor, whom Pylos' sandy Realms obey'd)   100
Princes of Greece, your faithful Ears incline,
Nor doubt the Vision of the Pow'rs Divine;
Sent by great Jove to him who rules the Host,
Forbid it Heav'n! this Warning should be lost!
Then let us haste, obey the Gods Alarms,
And join to rouze the Sons of Greece to Arms.
    Thus spoke the Sage: The Kings without Delay
Dissolve the Council, and their Chief obey:
The sceptred Rulers lead; the following Host
Pour'd forth in Millions, darkens all the Coast.   110
As from some Rocky Cleft the Shepherd sees
Clust'ring in Heaps on Heaps the driving Bees,
Rolling, and black'ning, Swarms succeeding Swarms,
With deeper Murmurs and more hoarse Alarms;
Dusky they spread, a close-embody'd Crowd,
And o'er the Vale descends the living Cloud.
So, from the Tents and Ships, a length'ning Train
Spreads all the Beach, and wide o'ershades the Plain:
Along the Region runs a deaf'ning Sound;
Beneath their Footsteps groans the trembling Ground.   120
Fame flies before, the Messenger of Jove,
And shining soars and claps her Wings above.

Nine sacred Heralds now proclaiming loud
The Monarch's Will, suspend[1] the list'ning Crowd.
Soon as the Throngs in Order rang'd appear,
And fainter Murmurs dy'd upon the Ear,
The King of Kings his awful Figure rais'd;
High in his Hand the Golden Sceptre blaz'd:
The Golden Sceptre, of Celestial Frame,
By Vulcan form'd, from Jove to Hermes came: 130
To Pelops He th' immortal Gift resign'd;
Th' immortal Gift great Pelops left behind,
In Atreus' Hand; which not with Atreus ends,
To rich Thyestes next the Prize descends;
And now the Mark of Agamemnon's Reign,
Subjects all Argos, and controuls the Main.
   On this bright Sceptre now the King reclin'd,
And artful thus pronounc'd the Speech design'd.
Ye Sons of Mars, partake your Leader's Care,
Heroes of Greece, and Brothers of the War!   140
Of partial Jove with Justice I complain,
And Heav'nly Oracles believ'd in vain.
A safe Return was promis'd to our Toils,
Renown'd, triumphant, and enrich'd with Spoils.
Now shameful Flight alone can save the Host,
Our Blood, our Treasure, and our Glory lost.
So Jove decrees, resistless Lord of All!
At whose Command whole Empires rise or fall:
He shakes the feeble Props of human Trust,
And Towns and Armies humbles to the Dust.   150
What Shame to Greece a fruitless War to wage,
Oh lasting Shame in ev'ry future Age!
Once great in Arms, the common Scorn we grow,
Repuls'd and baffled by a feeble Foe.
So small their Number, that if Wars were ceas'd,
And Greece triumphant held a gen'ral Feast,
All rank'd by Tens; whole Decads when they dine
Must want a Trojan Slave to pour the Wine.
But other Forces have our Hopes o'erthrown,
And Troy prevails by Armies not her own.   160

[1] Check their noise, compelling them to listen

Now nine long Years of mighty Jove are run,
Since first the Labours of this War begun:
Our Cordage torn, decay'd our Vessels lie,
And scarce ensure the wretched Pow'r to fly.
Haste then, for ever leave the Trojan Wall!
Our weeping Wives, our tender Children call:
Love, Duty, Safety, summon us away,
'Tis Nature's Voice, and Nature we obey.
Our shatter'd Barks may yet transport us o'er,
Safe and inglorious, to our native Shore.   170
Fly, Grecians fly, your Sails and Oars employ,
And dream no more of Heav'n-defended Troy.

His deep Design unknown, the Hosts approve
Atrides' Speech. The mighty Numbers move.
So roll the Billows to th' Icarian Shore,
From East and South when Winds begin to roar,
Burst their dark Mansions in the Clouds, and sweep
The whitening Surface of the ruffled Deep.
And as on Corn when Western Gusts descend,
Before the blast the lofty Harvests bend: 180
Thus o'er the Field the moving host appears,
With nodding Plumes and Groves of waving Spears.
The gath'ring Murmur spreads; their trampling Feet
Beat the loose Sands, and thicken to the Fleet.
With long-resounding Cries they urge the Train,
To fit the Ships, and launch into the Main.
They toil, they sweat, thick Clouds of Dust arise,
The doubling Clamours eccho to the Skies.
Ev'n then the Greeks had left the hostile Plain,
And Fate decreed the Fall of Troy in vain;   190
But Jove's Imperial Queen their Flight survey'd,
And sighing thus bespoke the blue-ey'd Maid.

Shall then the Grecians fly? Oh dire Disgrace!
And leave unpunish'd this perfidious Race?
Shall Troy, shall Priam, and th' Adult'rous Spouse,
In Peace enjoy the Fruits of broken Vows?
And bravest Chiefs, in Helen's Quarrel slain,
Lie unreveng'd on yon' detested Plain?
No—let my Greeks, unmov'd by vain Alarms,
Once more refulgent shine in Brazen Arms.   200

Haste, Goddess, haste! the flying Host detain,
Nor let one Sail be hoisted on the Main.
   Pallas obeys, and from Olympus' Height
Swift to the Ships precipitates her Flight;
Ulysses, first in publick Cares, she found,
For prudent Counsel like the Gods renown'd:
Oppress'd with gen'rous Grief the Heroe stood,
Nor drew his sable Vessels to the Flood.
And is it thus, divine Laertes' Son!
Thus fly the Greeks (the Martial Maid begun)   210
Thus to their Country bear their own Disgrace,
And Fame eternal leave to Priam's Race?
Shall beauteous Helen still remain unfreed,
Still unreveng'd a thousand Heroes bleed?
Haste gen'rous Ithacus! prevent the Shame,
Recall your Armies, and your Chiefs reclaim.
Your own resistless Eloquence employ,
And to th' Immortals trust the Fall of Troy.
   The Voice Divine confess'd the Warlike Maid,
Ulysses heard, nor uninspir'd obey'd.   220
Then meeting first Atrides, from his Hand
Receiv'd th' Imperial Sceptre of Command,
Thus grac'd, Attention and Respect to gain,
He runs, he flies, thro' all the Grecian Train,
Each Prince of Name, or Chief in Arms approv'd,
He fir'd with Praise or with Persuasion mov'd.
   Warriors like you, with Strength and Wisdom blest,
By brave examples should confirm the rest.
The Monarch's Will not yet reveal'd appears;
He tries our Courage, but resents our Fears.   230
Th' unwary Greeks his Fury may provoke;
Not thus the King in secret Council spoke.
Jove loves our Chief, from Jove his Honour springs;
Beware! for dreadful is the Wrath of Kings.
   But if a clam'rous vile Plebeian rose,
Him with Reproof he check'd, or tam'd with Blows.
Be still thou Slave! and to thy Betters yield;
Unknown alike in Council and in Field!
Ye Gods, what Dastards would our Host command?
Swept to the War, the Lumber of a Land.   240

Be silent Wretch, and think not here allow'd
That worst of Tyrants, an usurping Crowd.
To One sole Monarch Jove commits the Sway;
His are the Laws, and Him let all obey.
  With Words like these the Troops Ulysses rul'd,
The loudest silenc'd, and the fiercest cool'd.
Back to th' Assembly roll the thronging Train,
Desert the Ships, and pour upon the Plain.
Murm'ring they move, as when old Ocean roars,
And heaves huge Surges to the trembling Shores: 250
The groaning Banks are burst with bellowing Sound,
The Rocks remurmur, and the Deeps rebound.
At length the Tumult sinks, the Noises cease,
And a still Silence lulls the Camp to Peace.
  Thersites only clamour'd in the Throng,
Loquacious, loud, and turbulent of Tongue:
Aw'd by no Shame, by no Respect controuled,
In Scandal busie, in Reproaches bold:
With witty Malice, studious to defame,
Scorn all his Joy, and Laughter all his Aim.   260
But chief he glory'd with licentious Style
To lash the Great, and Monarchs to revile.
His Figure such as might his Soul proclaim;
One Eye was blinking, and one leg was lame:
His Mountain-Shoulders half his Breast o'erspread,
Thin Hairs bestrew'd his long mis-shapen Head.
Spleen to Mankind his envious Heart possest,
And much he hated All, but most the Best.
Ulysses or Achilles still his Theme;
But Royal Scandal his Delight supreme.   270
Long had he liv'd the Scorn of ev'ry Greek,
Vext when he spoke, yet still they heard him speak.
Sharp was his Voice; which in the shrillest Tone,
Thus with injurious Taunts attack'd the Throne.
  Amidst the Glories of so bright a Reign,
What moves the great Atrides to complain?
'Tis thine whate'er the Warrior's Breast inflames,
The golden Spoil, and thine the lovely Dames.
With all the Wealth our Wars and Blood bestow,
Thy Tents are crowded, and thy Chests o'erflow.   280

Thus at full Ease in Heaps of Riches roll'd,
What grieves the Monarch? Is it Thirst of Gold?
Say shall we march with our unconquer'd Pow'rs,
(The Greeks and I) to Ilion's hostile Tow'rs,
And bring the Race of Royal Bastards here,
For Troy to ransom at a Price too dear?
But safer Plunder thy own Host supplies;
Say would'st thou seize some valiant Leader's Prize?
Or, if thy Heart to gen'rous Love be led,
Some Captive Fair, to bless thy Kingly Bed?   290
Whate'er our Master craves, submit we must,
Plagu'd with his Pride, or punish'd for his Lust.
Oh Women of Achaia! Men no more!
Hence let us fly, and let him waste his Store
In Loves and Pleasures on the Phrygian Shore.
We may be wanted on some busie Day,
When Hector comes: So great Achilles may:
From him he forc'd the Prize we jointly gave,
From him, the fierce, the fearless, and the brave:
And durst he, as he ought, resent that Wrong,   300
This mighty Tyrant were no Tyrant long.

   Fierce from his Seat, at this, Ulysses springs,
In gen'rous Vengeance of the King of Kings.
With Indignation sparkling in his Eyes,
He views the Wretch, and sternly thus replies.
Peace, factious Monster, born to vex the State,
With wrangling Talents form'd for foul Debate:
Curb that impetuous Tongue, nor rashly vain
And singly mad, asperse the Sov'reign Reign.
Have we not known thee, Slave! of all our Host,   310
The Man who acts the least, upbraids the most?
Think not the Greeks to shameful Flight to bring,
Nor let those Lips profane the Name of King.
For our Return we trust the heav'nly Pow'rs;
Be that their Care; to fight like Men be ours.
But grant the Host with Wealth the Gen'ral load,
Except Detraction, what hast thou bestow'd?
Suppose some Hero should his Spoils resign,
Art thou that Hero, could those Spoils be thine?

Gods! let me perish on this hateful Shore,   320
And let these Eyes behold my Son no more;
If, on thy next Offence, this Hand forbear
To strip those Arms thou ill deserv'st to wear,
Expell the Council where our Princes meet,
And send thee scourg'd, and howling thro' the Fleet.

He said, and cow'ring as the Dastard bends,
The weighty Sceptre on his Back descends:
On the round Bunch the bloody Tumors rise;
The Tears spring starting from his haggard Eyes:
Trembling he sate, and shrunk in abject Fears,   330
From his vile Visage wip'd the scalding Tears.
While to his Neighbour each express'd his Thought;
Ye Gods! what Wonders has Ulysses wrought?
What Fruits his Conduct and his Courage yield?
Great in the Council, glorious in the Field.
Gen'rous he rises in the Crown's Defence,
To curb the factious Tongue of Insolence.
Such just Examples on Offenders shown,
Sedition silence, and assert[2] the Throne.

'Twas thus the gen'ral Voice the Heroe prais'd,   340
Who rising, high th' Imperial Sceptre rais'd:
The blue-ey'd Pallas, his Celestial Friend,
(In Form a Herald) bade the Crowds attend.
Th' expecting Crowds in still Attention hung,
To hear the Wisdom of his heav'nly Tongue.
Then deeply thoughtful, pausing e're he spoke,
His Silence thus the prudent Hero broke.

Unhappy Monarch! whom the Grecian Race
With Shame deserting, heap with vile Disgrace.
Not such at Argos was their gen'rous Vow,   350
Once all their Voice, but ah! forgotten now:
Ne'er to return, was then the common Cry,
'Till Troy's proud Structures shou'd in Ashes lie.
Behold them weeping for their native Shore!
What cou'd their Wives or helpless Children more?
What Heart but melts to leave the tender Train,
And, one short Month, endure the Wintry Main?

[2] Protect

Few Leagues remov'd, we wish our peaceful Seat,
When the Ship tosses, and the Tempests beat:
Then well may this long Stay provoke their Tears,   360
The tedious Length of nine revolving Years.
Not for their Grief the Grecian Host I blame;
But vanquish'd! baffled! oh eternal Shame!
Expect[3] the Time to Troy's Destruction giv'n,
And try the Faith of Calchas and of Heav'n.
What past at Aulis, Greece can witness bear,
And all who live to breathe this Phrygian Air.
Beside a Fountain's sacred Brink we rais'd
Our verdant Altars, and the Victims blaz'd;
('Twas where the Plane-tree spread its Shades around)   370
The Altars heav'd; and from the crumbling Ground
A mighty Dragon shot, of dire Portent;
From Jove himself the dreadful Sign was sent.
Strait to the Tree his sanguine Spires he roll'd,
And curl'd around in many a winding Fold.
The Topmost Branch a Mother-Bird possest;
Eight callow Infants fill'd the mossie Nest;
Herself the ninth: The Serpent as he hung,
Stretch'd his black Jaws, and crash'd the crying Young;
While hov'ring near, with miserable Moan,   380
The drooping Mother wail'd her Children gone.
The Mother last, as round the Nest she flew,
Seiz'd by the beating Wing, the Monster slew:
Nor long surviv'd; to Marble turn'd he stands
A lasting Prodigy on Aulis' Sands.
Such was the Will of Jove; and hence we dare
Trust in his Omen, and support the War.
For while around we gaz'd with wondring Eyes,
And trembling sought the Pow'rs with Sacrifice,
Full of his God, the rev'rend Calchas cry'd,   390
Ye Grecian Warriors! lay your Fears aside.
This wondrous Signal Jove himself displays,
Of long, long Labours, but Eternal Praise.
As many Birds as by the Snake were slain,
So many Years the Toils of Greece remain;

[3] Wait for

But wait the Tenth, for Ilion's Fall decreed:
Thus spoke the Prophet, thus the Fates succeed.[4]
Obey, ye Grecians! with Submission wait,
Nor let your flight avert the Trojan Fate.
  He said: the Shores with loud Applauses sound,   400
The hollow Ships each deaf'ning Shout rebound.
Then Nestor thus—These vain Debates forbear,
Ye talk like Children, not like Heroes dare.
Where now are all your high Resolves at last,
Your Leagues concluded, your Engagements past?
Vow'd with Libations and with Victims then,
Now vanish'd like their Smoke: The Faith of Men!
While useless Words consume th' unactive Hours,
No wonder Troy so long resists our Pow'rs.
Rise, great Atrides! and with Courage sway;   410
We march to War if thou direct the Way.
But leave the few that dare resist thy Laws,
The mean Deserters of the Grecian Cause,
To grudge the Conquests mighty Jove prepares,
And view, with Envy, our successful Wars.
On that great Day when first the martial Train
Big with the Fate of Ilion, plow'd the Main,
Jove, on the Right, a prosp'rous Signal sent,
And Thunder rolling shook the Firmament.
Encourag'd hence, maintain the glorious Strife   420
'Till ev'ry Soldier grasp a Phrygian Wife,
'Till Helen's Woes at full reveng'd appear,
And Troy's proud Matrons render Tear for Tear.
Before that Day, if any Greek invite
His Country's Troops to base, inglorious Flight,
Stand forth that Greek! and hoist his Sail to fly;
And dye the Dastard first, who dreads to dye.
But now, O Monarch! all thy Chiefs advise:
Nor what they offer, thou thy self despise.   430
Among those Counsels, let not mine be vain;
In Tribes and Nations to divide thy Train:
His sep'rate Troops let ev'ry Leader call,
Each strengthen each, and all encourage all.

[4] Follow, come to pass

What Chief, or Soldier, of the num'rous Band,
Or bravely fights, or ill obeys Command,
When thus distinct they war, shall soon be known,
And what the Cause of Ilion not o'erthrown?
If Fate resists, or if our Arms are slow,
If Gods above prevent, or Men below?   440
   To him the King: How much thy Years excell,
In Arts of Council, and in speaking well!
Oh would the Gods, in Love to Greece, decree
But ten such Sages as they grant in thee;
Such Wisdom soon should Priam's Force destroy,
And soon should fall the haughty Tow'rs of Troy!
But Jove forbids, who plunges those he hates
In fierce Contention and in vain Debates.
Now great Achilles from our Aid withdraws,
By me provok'd; a Captive Maid the Cause:
If e'er as Friends we join, the Trojan Wall   450
Must shake, and heavy will the Vengeance fall!
But now, ye Warriors, take a short Repast;
And, well refresh'd, to bloody Conflict haste.
His sharpen'd Spear let ev'ry Grecian wield,
And ev'ry Grecian fix his Brazen Shield,
Let all excite the fiery Steeds of War,
And all for Combate fit the ratling Car.
This Day, this dreadful Day, let each contend;
No rest, no Respite, 'till the Shades descend;
'Till Darkness, or 'till Death shall cover all: 460
Let the War bleed, and let the Mighty fall!
'Till bath'd in Sweat be ev'ry manly Breast,
With the huge Shield each brawny Arm deprest,
Each aking Nerve refuse the Lance to throw,
And each spent Courser at the Chariot blow.
Who dares, inglorious, in his Ships to stay,
Who dares to tremble on this signal Day,
That Wretch, too mean to fall by martial Pow'r,
The Birds shall mangle, and the Dogs devour.
   The Monarch spoke: and strait a Murmur rose,   470
Loud as the Surges when the Tempest blows,
That dash'd on broken Rocks tumultuous roar,
And foam and thunder on the stony Shore.

Strait to the Tents the Troops dispersing bend,
The Fires are kindled, and the Smokes ascend;
With hasty Feasts they sacrifice, and pray
T'avert the Dangers of the doubtful Day.
A Steer of five Year's Age, large limb'd, and fed,
To Jove's high Altars Agamemnon led:
There bade the noblest of the Grecian Peers;   480
And Nestor first, as most advanc'd in Years.
Next came Idomeneus and Tydeus' Son,
Ajax the less, and Ajax Telamon;
Then wise Ulysses in his Rank was plac'd;
And Menelaus came unbid, the last.
The Chiefs surround the destin'd Beast, and take
The sacred Off'ring of the salted Cake:
When thus the King prefers his solemn Pray'r.
Oh Thou! whose Thunder rends the clouded Air,
Who in the Heav'n of Heav'ns hast fix'd thy Throne,   490
Supreme of Gods! unbounded, and alone!
Hear! and before the burning Sun descends,
Before the Night her gloomy Veil extends,
Low in the Dust be laid yon' hostile Spires,
Be Priam's Palace sunk in Grecian Fires,
In Hector's Breast be plung'd this shining Sword,
And slaughter'd Heroes groan around their Lord!
    Thus pray'd the Chief: His unavailing Pray'r
Great Jove refus'd, and tost in empty Air:
The God averse, while yet the Fumes arose,   500
Prepar'd new Toils and doubled Woes on Woes.
Their Pray'rs perform'd, the Chiefs the Rite pursue,
The Barley sprinkled, and the Victim slew.
The Limbs they sever from th' inclosing Hyde,
The Thighs, selected to the Gods, divide.
On these, in double Cauls involv'd with Art,
The choicest Morsels lie from ev'ry Part.
From the cleft Wood the crackling Flames aspire,
While the fat Victim feeds the sacred Fire.
The Thighs thus sacrific'd and Entrails drest,   510
Th' Assistants part, transfix, and roast the rest;
Then spread the Tables, the Repast prepare,
Each takes his Seat, and each receives his Share.

Soon as the Rage of Hunger was supprest,
The gen'rous Nestor thus the Prince addrest.
Now bid thy Heralds sound the loud Alarms,
And call the Squadrons sheath'd in Brazen Arms:
Now seize th' Occasion, now the Troops survey,
And lead to War, when Heav'n directs the Way.
He said; the Monarch issu'd his Commands;   520
Strait the loud Heralds call the gath'ring Bands.
The Chiefs inclose their King; the Hosts divide,
In Tribes and Nations rank'd on either side.
High in the midst the blue-ey'd Virgin[5] flies;
From Rank to Rank she darts her ardent Eyes:
The dreadful Ægis, Jove's immortal Shield,
Blaz'd on her Arm, and lighten'd all the Field:
Round the vast Orb an hundred Serpents roll'd,
Form'd the bright Fringe, and seem'd to burn in Gold.
With this, each Grecian's manly Breast she warms,   530
Swells their bold Hearts, and strings their nervous[6] Arms;
No more they sigh, inglorious to return,
But breathe Revenge, and for the Combate burn.
As on some Mountain, thro' the lofty Grove
The crackling Flames ascend and blaze above,
The Fires expanding as the Winds arise,
Shoot their long Beams, and kindle half the Skies:
So from the polish'd Arms, and brazen Shields,
A gleamy Splendor flash'd along the Fields.
Not less their Number, than th' embody'd Cranes,   540
Or milk-white Swans in Asius' watry Plains,
That o'er the Windings of Cayster's Springs,
Stretch their long Necks, and clap their rustling Wings,
Now tow'r aloft, and course in airy Rounds;
Now light with Noise; with Noise the Field resounds.
Thus num'rous and confus'd, extending wide,
The Legions crowd Scamander's flow'ry Side,
With rushing Troops the Plains are cover'd o'er,
And thund'ring Footsteps shake the sounding Shore:
Along the River's level Meads they stand,   550
Thick as in Spring the Flow'rs adorn the Land,

[5] Minerva, Pallas
[6] Strong, from *nerve*, muscle

Or Leaves the Trees; or thick as Insects play,
The wandring Nation of a Summer's Day,
That drawn by milky Steams, at Ev'ning Hours,
In gather'd Swarms surround the Rural Bow'rs;
From Pail to Pail with busie Murmur run
The gilded Legions glitt'ring in the Sun.
So throng'd, so close, the Grecian Squadrons stood
In radiant Arms, and thirst for Trojan Blood.
Each Leader now his scatter'd Force conjoins   560
In close Array, and forms the deep'ning Lines.
Not with more Ease, the skilful Shepherd Swain
Collects his Flock from Millions on the Plain.
The King of Kings, majestically tall,
Tow'rs o'er his Armies, and outshines them all:
Like some proud Bull that round the Pastures leads
His Subject-Herds, the Monarch of the Meads.
Great as the Gods th' exalted Chief was seen,
His Strength like Neptune, and like Mars his Mien,
Jove o'er his Eyes celestial Glories spread,   570
And dawning Conquest play'd around his Head.
   Say, Virgins, seated round the Throne Divine,
All-knowing Goddesses! immortal Nine!
Since Earth's wide Regions, Heav'n's unmeasur'd Height,
And Hell's Abyss hide nothing from your sight,
(We, wretched Mortals! lost in Doubts below,
But guess by Rumour, and but boast we know)
Oh say what Heroes, fir'd by Thirst of Fame,
Or urg'd by Wrongs, to Troy's Destruction came?
To count them all, demands a thousand Tongues,   580
A Throat of Brass, and Adamantine Lungs.
Daughters of Jove assist! inspir'd by You
The mighty Labour dauntless I pursue:
What crowded Armies, from what Climes they bring,
Their Names, their Numbers, and their Chiefs I sing.

THE CATALOGUE OF THE SHIPS

The hardy Warriors whom Bœotia bred,
Peneleus, Leitus, Prothoënor led:

With these Arcesilaus and Clonius stand,
Equal in Arms, and equal in Command.
These head the Troops that Rocky Aulis yields,   590
And Eteon's Hills, and Hyrie's watry Fields,
And Schœnos, Scolos, Græa near the Main,
And Mycalessia's ample Piny Plain.
Those who in Peteon or Ilesion dwell,
Or Harma where Apollo's Prophet fell;
Heleon and Hylè, which the Springs o'erflow;
And Medeon lofty, and Ocalea low;
Or in the Meads of Haliartus stray,
Or Thespia sacred to the God of Day.
Onchestus, Neptune's celebrated Groves;   600
Copæ, and Thisbè, fam'd for silver Doves,
For Flocks Erythræ, Glissa for the Vine;
Platæa green, and Nisa the divine.
And they whom Thebè's well-built Walls inclose,
Where Mydè, Eutresis, Coronè rose;
And Arnè rich, with purple Harvests crown'd;
And Anthedon, Bœotia's utmost Bound.
Full fifty Ships they send, and each conveys
Twice sixty Warriors thro' the foaming Seas.
   To these succeed Aspledon's martial Train,   610
Who plow the spacious Orchomenian Plain.
Two valiant Brothers rule th' undaunted Throng,
Iälmen and Ascalaphus the strong:
Sons of Astyochè the Heav'nly Fair,
Whose Virgin Charms subdu'd the God of War:
(In Actor's Court as she retir'd to Rest,
The Strength of Mars the blushing Maid comprest)
Their Troops in thirty sable Vessels sweep
With equal Oars, the hoarse-resounding Deep.
   The Phocians next in forty Barks repair,   620
Epistrophus and Schedius head the War.
From those rich Regions where Cephisus leads
His silver Current thro' the flow'ry Meads;
From Panopëa, Chrysa the Divine,
Where Anemoria's stately Turrets shine,
Where Pytho, Daulis, Cyparissus stood,
And fair Lilæa views the rising Flood.

These rang'd in Order on the floating Tide,
Close, on the left, the bold Bœotians side.
  Fierce Ajax led the Locrian Squadrons on,   630
Ajax the less, Oïleus' valiant Son;
Skill'd to direct the flying Dart aright;
Swift in Pursuit, and active in the Fight.
Him, as their Chief, the chosen Troops attend,
Which Bessa, Thronus, and rich Cynos send:
Opus, Calliarus, and Scarphe's Bands;
And those who dwell where pleasing Augia stands,
And where Boägrius floats the lowly Lands,
Or in fair Tarphe's Sylvan Seats reside;
In forty Vessels cut the yielding Tide.   640
  Eubœa next her martial Sons prepares,
And sends the brave Abantes to the Wars:
Breathing Revenge, in Arms they take their Way
From Chalcis' Walls, and strong Eretria;
Th' Isteian Fields for gen'rous Vines renown'd,
The fair Carystos, and the Styrian Ground;
Where Dios from her Tow'rs o'erlooks the Plain,
And high Cerinthus views the neighb'ring Main.
Down their broad Shoulders falls a Length of Hair;
Their Hands dismiss not the long Lance in Air;   650
But with protended Spears in fighting Fields,
Pierce the tough Cors'lets and the brazen Shields.
Twice twenty Ships transport the warlike Bands,
Which bold Elphenor, fierce in Arms, commands.
  Full fifty more from Athens stem the Main,
Led by Menestheus thro' the liquid Plain,
(Athens the fair, where great Erectheus sway'd,
That ow'd his Nurture to the blue-ey'd Maid,
But from the teeming Furrow took his Birth,
The mighty Offspring of the foodful Earth.   660
Him Pallas plac'd amidst her wealthy Fane,
Ador'd with Sacrifice and Oxen slain;
Where as the Years revolve, her Altars blaze,
And all the Tribes resound the Goddess' Praise.)
No Chief like thee, Menestheus! Greece could yield,
To marshal Armies in the dusty Field,

Th' extended Wings of Battel to display,
Or close th' embody'd Host in firm Array.
Nestor alone, improv'd by Length of Days,
For martial Conduct bore an equal Praise.   670
  With these appear the Salaminian Bands,
Whom the Gigantic Telamon commands;
In twelve black Ships to Troy they steer their Course,
And with the great Athenians join their Force.
  Next move to War the gen'rous Argive Train,
From high Trœzenè, and Maseta's Plain,
And fair Ægina circled by the Main:
Whom strong Tyrinthè's lofty Walls surround,
And Epidaure with Viny Harvests crown'd:
And where fair Asinen and Hermion show   680
Their Cliffs above, and ample Bay below.
These by the brave Euryalus were led,
Great Sthenelus, and greater Diomed,
But chief Tydides bore the Sov'reign Sway;
In fourscore Barks they plow the watry Way.
  The proud Mycœnè arms her martial Pow'rs,
Cleonè, Corinth, with Imperial Tow'rs,
Fair Arethyrea, Ornia's fruitful Plain,
And Ægion, and Adrastus' ancient Reign;
And those who dwell along the sandy Shore,   690
And where Pellenè yields her fleecy Store,
Where Helicè and Hyperesia lie,
And Gonoëssa's Spires salute the Sky.
Great Agamemnon rules the num'rous Band,
A hundred Vessels in long Order stand,
And crowded Nations wait his dread Command.
High on the Deck the King of Men appears,
And his refulgent Arms in Triumph wears;
Proud of his Host, unrival'd in his Reign,
In silent Pomp he moves along the Main.   700
  His Brother follows, and to Vengeance warms
The hardy Spartans, exercis'd in Arms:
Phares and Brysia's valiant Troops, and those
Whom Lacedæmon's lofty Hills inclose:
Or Messè's Tow'rs for silver Doves renown'd,
Amyclæ, Laäs, Augia's happy Ground,

And those whom Œtylos' low Walls contain,
And Helos, on the Margin of the Main.
These, o'er the bending Ocean, Helen's Cause
In sixty Ships with Menelaus draws: 710
Eager and loud, from Man to Man he flies,
Revenge and Fury flaming in his Eyes;
While vainly fond, in Fancy oft he hears
The Fair one's Grief, and sees her falling Tears.

  In ninety Sail, from Pylos' sandy Coast,
Nestor the Sage conducts his chosen Host:
From Amphigenia's ever-fruitful Land;
Where Æpy high, and little Pteleon stand;
Where beauteous Arenè her Structures shows,
And Thryon's Walls Alphëus' Streams inclose: 720
And Dorion, fam'd for Thamyris' Disgrace,
Superior once of all the tuneful Race,
'Till vain of Mortal's empty Praise, he strove
To match the Seed of Cloud-compelling Jove.
Too daring Bard! whose unsuccessful Pride
Th' Immortal Muses in their Art defy'd.
Th' avenging Muses of the Light of Day
Depriv'd his Eyes, and snatch'd his Voice away;
No more his heav'nly Voice was heard to sing;
His Hand no more awak'd the silver String.   730
  Where under high Cyllenè crown'd with Wood,
The shaded Tomb of old Æpytus stood;
From Ripè, Stratie, Tegea's bord'ring Towns,
The Phenean Fields, and Orchomenian Downs,
Where the fat Herds in plenteous Pasture rove;
And Stymphelus with her surrounding Grove;
Parrhasia, on her snowy Cliffs reclin'd,
And high Enispè shook by wintry Wind,
And fair Mantinea's ever-pleasing Site;
In sixty Sail th' Arcadian Bands unite.   740
Bold Agapenor glorious at their Head,
(Ancœus' Son) the mighty Squadron led.
Their Ships, supply'd by Agamemnon's Care,
Thro' roaring Seas the wond'ring Warriors bear;
The first to battel on th' appointed Plain,
But new to all the Dangers of the Main.

Those, where fair Elis and Buprasium join;
Whom Hyrmin, here, and Myrsinus confine,
And bounded there, where o'er the Vallies rose
Th' Olenian Rock; and where Alisium flows;   750
Beneath four Chiefs (a num'rous Army) came:
The Strength and Glory of th' Epean Name.
In sep'rate Squadrons these their Train divide,
Each leads ten Vessels thro' the yielding Tide.
One was Amphimachus, and Thalpius one;
(Eurytus' this, and that Teätus' Son)
Diores sprung from Amarynceus' Line;
And great Polyxenus, of Force divine.
But those who view fair Elis o'er the Seas
From the blest Islands of th' Echinades,   760
In forty Vessels under Meges move,
Begot by Phyleus, the Belov'd of Jove.
To strong Dulichium from his Sire he fled,
And thence to Troy his hardy Warriors led.
Ulysses follow'd thro' the watry Road,
A Chief, in Wisdom equal to a God.
With those whom Cephalenia's Isle inclos'd,
Or till'd their Fields along the Coast oppos'd;
Or where fair Ithaca o'erlooks the Floods,
Where high Neritos shakes his waving Woods,   770
Where Ægilipa's rugged Sides are seen,
Crocylia rocky, and Zacynthus green.
These in twelve Galleys with Vermillion Prores,
Beneath his Conduct sought the Phrygian Shores.
Thoas came next, Andræmon's valiant Son,
From Pleuron's Walls and chalky Calydon,
And rough Pylenè, and th' Olenian Steep,
And Chalcis, beaten by the rolling Deep.
He led the Warriors from th' Ætolian Shore,
For now the Sons of Oeneus were no more!   780
The Glories of the mighty Race were fled!
Oeneus himself, and Meleager dead;
To Thoas' Care now trust the martial Train,
His forty Vessels follow thro' the Main.
Next eighty Barks the Cretan King commands,
Of Gnossus, Lyctus, and Gortyna's Bands,

And those who dwell where Rhytion's Domes arise,
Or white Lycastus glitters to the Skies,
Or where by Phœstus silver Jardan runs;
Crete's hundred Cities pour forth all her Sons.   790
These march'd, Idomeneus, beneath thy Care,
And Merion, dreadful as the God of War.

Tlepolemus, the Son of Hercules,
Led nine swift Vessels thro' the foamy Seas;
From Rhodes with everlasting Sunshine bright,
Jalyssus, Lindus, and Camirus white.
His captive Mother fierce Alcides[7] bore
From Ephyr's Walls, and Sellè's winding Shore,
Where mighty Towns in Ruins spread the Plain,
And saw their blooming Warriors early slain.   800
The Hero, when to Manly Years he grew,
Alcides' Uncle, old Lycimnius, slew;
For this, constrain'd to quit his native Place,
And shun the Vengeance of th' Herculean Race,
A Fleet he built, and with a num'rous Train
Of willing Exiles wander'd o'er the Main;
Where many Seas, and many Suff'rings past,
On happy Rhodes the Chief arriv'd at last:
There in three Tribes divides his native Band,
And rules them peaceful in a foreign Land: 810
Encreas'd and prosper'd in their new Abodes,
By mighty Jove, the Sire of Men and Gods;
With Joy they saw the growing Empire rise,
And Show'rs of Wealth descending from the Skies.

Three Ships with Nireus sought the Trojan Shore,
Nireus, whom Agläe to Charopus bore,
Nireus, in faultless Shape, and blooming Grace,
The loveliest Youth of all the Grecian Race;
Pelides only match'd his early Charms;
But few his Troops, and small his Strength in Arms.   820

Next thirty Galleys cleave the liquid Plain,
Of those Calydnœ's Sea-girt Isles contain;
With them the Youth of Nisyrus repair,
Casus the strong, and Crapathus the fair;

7 Hercules

Cos, where Eurypylus possest the Sway,
'Till great Alcides made the Realms obey:
These Antiphus and bold Phidippus bring,
Sprung from the God, by Thessalus the King.

Now Muse recount Pelasgic Argos'[8] Pow'rs,
From Alos, Alopè, and Trechin's Tow'rs;   830
From Pthia's spacious Vales; and Hella, blest
With Female Beauty far beyond the rest.
Full fifty Ships beneath Achilles' Care
Th' Achaians, Myrmidons, Helleneans bear,
Thessalians all, tho' various in their Name,
The same their Nation, and their Chief the same.
But now inglorious, stretch'd along the Shore,
They hear the brazen Voice of War no more;
No more the Foe they face in dire Array;
Close in his Fleet their angry Leader lay: 840
Since fair Briseïs from his Arms was torn,
The noblest Spoil from sack'd Lyrnessus born,
Then, when the Chief the Theban Walls o'erthrew,
And the bold Sons of great Evenus slew.
There mourn'd Achilles, plung'd in Depth of Care,
But soon to rise in Slaughter, Blood, and War.

To these the Youth of Phylacè succeed,
Itona, famous for her fleecy Breed,
And grassy Pteleon deck'd with chearful Greens,
The Bow'rs of Ceres, and the Sylvan Scenes,   850
Sweet Pyrrhasus, with blooming Flourets crown'd,
And Antron's watry Dens and cavern'd Ground.
These own'd as Chief Protesilas the brave,
Who now lay silent in the gloomy Grave:
The first who boldly touch'd the Trojan Shore,
And dy'd a Phrygian Lance with Grecian Gore:
There lies, far distant from his native Plain;
Unfinish'd his proud Palaces remain,
And his sad Consort beats her Breast in vain.
His Troops in forty Ships Podarces led,   860
Iphiclus' Son, and Brother to the Dead;
Nor he unworthy to command the Host;
Yet still they mourn'd their ancient Leader lost.

[8] Part of Achilles' domain, along with places named in lines 830-31

The Men who Glaphyra's fair Soil partake,
Where Hills encircle Bœbe's lowly Lake,
Where Pheræ hears the neighb'ring Waters fall,
Or proud Iölcus lifts her Airy Wall:
In ten black Ships embark'd for Ilion's Shore,
With bold Eumelus, whom Alcestè bore.
All Pelias' Race Alcestè far outshin'd,   870
The Grace and Glory of the beauteous Kind.
The Troops Methonè, or Thaumacia yields,
Olyzon's Rocks, or Mœlibæa's Fields,
With Philoctetes sail'd, whose matchless Art
From the tough Bow directs the feather'd Dart.
Sev'n were his Ships; each Vessel fifty row,
Skill'd in his Science of the Dart and Bow.
But he lay raging on the Lemnian Ground,
A pois'nous Hydra gave the burning Wound,
There groan'd the Chief in agonizing Pain;   880
Whom Greece at length shall wish, nor wish in vain.[9]
His Forces Medon led from Lemnos' Shore,
Oileus' Son whom beauteous Rhena bore.
    Th' Oechalian Race, in those high Tow'rs contain'd,
Where once Eurytus in proud Triumph reign'd,
Or where her humbler Turrets Trica rears,
Or where Ithomè, rough with Rocks, appears;
In thirty Sail the sparkling Waves divide,
Which Podalirius and Machaon guide.
To these his Skill their Parent-God[10] imparts,   890
Divine Professors of the Healing Arts.
    The bold Ormenian and Asterian Bands
In forty Barks Eurypilus commands,
Where Titan hides his hoary Head in Snow,
And where Hyperia's silver Fountains flow.
    Thy Troops, Argissa, Polyphætes leads,
And Eleon, shelter'd by Olympus' Shades,
Girtonè's Warriors; and where Orthè lies,
And Oloösson's Chalky Cliffs arise.
Sprung from Pirithoüs of immortal Race,   900
The Fruit of fair Hippodamè's Embrace,

---

[9] Troy was not to fall without Philoctetes' bow and arrows.
[10] Aesculapius

(That Day, when hurl'd from Pelion's cloudy Head,
To distant Dens the shaggy Centaurs fled)
With Polypætes join'd in equal Sway
Leonteus leads, and forty Ships obey.

  In twenty Sail the bold Perrhebians came
From Cyphus, Guneus was their Leader's Name.
With these the Ænians join'd, and those who freeze
Where cold Dodona lifts her Holy Trees;
Or where the pleasing Titaresius glides,   910
And into Peneus rolls his easy Tides;
Yet o'er the silver Surface pure they flow,
The sacred Stream unmix'd with Streams below,
Sacred and awful! From the dark Abodes
Styx pours them forth, the dreadful Oath of Gods!

  Last under Prothous the Magnesians stood,
Prothous the swift, of old Tenthredon's Blood;
Who dwell where Pelion crown'd with Piny Boughs
Obscures the Glade, and nods his shaggy Brows,
Or where thro' flow'ry Tempè Peneus stray'd,   920
(The Region stretch'd beneath his mighty Shade)
In forty sable Barks they stem'd the Main;
Such were the Chiefs, and such the Grecian Train.

  Say next O Muse! of all Achaïa breeds,
Who bravest fought, or rein'd the noblest Steeds?
Eumelus' Mares were foremost in the Chace,
As Eagles fleet, and of Pheretian Race;
Bred where Pieria's fruitful Fountains flow,
And train'd by Him who bears the Silver Bow.
Fierce in the Fight, their Nostrils breath'd a Flame,   930
Their Height, their Colour, and their Age the same;
O'er Fields of Death they whirl the rapid Car,
And break the Ranks, and thunder thro' the War.
Ajax in Arms the first Renown acquir'd,
While stern Achilles in his Wrath retir'd:
(His was the Strength that mortal Might exceeds,
And his, th' unrival'd Race of Heav'nly Steeds)
But Thetis' Son now shines in Arms no more;
His Troops, neglected on the sandy Shore,
In empty Air their sportive Jav'lins throw,   940
Or whirl the Disk, or bend an idle Bow:

Unstain'd with Blood his cover'd Chariots stand;
Th' Immortal Coursers graze along the Strand;
But the brave Chiefs th' inglorious Life deplor'd,
And wand'ring o'er the Camp, requir'd their Lord.
　　Now, like a Deluge, cov'ring all around,
The shining Armies swept along the Ground;
Swift as a Flood of Fire, when Storms arise,
Floats the wide Field, and blazes to the Skies.
Earth groan'd beneath them; as when angry Jove   950
Hurls down the forky Light'ning from above,
On Arimè when he the Thunder throws,
And fires Typhœus with redoubled Blows,
Where Typhon, prest beneath the burning Load,
Still feels the Fury of th' avenging God.
　　But various Iris, Jove's Commands to bear,
Speeds on the Wings of Winds thro' liquid Air;
In Priam's Porch the Trojan Chiefs she found,
The Old consulting, and the Youths around.
Polites' Shape, the Monarch's Son, she chose,   960
Who from Æsetes' Tomb observ'd the Foes;
High on the Mound; from whence in Prospect lay
The Fields, the Tents, the Navy, and the Bay.
In this dissembled Form, she hasts to bring
Th' unwelcome Message to the Phrygian King.
　　Cease to consult, the Time for Action calls,
War, horrid War, approaches to your Walls!
Assembled Armies oft' have I beheld;
But ne'er 'till now such Numbers charg'd a Field.
Thick as Autumnal Leaves, or driving Sand,   970
The moving Squadrons blacken all the Strand.
Thou, Godlike Hector! all thy Force employ,
Assemble all th' united Bands of Troy;
In just Array let ev'ry Leader call
The foreign Troops: This Day demands them all.
　　The Voice Divine the mighty Chief alarms;
The Council breaks, the Warriors rush to Arms.
The Gates unfolding pour forth all their Train,
Nations on Nations fill the dusky Plain,
Men, Steeds, and Chariots shake the trembling Ground;   980
The Tumult thickens, and the Skies resound.

Amidst the Plain in sight of Ilion stands
A rising Mount the Work of human Hands,
(This for Myrinnè's Tomb th' Immortals know,
Tho' call'd Bateïa in the World below)
Beneath their Chiefs in martial Order here,
Th' Auxiliar Troops and Trojan Hosts appear.

The Godlike Hector, high above the rest,
Shakes his huge Spear, and nods his Plumy Crest:
In Throngs around his native Bands repair,   990
And Groves of Lances glitter in the Air.

Divine Ænëas brings the Dardan Race,
Anchises' Son, by Venus' stol'n Embrace,
Born in the Shades of Ida's secret Grove,
(A Mortal mixing with the Queen of Love)
Archilochus and Achamas divide
The Warrior's Toils, and combate by his side.

Who fair Zeleia's wealthy Vallies till,
Fast by the Foot of Ida's sacred Hill:
Or drink, Æsepus, of thy sable Flood;   1000
Were led by Pandarus, of Royal Blood.
To whom his Art Apollo deign'd to show,
Grac'd with the Present of his Shafts and Bow.

From rich Apæsus and Adrestia's Tow'rs,
High Teree's Summits, and Pityea's Bow'rs;
From these the congregated Troops obey
Young Amphius and Adrastus' equal Sway;
Old Merops Sons; whom skill'd in Fate to come
The Sire forewarn'd, and prophecy'd their Doom:
Fate urg'd them on! the Sire forewarn'd in vain, 1010
They rush'd to War, and perish'd on the Plain.

From Practius' Stream, Percotè's Pasture Lands,
And Sestos and Abydos' neighb'ring Strands,
From great Arisba's Walls and Sellè's Coast,
Asius Hyrtacides conducts his Host:
High on his Car he shakes the flowing Reins,
His fiery Coursers thunder o'er the Plains.

The fierce Pelasgi next, in War renown'd,
March from Larissa's ever-fertile Ground:
In equal Arms their Brother-Leaders shine,   1020
Hippothous bold, and Pyleus the Divine.

Next Acamas and Pyrous lead their Hosts
In dread Array, from Thracia's wintry Coasts;
Round the bleak Realms where Hellespontus roars,
And Boreas beats the hoarse-resounding Shores.
  With great Euphemus the Ciconians move,
Sprung from Trezenian Ceus, lov'd by Jove.
  Pyrechmes the Pœonian Troops attend,
Skill'd in the Fight their crooked Bows to bend;
From Axius' ample Bed he leads them on,   1030
Axius, that laves the distant Amydon,
Axius, that swells with all his neighb'ring Rills,
And wide around the floated Region fills.
  The Paphlagonians Pylæmenes rules,
Where rich Henetia breeds her savage Mules,
Where Erythinus' rising Clifts are seen,
Thy Groves of Box, Cytorus! ever green;
And where Ægyalus and Cromna lie,
And lofty Sesamus invades the Sky;
And where Parthenius, roll'd thro' Banks of Flow'rs,   1040
Reflects her bord'ring Palaces and Bow'rs.
  Here march'd in Arms the Halizonian Band,
Whom Odius and Epistrophus command,
From those far Regions where the Sun refines
The ripening Silver in Alybean Mines.
  There, mighty Chromis led the Mysian Train,
And Augur Ennomus, inspir'd in vain,
For stern Achilles lopt his sacred Head,
Roll'd down Scamander with the Vulgar Dead.
  Phorcys and brave Ascanius here unite   1050
Th' Ascanian Phrygians, eager for the Fight.
  Of those who round Mœonia's Realms reside,
Or whom the Vales in Shade of Tmolus hide,
Mestles and Antiphus the Charge partake;
Born on the Banks of Gyges' silent Lake.
There, from the Fields where wild Mæander flows,
High Mycalè, and Latmos' shady Brows,
And proud Miletus; came the Carian Throngs,
With mingled Clamors, and with barb'rous Tongues.

Amphimachus and Naustes guide the Train, 1060
Naustes the bold, Amphimachus the vain,
Who trick'd with Gold, and glitt'ring on his Car,
Rode like a Woman to the Field of War.
Fool that he was! by fierce Achilles slain,
The River swept him to the briny Main:
There whelm'd with Waves the gawdy Warrior lies;
The valiant Victor seiz'd the golden Prize.
 The Forces last in fair Array succeed,
Which blameless Glaucus and Sarpedon lead;
The warlike Bands that distant Lycia yields, 1070
Where gulphy Xanthus foams along the Fields.

꧁꧂

THE THIRD BOOK
OF THE ILIAD

THE ARGUMENT

The Duel of Menelaus and Paris

THE ARMIES being ready to engage, a single Combate is agreed upon between Menelaus and Paris (by the Intervention of Hector) for the Determination of the War. Iris is sent to call Helena to behold the Fight. She leads her to the Walls of Troy, where Priam sate with his Counsellors observing the Græcian Leaders on the Plain below, to whom Helen gives an Account of the chief of them. The Kings on either Part take the solemn Oath for the Conditions of the Combate. The Duel ensues, wherein Paris being overcome is snatch'd away in a Cloud by Venus, and transported to his Apartment. She then calls Helen from the Walls, and brings the Lovers together. Agamemnon on the Part of the Græcians, demands the Restoration of Helen, and the Performance of the Articles.

The three and twentieth Day still continues throughout this Book. The Scene is sometimes in the Fields before Troy, and sometimes in Troy itself.

Thus by their Leader's Care each martial Band
Moves into Ranks, and stretches o'er the Land.
　With Shouts the Trojans rushing from afar
Proclaim their Motions, and provoke the War[1]:
So when inclement Winters vex the Plain
With piercing Frosts, or thick-descending Rain,
To warmer Seas the Cranes embody'd fly,
With Noise, and Order, thro' the mid-way Sky;

[1] Make known their emotions, and stir up the fighting

To Pygmy-Nations Wounds and Death they bring,
And all the War descends upon the Wing. 10
But silent, breathing Rage, resolv'd, and skill'd
By mutual Aids to fix a doubtful Field,
Swift march the Greeks: the rapid Dust around
Dark'ning arises from the labour'd Ground.
Thus from his flaggy Wings when Notus sheds
A Night of Vapors round the Mountain-Heads,
Swift-gliding Mists the dusky Fields invade,
To Thieves more grateful than the Midnight Shade;
While scarce the Swains their feeding Flocks survey,
Lost and confus'd amidst the thicken'd Day: 20
So wrapt in gath'ring Dust, the Grecian Train
A moving Cloud, swept on, and hid the Plain.
  Now Front to Front the hostile Armies stand,
Eager of Fight, and only wait Command:
When, to the Van, before the Sons of Fame
Whom Troy sent forth, the beauteous Paris came:
In Form a God! the Panther's speckled Hyde
Flow'd o'er his Armour with an easy Pride,
His bended Bow a-cross his Shoulders flung,
His Sword beside him negligently hung, 30
Two pointed Spears he shook with gallant Grace,
And dar'd the Bravest of the Grecian Race.
  As thus with glorious Air and proud Disdain,
He boldly stalk'd, the foremost on the Plain,
Him Menelaus, lov'd of Mars, espies,
With Heart elated, and with joyful Eyes:
So joys a Lion if the branching Deer
Or Mountain Goat, his bulky Prize, appear;
In vain the Youths oppose, the Mastives bay,
The Lordly Savage rends the panting Prey. 40
Thus fond of Vengeance, with a furious Bound,
In clanging Arms he leaps upon the Ground
From his proud Chariot: Him, approaching near,
The beauteous Champion views with Marks of Fear,
Smit with a conscious[2] Sense, retires behind,
And shuns the Fate he well deserv'd to find.

[2] Guilty

As when some Shepherd from the rustling Trees
Shot forth to View, a scaly Serpent sees;
Trembling and pale, he starts with wild Affright,
And all confus'd, precipitates his Flight.   50
So from the King the shining Warrior flies,
And plung'd amid the thickest Trojans lies.
    As Godlike Hector sees the Prince retreat,
He thus upbraids him with a gen'rous Heat.
Unhappy Paris! but to Women brave,
So fairly form'd, and only to deceive!
Oh had'st thou dy'd when first thou saw'st the Light,
Or dy'd at least before thy Nuptial Rite!
A better Fate, than vainly thus to boast,
And fly, the Scandal of thy Trojan Host.   60
Gods! how the scornful Greeks exult to see
Their Fears of Danger undeceiv'd in thee!
Thy Figure promis'd with a martial Air,
But ill thy Soul supplies a Form so fair.
In former Days, in all thy gallant Pride,
When thy tall Ships triumphant stem'd the Tide,
When Greece beheld thy painted Canvas flow,
And Crowds stood wond'ring at the passing Show;
Say, was it thus, with such a baffled Mien,
You met th' Approaches of the Spartan Queen,   70
Thus from her Realm convey'd the beauteous Prize,
And both[3] her warlike Lords outshin'd in Helen's Eyes?
This Deed, thy Foes Delight, thy own Disgrace,
Thy Father's Grief, and Ruin of thy Race;
This Deed recalls thee to the proffer'd Fight;
Or hast thou injur'd whom thou dar'st not right?
Soon to thy Cost the Field wou'd make thee know
Thou keep'st the Consort of a braver Foe.
Thy graceful Form instilling soft Desire,
Thy curling Tresses, and thy silver Lyre,   80
Beauty and Youth, in vain to these you trust,
When Youth and Beauty shall be laid in Dust:
Troy yet may wake, and one avenging Blow
Crush the dire Author of his Country's Woe.

[3] Identified by Pope as Theseus and Menelaus (no word for *both* in the Greek)

His Silence here, with Blushes, Paris breaks;
'Tis just, my Brother, what your Anger speaks:
But who like thee can boast a Soul sedate,
So firmly Proof to all the Shocks of Fate?
Thy Force like Steel a temper'd Hardness shows,
Still edg'd to wound, and still untir'd with Blows,   90
Like Steel, uplifted by some strenuous Swain,
With falling Woods to strow the wasted Plain.
Thy Gifts I praise, nor thou despise the Charms
With which a Lover golden Venus arms;
Soft moving Speech, and pleasing outward Show,
No Wish can gain 'em, but the Gods bestow.
Yet, wou'd'st thou have the proffer'd Combate stand,
The Greeks and Trojans seat on either Hand;
Then let a mid-way Space our Hosts divide,
And, on that Stage of War, the Cause be try'd: 100
By Paris there the Spartan King be fought,
For beauteous Helen and the Wealth she brought;
And who his Rival can in Arms subdue,
His be the Fair, and his the Treasure too.
Thus with a lasting League your Toils may cease,
And Troy possess her fertile Fields in Peace;
Thus may the Greeks review their native Shore,
Much fam'd for gen'rous Steeds, for Beauty more.
He said. The Challenge Hector heard with Joy,
Then with his Spear restrain'd the Youth of Troy,   110
Held by the midst, athwart; and near the Foe
Advanc'd with Steps majestically slow.
While round his dauntless Head the Grecians pour
Their Stones and Arrows in a mingled Show'r.
Then thus the Monarch great Atrides cry'd;
Forbear ye Warriors! lay the Darts aside:
A Parley Hector asks, a Message bears;
We know him by the various Plume he wears.
Aw'd by his high Command the Greeks attend,
The Tumult silence, and the Fight suspend.   120
While from the Centre Hector rolls his Eyes
On either Host, and thus to both applies.

Hear, all ye Trojans, all ye Grecian Bands!
What Paris, Author of the War, demands.
Your shining Swords within the Sheath restrain,
And pitch your Lances in the yielding Plain.
Here, in the midst, in either Army's sight,
He dares the Spartan King to single Fight;
And wills, that Helen and the ravish'd Spoil
That caus'd the Contest, shall reward the Toil.
Let these the brave triumphant Victor grace,   130
And diff'ring Nations part in Leagues of Peace.
  He spoke: in still Suspense on either side
Each Army stood: The Spartan Chief reply'd.
  Me too ye Warriors hear, whose fatal Right
A World engages in the Toils of Fight.
To me the Labour of the Field resign;
Me Paris injur'd; all the War be mine.
Fall he that must beneath his Rival's Arms,
And live the rest secure of future Harms.
Two Lambs, devoted by your Country's Rite,   140
To Earth a sable, to the Sun a white,
Prepare ye Trojans! while a third we bring
Select to Jove, th' Inviolable King.
Let rev'rend Priam in the Truce engage,
And add the Sanction of consid'rate Age;
His Sons are faithless, headlong in Debate,
And Youth itself an empty wav'ring State:
Cool Age advances venerably wise,
Turns on all hands its deep-discerning Eyes;   150
Sees what befell, and what may yet befall;
Concludes from both, and best provides for all.
  The Nations hear, with rising Hopes possest,
And peaceful Prospects dawn in ev'ry Breast.
Within the Lines they drew their Steeds around,
And from their Chariots issu'd on the Ground:
Next all unbuckling the rich Mail they wore,
Lay'd their bright Arms along the sable Shore.
On either side the meeting Hosts are seen,
With Lances fix'd, and close the Space between.   160

Two Heralds now dispatch'd to Troy, invite
The Phrygian Monarch to the Peaceful Rite;
Talthybius hastens to the Fleet, to bring
The Lamb for Jove th' Inviolable King.
  Meantime, to beauteous Helen from the Skies
The various Goddess of the Rain-bow flies:
(Like fair Laodicè in Form and Face,
The loveliest Nymph of Priam's Royal Race)
Her in the Palace, at her Loom she found;
The golden Web her own sad Story crown'd,   170
The Trojan Wars she weav'd (herself the Prize)
And the dire Triumphs of her fatal Eyes.
To whom the Goddess of the painted Bow;
Approach, and view the wond'rous Scene below!
Each hardy Greek and valiant Trojan Knight,
So dreadful late, and furious for the Fight,
Now rest their Spears, or lean upon their Shields;
Ceas'd is the War, and silent all the Fields.
Paris alone and Sparta's King advance,
In single Fight to toss the beamy Lance;   180
Each met in Arms the Fate of Combate tries,
Thy Love the Motive, and thy Charms the Prize.
  This said, the many-colour'd Maid inspires
Her Husband's Love, and wakes her former Fires;
Her Country, Parents, all that once were dear,
Rush to her Thought, and force a tender Tear.
O'er her fair Face a snowy Veil she threw,
And, softly sighing, from the Loom withdrew.
Her Handmaids Clymenè and Æthra wait
Her silent Footsteps to the Scæan Gate.   190
  There sate the Seniors of the Trojan Race,
(Old Priam's Chiefs, and most in Priam's Grace)
The King the first; Thymætes at his side;
Lampus and Clytius, long in Council try'd;
Panthus, and Hicetäon, once the strong,
And next the wisest of the Rev'rend Throng,
Antenor grave, and sage Ucalegon,
Lean'd on the Walls, and bask'd before the Sun.

Chiefs, who no more in bloody Fights engage,
But Wise thro' Time, and Narrative with Age,   200
In Summer-Days like Grashoppers rejoice,
A bloodless Race, that send a feeble Voice.
These, when the Spartan Queen approach'd the Tow'r,
In secret own'd resistless Beauty's Pow'r:
They cry'd, No wonder such Celestial Charms
For nine long Years have set the World in Arms;
What winning Graces! what majestick Mien!
She moves a Goddess, and she looks a Queen!
Yet hence oh Heav'n! convey that fatal Face,
And from Destruction save the Trojan Race.   210
   The good old Priam welcom'd her, and cry'd,
Approach my Child, and grace thy Father's Side.
See on the Plain thy Grecian Spouse appears,
The Friends and Kindred of thy former Years.
No Crime of thine our present Suff'rings draws,
Not Thou, but Heav'ns disposing Will, the Cause;
The Gods these Armies and this Force employ,
The hostile Gods conspire the Fate of Troy.
But lift thy Eyes, and say, What Greek is He
(Far as from hence these aged Orbs can see)   220
Around whose Brow such martial Graces shine,
So tall, so awful, and almost Divine?
Tho' some of larger Stature tread the Green,
None match his Grandeur and exalted Mien:
He seems a Monarch, and his Country's Pride.
Thus ceas'd the King, and thus the Fair reply'd.
   Before thy Presence, Father, I appear
With conscious Shame and reverential Fear.
Ah! had I dy'd, e're to these Walls I fled,
False to my Country and my Nuptial Bed,   230
My Brothers, Friends, and Daughter left behind,
False to them all, to Paris only kind!
For this I mourn, 'till Grief or dire Disease
Shall waste the Form whose Crime it was to please!
The King of Kings, Atrides, you survey,
Great in the War, and great in Arts of Sway.

My Brother once, before my Days of Shame;
And oh! that still he bore a Brother's Name!
  With Wonder Priam view'd the Godlike Man,
Extoll'd the happy Prince, and thus began.   240
O blest Atrides! born to prosp'rous Fate,
Successful Monarch of a mighty State!
How vast thy Empire? Of yon' matchless Train
What Numbers lost, what Numbers yet remain?
In Phrygia once were gallant Armies known,
In ancient Time, when Otreus' fill'd the Throne,
When Godlike Mygdon led their Troops of Horse,
And I, to join them, rais'd the Trojan Force:
Against the Manlike Amazons we stood,
And Sangar's Stream ran purple with their Blood.   250
But far inferior those, in manly Grace
And Strength of Numbers, to this Grecian Race.
  This said, once more he view'd the martial Train:
What's He, whose Arms lie scatter'd on the Plain?
Broad is his Breast, his Shoulders larger spread,
Tho' great Atrides overtops his Head.
Nor yet appear his Care and Conduct small;
From Rank to Rank he moves, and orders all.
The stately Ram thus measures o'er the Ground,
And, Master of the Flocks, surveys them round.   260
  Then Helen thus. Whom your discerning Eyes
Have singled out, is Ithacus the Wise:
A barren Island boasts his glorious Birth;
His Fame for Wisdom fills the spacious Earth.
  Antenor took the Word, and thus began:
My self, O King! have seen that wondrous Man;
When trusting Jove and hospitable Laws,
To Troy he came, to plead the Grecian Cause;
(Great Menelaus urg'd the same Request)
My House was honour'd with each Royal Guest: 270
I knew their Persons, and admir'd their Parts,
Both brave in Arms, and both approv'd in Arts.
Erect, the Spartan most engag'd our View,
Ulysses seated, greater Rev'rence drew.

When Atreus' Son harangu'd the list'ning Train,
Just was his Sense, and his Expression plain,
His Words succinct, yet full, without a Fault;
He spoke no more than just the Thing he ought.
But when Ulysses rose, in Thought profound,
His modest Eyes he fix'd upon the Ground,   280
As one unskill'd or dumb, he seem'd to stand,
Nor rais'd his Head, nor stretch'd his sceptred Hand;
But, when he speaks, what Elocution flows!
Soft as the Fleeces of descending Snows
The copious Accents fall, with easy Art;
Melting they fall, and sink into the Heart!
Wond'ring we hear, and fix'd in deep Surprize
Our Ears refute the Censure of our Eyes.
    The King then ask'd (as yet the Camp he view'd)
What Chief is that with Giant Strength endu'd,
Whose brawny Shoulders, and whose dwelling Chest,   290
And lofty Stature far exceed the rest?
Ajax the great (the beauteous Queen reply'd)
Himself an Host: the Grecian Strength and Pride.
See! bold Idomeneus superior tow'rs
Amidst yon' Circle of his Cretan Pow'rs,
Great as a God! I saw him once before,
With Menelaus, on the Spartan Shore.
The rest I know, and could in Order name;
All valiant Chiefs, and Men of mighty Fame.
Yet two are wanting of the num'rous Train,   300
Whom long my Eyes have sought, but sought in vain;
Castor and Pollux, first in martial Force,
One bold on Foot, and one renown'd for Horse.
My Brothers these; the same our native Shore,
One House contain'd us, as one Mother bore.
Perhaps the Chiefs, from warlike Toils at ease,
For distant Troy refus'd to sail the Seas:
Perhaps their Sword some nobler Quarrel draws,
Asham'd to combate in their Sister's Cause.   310
    So spoke the Fair, nor knew her Brothers Doom,
Wrapt in the cold Embraces of the Tomb;

Ador'd with Honours in their native Shore,
Silent they slept, and heard of Wars no more.
  Meantime the Heralds, thro' the crowded Town,
Bring the rich Wine and destin'd Victims down.
Idæus' Arms the golden Goblets prest,
Who thus the venerable King addrest.
Arise, O Father of the Trojan State!
The Nations call, thy joyful People wait,   320
To seal the Truce and end the dire Debate.
Paris thy Son, and Sparta's King advance,
In measur'd Lists to toss the weighty Lance;
And who his Rival shall in Arms subdue,
His be the Dame, and his the Treasure too.
Thus with a lasting League our Toils may cease,
And Troy possess her fertile Fields in Peace;
So shall the Greeks review their native Shore,
Much fam'd for gen'rous Steeds, for Beauty more.
  With Grief he heard, and bade the Chiefs prepare   330
To join his milk-white Coursers to the Car:
He mounts the Seat, Antenor at his side;
The gentle Steeds thro' Scæa's Gates they guide:
Next from the Car descending on the Plain,
Amid the Grecian Host and Trojan Train
Slow they proceed: The sage Ulysses then
Arose, and with him rose the King of Men.
On either side a sacred Herald stands,
The Wine they mix, and on each Monarch's Hands
Pour the full Urn; Then drew the Grecian Lord   340
His Cutlace sheath'd beside his pondrous Sword.
From the sign'd Victims crops the curling Hair,
The Heralds part it, and the Princes share;
Then loudly thus before th' attentive Bands
He calls the Gods, and spreads his lifted Hands.
O first and greatest Pow'r! whom all obey,
Who high on Ida's holy Mountain sway,
Eternal Jove! and you bright Orb that roll
From East to West, and view from Pole to Pole!
Thou Mother Earth! and all ye living Floods!   350
Infernal Furies, and Tartarean Gods,

Who rule the Dead, and horrid Woes prepare
For perjur'd Kings, and all who falsely swear!
Hear, and be Witness. If, by Paris slain,
Great Menelaus press the fatal Plain;
The Dame and Treasures let the Trojan keep,
And Greece returning plow the watry Deep.
If by my Brother's Lance the Trojan bleed;
Be his the Wealth and beauteous Dame decreed:
Th' appointed Fine let Ilion justly pay,   360
And ev'ry Age record the signal Day.
This if the Phrygians shall refuse to yield,
Arms must revenge, and Mars decide the Field.

  With that, the Chief the tender Victims slew,
And in the Dust their bleeding Bodies threw,
The vital Spirit issu'd at the Wound,
And left the Members quiv'ring on the Ground.
From the same Urn they drink the mingled Wine,
And add Libations to the Pow'rs Divine.
While thus their Pray'rs united mount the Sky;   370
Hear mighty Jove! and hear ye Gods on high!
And may their Blood who first the League confound,
Shed like this Wine, distain the thirsty Ground;
May all their Consorts serve promiscuous Lust,
And all their Race be scatter'd as the Dust!
Thus either Host their Imprecations join'd,
Which Jove refus'd, and mingled with the Wind.

  The Rites now finish'd, rev'rend Priam rose,
And thus express'd a Heart o'ercharg'd with Woes.
Ye Greeks and Trojans, let the Chiefs engage,   380
But spare the Weakness of my feeble Age:
In yonder Walls that Object let me shun,
Nor view the Danger of so dear a Son.
Whose Arms shall conquer, and what Prince shall fall,
Heav'n only knows, for Heav'n disposes all.

  This said, the hoary King no longer stay'd,
But on his Car the slaughter'd Victims laid,
Then seiz'd the Reins his gentle Steeds to guide,
And drove to Troy, Antenor at his Side.

    Bold Hector and Ulysses now dispose   390
The Lists of Combate, and the Ground inclose;
Next to decide by sacred Lots prepare,
Who first shall launce his pointed Spear in Air.
The People pray with elevated Hands,
And Words like these are heard thro' all the Bands.
Immortal Jove! high Heav'n's superior Lord,
On lofty Ida's holy Mount ador'd!
Whoe'er involv'd us in this dire Debate,
Oh give that Author of the War to Fate,
And Shades Eternal! Let Division cease,   400
And joyful Nations join in Leagues of Peace.
    With Eyes averted Hector hasts to turn
The Lots of Fight, and shakes the brazen Urn.
Then Paris, thine leap'd forth, by fatal Chance
Ordain'd the first to whirl the weighty Lance.
Both Armies sate, the Combate to survey,
Beside each Chief his Azure Armour lay,
And round the Lists the gen'rous Coursers neigh.
The beauteous Warrior now arrays for Fight,
In gilded Arms magnificently bright: 410
The Purple Cuishes clasp his Thighs around,
With Flow'rs adorn'd, and silver Buckles bound:
Lycaon's Cors'let his fair Body drest,
Brac'd in, and fitted to his softer Breast;
A radiant Baldric, o'er his Shoulder ty'd,
Sustains the Sword that glitters at his side.
His youthful Face a polish'd Helm o'erspread;
The waving Horse-hair nodded on his Head.
His figur'd Shield, a shining Orb, he takes,
And in his Hand a pointed Jav'lin shakes.   420
With equal Speed, and fir'd by equal Charms,
The Spartan Hero sheaths his Limbs in Arms.
    Now round the Lists th' admiring Armies stand,
With Jav'lins fix'd, the Greek and Trojan Band.
Amidst the dreadful Vale the Chiefs advance,
All pale with Rage, and shake the threat'ning Lance.
The Trojan first his shining Jav'lin threw;
Full on Atrides' ringing Shield it flew,

Nor pierc'd the brazen Orb, but with a Bound
Leap'd from the Buckler blunted on the Ground.   430
Atrides then his massy Lance prepares,
In Act to throw, but first prefers his Pray'rs.
    Give me, great Jove! to punish lawless lust,
And lay the Trojan gasping in the Dust:
Destroy th' Aggressor, aid my righteous Cause,
Avenge the Breach of hospitable Laws!
Let this Example future Times reclaim,
And guard from Wrong fair Friendship's holy Name.
    He said, and poiz'd in Air the Jav'lin sent,
Thro' Paris' Shield the forceful Weapon went,   440
His Cors'let pierces, and his Garment rends,
And glancing downward, near his Flank descends.
The wary Trojan, bending from the Blow,
Eludes the Death, and disappoints his Foe:
But fierce Atrides wav'd his Sword and strook
Full on his Casque; the crested Helmet shook;
The brittle Steel, unfaithful to his Hand,
Broke short: the Fragments glitter'd on the Sand.
The raging Warrior to the spacious Skies
Rais'd his upbraiding Voice, and angry Eyes: 450
Then is it vain in Jove himself to trust?
And is it thus the Gods assist the Just?
When Crimes provoke us, Heav'n Success denies;
The Dart falls harmless, and the Faulchion flies.
Furious he said, and tow'rd the Grecian Crew
(Seiz'd by the Crest) th' unhappy Warrior drew;
Struggling he follow'd, while th' embroider'd Thong
That ty'd his Helmet, dragg'd the Chief along.
Then had his Ruin crown'd Atrides' Joy,
But Venus trembl'd for the Prince of Troy: 460
Unseen she came, and burst the golden Band;
And left an empty Helmet in his Hand.
The Casque, enrag'd, amidst the Greeks he threw;
The Greeks with Smiles the polish'd Trophy view.
Then, as once more he lifts the deadly Dart,
In Thirst of Vengeance, at his Rival's Heart,

The Queen of Love her favour'd Champion shrouds
(For Gods can all things) in a Veil of Clouds.
Rais'd from the Field the panting Youth she led,
And gently laid him on the Bridal Bed,   470
With pleasing Sweets his fainting Sense renews,
And all the Dome perfumes with Heav'nly Dews.
  Meantime the brightest of the Female Kind,
The matchless Helen o'er the Walls reclin'd:
To her, beset with Trojan Beauties, came
In Grœa's Form, the Laughter-loving Dame.[4]
(Grœa, her Fav'rite Maid, well-skill'd to cull
The snowie Fleece, and wind the twisted Wool.)
The Goddess softly shook her silken Vest
That shed Perfumes, and whisp'ring thus addrest.   480
  Haste, happy Nymph! for thee thy Paris calls,
Safe from the Fight, in yonder lofty Walls,
Fair as a God with Odours round him spread
He lies, and waits thee on the well-known Bed:
Not like a Warrior parted from the Foe,
But some gay Dancer in the publick Show.
  She spoke, and Helen's secret Soul was mov'd;
She scorn'd the Champion, but the Man she lov'd.
Fair Venus' Neck, her Eyes that sparkled Fire,
And Breast, reveal'd the Queen of soft Desire.   490
Struck with her Presence, strait the lively Red
Forsook her Cheek; and, trembling, thus she said.
Then is it still thy Pleasure to deceive?
And Woman's Frailty always to believe?
Say, to new Nations must I cross the Main,
Or carry Wars to some soft Asian Plain?
For whom must Helen break her second Vow?
What other Paris is thy Darling now?
Left to Atrides, (Victor in the Strife)
An odious Conquest and a Captive Wife,   500
Hence let me sail: And if thy Paris bear
My absence ill, let Venus ease his Care.
A Hand-maid Goddess at his Side to wait,
Renounce the Glories of thy Heav'nly State,

[4] Venus

Be fix'd for ever to the Trojan Shore,
His Spouse, or Slave; and mount the Skies no more.
For me, to lawless Love no longer led,
I scorn the Coward, and detest his Bed;
Else should I merit everlasting Shame,
And keen Reproach, from ev'ry Phrygian Dame: 510
Ill suits it now the Joys of Love to know,
Too deep my Anguish, and too wild my Woe.

   Then thus, incens'd, the Paphian Queen replies;
Obey the Pow'r from whom thy Glories rise:
Should Venus leave thee, ev'ry Charm must fly,
Fade from thy Cheek, and languish in thy Eye.
Cease to provoke me, lest I make thee more
The World's Aversion, than their Love before;
Now the bright Prize for which Mankind engage,
Then, the sad Victim of the Publick Rage.   520

   At this, the Fairest of her Sex obey'd,
And veil'd her Blushes in a silken Shade;
Unseen, and silent, from the Train she moves,
Led by the Goddess of the Smiles and Loves.

   Arriv'd, and enter'd at the Palace Gate,
The Maids officious round their Mistress wait,
Then all dispersing, various Tasks attend;
The Queen and Goddess to the Prince ascend.
Full in her Paris' Sight the Queen of Love
Had plac'd the beauteous Progeny of Jove;   530
Where, as he view'd her Charms, she turn'd away
Her glowing Eyes, and thus began to say.

   Is this the Chief, who lost to Sense of Shame
Late fled the Field, and yet survives his Fame?
Oh hadst thou dy'd beneath the righteous Sword
Of that brave Man whom once I call'd my Lord!
The Boaster Paris oft' desir'd the Day
With Sparta's King to meet in single Fray:
Go now, once more thy Rival's Rage excite,
Provoke Atrides and renew the Fight: 540
Yet Helen bids thee stay, lest thou unskill'd
Should'st fall an easy Conquest on the Field.

The Prince replies; Ah cease, divinely fair,
Nor add Reproaches to the Wounds I bear,
This Day the Foe prevail'd by Pallas' Pow'r;
We yet may vanquish in a happier Hour:
There want not Gods to favour us above;
But let the Business of our Life be Love:
These softer Moments let Delights employ,
And kind Embraces snatch the hasty Joy.   550
Not thus I lov'd thee, when from Sparta's Shore
My forc'd, my willing Heav'nly Prize I bore,
When first entranc'd in Cranaë's Isle I lay,
Mix'd with thy Soul, and all dissolv'd away.
Thus having spoke, th' enamour'd Phrygian Boy
Rush'd to the Bed, impatient for the Joy.
Him Helen follow'd slow with bashful Charms,
And clasp'd the blooming Hero in her Arms.

   While these to Love's delicious Rapture yield,
The stern Atrides rages round the Field: 560
So some fell Lion whom the Woods obey,
Roars thro' the Desart, and demands his Prey.
Paris he seeks, impatient to destroy,
But seeks in vain along the Troops of Troy;
Ev'n those had yielded to a Foe so brave
The recreant Warrior, hateful as the Grave.
Then speaking thus the King of Kings arose;
Ye Trojans, Dardans, all our gen'rous Foes!
Hear and attest! From Heav'n with Conquest crown'd,
Our Brother's Arms the just Success have found: 570
Be therefore now the Spartan Wealth restor'd,
Let Argive Helen own her lawful Lord,
Th' appointed Fine let Ilion justly pay,
And Age to Age record this signal Day.

   He ceas'd; His Army's loud Applauses rise,
And the Long Shout runs ecchoing thro' the Skies.

᠃᠃᠃᠃

THE FOURTH BOOK
OF THE ILIAD

THE ARGUMENT

The Breach of the Truce, and the First Battel

THE GODS DELIBERATE in Council concerning the Trojan War: They agree
upon the Continuation of it, and Jupiter sends down Minerva to break
the Truce. She persuades Pandarus to aim an Arrow at Menelaus, who is
wounded, but cured by Machaon. In the mean time some of the Trojan
Troops attack the Greeks. Agamemnon is distinguished in all the Parts of
a good General; he reviews the Troops and exhorts the Leaders, some by
Praises and others by Reproofs. Nestor is particularly celebrated for his
military Discipline. The Battel joins, and great Numbers are slain on both
sides.

The same Day continues thro' this, as thro' the last Book (as it does
also thro' the two following, and almost to the end of the seventh Book.)
The Scene is wholly in the Field before Troy.

And now Olympus' shining Gates unfold;
The Gods, with Jove, assume their Thrones of Gold:
Immortal Hebè, fresh with Bloom Divine,
The golden Goblets crowns with Purple Wine:
While the full Bowls flow round, the Pow'rs employ
Their careful Eyes on long-contended Troy.
    When Jove, dispos'd to tempt Saturnia's Spleen,
Thus wak'd the Fury of his partial Queen.

Two Pow'rs Divine the Son of Atreus aid,
Imperial Juno, and the Martial Maid[1];   10
But high in Heav'n they sit, and gaze from far,
The tame Spectators of his Deeds of War.
Not thus fair Venus helps her favour'd Knight,
The Queen of Pleasures shares the Toils of Fight,
Each Danger wards, and constant in her Care
Saves in the Moment of the last Despair.
Her Act has rescu'd Paris' forfeit Life,
Tho' great Atrides gain'd the glorious Strife.
Then say ye Pow'rs! what signal Issue waits
To crown this Deed, and finish all the Fates?   20
Shall Heav'n by Peace the bleeding Kingdoms spare,
Or rowze the Furies and awake the War?
Yet, would the Gods for human Good provide,
Atrides soon might gain his beauteous Bride,
Still Priam's Walls in peaceful Honours grow,
And thro' his Gates the crowding Nations flow.
     Thus while he spoke, the Queen of Heav'n enrag'd
And Queen of War, in close Consult engag'd.
Apart they sit, their deep Designs employ,
And meditate the future Woes of Troy.   30
Tho' secret Anger swell'd Minerva's Breast,
The prudent Goddess yet her Wrath supprest,
But Juno, impotent of Passion, broke
Her sullen Silence, and with Fury spoke.
     Shall then, O Tyrant of th' Æthereal Reign!
My Schemes, my Labours, and my Hopes be vain?
Have I, for this, shook Ilion with Alarms,
Assembled Nations, set two Worlds in Arms?
To spread the War, I flew from Shore to Shore;
Th' Immortal Coursers scarce the Labour bore.   40
At length, ripe Vengeance o'er their Heads impends,
But Jove himself the faithless Race defends:
Loth as thou art to punish lawless Lust,
Not all the Gods are partial and unjust.
     The Sire whose Thunder shakes the Cloudy Skies,
Sighs from his inmost Soul, and thus replies;

[1] Minerva

Oh lasting Rancour! oh insatiate Hate
To Phrygia's Monarch, and the Phrygian State!
What high Offence has fir'd the Wife of Jove,
Can wretched Mortals harm the Pow'rs above,   50
That Troy, and Troy's whole Race thou woud'st confound,
And yon' fair Structures level with the Ground?
Haste, leave the Skies, fulfil thy stern Desire,
Burst all her Gates, and wrap her Walls in Fire!
Let Priam bleed! If yet thou thirst for more,
Bleed all his Sons, and Ilion float with Gore,
To boundless Vengeance the wide Realm be giv'n,
'Till vast Destruction glut the Queen of Heav'n!
So let it be, and Jove his Peace enjoy,
When Heav'n no longer hears the Name of Troy.   60
But should this Arm prepare to wreak our Hate
On thy lov'd Realms whose Guilt demands their Fate,
Presume not thou the lifted Bolt to stay,
Remember Troy, and give the Vengeance way.
For know, of all the num'rous Towns that rise
Beneath the rowling Sun, and starry Skies,
Which Gods have rais'd, or Earth-born Men enjoy;
None stands so dear to Jove as sacred Troy.
No Mortals merit more distinguish'd Grace
Than Godlike Priam, or than Priam's Race.   70
Still to our Name their Hecatombs expire,
And Altars blaze with unextinguish'd Fire.
   At this the Goddess roll'd her radiant Eyes,
Then on the Thund'rer fix'd them, and replies.
Three Towns are Juno's on the Grecian Plains,
More dear than all th' extended Earth contains,
Mycenæ, Argos, and the Spartan Wall;
These thou may'st raze, nor I forbid their Fall:
'Tis not in me the Vengeance to remove;
The Crime's sufficient that they share my Love.   80
Of Pow'r superior why should I complain?
Resent I may, but must resent in vain.
Yet some Distinction Juno might require,
Sprung, with thy self, from one Celestial Sire,

A Goddess born to share the Realms above,
And styl'd the consort of the thund'ring Jove.
Nor thou a Wife and Sister's Right deny;
Let both consent, and both by turns comply:
So shall the Gods our joint Decrees obey,
And Heav'n shall act as we direct the way.   90
See ready Pallas waits thy high Commands,
To raise in Arms the Greek and Phrygian Bands;
Their sudden Friendship by her Arts may cease,
And the proud Trojans first infringe the Peace.
  The Sire of Men and Monarch of the Sky
Th' Advice approv'd, and bade Minerva fly,
Dissolve the League, and all her Arts employ
To make the Breach the faithless Act of Troy.
  Fir'd with the Charge, she head-long urg'd her Flight,
And shot like Light'ning from Olympus' Height.   100
As the red Comet from Saturnius sent
To fright the Nations with a dire Portent,
(A fatal Sign to Armies on the Plain,
Or trembling Sailors on the wintry Main)
With sweeping Glories glides along in Air,
And shakes the Sparkles from its blazing Hair:
Between both Armies thus, in open Sight,
Shot the bright Goddess in a Trail of Light.
With Eyes erect the gazing Hosts admire
The Pow'r descending, and the Heav'ns on Fire!   110
The Gods (they cry'd) the Gods this Signal sent,
And Fate now labours with some vast Event:
Jove seals the League, or bloodier Scenes prepares;
Jove, the great Arbiter of Peace and Wars!
  They said, while Pallas thro' the Trojan Throng
(In Shape a Mortal) pass'd disguis'd along.
Like bold Laödocus, her Course she bent,
Who from Antenor trac'd his high Descent.
Amidst the Ranks Lycaön's Son she found,
The warlike Pandarus, for Strength renown'd;   120
Whose Squadrons, led from black Æsepus' Flood,
With flaming Shields in martial Circle stood.

To him the Goddess: Phrygian! can'st thou hear
A well-tim'd Counsel with a willing Ear?
What Praise were thine, cou'd'st thou direct thy Dart
Amidst his Triumph to the Spartan's Heart?
What Gifts from Troy, from Paris wou'd'st thou gain,
Thy Country's Foe, the Grecian Glory slain?
Then seize th' Occasion, dare the mighty Deed,
Aim at his Breast, and may that Aim succeed!   130
But first, to speed the Shaft, address thy Vow
To Lycian Phœbus with the Silver Bow,
And swear the Firstlings of thy Flock to pay
On Zelia's Altars, to the God of Day.
   He heard, and madly at the Motion pleas'd,
His polish'd Bow with hasty Rashness seiz'd.
'Twas form'd of Horn, and smooth'd with artful Toil;
A Mountain Goat resign'd the shining Spoil,
Who pierc'd long since beneath his Arrows bled;
The stately Quarry on the Cliffs lay dead,   140
And sixteen Palms his Brows large Honours spread:
The Workman join'd, and shap'd the bended Horns,
And beaten Gold each taper Point adorns.
This, by the Greeks unseen, the Warrior bends,
Screen'd by the Shields of his surrounding Friends.
There meditates the Mark; and couching low,
Fits the sharp Arrow to the well-strung Bow.
One from a hundred feather'd Deaths he chose,
Fated to wound, and Cause of future Woes.
Then offers Vows with Hecatombs to crown   150
Apollo's Altars in his Native Town.
   Now with full Force the yielding Horn he bends,
Drawn to an Arch, and joins the doubling Ends;
Close to his Breast he strains the Nerve below,
'Till the barb'd Point approach the circling Bow;
Th' impatient Weapon whizzes on the Wing,
Sounds the tough Horn, and twangs the quiv'ring String.
   But Thee, Atrides! in that dang'rous Hour
The Gods forget not, nor thy Guardian Pow'r.
Pallas assists, and (weaken'd in its Force)   160
Diverts the Weapon from the destin'd Course.

So from her Babe, when Slumber seals his Eye,
The watchful Mother wafts th' envenom'd Fly.
Just where his Belt with golden Buckles join'd,
Where Linen Folds the double Corslet lin'd,
She turn'd the Shaft, which hissing from above,
Pass'd the broad Belt, and thro' the Corslet drove;
The Folds it pierc'd, the plaited Linen tore,
And raz'd the Skin and drew the Purple Gore.
As when some stately Trappings are decreed,   170
To grace a Monarch on his bounding Steed,
A Nymph in Caria or Meönia bred,
Stains the pure Iv'ry with a lively Red;
With equal Lustre various Colours vie,
The shining Whiteness and the Tyrian Dye.
So, great Atrides! show'd thy sacred Blood,
As down thy snowie Thigh distill'd the streaming Flood.
With Horror seiz'd, the King of Men descry'd
The Shaft infix'd, and saw the gushing Tide:
Nor less the Spartan fear'd, before he found   180
The shining Barb appear above the Wound.
Then, with a Sigh that heav'd his manly Breast,
The Royal Brother thus his Grief exprest,
And grasp'd his Hand; while all the Greeks around
With answering Sighs return'd the plaintive Sound.
    Oh dear as Life! did I for this agree
The solemn Truce, a fatal Truce to thee!
Wert thou expos'd to all the hostile Train,
To fight for Greece, and conquer to be slain?
The Race of Trojans in thy Ruin join,   190
And Faith is scorn'd by all the perjur'd Line.
Not thus our Vows, confirm'd with Wine and Gore,
Those Hands we plighted, and those Oaths we swore,
Shall all be vain: When Heav'n's Revenge is slow,
Jove but prepares to strike the fiercer Blow.
The Day shall come, that great avenging Day,
Which Troy's proud Glories in the Dust shall lay,
When Priam's Pow'rs and Priam's self shall fall,
And one prodigious Ruin swallow All.

I see the God, already, from the Pole   200
Bare his red Arm, and bid the Thunder roll;
I see th' Eternal all his Fury shed,
And shake his Ægis o'er their guilty Head.
Such mighty Woes on perjur'd Princes wait;
But thou, alas! deserv'st a happier Fate.
Still must I mourn the Period of thy Days,
And only mourn, without my Share of Praise?
Depriv'd of thee, the heartless Greeks no more
Shall dream of Conquests on the hostile Shore;
Troy seiz'd of Helen, and our Glory lost,   210
Thy Bones shall moulder on a foreign Coast:
While some proud Trojan thus insulting cries,
(And spurns the Dust where Menelaus lies)
"Such are the Trophies Greece from Ilion brings,
"And such the Conquests of her King of Kings!
"Lo his proud Vessels scatter'd o'er the Main,
"And unreveng'd, his mighty Brother slain.
Oh! e're that dire Disgrace shall blast my Fame,
O'erwhelm me, Earth! and hide a Monarch's Shame.
     He said: A Leader's and a Brother's Fears   220
Possess his Soul, which thus the Spartan chears:
Let not thy Words the Warmth of Greece abate;
The feeble Dart is guiltless of my Fate:
Stiff with the rich embroider'd Work around,
My vary'd Belt repell'd the flying Wound.
     To whom the King. My Brother and my Friend,
Thus, always thus, may Heav'n thy Life defend!
Now seek some skilful Hand whose pow'rful Art
May stanch th' Effusion and extract the Dart.
Herald be swift, and bid Machaön bring   230
His speedy Succour to the Spartan King;
Pierc'd with a winged Shaft (the Deed of Troy)
The Grecian's Sorrow, and the Dardan's Joy.
     With hasty Zeal the swift Talthybius flies;
Thro' the thick Files he darts his searching Eyes,
And finds Machaön, where sublime he stands
In Arms encircled with his native Bands.

Then thus: Machaön, to the King repair,
His wounded Brother claims thy timely Care;
Pierc'd by some Lycian or Dardanian Bow,   240
A Grief to us, a Triumph to the Foe.
The heavy Tidings griev'd the Godlike Man;
Swift to his Succour thro' the Ranks he ran:
The dauntless King yet standing firm he found,
And all the Chiefs in deep Concern around.
Where to the steely Point the Reed was join'd,
The Shaft he drew, but left the Head behind.
Strait the broad Belt with gay Embroid'ry grac'd
He loos'd; the Corslet from his Breast unbrac'd;
Then suck'd the Blood, and Sov'reign Balm infus'd,   250
Which Chiron gave, and Æsculapius us'd.
While round the Prince the Greeks employ their Care,
The Trojans rush tumultuous to the War;
Once more they glitter in refulgent Arms,
Once more the Fields are fill'd with dire Alarms.
Nor had you seen the King of Men appear
Confus'd, unactive, or surpriz'd with Fear;
But fond of Glory, with severe Delight,
His beating Bosom claim'd the rising Fight.
No longer with his warlike Steeds he stay'd,   260
Or press'd the Car with polish'd Brass inlay'd,
But left Eurymedon the Reins to guide;
The fiery Coursers snorted at his side.
On Foot thro' all the martial Ranks he moves,
And these encourages, and those reproves.
Brave Men! he cries (to such who boldly dare
Urge their swift Steeds to face the coming War)
Your ancient Valour on the Foes approve;
Jove is with Greece, and let us trust in Jove.
'Tis not for us, but guilty Troy to dread,   270
Whose Crimes sit heavy on her perjur'd Head;
Her Sons and Matrons Greece shall lead in Chains,
And her dead Warriors strow the mournful Plains.
    Thus with new Ardour he the Brave inspires,
Or thus the fearful with Reproaches fires.

Shame to your Country, Scandal of your Kind!
Born to the Fate ye well deserve to find!
Why stand ye gazing round the dreadful Plain,
Prepar'd for Flight, but doom'd to fly in vain?
Confus'd and panting, thus, the hunted Deer   280
Falls as he flies, a Victim to his Fear.
Still must ye wait the Foes, and still retire,
'Till yon' tall Vessels blaze with Trojan Fire?
Or trust ye, Jove a valiant Foe shall chace,
To save a trembling, heartless, dastard Race?
    This said, he stalk'd with ample Strides along,
To Crete's brave Monarch and his martial Throng;
High at their Head he saw the Chief appear,
And bold Meriones excite the Rear.
At this the King his gen'rous Joy exprest,   290
And clasp'd the Warrior to his armed Breast.
Divine Idomeneus! what Thanks we owe
To Worth like thine? what Praise shall we bestow?
To thee the foremost Honours are decreed,
First in the Fight, and ev'ry graceful Deed.
For this, in Banquets when the gen'rous Bowls
Restore our Blood, and raise the Warrior's Souls,
Tho' all the rest with stated Rules we bound,
Unmix'd, unmeasur'd are thy Goblets crown'd.
Be still thy self; in Arms a mighty Name;   300
Maintain thy Honours, and enlarge thy Fame.
    To whom the Cretan thus his Speech addrest;
Secure of me, O King! exhort the rest:
Fix'd to thy Side, in ev'ry Toil I share,
Thy firm Associate in the Day of War.
But let the Signal be this Moment giv'n;
To mix in Fight is all I ask of Heav'n.
The Field shall prove how Perjuries succeed,
And Chains or Death avenge their impious Deed.
    Charm'd with this Heat, the King his Course pursues,   310
And next the Troops of either Ajax views:
In one firm Orb the Bands were rang'd around,
A Cloud of Heroes blacken'd all the Ground.

Thus from the lofty Promontory's Brow
A Swain surveys the gath'ring Storm below;
Slow from the Main the heavy Vapours rise,
Spread in dim Streams, and sail along the Skies,
'Till black as Night the swelling Tempest shows,
The Cloud condensing as the West-Wind blows:
He dreads th' impending Storm, and drives his Flock   320
To the close Covert of an arching Rock.

Such, and so thick, th' embattel'd Squadrons stood,
With Spears erect, a moving Iron Wood;
A shady Light was shot from glimm'ring Shields,
And their brown Arms obscur'd the dusky Fields.

O Heroes! worthy such a dauntless Train,
Whose Godlike Virtue we but urge in vain,
(Exclaim'd the King) who raise your eager Bands
With great Examples more than loud Commands.
Ah would the Gods but breathe in all the rest   330
Such Souls as burn in your exalted Breast!
Soon should our Arms with just Success be crown'd,
And Troy's proud Walls lie smoking on the Ground.

Then to the next the Gen'ral bends his Course;
(His Heart exults, and glories in his Force)
There rev'rend Nestor ranks his Pylian Bands,
And with inspiring Eloquence commands,
With strictest Order sets his Train in Arms,
The Chiefs advises, and the Soldiers warms.
Alastor, Chromius, Hæmon round him wait,   340
Bias the good, and Pelagon the great.
The Horse and Chariots to the Front assign'd,
The Foot (the Strength of War) he rang'd behind;
The middle Space suspected Troops supply,
Inclos'd by both, nor left the Pow'r to fly:
He gives Command to curb the fiery Steed,
Nor cause Confusion, nor the Ranks exceed;
Before the rest let none too rashly ride;
No Strength or Skill, but just in Time, be try'd:
The Charge once made, no Warrior turn the Rein,   350
But fight, or fall; a firm, embody'd Train.

He whom the Fortune of the Field shall cast
From forth his Chariot, mount the next in haste;
Nor seek unpractis'd to direct the Car,
Content with Jav'lins to provoke the War.
Our great Fore-fathers held this prudent Course,
Thus rul'd their Ardour, thus preserv'd their Force,
By Laws like these Immortal Conquests made,
And Earth's proud Tyrants low in Ashes laid.
  So spoke the Master of the martial Art,   360
And touch'd with Transport great Atrides' Heart.
Oh! had'st thou Strength to match thy brave Desires,
And Nerves to second what thy Soul inspires!
But wasting Years that wither human Race,
Exhaust thy Spirits, and thy Arms unbrace.
What once thou wert, oh ever might'st thou be!
And Age the Lot of any Chief but thee.
  Thus to th' experienc'd Prince Atrides cry'd;
He shook his hoary Locks, and thus reply'd.
Well might I wish, could Mortal Wish renew   370
That Strength which once in boiling Youth I knew;
Such as I was, when Ereuthalion slain
Beneath this Arm fell prostrate on the Plain.
But Heav'n its Gifts not all at once bestows,
These Years with Wisdom crowns, with Action those:
The Field of Combate fits the Young and Bold,
The solemn Council best becomes the Old:
To you the glorious Conflict I resign,
Let sage Advice, the Palm of Age, be mine.
  He said. With Joy the Monarch march'd before,   380
And found Menestheus on the dusty Shore,
With whom the firm Athenian Phalanx stands;
And next Ulysses, with his Subject Bands.
Remote their Forces lay, nor knew so far
The Peace infring'd, nor heard the Sounds of War;
The Tumult late begun, they stood intent
To watch the Motion, dubious of th' Event.
The King, who saw their Squadrons yet unmov'd,
With hasty Ardour thus the Chiefs reprov'd.

Can Peteus' Son forget a Warrior's Part,   390
And fears Ulysses, skill'd in ev'ry Art?
Why stand you distant, and the rest expect
To mix in Combate which your selves neglect?
From you 'twas hop'd among the first to dare
The Shock of Armies, and commence the War.
For this your Names are call'd, before the rest,
To share the Pleasures of the Genial Feast:
And can you, Chiefs! without a Blush survey
Whole Troops before you lab'ring in the Fray?
Say, is it thus those Honours you requite?   400
The first in Banquets, but the last in Fight.

   Ulysses heard; The Hero's Warmth o'erspread
His Cheek with Blushes; and severe, he said.
Take back th' unjust Reproach! Behold we stand
Sheath'd in bright Arms, and but expect Command.
If glorious Deeds afford thy Soul delight,
Behold me plunging in the thickest Fight.
Then give thy Warrior-Chief a Warrior's Due,
Who dares to act whate'er thou dar'st to view.

   Struck with his gen'rous Wrath, the King replies;   410
Oh great in Action, and in Council wise!
With ours, thy Care and Ardour are the same,
Nor need I to command, nor ought to blame.
Sage as thou art, and learn'd in Humankind,
Forgive the Transport of a martial Mind.
Haste to the Fight, secure of just Amends;
The Gods that make, shall keep the Worthy, Friends.

   He said, and pass'd where great Tydides lay,
His Steeds and Chariots wedg'd in firm Array:
(The warlike Sthenelus attends his side)   420
To whom with stern Reproach the Monarch cry'd.
Oh Son of Tydeus! (He, whose Strength could tame
The bounding Steed, in Arms a mighty Name)
Can'st thou, remote, the mingling Hosts descry
With Hands unactive, and a careless Eye?
Not thus thy Sire the fierce Encounter fear'd;
Still first in Front the matchless Prince appear'd:

What glorious Toils, what Wonders they recite,
Who view'd him lab'ring thro' the Ranks of Fight!
I saw him once, when gath'ring martial Pow'rs   430
A peaceful Guest, he sought Mycenæ's Tow'rs;
Armies he ask'd, and Armies had been giv'n,
Not we deny'd, but Jove forbad from Heav'n;
While dreadful Comets glaring from afar
Forewarn'd the Horrors of the Theban War.[2]
Next, sent by Greece from where Asopus flows,
A fearless Envoy he approach'd the Foes;
Thebes' hostile Walls, unguarded and alone,
Dauntless he enters, and demands the Throne.
The Tyrant feasting with his Chiefs he found,   440
And dar'd to Combate all those Chiefs around;
Dar'd and subdu'd, before their haughty Lord;
For Pallas strung his Arm, and edg'd his Sword.
Stung with the Shame, within the winding Way,
To bar his Passage fifty Warriors lay;
Two Heroes led the secret Squadron on,
Mœon the fierce, and hardy Lycophon;
Those fifty slaughter'd in the gloomy Vale,
He spar'd but one to bear the dreadful Tale.
Such Tydeus was, and such his martial Fire;   450
Gods! how the Son degen'rates from the Sire?
    No Words the Godlike Diomed return'd,
But heard respectful, and in secret burn'd:
Not so fierce Capaneus' undaunted Son,
Stern as his Sire, the Boaster thus begun.
    What needs, O Monarch, this invidious Praise,
Our selves to lessen, while our Sires you raise?
Dare to be just, Atrides! and confess
Our Valour equal, tho' our Fury less.
With fewer Troops we storm'd the Theban Wall,[3]   460
And happier, saw the Sev'nfold City fall.
In impious Acts the guilty Fathers dy'd;
The Sons subdu'd, for Heav'n was on their side.

[2] War of "The Seven against Thebes"
[3] War of the sons of "The Seven"

Far more than Heirs of all our Parent's Fame,
Our Glories darken their diminish'd Name.
  To him Tydides thus. My Friend forbear,
Suppress thy Passion, and the King revere:
His high Concern may well excuse this Rage,
Whose Cause we follow, and whose War we wage;
His the first Praise were Ilion's Tow'rs o'erthrown,   470
And, if we fail, the chief Disgrace his own.
Let him the Greeks to hardy Toils excite,
'Tis ours, to labour in the glorious Fight.
  He spoke, and ardent, on the trembling Ground
Sprung from his Car; his ringing Arms resound.
Dire was the Clang, and dreadful from afar,
Of arm'd Tydides rushing to the War.
As when the Winds, ascending by degrees,
First move the whitening Surface of the Seas,
The Billows float in order to the Shore,   480
The Wave behind rolls on the Wave before;
Till, with the growing Storm, the Deeps arise,
Foam o'er the Rocks, and thunder to the Skies.
So to the Fight the thick Battalions throng,
Shields urg'd on Shields, and Men drove Men along.
Sedate and silent move the num'rous Bands;
No Sound, no Whisper, but their Chief's Commands,
Those only heard; with Awe the rest obey,
As if some God had snatch'd their Voice away.
No so the Trojans, from their Host ascends   490
A gen'ral Shout that all the Region rends.
As when the fleecy Flocks unnumber'd stand
In wealthy Folds, and wait the Milker's Hand,
The hollow Vales incessant Bleating fills,
The Lambs reply from all the neighb'ring Hills:
Such Clamours rose from various Nations round,
Mix'd was the Murmur, and confus'd the Sound.
Each Host now joins, and each a God inspires,
These Mars incites, and those Minerva fires.
Pale Flight around, and dreadful Terror reign;   500
And Discord raging bathes the purple Plain:

Discord! dire Sister of the slaught'ring Pow'r,
Small at her Birth, but rising ev'ry Hour,
While scarce the Skies her horrid Head can bound,
She stalks on Earth, and shakes the World around;
The Nations bleed, where-e'er her Steps she turns,
The Groan still deepens, and the Combate burns.
   Now Shield with Shield, with Helmet Helmet clos'd,
To Armour Armour, Lance to Lance oppos'd,
Host against Host with shadowy Squadrons drew,   510
The sounding Darts in Iron Tempests flew,
Victors and Vanquish'd join promiscuous Cries,
And shrilling Shouts and dying Groans arise;
With streaming Blood the slipp'ry Fields are dy'd,
And slaughter'd Heroes swell the dreadful Tide.
   As Torrents roll, increas'd by num'rous Rills,
With Rage impetuous down their ecchoing Hills;
Rush to the Vales, and pour'd along the Plain,
Roar thro' a thousand Chanels to the Main;
The distant Shepherd trembling hears the Sound: 520
So mix both Hosts, and so their Cries rebound.
   The bold Antilochus the Slaughter led,
The first who strook a valiant Trojan dead:
At great Echepolus the Lance arrives,
Raz'd his high Crest, and thro' his Helmet drives,
Warm'd in the Brain the brazen Weapon lies,
And Shades Eternal settle o'er his Eyes.
So sinks a Tow'r, that long Assaults had stood
Of Force and Fire; its Walls besmear'd with Blood.
Him, the bold Leader of th' Abantian Throng   530
Seiz'd to despoil, and dragg'd the Corps along:
But while he strove to tug th' inserted Dart,
Agenor's Jav'lin reach'd the Hero's Heart.
His Flank, unguarded by his ample Shield,
Admits the Lance: He falls, and spurns the Field;
The Nerves unbrac'd support his Limbs no more;
The Soul comes floating in a Tide of Gore.
Trojans and Greeks now gather round the Slain;
The War renews, the Warriors bleed again;

As o'er their Prey rapacious Wolves engage,   540
Man dies on Man, and all is Blood and Rage.
    In blooming Youth fair Simoïsius fell,
Sent by great Ajax to the Shades of Hell;
Fair Simoïsius, whom his Mother bore
Amid the Flocks on silver Simois' Shore:
The Nymph descending from the Hills of Ide,
To seek her Parents on his flow'ry Side,
Brought forth the Babe, their common Care and Joy,
And thence from Simois nam'd the lovely Boy.
Short was his Date! by dreadful Ajax slain   550
He falls, and renders all their Cares in vain!
So falls a Poplar, that in watry Ground
Rais'd high the Head, with stately Branches crown'd,
(Fell'd by some Artist with his shining Steel,
To shape the Circle of the bending Wheel)
Cut down it lies, tall, smooth, and largely spread,
With all its beauteous Honours on its Head;
There left a Subject to the Wind and Rain
And scorch'd by Suns, it withers on the Plain.
Thus pierc'd by Ajax, Simoïsius lies   560
Stretch'd on the Shore, and thus neglected dies.
    At Ajax, Antiphus his Jav'lin threw;
The pointed Lance with erring Fury flew,
And Leucus, lov'd by wise Ulysses, slew.
He drops the Corps of Simoïsius slain,
And sinks a breathless Carcass on the Plain.
This saw Ulysses, and with Grief enrag'd
Strode where the foremost of the Foes engag'd;
Arm'd with his Spear, he meditates the Wound,
In Act to throw; but cautious, look'd around.   570
Struck at his Sight the Trojans backward drew,
And trembling heard the Jav'lin as it flew.
A Chief stood nigh who from Abydos came,
Old Priam's Son, Democoon was his Name;
The Weapon enter'd close above his Ear,
Cold thro' his Temples glides the whizzing Spear;
With piercing Shrieks the Youth resigns his Breath,
His Eye-balls darken with the Shades of Death;

Down sinks the Chief: his clanging Arms resound;
And his broad Buckler rings against the Ground.   580
    Seiz'd with Affright the boldest Foes appear;
Ev'n Godlike Hector seems himself to fear;
Slow he gave way, the rest tumultuous fled;
The Greeks with Shouts press on, and spoil the Dead,
But Phœbus now from Ilion's tow'ring Height
Shines forth reveal'd, and animates the Fight.
Trojans be bold, and Force with Force oppose;
Your foaming Steeds urge headlong on the Foes!
Nor are their Bodies Rocks, nor ribb'd with Steel;
Your Weapons enter, and your Strokes they feel.   590
Have ye forgot what seem'd your Dread before?
The great, the fierce Achilles fights no more.
    Apollo thus from Ilion's lofty Tow'rs
Array'd in Terrors, rowz'd the Trojan Pow'rs:
While War's fierce Goddess fires the Grecian Foe,
And shouts and thunders in the Fields below.
    Then great Diores[4] fell, by Doom Divine,
In vain his Valour, and illustrious Line.
A broken Rock the Force of Pirus threw,
(Who from cold Ænus led the Thracian Crew)   600
Full on his Ankle dropt the pond'rous Stone,
Burst the strong Nerves, and crash'd the solid Bone:
Supine he tumbles on the crimson'd Sands,
Before his helpless Friends, and native Bands,
And spreads for Aid his unavailing Hands.
The Foe rush'd furious as he pants for Breath,
And thro' his Navel drove the pointed Death:
His gushing Entrails smoak'd upon the Ground,
And the warm Life came issuing from the Wound.
    His Lance bold Thoas at the Conqu'ror sent,   610
Deep in his Breast above the Pap it went,
Amid the Lungs was fix'd the winged Wood,
And quiv'ring in his heaving Bosom stood:
'Till from the dying Chief, approaching near,
Th' Ætolian[5] Warrior tugg'd his weighty Spear:

---

[4] On the Greek side, leader of the Epeians
[5] Thoas, a Greek

Then sudden wav'd his flaming Faulchion round,
And gash'd his Belly with a ghastly Wound.
The Corps now breathless on the bloody Plain,
To spoil his Arms the Victor strove in vain;
The Thracian Bands against the Victor prest;   620
A Grove of Lances glitter'd at his Breast.
Stern Thoas, glaring with revengeful Eyes,
In sullen Fury slowly quits the Prize.
    Thus fell two Heroes; one the Pride of Thrace,
And one the Leader of th' Epeian Race;
Death's sable Shade at once o'ercast their Eyes,
In Dust the Vanquish'd, and the Victor lies.
With copious Slaughter all the Fields are red,
And heap'd with growing Mountains of the Dead.
    Had some brave Chief this martial Scene beheld,   630
By Pallas guarded thro' the dreadful Field,
Might Darts be bid to turn their Points away,
And Swords around him innocently play,
The War's whole Art with Wonder had he seen,
And counted Heroes where he counted Men.
    So fought each Host, with Thirst of Glory fir'd,
And Crowds on Crowds triumphantly expir'd.

THE FIFTH BOOK
OF THE ILIAD

THE ARGUMENT

The Acts of Diomed

DIOMED, ASSISTED BY PALLAS, performs Wonders in this Day's Battel.
Pandarus wounds him with an Arrow, but the Goddess cures him, enables
him to discern Gods from Mortals, and prohibits him from contending
with any of the former, excepting Venus. Æneas joins Pandarus to oppose
him, Pandarus is killed, and Æneas in great danger but for the Assistance
of Venus; who, as she is removing her Son from the Fight, is wounded
on the Hand by Diomed. Apollo seconds her in his Rescue, and at length
carries off Æneas to Troy, where he is heal'd in the Temple of Pergamus.
Mars rallies the Trojans, and assists Hector to make a Stand. In the mean
time Æneas is restor'd to the Field, and they overthrow several of the
Greeks; among the rest Tlepolemus is slain by Sarpedon. Juno and
Minerva descend to resist Mars; the latter incites Diomed to go against
that God; he wounds him, and sends him groaning to Heaven.

The first Battel continues thro' this Book. The Scene is the same as in
the former.

But Pallas now Tydides Soul inspires,
Fills with her Force, and warms with all her Fires,
Above the Greeks his deathless Fame to raise,
And crown her Hero with distinguish's Praise.
High on his Helm Celestial Lightnings play,
His beamy Shield emits a living Ray;
Th' unweary'd Blaze incessant Streams supplies,
Like the red Star that fires th' Autumnal Skies,

When fresh he rears his radiant Orb to Sight,
And bath'd in Ocean, shoots a keener Light.   10
Such Glories Pallas on the Chief bestowed,
Such, from his Arms, the fierce Effulgence flow'd:
Onward she drives him, furious to engage,
Where the Fight burns, and where the thickest rage.
    The Sons of Dares first the Combate sought,
A wealthy Priest, but rich without a Fault;
In Vulcan's Fane the Father's Days were led,
The Sons to Toils of glorious Battel bred;
These singled from their Troops the Fight maintain,
These from their Steeds, Tydides on the Plain.   20
Fierce for Renown the Brother Chiefs draw near,
And first bold Phegeus cast his sounding Spear,
Which o'er the Warrior's Shoulder took its Course,
And spent in empty Air its erring Force.
Not so, Tydides, flew thy Lance in vain,
But pierc'd his Breast, and stretch'd him on the Plain.
Seiz'd with unusual Fear Idæus fled,
Left the rich Chariot, and his Brother dead;
And had not Vulcan lent Celestial Aid,
He too had sunk to Death's Eternal Shade;   30
But in a smoaky Cloud the God of Fire
Preserv'd the Son, in Pity to the Sire.
The Steeds and Chariot, to the Navy led,
Encreas'd the Spoils of gallant Diomed.
    Struck with Amaze, and Shame, the Trojan Crew
Or slain, or fled, the Sons of Dares view:
When by the blood-stain'd Hand Minerva prest
The God of Battels, and this Speech addrest.
    Stern Pow'r of War! by whom the Mighty fall,
Who bath'st in Blood, and shak'st the lofty Wall!   40
Let the brave Chiefs their glorious Toils divide;
And whose the Conquest, mighty Jove decide:
While we from interdicted Fields retire,
Nor tempt the Wrath of Heav'ns avenging Sire.
    Her Words allay th' impetuous Warrior's Heat,
The God of Arms and Martial Maid retreat;
Remov'd from Fight, on Xanthus flow'ry Bounds
They sate, and listen'd to the dying Sounds.

Meantime the Greeks the Trojan Race pursue,
And some bold Chieftain ev'ry Leader slew: 50
First Odius falls, and bites the bloody Sand,
His Death ennobled by Atrides' Hand;
As he to Flight his wheeling Car addrest,
The speedy Javelin drove from Back to Breast.
In Dust the mighty Halizonian lay,
His Arms resound, the Spirit wings its way.
    Thy Fate was next, O Phæstus! doom'd to feel
The great Idomeneus' protended Steel;
Whom Borus sent (his Son and only Joy)
From fruitful Tarnè to the Fields of Troy.   60
The Cretan Javelin reach'd him from afar,
And pierc'd his Shoulder as he mounts his Car;
Back from the Car he tumbles to the Ground,
And everlasting Shades his Eyes surround.
    Then dy'd Scamandrius, expert in the Chace,
In Woods and Wilds to wound the Savage Race;
Diana taught him all her Sylvan Arts,
To bend the Bow and aim unerring Darts:
But vainly here Diana's Arts he tries,
The fatal Lance arrests him as he flies;   70
From Menelaus' Arm the Weapon sent,
Thro' his broad Back and heaving Bosom went:
Down sinks the Warrior with a thundring Sound,
His Brazen Armor rings against the Ground.
    Next artful Phereclus untimely fell;
Bold Merion sent him to the Realms of Hell.
Thy Father's Skill, O Phereclus, was thine,
The graceful Fabrick and the fair Design;
For lov'd by Pallas, Pallas did impart
To him the Shipwright's and the Builder's Art.   80
Beneath his Hand the Fleet of Paris rose,
The fatal Cause of all his Country's Woes,
But he, the mystick Will of Heav'n unknown,
Nor saw his Country's Peril, nor his own.
The hapless Artist, while confus'd he fled,
The Spear of Merion mingled with the Dead.
Thro' his right Hip with forceful Fury cast,
Between the Bladder and the Bone it past:

Prone on his Knees he falls with fruitless Cries,
And Death in lasting Slumber seals his Eyes. 90
　From Meges' Force the swift Pedæus fled,
Antenor's Offspring from a foreign Bed,
Whose gen'rous Spouse, Theano, heav'nly Fair,
Nurs'd the young Stranger with a Mother's Care.
How vain those Cares! when Meges in the Rear
Full in his Nape infix'd the fatal Spear;
Swift thro' his crackling Jaws the Weapon glides,
And the cold Tongue and grinning Teeth divides.
　Then dy'd Hypsenor, gen'rous and divine,
Sprung from the brave Dolopion's mighty Line, 100
Who near ador'd Scamander made Abode,
Priest of the Stream, and honour'd as a God.
On him, amidst the flying Numbers found,
Eurypilus inflicts a deadly Wound;
On his broad Shoulder fell the forceful Brand,
Thence glancing downward lopp'd his Holy Hand,
Which stain'd with sacred Blood the blushing Sand.
Down sunk the Priest: the Purple Hand of Death
Clos'd his dim Eye, and Fate suppress'd his Breath.
　Thus toil'd the Chiefs in diff'rent Parts engag'd, 110
In ev'ry Quarter fierce Tydides rag'd,
Amid the Greek, amid the Trojan Train,
Rapt thro' the Ranks he thunders o'er the Plain,
Now here, now there, he darts from Place to Place,
Pours on the Rear, or lightens in their Face.
Thus from high Hills the Torrents swift and strong
Deluge whole Fields, and sweep the Trees along,
Thro' ruin'd Moles the rushing Wave resounds,
O'erwhelms the Bridge, and bursts the lofty Bounds;
The yellow Harvests of the ripen'd Year, 120
And flatted Vineyards, one sad Waste appear;
While Jove descends in sluicy Sheets of Rain,
And all the Labours of Mankind are vain.
　So rag'd Tydides, boundless in his Ire,
Drove Armies back, and made all Troy retire.
With Grief the Leader of the Lycian Band
Saw the wide Waste of his destructive Hand:

His bended Bow against the Chief he drew;
Swift to the Mark the thirsty Arrow flew,
Whose forky Point the hollow Breastplate tore,   130
Deep in his Shoulder pierc'd, and drank the Gore:
The rushing Stream his Brazen Armor dy'd,
While the proud Archer thus exulting cry'd.
    Hither ye Trojans, hither drive your Steeds!
Lo! by our Hand the bravest Grecian bleeds.
Not long the deathful Dart he can sustain;
Or Phœbus urg'd me to these Fields in vain.
    So spoke he, boastful; but the winged Dart
Stopt short of Life, and mock'd the Shooter's Art.
The wounded Chief behind his Car retir'd,   140
The helping Hand of Sthenelus requir'd;
Swift from his Seat he leap'd upon the Ground,
And tugg'd the Weapon from the gushing Wound;
When thus the King his Guardian Pow'r addrest,
The purple Current wand'ring o'er his Vest.
    O Progeny of Jove! unconquer'd Maid!
If e'er my Godlike Sire deserv'd thy Aid,
If e'er I felt thee in the fighting Field;
Now, Goddess, now, thy sacred Succour yield.
Oh give my Lance to reach the Trojan Knight,   150
Whose Arrow wounds the Chief thou guard'st in Fight;
And lay the Boaster grov'ling on the Shore,
That vaunts these Eyes shall view the Light no more.
    Thus pray'd Tydides, and Minerva heard,
His Nerves confirm'd, his languid Spirits chear'd;
He feels each Limb with wonted Vigor light;
His beating Bosom claims the promis'd Fight.
Be bold (she cry'd) in ev'ry Combate shine,
War be thy Province, thy Protection mine;
Rush to the Fight, and ev'ry Foe controul;   160
Wake each Paternal Virtue in thy Soul:
Strength swells thy boiling Breast, infus'd by me,
And all thy Godlike Father breathes in thee!
Yet more, from mortal Mists I purge thy Eyes,
And set to View the warring Deities.
These see thou shun, thro' all th' embattled Plain,
Nor rashly strive where human Force is vain.

If Venus mingle in the martial Band,
Her shalt thou wound: So Pallas gives Command.
   With that, the blue-ey'd Virgin wing'd her Flight; 170
The Hero rush'd impetuous to the Fight;
With tenfold Ardor now invades the Plain,
Wild with Delay, and more enrag'd by Pain.
As on the fleecy Flocks, when Hunger calls,
Amidst the Field a brindled Lyon falls;
If chance some Shepherd with a distant Dart
The Savage wound, he rowzes at the Smart,
He foams, he roars; The Shepherd dares not stay,
But trembling leaves the scatt'ring Flocks a Prey.
Heaps fall on Heaps; he bathes with Blood the Ground, 180
Then leaps victorious o'er the lofty Mound.
Not with less Fury stern Tydides flew,
And two brave Leaders at an Instant slew;
Astynous breathless fell, and by his side
His People's Pastor, good Hypenor, dy'd;
Astynous' Breast the deadly Lance receives,
Hypenor's Shoulder his broad Faulchion cleaves.
Those slain he left; and sprung with noble Rage
Abas, and Polyidus to engage;
Sons of Eurydamas, who wise and old, 190
Could Fates foresee, and mystic Dreams unfold;
The Youths return'd not from the doubtful Plain,
And the sad Father try'd his Arts in vain;
No mystic Dream could make their Fates appear,
Tho' now determin'd by Tydides' Spear.
   Young Xanthus next and Thoon felt his Rage,
The Joy and Hope of Phœnops feeble Age,
Vast was his Wealth, and these the only Heirs
Of all his Labours, and a Life of Cares;
Cold Death o'ertakes them in their blooming Years, 200
And leaves the Father unavailing Tears:
To Strangers now descends his heapy Store,
The Race forgotten, and the Name no more.
   Two Sons of Priam in one Chariot ride,
Glitt'ring in Arms, and combate Side by Side.
As when the lordly Lyon seeks his Food
Where grazing Heifers range the lonely Wood,

He leaps amidst them with a furious Bound,
Bends their strong Necks, and tears them to the Ground.
So from their Seats the Brother-Chiefs are torn,   210
Their Steeds and Chariot to the Navy born.
  With deep Concern divine Æneas view'd
The Foe prevailing, and his Friends pursu'd,
Thro' the thick Storm of singing Spears he flies,
Exploring Pandarus with careful Eyes.
At length he found Lycaon's mighty Son;
To whom the Chief of Venus' Race begun.
  Where, Pandarus, are all thy Honours now,
Thy winged Arrows and unerring Bow,
Thy matchless Skill, thy yet-unrival'd Fame,   220
And boasted Glory of the Lycian Name?
Oh pierce that Mortal, if we Mortal call
That wondrous Force by which whole Armies fall,
Or God incens'd, who quits the distant Skies
To punish Troy for slighted Sacrifice;
(Which oh avert from our unhappy State!
For what so dreadful as Celestial Hate?)
Whoe'er he be, propitiate Jove with Pray'r;
If Man, destroy; if God, entreat to spare.
  To him the Lycian. Whom your Eyes behold,   230
If right I judge, is Diomed the bold.
Such Coursers whirl him o'er the dusty Field,
So tow'rs his Helmet, and so flames his Shield.
If 'tis a God, he wears that Chief's Disguise;
Or if that Chief, some Guardian of the Skies
Involv'd in Clouds, protects him in the Fray,
And turns unseen the frustrate Dart away.
I wing'd an Arrow, which not idly fell,
The Stroke had fix'd him to the Gates of Hell,
And, but some God, some angry God withstands,   240
His Fate was due to these unerring Hands.
  Skill'd in the Bow, on Foot I sought the War,
Nor join'd swift Horses to the rapid Car.
Ten polish'd Chariots I possess'd at home,
And still they grace Lycaon's Princely Dome:
There veil'd in spacious Coverlets they stand;
And twice ten Coursers wait their Lord's Command.

The good old Warrior bade me trust to these,
When first for Troy I sail'd the sacred Seas,
In Fields, aloft, the whirling Car to guide, 250
And thro' the Ranks of Death triumphant ride.
But vain with Youth, and yet to Thrift inclin'd,
I heard his Counsels with unheedful Mind,
And thought the Steeds (your large Supplies unknown)
Might fail of Forage in the straiten'd Town:
So took my Bow and pointed Darts in hand,
And left the Chariots in my Native Land.
    Too late, O Friend! my Rashness I deplore;
These Shafts, once fatal, carry Death no more.
Tydeus' and Atreus' Sons their Points have found, 260
And undissembled Gore pursu'd the Wound.
In vain they bled: This unavailing Bow
Serves not to slaughter, but provoke the Foe.
In evil Hour these bended Horns I strung,
And seiz'd the Quiver where it idly hung.
Curs'd be the Fate that sent me to the Field,
Without a Warrior's Arms, the Spear and Shield!
If e'er with Life I quit the Trojan Plain,
If e'er I see my Spouse and Sire again,
This Bow, unfaithful to my glorious Aims, 270
Broke by my Hand, shall feed the blazing Flames.
    To whom the Leader of the Dardan Race:
Be calm, nor Phœbus' honour'd Gift disgrace.
The distant Dart be prais'd, tho' here we need
The rushing Chariot, and the bounding Steed.
Against yon' Hero let us bend our Course,
And, Hand to Hand, encounter Force with Force.
Now haste, ascend my Seat, and from the Car
Observe my Father's Steeds, renown'd in War,
Practis'd alike to turn, to stop, to chace, 280
To dare the Shock, or urge the rapid Race:
Secure with these, thro' fighting Fields we go,
Or safe to Troy, if Jove assist the Foe.
Haste, seize the Whip, and snatch the guiding Rein;
The Warrior's Fury let this Arm sustain;
Or if to Combate thy bold Heart incline,
Take thou the Spear, the Chariot's Care be mine.

O Prince! (Lycaon's valiant Son reply'd)
As thine the Steeds, be thine the Task to guide.
The Horses practis'd to their Lord's Command,   290
Shall hear the Rein, and answer to thy Hand.
But if unhappy, we desert the Fight,
Thy Voice alone can animate their Flight:
Else shall our Fates be number'd with the Dead,
And these, the Victor's Prize, in Triumph led.
Thine be the Guidance then: With Spear and Shield
My self will charge this Terror of the Field.
   And now both Heroes mount the glitt'ring Car;
The bounding Coursers rush amidst the War.
Their fierce Approach bold Sthenelus espy'd,   300
Who thus, alarm'd, to great Tydides cry'd.
   O Friend! two Chiefs of Force immense I see,
Dreadful they come, and bend their Rage on thee:
Lo the brave Heir of old Lycaon's Line,
And great Æneas, sprung from Race Divine!
Enough is giv'n to Fame. Ascend thy Car;
And save a Life, the Bulwark of our War.
   At this the Hero cast a gloomy Look,
Fix'd on the Chief with Scorn, and thus he spoke.
Me dost thou bid to shun the coming Fight,   310
Me would'st thou move to base inglorious Flight?
Know, 'tis not honest in my Soul to fear,
Nor was Tydides born to tremble here.
I loath in lazy Fights to press the Car,
At distance wound, or wage a flying War;
But while my Nerves are strung, my Force entire,
Thus front the Foe, and emulate my Sire.
Nor shall yon' Steeds that fierce to Fight convey
Those threatning Heroes, bear them both away;
One Chief at least beneath this Arm shall die;   320
So Pallas tells me, and forbids to fly.
But if she dooms, and if no God withstand,
That both shall fall by one victorious Hand;
Then heed my Words: My Horses here detain,
Fix'd to the Chariot by the straiten'd Rein;
Swift to Æneas' empty Seat proceed,
And seize the Coursers of Ætherial Breed.

The Race of those which once the thund'ring God
For ravish'd Ganymede on Tros bestow'd,
The best that e'er on Earth's broad Surface run,   330
Beneath the rising or the setting Sun.
Hence great Anchises stole a Breed unknown
By mortal Mares, from fierce Laomedon.
Four of this Race his ample Stalls contain,
And two transport Æneas o'er the Plain.
These, were the rich immortal Prize our own,
Thro' the wide World should make our Glory known.
   Thus while they spoke, the Foe came furious on,
And stern Lycaon's warlike Race begun.
   Prince, thou art met. Tho' late in vain assail'd,   340
The Spear may enter where the Arrow fail'd.
   He said, then shook the pondrous Lance and flung,
On his broad Shield the sounding Weapon rung,
Pierc'd the tough Orb, and in his Cuirass hung.
He bleeds! The Pride of Greece! (the Boaster cries)
Our Triumph now, the mighty Warrior lies!
Mistaken Vaunter! Diomed reply'd;
Thy Dart has err'd, and now my Spear be try'd:
Ye scape not both; One, headlong from his Car,
With hostile Blood shall glut the God of War.   350
   He spoke, and rising hurl'd his forceful Dart,
Which driv'n by Pallas, pierc'd a vital Part;
Full in his Face it enter'd, and betwixt
The Nose and Eye-ball the proud Lycian fixt;
Crash'd all his Jaws, and cleft the Tongue within,
'Till the bright Point look'd out beneath the Chin.
Headlong he falls, his Helmet knocks the Ground;
Earth groans beneath him, and his Arms resound;
The starting Coursers tremble with Affright;
The Soul indignant seeks the Realms of Night.   360
   To guard his slaughter'd Friend, Æneas flies,
His Spear extending where the Carcass lies;
Watchful he wheels, protects it ev'ry way,
As the grim Lyon stalks around his Prey.
O'er the fall'n Trunk his ample Shield display'd,
He hides the Hero with his mighty Shade.

And threats aloud: The Greeks with longing Eyes
Behold at distance, but forbear the Prize.
Then fierce Tydides stoops; and from the Fields
Heav'd with vast Force, a Rocky Fragment wields.   370
Not two strong Men th' enormous Weight could raise,
Such Men as live in these degen'rate Days.
He swung it round; and gath'ring Strength to throw,
Discharg'd the pond'rous Ruin at the Foe.
Where to the Hip th' inserted Thigh unites,
Full on the Bone the pointed Marble lights;
Thro' both the Tendons broke the rugged Stone,
And stripp'd the Skin, and crack'd the solid Bone.
Sunk on his Knees and stagg'ring with his Pains,
His falling Bulk his bended Arm sustains;   380
Lost in a dizzy Mist the Warrior lies;
A sudden Cloud comes swimming o'er his Eyes.
There the brave Chief who mighty Numbers sway'd
Oppress'd had sunk to Death's Eternal Shade,
But Heav'nly Venus, mindful of the Love
She bore Anchises in th' Idæan Grove,
His Danger views with Anguish and Despair,
And guards her Offspring with a Mother's Care.
About her much-lov'd Son her Arms she throws,
Her Arms whose Whiteness match'd the falling Snows.   390
Screen'd from the Foe behind her shining Veil,
The Swords wave harmless, and the Javelins fail:
Safe thro' the rushing Horse and feather'd Flight
Of sounding Shafts, she bears him from the Fight.
   Nor Sthenelus, with unassisting Hands,
Remain'd unheedful of his Lord's Commands:
His panting Steeds, remov'd from out the War,
He fix'd with straiten'd Traces to the Car.
Next rushing to the Dardan Spoil, detains
The heav'nly Coursers with the flowing Manes.   400
These in proud Triumph to the Fleet convey'd,
No longer now a Trojan Lord obey'd.
That Charge to bold Deipylus he gave,
(Whom most he lov'd, as brave Men love the Brave)
Then mounting on his Car, resum'd the Rein,
And follow'd where Tydides swept the Plain.

Meanwhile (his Conquest ravish'd from his Eyes)
The raging Chief in chace of Venus flies:
No Goddess She, commission'd to the Field,
Like Pallas dreadful with her sable Shield, 410
Or fierce Bellona thund'ring at the Wall,
While Flames ascend, and mighty Ruins fall.
He knew soft Combates suit the tender Dame,
New to the Field, and still a Foe to Fame.
Thro' breaking Ranks his furious Course he bends,
And at the Goddess his broad Lance extends;
Thro' her bright Veil the daring Weapon drove
Th' Ambrosial Veil which all the Graces wove:
Her snowie Hand the razing Steel profan'd,
And the transparent Skin with Crimson stain'd. 420
From the clear Vein a Stream immortal flow'd,
Such Stream as issues from a wounded God;
Pure Emanation! uncorrupted Flood;
Unlike our gross, diseas'd, terrestrial Blood:
(For not the Bread of Man their Life sustains,
Nor Wine's inflaming Juice supplies their Veins.)
With tender Shrieks the Goddess fill'd the Place,
And dropt her Offspring from her weak Embrace.
Him Phæbus took: He casts a Cloud around
The fainting Chief, and wards the mortal Wound. 430
  Then with a Voice that shook the vaulted Skies,
The King insults the Goddess as she flies.
Ill with Jove's Daughter bloody Fights agree,
The Field of Combate is no Scene for thee:
Go, let thy own soft Sex employ thy Care,
Go lull the Coward, or delude the Fair.
Taught by this Stroke, renounce the War's Alarms,
And learn to tremble at the Name of Arms.
  Tydides thus. The Goddess, seiz'd with Dread,
Confus'd, distracted, from the Conflict fled. 440
To aid her, swift the winged Iris flew,
Wrapt in a Mist above the warring Crew.
The Queen of Love with faded Charms she found,
Pale was her Cheek, and livid look'd the Wound.
To Mars, who sate remote, they bent their way;
Far on the left, with Clouds involv'd, he lay;

Beside him stood his Lance, distain'd with Gore,
And, rein'd with Gold, his foaming Steeds before.
Low at his Knee, she begg'd, with streaming Eyes,
Her Brother's Car, to mount the distant Skies,   450
And shew'd the Wound by fierce Tydides giv'n,
A mortal Man, who dares encounter Heav'n.
    Stern Mars attentive hears the Queen complain,
And to her Hand commits the golden Rein:
She mounts the Seat oppress'd with silent Woe,
Driv'n by the Goddess of the painted Bow.
The Lash resounds, the rapid Chariot flies,
And in a Moment scales the lofty Skies.
There stopp'd the Car, and there the Coursers stood,
Fed by fair Iris with Ambrosial Food.   460
Before her Mother Love's bright Queen appears,
O'erwhelm'd with Anguish and dissolv'd in Tears;
She rais'd her in her Arms, beheld her bleed,
And ask'd, what God had wrought this guilty Deed?
    Then she: This Insult from no God I found,
An impious Mortal gave the daring Wound!
Behold the Deed of haughty Diomed!
'Twas in the Son's Defence the Mother bled.
The War with Troy no more the Grecians wage;
But with the Gods (th' immortal Gods) engage.   470
    Dione then. Thy Wrongs with Patience bear,
And share those Griefs inferior Pow'rs must share;
Unnumber'd Woes Mankind from us sustain,
And Men with Woes afflict the Gods again.
The mighty Mars in mortal Fetters bound,
And lodg'd in Brazen Dungeons under Ground,
Full thirteen Moons imprison'd roar'd in vain;
Otus and Ephialtes held the Chain:
Perhaps had perish'd; had not Hermes' Care
Restor'd the groaning God to upper Air.   480
Great Juno's self has born her Weight of Pain,
Th' imperial Partner of the heav'nly Reign;
Amphitryon's Son[1] infix'd the deadly Dart,
And fill'd with Anguish her immortal Heart.

[1] Hercules, *Alcides* (485)

Ev'n Hell's grim King Alcides' Pow'r confest,
The Shaft found Entrance in his Iron Breast,
To Jove's high Palace for a Cure he fled,
Pierc'd in his own Dominions of the Dead;
Where Pæon sprinkling heav'nly Balm around,
Asswag'd the glowing Pangs, and clos'd the Wound. 490
Rash, impious Man! to stain the blest Abodes,
And drench his Arrows in the Blood of Gods!
　But thou (tho' Pallas urg'd thy frantic Deed)
Whose Spear ill-fated makes a Goddess bleed,
Know thou, whoe'er with heav'nly Pow'r contends,
Short is his Date, and soon his Glory ends;
From Fields of Death when late he shall retire,
No Infant on his Knees shall call him Sire.
Strong as thou art, some God may yet be found,
To stretch thee pale and gasping on the Ground; 500
Thy distant Wife, Ægiale the Fair,
Starting from Sleep with a distracted Air,
Shall rowze thy Slaves, and her lost Lord deplore,
The brave, the great, the glorious, now no more!
　This said, she wip'd from Venus' wounded Palm
The sacred Ichor, and infus'd the Balm.
Juno and Pallas with a Smile survey'd,
And thus to Jove began the blue-ey'd Maid.
　Permit thy Daughter, gracious Jove! to tell
How this Mischance the Cyprian Queen[2] befell. 510
As late she try'd with Passion to inflame
The tender Bosome of a Grecian Dame,
Allur'd the Fair with moving Thoughts of Joy,
To quit her Country for some Youth of Troy;
The clasping Zone, with golden Buckles bound,
Raz'd her soft Hand with this lamented Wound.
　The Sire of Gods and Men superior smil'd,
And, calling Venus, thus addrest his Child.
Not these, O Daughter, are thy proper Cares,
Thee milder Arts befit, and softer Wars, 520
Sweet Smiles are thine and kind endearing Charms,
To Mars and Pallas leave the Deeds of Arms.

[2] Venus

Thus they in Heav'n: While on the Plain below
The fierce Tydides charg'd his Dardan Foe[3]:
Flush'd with Celestial Blood pursu'd his way,
And fearless dar'd the threatning God of Day;
Already in his Hopes he saw him kill'd,
Tho' screen'd behind Apollo's mighty Shield.
Thrice rushing furious, at the Chief he strook;
His blazing Buckler thrice Apollo shook: 530
He try'd the fourth: When breaking from the Cloud,
A more than mortal Voice was heard aloud.

O Son of Tydeus, cease! be wise and see
How vast the Diff'rence of the Gods and Thee;
Distance immense! between the Pow'rs that shine
Above, Eternal, Deathless, and Divine,
And mortal Man! a Wretch of humble Birth,
A short-liv'd Reptile in the Dust of Earth.

So spoke the God who darts Celestial Fires;
He dreads his Fury, and some Steps retires.   540
Then Phœbus bore the Chief of Venus' Race
To Troy's high Fane, and to his Holy Place;
Latona there and Phœbe heal'd the Wound,
With Vigor arm'd him, and with Glory crown'd.
This done, the Patron of the Silver Bow
A Phantom rais'd, the same in Shape and Show
With great Æneas; such the Form he bore,
And such in Fight the radiant Arms he wore.
Around the Spectre bloody Wars are wag'd,
And Greece and Troy with clashing Shields engag'd.   550
Meantime on Ilion's Tow'r Apollo stood,
And calling Mars, thus urg'd the raging God.

Stern Pow'r of Arms! by whom the Mighty fall,
Who bathe in Blood, and shake th' embattel'd Wall!
Rise in thy Wrath! To Hell's abhorr'd Abodes
Dispatch yon' Greek, and vindicate the Gods.
First rosie Venus felt his brutal Rage;
Me next he charg'd, and dares all Heav'n engage:
The Wretch would brave high Heav'ns immortal Sire,
His triple Thunder, and his Bolts of Fire.   560

[3] Aeneas

The God of Battel issues on the Plain,
Stirs all the Ranks, and fires the Trojan Train;
In Form like Acamas, the Thracian Guide,
Enrag'd, to Troy's retiring Chiefs he cry'd.
How long, ye Sons of Priam! will ye fly,
And unreveng'd see Priam's People die?
Still unresisted shall the Foe destroy,
And stretch the Slaughter to the Gates of Troy?
Lo brave Æneas sinks beneath his Wound,
Not Godlike Hector more in Arms renown'd: 570
Haste all, and take the gen'rous Warrior's Part.
He said; new Courage swell'd each Hero's Heart.
Sarpedon first his ardent Soul express'd,
And, turn'd to Hector, these bold Words address'd.
    Say, Chief, is all thy ancient Valor lost,
Where are thy Threats, and where thy glorious Boast,
That propt alone by Priam's Race should stand
Troy's sacred Walls, nor need a foreign Hand?
Now, now thy Country calls her wanted Friends,
And the proud Vaunt in just Derision ends.   580
Remote they stand, while Alien Troops engage,
Like trembling Hounds before the Lion's Rage.
Far distant hence I held my wide Command,
Where foaming Xanthus laves the Lycian Land,
With ample Wealth (the Wish of Mortals) blest,
A beauteous Wife, and Infant at her Breast;
With those I left whatever dear could be;
Greece, if she conquers, nothing wins from me.
Yet first in Fight my Lycian Bands I chear,
And long to meet this mighty Man ye fear.   590
While Hector idle stands, nor bids the Brave
Their Wives, their Infants, and their Altars save.
Haste, Warrior, haste! preserve thy threaten'd State;
Or one vast Burst of all-involving Fate
Full o'er your Tow'rs shall fall, and sweep away
Sons, Sires, and Wives, an undistinguish'd Prey.
Rowze all thy Trojans, urge thy Aids to fight;
These claim thy Thoughts by Day, thy Watch by Night:
With Force incessant the brave Greeks oppose;
Such Cares thy Friends deserve, and such thy Foes.   600

Stung to the Heart the gen'rous Hector hears,
But just Reproof with decent Silence bears.
From his proud Car the Prince impetuous springs;
On Earth he leaps; his Brazen Armor rings.
Two shining Spears are brandish'd in his Hands;
Thus arm'd, he animates his drooping Bands,
Revives their Ardor, turns their Steps from Flight,
And wakes anew the dying Flames of Fight.
They turn, they stand: The Greeks their Fury dare,
Condense their Pow'rs, and wait the growing War. 610
  As when on Ceres' sacred Floor the Swain
Spreads the wide Fan to clear the golden Grain,
And the light Chaff, before the Breezes born,
Ascends in Clouds from off the heapy Corn;
The grey Dust, rising with collected Winds,
Drives o'er the Barn, and whitens all the Hinds.
So white with Dust the Grecian Host appears,
From trampling Steeds, and thundring Charioteers,
The dusky Clouds from labour'd Earth arise,
And roll in smoaking Volumes to the Skies. 620
Mars hovers o'er them with his sable Shield,
And adds new Horrors to the darken'd Field;
Pleas'd with his Charge, and ardent to fulfill
In Troy's Defence Apollo's heav'nly Will:
Soon as from Fight the blue-ey'd Maid retires,
Each Trojan Bosom with new Warmth he fires.
And now the God, from forth his sacred Fane,
Produc'd Æneas to the shouting Train;
Alive, unharm'd, with all his Peers around,
Erect he stood, and vig'rous from his Wound: 630
Enquiries none they made; the dreadful Day
No Pause of Words admits, no dull Delay;
Fierce Discord storms, Apollo loud exclaims,
Fame calls, Mars thunders, and the Field's in Flames.
  Stern Diomed with either Ajax stood,
And great Ulysses, bath'd in hostile Blood.
Embodied Close, the lab'ring Grecian Train
The fiercest Shock of charging Hosts sustain;
Unmov'd and silent, the whole War they wait,
Serenely dreadful, and as fix'd as Fate. 640

So when th' embattel'd Clouds in dark Array
Along the Skies their gloomy Lines display,
When now the North his boist'rous Rage has spent,
And peaceful sleeps the liquid Element,
The low-hung Vapors, motionless and still,
Rest on the Summits of the shaded Hill;
'Till the Mass scatters as the Winds arise,
Dispers'd and broken thro' the ruffled Skies.
 Nor was the Gen'ral wanting to his Train,
From Troop to Troop he toils thro' all the Plain. 650
Ye Greeks be Men! the Charge of Battel bear;
Your brave Associates, and Your-selves revere!
Let glorious Acts more glorious Acts inspire,
And catch from Breast to Breast the noble Fire!
On Valor's side the Odds of Combate lie,
The Brave live glorious, or lamented die;
The Wretch who trembles in the Field of Fame,
Meets Death, and worse than Death, Eternal Shame.
 These Words he seconds with his flying Lance,
To meet whose Point was strong Deicoon's Chance; 660
Æneas' Friend, and in his native Place
Honour'd and lov'd like Priam's Royal Race:
Long had he fought the foremost in the Field;
But now the Monarch's Lance transpierc'd his Shield,
His Shield too weak the furious Dart to stay,
Thro' his broad Belt the Weapon forc'd its way;
The grizly Wound dismiss'd his Soul to Hell,
His Arms around him rattled as he fell.
 Then fierce Æneas brandishing his Blade,
In Dust Orsilochus and Crethon laid, 670
Whose Sire Diöcleus, wealthy, brave and great,
In well-built Pheræ held his lofty Seat:
Sprung from Alpheus, plenteous Stream! that yields
Encrease of Harvests to the Pylian Fields:
He got Orsilochus, Diöcleus He,
And these descended in the third Degree.
Too early expert in the martial Toil,
In sable Ships they left their native Soil,
T'avenge Atrides: Now, untimely slain,
They fell with Glory on the Phrygian Plain. 680

So two young Mountain Lions, nurs'd with Blood
In deep Recesses of the gloomy Wood,
Rush fearless to the Plains, and uncontroul'd
Depopulate the Stalls and waste the Fold;
'Till pierc'd at distance from their native Den,
O'erpow'r'd they fall beneath the Force of Men.
Prostrate on Earth their beauteous Bodies lay,
Like Mountain Firs, as tall and strait as they.
Great Menelaus views with pitying Eyes,
Lifts his bright Lance, and at the Victor flies;   690
Mars urg'd him on; yet, ruthless in his Hate,
The God but urg'd him to provoke his Fate.
He thus advancing, Nestor's valiant Son
Shakes for his Danger, and neglects his own;
Struck with the Thought, should Helen's Lord be slain,
And all his Country's glorious Labours vain.
Already met the threat'ning Heroes stand;
The Spears already tremble in their Hand;
In rush'd Antilochus, his Aid to bring,
And fall or conquer by the Spartan King.   700
These seen, the Dardan backward turn'd his Course,
Brave as he was, and shunn'd unequal Force.
The breathless Bodies to the Greeks they drew;
Then mix in Combate and their Toils renew.
    First Pylæmenes, great in Battel, bled,
Who sheath'd in Brass the Paphlagonians led.
Atrides mark'd him where sublime he stood;
Fix'd in his Throat, the Javelin drank his Blood.
The faithful Mydon as he turn'd from Fight
His flying Coursers, sunk to endless Night: 710
A broken Rock by Nestor's Son was thrown,
His bended Arm receiv'd the falling Stone,
From his numb'd Hand the Iv'ry-studded Reins
Dropt in the Dust are trail'd along the Plains.
Meanwhile his Temples feel a deadly Wound;
He groans in Death, and pondrous sinks to Ground:
Deep drove his Helmet in the Sands, and there
The Head stood fix'd, the quiv'ring Legs in Air:

'Till trampled flat beneath the Courser's Feet,
The youthful Victor mounts his empty Seat,   720
And bears the Prize in Triumph to the Fleet.
　Great Hector saw, and raging at the View
Pours on the Greeks: The Trojan Troops pursue:
He fires his Host with animating Cries,
And brings along the Furies of the Skies.
Mars, stern Destroyer! and Bellona dread,
Flame in the Front, and thunder at their Head:
This swells the Tumult and the Rage of Fight;
That shakes a Spear that casts a dreadful Light;
Where Hector march'd, the God of Battels shin'd,   730
Now storm'd before him, and now rag'd behind.
　Tydides paus'd amidst his full Carrier;
Then first the Hero's manly Breast knew Fear.
As when some simple Swain his Cot forsakes,
And wide thro' Fens an unknown Journey takes;
If chance a swelling Brook his Passage stay,
And foam impervious cross the Wand'rer's way,
Confus'd he stops, a Length of Country past,
Eyes the rough Waves, and tir'd returns at last.
Amaz'd no less the great Tydides stands;   740
He stay'd, and turning, thus address'd his Bands.
　No wonder, Greeks! that all to Hector yield,
Secure of fav'ring Gods, he takes the Field;
His Strokes they second, and avert our Spears:
Behold where Mars in mortal Arms appears!
Retire then Warriors, but sedate and slow;
Retire, but with your Faces to the Foe.
Trust not too much your unavailing Might;
'Tis not with Troy, but with the Gods ye fight.
　Now near the Greeks the black Battalions drew,   750
And first two Leaders valiant Hector slew,
His Force Anchialus and Mnesthes found,
In ev'ry Art of glorious War renown'd;
In the same Car the Chiefs to Combate ride,
And fought united, and united dy'd.
Struck at the Sight, the mighty Ajax glows
With Thirst of Vengeance, and assaults the Foes.

His massy Spear with matchless Fury sent
Thro' Amphius' Belt and heaving Belly went:
Amphius Apæsus' happy Soil posses'd,   760
With Herds abounding, and with Treasure bless'd;
But Fate resistless from his Country led
The Chief, to perish at his People's Head.
Shook with his Fall his Brazen Armor rung,
And fierce, to seize it, conqu'ring Ajax sprung:
Around his Head an Iron Tempest rain'd;
A Wood of Spears his ample Shield sustain'd;
Beneath one Foot the yet-warm Corps he prest,
And drew his Javelin from the bleeding Breast:
He could no more; The show'ring Darts deny'd   770
To spoil his glitt'ring Arms, and Plumy Pride.
Now Foes on Foes came pouring on the Fields,
With bristling Lances, and compacted Shields;
'Till in the Steely Circle straiten'd round,
Forc'd he gives way, and sternly quits the Ground.

  While thus they strive, Tlepolemus the great,
Urg'd by the Force of unresisted Fate,
Burns with Desire Sarpedon's Strength to prove;
Alcides' Offspring meets the Son of Jove.
Sheath'd in bright Arms each adverse Chief came on,   780
Jove's great Descendent, and his greater Son.
Prepar'd for Combate, e're the Lance he tost,
The daring Rhodian vents his haughty Boast.

  What brings this Lycian Counsellor so far,
To tremble at our Arms, not mix in War?
Know thy vain self, nor let their Flatt'ry move
Who style thee Son of Cloud-compelling Jove.
How far unlike those Chiefs of Race divine,
How vast the Diff'rence of their Deeds and thine?
Jove got such Heroes as my Sire, whose Soul   790
No Fear could daunt, nor Earth, nor Hell controul.
Troy felt his Arm, and yon' proud Ramparts stand
Rais'd on the Ruins of his vengeful Hand:
With six small Ships, and but a slender Train,
He left the Town a wide, deserted Plain.
But what art thou? who deedless look'st around,
While unreveng'd thy Lycians bite the Ground:

Small Aid to Troy thy feeble Force can be,
But wert thou greater, thou must yield to me.
Pierc'd by my Spear to endless Darkness go!   800
I make this Present to the Shades below.
The Son of Hercules, the Rhodian Guide,
Thus haughty spoke. The Lycian King reply'd.
Thy Sire, O Prince! o'erturn'd the Trojan State,
Whose perjur'd Monarch well deserv'd his Fate;
Those heav'nly Steeds the Hero sought so far,
False he detain'd, the just Reward of War:
Nor so content, the gen'rous Chief defy'd,
With base Reproaches and unmanly Pride.
But you, unworthy the high Race you boast,   810
Shall raise my Glory when thy own is lost:
Now meet thy Fate, and by Sarpedon slain
Add one more Ghost to Pluto's gloomy Reign.
He said: Both Javelins at an Instant flew:
Both strook, both wounded, but Sarpedon's slew:
Full in the Boaster's Neck the Weapon stood,
Transfix'd his Throat, and drank the vital Blood;
The Soul disdainful seeks the Caves of Night,
And his seal'd Eyes for ever lose the Light.
Yet not in vain, Tlepolemus, was thrown   820
Thy angry Lance; which piercing to the Bone
Sarpedon's Thigh, had robb'd the Chief of Breath;
But Jove was present, and forbad the Death.
Born from the Conflict by his Lycian Throng,
The wounded Hero dragg'd the Lance along.
(His Friends, each busy'd in his sev'ral Part,
Thro' Haste, or Danger, had not drawn the Dart)
The Greeks with slain Tlepolemus retir'd;
Whose Fall Ulysses view'd, with Fury fir'd;
Doubtful if Jove's great Son he should pursue,   830
Or pour his Vengeance on the Lycian Crew.
But Heav'n and Fate the first Design withstand,
Nor this great Death must grace Ulysses' Hand.
Minerva drives him on the Lycian Train;
Alastor, Chromius, Halius strow'd the Plain,
Alcander, Prytanis, Noëmon fell,
And Numbers more his Sword had sent to Hell:

But Hector saw; and furious at the Sight,
Rush'd terrible amidst the Ranks of Fight.
With Joy Sarpedon view'd the wish'd Relief,   840
And faint, lamenting, thus implor'd the Chief.
   Oh suffer not the Foe to bear away
My helpless Corps, an unassisted Prey.
If I, unblest, must see my Son no more,
My much-lov'd Consort, and my native Shore,
Yet let me die in Ilion's sacred Wall;
Troy, in whose Cause I fell, shall mourn my Fall.
   He said, nor Hector to the Chief replies,
But shakes his Plume, and fierce to Combate flies,
Swift as a Whirlwind drives the scatt'ring Foes,   850
And dyes the Ground in Purple as he goes.
   Beneath a Beech, Jove's consecrated Shade,
His mournful Friends divine Sarpedon laid:
Brave Pelagon, his fav'rite Chief, was nigh,
Who wrench'd the Javelin from his sinewy Thigh.
The fainting Soul stood ready wing'd for Flight,
And o'er his Eye-balls swum the Shades of Night.
But Boreas rising fresh, with gentle Breath,
Recall'd his Spirit from the Gates of Death.
   The gen'rous Greeks recede with tardy Pace,   860
Tho Mars and Hector thunder in their Face;
None turn their Backs to mean ignoble Flight,
Slow they retreat, and ev'n retreating fight.
Who first, who last, by Mars and Hector's Hand
Stretch'd in their Blood lay gasping on the Sand?
Teuthras the great, Orestes the renown'd
For manag'd Steeds, and Trechus press'd the Ground;
Next Oenomaus, and Oenops' Offspring dy'd;
Oresbius last fell groaning at their side:
Oresbius, in his painted Mitre gay,   870
In fat Bœotia held his wealthy Sway,
Where Lakes surround low Hylè's watry Plain;
A Prince and People studious of their Gain.
   The Carnage Juno from the Skies survey'd,
And touch'd with Grief bespoke the blue-ey'd Maid.
Oh Sight accurst! Shall faithless Troy prevail,
And shall our Promise to our People fail?

How vain the Word to Menelaus giv'n
By Jove's great Daughter and the Queen of Heav'n,
Beneath his Arms that Priam's Tow'rs should fall; 880
If warring Gods for ever guard the Wall?
Mars, red with Slaughter, aids our hated Foes:
Haste, let us arm, and Force with Force oppose!
   She spoke; Minerva burns to meet the War:
And now Heav'ns Empress calls her blazing Car.
At her Command rush forth the Steeds Divine;
Rich with immortal Gold their Trappings shine.
Bright Hebè waits; by Hebè, ever young,
The whirling Wheels are to the Chariot hung.
On the bright Axle turns the bidden Wheel, 890
Of sounding Brass; the polish'd Axle Steel.
Eight brazen Spokes in radiant Order flame;
The Circles Gold, of uncorrupted Frame,
Such as the Heav'ns produce: and round the Gold
Two brazen Rings of Work divine were roll'd.
The bossie Naves of solid Silver shone;
Braces of Gold suspend the moving Throne:
The Car behind an arching Figure bore;
The bending Concave form'd an Arch before.
Silver the Beam, th' extended Yoke was Gold, 900
And golden Reins th' immortal Coursers hold.
Herself, impatient, to the ready Car
The Coursers joins, and breathes Revenge and War.
   Pallas disrobes; Her radiant Veil unty'd,
With Flow'rs adorn'd, with Art diversify'd,
(The labour'd Veil her heav'nly Fingers wove)
Flows on the Pavement of the Court of Jove.
Now Heav'ns dread Arms her mighty Limbs invest,
Jove's Cuirass blazes on her ample Breast;
Deck'd in sad Triumph for the mournful Field, 910
O'er her broad Shoulders hangs his horrid Shield,
Dire, black, tremendous! Round the Margin roll'd,
A Fringe of Serpents hissing guards the Gold:
Here all the Terrors of grim War appear,
Here rages Force, here tremble Flight and Fear,
Here storm'd Contention, and here Fury frown'd;
And the dire Orb Portentous Gorgon crown'd.

The massy golden Helm she next assumes,
That dreadful nods with four o'ershading Plumes;
So vast, the broad Circumference contains   920
A hundred Armies on a hundred Plains.
The Goddess thus th' imperial Car ascends;
Shook by her Arm the mighty Javelin bends,
Pond'rous and huge; that when her Fury burns,
Proud Tyrants humbles, and whole Hosts o'erturns.
  Swift at the Scourge th' Ethereal Coursers fly,
While the smooth Chariot cuts the liquid Sky.
Heav'n Gates spontaneous open to the Pow'rs,
Heav'ns golden Gates, kept by the winged Hours;
Commission'd in alternate Watch they stand,   930
The Sun's bright Portals and the Skies command,
Involve in Clouds th' Eternal Gates of Day,
Or the dark Barrier roll with Ease away.
The sounding Hinges ring: On either side
The gloomy Volumes, pierc'd with Light, divide.
The Chariot mounts, where deep in ambient Skies,
Confus'd, Olympus' hundred Heads arise;
Where far apart the Thund'rer fills his Throne,
O'er all the Gods, superior and alone.
  There with her snowy Hand the Queen restrains   940
The fiery Steeds, and thus to Jove complains.
  O Sire! can no Resentment touch thy Soul?
Can Mars rebel, and does no Thunder roll?
What lawless Rage on yon' forbidden Plain,
What rash Destruction! and what Heroes slain?
Venus, and Phœbus with the dreadful Bow,
Smile on the Slaughter, and enjoy my Woe.
Mad, furious Pow'r! whose unrelenting Mind
No God can govern, and no Justice bind.
Say, mighty Father! Shall we scourge his Pride,   950
And drive from Fight th' impetuous Homicide?
  To whom assenting, thus the Thund'rer said:
Go! and the great Minerva be thy Aid.
To tame the Monster-God Minerva knows,
And oft' afflicts his Brutal Breast with Woes.
  He said; Saturnia, ardent to obey,
Lash'd her white Steeds along th' Aerial Way.

Swift down the Steep of Heav'n the Chariot rolls,
Between th' expanded Earth and starry Poles.
Far as a Shepherd, from some Point on high,   960
O'er the wide Main extends his boundless Eye,
Thro' such a Space of Air, with thund'ring Sound,
At ev'ry Leap th' Immortal Coursers bound.
Troy now they reach'd, and touch'd those Banks Divine
Where Silver Simois and Scamander join.
There Juno stop'd, and (her fair Steeds unloos'd)
Of Air condens'd a Vapor circumfus'd:
For these, impregnate with Celestial Dew
On Simois' Brink Ambrosial Herbage grew.
Thence, to relieve the fainting Argive Throng,   970
Smooth as the sailing Doves they glide along.
The best and bravest of the Grecian Band
(A warlike Circle) round Tydides stand:
Such was their Look as Lions bath'd in Blood,
Or foaming Boars, the Terror of the Wood.
Heav'ns Empress mingles with the mortal Crowd,
And shouts, in Stentor's sounding Voice, aloud:
Stentor the strong, endu'd with Brazen Lungs,
Whose Throat surpass'd the Force of fifty Tongues.

    Inglorious Argives! to your Race a Shame,   980
And only Men in Figure and in Name!
Once from their Walls your tim'rous Foes engag'd,
While fierce in War divine Achilles rag'd;
Now issuing fearless they possess the Plain,
Now win the Shores, and scarce the Seas remain.

    Her Speech new Fury to their Hearts convey'd;
While near Tydides stood th' Athenian Maid:
The King beside his panting Steeds she found,
O'erspent with Toil, reposing on the Ground;
To cool his glowing Wound he sate apart,   990
(The Wound inflicted by the Lycian Dart)
Large Drops of Sweat from all his Limbs descend,
Beneath his pond'rous Shield his Sinews bend,
Whose ample Belt that o'er his Shoulder lay,
He eas'd; and wash'd the clotted Gore away.
The Goddess leaning o'er the bending Yoke,
Beside his Coursers, thus her Silence broke.

Degen'rate Prince! and not of Tydeus' Kind,
Whose little Body lodg'd a mighty Mind.
Foremost he press'd, in glorious Toils to share,   1000
And scarce refrain'd when I forbad the War.
Alone, unguarded, once he dar'd to go,
And feast encircled by the Theban Foe;
There brav'd, and vanquish'd, many a hardy Knight;
Such Nerves I gave him, and such Force in Fight.
Thou too no less hast been my constant Care;
Thy Hands I arm'd, and sent thee forth to War:
But Thee or Fear deterrs, or Sloth detains;
No Drop of all thy Father warms thy Veins.
The Chief thus answer'd mild. Immortal Maid!   1010
I own thy Presence, and confess thy Aid.
Not Fear, thou know'st, withholds me from the Plains,
Nor Sloth hath seiz'd me, but thy Word restrains:
From warring Gods thou bad'st me turn my Spear,
And Venus only found Resistance here.
Hence, Goddess! heedful of thy high Commands,
Loth I gave way, and warn'd our Argive Bands:
For Mars, the Homicide, these Eyes beheld,
With Slaughter red, and raging round the Field.
Then thus Minerva. Grave Tydides hear!   1020
Not Mars himself, nor ought Immortal fear.
Full on the God impell thy foaming Horse:
Pallas commands, and Pallas lends thee Force.
Rash, furious, blind, from these to those he flies,
And ev'ry side of wav'ring Combate tries;
Large Promise makes, and breaks the Promise made;
Now gives the Grecians, now the Trojans Aid.
She said, and to the Steeds approaching near,
Drew from his Seat the martial Charioteer.
The vig'rous Pow'r the trembling Car ascends,   1030
Fierce for Revenge; and Diomed attends.
The groaning Axle bent beneath the Load;
So great a Hero, and so great a God.
She snatch'd the Reins, she lash'd with all her Force,
And full on Mars impell'd the foaming Horse:
But first, to hide her Heav'nly Visage, spread
Black Orcus' Helmet o'er her radiant Head.

Just then Gigantic Periphas lay slain,
The strongest Warrior of th' Ætolian Train;
The God who slew him, leaves his prostrate Prize   1040
Stretch'd where he fell, and at Tydides flies.
Now rushing fierce, in equal Arms appear,
The daring Greek; the dreadful God of War!
Full at the Chief, above his Courser's Head,
From Mars his Arm th' enormous Weapon fled:
Pallas oppos'd her Hand, and caus'd to glance
Far from the Car, the strong immortal Lance.
Then threw the Force of Tydeus' warlike Son;
The Javelin hiss'd; the Goddess urg'd it on:
Where the broad Cincture girt his Armor round,   1050
It pierc'd the God: His Groin receiv'd the Wound.
From the rent Skin the Warrior tuggs again
The smoaking Steel. Mars bellows with the Pain:
Loud, as the Roar encountring Armies yield,
When shouting Millions shake the thund'ring Field.
Both Armies start, and trembling gaze around;
And Earth and Heav'n rebellow to the Sound.
As Vapors blown by Auster's sultry Breath,
Pregnant with Plagues, and shedding Seeds of Death,
Beneath the Rage of burning Sirius rise,   1060
Choak the parch'd Earth, and blacken all the Skies;
In such a Cloud the God from Combate driv'n,
High o'er the dusty Whirlwind scales the Heav'n.
Wild with his Pain, he sought the bright Abodes,
There sullen sate beneath the Sire of Gods,
Show'd the Celestial Blood, and with a Groan
Thus pour'd his Plaints before th' immortal Throne.
  Can Jove, supine, flagitious Facts survey,
And brook the Furies of this daring Day?
For mortal Men Celestial Pow'rs engage,   1070
And Gods on Gods exert Eternal Rage.
From thee, O Father! all these Ills we bear,
And thy fell Daughter with the Shield and Spear:
Thou gav'st that Fury to the Realms of Light,
Pernicious, wild, regardless of the Right.
All Heav'n beside revere thy Sov'reign Sway,
Thy Voice we hear, and thy Behests obey:

'Tis hers t'offend; and ev'n offending share
Thy Breast, thy Counsels, thy distinguish'd Care:
So boundless she, and thou so partial grown,   1080
Well may we deem the wond'rous Birth thy own.
Now frantic Diomed, at her Command,
Against th' Immortals lifts his raging Hand:
The heav'nly Venus first his Fury found,
Me next encount'ring, me he dar'd to wound;
Vanquish'd I fled: Ev'n I, the God of Fight,
From mortal Madness scarce was sav'd by Flight.
Else had'st thou seen me sink on yonder Plain,
Heap'd round, and heaving under Loads of slain;
Or pierc'd with Grecian Darts, for Ages lie,   1090
Condemn'd to Pain, tho' fated not to die.
   Him thus upbraiding, with a wrathful Look
The Lord of Thunders view'd, and stern bespoke.
To me, Perfidious! this lamenting Strain?
Of lawless Force shall lawless Mars complain?
Of all the Gods who tread the spangled Skies,
Thou most unjust, most odious in our Eyes!
Inhuman Discord is thy dire Delight,
The Waste of Slaughter, and the Rage of Fight.
No Bound, no Law thy fiery Temper quells,   1100
And all thy Mother in thy Soul rebells.
In vain our Threats, in vain our Pow'r we use;
She gives th' Example, and her Son pursues.
Yet long th' inflicted Pangs thou shalt not mourn,
Sprung since thou art from Jove, and Heav'nly born.
Else, sing'd with Light'ning, had'st thou hence been thrown,
Where chain'd on burning Rocks the Titans groan.
   Thus He who shakes Olympus with his Nod;
Then gave to Pœon's Care the bleeding God.
With gentle Hand the Balm he pour'd around,   1110
And heal'd th' immortal Flesh, and clos'd the Wound.
As when the Fig's prest Juice, infus'd in Cream,
To Curds coagulates the liquid Stream,
Sudden the Fluids fix, the Parts combin'd;
Such, and so soon, th' Ætherial Texture join'd.

Cleans'd from the Dust and Gore, fair Hebè drest
His mighty Limbs in an immortal Vest.
Glorious he sate, in Majesty restor'd,
Fast by the Throne of Heav'ns superior Lord.
Juno and Pallas mount the blest Abodes,   1120
Their Task perform'd, and mix among the Gods.

ᒲᒲᒲᒲ

THE SIXTH BOOK
OF THE ILIAD

THE ARGUMENT

The Episodes of Glaucus and Diomed,
and of Hector and Andromache

THE GODS having left the Field, the Grecians prevail. Helenus, the chief
Augur of Troy, commands Hector to return to the City in order to ap-
point a solemn Procession of the Queen and the Trojan Matrons to the
Temple of Minerva, to entreat her to remove Diomed from the Fight.
The Battel relaxing during the Absence of Hector, Glaucus and Diomed
have an Interview between the two Armies; where coming to the Knowl-
edge of the Friendship and Hospitality past between their Ancestors, they
make exchange of their Arms. Hector having performed the Orders of
Helenus, prevail'd upon Paris to return to the Battel, and taken a tender
Leave of his Wife Andromache, hastens again to the Field.

The Scene is first in the Field of Battel, between the Rivers Simois and
Scamander, and then changes to Troy.

Now Heav'n forsakes the Fight: Th' Immortals yield
To human Force and human Skill, the Field:
Dark Show'rs of Javelins fly from Foes to Foes;
Now here, now there, the Tyde of Combate flows;
While Troy's fam'd Streams that bound the deathful Plain
On either side run purple to the Main.
  Great Ajax first to Conquest led the way,
Broke the thick Ranks, and turn'd the doubtful Day.

The Thracian Acamas his Faulchion found,
That hew'd th' enormous Giant to the Ground; 10
His thundring Arm a deadly Stroke imprest
Where the black Horse-hair nodded o'er his Crest:
Fix'd in his Front the brazen Weapon lies,
And seals in endless Shades his swimming Eyes.
Next Teuthras' Son distain'd the Sands with Blood,
Axylus, hospitable, rich and good:
In fair Arisba's Walls (his native Place)
He held his Seat; a Friend to Human Race.
Fast by the Road, his ever-open Door
Oblig'd the Wealthy, and reliev'd the Poor. 20
To stern Tydides now he falls a Prey,
No Friend to guard him in the dreadful Day!
Breathless the good Man fell, and by his side
His faithful Servant, old Calesius dy'd.
    By great Euryalus was Dresus slain,
And next he lay'd Opheltius on the Plain.
Two Twins were near, bold, beautiful and young,
From a fair Naiad and Bucolion sprung:
(Laomedon's white Flocks Bucolion fed,
That Monarch's First-born by a foreign Bed; 30
In secret Woods he won the Naiad's Grace,
And two fair Infants crown'd his strong Embrace.)
Here dead they lay in all their youthful Charms;
The ruthless Victor stripp'd their shining Arms.
    Astyalus by Polypætes fell;
Ulysses' Spear Pidytes sent to Hell;
By Teucer's Shaft brave Aretäon bled,
And Nestor's Son laid stern Ablerus dead.
Great Agamemnon, Leader of the Brave,
The mortal Wound of rich Elatus gave, 40
Who held in Pedasus his proud Abode,
And till'd the Banks where silver Satnio flow'd.
Melanthius by Eurypylus was slain;
And Phylacus from Leitus flies in vain.
    Unblest Adrastus next at Mercy lies
Beneath the Spartan[1] Spear, a living Prize.

[1] Of Menelaus

Scar'd with the Din and Tumult of the Fight,
His headlong Steeds, precipitate in Flight,
Rush'd on a Tamarisk's strong Trunk, and broke
The shatter'd Chariot from the crooked Yoke: 50
Wide o'er the Field, resistless as the Wind,
For Troy they fly, and leave their Lord behind.
Prone on his Face he sinks beside the Wheel;
Atrides o'er him shakes his vengeful Steel;
The fallen Chief in suppliant Posture press'd
The Victor's Knees, and thus his Pray'r address'd.
    Oh spare my Youth, and for the Life I owe
Large Gifts of Price my Father shall bestow;
When Fame shall tell, that not in Battel slain
Thy hollow Ships his Captive Son detain,   60
Rich Heaps of Brass shall in thy Tent be told,
And Steel well-temper'd, and persuasive Gold.
    He said: Compassion touch'd the Hero's Heart,
He stood suspended with the lifted Dart:
As Pity pleaded for his vanquish'd Prize,
Stern Agamemnon swift to Vengeance flies,
And furious, thus. Oh impotent of Mind!
Shall these, shall these Atrides' Mercy find?
Well hast thou known proud Troy's perfidious Land,
And well her Natives merit at thy Hand!   70
Not one of all the Race, not Sex, nor Age,
Shall save a Trojan from our boundless Rage:
Ilion shall perish whole, and bury All;
Her Babes, her Infants at the Breast, shall fall.
A dreadful Lesson of exampled Fate,
To warn the Nations, and to curb the Great!
    The Monarch spoke: the Words with Warmth addrest
To rigid Justice steel'd his Brother's Breast.
Fierce from his Knees the hapless Chief he thrust;
The Monarch's Javelin stretch'd him in the Dust.   80
Then pressing with his Foot his panting Heart,
Forth from the slain he tugg'd the reeking Dart.
Old Nestor saw, and rowz'd the Warrior's Rage;
Thus, Heroes! thus the vig'rous Combate wage!

No Son of Mars descend, for servile Gains,
To touch the Booty, while a Foe remains.
Behold yon' glitt'ring Host, your future Spoil!
First gain the Conquest, then reward the Toil.
  And now had Greece Eternal Fame acquir'd.
And frighted Troy within her Walls retir'd;   90
Had not sage Helenus her State redrest,
Taught by the Gods that mov'd his sacred Breast:
Where Hector stood, with great Æneas join'd,
The Seer reveal'd the Counsels of his Mind.
  Ye gen'rous Chiefs! on whom th' Immortals lay
The Cares and Glories of this doubtful Day,
On whom your Aid's, your Country's Hopes depend,
Wise to consult, and active to defend!
Here, at our Gates, your brave Efforts unite,
Turn back the Routed, and forbid the Flight;   100
E're yet their Wives soft Arms the Cowards gain,
The Sport and Insult of the Hostile Train.
When your Commands have hearten'd ev'ry Band,
Our selves, here fix'd, will make the dang'rous Stand:
Press'd as we are, and sore of former Fight,
These Straits demand our last Remains of Might.
Meanwhile, thou Hector to the Town retire,
And teach our Mother what the Gods require:
Direct the Queen to lead th' assembled Train
Of Troy's chief Matrons to Minerva's Fane;   110
Unbar the sacred Gates; and seek the Pow'r
With offer'd Vows, in Ilion's topmost Tow'r.
The largest Mantle her rich Wardrobes hold,
Most priz'd for Art, and labour'd o'er with Gold,
Before the Goddess' honour'd Knees be spread;
And twelve young Heifers to her Altars led.
If so the Pow'r, atton'd by fervent Pray'r,
Our Wives, our Infants, and our City spare,
And far avert Tydides' wastful Ire,
That mows whole Troops, and makes all Troy retire.   120
Not thus Achilles taught our Hosts to dread,
Sprung tho' he was from more than mortal Bed;

Not thus resistless rul'd the Stream of Fight,
In Rage unbounded, and unmatch'd in Might.
Hector obedient heard; and, with a Bound,
Leap'd from his trembling Chariot to the Ground;
Thro' all his Host, inspiring Force he flies,
And bids the Thunder of the Battel rise.
With Rage recruited the bold Trojans glow,
And turn the Tyde of Conflict on the Foe: 130
Fierce in the Front he shakes two dazling Spears;
All Greece recedes, and 'midst her Triumph fears.
Some God, they thought, who rul'd the Fate of Wars,
Shot down avenging, from the Vault of Stars.

Then thus, aloud. Ye dauntless Dardans hear!
And you whom distant Nations send to War!
Be mindful of the Strength your Fathers bore;
Be still your selves, and Hector asks no more.
One Hour demands me in the Trojan Wall,
To bid our Altars flame, and Victims fall: 140
Nor shall, I trust, the Matron's holy Train
And rev'rend Elders, seek the Gods in vain.

This said, with ample Strides the Hero past;
The Shield's large Orb behind his Shoulder cast,
His Neck o'ershading, to his Ancle hung;
And as he march'd, the brazen Buckler rung.

Now paus'd the Battel, (Godlike Hector gone)
When daring Glaucus and great Tydeus' Son
Between both Armies met: The Chiefs from far
Observ'd each other, and had mark'd for War. 150
Near as they drew, Tydides thus began.

What art thou, boldest of the Race of Man?
Our Eyes, till now, that Aspect ne'er beheld,
Where Fame is reap'd amid th' embattel'd Field;
Yet far before the Troops thou dar'st appear,
And meet a Lance the fiercest Heroes fear.
Unhappy they, and born of luckless Sires,
Who tempt our Fury when Minerva fires!
But if from Heav'n, Celestial thou descend;
Know, with Immortals we no more contend. 160

Not long Lycurgus view'd the Golden Light,
That daring Man who mix'd with Gods in Fight;
Bacchus, and Bacchus' Votaries he drove
With brandish'd Steel from Nyssa's sacred Grove,
Their consecrated Spears lay scatter'd round,
With curling Vines and twisted Ivy bound;
While Bacchus headlong sought the briny Flood,
And Thetis' Arms receiv'd the trembling God.
Nor fail'd the Crime th' Immortals Wrath to move,
(Th' Immortals blest with endless Ease above)   170
Depriv'd of Sight by their avenging Doom,
Chearless he breath'd, and wander'd in the Gloom,
Then sunk unpity'd to the dire Abodes,
A Wretch accurst, and hated by the Gods!
I brave not Heav'n: But if the Fruits of Earth
Sustain thy Life, and Human be thy Birth;
Bold as thou art, too prodigal of Breath,
Approach, and enter the dark Gates of Death.
    What, or from whence I am, or who my Sire,
(Reply'd the Chief) can Tydeus' Son enquire?   180
Like Leaves on Trees the Race of Man is found,
Now green in Youth, now with'ring on the Ground,
Another Race the following Spring supplies,
They fall successive, and successive rise;
So Generations in their Course decay,
So flourish these, when those are past away.
But if thou still persist to search my Birth,
Then hear a Tale that fills the spacious Earth.
    A City stands on Argos' utmost Bound,
(Argos the fair for warlike Steeds renown'd)   190
Æolian Sysiphus, with Wisdom blest,
In ancient Time the happy Walls possest,
Then call'd Ephyre: Glaucus was his Son;
Great Glaucus Father of Bellerophon,
Who o'er the Sons of Men in Beauty shin'd,
Lov'd for that Valour which preserves Mankind.
Then mighty Prætus Argos' Sceptres sway'd,
Whose hard Commands Bellerophon obey'd.

With direful Jealousy the Monarch rag'd,
And the brave Prince in num'rous Toils engag'd.   200
For him, Antæa[2] burn'd with lawless Flame,
And strove to tempt him from the Paths of Fame:
In vain she tempted the relentless Youth,
Endu'd with Wisdom, sacred Fear, and Truth.
Fir'd at his Scorn the Queen to Prætus fled,
And beg'd Revenge for her insulted Bed:
Incens'd he heard, resolving on his Fate;
But Hospitable Laws restrain'd his Hate:
To Lycia the devoted Youth he sent,
With Tablets seal'd, that told his dire Intent.   210
Now blest by ev'ry Pow'r who guards the Good,
The Chief arriv'd at Xanthus' silver Flood:
There Lycia's Monarch paid him Honours due;
Nine Days he feasted, and nine Bulls he slew.
But when the tenth bright Morning Orient glow'd,
The faithful Youth his Monarch's Mandate show'd:
The fatal Tablets, till that Instant seal'd,
The deathful Secret to the King reveal'd.
First, dire Chymæra's Conquest was enjoin'd;
A mingled Monster, of no mortal Kind;   220
Behind, a Dragon's fiery Tail was spread;
A Goat's rough Body bore a Lion's Head;
Her pitchy Nostrils flaky Flames expire;
Her gaping Throat emits infernal Fire.
    This Pest he slaughter'd (for he read the Skies,
And trusted Heav'ns informing Prodigies)
Then met in Arms the Solymæan Crew,
(Fiercest of Men) and those the Warrior slew.
Next the bold Amazon's whole Force defy'd;
And conquer'd still, for Heav'n was on his side.   230
    Nor ended here his Toils: His Lycian Foes
At his Return, a treach'rous Ambush, rose,
With levell'd Spears along the winding Shore;
There fell they breathless, and return'd no more.
    At length the Monarch with repentant Grief
Confess'd the Gods, and God-descended Chief;

[2] Wife of *Praetus* (205)

His Daughter gave, the Stranger to detain,
With half the Honours of his ample Reign.
The Lycians grant a chosen Space of Ground,
With Woods, with Vineyards, and with Harvests crown'd.   240
There long the Chief his happy Lot posses'd,
With two brave Sons and one fair Daughter bless'd;
(Fair ev'n in heav'nly Eyes; her fruitful Love
Crown'd with Sarpedon's Birth th' Embrace of Jove)
But when at last, distracted in his Mind,
Forsook by Heav'n, forsaking Human-kind,
Wide o'er th' Aleian Field he chose to stray,
A long, forlorn, uncomfortable Way!
Woes heap'd on Woes oppress'd his wasted Heart;
His beauteous Daughter fell by Phœbè's Dart;   250
His Eldest-born by raging Mars was slain,
In Combate on the Solymæan Plain.
Hippolochus surviv'd; from him I came,
The honour'd Author of my Birth and Name;
By his Decree I sought the Trojan Town,
By his Instructions learn to win Renown,
To stand the first in Worth as in Command,
To add new Honours to my native Land,
Before my Eyes my mighty Sires to place,
And emulate the Glories of our Race.   260
    He spoke, and Transport fill'd Tydides' Heart;
In Earth the gen'rous Warrior fix'd his Dart,
Then friendly, thus, the Lycian Prince addrest.
Welcome, my brave Hereditary Guest!
Thus ever let us meet, with kind Embrace,
Nor stain the sacred Friendship of our Race.
Know, Chief, our Grandsires have been Guests of old;
Oeneus the strong, Bellerophon the bold:
Our ancient Seat his honour'd Presence grac'd,
Where twenty Days in Genial Rites he pass'd.   270
The parting Heroes mutual Presents left;
A golden Goblet was thy Grandsire's Gift;
Oeneus a Belt of matchless Work bestow'd,
That rich with Tyrian Dye refulgent glow'd.

(This from his Pledge I learn'd, which safely stor'd
Among my Treasures, still adorns my Board:
For Tydeus left me young, when Thebè's Wall
Beheld the Sons of Greece untimely fall.)
Mindful of this, in Friendship let us join;
If Heav'n our Steps to foreign Lands incline,   280
My Guest in Argos thou, and I in Lycia thine.
Enough of Trojans to this Lance shall yield,
In the full Harvest of yon' ample Field;
Enough of Greeks shall die thy Spear with Gore;
But Thou and Diomed be Foes no more.
Now change we Arms, and prove to either Host
We guard the Friendship of the Line we boast.
  Thus having said, the gallant Chiefs alight,
Their Hands they join, their mutual Faith they plight,
Brave Glaucus then each narrow Thought resign'd,   290
(Jove warm'd his Bosom and enlarg'd his Mind)
For Diomed's Brass Arms, of mean Device,
For which nine Oxen paid (a vulgar Price)
He gave his own, of Gold divinely wrought,
A hundred Beeves the shining Purchase bought.
  Meantime the Guardian of the Trojan State,
Great Hector enter'd at the Scæan Gate.
Beneath the Beech-Tree's consecrated Shades,
The Trojan Matrons and the Trojan Maids
Around him flock'd, all press'd with pious Care   300
For Husbands, Brothers, Sons, engag'd in War.
He bids the Train in long Procession go,
And seek the Gods, t' avert th' impending Woe.
And now to Priam's stately Courts he came,
Rais'd on arch'd Columns of stupendous Frame;
O'er these a Range of Marble Structure runs,
The rich Pavillions of his fifty Sons,
In fifty Chambers lodg'd; and Rooms of State
Oppos'd to those, where Priam's Daughters sate:
Twelve Domes for them and their lov'd Spouses shone,   310
Of equal Beauty, and of polish'd Stone.
Hither great Hector pass'd, nor pass'd unseen
Of Royal Hecuba, his Mother Queen.

(With her Laodicè, whose beauteous Face
Surpass'd the Nymphs of Troy's illustrious Race)
Long in a strict Embrace she held her Son,
And press'd his Hand, and tender thus begun.

   O Hector! say, what great Occasion calls
My Son from Fight, when Greece surrounds our Walls?
Com'st thou to supplicate th' Almighty Pow'r,   320
With lifted Hands from Ilion's lofty Tow'r?
Stay, till I bring the Cup with Bacchus crown'd,
In Jove's high Name to sprinkle on the Ground,
And pay due Vows to all the Gods around.
Then with a plenteous Draught refresh thy Soul,
And draw new Spirits from the gen'rous Bowl;
Spent as thou art with long laborious Fight,
The brave Defender of thy Country's Right.

   Far hence be Bacchus' Gifts (the Chief rejoin'd)
Inflaming Wine, pernicious to Mankind,   330
Unnerves the Limbs, and dulls the noble Mind.
Let Chiefs abstain, and spare the sacred Juice
To sprinkle to the Gods, its better Use.
By me that holy Office were prophan'd;
Ill fits it me, with human Gore distain'd,
To the pure Skies these horrid Hands to raise,
Or offer Heav'n's great Sire polluted Praise.
You, with your Matrons, go! a spotless Train,
And burn rich Odors in Minerva's Fane.
The largest Mantle your full Wardrobes hold,   340
Most Priz'd for Art, and labour'd o'er with Gold,
Before the Goddess' honour'd Knees be spread,
And twelve young Heifers to her Altar led.
So may the Pow'r, atton'd by fervent Pray'r,
Our Wives, our Infants, and our City spare,
And far avert Tydides' wastful Ire,
Who mows whole Troops and makes all Troy retire.
Be this, O Mother, your religious Care;
I go to rowze soft Paris to the War;
If yet not lost to all the Sense of Shame,   350
The recreant Warrior hear the Voice of Fame.

Oh would kind Earth the hateful Wretch embrace,
That pest of Troy, that Ruin of our Race!
Deep to the dark Abyss might he descend,
Troy yet should flourish, and my Sorrows end.
   This heard, she gave Command; and summon'd came
Each noble Matron, and illustrious Dame.
The Phrygian Queen to her rich Wardrobe went,
Where treasur'd Odors breath'd a costly Scent.
There lay the Vestures, of no vulgar Art,   360
Sidonian Maids embroider'd ev'ry Part,
Whom from soft Sidon youthful Paris bore,
With Helen touching on the Tyrian Shore.
Here as the Queen revolv'd with careful Eyes
The Various Textures and the various Dies,
She chose a Veil that shone superior far,
And glow'd refulgent as the Morning Star.
Herself with this the long Procession leads;
The Train majestically slow proceeds.
Soon as to Ilion's topmost Tow'r they come,   370
And awful reach the high Palladian Dome,
Antenor's Consort, fair Theano, waits
As Pallas' Priestess, and unbars the Gates.
With Hands uplifted and imploring Eyes,
They fill the Dome with supplicating Cries.
The Priestess then the shining Veil displays,
Plac'd on Minerva's Knees, and thus she prays.
   Oh awful Goddess! ever-dreadful Maid,
Troy's strong Defence, unconquer'd Pallas, aid!
Break thou Tydides' Spear, and let him fall   380
Prone on the Dust before the Trojan Wall.
So twelve young Heifers, guiltless of the Yoke,
Shall fill thy Temple with a grateful Smoke.
But thou, atton'd by Penitence and Pray'r,
Our selves, our Infants, and our City spare!
So pray'd the Priestess in her holy Fane;
So vow'd the Matrons, but they vow'd in vain.
   While these appear before the Pow'r with Pray'rs,
Hector to Paris' lofty Dome repairs.

Himself the Mansion rais'd, from ev'ry Part   390
Assembling Architects of matchless Art.
Near Priam's Court and Hector's Palace stands
The pompous Structure, and the Town commands.
A Spear the Hero bore of wondrous Strength,
Of full ten Cubits was the Lance's Length,
The steely Point with golden Ringlets join'd,
Before him brandish'd, at each Motion shin'd.
Thus entring in the glitt'ring Rooms, he found
His Brother-Chief, whose useless Arms lay round,
His Eyes delighting with their splendid Show,   400
Bright'ning the Shield, and polishing the Bow.
Beside him, Helen with her Virgins stands,
Guides their rich Labours, and instructs their Hands.
      Him thus unactive, with an ardent Look
The Prince beheld, and high-resenting spoke.
Thy Hate to Troy, is this the Time to show?
(Oh Wretch ill-fated, and thy Country's Foe!)
Paris and Greece against us both conspire;
Thy close Resentment, and their vengeful Ire.
For thee great Ilion's Guardian Heroes fall,   410
Till Heaps of Dead alone defend her Wall;
For thee the Soldier bleeds, the Matron mourns,
And wastful War in all its Fury burns.
Ungrateful Man! deserves not this thy Care,
Our Troops to hearten, and our Toils to share?
Rise, or behold the conqu'ring Flames ascend,
And all the Phrygian Glories at an End.
      Brother, 'tis just (reply'd the beauteous Youth)
Thy free Remonstrance proves thy Worth and Truth:
Yet charge my Absence less, oh gen'rous Chief!   420
On Hate to Troy, than conscious Shame and Grief:
Here, hid from human Eyes, thy Brother sate,
And mourn'd in secret, his, and Ilion's Fate.
'Tis now enough: now Glory spreads her Charms,
And beauteous Helen calls her Chief to Arms.
Conquest to-Day my happier Sword may bless,
'Tis Man's to fight, but Heav'ns to give Success.

But while I arm, contain thy ardent Mind;
Or go, and Paris shall not lag behind.
 He said, nor answer'd Priam's warlike Son;   430
When Helen thus with lowly Grace begun.
 Oh gen'rous Brother! if the guilty Dame
That caus'd these Woes, deserve a Sister's Name!
Would Heav'n, e're all these dreadful Deeds were done,
The Day, that show'd me to the golden Sun,
Had seen my Death! Why did not Whirlwinds bear
The fatal Infant to the Fowls of Air?
Why sunk I not beneath the whelming Tyde,
And 'midst the Roarings of the Waters dy'd?
Heav'n fill'd up all my Ills, and I accurst.   440
Bore all, and Paris of those Ills the worst.
Helen at least a braver Spouse might claim,
Warm'd with some Virtue, some Regard of Fame!
Now tir'd with Toils, thy fainting Limbs recline,
With Toils, sustain'd for Paris' sake and mine:
The Gods have link'd our miserable Doom,
Our present Woe, and Infamy to come:
Wide shall it spread, and last thro' Ages long,
Example sad! and Theme of future Song.
 The Chief reply'd: This Time forbids to rest: 450
The Trojan Bands, by hostile Fury prest,
Demand their Hector, and his Arm require;
The Combate urges, and my Soul's on fire.
Urge thou thy Knight to march where Glory calls,
And timely join me, e're I leave the Walls.
E're yet I mingle in the direful Fray,
My Wife, my Infant, claim a Moment's Stay;
This Day (perhaps the last that sees me here)
Demands a parting Word, a tender Tear:
This Day, some God who hates our Trojan Land 460
May vanquish Hector by a Grecian Hand.
 He said, and past with sad presaging Heart
To seek his Spouse,[3] his Soul's far dearer Part;
At home he sought her, but he sought in vain;
She, with one Maid of all her Menial Train,

[3] Andromache

Had thence retir'd; and with her second Joy,
The young Astyanax, the Hope of Troy.
Pensive she stood on Ilion's Tow'ry Height,
Beheld the War, and sicken'd at the sight;
There her sad Eyes in vain her Lord explore,   470
Or weep the Wounds her bleeding Country bore.
  But he who found not whom his Soul desir'd,
Whose Virtue charm'd him as her Beauty fir'd,
Stood in the Gates, and ask'd what way she bent
Her parting Step? If to the Fane she went,
Where late the mourning Matrons made Resort;
Or sought her Sisters in the Trojan Court?
Not to the Court (reply'd th' Attendant Train)
Nor mix'd with Matrons to Minerva's Fane:
To Ilion's steepy Tow'r she bent her way,   480
To mark the Fortunes of the doubtful Day.
Troy fled, she heard, before the Grecian Sword;
She heard, and trembled for her absent Lord:
Distracted with Surprize, she seem'd to fly,
Fear on her Cheek, and Sorrow in her Eye.
The Nurse attended with her Infant Boy,
The young Astyanax, the Hope of Troy.
  Hector, this heard, return'd without Delay;
Swift thro' the Town he trod his former way,
Thro' Streets of Palaces and Walks of State;   490
And met the Mourner at the Scæan Gate.
With haste to meet him sprung the joyful Fair,
His blameless Wife, Aëtion's wealthy Heir:
(Cilician Thebè great Aëtion sway'd,
And Hippoplacus'[4] wide-extended Shade)
The Nurse stood near, in whose Embraces prest
His only Hope hung smiling at her Breast,
Whom each soft Charm and early Grace adorn,
Fair as the new-born Star that gilds the Morn.
To this lov'd Infant Hector gave the Name   500
Scamandrius, from Scamander's honour'd Stream;
Astyanax the Trojans call'd the Boy,
From his great Father, the Defence of Troy.

[4] Mistranslation of the Greek for *under Placus*, a mountain near Thebè

Silent the Warrior smil'd, and pleas'd resign'd
To tender Passions all his mighty Mind:
His beauteous Princess cast a mournful Look,
Hung on his Hand, and then dejected spoke;
Her Bosom labour'd with a boding Sigh,
And the big Tear stood trembling in her Eye.
　　Too daring Prince! ah whither dost thou run?　　510
Ah too forgetful of thy Wife and Son!
And think'st thou not how wretched we shall be,
A Widow I, an helpless Orphan He!
For sure such Courage Length of Life denies,
And thou must fall, thy Virtue's Sacrifice.
Greece in her single Heroes strove in vain;
Now Hosts oppose thee, and thou must be slain!
Oh grant me Gods! e're Hector meets his Doom,
All I can ask of Heav'n, an early Tomb!
　　So shall my Days in one sad Tenor run,　　520
And end with Sorrows as they first begun.
No Parent now remains, my Griefs to share,
No Father's Aid, no Mother's tender Care.
The fierce Achilles wrapt our Walls in Fire,
Lay'd Thebè waste, and slew my warlike Sire!
His Fate Compassion in the Victor bred;
Stern as he was, he yet rever'd the Dead,
His radiant Arms preserv'd from hostile Spoil,
And lay'd him decent on the Fun'ral Pyle;
Then rais'd a Mountain where his Bones were burn'd,　　530
The Mountain Nymphs the rural Tomb adorn'd,
Jove's Sylvan Daughters bade their Elms bestow
A barren Shade, and in his Honour grow.
　　By the same Arm my sev'n brave Brothers fell,
In one sad Day beheld the Gates of Hell;
While the fat Herds and snowie Flocks they fed,
Amid their Fields the hapless Heroes bled!
My Mother liv'd to bear the Victor's Bands,
The Queen of Hippoplacia's[5] Sylvan Lands:
Redeem'd too late, she scarce beheld again　　540
Her pleasing Empire and her native Plain,

[5] Thebè

When ah! opprest by Life-consuming Woe,
She fell a Victim to Diana's Bow.
　Yet while my Hector still survives, I see
My Father, Mother, Brethren, all, in thee.
Alas! my Parents, Brothers, Kindred, all,
Once more will perish if my Hector fall.
Thy Wife, thy Infant, in thy Danger share:
Oh prove a Husband's and a Father's Care!
That Quarter most the skillful Greeks annoy,   550
Where yon' wild Fig-Trees join the Wall of Troy:
Thou, from this Tow'r defend th' important Post;
There Agamemnon points his dreadful Host,
That Pass Tydides, Ajax strive to gain,
And there the vengeful Spartan fires his Train.
Thrice our bold Foes the fierce Attack have giv'n,
Or led by Hopes, or dictated from Heav'n.
Let others in the Field their Arms employ,
But stay my Hector here, and guard his Troy.
　The Chief reply'd: That Post shall be my Care,   560
Nor that alone, but all the Works of War.
How would the Sons of Troy, in Arms renown'd,
And Troy's proud Dames whose Garments sweep the Ground,
Attaint the Lustre of my former Name,
Should Hector basely quit the Field of Fame?
My early Youth was bred to martial Pains,
My Soul impells me to th' embattel'd Plains;
Let me be foremost to defend the Throne,
And guard my Father's Glories, and my own.
　Yet come it will, the Day decreed by Fates;   570
(How my Heart trembles while my Tongue relates!)
The Day when thou, Imperial Troy! must bend,
And see thy Warriors fall, thy Glories end.
And yet no dire Presage so wounds my Mind,
My Mother's Death, the Ruin of my Kind,
Not Priam's hoary Hairs defil'd with Gore,
Not all my Brothers gasping on the Shore;
As thine, Andromache! thy Griefs I dread;
I see thee trembling, weeping, Captive led!

In Argive Looms our Battels to design,   580
And Woes, of which so large a Part was thine!
To bear the Victor's hard Commands, or bring
The Weight of Waters from Hyperia's Spring.
There, while you groan beneath the Load of Life,
They cry, Behold the mighty Hector's Wife!
Some haughty Greek who lives thy Tears to see,
Embitters all thy Woes, by naming me.
The Thoughts of Glory past, and present Shame,
A thousand Griefs shall waken at the Name!
May I lie cold before that dreadful Day,   590
Press'd with a Load of Monumental Clay!
Thy Hector wrapt in everlasting Sleep,
Shall neither hear thee sigh, nor see thee weep.
  Thus having spoke, th' illustrious Chief of Troy
Stretch'd his fond Arms to clasp the lovely Boy.
The Babe clung crying to his Nurse's Breast,
Scar'd at the dazling Helm, and nodding Crest.
With secret Pleasure each fond Parent smil'd,
And Hector hasted to relieve his Child,
The glitt'ring Terrors from his Brows unbound,   600
And plac'd the beaming Helmet on the Ground.
Then kist the Child, and lifting high in Air,
Thus to the Gods prefer'd a Father's Pray'r.
  O Thou! whose Glory fills th' Ætherial Throne,
And all ye deathless Pow'rs! protect my Son!
Grant him, like me, to purchase just Renown,
To guard the Trojans, to defend the Crown,
Against his Country's Foes the War to wage,
And rise the Hector of the future age!
So when triumphant from successful Toils,   610
Of Heroes slain he bears the reeking Spoils,
Whole Hosts may hail him with deserv'd Acclaim,
And say, This Chief transcends his Father's Fame:
While pleas'd amidst the gen'ral Shouts of Troy,
His Mother's conscious Heart o'erflows with Joy.
  He spoke, and fondly gazing on her Charms
Restor'd the pleasing Burden to her Arms;

Soft on her fragrant Breast the Babe she laid,
Hush'd to Repose, and with a Smile survey'd.
The troubled Pleasure soon chastis'd by Fear,   620
She mingled with the Smile a tender Tear.
The soften'd Chief with kind Compassion view'd,
And dry'd the falling Drops, and thus pursu'd.
   Andromache! my Soul's far better Part,
Why with untimely Sorrows heaves thy Heart?
No hostile Hand can antedate my Doom,
Till Fate condemns me to the silent Tomb.
Fix'd is the Term to all the Race of Earth,
And such the hard Condition of our Birth.
No Force can then resist, no Flight can save,   630
All sink alike, the Fearful and the Brave.
No more—but hasten to thy Tasks at home,
There guide the Spindle, and direct the Loom:
Me Glory summons to the martial Scene,
The Field of Combate is the Sphere for Men.
Where Heroes war, the foremost Place I claim,
The first in Danger as the first in Fame.
   Thus having said, the glorious Chief resumes
His Tow'ry Helmet, black with shading Plumes.
His Princess parts with a prophetick Sigh,   640
Unwilling parts, and oft' reverts her Eye
That stream'd at ev'ry Look: then, moving slow,
Sought her own Palace, and indulg'd her Woe.
There, while her Tears deplor'd the Godlike Man,
Thro' all her Train the soft Infection ran,
The pious Maids their mingled Sorrows shed,
And mourn the living Hector, as the dead.
   But now, no longer deaf to Honour's Call,
Forth issues Paris from the Palace Wall.
In Brazen Arms that cast a gleamy Ray,   650
Swift thro' the Town the Warrior bends his way.
The wanton Courser thus, with Reins unbound,
Breaks from his Stall, and beats the trembling Ground;
Pamper'd and proud, he seeks the wonted Tides,
And laves, in Height of Blood, his shining Sides;

His Head now freed, he tosses to the Skies;
His Mane dishevel'd o'er his Shoulders flies;
He snuffs the Females in the distant Plain,
And springs, exulting, to his Fields again.
With equal Triumph, sprightly, bold and gay,   660
In Arms refulgent as the God of Day,
The Son of Priam, glorying in his Might,
Rush'd forth with Hector to the Fields of Fight.
  And now the Warriors passing on the way,
The graceful Paris first excus'd his Stay.
To whom the noble Hector thus reply'd:
O Chief! in Blood, and now in Arms, ally'd!
Thy Pow'r in War with Justice none contest;
Known is thy Courage, and thy Strength confest.
What Pity, Sloath should seize a Soul so brave,   670
Or Godlike Paris live a Woman's Slave!
My Heart weeps Blood at what the Trojans say,
And hopes, thy Deeds shall wipe the Stain away.
Haste then, in all their glorious Labours share;
For much they suffer, for thy sake, in War.
These Ills shall cease, whene'er by Jove's Decree
We crown the Bowl to Heav'n and Liberty:
While the proud Foe his frustrate Triumphs mourns,
And Greece indignant thro' Seas returns.

THE SEVENTH BOOK
OF THE ILIAD

THE ARGUMENT

The Single Combate of Hector and Ajax

THE BATTEL renewing with double Ardour upon the Return of Hector, Minerva is under Apprehensions for the Greeks. Apollo seeing her descend from Olympus, joins her near the Scæan Gate. They agree to put off the general Engagement for that Day, and incite Hector to challenge the Greeks to a single Combate. Nine of the Princes accepting the Challenge, the Lot is cast, and falls upon Ajax. These Heroes, after several Attacks, are parted by the Night. The Trojans calling a Council, Antenor proposes the Delivery of Helen to the Greeks, to which Paris will not consent, but offers to restore them her Riches. Priam sends a Herald to make this Offer, and to demand a Truce for burning the Dead, the last of which only is agreed to by Agamemnon. When the Funerals are performed, the Greeks, pursuant to the Advice of Nestor, erect a Fortification to protect their Fleet and Camp, flank'd with Towers, and defended by a Ditch and Palisades. Neptune testifies his Jealousy at this Work, but is pacified by a Promise from Jupiter. Both Armies pass the Night in Feasting, but Jupiter disheartens the Trojans with Thunder and other signs of his Wrath.

The three and twentieth Day ends with the Duel of Hector and Ajax: The next Day the Truce is agreed: Another is taken up in the Funeral Rites of the Slain; and one more in building the Fortification before the Ships: So that somewhat above three Days is employed in this Book. The Scene lies wholly in the Field.

So spoke the Guardian of the Trojan State,
Then rush'd impetuous thro' the Scæan Gate.

Him Paris follow'd to the dire Alarms;
Both breathing Slaughter, both resolv'd in Arms.
As when to Sailors lab'ring thro' the Main,
That long had heav'd the weary Oar in vain,
Jove bids at length th' expected Gales arise;
The Gales blow grateful, and the Vessel flies:
So welcome these to Troy's desiring Train;
The Bands are chear'd, the War awakes again.   10
  Bold Paris first the Work of Death begun,
On great Menesthius, Areïthous' Son;
Sprung from the fair Philomeda's Embrace,
The pleasing Arnè was his native Place.
Then sunk Eioneus to the Shades below,
Beneath his steely Casque he felt the Blow
Full on his Neck, from Hector's weighty Hand;
And roll'd, with Limbs relax'd, along the Land.
By Glaucus' Spear the bold Iphinous bleeds,
Fix'd in the Shoulder as he mounts his Steeds;   20
Headlong he tumbles: His slack Nerves unbound
Drop the cold useless Members on the Ground.
  When now Minerva saw her Argives slain,
From vast Olympus to the gleaming Plain
Fierce she descends: Apollo mark'd her Flight,
Nor shot less swift from Ilion's Tow'ry Height:
Radiant they met, beneath the Beechen Shade;
When thus Apollo to the blue-ey'd Maid.
  What cause, O Daughter of Almighty Jove!
Thus wings thy Progress from the Realms above?   30
Once more impetuous dost thou bend thy way,
To give to Greece the long-divided Day?
Too much has Troy already felt thy Hate,
Now breathe thy Rage, and hush the stern Debate:
This Day, the Business of the Field suspend;
War soon shall kindle, and great Ilion bend;
Since vengeful Goddesses confed'rate join
To raze her Walls, tho' built by Hands Divine.
  To whom the Progeny of Jove replies.
I left, for this, the Council of the Skies: 40
But who shall bid conflicting Hosts forbear,
What Art shall calm the furious Sons of War?

To her the God: Great Hector's Soul incite
To dare the boldest Greek to single Fight,
Till Greece, provok'd, from all her Numbers show
A Warrior worthy to be Hector's Foe.
At this agreed, the Heav'nly Pow'rs withdrew;
Sage Helenus their secret Counsels knew:
Hector inspir'd he sought: To him addrest,
Thus told the Dictates of his sacred Breast.   50
O Son of Priam! let thy faithful Ear
Receive my Words; thy Friend and Brother hear!
Go forth persuasive, and a while engage
The warring Nations to suspend their Rage;
Then dare the boldest of the hostile Train
To mortal Combate on the listed Plain.
For not this Day shall end thy glorious Date;
The Gods have spoke it, and their Voice is Fate.
He said: The Warrior heard the Word with Joy.
Then with his Spear restrain'd the Youth of Troy,   60
Held by the midst athwart. On either Hand
The Squadrons part; th' expecting Trojans stand.
Great Agamemnon bids the Greeks forbear;
They breathe, and hush the Tumult of the War.
Th' Athenian Maid, and glorious God of Day,
With silent Joy the settling Hosts survey:
In Form like Vulturs, on the Beeche's Height
They sit conceal'd, and wait the future Fight.
The thronging Troops obscure the dusky Fields,
Horrid with bristling Spears, and gleaming Shields.   70
As when a gen'ral Darkness veils the Main,
(Soft Zephyr curling the wide wat'ry Plain)
The Waves scarce heave, the Face of Ocean sleeps,
And a still Horror saddens all the Deeps:
Thus in thick Orders settling wide around,
At length compos'd they sit, and shade the Ground.
Great Hector first amidst both Armies broke
The solemn Silence, and their Pow'rs bespoke.
Hear all ye Trojan, all ye Grecian Bands,
What my Soul prompts, and what some God commands.   80
Great Jove averse our Warfare to compose,
O'erwhelms the Nations with new Toils and Woes;

War with a fiercer Tide once more returns,
Till Ilion falls, or till yon' Navy burns.
You then, O Princes of the Greeks! appear,
'Tis Hector speaks, and calls the Gods to hear:
From all your Troops select the boldest Knight,
And him, the boldest, Hector dares to Fight.
Here if I fall, by chance of Battel slain,
Be his my Spoil, and his these Arms remain;   90
But let my Body, to my Friends return'd,
By Trojan Hands and Trojan Flames be burn'd.
And if Apollo, in whose Aid I trust,
Shall stretch your daring Champion in the Dust;
If mine the Glory to despoil the Foe;
On Phœbus' Temple I'll his Arms bestow:
The breathless Carcase to your Navy sent,
Greece on the Shore shall raise a Monument;
Which when some future Mariner surveys,
Wash'd by broad Hellespont's resounding Seas,   100
Thus shall he say. "A valiant Greek lies there,
"By Hector slain, the mighty Man of War.
The Stone shall tell your vanquish'd Hero's Name,
And distant Ages learn the Victor's Fame.

This fierce Defiance Greece astonish'd heard,
Blush'd to refuse, and to accept it fear'd.
Stern Menelaus first the Silence broke,
And inly groaning, thus opprobrious spoke.
Women of Greece! Oh Scandal of your Race,
Whose Coward Souls your manly Form disgrace.   110
How great the Shame, when ev'ry Age shall know
That not a Grecian met this noble Foe!
Go then! resolve to Earth from whence ye grew,
A heartless, spiritless, inglorious Crew:
Be what ye seem, unanimated Clay!
My self will dare the Danger of the Day.
'Tis Man's bold Task the gen'rous Strife to try,
But in the Hands of God is Victory.

These Words scarce spoke, with gen'rous Ardour prest,
His manly Limbs in Azure Arms he drest: 120
That Day, Atrides! a superior Hand
Had stretch'd thee breathless on the hostile Strand;

But all at once, thy Fury to compose,
The Kings of Greece, an awful Band, arose:
Ev'n He their Chief, great Agamemnon press'd
Thy daring Hand, and this Advice address'd.
Whither, O Menelaus! would'st thou run,
And tempt a Fate which Prudence bids thee shun?
Griev'd tho' thou art, forbear the rash Design;
Great Hector's Arm is mightier far than thine.   130
Ev'n fierce Achilles learn'd its Force to fear,
And trembling met this dreadful Son of War.
Sit thou secure amidst thy social Band;
Greece in our Cause shall arm some pow'rful Hand.
The mightiest Warrior of th' Achaian Name,
Tho' bold, and burning with Desire of Fame,
Content, the doubtful Honour might foregoe,
So great the Danger, and so brave the Foe.
    He said, and turn'd his Brother's vengeful Mind,
He stoop'd to Reason, and his Rage resign'd.   140
No longer bent to rush on certain Harms,
His joyful Friends unbrace his Azure Arms.
    He, from whose Lips divine Persuasion flows,
Grave Nestor, then, in graceful Act arose.
Thus to the Kings he spoke. What Grief, what Shame
Attend on Greece, and all the Grecian Name?
How shall, alas! her hoary Heroes mourn,
Their Sons degen'rate, and their Race a Scorn?
What Tears shall down thy silver Beard be roll'd,
Oh Peleus, old in Arms, in Wisdom old!   150
Once with what Joy the gen'rous Prince would hear
Of ev'ry Chief who sought this glorious War,
Participate their Fame, and pleas'd enquire
Each Name, each Action, and each Hero's Sire?
Gods! should he see our Warriors trembling stand,
And trembling all before one hostile Hand;
How would he lift his aged Arms on high,
Lament inglorious Greece, and beg to die!
Oh would to all th' immortal Pow'rs above,
Minerva, Phœbus, and Almighty Jove!   160
Years might again roll back, my Youth renew,
And give this Arm the Spring which once it knew:

When fierce in War, where Jardan's Waters fall,
I led my Troops to Phea's trembling Wall,
And with th' Arcadian Spears my Prowess try'd,
Where Celadon rolls down his rapid Tide.
There Ereuthalion brav'd us in the Field,
Proud, Areïthous' dreadful Arms to wield;
Great Areïthous, known from Shore to Shore
By the huge, knotted Iron-Mace he bore;   170
No Lance he shook, nor bent the twanging Bow,
But broke, with this, the Battel of the Foe.
Him not by manly Force Lycurgus slew,
Whose guileful Javelin from the Thicket flew,
Deep in a winding Way his Breast assail'd,
Nor ought the Warrior's thund'ring Mace avail'd.
Supine he fell: Those Arms which Mars before
Had giv'n the Vanquish'd, now the Victor bore.
But when old Age had dim'd Lycurgus Eyes,
To Ereuthalion he consign'd the Prize.   180
Furious with this, he crush'd our levell'd Bands,
And dar'd the Trial of the strongest Hands;
Nor cou'd the strongest Hands his Fury stay;
All saw, and fear'd, his huge, tempestuous Sway.
Till I, the youngest of the Host, appear'd,
And youngest, met whom all our Army fear'd.
I fought the Chief: my Arms Minerva crown'd:
Prone fell the Giant o'er a Length of Ground.
What then I was, Oh were your Nestor now!
Not Hector's self should want an equal Foe.   190
But Warriors, you, that youthful Vigour boast,
The Flow'r of Greece, th' Examples of our Host,
Sprung from such Fathers, who such Numbers sway;
Can you stand trembling, and desert the Day?
   His warm Reproofs the list'ning Kings inflame,
And nine, the noblest of the Grecian Name,
Up-started fierce: But far before the rest
The King of Men advanc'd his dauntless Breast:
Then bold Tydides, great in Arms, appear'd;
And next his Bulk gigantic Ajax rear'd: 200
Oïleus follow'd, Idomen was there,
And Merion, dreadful as the God of War:

With these Eurypylus and Thoas stand,
And wise Ulysses clos'd the daring Band.
All these, alike inspir'd with noble Rage,
Demand the Fight. To whom the Pylian Sage:
  Lest Thirst of Glory your brave Souls divide,
What Chief shall combate, let the Lots decide.
Whom Heav'n shall chuse, be his the Chance to raise
His Country's Fame, his own immortal Praise.   210
  The Lots produc'd, each Hero signs his own,
Then in the Gen'rals Helm the Fates are thrown.
The People pray with lifted Eyes and Hands,
And Vows like these ascend from all the Bands.
Grant thou Almighty! in whose Hand is Fate,
A worthy Champion for the Grecian State.
This Task let Ajax or Tydides prove,
Or He, the King of Kings, belov'd by Jove.
  Old Nestor shook the Casque. By Heav'n inspir'd,
Leap'd forth the Lot of ev'ry Greek desir'd.   220
This from the Right to Left the Herald bears,
Held out in Order to the Grecian Peers.
Each to his Rival yields the Mark unknown,
Till Godlike Ajax finds the Lot his own;
Surveys th' Inscription with rejoicing Eyes,
Then casts before him, and with Transport cries:
  Warriors! I claim the Lot, and arm with Joy;
Be mine the Conquest of this Chief of Troy.
Now, while my brightest Arms my Limbs invest,
To Saturn's Son be all your Vows addrest: 230
But pray in secret, lest the Foes should hear,
And deem your Pray'rs the mean Effect of Fear.
Said I in secret? No, your Vows declare,
In such a Voice as fills the Earth and Air.
Lives there a Chief whom Ajax ought to dread,
Ajax, in all the Toils of Battel bred?
From warlike Salamis I drew my Birth,
And born to Combates, fear no Force of Earth.
  He said. The Troops with elevated Eyes,
Implore the God whose Thunder rends the Skies.   240
O Father of Mankind, Superior Lord!
On lofty Ida's holy Hill ador'd;

Who in the highest Heav'n hast fix'd thy Throne,
Supreme of Gods! unbounded, and alone:
Grant thou, that Telamon may bear away
The Praise and Conquest of this doubtful Day.
Or if illustrious Hector be thy Care,
That both may claim 'em, and that both may share.

Now Ajax brac'd his dazling Armour on;
Sheath'd in bright Steel the Giant-Warrior shone: 250
He moves to Combate with majestic Pace;
So stalks in Arms the grizly God of Thrace,
When Jove to punish faithless Men prepares,
And gives whole Nations to the Waste of Wars.
Thus march'd the Chief, tremendous as a God;
Grimly he smil'd; Earth trembled as he strode:
His massy Javelin quiv'ring in his Hand,
He stood, the Bulwark of the Grecian Band.
Thro' ev'ry Argive Heart new Transport ran,
All Troy stood trembling at the mighty Man.   260
Ev'n Hector paus'd, and with new Doubt opprest
Felt his great Heart suspended in his Breast:
'Twas vain to seek Retreat, and vain to fear;
Himself had challeng'd, and the Foe drew near.

Stern Telamon behind his ample Shield
As from a Brazen Tow'r, o'erlook'd the Field.
Huge was its Orb, with sev'n thick Folds o'ercast,
Of tough Bull-hides; of solid Brass the last.
(The Work of Tychius, who in Hylè dwell'd,
And All in Arts of Armoury excell'd.)   270
This Ajax bore before his manly Breast,
And threat'ning, thus his adverse Chief addrest.

Hector! approach my Arm, and singly know
What Strength thou hast, and what the Grecian Foe.
Achilles shuns the Fight; yet some there are
Not void of Soul, and not unskill'd in War:
Let him, unactive on the Sea-beat Shore,
Indulge his Wrath, and aid our Arms no more;
Whole Troops of Heroes, Greece has yet to boast,
And sends thee One, a Sample of her Host.   280
Such as I am, I come to prove thy Might;
No more—be sudden, and begin the Fight.

O Son of Telamon, thy Country's Pride!
(To Ajax thus the Trojan Prince reply'd)
Me, as a Boy or Woman would'st thou fright,
New to the Field, and trembling at the Fight?
Thou meet'st a Chief deserving of thy Arms,
To Combate born, and bred amidst Alarms:
I know to shift my Ground, remount the Car,
Turn, charge, and answer ev'ry Call of War,   290
To right, to left, the dext'rous Lance I wield,
And bear thick Battel on my sounding Shield.
But open be our Fight, and bold each Blow;
I steal no Conquest from a noble Foe.
    He said, and rising, high above the Field
Whirl'd the long Lance against the sev'nfold Shield.
Full on the Brass descending from above
Thro' six Bull-hides the furious Weapon drove,
Till in the sev'nth it fix'd. Then Ajax threw,
Thro' Hector's Shield the forceful Javelin flew,   300
His Corslet enters, and his Garment rends,
And glancing downwards near his Flank descends.
The wary Trojan shrinks, and bending low
Beneath his Buckler, disappoints the Blow.
From their bor'd Shields the Chiefs the Javelins drew,
Then close impetuous, and the Charge renew:
Fierce as the Mountain-Lions bath'd in Blood,
Or foaming Boars, the Terror of the Wood.
At Ajax Hector his long Lance extends;
The blunted Point against the Buckler bends.   310
But Ajax watchful as his Foe drew near,
Drove thro' the Trojan Targe the knotty Spear;
It reach'd his Neck, with matchless Strength impell'd;
Spouts the black Gore, and dimms his shining Shield.
Yet ceas'd not Hector thus; but, stooping down,
In his strong Hand up-heav'd a flinty Stone,
Black, craggy, vast: To this his Force he bends;
Full on the Brazen Boss the Stone descends;
The hollow Brass resounded with the Shock.
Then Ajax seiz'd the Fragment of a Rock,   320
Apply'd each Nerve, and swinging round on high,
With Force tempestuous let the Ruin fly:

The huge Stone thund'ring thro' his Buckler broke;
His slacken'd Knees receiv'd the numbing Stroke;
Great Hector falls extended on the Field,
His Bulk supporting on the shatter'd Shield.
Nor wanted heav'nly Aid: Apollo's Might
Confirm'd his Sinews, and restor'd to Fight.
And now both Heroes their broad Faulchions drew,
In flaming Circles round their Heads they flew,   330
But then by Heralds Voice the Word was giv'n,
The sacred Ministers of Earth and Heav'n:
Divine Talthybius whom the Greeks employ,
And sage Idæus on the Part of Troy,
Between the Swords their peaceful Sceptres rear'd;
When thus Idæus' awful Voice was heard.
    Forbear, my Sons! your farther Force to prove,
Both dear to Men, and both belov'd of Jove.
To either Host your matchless Worth is known,
Each sounds your Praise, and War is all your own.   340
But now the Night extends her awful Shade;
The Goddess parts you: Be the Night obey'd.
    To whom great Ajax his high Soul express'd.
O Sage! to Hector be these Words address'd.
Let him, who first provok'd our Chiefs to fight,
Let him demand the Sanction of the Night:
If first he ask it, I content obey,
And cease the Strife when Hector shows the way.
    Oh first of Greeks! (his noble Foe rejoin'd)
Whom Heav'n adorns, superior to thy Kind,   350
With Strength of Body, and with Worth of Mind!
Now Martial Law commands us to forbear,
Hereafter we shall meet in glorious War,
Some future Day shall lengthen out the Strife,
And let the Gods decide of Death or Life!
Since then the Night extends her gloomy Shade,
And Heav'n enjoins it, be the Night obey'd.
Return, brave Ajax, to thy Grecian Friends,
And joy the Nations whom thy Arm defends;
As I shall glad each Chief, and Trojan Wife,   360
Who wearies Heav'n with Vows for Hector's Life.

But let us, on this memorable Day,
Exchange some Gift; that Greece and Troy may say,
"Not Hate, but Glory, made these Chiefs contend;
"And each brave Foe was in his Soul a Friend.
   With that, a Sword with Stars of Silver grac'd,
The Baldric studded, and the Sheath enchas'd,
He gave the Greek. The gen'rous Greek bestow'd
A radiant Belt that rich with Purple glow'd.
Then with majestic Grace they quit the Plain;   370
This seeks the Grecian, that the Phrygian Train.
   The Trojan Bands returning Hector wait,
And hail with Joy the Champion of their State:
Escap'd great Ajax, they survey'd him round,
Alive, unharm'd, and vig'rous from his Wound.
To Troy's high Gates the God-like Chief they bear,
Their present Triumph, as their late Despair.
   But Ajax, glorying in his hardy Deed,
The well-arm'd Greeks to Agamemnon lead.
A Steer for Sacrifice the King design'd,   380
Of full five Years, and of the nobler Kind.
The Victim falls, they strip the smoking Hide,
The Beast they quarter, and the Joints divide,
Then spread the Tables, the Repast prepare,
Each takes his Seat, and each receives his Share.
The King himself (an Honorary Sign)
Before great Ajax plac'd the mighty Chine.
When now the Rage of Hunger was remov'd;
Nestor, in each persuasive Art approv'd,
The Sage whose Counsels long had sway'd the rest,   390
In Words like these his prudent Thought exprest.
   How dear, O Kings! this fatal Day has cost,
What Greeks are perish'd! what a People lost!
What Tides of Blood have drench'd Scamander's Shore?
What Crowds of Heroes sunk, to rise no more?
Then hear me, Chief! nor let the Morrow's Light
Awake thy Squadrons to new Toils of Fight.
Some Space at least permit the War to breathe,
While we to Flames our slaughter'd Friends bequeathe,
From the red Field their scatter'd Bodies bear,   400
And nigh the Fleet a Fun'ral Structure rear:

So decent Urns their snowy Bones may keep,
And pious Children o'er their Ashes weep.
Here, where on one promiscuous Pile they blaz'd,
High o'er them all a gen'ral Tomb be rais'd.
Next, to secure our Camp, and Naval Pow'rs,
Raise an embattel'd Wall, with lofty Tow'rs;
From Space to Space be ample Gates around,
For passing Chariots, and a Trench profound.
So Greece to Combate shall in Safety go,   410
Nor fear the fierce Incursions of the Foe.
'Twas thus the Sage his wholsome Counsel mov'd;
The sceptred Kings of Greece his Words approv'd.

Meanwhile, conven'd at Priam's Palace Gate,
The Trojan Peers in nightly Council sate:
A Senate void of Union as of Choice,
Their Hearts were fearful, and confus'd their Voice.
Antenor rising, thus demands their Ear:
Ye Trojans, Dardans, and Auxiliars hear!
'Tis Heav'n the Counsel of my Breast inspires,   420
And I but move what ev'ry God requires,
Let Sparta's Treasures be this Hour restor'd,
And Argive Helen own her ancient Lord.
The Ties of Faith, the sworn Alliance broke,
Our impious Battels the just Gods provoke.
As this Advice ye practice, or reject,
So hope Success, or dread the dire Effect.
The Senior spoke, and sate. To whom reply'd
The Graceful Husband of the Spartan Bride.
Cold Counsels, Trojan, may become thy Years,   430
But sound ungrateful in a Warrior's Ears:
Old Man, if void of Fallacy or Art
Thy Words express the Purpose of thy Heart,
Thou, in thy Time, more sound advice hast giv'n;
But Wisdom has its Date, assign'd by Heav'n.
Then hear me, Princes of the Trojan Name!
Their Treasures I'll restore, but not the Dame;
My Treasures too, for Peace, I will resign;
But be this bright Possession ever mine.

'Twas then, the growing Discord to compose,   440
Slow from his Seat the rev'rend Priam rose.

His God-like Aspect deep Attention drew:
He paus'd, and these pacific Words ensue.
Ye Trojans, Dardans, and Auxiliar Bands!
Now take Refreshment as the Hours demands:
Guard well the Walls, relieve the Watch of Night,
Till the new Sun restores the chearful Light:
Then shall our Herald to th' Atrides sent,
Before their Ships, proclaim my Son's Intent:
Next let a Truce be ask'd, that Troy may burn   450
Her slaughter'd Heroes, and their Bones in-urn.
That done, once more the Fate of War be try'd,
And whose the Conquest, mighty Jove decide!
   The Monarch spoke: the Warriors snatch'd with haste
(Each at his Post in Arms) a short Repaste.
Soon as the rosy Morn had wak'd the Day,
To the black Ships Idæus bent his way:
There, to the Sons of Mars, in Council found,
He rais'd his Voice: The Hosts stood list'ning round.
Ye Sons of Atreus, and ye Greeks, give ear!   460
The Words of Troy, and Troy's great Monarch hear.
Pleas'd may ye hear (so Heav'n succeed my Pray'rs)
What Paris, Author of the War, declares.
The Spoils and Treasures he to Ilion bore,
(Oh had he perish'd e'er they touch'd our Shore)
He proffers injur'd Greece; with large Encrease
Of added Trojan Wealth to buy the Peace.
But to restore the beauteous Bride again,
This Greece demands, and Troy requests in vain.
Next, O ye Chiefs! we ask a Truce to burn   470
Our slaughter'd Heroes, and their Bones in-urn.
That done, once more the Fate of War be try'd,
And whose the Conquest, mighty Jove decide!
   The Greeks gave ear, but none the Silence broke,
At length Tydides rose, and rising spoke.
Oh take not, Friends! defrauded of your Fame,
Their proffer'd Wealth, nor ev'n the Spartan Dame.
Let Conquest make them ours: Fate shakes their Wall,
And Troy already totters to her Fall.
   Th' admiring Chiefs, and all the Grecian Name,   480
With gen'ral Shouts return'd him loud Acclaim.

Then thus the King of Kings rejects the Peace:
Herald! in him thou hear'st the Voice of Greece.
For what remains; let Fun'ral Flames be fed
With Heroes Corps: I war not with the Dead:
Go search your slaughter'd Chiefs on yonder Plain,
And gratify the Manes of the slain.
Be witness, Jove! whose Thunder rolls on high.
He said, and rear'd his Sceptre to the Sky.

  To sacred Troy, where all her Princes lay   490
To wait th' Event, the Herald bent his way.
He came, and standing in the midst, explain'd
The Peace rejected, but the Truce obtain'd.
Strait to their sev'ral Cares the Trojans move,
Some search the Plain, some fell the sounding Grove:
Nor less the Greeks, descending on the Shore,
Hew'd the green Forests, and the Bodies bore.
And now from forth the Chambers of the Main,
To shed his sacred Light on Earth again,
Arose the golden Chariot of the Day,   500
And tipt the Mountains with a purple Ray.
In mingled Throngs, the Greek and Trojan Train
Thro' Heaps of Carnage search'd the mournful Plain.
Scarce could the Friend his slaughter'd Friend explore,
With Dust dishonour'd, and deform'd with Gore.
The Wounds they wash'd, their pious Tears they shed,
And, lay'd along their Cars, deplor'd the dead.
Sage Priam check'd their Grief: With silent Haste
The Bodies decent on the Piles were plac'd:
With melting Hearts the cold Remains they burn'd;   510
And sadly slow, to sacred Troy return'd.
Nor less the Greeks their pious Sorrows shed,
And decent on the Pile dispose the dead;
The cold Remains consume with equal Care;
And slowly, sadly, to their Fleet repair.
Now, e're the Morn had streak'd with red'ning Light
The doubtful Confines of the Day and Night;
About the dying Flames the Greeks appear'd,
And round the Pile a gen'ral Tomb they rear'd.
Then, to secure the Camp and Naval Pow'rs,   520
They rais'd embattel'd Walls with lofty Tow'rs:

From Space to Space were ample Gates around,
For passing Chariots; and a Trench profound,
Of large Extent, and deep in Earth below
Strong Piles infix'd stood adverse to the Foe.
  So toil'd the Greeks: Meanwhile the Gods above
In shining Circle round their Father Jove,
Amaz'd beheld the wondrous Works of Man:
Then He, whose Trident shakes the Earth, began.
  What Mortals henceforth shall our Pow'r adore,   530
Our Fanes frequent, our Oracles implore,
If the proud Grecians thus successful boast
Their rising Bulwarks on the Sea-beat Coast?
See the long Walls extending to the Main,
No God consulted, and no Victim slain!
Their Fame shall fill the World's remotest Ends,
Wide, as the Morn her golden Beam extends.
While old Laömedon's divine Abodes,
Those radiant Structures rais'd by lab'ring Gods,[1]
Shall, raz'd and lost, in long Oblivion sleep.   540
Thus spoke the hoary Monarch of the Deep.
  Th' Almighty Thund'rer with a Frown replies,
That clouds the World, and blackens half the Skies.
Strong God of Ocean! Thou, whose Rage can make
The solid Earth's eternal Basis shake!
What Cause of Fear from mortal Works, cou'd move
The meanest Subject of our Realms above?
Where-e'er the Sun's refulgent Rays are cast,
Thy Pow'r is honour'd, and thy Fame shall last.
But yon' proud Work no future Age shall view,   550
No Trace remain where once the Glory grew.
The sapp'd Foundations by thy Force shall fall,
And whelm'd beneath thy Waves, drop the huge Wall:
Vast Drifts of Sand shall change the former Shore;
The Ruin vanish'd, and the Name no more.
   Thus they in Heav'n: while, o'er the Grecian Train,
The rolling Sun descending to the Main
Beheld the finish'd Work. Their Bulls they slew;
Black from the Tents the sav'ry Vapors flew.

---

[1] The walls of Troy were built by Apollo and Neptune (or Neptune alone, XXI, 516-30). When the work was done, Laomedon cheated the gods of their pay.

And now the Fleet, arriv'd from Lemnos' Strands,   560
With Bacchus' Blessings chear'd the gen'rous Bands.
Of fragrant Wines the rich Eunæus sent
A thousand Measures to the Royal Tent.
(Eunæus, whom Hypsipyle of yore
To Jason, Shepherd of his People, bore)
The rest they purchas'd at their proper Cost,
And well the plenteous Freight supply'd the Host:
Each, in exchange, proportion'd Treasures gave;
Some Brass or Iron, some an Oxe, or Slave.
All Night they feast, the Greek and Trojan Pow'rs;   570
Those on the Fields, and these within their Tow'rs.
But Jove averse the Signs of Wrath display'd,
And shot red Light'nings thro' the gloomy Shade:
Humbled they stood; pale Horror seiz'd on all,
While the deep Thunder shook th' Aerial Hall.
Each pour'd to Jove before the Bowl was crown'd,
And large Libations drench'd the thirsty Ground;
Then late refresh'd with Sleep from Toils of Fight,
Enjoy'd the balmy Blessings of the Night.

꙳꙳꙳

THE EIGHTH BOOK
OF THE ILIAD

THE ARGUMENT

The second Battel, and the Distress of the Greeks

JUPITER ASSEMBLES A COUNCIL of the Deities, and threatens them with the Pains of Tartarus if they assist either side: Minerva only obtains of him that she may direct the Greeks by her Counsels. The Armies join Battel; Jupiter on Mount Ida weighs in his Balances the Fates of both, and affrights the Greeks with his Thunders and Lightnings. Nestor alone continues in the Field in great Danger; Diomed relieves him; whose Exploits, and those of Hector, are excellently described. Juno endeavours to animate Neptune to the Assistance of the Greeks, but in vain. The Acts of Teucer, who is at length wounded by Hector and carry'd off. Juno and Minerva prepare to aid the Grecians, but are restrained by Iris, sent from Jupiter. The Night puts an end to the Battel. Hector keeps the Field (the Greeks being driven to their Fortification before the Ships) and gives Orders to keep the Watch all Night in the Camp, to prevent the Enemy from reimbarking and escaping by Flight. They kindle Fires through all the Field, and pass the Night under Arms.

The Time of seven and twenty Days is employed from the Opening of the Poem to the End of this Book. The Scene here (except of the Celestial Machines) lies in the Field toward the Sea Shore.

Aurora now, fair Daughter of the Dawn,
Sprinkled with rosy Light the dewy Lawn;
When Jove conven'd the Senate of the Skies,
Where high Olympus' cloudy Tops arise.

The Sire of Gods his awful Silence broke;
The Heav'ns attentive trembled as he spoke.
   Celestial States, Immortal Gods! give ear,
Hear our Decree, and rev'rence what ye hear;
The fix'd Decree which not all Heav'n can move;
Thou Fate! fulfill it; and ye Pow'rs! approve.   10
What God but enters yon' forbidden Field,
Who yields Assistance, or but wills to yield;
Back to the Skies with Shame he shall be driv'n,
Gash'd with dishonest Wounds, the Scorn of Heav'n:
Or far, oh far from steep Olympus thrown,
Low in the dark, Tartarean Gulf shall groan,
With burning Chains fix'd to the Brazen Floors,
And lock'd by Hell's inexorable Doors;
As deep beneath th' Infernal Centre hurl'd,
As from that Centre to th' Æthereal World.   20
Let him who tempts me, dread those dire Abodes;
And know, th' Almighty is the God of Gods.
League all your Forces then, ye Pow'rs above,
Join all, and try th' Omnipotence of Jove:
Let down our golden everlasting Chain,
Whose strong Embrace holds Heav'n, and Earth, and Main:
Strive all, of mortal and immortal Birth,
To drag, by this, the Thund'rer down to Earth:
Ye strive in vain! If I but stretch this Hand,
I heave the Gods, the Ocean, and the Land,   30
I fix the Chain to great Olympus' Height,
And the vast World hangs trembling in my Sight!
For such I reign, unbounded and above;
And such are Men, and Gods, compar'd to Jove.
   Th' Almighty spoke, nor durst the Pow'rs reply,
A rev'rend Horror silenc'd all the Sky;
Trembling they stood before their Sov'reign's Look;
At length his Best-belov'd, the Pow'r of Wisdom, spoke.
   Oh First and Greatest! God by Gods ador'd!
We own thy Might, our Father and our Lord!   40
But ah! permit to pity human State;
If not to help, at least lament their Fate.

From Fields forbidden we submiss refrain,
With Arms unaiding mourn our Argives slain;
Yet grant my Counsels still their Breasts may move,
Or all must perish in the Wrath of Jove.
　The Cloud-compelling God her Suit approv'd,
And smil'd superior on his Best-belov'd.
Then call'd his Coursers, and his Chariot took;
The stedfast Firmament beneath them shook:　　　　50
Rapt by th' Æthereal Steeds the Chariot roll'd;
Brass were their Hoofs, their curling Manes of Gold.
Of Heav'ns undrossy Gold the God's Array
Refulgent, flash'd intolerable Day.
High on the Throne he shines: His Coursers fly,
Between th' extended Earth and starry Sky.
But when to Ida's topmost Height he came,
(Fair Nurse of Fountains, and of Savage Game)
Where o'er her pointed Summits proudly rais'd,
His Fane breath'd Odours, and his Altar blaz'd:　　　60
There, from his radiant Car, the sacred Sire
Of Gods and Men releas'd the Steeds of Fire:
Blue ambient Mists th' immortal Steeds embrac'd;
High on the cloudy Point his Seat he plac'd.
Thence his broad Eye the subject World surveys,
The Town, the Tents, and navigable Seas.
　Now had the Grecians snatch'd a short Repaste,
And buckled on their shining Arms with Haste.
Troy rowz'd as soon; for on this dreadful Day
The Fate of Fathers, Wives, and Infants lay.　　　70
The Gates unfolding pour forth all their Train;
Squadrons on Squadrons cloud the dusky Plain:
Men, Steeds, and Chariots shake the trembling Ground;
The Tumult thickens, and the Skies resound.
And now with Shouts the shocking Armies clos'd,
To Lances, Lances, Shields to Shields oppos'd,
Host against Host with shadowy Legions drew,
The sounding Darts in Iron Tempests flew,
Victors and Vanquish'd join promiscuous Cries,
Triumphant Shouts and dying Groans arise;　　　80

With streaming Blood the slipp'ry Fields are dy'd,
And slaughter'd Heroes swell the dreadful Tide.
Long as the Morning Beams encreasing bright,
O'er Heav'ns clear Azure spread the sacred Light;
Commutual Death the Fate of War confounds,
Each adverse Battel goar'd with equal Wounds.
But when the Sun the Height of Heav'n ascends;
The Sire of Gods his golden Scales suspends,
With equal Hand: In these explor'd the Fate
Of Greece and Troy, and pois'd the mighty Weight.   90
Press'd with its Load the Grecian Balance lies
Low sunk on Earth, the Trojan strikes the Skies.
Then Jove from Ida's Top his Horrors spreads;
The Clouds burst dreadful o'er the Grecian Heads;
Thick Light'nings flash; the mutt'ring Thunder rolls;
Their Strength he withers, and unmans their Souls.
Before his Wrath the Trembling Host retire;
The God in Terrors, and the Skies on fire.
Nor great Idomeneus that Sight could bear,
Nor each stern Ajax, Thunderbolts of War: 100
Nor He, the King of Men, th' Alarm sustain'd;
Nestor alone amidst the Storm remain'd.
Unwilling he remain'd, for Paris' Dart
Had pierc'd his Courser in a mortal Part;
Fix'd in the Forehead where the springing Mane
Curl'd o'er the Brow, it stung him to the Brain;
Mad with his Anguish, he begins to rear,
Paw with his Hoofs aloft, and lash the Air.
Scarce had his Falchion cut the Reins, and freed
Th' incumber'd Chariot from the dying Steed,   110
When dreadful Hector, thund'ring thro' the War,
Pour'd to the Tumult on his whirling Car.
That Day had stretch'd beneath his matchless Hand
The hoary Monarch of the Pylian Band,
But Diomed beheld; from forth the Crowd
He rush'd, and on Ulysses call'd aloud.
    Whither, oh whither does Ulysses run?
Oh Flight unworthy great Laertes' Son!

Mix'd with the Vulgar shall thy Fate be found,
Pierc'd in the Back, a vile, dishonest Wound?   120
Oh turn and save from Hector's direful Rage
The Glory of the Greeks, the Pylian Sage.
His fruitless Words are lost unheard in Air;
Ulysses seeks the Ships, and shelters there.
But bold Tydides to the Rescue goes,
A single Warrior 'midst a Host of Foes;
Before the Coursers with a sudden Spring
He leap'd, and anxious thus bespoke the King.
  Great Perils, Father! wait th' unequal Fight;
These younger Champions will oppress thy Might.   130
Thy Veins no more with ancient Vigour glow,
Weak is thy Servant, and thy Coursers slow.
Then haste, ascend my Seat, and from the Car
Observe the Steeds of Tros, renown'd in War,
Practis'd alike to turn, to stop, to chace,
To dare the Fight, or urge the rapid Race;
These late obey'd Æneas' guiding Rein;
Leave thou thy Chariot to our faithful Train:
With these against yon' Trojans will we go,
Nor shall great Hector want an equal Foe;   140
Fierce as he is, ev'n He may learn to fear
The thirsty Fury of my flying Spear.
  Thus said the Chief; and Nestor, skill'd in War,
Approves his Counsel, and ascends the Car:
The Steeds he left, their trusty Servants hold;
Eurymedon and Sthenelus the bold.
The rev'rend Charioteer directs the Course,
And strains his aged Arm to lash the Horse.
Hector they face; unknowning how to fear,
Fierce he drove on; Tydides whirl'd his Spear.   150
The Spear with erring Haste mistook its way,
But plung'd in Eniopeus' Bosom lay.
His opening Hand in Death forsakes the Rein;
The Steeds fly back: He falls, and spurns the Plain.
Great Hector sorrows for his Servant kill'd,
Yet unreveng'd permits to press the Field;

Till to supply his Place and rule the Car,
Rose Archeptolemus, the fierce in War.
And now had Death and Horror cover'd all;
Like tim'rous Flocks the Trojans in their Wall   160
Inclos'd had bled: but Jove with awful Sound
Roll'd the big Thunder o'er the vast Profound:
Full in Tydides' Face the Light'ning flew;
The Ground before him flam'd with Sulphur blew;
The quiv'ring Steeds fell prostrate at the Sight;
And Nestor's trembling Hand confess'd his Fright.
He drop'd the Reins; and shook with sacred Dread,
Thus, turning, warn'd th' intrepid Diomed.
   O Chief! too daring in thy Friend's Defence,
Retire advis'd, and urge the Chariot hence.   170
This Day, averse, the Sov'reign of the Skies
Assists great Hector, and our Palm denies.
Some other Sun may see the happier Hour,
When Greece shall conquer by his heav'nly Pow'r.
'Tis not in Man his fix'd Decree to move:
The Great will glory to submit to Jove.
   O rev'rend Prince! (Tydides thus replies)
Thy Years are awful, and thy Words are wise.
But ah! what Grief? should haughty Hector boast,
I fled inglorious to the guarded Coast.   180
Before that dire Disgrace shall blast my Fame,
O'erwhelm me Earth! and hide a Warrior's Shame.
   To whom Gerenian Nestor thus reply'd,
Gods! can thy Courage fear the Phrygian's Pride?
Hector may vaunt, but who shall heed the Boast?
Not those who felt thy Arm, the Dardan Host,
Nor Troy, yet bleeding in her Heroes lost;
Not ev'n a Phrygian Dame, who dreads the Sword
That lay'd in Dust her lov'd, lamented Lord.
He said; and hasty, o'er the gasping Throng   190
Drives the swift Steeds; the Chariot smoaks along.
The Shouts of Trojans thicken in the Wind;
The Storm of hissing Javelins pours behind.
Then with a Voice that shakes the solid Skies,
Pleas'd Hector braves the Warrior as he flies.

Go, mighty Hero! grac'd above the rest
In Seats of Council and the sumptuous Feast:
Now hope no more those Honours from thy Train;
Go, less than Woman in the Form of Man!
To scale our Walls, to wrap our Tow'rs in Flames,   200
To lead in Exile the fair Phrygian Dames,
Thy once-proud Hopes, presumptuous Prince! are fled;
This Arm shall reach thy Heart, and stretch thee dead.

Now Fears dissuade him, and now Hopes invite,
To stop his Coursers, and to stand the Fight;
Thrice turn'd the Chief, and thrice imperial Jove
On Ida's Summits thunder'd from above.
Great Hector heard; he saw the flashing Light,
(The Sign of Conquest) and thus urg'd the Fight.

Hear ev'ry Trojan, Lycian, Dardan Band,   210
All fam'd in War, and dreadful hand to hand.
Be mindful of the Wreaths your Arms have won,
Your great Forefathers Glories, and your own.
Heard ye the Voice of Jove? Success and Fame
Await on Troy, on Greece eternal Shame.
In vain they skulk behind their boasted Wall,
Weak Bulwarks! destin'd by this Arm to fall.
High o'er their slighted Trench our Steeds shall bound,
And pass victorious o'er the levell'd Mound.
Soon as before yon' hollow Ships we stand,   220
Fight each with Flames, and toss the blazing Brand;
Till their proud Navy wrapt in Smoak and Fires,
All Greece, encompass'd, in one Blaze expires.

Furious he said; then, bending o'er the Yoke,
Encourag'd his proud Steeds, while thus he spoke.
Now Xanthus, Æthon, Lampus! urge the Chace,
And thou, Podargus! prove thy gen'rous Race:
Be fleet, be fearless, this important Day,
And all your Masters well-spent Care repay.
For this, high fed in plenteous Stalls ye stand,   230
Serv'd with pure Wheat, and by a Princess' Hand;
For this my Spouse of great Aëtion's Line
So oft' has steep'd the strength'ning Grain in Wine.

Now swift pursue, now thunder uncontroll'd;
Give me to seize rich Nestor's Shield of Gold;
From Tydeus' Shoulders strip the costly Load,
Vulcanian Arms, the Labour of a God:
These if we gain, then Victory, ye Pow'rs!
This Night, this glorious Night, the Fleet is ours.

That heard, deep Anguish stung Saturnia's Soul;   240
She shook her Throne that shook the starry Pole:
And thus to Neptune: Thou! whose Force can make
The stedfast Earth from her Foundations shake,
See'st thou the Greeks by Fates unjust opprest,
Nor swells thy Heart in that immortal Breast?
Yet Ægæ, Helicè, thy Pow'r obey,
And Gifts unceasing on thine Altars lay.
Would all the Deities of Greece combine,
In vain the gloomy Thund'rer might repine:
Sole should he sit, with scarce a God to Friend,   250
And see his Trojans to the Shades descend.
Such be the Scene from his Idæan Bow'r;
Ungrateful Prospect to the sullen Pow'r!

Neptune with Wrath rejects the rash Design:
What Rage, what Madness, furious Queen! is thine?
I war not with the Highest. All above
Submit and tremble at the Hand of Jove.

Now Godlike Hector, to whose matchless Might:
Jove gave the Glory of the destin'd Fight,
Squadrons on Squadrons drives, and fills the Fields   260
With close-rang'd Chariots, and with thicken'd Shields.
Where the deep Trench in Length extended lay,
Compacted Troops stand wedg'd in firm Array,
A dreadful Front! they shake the Brands, and threat
With long-destroying Flames, the hostile Fleet.
The King of Men, by Juno's self inspir'd,
Toil'd thro' the Tents, and all his Army fir'd,
Swift as he mov'd he lifted in his Hand
His Purple Robe, bright Ensign of Command.
High on the midmost Bark the King appear'd;   270
There, from Ulysses' Deck, his Voice was heard.

To Ajax and Achilles reach'd the Sound,
Whose distant Ships the guarded Navy bound.
Oh Argives! Shame of human Race; he cry'd,
(The hollow Vessels to his Voice reply'd)
Where now are all our glorious Boasts of yore,
Our hasty Triumphs on the Lemnian Shore?
Each fearless Hero dares an hundred Foes,
While the Feast lasts, and while the Goblet flows;
But who to meet one martial Man is found,   280
When the Fight rages, and the Flames surround?
Oh mighty Jove! oh Sire of the distress'd!
Was ever King like me, like me oppress'd?
With Pow'r immense, with Justice arm'd in vain;
My Glory ravish'd, and my People slain!
To thee my Vows were breath'd from ev'ry Shore;
What Altar smoak'd not with our Victims Gore?
With Fat of Bulls I fed the constant Flame,
And ask'd Destruction to the Trojan Name.
Now, gracious God! far humbler our Demand;   290
Give these at least to 'scape from Hector's Hand,
And save the Reliques of the Grecian Land!
    Thus pray'd the King, and Heav'ns great Father heard
His Vows, in Bitterness of Soul preferr'd;
The Wrath appeas'd, by happy Signs declares,
And gives the People to their Monarch's Pray'rs.
His Eagle, sacred Bird of Heav'n! he sent,
A Fawn his Talons truss'd (divine Portent)
High o'er the wond'ring Hosts he soar'd above,
Who paid their Vows to Panomphæan[1] Jove;   300
Then let the Prey before his Altar fall;
The Greeks beheld, and Transport seiz'd on all:
Encourag'd by the Sign, the Troops revive,
And fierce on Troy with doubled Fury drive.
Tydides first, of all the Grecian Force,
O'er the broad Ditch impell'd his foaming Horse;
Pierc'd the deep Ranks; their strongest Battel tore;
And dy'd his Javelin red with Trojan Gore.

[1] Jove as god of omens sent through sounds or voices

Young Ageläus (Phradmon was his Sire)
With flying Coursers shun'd his dreadful Ire: 310
Strook thro' the Back the Phrygian fell opprest;
The Dart drove on, and issu'd at his Breast:
Headlong he quits the Car; his Arms resound;
His pond'rous Buckler thunders on the Ground.
Forth rush a Tide of Greeks, the Passage freed;
Th' Atridæ first, th' Ajaces next succeed:
Meriones, like Mars in Arms renown'd,
And Godlike Idomen, now pass the Mound;
Euæmon's Son next issues to the Foe,
And last young Teucer with his bended Bow.   320
Secure behind the Telamonian Shield
The skilful Archer wide survey'd the Field,
With ev'ry Shaft some hostile Victim slew,
Then close beneath the sev'nfold Orb withdrew.
The conscious Infant so, when Fear alarms,
Retires for Safety to the Mother's Arms.
Thus Ajax guards his Brother in the Field,
Moves as he moves, and turns the shining Shield.
Who first by Teucer's mortal Arrows bled?
Orsilochus; then fell Ormenus dead: 330
The Godlike Lycophon next press'd the Plain,
With Chromius, Dætor, Ophelestes slain:
Bold Hamopäon breathless sunk to Ground;
The bloody Pile great Melanippus crown'd.
Heaps fell on Heaps, sad Trophies of his Art,
A Trojan Ghost attending ev'ry Dart.
Great Agamemnon views with joyful Eye
The Ranks grow thinner as his Arrows fly,
Oh Youth for ever dear! (the Monarch cry'd)
Thus, always thus, thy early Worth be try'd.   340
Thy brave example shall retrieve our Host,
Thy Country's Saviour, and thy Father's Boast!
Sprung from an Alien's Bed thy Sire to grace,
The vig'rous Offspring of a stol'n Embrace,
Proud of his Boy, he own'd the gen'rous Flame,
And the brave Son repays his Cares with Fame.

Now hear a Monarchs Vow: If Heav'ns high Pow'rs
Give me to raze Troy's long-defended Tow'rs;
Whatever Treasures Greece for me design,
The next rich Honorary Gift be thine: 350
Some golden Tripod, or distinguish'd Car,
With Coursers dreadful in the Ranks of War;
Or some fair Captive whom thy Eyes approve
Shall recompence the Warrior's Toils with Love.
    To this the Chief: With Praise the rest inspire,
Nor urge a Soul already fill'd with fire.
What Strength I have, be now in Battel try'd,
Till ev'ry Shaft in Phrygian Blood be dy'd.
Since rallying from our Wall we forc'd the Foe,
Still aim'd at Hector have I bent my Bow;   360
Eight forky Arrows from this Hand have fled,
And eight bold Heroes by their Points lie dead:
But sure some God denies me to destroy
This Fury of the Field, this Dog of Troy.
    He said, and twang'd the String. The Weapon flies
At Hector's Breast, and sings along the Skies:
He miss'd the Mark; but pierc'd Gorgythio's Heart,
And drench'd in Royal Blood the thirsty Dart.
(Fair Castianira, Nymph of Form Divine,
This Offspring added to King Priam's Line)   370
As full blown Poppies overcharg'd with Rain
Decline the Head, and drooping kiss the Plain;
So sinks the Youth: his beauteous Head, depress'd
Beneath his Helmet, drops upon his Breast.
Another Shaft the raging Archer drew;
That other Shaft with erring Fury flew,
(From Hector Phœbus turn'd the flying Wound)
Yet fell not dry, or guiltless to the Ground:
Thy Breast, brave Archeptolemus! it tore,
And dipp'd its Feathers in no vulgar Gore.   380
Headlong he falls; his sudden Fall alarms
The Steeds that startle at his sounding Arms.
Hector with Grief his Charioteer beheld,
And ey'd him breathless on the sanguin Field.

Then bids Cebriones direct the Rein,
Quits his bright Car, and issues on the Plain.
Dreadful he shouts: from Earth a Stone he took,
And rush'd on Teucer with the lifted Rock.
The Youth already strain'd the forceful Yew;
The Shaft already to his Shoulder drew;   390
The Feather in his Hand, just wing'd for flight,
Touch'd where the Neck and hollow Chest unite:
There, where the Juncture knits the Channel Bone,
The furious Chief discharg'd the craggy Stone.
The Tendon burst beneath the Pondrous Blow,
And his numb'd Hand dismiss'd his useless Bow.
He fell: But Ajax his broad Shield display'd,
And screen'd his Brother with the mighty Shade;
Till great Alastor, and Mecistheus, bore
The batter'd Archer groaning to the Shore.   400
    Troy yet found Grace before th' Olympian Sire,
He arm'd their Hands, and fill'd their Breasts with Fire.
The Greeks, repuls'd, retreat behind their Wall,
Or in the Trench on Heaps confus'dly fall.
First of the Foe great Hector march'd along,
With Terror cloath'd, and more than mortal strong.
As the bold Hound that gives the Lion chace,
With beating Bosom, and with eager Pace,
Hangs on his Haunch, or fastens on his Heels,
Guards as he turns, and circles as he wheels: 410
Thus oft' the Grecians turn'd, but still they flew;
Thus following Hector still the hindmost slew.
When flying they had pass'd the Trench profound,
And many a Chief lay gasping on the Ground;
Before the Ships a desp'rate Stand they made,
And fir'd the Troops, and call'd the Gods to aid.
Fierce on his ratt'ling Chariot Hector came;
His Eyes like Gorgon shot a sanguin Flame
That wither'd all their Host: Like Mars he stood,
Dire as the Monster, dreadful as the God!   420
Their strong Distress the Wife of Jove survey'd;
Then pensive thus, to War's triumphant Maid.

Oh Daughter of that God, whose Arm can wield
Th' avenging Bolt, and shake the sable Shield!
Now, in this Moment of her last Despair,
Shall wretched Greece no more confess our Care,
Condemn'd to suffer the full Force of Fate,
And drain the Dregs of Heav'ns relentless Hate?
Gods! shall one raging Hand thus level All?
What Numbers fell! what Numbers yet shall fall!   430
What Pow'r Divine shall Hector's Wrath asswage?
Still swells the Slaughter, and still grows the Rage!
   So spoke th' imperial Regent of the Skies;
To whom the Goddess with the Azure Eyes.
Long since had Hector stain'd these Fields with Gore,
Stretch'd by some Argive on his native Shore:
But He above, the Sire of Heav'n withstands,
Mocks our Attempts, and slights our just Demands.
The stubborn God, inflexible and hard,
Forgets my Service and deserv'd Reward.   440
Sav'd I, for this, his Fav'rite Son[2] distress'd,
By stern Eurystheus with long Labours press'd?
He begg'd, with Tears he begg'd, in deep Dismay;
I shot from Heav'n, and gave his Arm the Day.
Oh had my Wisdom known this dire Event,
When to grim Pluto's gloomy Gates he went;
The Triple Dog had never felt his Chain,
Nor Styx been cross'd, nor Hell explor'd in vain.
Averse to me of all his Heav'n of Gods;
At Thetis' Suit the partial Thund'rer nods.   450
To grace her gloomy, fierce, resenting Son,
My Hopes are frustrate, and my Greeks undone.
Some future Day, perhaps he may be mov'd
To call his blue-ey'd Maid his Best-belov'd.
Haste, launch thy Chariot, thro' yon' Ranks to ride;
My self will arm, and thunder at thy side.
Then Goddess! say, shall Hector glory then,
(That Terror of the Greeks, that Man of Men)
When Juno's self, and Pallas shall appear,
All dreadful in the crimson Walks of War?   460

2 Hercules

What mighty Trojan then, on yonder Shore,
Expiring, pale, and terrible no more,
Shall feast the Fowls, and glut the Dogs with Gore?
   She ceas'd, and Juno rein'd her Steeds with Care;
(Heav'ns awful Empress, Saturn's other Heir)
Pallas, meanwhile, her various Veil unbound,
With Flow'rs adorn'd, with Art immortal crown'd;
The radiant Robe her sacred Fingers wove,
Floats in rich Waves, and spreads the Court of Jove.
Her Father's Arms her mighty Limbs invest,   470
His Cuirass blazes on her ample Breast.
The vig'rous Pow'r the trembling Car ascends;
Shook by her Arm, the massy Javelin bends;
Huge, pond'rous, strong! that when her Fury burns,
Proud Tyrants humbles, and whole Hosts o'erturns.
   Saturnia lends the Lash; the Coursers fly;
Smooth glides the Chariot thro' the liquid Sky.
Heav'n-Gates spontaneous open to the Pow'rs,
Heav'ns golden Gates, kept by the winged Hours,
Commission'd in alternate Watch they stand,   480
The Sun's bright Portals and the Skies command;
Close, or unfold, th' Eternal Gates of Day;
Bar Heav'n with Clouds, or roll those Clouds away.
The sounding Hinges ring, the Clouds divide;
Prone down the Steep of Heav'n their Course they guide.
But Jove incens'd from Ida's Top survey'd,
And thus enjoin'd the many-colour'd Maid.
   Thaumantia![3] mount the Winds, and stop their Car;
Against the Highest who shall wage the War?
If furious yet they dare the vain Debate,   490
Thus have I spoke, and what I spake is Fate.
Their Coursers crush'd beneath the Wheels shall lie,
Their Car in Fragments scatter'd o'er the Sky;
My Light'ning these Rebellious shall confound,
And hurl them flaming, headlong to the Ground,
Condemn'd for ten revolving Years to weep
The Wounds impress'd by burning Thunder deep.

[3] Iris, daughter of the Titan Thaumas

So shall Minerva learn to fear our Ire,
Nor dare to combate her's and Natures Sire.
For Juno, headstrong and imperious still,   500
She claims some Title to transgress our Will.
  Swift as the Wind, the various-colour'd Maid
From Ida's Top her golden Wings display'd;
To great Olympus' shining Gates she flies,
There meets the Chariot rushing down the Skies,
Restrains their Progress from the bright Abodes,
And speaks the Mandate of the Sire of Gods.
  What Frenzy, Goddesses! what Rage can move
Celestial Minds to tempt the Wrath of Jove?
Desist, obedient to his high Command;   510
This is his Word; and know his Word shall stand.
His Light'ning your Rebellion shall confound,
And hurl ye headlong, flaming to the Ground:
Your Horses crush'd beneath the Wheels shall lie
Your Car in Fragments scatter'd o'er the Sky;
Your selves condemn'd ten rolling Years to weep
The Wounds impress'd by burning Thunder deep.
So shall Minerva learn to fear his Ire,
Nor dare to combate her's and Nature's Sire.
For Juno, headstrong and imperious still,   520
She claims some Title to transgress his Will:
But Thee what desp'rate Insolence has driv'n,
To lift thy Lance against the Sire of Heav'n?
  Then mounting on the Pinions of the Wind,
She flew; and Juno thus her Rage resign'd.
  O Daughter of that God, whose Arm can wield
Th' avenging Bolt, and shake the dreadful Shield!
No more let Beings of superior Birth
Contend with Jove for this low Race of Earth:
Triumphant now, now miserably slain,   530
They breathe or perish, as the Fates ordain.
But Jove's high Counsels full Effect shall find,
And ever constant, ever rule Mankind.
  She spoke, and backward turn'd her Steeds of Light,
Adorn'd with Manes of Gold, and Heav'nly bright.

The Hours unloos'd them, panting as they stood,
And heap'd their Mangers with Ambrosial Food.
There ty'd, they rest in high Celestial Stalls;
The Chariot propt against the Crystal Walls.
The pensive Goddesses, abash'd, controul'd,   540
Mix with the Gods, and fill their Seats of Gold.
   And now the Thund'rer meditates his Flight
From Ida's Summits to th' Olympian Height.
Swifter than Thought the Wheels instinctive fly,
Flame thro' the Vast of Air, and reach the Sky.
'Twas Neptune's Charge his Coursers to unbrace,
And fix the Car on its immortal Base;
There stood the Chariot beaming forth its Rays,
Till with a snowy Veil he screen'd the Blaze.
He, whose all-conscious Eyes the World behold,   550
Th' Eternal Thunderer, sate thron'd in Gold.
High Heav'n the Footstool of his Feet he makes,
And wide beneath him, all Olympus shakes.
Trembling afar th' offending Pow'rs appear'd,
Confus'd and silent, for his Frown they fear'd.
He saw their Soul, and thus his Word imparts.
Pallas and Juno! say, why heave your Hearts?
Soon was your Battel o'er: Proud Troy retir'd
Before your Face, and in your Wrath expir'd.
But know, whoe'er Almighty Pow'r withstand!   560
Unmatch'd our Force, unconquer'd is our Hand:
Who shall the Sov'reign of the Skies controul?
Not all the Gods that crown the starry Pole.
Your Hearts shall tremble, if our Arms we take,
And each immortal Nerve with Horror shake.
For thus I speak, and what I speak shall stand;
What Pow'r soe'er provokes our lifted Hand,
On this our Hill no more shall hold his Place,
Cut off, and exil'd from th' Æthereal Race.
   Juno and Pallas grieving hear the Doom,   570
But feast their Souls on Ilion's Woes to come.
Tho' secret Anger swell'd Minerva's Breast,
The prudent Goddess yet her Wrath represt,

But Juno, impotent of Rage, replies.
What hast thou said, Oh Tyrant of the Skies!
Strength and Omnipotence invest thy Throne;
'Tis thine to punish; ours to grieve alone.
For Greece we grieve, abandon'd by her Fate
To drink the Dregs of thy unmeasur'd Hate:
From Fields forbidden we submiss refrain,   580
With Arms unaiding see our Argives slain;
Yet grant our Counsels still their Breasts may move,
Lest all should perish in the Rage of Jove.
  The Goddess thus: and thus the God replies
Who swells the Clouds, and blackens all the Skies.
The Morning Sun, awak'd by loud Alarms,
Shall see th' Almighty Thunderer in Arms.
What Heaps of Argives then shall load the Plain,
These radiant Eyes shall view, and view in vain.
Nor shall great Hector cease the Rage of Fight,   590
The Navy Flaming, and thy Greeks in Flight,
Ev'n till the Day, when certain Fates ordain
That stern Achilles (his Patroclus slain)
Shall rise in Vengeance, and lay waste the Plain.
For such is Fate, nor can'st thou turn its Course
With all thy Rage, with all thy Rebel Force.
Fly, if thou wilt, to Earth's remotest Bound,
Where on her utmost Verge the Seas resound;
Where curs'd Iäpetus and Saturn dwell,
Fast by the Brink, within the Steams of Hell;   600
No Sun e'er gilds the gloomy Horrors there,
No Chearful Gales refresh the lazy Air:
There arm once more the bold Titanian Band;
And arm in vain: For what I will, shall stand.
  Now deep in Ocean sunk the Lamp of Light,
And drew behind the cloudy Veil of Night:
The conqu'ring Trojans mourn his Beams decay'd;
The Greeks rejoicing bless the friendly Shade.
  The Victors keep the Field; and Hector calls
A martial Council near the Navy-Walls: 610
These to Scamander's Bank apart he led,
Where thinly scatter'd lay the Heaps of Dead.

Th' assembled Chiefs, descending on the Ground,
Attend his Order, and their Prince surround.
A massy Spear he bore of mighty Strength,
Of full ten Cubits was the Lance's Length;
The Point was Steel, refulgent to behold,
Fix'd to the Wood with circling Rings of Gold:
The noble Hector on this Lance reclin'd,
And bending forward, thus reveal'd his Mind.   620
 Ye valiant Trojans, with Attention hear!
Ye Dardan Bands, and gen'rous Aids give ear!
This Day, we hop'd, would wrap in conq'ring Flame
Greece with her Ships, and crown our Toils with Fame:
But Darkness now, to save the Cowards, falls,
And guards them trembling in their wooden Walls.
Obey the Night, and use her peaceful Hours
Our Steeds to forage, and refresh our Pow'rs.
Strait from the Town be Sheep and Oxen sought,
And strength'ning Bread, and gen'rous Wine be brought.   630
Wide o'er the Field, high-blazing to the Sky,
Let num'rous Fires the absent Sun supply;
The flaming Piles with plenteous Fuel raise,
Till the bright Morn her purple Beam displays:
Lest in the Silence and the Shades of Night,
Greece on her sable Ships attempt her Flight.
Not unmolested let the Wretches gain
Their lofty Decks, and safely cleave the Main;
Some hostile Wound let ev'ry Dart bestow,
Some lasting Token of the Phrygian Foe,   640
Wounds, that long hence may ask their Spouses Care,
And warn their Children from a Trojan War.
Now thro' the Circuit of our Ilian Wall,
Let sacred Heralds sound the solemn Call;
To bid the Sires with hoary Honours crown'd,
And beardless Youths, the Battlements surround.
Firm be the Guard, while distant lie our Pow'rs,
And let the Matrons hang with Lights the Tow'rs:
Lest under Covert of the Midnight Shade,
Th' insidious Foe the naked Town invade.   650

Suffice, to Night, these Orders to obey;
A nobler Charge shall rowze the dawning Day.
The Gods, I trust, shall give to Hector's Hand,
From these detested Foes to free the Land,
Who plow'd, with Fates averse, the wat'ry way;
For Trojan Vulturs a predestin'd Prey.
Our common Safety must be now the Care;
But soon as Morning paints the Fields of Air,
Sheath'd in bright Arms let ev'ry Troop engage,
And the fir'd Fleet behold the Battel rage.   660
Then, then shall Hector and Tydides prove,
Whose Fates are heaviest in the Scale of Jove.
To Morrow's Light (oh haste the glorious Morn!)
Shall see his bloody Spoils in Triumph born,
With this keen Javelin shall his Breast be gor'd,
And prostrate Heroes bleed around their Lord.
Certain as this, oh might my Days endure,
From Age inglorious and black Death secure;
So might my Life and Glory know no bound,
Like Pallas worship'd, like the Sun renown'd;   670
As the next Dawn, the last they shall enjoy,
Shall crush the Greeks, and end the Woes of Troy.
   The Leader spoke. From all his Hosts around
Shouts of Applause along the Shores resound.
Each from the Yoke the smoking Steeds unty'd,
And fix'd their Headstalls to his Chariot-side.
Fat Sheep and Oxen from the Town are led,
With gen'rous Wine, and all-sustaining Bread.
Full Hecatombs lay burning on the Shore;
The Winds to Heav'n the curling Vapours bore.   680
Ungrateful Off'ring to th' immortal Pow'rs,
Whose Wrath hung heavy o'er the Trojan Tow'rs;
Nor Priam, nor his Sons obtain'd their Grace;
Proud Troy they hated, and her guilty Race.
   The Troops exulting sate in order round,
And beaming Fires illumin'd all the Ground.
As when the Moon, refulgent Lamp of Night!
O'er Heav'ns clear Azure spreads her sacred Light,

When not a breath disturbs the deep Serene;
And not a Cloud o'ercasts the Solemn Scene;   690
Around her Throne the vivid Planets roll,
And Stars unnumber'd gild the glowing Pole,
O'er the dark Trees a yellower Verdure shed,
And tip with Silver ev'ry Mountain's Head;
Then shine the Vales, the Rocks in Prospect rise,
A Flood of Glory bursts from all the Skies:
The conscious Swains, rejoicing in the Sight,
Eye the blue Vault, and bless the useful Light.
So many Flames before proud Ilion blaze,
And lighten glimm'ring Xanthus with their Rays.   700
The long Reflections of the distant Fires
Gleam on the Walls, and tremble on the Spires.
A thousand Piles[4] the dusky Horrors[5] gild,
And shoot a shady Lustre o'er the Field.
Full fifty Guards each flaming Pile attend,
Whose umber'd Arms, by fits, thick Flashes send.
Loud neigh the Coursers o'er their Heaps of Corn,
And ardent Warriors wait the rising Morn.

[4] Fires, as in *funeral piles* (pyres)
[5] Trembling, *horrid*, shadows, gilded by the firelight

THE NINTH BOOK
OF THE ILIAD

THE ARGUMENT

The Embassy to Achilles

AGAMEMNON AFTER THE LAST DAY'S DEFEAT, proposes to the Greeks to quit the Siege, and return to their Country. Diomed opposes this, and Nestor seconds him, praising his Wisdom and Resolution. He orders the Guard to be strengthen'd, and a Council summon'd to deliberate what Measures were to be follow'd in this Emergency. Agamemnon pursues this Advice, and Nestor farther prevails upon him to send Ambassadors to Achilles, in order to move him to a Reconciliation. Ulysses and Ajax are made choice of, who are accompanied by old Phœnix. They make, each of them, very moving and pressing Speeches, but are rejected with Roughness by Achilles, who notwithstanding retains Phœnix in his Tent. The Ambassadors return unsuccessfully to the Camp, and the Troops betake themselves to sleep.

This Book, and the next following, take up the Space of one Night, which is the twenty seventh from the beginning of the Poem. The Scene lies on the Sea-shore, the Station of the Grecian Ships.

Thus joyful Troy maintain'd the Watch of Night,
While Fear, pale Comrade of inglorious Flight,
And heav'n-bred Horror, on the Grecian part,
Sate on each Face, and sadden'd ev'ry heart.
As from its cloudy Dungeon issuing forth,
A double Tempest of the West and North
Swells o'er the Sea, from Thracia's frozen Shore,
Heaps Waves on Waves, and bids th' Ægean roar;

This way and that, the boiling Deeps are tost;
Such various Passions urg'd the troubled Host.   10
Great Agamemnon griev'd above the rest;
Superior Sorrows swell'd his Royal Breast;
Himself his Orders to the Heralds bears,
To bid to Council all the Grecian Peers,
But bid in Whispers: These surround their Chief,
In solemn Sadness, and majestic Grief.
The King amidst the mournful Circle rose;
Down his wan Cheek a briny Torrent flows;
So silent Fountains, from a Rock's tall Head,
In sable Streams soft-trickling Waters shed.   20
With more than vulgar Grief he stood opprest;
Words, mixt with Sighs, thus bursting from his Breast.
    Ye Sons of Greece! partake your Leader's Care,
Fellows in Arms, and Princes of the War!
Of partial Jove too justly we complain,
And heav'nly Oracles believ'd in vain;
A safe Return was promis'd to our toils,
With Conquest honour'd, and enrich'd with Spoils:
Now shameful flight alone can save the Host;
Our Wealth, our People, and our Glory lost.   30
So Jove decrees, Almighty Lord of all!
Jove, at whose Nod whole Empires rise or fall,
Who shakes the feeble Props of human Trust,
And Tow'rs and Armies humbles to the Dust.
Haste then, for ever quit these fatal Fields,
Haste to the Joys our native Country yields;
Spread all your Canvas, all your Oars employ,
Nor hope the Fall of heav'n-defended Troy.
    He said; deep Silence held the Grecian Band,
Silent, unmov'd, in dire Dismay they stand,   40
A pensive Scene! 'till Tydeus' warlike Son
Roll'd on the King his Eyes, and thus begun.
    When Kings advise us to renounce our Fame,
First let him speak, who first has suffer'd Shame.
If I oppose thee, Prince! thy Wrath with-hold,
The Laws of Council bid my Tongue be bold.

Thou first, and thou alone, in Fields of Fight,
Durst brand my courage, and defame my might;
Nor from a Friend th' unkind Reproach appear'd,
The Greeks stood witness, all our Army heard.　　　　50
The Gods, O Chief! from whom our honours spring,
The Gods have made thee but by halves a King;
They gave thee Scepters, and a wide Command,
They gave Dominion o'er the Seas and Land,
The noblest Pow'r that might the World controul
They gave thee not—a brave and virtuous Soul.
Is this a Gen'ral's Voice, that would suggest
Fears like his own to ev'ry Grecian Breast?
Confiding in our want of Worth, he stands,
And if we fly, 'tis what our King commands.　　　　60
Go thou inglorious! from th' embattel'd Plain;
Ships thou hast store, and nearest to the Main,
A nobler Care the Grecians shall employ,
To combate, conquer, and extirpate Troy.
Here Greece shall stay; or if all Greece retire,
My self will stay, 'till Troy or I expire;
My self, and Sthenelus, will fight for Fame;
God bad us fight, and 'twas with God we came.
　　He ceas'd: the Greeks loud Acclamations raise,
And Voice to Voice resounds Tydides' Praise.　　　　70
Wise Nestor then his Rev'rend Figure rear'd;
He spoke: the Host in still Attention heard.
　　O truly great! in whom the Gods have join'd
Such Strength of Body, with such Force of Mind;
In Conduct, as in Courage, you excell,
Still first to act what you advise so well.
Those wholsome Counsels which thy Wisdom moves,
Applauding Greece with common Voice approves.
Kings thou canst blame; a bold, but prudent Youth;
And blame ev'n Kings with Praise, because with Truth.　　　　80
And yet those Years that since thy Birth have run,
Would hardly stile thee Nestor's youngest Son.
Then let me add what yet remains behind,
A Thought unfinish'd in that gen'rous Mind;

Age bids me speak; nor shall th' Advice I bring
Distast the People, or offend the King.
  Curs'd is the Man, and void of Law and Right,
Unworthy Property, unworthy Light,
Unfit for publick Rule, or private Care;
That Wretch, that Monster, who delights in War: 90
Whose Lust is Murder, and whose horrid Joy,
To tear his Country, and his Kind destroy!
This Night, refresh and fortify thy Train;
Between the Trench and Wall, let Guards remain:
Be that the Duty of the young and bold;
But thou, O King, to Council call the old:
Great is thy Sway, and weighty are thy Cares;
Thy high Commands must spirit all our Wars.
With Thracian Wines recruit thy honour'd Guests,
For happy Counsels flow from sober Feasts.   100
Wise, weighty Counsels aid a State distrest,
And such a Monarch as can chuse the best.
See! what a Blaze from hostile Tents aspires,
How near our Fleet approach the Trojan Fires?
Who can, unmov'd, behold the dreadful Light,
What Eye beholds 'em, and can close to night?
This dreadful Interval determines all;
To morrow, Troy must flame, or Greece must fall.
  Thus spoke the hoary Sage: the rest obey;
Swift thro' the Gates the Guards direct their way.   110
His Son was first to pass the lofty Mound,
The gen'rous Thrasymed, in Arms renown'd:
Next him Ascalaphus, Iälmen, stood,
The double Offspring of the Warrior-God.
Deipyrus, Aphareus, Merion join,
And Lycomed, of Creon's noble Line.
Sev'n were the Leaders of the nightly Bands,
And each bold Chief a hundred Spears commands.
The Fires they light, to short Repasts they fall,
Some line the Trench, and others man the Wall.   120
  The King of Men, on publick Counsels bent,
Conven'd the Princes in his ample Tent;

Each seiz'd a Portion of the Kingly Feast,
But stay'd his Hand when Thirst and Hunger ceast.
Then Nestor spoke, for Wisdom long approv'd,
And slowly rising, thus the Council mov'd.
  Monarch of Nations! whose superior Sway
Assembled States, and Lords of Earth obey,
The Laws and Scepters to thy Hand are giv'n,
And Millions own the Care of thee and Heav'n.   130
O King! the Counsels of my Age attend;
With thee my Cares begin, in thee must end;
Thee, Prince! it fits alike to speak and hear,
Pronounce with Judgment, with Regard give ear,
To see no wholsom Motion be withstood,
And ratify the best, for publick Good.
Nor, tho' a meaner give Advice, repine,
But follow it, and make the Wisdom thine.
Hear then a Thought, not now conceiv'd in hast,
At once my present Judgment, and my past;   140
When from Pelides' Tent you forc'd the Maid,
I first oppos'd, and faithful, durst dissuade;
But bold of Soul, when headlong Fury fir'd,
You wrong'd the Man, by Men and Gods admir'd:
Now seek some means his fatal wrath to end,
With Pray'rs to move him, or with Gifts to bend.
  To whom the King. With Justice has thou shown
A Prince's Faults, and I with Reason own.
That happy Man whom Jove still honours most,
Is more than Armies, and himself an Host.   150
Blest in his Love, this wond'rous Hero stands;
Heav'n fights his War, and humbles all our Bands.
Fain wou'd my Heart, which err'd thro' frantic Rage,
The wrathful Chief and angry Gods assuage.
If Gifts immense his mighty Soul can bow,
Hear all ye Greeks, and witness what I vow.
Ten weighty Talents of the purest Gold,
And twice ten Vases of refulgent Mold;
Sev'n sacred Tripods, whose unsully'd Frame
Yet knows no Office, nor has felt the Flame: 160

Twelve Steeds unmatch'd in Fleetness and in Force,
And still victorious in the dusty Course:
(Rich were the Man, whose ample Stores exceed
The Prizes purchas'd by their winged Speed)
Sev'n lovely Captives of the Lesbian Line,
Skill'd in each Art, unmatch'd in Form divine,
The same I chose for more than vulgar Charms,
When Lesbos sunk beneath the Hero's Arms.
All these, to buy his Friendship, shall be paid,
And join'd with these, the long contested Maid;   170
With all her Charms, Briseis I resign,
And solemn swear those Charms were never mine;
Untouch'd she stay'd, uninjur'd she removes,
Pure from my Arms, and guiltless of my Loves,
These instant shall be his; and if the Pow'rs
Give to our Arms proud Ilion's hostile Tow'rs,
Then shall he store (when Greece the Spoil divides)
With Gold and Brass his loaded Navy's sides.
Besides full twenty Nymphs of Trojan Race,
With copious Love shall crown his warm Embrace;   180
Such as himself will chuse; who yield to none,
Or yield to Helen's heav'nly Charms alone.
Yet hear me farther: When our Wars are o'er,
If safe we land on Argos fruitful Shore,
There shall he live my Son, our Honours share,
And with Orestes' self divide my Care.
Yet more—three Daughters in my Court are bred,
And each well worthy of a Royal Bed;
Laodice and Iphigenia fair,
And bright Chrysothemis with golden Hair;   190
Her let him choose, whom most his Eyes approve,
I ask no Presents, no Reward for Love.
My self will give the Dow'r; so vast a Store,
As never Father gave a Child before.
Sev'n ample Cities shall confess his Sway,
Him Enope, and Phæræ him obey,
Cardamyle with ample Turrets crown'd,
And sacred Pedasus, for Vines renown'd;

Æpea fair, the Pastures Hyra yields,
And rich Antheia with her flow'ry Fields: 200
The whole Extent to Pylos' sandy Plain
Along the verdant Margin of the Main.
There Heifers graze, and lab'ring Oxen toil;
Bold are the Men, and gen'rous is the Soil;
There shall he reign with Pow'r and Justice crown'd,
And rule the tributary Realms around.
All this I give, his Vengeance to controul,
And sure all this may move his mighty Soul.
Pluto, the grizly God who never spares,
Who feels no Mercy, and who hears no Pray'rs,   210
Lives dark and dreadful in deep Hell's Abodes,
And Mortals hate him, as the worst of Gods.
Great tho' he be, it fits him to obey;
Since more than his my Years, and more my Sway.
    The Monarch thus: the Rev'rend Nestor then:
Great Agamemnon! glorious King of Men!
Such are thy Offers as a Prince may take,
And such as fits a gen'rous King to make.
Let chosen Delegates this Hour be sent,
(My self will name them) to Pelides' Tent: 220
Let Phænix lead, rever'd for hoary Age,
Great Ajax next, and Ithacus the sage.
Yet more to sanctify the Word you send,
Let Hodius and Eurybates attend.
Now pray to Jove to grant what Greece demands;
Pray, in deep Silence, and with purest Hands.
    He said, and all approv'd. The Heralds bring
The cleansing Water from the living Spring.
The Youth with Wine the sacred Goblets crown'd,
And large Libations drench'd the Sands around.   230
The Rite perform'd, the Chiefs their Thirst allay,
Then from the Royal Tent they took their way;
Wise Nestor turns on each his careful Eye,
Forbids t' offend, instructs them to apply:
Much he advis'd them all, Ulysses most,
To deprecate the Chief, and save the Host.

Thro' the still Night they march, and hear the roar
Of murm'ring Billows on the sounding Shore.
To Neptune, Ruler of the Seas profound,
Whose liquid Arms the mighty Globe surround,   240
They pour forth Vows their Embassy to bless,
And calm the Rage of stern Æacides.
And now arriv'd, where, on the sandy Bay
The Myrmidonian Tents and Vessels lay;
Amus'd at Ease, the godlike Man they found,
Pleas'd with the solemn Harp's harmonious Sound.
(The well-wrought Harp from conquer'd Thebæ came,
Of polish'd Silver was its costly Frame)
With this he sooths his angry Soul, and sings
Th' immortal Deeds of Heroes and of Kings.   250
Patroclus only of the Royal Train,
Plac'd in his Tent, attends the lofty Strain:
Full opposite he sate, and listen'd long,
In Silence waiting till he ceas'd the Song.
Unseen the Grecian Embassy proceeds
To his high Tent; the great Ulysses leads.
Achilles, starting as the Chiefs he spy'd,
Leap'd from his Seat, and laid the Harp aside.
With like Surprize arose Menætius' Son:
Pelides grasp'd their Hands, and thus begun.   260
    Princes all hail! whatever brought ye here,
Or strong Necessity, or urgent Fear:
Welcome, tho' Greeks! for not as Foes ye came;
To me more dear than all that bear the Name.
    With that, the Chiefs beneath his Roof he led,
And plac'd in Seats with purple Carpets spread.
Then thus—Patroclus; crown a larger Bowl,
Mix purer Wine, and open ev'ry Soul.
Of all the Warriors yonder Host can send,
Thy Friend most honours these, and these thy Friend.   270
    He said; Patroclus o'er the blazing Fire
Heaps in a Brazen Vase three Chines entire:
The Brazen Vase Automedon sustains,
Which Flesh of Porker, Sheep, and Goat contains:

Achilles at the genial Feast presides,
The Parts transfixes, and with Skill divides.
Mean while Patroclus sweats the Fire to raise;
The Tent is brightned with the rising Blaze:
Then, when the languid Flames at length subside,
He strows a Bed of glowing Embers wide,   280
Above the Coals the smoaking Fragments turns,
And sprinkles sacred Salt from lifted Urns;
With Bread the glitt'ring Canisters they load,
Which round the Board Menætius' Son bestow'd;
Himself, oppos'd t' Ulysses full in sight,
Each Portion parts, and orders ev'ry Rite.
The first fat Off'rings, to th' Immortals due,
Amidst the greedy Flames Patroclus threw;
Then each, indulging in the social Feast,
His Thirst and Hunger soberly represt.   290
That done, to Phænix Ajax gave the Sign;
Not unperceiv'd; Ulysses crown'd with Wine
The foaming Bowl, and instant thus began,
His Speech addressing to the Godlike Man.
    Health to Achilles! happy are thy Guests!
Not those more honour'd whom Atrides feasts:
Tho' gen'rous Plenty crown thy loaded Boards,
That, Agamemnon's regal Tent affords;
But greater Cares sit heavy on our Souls,
Not eas'd by Banquets or by flowing Bowls.   300
What Scenes of Slaughter in yon Fields appear!
The dead we mourn, and for the living fear;
Greece on the Brink of Fate all doubtful stands,
And owns no Help but from thy saving Hands:
Troy and her Aids for ready Vengeance call;
Their threat'ning Tents already shade our Wall,
Hear how with Shouts their Conquest they proclaim,
And point at ev'ry Ship their vengeful Flame!
For them, the Father of the Gods declares,
Theirs are his Omens, and his Thunder theirs,   310
See, full of Jove, avenging Hector rise!
See! Heav'n and Earth the raging Chief defies;
What Fury in his Breast, what Light'ning in his Eyes!

He waits but for the Morn, to sink in Flame
The Ships, the Greeks, and all the Grecian Name.
Heav'ns! how my Country's Woes distract my Mind!
Lest Fate accomplish all his Rage design'd.
And must we, Gods! our Heads inglorious lay
In Trojan Dust, and this the fatal Day?
Return, Achilles! oh return, tho' late,   320
To save thy Greeks, and stop the Course of Fate;
If in that Heart, or Grief, or Courage lies,
Rise to redeem; ah yet, to conquer, rise!
The Day may come, when all our Warriors slain,
That Heart shall melt, that Courage rise in vain.
Regard in time, O Prince divinely brave!
Those wholesome Counsels which thy Father gave.
When Peleus in his aged Arms embrac'd
His parting Son, these Accents were his last.
My Child! with Strength, with Glory and Success,   330
Thy Arms may Juno and Minerva bless!
Trust that to Heav'n—but thou, thy Cares engage
To calm thy Passions, and subdue thy Rage:
From gentler Manners let thy Glory grow,
And shun Contention, the sure Source of Woe;
That young and old may in thy Praise combine,
The Virtues of Humanity be thine—
This, now despis'd Advice, thy Father gave;
Ah! check thy Anger, and be truly brave,
If thou wilt yield to great Atrides' Pray'rs,   340
Gifts worthy thee, his Royal Hand prepares;
If not—but hear me, while I number o'er
The proffer'd Presents, an exhaustless Store.
Ten weighty Talents of the purest Gold,
And twice ten Vases of refulgent Mold;
Sev'n sacred Tripods, whose unsully'd Frame
Yet knows no Office, nor has felt the Flame:
Twelve Steeds unmatch'd in Fleetness and in Force,
And still victorious in the dusty Course:
(Rich were the Man, whose ample Stores exceed   350
The Prizes purchas'd by their winged Speed)

Sev'n lovely Captives of the Lesbian Line,
Skill'd in each Art, unmatch'd in Form divine,
The same he chose for more than vulgar Charms,
When Lesbos sunk beneath thy conqu'ring Arms.
All these, to buy thy Friendship, shall be paid,
And join'd with these, the long contested Maid;
With all her Charms, Briseis he'll resign,
And solemn swear those Charms were only thine;
Untouch'd she stay'd, uninjur'd she removes,   360
Pure from his Arms, and guiltless of his Loves.
These instant shall be thine; and if the Pow'rs
Give to our Arms proud Ilion's hostile Tow'rs,
Then shalt thou store (when Greece the Spoil divides)
With Gold and Brass thy loaded Navy's sides.
Besides full twenty Nymphs of Trojan Race,
With copious Love shall crown thy warm Embrace;
Such as thy self shall chuse; who yield to none,
Or yield to Helen's heav'nly Charms alone.
Yet hear me farther: When our Wars are o'er,   370
If safe we land on Argos fruitful Shore,
There shalt thou live his Son, his Honours share,
And with Orestes' self divide his Care.
Yet more—three Daughters in his Court are bred,
And each well worthy of a Royal Bed;
Laodice and Iphigenia fair,
And bright Chrysothemis with golden Hair;
Her shalt thou wed whom most thy Eyes approve,
He asks no Presents, no Reward for Love.
Himself will give the Dow'r; so vast a Store,   380
As never Father gave a Child before.
Sev'n ample Cities shall confess thy Sway,
Thee Enope, and Phæræ thee obey,
Cardamyle with ample Turrets crown'd,
And sacred Pedasus, for Vines renown'd;
Æpea fair, the Pastures Hyra yields,
And rich Antheia with her flow'ry Fields:
The whole Extent to Pylos' sandy Plain
Along the verdant Margin of the Main.

There Heifers graze, and lab'ring Oxen toil;   390
Bold are the Men, and gen'rous is the Soil;
There shalt thou reign with Pow'r and Justice crown'd,
And rule the tributary Realms around.
Such are the Proffers which this Day we bring,
Such the Repentance of a suppliant King.
But if all this relentless thou disdain,
If Honour, and if Int'rest plead in vain;
Yet some Redress to suppliant Greece afford,
And be, amongst her guardian Gods, ador'd.
If no Regard thy suff'ring Country claim,   400
Hear thy own Glory, and the Voice of Fame:
For now that Chief, whose unresisted Ire,
Made Nations tremble, and whole Hosts retire,
Proud Hector, now, th' unequal Fight demands,
And only triumphs to deserve thy Hands.
    Then thus the Goddess-born. Ulysses, hear
A faithful Speech, that knows nor Art, nor Fear;
What in my secret Soul is understood,
My Tongue shall utter, and my Deeds make good.
Let Greece then know, my Purpose I retain,   410
Nor with new Treaties vex my Peace in vain.
Who dares think one thing, and another tell,
My Heart detests him as the Gates of Hell.
    Then thus in short my fixt Resolves attend,
Which nor Atrides, nor his Greeks can bend;
Long Toils, long Perils in their Cause I bore,
But now th' unfruitful Glories charm no more.
Fight or not fight, a like Reward we claim,
The Wretch and Hero find their Prize the same;
Alike regretted in the Dust he lies,   420
Who yields ignobly, or who bravely dies.
Of all my Dangers, all my glorious Pains,
A Life of Labours, lo! what Fruit remains.
As the bold Bird her helpless Young attends,
From Danger guards them, and from Want defends;
In Search of Prey she wings the spacious Air,
And with th' untasted Food supplies her Care:

For thankless Greece such Hardships have I brav'd,
Her Wives, her Infants by my Labours sav'd;
Long sleepless Nights in heavy Arms I stood,   430
And sweat laborious Days in Dust and Blood.
I sack'd twelve ample Cities on the Main,
And twelve lay smoaking on the Trojan Plain:
Then at Atrides' haughty Feet were laid
The Wealth I gather'd, and the Spoils I made.
Your mighty Monarch these in Peace possest;
Some few my Soldiers had, himself the rest.
Some Present too to ev'ry Prince was paid;
And ev'ry Prince enjoys the Gift he made;
I only must refund, of all his Train;   440
See what Preheminence our Merits gain!
My Spoil alone his greedy Soul delights;
My Spouse alone must bless his lustful Nights:
The Woman, let him (as he may) enjoy;
But what's the Quarrel then of Greece to Troy?
What to these Shores th' assembled Nations draws,
What calls for Vengeance but a Woman's Cause?
Are fair Endowments and a beauteous Face
Belov'd by none but those of Atreus' Race?
The Wife whom Choice and Passion both approve,   450
Sure ev'ry wise and worthy Man will love.
Nor did my fair one less Distinction claim;
Slave as she was, my Soul ador'd the Dame.
Wrong'd in my Love, all Proffers I disdain;
Deceiv'd for once, I trust not Kings again.
Ye have my Answer—what remains to do,
Your King, Ulysses, may consult with you.
What needs he the Defence this Arm can make?
Has he not Walls no human Force can shake?
Has he not fenc'd his guarded Navy round,   460
With Piles, with Ramparts, and a Trench profound?
And will not these (the Wonders he has done)
Repell the Rage of Priam's single Son?
There was a time ('twas when for Greece I fought)
When Hector's Prowess no such Wonders wrought;

He kept the Verge of Troy, nor dar'd to wait
Achilles' Fury at the Scæan Gate;
He try'd it once, and scarce was sav'd by Fate.
But now those ancient Enmities are o'er;
To morrow we the fav'ring Gods implore,   470
Then shall you see our parting Vessels crown'd,
And hear with Oars the Hellespont resound.
The third Day hence, shall Pthia greet our Sails,
If mighty Neptune send propitious Gales;
Pthia to her Achilles shall restore
The Wealth he left for this detected Shore:
Thither the Spoils of this long War shall pass,
The ruddy Gold, the Steel, and shining Brass;
My beauteous Captives thither I'll convey,
And all that rests of my unravish'd Prey.   480
One only valu'd Gift your Tyrant gave,
And that resum'd; the fair Lyrnessian Slave.
Then tell him; loud, that all the Greeks may hear,
And learn to scorn the Wretch they basely fear.
(For arm'd in Impudence, Mankind he braves,
And meditates new Cheats on all his Slaves:
Tho' shameless as he is, to face these Eyes
Is what he dares not; if he dares, he dies)
Tell him, all Terms, all Commerce I decline,
Nor share his Council, nor his Battel join;   490
For once deceiv'd, was his; but twice, were mine.[1]
No—let the stupid Prince, whom Jove deprives
Of Sense and Justice, run where Frenzy drives;
His Gifts are hateful: Kings of such a Kind
Stand but as Slaves before a noble Mind.
Not tho' he proffer'd all himself possest;
And all his Rapine cou'd from others wrest;
Not all the golden Tydes of Wealth that crown
The many-peopled Orchomenian Town;[2]
Not all proud Thebes' unrival'd Walls contain,   500
The World's great Empress on th' Ægyptian Plain,

---

[1] Pope's dark translation of the Greek for 'nor shall he deceive me a second time'
[2] Orchomenus, town of the Minyans, in Boeotia

(That spreads her Conquests o'er a thousand States,
And pours her Heroes thro' a hundred Gates,
Two hundred Horsemen, and two hundred Cars
From each wide Portal issuing to the Wars)
Tho' Bribes were heap'd on Bribes, in Number more
Than Dust in Fields, or Sands along the Shore;
Should all these Offers for my Friendship call;
'Tis he that offers, and I scorn them all.
Atrides' Daughter never shall be led   510
(An ill-match'd Consort) to Achilles' Bed;
Like golden Venus tho' she charm'd the Heart,
And vy'd with Pallas in the Works of Art.
Some greater Greek let those high Nuptials grace,
I hate Alliance with a Tyrant's Race.
If Heav'n restore me to my Realms with Life,
The rev'rend Peleus shall elect my Wife;
Thessalian Nymphs there are, of Form divine,
And Kings that sue to mix their Blood with mine.
Blest in kind Love, my Years shall glide away,   520
Content with just hereditary Sway;
There deaf for ever to the martial Strife,
Enjoy the dear Prerogative of Life.
Life is not to be bought with Heaps of Gold;
Not all Apollo's Pythian Treasures hold,
Or Troy once held, in Peace and Pride of Sway,
Can bribe the poor Possession of a Day!
Lost Herds and Treasures, we by Arms regain,
And Steeds unrival'd on the dusty Plain;
But from our Lips the vital Spirit fled,   530
Returns no more to wake the silent dead.
My Fates long since by Thetis were disclos'd,
And each alternate, Life or Fame propos'd:
Here, if I stay, before the Trojan Town,
Short is my Date, but deathless my Renown;
If I return, I quit immortal Praise
For Years on Years, and long-extended Days.
Convinc'd, tho' late, I find my fond Mistake,
And warn the Greeks the wiser Choice to make:

To quit these Shores, their native Seats enjoy,   540
Nor hope the Fall of Heav'n-defended Troy.
Jove's Arm, display'd, asserts her from the Skies;
Her Hearts are strengthen'd, and her Glories rise.
Go then, to Greece report our fixt Design;
Bid all your Counsels, all your Armies join,
Let all your Forces, all your Arts conspire,
To save the Ships, the Troops, the Chiefs from Fire.
One Stratagem has fail'd, and others will:
Ye find, Achilles is unconquer'd still.
Go then—digest my Message as ye may—   550
But here this Night let rev'rend Phænix stay:
His tedious Toils, and hoary Hairs demand
A peaceful Death in Pthia's friendly Land.
But whether he remain, or sail with me,
His Age be sacred, and his Will be free.
    The Son of Peleus ceas'd: The Chiefs around
In Silence wrapt, in Consternation drown'd,
Attend the stern Reply. Then Phænix rose;
(Down his white Beard a Stream of Sorrow flows)
And while the Fate of suff'ring Greece he mourn'd,   560
With Accents weak these tender Words return'd.
    Divine Achilles! wilt thou then retire,
And leave our Hosts in Blood, our Fleets on Fire?
If Wrath so dreadful fill thy ruthless Mind,
How shall thy Friend, thy Phænix, stay behind?
The Royal Peleus, when from Pthia's Coast
He sent thee early to th' Achaian Hoast;
Thy Youth as then in sage Debates unskill'd,
And new to Perils of the direful Field:
He bade me teach thee all the ways of War.   570
To shine in Councils, and in Camps to dare.
Never, ah never let me leave thy side!
No Time shall part us, and no Fate divide.
Not tho' the God that breath'd my Life, restore
The Bloom I boasted, and the Port I bore,
When Greece of old beheld my youthful Flames,
(Delightful Greece, the Land of Lovely Dames.)

My Father, faithless to my Mother's Arms,
Old as he was, ador'd a Stranger's Charms.
I try'd what Youth could do (at her Desire)   580
To win the Damsel, and prevent my Sire.
My Sire with Curses loads my hated Head,
And cries, Ye Furies! barren be his Bed.
Infernal Jove, the vengeful Fiends below,
And ruthless Proserpine, confirm'd his Vow.
Despair and Grief distract my lab'ring Mind;
Gods! what a Crime my impious Heart design'd?
I thought (but some kind God that Thought supprest)
To plunge the Ponyard in my Father's Breast:
Then meditate my Flight; my Friends in vain   590
With Pray'rs entreat me, and with Force detain.
On fat of Rams, black Bulls, and brawny Swine,
They daily feast, with Draughts of fragrant Wine.
Strong Guards they plac'd, and watch'd nine Nights entire;
The Roofs and Porches flam'd with constant Fire.
The tenth, I forc'd the Gates, unseen of all;
And favour'd by the Night, o'er leap'd the Wall.
My Travels thence thro' spacious Greece extend;
In Pthia's Court at last my Labours end.
Your Sire receiv'd me, as his Son caress'd,   600
With Gifts enrich'd, and with Possessions bless'd.
The strong Dolopians thenceforth own'd my Reign,
And all the Coast that runs along the Main.
By Love to thee his Bounties I repay'd,
And early Wisdom to thy Soul convey'd:
Great as thou art, my Lessons made thee brave,
A Child I took thee, but a Hero gave.
Thy Infant Breast a like Affection show'd;
Still in my Arms (an ever-pleasing Load)
Or at my Knee, by Phœnix wouldst thou stand;   610
No Food was grateful but from Phœnix' Hand.
I pass my Watchings o'er thy helpless Years,
The tender Labours, the compliant Cares;
The Gods (I thought) revers'd their hard Decree,
And Phœnix felt a Father's Joys in thee:

Thy growing Virtues justify'd my Cares,
And promis'd Comfort to my silver Hairs.
Now by thy Rage, thy fatal Rage, resign'd;
A cruel Heart ill suits a manly Mind:
The Gods (the only great, and only wise)   620
Are mov'd by Off'rings, Vows, and Sacrifice;
Offending Man their high Compassion wins,
And daily Pray'rs attone for daily Sins.
Pray'rs are Jove's Daughters, of celestial Race,
Lame are their Feet, and wrinkled is their Face;
With humble Mien, and with dejected Eyes,
Constant they follow where Injustice[3] flies:
Injustice swift, erect, and unconfin'd,
Sweeps the wide Earth, and tramples o'er Mankind,
While Pray'rs, to heal her Wrongs, move slow behind.   630
Who hears these Daughters of Almighty Jove,
For him they mediate to the Throne above:
When Man rejects the humble Suit they make,
The Sire revenges for the Daughter's sake,
From Jove commission'd fierce Injustice then
Descends, to punish unrelenting Men.
Oh let not headlong Passion bear the Sway;
These reconciling Goddesses obey:
Due Honours to the Seed of Jove belong;
Due Honours calm the fierce, and bend the strong.   640
Were these not paid thee by the Terms we bring,
Were Rage still harbour'd in the haughty King,
Nor Greece, nor all her Fortunes, should engage
Thy Friend to plead against so just a Rage.
But since what Honour asks, the Gen'ral sends,
And sends by those whom most thy Heart commends,
The best and noblest of the Grecian Train;
Permit not these to sue, and sue in vain!
Let me (my Son) an ancient Fact unfold,
A great Example drawn from Times of old;   650
Hear what our Fathers were, and what their Praise,
Who conquer'd their Revenge in former Days.

[3] Pope's translation of *Atè*, moral blindness, that brings men to ruin

Where Calydon[4] on rocky Mountains stands,
Once fought th' Ætolian and Curetian Bands;
To guard it those, to conquer, these advance;
And mutual Deaths were dealt with mutual Chance.
The silver Cynthia bade Contention rise,
In Vengeance of neglected Sacrifice;
On Oeneus' Fields she sent a monstrous Boar,
That levell'd Harvests, and whole Forests tore: 660
This Beast (when many a Chief his Tusks had slain)
Great Meleager stretch'd along the Plain.[5]
Then, for his Spoils, a new Debate arose,
The Neighbour Nations thence commencing Foes.
Strong as they were, the bold Curetes fail'd,
While Meleager's thund'ring Arm prevail'd:
Till Rage at length inflam'd his lofty Breast,
(For Rage invades the wisest and the best.)
Curs'd by Althæa, to his Wrath he yields,
And in his Wife's Embrace forgets the Fields.   670
"(She from Marpessa sprung, divinely fair,
"And matchless Idas, more than Man in War;
"The God of Day ador'd the Mother's Charms;
"Against the God the Father bent his Arms:
"Th' afflicted Pair, their Sorrows to proclaim,
"From Cleopatra chang'd this Daughter's Name,
"And call'd Alcyone; a Name to show
"The Father's Grief, the mourning Mother's Woe.)
To her the Chief retir'd from stern Debate,
But found no Peace from fierce Althæa's Hate: 680
Althæa's Hate th' unhappy Warrior drew,
Whose luckless Hand his Royal Uncle slew;
She beat the Ground, and call'd the Pow'rs beneath
On her own Son to wreak her Brother's Death:
Hell heard her Curses from the Realms profound,
And the red Fiends that walk the nightly Round.

---

[4] Phoenix tells the story of Meleager, son of Oeneus, of Calydon in Aetolia.
When the Curetes attacked the Aetolians, Meleager, angered by his mother's
curse (669), refused his aid. He was finally moved to renounce his wrath
by the pleas of his wife, Cleopatra-Alcyone (676-77).
[5] Meleager killed the boar sent by Cynthia (Diana).

In vain Ætolia her Deliv'rer waits,
War shakes her Walls, and thunders at her Gates.
She sent Embassadors, a chosen Band,
Priests of the Gods, and Elders of the Land;   690
Besought the Chief to save the sinking State;
Their Pray'rs were urgent, and their Proffers great:
(Full fifty Acres of the richest Ground,
Half Pasture green, and half with Vin'yards crown'd.)
His suppliant Father, aged Oeneus, came;
His Sisters follow'd; ev'n the vengeful Dame,
Althæa sues; His Friends before him fall:
He stands relentless, and rejects 'em all.
Mean while the Victor's Shouts ascend the Skies;
The Walls are scal'd; the rolling Flames arise;   700
At length his Wife (a Form divine) appears,
With piercing Cries, and supplicating Tears:
She paints the Horrors of a conquer'd Town,
The Heroes slain, the Palaces o'erthrown,
The Matrons ravish'd, the whole Race enslav'd:
The Warrior heard, he vanquish'd, and he sav'd.
Th' Ætolians, long disdain'd, now took their turn,
And left the Chief their broken Faith to mourn.
Learn hence, betimes to curb pernicious Ire,
Nor stay, till yonder Fleets ascend in Fire: 710
Accept the Presents; draw thy conqu'ring Sword;
And be amongst our guardian Gods ador'd.
    Thus he: The stern Achilles thus reply'd.
My second Father, and my rev'rend Guide!
Thy Friend, believe me, no such Gifts demands,
And asks no Honours from a Mortal's Hands:
Jove honours me, and favours my Designs;
His Pleasure guides me, and his Will confines:
And here I stay, (if such his high Behest)
While Life's warm Spirit beats within my Breast.   720
Yet hear one word, and lodge it in thy Heart,
No more molest me on Atrides' Part:
Is it for him these Tears are taught to flow,
For him these Sorrows? for my mortal Foe?

A gen'rous Friendship no cold Medium knows,
Burns with one Love, with one Resentment glows;
One should our Int'rests, and our Passions be;
My Friend must hate the Man that injures me.
Do this, my Phœnix, 'tis a gen'rous Part,
And share my Realms, my Honours, and my Heart. 730
Let these return: Our Voyage, or our Stay,
Rest undetermin'd till the dawning Day.
  He ceas'd; then order'd for the Sage's Bed
A warmer Couch with num'rous Carpets spread.
With that, stern Ajax his long Silence broke,
And thus, impatient, to Ulysses spoke.
  Hence, let us go—why waste we Time in vain?
See what Effect our low Submissions gain!
Lik'd or not lik'd, his Words we must relate,
The Greeks expect them, and our Heroes wait. 740
Proud as he is, that Iron-heart retains
Its stubborn Purpose, and his Friends disdains.
Stern, and unpitying! if a Brother bleed,
On just Attonement, we remit the Deed;
A Sire the Slaughter of his Son forgives;
The Price of Blood discharg'd, the Murd'rer lives:
The haughtiest Hearts at length their Rage resign,
And Gifts can conquer ev'ry Soul but thine.
The Gods that unrelenting Breast have steel'd,
And curs'd thee with a Mind that cannot yield. 750
One Woman-Slave was ravish'd from thy Arms:
Lo, sev'n are offer'd, and of equal Charms.
Then hear, Achilles! be of better Mind;
Revere thy Roof, and to thy Guests be kind;
And know the Men, of all the Grecian Host,
Who honour Worth, and prize thy Valour most.
  Oh Soul of Battels, and thy People's Guide!
(To Ajax thus the first of Greeks reply'd)
Well hast thou spoke; but at the Tyrant's Name,
My Rage rekindles, and my Soul's on flame, 760
'Tis just Resentment, and becomes the brave;
Disgrac'd, dishonour'd, like the vilest Slave!

Return then Heroes! and our Answer bear,
The glorious Combat is no more my Care;
Not till amidst yon' sinking Navy slain,
The Blood of Greeks shall dye the sable Main;
Not till the Flames, by Hector's Fury thrown,
Consume your Vessels, and approach my own;
Just there, th' impetuous Homicide shall stand,
There cease his Battel, and there feel our Hand.   770
     This said, each Prince a double Goblet crown'd,
And cast a large Libation on the Ground;
Then to their Vessels, thro' the gloomy Shades,
The Chiefs return; divine Ulysses leads.
Meantime Achilles' Slaves prepar'd a Bed,
With Fleeces, Carpets, and soft Linen spread:
There, till the sacred Morn restor'd the Day,
In Slumbers sweet the rev'rend Phœnix lay.
But in his inner Tent, an ampler Space,
Achilles slept; and in his warm Embrace   780
Fair Diomedè of the Lesbian Race.
Last, for Patroclus was the Couch prepar'd,
Whose nightly Joys the beauteous Iphis shar'd:
Achilles to his Friend consign'd her Charms,
When Scyros fell before his conqu'ring Arms.
     And now th' elected Chiefs whom Greece had sent,
Pass'd thro' the Hosts, and reach'd the Royal Tent.
Then rising all, with Goblets in their Hands,
The Peers and Leaders of th' Achaian Bands
Hail'd their Return: Atrides first begun.   790
     Say what Success? divine Laertes Son!
Achilles' high Resolves declare to all;
Returns the Chief, or must our Navy fall?
     Great King of Nations! (Ithacus reply'd)
Fixt is his Wrath, unconquer'd is his Pride;
He slights thy Friendship, thy Proposals scorns,
And thus implor'd, with fiercer Fury burns.
To save our Army, and our Fleets to free,
Is not his Care; but left to Greece and thee.
Your Eyes shall view, when Morning paints the Sky,   800
Beneath his Oars the whitening Billows fly.

Us too he bids our Oars and Sails employ,
Nor hope the Fall of Heav'n-protected Troy;
For Jove o'ershades her with his Arm divine,
Inspires her War, and bids her Glory shine.
Such was his Word: What farther he declar'd,
These sacred Heralds and great Ajax heard.
But Phœnix in his Tent the Chief retains,
Safe to transport him to his native Plains,
When Morning dawns: if other he decree,   810
His Age is sacred, and his Choice is free.
   Ulysses ceas'd: The great Achaian Host,
With Sorrow seiz'd, in Consternation lost,
Attend the stern Reply. Tydides broke
The gen'ral Silence, and undaunted spoke.
Why shou'd we Gifts to proud Achilles send,
Or strive with Pray'rs his haughty Soul to bend?
His Country's Woes he glories to deride,
And Pray'rs will burst that swelling Heart with Pride.
Be the fierce Impulse of his Rage obey'd;   820
Our Battels let him, or desert, or aid;
Then let him arm when Jove or he think fit;
That, to his Madness, or to Heav'n commit.
What for our selves we can, is always ours;
This Night, let due Repast refresh our Pow'rs;
(For Strength consists in Spirits and in Blood,
And those are ow'd to gen'rous Wine and Food)
But when the rosy Messenger of Day
Strikes the blue Mountains with her golden Ray,
Rang'd at the Ships let all our Squadrons shine,   830
In flaming Arms, a long-extended Line:
In the dread Front let great Atrides stand,
The first in Danger, as in high Command.
   Shouts of Acclaim the list'ning Heroes raise,
Then each to Heav'n the due Libations pays;
Till Sleep descending o'er the Tents, bestows
The grateful Blessings of desir'd Repose.

ܕܖܖܖ

THE TENTH BOOK
OF THE ILIAD

THE ARGUMENT

The Night-Adventure of Diomed and Ulysses

Upon the refusal of Achilles to return to the Army, the Distress of
Agamemnon is describ'd in the most lively manner. He takes no Rest that
Night, but passes thro' the Camp, awaking the Leaders, and contriving
all possible Methods for the publick Safety. Menelaus, Nestor, Ulysses
and Diomed are employ'd in raising the rest of the Captains. They call a
Council of War, and determine to send Scouts into the Enemy's Camp
to learn their Posture and discover their Intentions. Diomed undertakes
this hazardous Enterprize, and makes choice of Ulysses for his Companion. In their Passage they surprize Dolon, whom Hector had sent on
a like Design to the Camp of the Grecians. From him they are inform'd
of the Situation of the Trojan and Auxiliary Forces, and particularly of
Rhesus and the Thracians who were lately arrived. They pass on with
Success, kill Rhesus, with several of his Officers, and seize the famous
Horses of that Prince with which they return in Triumph to the Camp.
The same Night continues; the Scene lies in the two Camps.

All Night the Chiefs before their Vessels lay,
And lost in Sleep the Labours of the Day:
All but the King; with various Thoughts opprest,
His Country's Cares lay rowling in his Breast.
As when by Light'nings Jove's Ætherial Pow'r
Foretells the ratling Hail, or weighty Show'r,
Or sends soft Snows to whiten all the Shore,
Or bids the brazen Throat of War to roar;

By fits one Flash succeeds, as one expires,
And Heav'n flames thick with momentary Fires.   10
So bursting frequent from Atrides' Breast,
Sighs following Sighs his inward Fears confest.
Now o'er the Fields, dejected, he surveys
From thousand Trojan Fires the mounting Blaze;
Hears in the passing Wind their Music blow,
And marks distinct the Voices of the Foe.
Now looking backwards to the Fleet and Coast,
Anxious he sorrows for th' endanger'd Host.
He rends his Hairs, in sacrifice to Jove,
And sues to Him that ever lives above: 20
Inly he groans; while Glory and Despair
Divide his Heart, and wage a doubtful War.
   A thousand Cares his lab'ring Breast revolves;
To seek sage Nestor now the Chief resolves,
With him, in wholsome Counsels, to debate
What yet remains to save th' afflicted State.
He rose, and first he cast his Mantle round,
Next on his Feet the shining Sandals bound;
A Lion's yellow Spoils his Back conceal'd;
His warlike Hand a pointed Javelin held.   30
Meanwhile his Brother, prest with equal Woes,
Alike deny'd the Gifts of soft Repose,
Laments for Greece; that in his Cause before
So much had suffer'd, and must suffer more.
A Leopard's spotted Hide his Shoulders spread;
A brazen Helmet glitter'd on his Head:
Thus (with a Javelin in his Hand) he went,
To wake Atrides in the Royal Tent.
Already wak'd, Atrides he descry'd,
His Armour buckling at his Vessel's side.   40
Joyful they met; the Spartan thus begun:
Why puts my Brother his bright Armour on?
Sends he some Spy, amidst these silent Hours,
To try yon' Camp, and watch the Trojan Pow'rs?
But say, what Hero shall sustain that Task?
Such bold Exploits uncommon Courage ask,

Guideless, alone, through Night's dark Shade to go,
And 'midst a hostile Camp explore the Foe?
　To whom the King. In such Distress we stand,
No vulgar Counsels our Affairs demand;　　　　　　　　　50
Greece to preserve, is now no easy part,
But asks high Wisdom, deep Design, and Art.
For Jove, averse, our humble Vows denies,
And bows his Head to Hector's Sacrifice.
What Eye has witness'd, or what Ear believ'd,
In one great Day, by one great Arm atchiev'd,
Such wond'rous Deeds as Hector's Hand has done,
And we beheld, the last revolving Sun?
What Honours the belov'd of Jove adorn!
Sprung from no God, and of no Goddess born,　　　　60
Yet such his Acts, as Greeks unborn shall tell,
And curse the Battel where their Fathers fell.
　Now speed thy hasty Course along the Fleet,
There call great Ajax, and the Prince of Crete.[1]
Our self to hoary Nestor will repair;
To keep the Guards on Duty, be his Care;
(For Nestor's Influence best that Quarter guides;
Whose Son, with Merion, o'er the Watch presides.)
To whom the Spartan: These thy Orders born,
Say shall I stay, or with Dispatch return?　　　　　70
There shalt thou stay (the King of Men reply'd)
Else may we miss to meet, without a Guide,
The Paths so many, and the Camp so wide.
Still, with your Voice, the sloathful Soldiers raise,
Urge by their Father's Fame, their future Praise.
Forget we now our State and lofty Birth;
Not Titles here, but Works, must prove our Worth.
To labour is the Lot of Man below;
And when Jove gave us Life, he gave us Woe.
　This said, each parted to his sev'ral Cares;　　　　80
The King to Nestor's sable Ship repairs;
The sage Protector of the Greeks he found
Stretch'd in his Bed, with all his Arms around;

---

[1] Idomeneus

The various-colour'd Scarf, the Shield he rears,
The shining Helmet, and the pointed Spears:
The dreadful Weapons of the Warrior's Rage,
That old in Arms, disdain'd the Peace of Age.
Then leaning on his Hand his watchful Head,
The hoary Monarch rais'd his Eyes, and said.
    What art thou, speak, that on Designs unknown   90
While others sleep, thus range the Camp alone?
Seek'st thou some Friend, or nightly Centinel?
Stand off, approach not, but thy Purpose tell.
    O Son of Neleus (thus the King rejoin'd)
Pride of the Greeks, and Glory of thy Kind!
Lo here the wretched Agamemnon stands,
Th' unhappy Gen'ral of the Grecian Bands;
Whom Jove decrees with daily Cares to bend,
And Woes, that only with his Life shall end!
Scarce can my Knees these trembling Limbs sustain,   100
And scarce my Heart support its Load of Pain.
No Taste of Sleep these heavy Eyes have known;
Confus'd, and sad, I wander thus alone,
With Fears distracted, with no fix'd Design;
And all my People's Miseries are mine.
If ought of use thy waking Thoughts suggest,
(Since Cares, like mine, deprive thy Soul of Rest)
Impart thy Counsel, and assist thy Friend:
Now let us jointly to the Trench descend,
At ev'ry Gate the fainting Guard excite,   110
Tir'd with the Toils of Day, and Watch of Night:
Else may the sudden Foe our Works invade,
So near, and favour'd by the gloomy Shade.
    To him thus Nestor. Trust the Pow'rs above,
Nor think proud Hector's Hopes confirm'd by Jove:
How ill agree the Views of vain Mankind,
And the wise Counsels of th' eternal Mind?
Audacious Hector, if the Gods ordain
That great Achilles rise and rage again,
What Toils attend thee, and what Woes remain?   120
Lo faithful Nestor thy Command obeys;
The Care is next our other Chiefs to raise:

Ulysses, Diomed we chiefly need;
Mages for Strength, Oïleus² fam'd for Speed.
Some other be dispatch'd, of nimbler Feet,
To those tall Ships, remotest of the Fleet,
Where lie great Ajax and the King of Crete.
To rouse the Spartan I my self decree;
Dear as he is to us, and dear to thee,
Yet must I tax his Sloath, that Claims no share   130
With his great Brother in this martial Care:
Him it behov'd to ev'ry Chief to sue,
Preventing ev'ry Part perform'd by you;
For strong Necessity our Toils demands,
Claims all our Hearts, and urges all our Hands.

   To whom the King: With Rev'rence we allow
Thy just Rebukes, yet learn to spare them now.
My gen'rous Brother is of gentle kind,
He seems remiss but bears a valiant Mind;
Thro' too much Def'rence to our Sov'reign Sway,   140
Content to follow when we lead the way.
But now our Ills industrious to prevent,
Long e'er the rest, he rose, and sought my Tent.
The Chiefs you nam'd, already, at his Call,
Prepare to meet us near the Navy-wall;
Assembling there, between the Trench and Gates,
Near the Night-Guards, our chosen Council waits.

   Then none (said Nestor) shall his Rule withstand,
For great Examples justify Command.

   With that, the venerable Warrior rose;   150
The shining Greaves his manly Legs inclose;
His purple Mantle golden Buckles join'd,
Warm with the softest Wool, and doubly lin'd.
Then rushing from his Tent, he snatch'd in hast
His steely Lance, that lighten'd as he past.
The Camp he travers'd thro' the sleeping Crowd,
Stopp'd at Ulysses' Tent, and call'd aloud.
Ulysses, sudden as the Voice was sent,
Awakes, starts up, and issues from his Tent.

² More correctly, Ajax, the son of Oïleus

What new Distress, what sudden Cause of Fright   160
Thus leads you wandring in the silent Night?
O prudent Chief! (the Pylian Sage reply'd)
Wise as thou art, be now thy Wisdom try'd:
Whatever means of Safety can be sought,
Whatever Counsels can inspire our Thought,
Whatever Methods, or to fly, or fight;
All, all depend on this important Night!

He heard, return'd, and took his painted Shield:
Then join'd the Chiefs, and follow'd thro' the Field.
Without his Tent, bold Diomed they found,   170
All sheath'd in Arms; his brave Companions round:
Each sunk in Sleep, extended on the Field,
His Head reclining on his bossy Shield.
A Wood of Spears stood by, that fixt upright,
Shot from their flashing Points a quiv'ring Light.
A Bull's black Hide compos'd the Hero's Bed;
A splendid Carpet roll'd beneath his Head.
Then, with his Foot, old Nestor gently shakes
The slumb'ring Chief, and in these Words awakes.

Rise, Son of Tydeus! to the brave and strong   180
Rest seems inglorious, and the Night too long.
But sleep'st thou now? when from yon' Hills the Foe
Hangs o'er the Fleet, and shades our Walls below?

At this, soft Slumber from his Eyelids fled;
The Warrior saw the hoary Chief, and said.
Wond'rous old Man! whose Soul no Respite knows,
Tho' Years and Honours bid thee seek Repose.
Let younger Greeks our sleeping Warriors wake;
Ill fits thy Age these Toils to undertake.
My Friend, (he answer'd) gen'rous is thy Care,   190
These Toils, my Subjects and my Sons might bear,
Their loyal Thoughts and pious Loves conspire
To ease a Sov'reign, and relieve a Sire.
But now the last Despair surrounds our Host;
No Hour must pass, no Moment must be lost;
Each single Greek, in this conclusive Strife,
Stands on the sharpest Edge of Death or Life:

Yet if my Years thy kind Regard engage,
Employ thy Youth as I employ my Age;
Succeed to these my Cares, and rouze the rest;   200
He serves me most, who serves his Country best.
   This said, the Hero o'er his Shoulders flung
A Lion's Spoils, that to his Ankles hung;
Then seiz'd his pond'rous Lance, and strode along.
Meges the bold, with Ajax fam'd for speed,
The Warrior rouz'd, and to th' Entrenchments led.
   And now the Chiefs approach the nightly Guard;
A wakeful Squadron, each in Arms prepar'd:
Th' unweary'd Watch their list'ning Leaders keep,
And couching close, repell invading Sleep.   210
So faithful Dogs their fleecy Charge maintain,
With Toil protected from the prowling Train;
When the gaunt Lioness, with Hunger bold,
Springs from the Mountains tow'rd the guarded Fold:
Thro' breaking Woods her rust'ling Course they hear;
Loud, and more loud, the Clamours strike their Ear
Of Hounds and Men; they start, they gaze around;
Watch ev'ry Side, and turn to ev'ry Sound.
Thus watch'd the Grecians, cautious of Surprize,
Each Voice, each Motion, drew their Ears and Eyes;   220
Each step of passing Feet increas'd th' Affright;
And hostile Troy was ever full in Sight.
Nestor with Joy the wakeful Band survey'd,
And thus accosted thro' the gloomy Shade.
'Tis well, my Sons, your nightly Cares employ,
Else must our Host become the Scorn of Troy.
Watch thus, and Greece shall live—the Hero said;
Then o'er the Trench the following Chieftains led.
His Son, and godlike Merion march'd behind,
(For these the Princes to their Council join'd)   230
The Trenches past, th' assembl'd Kings around
In silent State the Consistory crown'd.[3]
A Place there was, yet undefil'd with Gore,
The Spot, where Hector stop'd his Rage before,

[3] Filled to overflowing (also of a bowl of wine)

When Night descending, from his vengeful Hand
Repriev'd the Relicks of the Grecian Band:
(The Plain beside with mangled Corps was spread,
And all his Progress mark'd by Heaps of dead.)
There sate the mournful Kings: when Neleus' Son,
The Council opening, in these Words begun.   240
  Is there (he said) a Chief so greatly brave,
His Life to hazard, and his Country save?
Lives there a Man, who singly dares to go
To yonder Camp, or seize some stragling Foe?
Or favour'd by the Night, approach so near,
Their Speech, their Counsels, and Designs to hear?
If to besiege our Navies they prepare,
Or Troy once more must be the Seat of War?
This could he learn, and to our Peers recite,
And pass unharm'd the Dangers of the Night;   250
What Fame were his thro' all succeeding Days,
While Phœbus shines, or Men have tongues to praise?
What Gifts his grateful Country would bestow?
What must not Greece to her Deliv'rer owe?
A sable Ewe each Leader should provide,
With each a sable Lambkin by her side;
At ev'ry Rite his Share should be increas'd,
And his the foremost Honours of the Feast.
  Fear held them mute: Alone, untaught to fear,
Tydides spoke—The Man you seek, is here.   260
Thro' yon' black Camps to bend my dang'rous way,
Some God within commands, and I obey.
But let some other chosen Warrior join,
To raise my Hopes, and second my Design.
By mutual Confidence, and mutual Aid,
Great Deeds are done, and great Discov'ries made;
The Wise new Prudence from the Wise acquire,
And one brave Hero fans another's Fire.
  Contending Leaders at the Word arose;
Each gen'rous Breast with Emulation glows: 270
So brave a Task each Ajax strove to share,
Bold Merion strove, and Nestor's valiant Heir;

The Spartan wish'd the second Place to gain,
And great Ulysses wish'd, nor wish'd in vain.
Then thus the King of Men the Contest ends:
Thou first of Warriors, and thou best of Friends,
Undaunted Diomed! what Chief to join
In this great Enterprize, is only thine.
Just be thy Choice, without Affection made,
To Birth, or Office, no respect be paid;   280
Let Worth determine here. The Monarch spake,
And inly trembled for his Brother's sake.

Then thus (the Godlike Diomed rejoin'd)
My Choice declares the Impulse of my Mind.
How can I doubt, while great Ulysses stands
To lend his Counsels, and assist our Hands?
A Chief, whose Safety is Minerva's Care;
So fam'd, so dreadful, in the Works of War?
Blest in his Conduct, I no Aid require,
Wisdom like his might pass thro' Flames of Fire.   290

It fits thee not, before these Chiefs of Fame,
(Reply'd the Sage) to praise me, or to blame:
Praise from a Friend, or Censure from a Foe,
Are lost on Hearers that our Merits know.
But let us haste—Night rolls the Hours away,
The red'ning Orient shows the coming Day,
The Stars shine fainter on th' Ætherial Plains,
And of Night's Empire but a third remains.

Thus having spoke, with gen'rous Ardour prest,
In Arms Terrific their huge Limbs they drest.   300
A two-edg'd Faulchion Thrasymed the brave,
And ample Buckler, to Tydides gave:
Then in a leathern Helm he cas'd his Head,
Short of its Crest, and with no Plume o'erspread;
(Such as by Youths unus'd to Arms, are worn;
No Spoils enrich it, and no Studs adorn.)
Next him Ulysses took a shining Sword,
A Bow and Quiver, with bright Arrows stor'd:
A well-prov'd Casque with Leather Braces bound
(Thy Gift, Meriones) his Temples crown'd;   310

Soft Wool within; without, in order spread,
A Boar's white Teeth grinn'd horrid o'er his Head.
This from Amyntor, rich Ormenus' Son,
Autolychus by fraudful Rapine won,
And gave Amphydamas; from him the Prize
Molus receiv'd, the Pledge of social Ties;
The Helmet next by Merion was possess'd,
And now Ulysses' thoughtful Temples press'd.
Thus sheath'd in Arms, the Council they forsake,
And dark thro' Paths oblique their Progress take.   320
Just then, in sign she favour'd their Intent,
A long-wing'd Heron great Minerva sent;
This, tho' surrounding Shades obscur'd their View,
By the shrill Clang and whistling Wings, they knew.
As from the Right she soar'd, Ulysses pray'd,
Hail'd the glad Omen, and address'd the Maid.

   O Daughter of that God, whose Arm can wield
Th' avenging Bolt, and shake the dreadful Shield.
O thou! for ever present in my way,
Who, all my Motions, all my Toils survey!   330
Safe may we pass beneath the gloomy Shade,
Safe by thy Succour to our Ships convey'd;
And let some Deed this signal Night adorn,
To claim the Tears of Trojans yet unborn.

   Then Godlike Diomed prefer'd his Pray'r:
Daughter of Jove, unconquer'd Pallas! hear.
Great Queen of Arms, whose Favour Tydeus won,
As thou defend'st the Sire, defend the Son.
When on Æsopus' Banks the banded Pow'rs
Of Greece he left, and sought the Theban Tow'rs,[4]   340
Peace was his Charge; receiv'd with peaceful Show,
He went a Legat, but return'd a Foe:
Then help'd by thee, and cover'd by thy Shield,
He fought with numbers, and made numbers yield.
So now be present, Oh celestial Maid!
So still continue to the Race thine Aid!
A youthful Steer shall fall beneath the Stroke,
Untam'd, unconscious of the galling Yoke,

[4] IV, 435 n.

With ample Forehead, and with spreading Horns,
Whose taper tops refulgent Gold adorns.   350
   The Heroes pray'd, and Pallas from the Skies,
Accords their Vow, succeeds their Enterprize.
Now, like two Lions panting for the Prey,
With deathful Thoughts they trace the dreary way,
Thro' the black Horrors of th' ensanguin'd Plain,
Thro' Dust, thro' Blood, o'er Arms, and Hills of Slain.
   Nor less bold Hector, and the Sons of Troy,
On high Designs the wakeful Hours employ;
Th' assembled Peers their lofty Chief inclos'd;
Who thus the Counsels of his Breast propos'd.   360
   What glorious Man, for high Attempts prepar'd,
Dares greatly venture for a rich Reward?
Of yonder Fleet a bold Discov'ry make,
What Watch they keep, and what Resolves they take:
If now subdu'd they meditate their Flight,
And spent with Toil neglect the Watch of Night?
His be the Chariot that shall please him most,
Of all the Plunder of the vanquish'd Host;
His the fair Steeds that all the rest excell,
And his the Glory to have serv'd so well.   370
   A Youth there was among the Tribes of Troy,
Dolon his Name, Eumedes' only Boy,
(Five Girls beside the rev'rend Herald told)
Rich was the Son in Brass, and rich in Gold;
Not blest by Nature with the Charms of Face,
But swift of Foot, and matchless in the Race.
Hector! (he said) my Courage bids me meet
This high Atchievement, and explore the Fleet:
But first exalt thy Sceptre to the Skies,
And swear to grant me the demanded Prize;   380
Th' immortal Coursers, and the glitt'ring Car,
That bear Pelides thro' the Ranks of War.
Encourag'd thus, no idle Scout I go,
Fulfill thy Wish, their whole Intention know,
Ev'n to the Royal Tent pursue my way,
And all their Counsels, all their Aims betray.

The Chief then heav'd the golden Sceptre high,
Attesting thus the Monarch of the Sky.
Be witness thou! immortal Lord of all!
Whose Thunder shakes the dark aerial Hall.   390
By none but Dolon shall this Prize be born,
And him alone th' immortal Steeds adorn.
　Thus Hector swore: the Gods were call'd in vain;
But the rash Youth prepares to scour the Plain:
A-cross his Back the bended Bow he flung,
A Wolf's grey Hide around his Shoulders hung.
A Ferret's downy Fur his Helmet lin'd,
And in his Hand a pointed Javelin shin'd.
Then (never to return) he sought the Shore,
And trod the Path his Feet must tread no more.   400
Scarce had he pass'd the Steeds and Trojan Throng,
(Still bending forward as he cours'd along)
When, on the hollow way, th' approaching Tread
Ulysses mark'd, and thus to Diomed.
　O Friend! I hear some Step of hostile Feet,
Moving this way, or hast'ning to the Fleet;
Some Spy perhaps, to lurk beside the Main;
Or nightly Pillager that strips the slain.
Yet let him pass, and win a little Space;
Then rush behind him, and prevent his Pace.   410
But if too swift of Foot he flies before,
Confine his Course along the Fleet and Shore,
Betwixt the Camp and him our Spears employ,
And intercept his hop'd return to Troy.
　With that, they step'd aside, and stoop'd their head,
(As Dolon pass'd) behind a Heap of dead:
Along the Path the Spy unwary flew;
Soft, at just distance, both the Chiefs pursue.
So distant they, and such the Space between,
As when two Teams of Mules divide the Green,   420
(To whom the Hind like Shares of Land allows)
When now few Furrows part th' approaching Ploughs.
Now Dolon list'ning, heard them as they past;
Hector (he thought) had sent, and check'd his hast,

Till scarce at distance of a Javelin's throw,
No Voice succeeding, he perceiv'd the Foe.
As when two skilful Hounds the Lev'ret winde,
Or chase thro' Woods obscure the trembling Hinde;
Now lost, now seen, they intercept his way,
And from the Herd still turn the flying Prey: 430
So fast, and with such Fears, the Trojan flew;
So close, so constant, the bold Greeks pursue.
Now almost on the Fleet the Dastard falls,
And mingles with the Guards that watch the Walls;
When brave Tydides stopp'd; a gen'rous Thought
(Inspir'd by Pallas) in his Bosom wrought,
Lest on the Foe some forward Greek advance,
And snatch the Glory from his lifted Lance.
Then thus aloud: Whoe'er thou art, remain;
This Javelin else shall fix thee to the Plain.   440
He said, and high in Air the Weapon cast,
Which wilful err'd, and o'er his Shoulder past;
Then fix'd in Earth. Against the trembling Wood
The Wretch stood prop'd, and quiver'd as he stood;
A sudden Palsy seiz'd his turning Head;
His loose Teeth chatter'd, and his Colour fled:
The panting Warriors seize him as He stands,
And with unmanly Tears his Life demands.
      O spare my Youth, and for the Breath I owe,
Large Gifts of Price my Father shall bestow: 450
Vast Heaps of Brass shall in your Ships be told,
And Steel well temper'd, and refulgent Gold.
      To whom Ulysses made this wise Reply;
Whoe'er thou art, be bold, nor fear to die.
What moves thee, say, when Sleep has clos'd the Sight,
To roam the silent Fields in dead of Night?
Cam'st thou the Secrets of our Camp to find,
By Hector prompted, or thy daring Mind,
Or art some Wretch by hopes of Plunder led,
Thro' Heaps of Carnage to despoil the dead?   460
      Then thus pale Dolon with a fearful Look,
(Still, as he spoke, his Limbs with Horror shook)

Hither I came, by Hector's Words deceiv'd;
Much did he promise, rashly I believ'd:
No less a Bribe than great Achilles' Car,
And those swift Steeds that sweep the Ranks of War,
Urg'd me, unwilling, this Attempt to make;
To learn what Counsels, what Resolves you take,
If now subdu'd, you fix your Hopes on Flight,
And tir'd with Toils, neglect the Watch of Night?   470
  Bold was thy Aim, and glorious was the Prize,
(Ulysses, with a scornful Smile, replies)
Far other Rulers those proud Steeds demand,
And scorn the Guidance of a vulgar Hand;
Ev'n great Achilles scarce their Rage can tame,
Achilles sprung from an immortal Dame.
But say, be faithful, and the Truth recite!
Where lies encamp'd the Trojan Chief to Night?
Where stand his Coursers? In what Quarter sleep
Their other Princes? tell what Watch they keep?   480
Say, since this Conquest, what their Counsels are?
Or here to combat, from their City far,
Or back to Ilion's Walls transfer the War?
  Ulysses thus, and thus Eumedes' Son:
What Dolon knows, his faithful Tongue shall own.
Hector, the Peers assembling in his Tent,
A Council holds at Ilus' Monument.
No certain Guards the nightly Watch partake;
Where e'er yon' Fires ascend, the Trojans wake:
Anxious for Troy, the Guard the Natives keep;   490
Safe in their Cares, th' auxiliar Forces sleep,
Whose Wives and Infants, from the Danger far,
Discharge their Souls of half the Fears of War.
  Then sleep those aids among the Trojan Train,
(Enquir'd the Chief) or scatter'd o'er the Plain?
  To whom the Spy: Their Pow'rs they thus dispose:
The Pæons, dreadful with their bended Bows,
The Carians, Caucons, the Pelasgian Host,
And Leleges, encamp along the Coast.
Not distant far, lie higher on the Land   500
The Lycian, Mysian, and Mæonian Band,

And Phrygia's Horse, by Thymbras' ancient Wall;
The Thracians utmost, and a-part from all.
These Troy but lately to her Succour won,
Led on by Rhesus, great Eioneus' Son:
I saw his Coursers in proud Triumph go,
Swift as the Wind, and white as Winter-Snow:
Rich silver Plates his shining Car infold;
His solid Arms, refulgent, flame with Gold;
No mortal Shoulders suit the glorious Load,   510
Celestial Panoply, to grace a God!
Let me, unhappy, to your Fleet be born,
Or leave me here, a Captive's Fate to mourn,
In cruel Chains; till your Return reveal
The Truth or Falshood of the News I tell.
  To this Tydides, with a gloomy Frown:
Think not to live, tho' all the Truth be shown:
Shall we dismiss thee, in some future Strife
To risk more bravely thy now forfeit Life?
Or that again our Camps thou may'st explore?   520
No—once a Traytor, thou betray'st no more.
  Sternly he spoke, and as the Wretch prepar'd
With humble Blandishment to stroke his Beard,
Like Light'ning swift the wrathful Faulchion flew,
Divides the Neck, and cuts the Nerves in two;
One Instant snatch'd his trembling Soul to Hell,
The Head, yet speaking, mutter'd as it fell.
The furry Helmet from his Brow they tear,
The Wolf's grey Hide, th' unbended Bow and Spear;
These great Ulysses lifting to the Skies,   530
To fav'ring Pallas dedicates the Prize.
  Great Queen of Arms! receive this hostile Spoil,
And let the Thracian Steeds reward our Toil:
Thee first of all the heav'nly Host we praise;
Oh speed our Labours, and direct our ways!
This said, the Spoils with dropping Gore defac'd,
High on a spreading Tamarisk he plac'd;
Then heap'd with Reeds and gather'd Boughs the Plain,
To guide their Footsteps to the Place again.

Thro' the still Night they cross the devious Fields,   540
Slipp'ry with Blood, o'er Arms and Heaps of Shields.
Arriving where the Thracian Squadrons lay,
And eas'd in Sleep the Labours of the Day,
Rang'd in three Lines they view the prostrate Band;
The Horses yok'd beside each Warrior stand.
Their Arms in order on the Ground reclin'd,
Thro' the brown Shade the fulgid Weapons shin'd.
Amidst, lay Rhesus, stretch'd in Sleep profound,
And the white Steeds behind his Chariot bound.
The welcome Sight Ulysses first decries,   550
And points to Diomed the tempting Prize.
The Man, the Coursers, and the Car behold!
Describ'd by Dolon, with the Arms of Gold.
Now, brave Tydides! now thy Courage try,
Approach the Chariot, and the Steeds untye;
Or if thy Soul aspire to fiercer Deeds,
Urge thou the Slaughter, while I seize the Steeds.
Pallas (this said) her Hero's Bosom warms,
Breath'd in his Heart, and strung his nervous Arms;
Where e'er he pass'd, a purple Stream pursu'd;   560
His thirsty Faulchion, fat with hostile Blood,
Bath'd all his Footsteps, dy'd the Fields with Gore,
And a low Groan remurmur'd thro' the Shore.
So the grim Lion, from his nightly Den,
O'erleaps the fences, and invades the Pen;
On Sheep or Goats, resistless in his way,
He falls, and foaming rends the guardless Prey.
Nor stopp'd the Fury of his vengeful Hand,
Till twelve lay breathless of the Thracian Band.
Ulysses following, as his Part'ner slew,   570
Back by the Foot each slaughter'd Warrior drew;
The milk-white Coursers studious to convey
Safe to the Ships, he wisely clear'd the way,
Lest the fierce Steeds, not yet to Battels bred,
Should start, and tremble at the Heaps of dead.
Now twelve dispatch'd, the Monarch last they found;
Tydides' Faulchion fix'd him to the Ground.

Just then a deathful Dream Minerva sent;
A warlike Form appear'd before his Tent,
Whose visionary Steel his Bosom tore: 580
So dream'd the Monarch, and awak'd no more.
  Ulysses now the snowy Steeds detains,
And leads them, fasten'd by the silver Reins;
These, with his Bow unbent, he lash'd along;
(The Scourge forgot, on Rhesus Chariot hung.)
Then gave his Friend the Signal to retire;
But him, new Dangers, new Atchievements fire:
Doubtful he stood, or with his reeking Blade
To send more Heroes to th' infernal Shade,
Drag off the Car where Rhesus Armour lay,   590
Or heave with manly Force, and lift away.
While unresolv'd the Son of Tydeus stands,
Pallas appears, and thus her Chief commands.
  Enough, my Son, from Farther Slaughter cease,
Regard thy Safety, and depart in Peace;
Haste to the Ships, the gotten Spoils enjoy,
Nor tempt too far the hostile Gods of Troy.
  The Voice divine confess'd the martial Maid;
In haste he mounted, and her Word obey'd;
The Coursers fly before Ulysses' Bow,   600
Swift as the Wind, and white as Winter-Snow.
  Not unobserv'd they pass'd: the God of Light
Had watch'd his Troy, and mark'd Minerva's Flight;
Saw Tydeus' Son with heav'nly Succour blest,
And vengeful Anger fill'd his sacred Breast.
Swift to the Trojan Camp descends the Pow'r,
And wakes Hippocoon in the Morning-Hour,
(On Rhesus' side accustom'd to attend,
A faithful Kinsman, and instructive Friend.)
He rose, and saw the Field deform'd with Blood,   610
An empty Space where late the Coursers stood,
The yet-warm Thracians panting on the Coast;
For each he wept, but for his Rhesus most:
Now while on Rhesus' Name he calls in vain,
The gath'ring Tumult spreads o'er all the Plain;

On Heaps the Trojans rush, with wild affright,
And wond'ring view the Slaughters of the Night.
  Mean while the Chiefs, arriving at the Shade
Where late the Spoils of Hector's Spy were laid,
Ulysses stopp'd; to him Tydides bore   620
The Trophee, dropping yet with Dolon's Gore:
Then mounts again; again their nimble Feet
The Coursers ply, and thunder tow'rds the Fleet.
  Old Nestor first perceiv'd th' approaching Sound,
Bespeaking thus the Grecian Peers around.
Methinks the Noise of tramp'ling Steeds I hear
Thick'ning this way, and gath'ring on my Ear;
Perhaps some Horses of the Trojan Breed
(So may, ye Gods! my pious Hopes succeed)
The great Tydides and Ulysses bear,   630
Return'd Triumphant with this Prize of War.
Yet much I fear (ah may that Fear be vain)
The Chiefs out-number'd by the Trojan Train:
Perhaps, ev'n now pursu'd, they seek the Shore;
Or oh! perhaps those Heroes are no more.
  Scarce had he spoke, when lo! the Chiefs appear,
And spring to Earth: the Greeks dismiss their Fear:
With Words of Friendship and extended Hands
They greet the Kings; and Nestor first demands:
  Say thou, whose Praises all our Host proclaim,   640
Thou living Glory of the Grecian Name!
Say whence these Coursers? by what Chance bestow'd,
The Spoil of Foes, or Present of a God?
Not those fair Steeds so radiant and so gay,
That draw the burning Chariot of the Day.
Old as I am, to Age I scorn to yield,
And daily mingle in the martial Field;
But sure till now no Coursers struck my Sight
Like these, conspicuous thro' the Ranks of Fight.
Some God, I deem, conferr'd the glorious Prize,   650
Blest as ye are, and fav'rites of the Skies;
The Care of him who bids the Thunder roar,
And her, whose Fury bathes the World with Gore.

Father! not so, (sage Ithacus rejoin'd)
The Gifts of Heav'n are of a nobler kind.
Of Thracian Lineage are the Steeds ye view,
Whose hostile King the brave Tydides slew;
Sleeping he dy'd, with all his Guards around,
And twelve beside lay gasping on the Ground.
These other Spoils from conquer'd Dolon came,   660
A Wretch, whose Swiftness was his only Fame,
By Hector sent our Forces to explore,
He now lies headless on the sandy Shore.
  Then o'er the Trench the bounding Coursers flew;
The joyful Greeks with loud Acclaim pursue.
Strait to Tydides' high Pavilion born,
The matchless Steeds his ample Stalls adorn:
The neighing Coursers their new Fellows greet,
And the full Racks are heap'd with gen'rous Wheat.
But Dolon's Armour, to his Ships convey'd,   670
High on the painted Stern Ulysses laid,
A Trophy destin'd to the blue-ey'd Maid.
  Now from nocturnal Sweat, and sanguine Stain,
They cleanse their Bodies in the neighb'ring Main:
Then in the polish'd Bath, refresh'd from Toil,
Their Joints they supple with dissolving Oil,
In due Repast indulge the genial Hour,
And first to Pallas the Libations pour:
They sit, rejoicing in her Aid divine,
And the crown'd Goblet foams with Floods of Wine.   680

THE ELEVENTH BOOK
OF THE ILIAD

THE ARGUMENT

The third Battel, and the Acts of Agamemnon

AGAMEMNON HAVING ARM'D HIMSELF, leads the Grecians to Battel: Hector prepares the Trojans to receive them; while Jupiter, Juno, and Minerva give the Signals of War. Agamemnon bears all before him; and Hector is commanded by Jupiter (who sends Iris for that purpose) to decline the Engagement, till the King shall be wounded and retire from the Field. He then makes a great Slaughter of the Enemy; Ulysses and Diomed put a stop to him for a while; but the latter being wounded by Paris is obliged to desert his Companion, who is encompass'd by the Trojans, wounded, and in the utmost danger, till Menelaus and Ajax rescue him. Hector comes against Ajax, but that Hero alone opposes Multitudes, and rallies the Greeks. In the mean time Machaon, in the other Wing of the Army, is pierced with an Arrow by Paris, and carry'd from the Fight in Nestor's Chariot. Achilles (who overlook'd the Action from his Ship) sends Patroclus to enquire which of the Greeks was wounded in that manner? Nestor entertains him in his Tent with an Account of the Accidents of the Day, and a long Recital of some former Wars which he remember'd, tending to put Patroclus upon persuading Achilles to fight for his Countrymen, or at least to permit him to do it, clad in Achilles's Armour. Patroclus in his Return meets Eurypilus also wounded, and assists him in that Distress.

This Book opens with the eight and twentieth Day of the Poem; and the same Day, with its various Actions and Adventures, is extended thro' the twelfth, thirteenth, fourteenth, fifteenth, sixteenth, seventeenth, and part of the eighteenth, Books. The Scene lies in the Field near the Monument of Ilus.

The Saffron Morn, with early Blushes spread,
Now rose refulgent from Tithonus' Bed;

With new-born Day to gladden mortal Sight,
And gild the Courts of Heav'n with sacred Light.
When baleful Eris, sent by Jove's Command,
The Torch of Discord blazing in her Hand,
Thro' the red Skies her bloody Sign extends,
And, wrapt in Tempests, o'er the Fleets descends.
High on Ulysses' Bark her horrid Stand
She took, and thunder'd thro' the Seas and Land.   10
Ev'n Ajax and Achilles heard the Sound,
Whose Ships remote the guarded Navy bound.
Thence the black Fury thro' the Grecian Throng
With Horror sounds the loud Orthian Song:[1]
The Navy shakes, and at the dire Alarms
Each Bosom boils, each Warrior starts to Arms.
No more they sigh, inglorious to return,
But breathe Revenge, and for the Combat burn.
   The King of Men his hardy Host inspires
With loud Command, with great Example fires;   20
Himself first rose, himself before the rest
His mighty Limbs in radiant Armour drest.
And first he cas'd his manly Legs around
In shining Greaves, with silver Buckles bound:
The beaming Cuirass next adorn'd his Breast,
The same which once King Cinyras possest:
(The Fame of Greece and her assembled Host
Had reach'd that Monarch on the Cyprian Coast;
'Twas then, the Friendship of the Chief to gain,
This glorious Gift he sent, nor sent in vain.)   30
Ten Rows of azure Steel the Work infold,
Twice ten of Tin, and twelve of ductile Gold;
Three glitt'ring Dragons to the Gorget rise,
Whose imitated Scales against the Skies
Reflected various Light, and arching bow'd,
Like colour'd Rainbows o'er a show'ry Cloud:
(Jove's wond'rous Bow, of three celestial Dyes,
Plac'd as a Sign to Man amid the Skies.)
A radiant Baldrick, o'er his Shoulder ty'd,
Sustain'd the Sword that glitter'd at his side: 40

[1] Shrill cry of battle

Gold was the Hilt, a silver Sheath encas'd
The shining Blade, and golden Hangers grac'd.
His Buckler's mighty Orb was next display'd,
That round the Warrior cast a dreadful Shade;
Ten Zones of Brass its ample Brims surround,
And twice ten Bosses the bright Convex crown'd;
Tremendous Gorgon frown'd upon its Field,
And circling Terrors fill'd th' expressive Shield:
Within its Concave hung a silver Thong,
On which a mimic Serpent creeps along,   50
His azure Length in easy Waves extends,
Till in three Heads th' embroider'd Monster ends.
Last o'er his Brows his fourfold Helm he plac'd,
With nodding Horse-hair formidably grac'd;
And in his Hands two steely Javelins wields,
That blaze to Heav'n, and lighten all the Fields.
    That instant, Juno and the martial Maid
In happy Thunders promis'd Greece their Aid;
High o'er the Chief they clash'd their Arms in Air,
And leaning from the Clouds, expect the War.   60
    Close to the Limits of the Trench and Mound,
The fiery Coursers to their Chariots bound
The Squires restrain'd: The Foot, with those who wield
The lighter Arms, rush'd forward to the Field.
To second these, in close Array combin'd,
The Squadrons spread their sable Wings behind.
Now Shouts and Tumults wake the tardy Sun,
As with the Light the Warriors Toils begun.
Ev'n Jove, whose Thunder spoke his Wrath, distill'd
Red Drops of Blood o'er all the fatal Field;   70
The Woes of Men unwilling to survey,
And all the Slaughters that must stain the Day.
    Near Ilus' Tomb, in Order rang'd around,
The Trojan Lines possess'd the rising Ground.
There wise Polydamas and Hector stood;
Æneas, honour'd as a guardian God;
Bold Polybus, Agenor the divine;
The Brother-Warriors of Antenor's Line;

With youthful Acamas, whose beauteous Face
And fair Proportion match'd th' etherial Race.   80
Great Hector, cover'd with his spacious Shield,
Plies all the Troops, and orders all the Field.
As the red Star now shows his sanguine Fires
Thro' the dark Clouds, and now in Night retires;
Thus thro' the Ranks appear'd the Godlike Man,
Plung'd in the Rear, or blazing in the Van;
While streamy Sparkles, restless as he flies,
Flash from his Arms as Light'ning from the Skies.
As sweating Reapers in some wealthy Field,
Rang'd in two Bands, their crooked Weapons wield,   90
Bear down the Furrows, till their Labours meet;
Thick fall the heapy Harvests at their Feet.
So Greece and Troy the Field of War divide,
And falling Ranks are strow'd on ev'ry side.
None stoop'd a Thought to base inglorious Flight;
But Horse to Horse, and Man to Man they fight.
Not rabid Wolves more fierce contest their Prey;
Each wounds, each bleeds, but none resign the Day.
Discord with Joy the Scene of Death descries,
And drinks large Slaughter at her sanguin Eyes: 100
Discord alone, of all th' immortal Train,
Swells the red Horrors of this direful Plain:
The Gods in peace their golden Mansions fill,
Rang'd in bright Order on th' Olympian Hill;
But gen'ral Murmurs told their Griefs above,
And each accus'd the partial Will of Jove.
Mean-while apart, superior, and alone,
Th' eternal Monarch, on his awful Throne,
Wrapt in the Blaze of boundless Glory sate;
And fix'd, fulfill'd the just Decrees of Fate.   110
On Earth he turn'd his all-consid'ring Eyes,
And mark'd the Spot where Ilion's Tow'rs arise;
The Sea with Ships, the Fields with Armies spread,
The Victor's Rage, the dying, and the dead.
   Thus while the Morning-Beams increasing bright
O'er Heav'ns pure Azure spread the growing Light,

Commutual Death the Fate of War confounds,
Each adverse Battel goar'd with equal Wounds.
But now (what time in some sequester'd Vale
The weary Wood-man spreads his sparing Meal,   120
When his tir'd Arms refuse the Axe to rear,
And claim a Respite from the Sylvan War;
But not till half the prostrate Forests lay
Stretch'd in long Ruin, and expos'd to Day)
Then, nor till then, the Greeks impulsive Might
Pierc'd the black Phalanx, and let in the Light.
Great Agamemnon then the Slaughter led,
And slew Bienor at his People's Head:
Whose Squire Oïleus, with a sudden spring,
Leap'd from the Chariot to revenge his King,   130
But in his Front he felt the fatal Wound,
Which pierc'd his Brain, & stretch'd him on the Ground:
Atrides spoil'd, and left them on the Plain;
Vain was their Youth, their glitt'ring Armour vain:
Now soil'd with Dust, and naked to the Sky,
Their snowy Limbs and beauteous Bodies lie.
    Two Sons of Priam next to Battel move,
The Product one of Marriage, one of Love;
In the same Car the Brother-Warriors ride,
This took the charge to combat, that to guide: 140
Far other Task! than when they wont to keep
On Ida's Tops, their Father's fleecy Sheep.
These on the Mountains once Achilles found,
And captive led, with pliant Osiers bound;
Then to their Sire for ample Sums restor'd;
But now to perish by Atrides' Sword:
Pierc'd in the Breast the base-born Isus bleeds;
Cleft thro' the Head, his Brother's Fate succeeds.
Swift to the Spoil the hasty Victor falls,
And stript, their Features to his Mind recalls.   150
The Trojans see the Youths untimely die,
But helpless tremble for themselves, and fly.
So when a Lion, ranging o'er the Lawns,
Finds, on some grassy Lare, the couching Fawns,

Their Bones he cracks, their reeking Vitals draws,
And grinds the quiv'ring Flesh with bloody Jaws;
The frighted Hind beholds, and dares not stay,
But swift thro' rustling Thickets bursts her way;
All drown'd in Sweat the panting Mother flies,
And the big Tears roll trickling from her Eyes.   160
　　Amidst the Tumult of the routed Train,
The Sons of false Antimachus were slain;
He, who for Bribes his faithless Counsels sold,
And voted Helen's Stay, for Paris' Gold.
Atrides mark'd as these their Safety sought,
And slew the Children for the Father's Fault;
Their headstrong Horse unable to restrain,
They shook with Fear, and drop'd the silken Rein;
Then in their Chariot, on their Knees they fall,
And thus with lifted Hands for Mercy call.   170
　　Oh spare our Youth, and for the Life we owe,
Antimachus shall copious Gifts bestow;
Soon as he hears, that not in Battel slain,
The Grecian Ships his captive Sons detain,
Large Heaps of Brass in Ransome shall be told,
And Steel well-temper'd, and persuasive Gold.
　　These Words, attended with a Flood of Tears,
The Youths address'd to unrelenting Ears:
The vengeful Monarch gave this stern Reply;
If from Antimachus ye spring, ye die: 180
The daring Wretch who once in Council stood
To shed Ulysses' and my Brother's Blood,
For proffer'd Peace! And sues his Seed for Grace?
No, die, and pay the Forfeit of your Race.
　　This said, Pisander from the Car he cast,
And pierc'd his Breast: supine he breath'd his last.
His Brother leap'd to Earth; but as he lay,
The trenchant Faulchion lopp'd his Hands away;
His sever'd Head was toss'd among the Throng,
And rolling, drew a bloody Trail along.   190
Then, where the thickest fought, the Victor flew;
The King's Example all his Greeks pursue.

Now by the Foot the flying Foot were slain,
Horse trod by Horse, lay foaming on the Plain.
From the dry Fields thick Clouds of Dust arise,
Shade the black Host, and intercept the Skies.
The brass-hoof'd Steeds tumultuous plunge and bound,
And the thick Thunder beats the lab'ring Ground.
Still slaught'ring on, the King of Men proceeds;
The distanc'd Army wonders at his Deeds.   200
As when the Winds with raging Flames conspire,
And o'er the Forests roll the Flood of Fire,
In blazing heaps the Grove's old Honours fall,
And one refulgent Ruin levells all.
Before Atrides' Rage so sinks the Foe,
Whole Squadrons vanish, and proud Heads lie low.
The Steeds fly trembling from his waving Sword;
And many a Car, now lighted of its Lord,
Wide o'er the Field with guideless Fury rolls,
Breaking their Ranks, and crushing out their Souls;   210
While his keen Faulchion drinks the Warriors Lives;
More grateful, now, to Vulturs than their Wives!
    Perhaps great Hector then had found his Fate,
But Jove and Destiny prolong'd his Date.
Safe from the Darts, the Care of Heav'n he stood,
Amidst Alarms, and Deaths, and Dust, and Blood.
    Now past the Tomb where ancient Ilus lay,
Thro' the mid Field the routed urge their way.
Where the wild Figs th' adjoining Summit crown,
That Path they take, and speed to reach the Town.   220
As swift Atrides, with loud Shouts pursu'd,
Hot with his Toil, and bath'd in hostile Blood.
Now near the Beech-tree, and the Scæan Gates,
The Hero haults, and his Associates waits.
Mean-while on ev'ry side, around the Plain,
Dispers'd, disorder'd, fly the Trojan Train.
So flies a Herd of Beeves, that hear dismay'd
The Lion's roaring thro' the mid-night Shade;
On Heaps they tumble with successless haste;
The Savage seizes, draws, and rends the last: 230

Not with less Fury stern Atrides flew,
Still press'd the Rout, and still the hindmost slew;
Hurl'd from their Cars the bravest Chiefs are kill'd,
And Rage, and Death, and Carnage, load the Field.
   Now storms the Victor at the Trojan Wall;
Surveys the Tow'rs, and meditates their Fall.
But Jove descending shook th' Idæan Hills,
And down their Summits pour'd a hundred Rills:[2]
Th' unkindled Light'ning in his Hand he took,
And thus the many-colour'd Maid bespoke.   240
   Iris, with haste thy golden Wings display,
To God-like Hector this our Word convey.
While Agamemnon wastes the Ranks around,
Fights in the Front, and bathes with Blood the Ground,
Bid him give way; but issue forth Commands,
And trust the War to less important Hands:
But when, or wounded by the Spear, or Dart,
That Chief shall mount his Chariot, and depart;
Then Jove shall string his Arm, and fire his Breast,
Then to her Ships shall flying Greece be press'd,   250
Till to the Main the burning Sun descend,
And sacred Night her awful Shade extend.
   He spoke, and Iris at his Word obey'd;
On Wings of Winds descends the various Maid.
The Chief she found amidst the Ranks of War,
Close to the Bulwarks, on his glitt'ring Car.
The Goddess then: O Son of Priam hear!
From Jove I come, and his high Mandate bear.
While Agamemnon wastes the Ranks around,
Fights in the Front, and bathes with Blood the Ground,   260
Abstain from Fight; yet issue forth Commands,
And trust the War to less important Hands.
But when, or wounded by the Spear, or Dart,
The Chief shall mount his Chariot, and depart;
Then Jove shall string thy Arm, and fire thy Breast,
Then to her Ships shall flying Greece be prest,
Till to the Main the burning Sun descend,
And sacred Night her awful Shade extend.

[2] Pope's translation of Ida, *rich in springs*

She said, and vanish'd: Hector, with a Bound,
Vaults from his Chariot on the trembling Ground,   270
In clanging Arms: He grasps in either Hand
A pointed Lance, and speeds from Band to Band;
Revives their Ardour, turns their Steps from flight,
And wakes anew the dying Flames of Fight.
They stand to Arms: the Greeks their Onset dare,
Condense their Pow'rs, and wait the coming War.
New Force, new Spirit to each Breast returns;
The Fight renew'd with fiercer Fury burns:
The King leads on; all fix on him their Eye,
And learn from him, to conquer, or to die.   280
    Ye sacred Nine, Celestial Muses! tell,
Who fac'd him first, and by his Prowess fell?
The great Iphidamas, the bold and young;
From sage Antenor and Theano sprung;
Whom from his Youth his Grandsire Cisseus bred,
And nurs'd in Thrace where snowy Flocks are fed.
Scarce did the Down his rosy Cheeks invest,
And early Honour warm his gen'rous Breast,
When the kind Sire consign'd his Daughter's Charms
(Theano's Sister) to his youthful Arms.   290
But call'd by Glory to the Wars of Troy,
He leaves untasted the first Fruits of Joy;
From his lov'd Bride departs with melting Eyes,
And swift to aid his dearer Country flies.
With twelve black Ships he reach'd Percope's Strand,
Thence took the long, laborious March by Land.
Now fierce for Fame, before the Ranks he springs,
Tow'ring in Arms, and braves the King of Kings.
Atrides first discharg'd the missive Spear;
The Trojan stoop'd, the Javelin pass'd in Air.   300
Then near the Corselet, at the Monarch's Heart,
With all his Strength the Youth directs his Dart;
But the broad Belt, with Plates of Silver bound,
The Point rebated, and repell'd the Wound.
Encumber'd with the Dart, Atrides stands,
Till grasp'd with Force, he wrench'd it from his Hands.

At once, his weighty Sword discharg'd a Wound
Full on his Neck, that fell'd him to the Ground.
Stretch'd in the Dust th' unhappy Warrior lies,
And Sleep eternal seals his swimming Eyes.   310
Oh worthy better Fate! oh early slain!
Thy Country's Friend; and virtuous, tho' in vain!
No more the Youth shall join his Consort's side,
At once a Virgin, and at once a Bride!
No more with Presents her Embraces meet,
Or lay the Spoils of Conquest at her Feet,
On whom his Passion, lavish of his Store,
Bestow'd so much, and vainly promis'd more!
Unwept, uncover'd, on the Plain he lay,
While the proud Victor bore his Arms away.   320
    Coon, Antenor's eldest Hope, was nigh:
Tears, at the Sight, came starting from his Eye,
While pierc'd with Grief the much-lov'd Youth he view'd,
And the pale Features now deform'd with Blood.
Then with his Spear, unseen, his Time he took,
Aim'd at the King, and near his Elbow strook.
The thrilling Steel transpierc'd the brawny Part,
And thro' his Arm stood forth the barbed Dart.
Surpriz'd the Monarch feels, yet void of Fear
On Coon rushes with his lifted Spear: 330
His Brother's Corps the pious Trojan draws,
And calls his Country to assert his Cause,
Defends him breathless on the smoaking Field,
And o'er the Body spreads his ample Shield.
Atrides, marking an unguarded Part,
Transfix'd the Warrior with his brazen Dart;
Prone on his Brother's bleeding Breast he lay,
The Monarch's Faulchion lopp'd his Head away:
The social Shades the same dark Journey go,
And join each other in the Realms below.   340
    The vengeful Victor rages round the Fields
With ev'ry Weapon, Art or Fury yields:
By the long Lance, the Sword, or pond'rous Stone,
Whole Ranks are broken, and whole Troops o'erthrown.

This, while yet warm, distill'd the purple Flood;
But when the Wound grew stiff with clotted Blood,
Then grinding Tortures his strong Bosom rend,
Less keen those Darts the fierce Ilythiæ[3] send,
(The Pow'rs that cause the teeming Matron's Throes,
Sad Mothers of unutterable Woes!)   350
Stung with the Smart, all panting with the Pain,
He mounts the Car, and gives his Squire the Rein:
Then with a Voice which Fury made more strong,
And Pain augmented, thus exhorts the Throng.

   O Friends! O Greeks! assert your Honours won;
Proceed, and finish what this Arm begun:
Lo! angry Jove forbids your Chief to stay,
And envies half the Glories of the Day.

   He said; the Driver whirls his lengthful Thong;
The Horses fly; the Chariot smoaks along.   360
Clouds from their Nostrils the fierce Coursers blow,
And from their Sides the Foam descends in Snow;
Shot thro' the Battel in a Moment's Space,
The wounded Monarch at his Tent they place.

   No sooner Hector saw the King retir'd,
But thus his Trojans and his Aids he fir'd.
Hear all ye Dardan, all ye Lycian Race!
Fam'd in close Fight, and dreadful Face to Face;
Now call to Mind your ancient Trophies won,
Your great Forefathers Virtues, and your own.   370
Behold, the Gen'ral flies! deserts his Pow'rs!
Lo Jove himself declares the Conquest ours!
Now on yon' Ranks impell your foaming Steeds;
And, sure of Glory, dare immortal Deeds.

   With Words like these the fiery Chief alarms
His fainting Host, and ev'ry Bosom warms.
As the bold Hunter chears his Hounds to tear
The brindled Lion, or the tusky Bear,
With Voice and Hand provokes their doubting Heart,
And springs the foremost with his lifted Dart: 380
So God-like Hector prompts his Troops to dare,
Nor prompts alone, but leads himself the War.

[3] "Goddesses that Homer supposes to preside over Child-Birth" (P)

On the black Body of the Foes he pours:
As from the Cloud's deep Bosom swell'd with Show'rs,
A sudden Storm the purple Ocean sweeps,
Drives the wild Waves, and tosses all the Deeps.
Say Muse! when Jove the Trojan's Glory crown'd,
Beneath his Arm what Heroes bit the Ground?
Assæus, Dolops, and Autonous dy'd,
Opites next was added to their side,   390
Then brave Hipponous fam'd in many a Fight,
Opheltius, Orus, sunk to endless Night,
Æsymnus, Agelaus; all Chiefs of Name;
The rest were vulgar Deaths, unknown to Fame.
As when a western Whirlwind, charg'd with Storms,
Dispells the gather'd Clouds that Notus forms;
The Gust continu'd, violent, and strong,
Rolls sable Clouds in Heaps on Heaps along;
Now to the Skies the foaming Billows rears,
Now breaks the Surge, and wide the bottom bares.   400
Thus raging Hector, with resistless Hands,
O'erturns, confounds, and scatters all their Bands.
Now the last Ruin the whole Host appalls;
Now Greece had trembled in her wooden Walls;
But wise Ulysses call'd Tydides forth,
His Soul rekindled, and awak'd his Worth.
And stand we deedless, O eternal Shame!
Till Hector's Arm involve the Ships in Flame?
Haste, let us join, and combat side by side.
The Warrior thus, and thus the Friend reply'd.   410
    No martial Toil I shun, no Danger fear;
Let Hector come; I wait his Fury here.
But Jove with Conquest crowns the Trojan Train;
And, Jove our Foe, all human Force is vain.
    He sigh'd; but sighing, rais'd his vengeful Steel,
And from his Car the proud Thymbræus fell:
Molion, the Charioteer, pursu'd his Lord,
His Death ennobled by Ulysses' Sword.
There slain, they left them in eternal Night;
Then plung'd amidst the thickest Ranks of Fight.   420

So two wild Boars outstrip the foll'owing Hounds,
Then swift revert, and Wounds return for Wounds.
Stern Hector's Conquests in the middle Plain
Stood check'd a while, and Greece respir'd again.
  The Sons of Merops shone amidst the War;
Tow'ring they rode in one refulgent Car:
In deep Prophetic Arts their Father skill'd,
Had warn'd his Children from the Trojan Field;
Fate urg'd them on; the Father warn'd in vain,
They rush'd to Fight, and perish'd on the Plain!   430
Their Breasts no more the vital Spirit warms;
The stern Tydides strips their shining Arms.
Hypirochus by great Ulysses dies,
And rich Hippodamus becomes his Prize.
Great Jove from Ide with Slaughter fills his Sight,
And level hangs the doubtful Scale of Fight.
By Tydeus' Lance Agastrophus was slain,
The far-fam'd Hero of Pæonian Strain;
Wing'd with his Fears, on Foot he strove to fly,
His Steeds too distant, and the Foe too nigh;   440
Thro' broken Orders, swifter than the Wind,
He fled, but flying, left his Life behind.
This Hector sees, as his experienc'd Eyes
Traverse the Files, and to the Rescue flies;
Shouts, as he past, the crystal Regions rend,
And moving Armies on his March attend.
Great Diomed himself was seiz'd with Fear,
And thus bespoke his Brother of the War.
  Mark how this way yon' bending Squadrons yield!
The Storm rolls on, and Hector rules the Field: 450
Here stand his utmost Force—The Warrior said;
Swift at the Word, his pondrous Javelin fled;
Nor miss'd its Aim, but where the Plumage danc'd,
Raz'd the smooth Cone, and thence obliquely glanc'd.
Safe in his Helm (the Gift of Phœbus' Hands)
Without a Wound the Trojan Hero stands;
But yet so stunn'd, that stagg'ring on the Plain,
His Arm and Knee his sinking Bulk sustain;

O'er his dim Sight the misty Vapours rise,
And a short Darkness shades his swimming Eyes.　　460
Tydides follow'd to regain his Lance;
While Hector rose, recover'd from the Trance,
Remounts his Car, and herds amidst the Crowd;
The Greek pursues him, and exults aloud.
　Once more thank Phœbus for thy forfeit Breath,
Or thank that Swiftness which outstrips the Death.
Well by Apollo are thy Pray'rs repaid,
And oft' that partial Pow'r has lent his Aid.
Thou shalt not long the Death deserv'd withstand,
If any God assist Tydides' Hand.　　470
Fly then, inglorious! but thy Flight, this Day,
Whole Hecatombs of Trojan Ghosts shall pay.
　Him, while he triumph'd, Paris ey'd from far,
(The Spouse of Helen, the fair Cause of War)
Around the Field his Feather'd Shafts he sent,
From ancient Ilus' ruin'd Monument;
Behind the Column plac'd, he bent his Bow,
And wing'd an Arrow at th' unwary Foe;
Just as he stoop'd, Agastrophus's Crest
To seize, and drew the Corselet from his Breast.　　480
The Bow-string twang'd; nor flew the Shaft in vain,
But pierc'd his Foot, and nail'd it to the Plain.
The laughing Trojan, with a joyful Spring
Leaps from his Ambush, and insults the King.
　He bleeds! (he cries) some God has sped my Dart;
Would the same God had fixt it in his Heart!
So Troy reliev'd from that wide-wasting Hand
Shall breathe from Slaughter, and in combat stand,
Whose Sons now tremble at his darted Spear,
As scatter'd Lambs the rushing Lion fear.　　490
　He, dauntless, thus: Thou Conqu'ror of the Fair,
Thou Woman-warrior with the curling Hair;
Vain Archer! trusting to the distant Dart,
Unskill'd in Arms to act a manly Part!
Thou hast but done what Boys or Women can;
Such Hands may wound, but not incense a Man.

Nor boast the Scratch thy feeble Arrow gave,
A Coward's Weapon never hurts the Brave.
Not so this Dart, which thou may'st one Day feel;
Fate wings its Flight, and Death is on the Steel, 500
Where this but lights, some noble Life expires,
Its Touch makes Orphans, bathes the cheeks of Sires,
Steeps Earth in purple, gluts the Birds of Air,
And leaves such Objects as distract the Fair.
  Ulysses hastens with a trembling Heart,
Before him steps, and bending draws the Dart:
Forth flows the Blood; an eager Pang succeeds;
Tydides mounts, and to the Navy speeds.
  Now on the Field Ulysses stands alone,
The Greeks all fled, the Trojans pouring on: 510
But stands collected in himself and whole,
And questions thus his own unconquer'd Soul.
  What farther Subterfuge, what Hopes remain?
What Shame, inglorious if I quit the Plain;
What Danger, singly if I stand the Ground,
My Friends all scatter'd, all the Foes around?
Yet wherefore doubtful? Let this Truth suffice;
The Brave meets Danger, and the Coward flies:
To die, or conquer, proves a Hero's Heart;
And knowing this, I know a Soldier's Part. 520
  Such Thoughts revolving in his careful Breast,
Near, and more near, the shady Cohorts prest;
These, in the Warrior, their own Fate inclose;[4]
And round him deep the steely Circle grows.
So fares a Boar, whom all the Troop surrounds
Of shouting Huntsmen and of clam'rous Hounds;
He grinds his Iv'ry Tusks; he foams with Ire;
His sanguine Eyeballs glare with living Fire;
By these, by those, on ev'ry Part is ply'd;
And the red Slaughter spreads on ev'ry side. 530
Pierc'd thro' the Shoulder, first Deiopis fell;
Next Ennomus and Thoon sunk to Hell;
Chersidamas, beneath the Navel thrust,
Supinely falls, and grasps the bloody Dust.

[4] Bring about their own death by surrounding Ulysses

Charops, the Son of Hippasus, was near;
Ulysses reach'd him with the fatal Spear;
But to his Aid his Brother Socus flies,
Socus, the brave, the gen'rous, and the wise:
Near as he drew, the Warrior thus began.
O great Ulysses, much-enduring Man!   540
Not deeper skill'd in ev'ry martial Slight,
Than worn to Toils, and active in the Fight!
This Day, two Brothers shall thy Conquest grace,
And end at once the great Hippasian Race,
Or thou beneath this Lance must press the Field—
He said, and forceful pierc'd his spacious Shield;
Thro' the strong Brass the ringing Javelin thrown,
Plow'd half his side, and bar'd it to the Bone.
By Pallas' Care, the Spear, tho' deep infix'd,
Stop'd short of Life, nor with his Entrails mix'd.   550
   The Wound not mortal wise Ulysses knew,
Then furious thus, (but first some Steps withdrew.)
Unhappy Man! whose Death our Hand shall grace!
Fate calls thee hence, and finish'd is thy Race.
No longer check my Conquests on the Foe;
But pierc'd by this, to endless Darkness go,
And add one Spectre to the Realms below!
   He spoke, while Socus seiz'd with sudden Fright,
Trembling gave way, and turn'd his Back to Flight,
Between his Shoulders pierc'd the following Dart,   560
And held its Passage thro' the panting Heart.
Wide in his Breast appear'd the grizly Wound;
He falls; his Armour rings against the Ground.
Then thus Ulysses, gazing on the Slain.
Fam'd Son of Hippasus! there press the Plain;
There ends thy narrow Span assign'd by Fate,
Heav'n owes Ulysses yet a longer Date.
Ah Wretch! no Father shall thy Corps compose,
Thy dying Eyes no tender Mother close,
But hungry Birds shall tear those Balls away,   570
And hov'ring Vulturs scream around their Prey.
Me Greece shall honour, when I meet my Doom,
With solemn Fun'rals and a lasting Tomb.

Then raging with intolerable Smart,
He writhes his Body, and extracts the Dart.
The Dart a Tyde of spouting Gore pursu'd,
And gladden'd Troy with Sight of hostile Blood.
Now Troops on Troops the fainting Chief invade,
Forc'd he recedes, and loudly calls for Aid.
Thrice to its pitch his lofty Voice he rears;   580
The well-known Voice thrice Menelaus hears:
Alarm'd, to Ajax Telamon he cry'd,
Who shares his Labours, and defends his side.
O Friend! Ulysses' Shouts invade my Ear;
Distress'd he seems, and no Assistance near:
Strong as he is; yet, one oppos'd to all,
Oppress'd by Multitudes, the best may fall.
Greece, robb'd of him, must bid her Hosts despair,
And feel a Loss not Ages can repair.
    Then, where the Cry directs, his Course he bends;   590
Great Ajax, like the God of War, attends.
The prudent Chief in sore Distress they found,
With Bands of furious Trojans compass'd round.
As when some Huntsman with a flying Spear,
From the blind Thicket wounds a stately Deer;
Down his cleft Side while fresh the Blood distills,
He bounds aloft, and scuds from Hills to Hills,
Till Life's warm Vapour issuing thro' the Wound,
Wild Mountain-Wolves the fainting Beast surround;
Just as their Jaws his prostrate Limbs invade,   600
The Lion rushes thro' the woodland Shade,
The Wolves, tho' hungry, scour dispers'd away;
The Lordly Savage vindicates his Prey.
Ulysses thus, unconquer'd by his Pains,
A single Warrior, half an Host sustains:
But soon as Ajax heaves his Tow'r-like Shield,
The scatter'd Crowds fly frighted o'er the Field;
Atrides' Arm the sinking Hero stays,
And sav'd from Numbers, to his Car conveys.
    Victorious Ajax plies the routed Crew;   610
And first Doryclus, Priam's Son, he slew,

On strong Pandocus next inflicts a Wound,
And lays Lysander bleeding on the Ground.
As when a Torrent, swell'd with wintry Rains,
Pours from the Mountains o'er the delug'd Plains,
And Pines and Oaks, from their Foundations torn,
A Country's Ruins! to the Seas are born:
Fierce Ajax thus o'erwhelms the yielding Throng,
Men, Steeds, and Chariots, roll in Heaps along.
But Hector, from this Scene of Slaughter far,   620
Rag'd on the left, and rul'd the Tyde of War:
Loud Groans proclaim his Progress thro' the Plain,
And deep Scamander swells with Heaps of Slain.
There Nestor and Idomeneus oppose
The Warrior's Fury, there the Battel glows;
There fierce on Foot, or from the Chariot's Height,
His Sword deforms the beauteous Ranks of Fight.
The Spouse of Helen dealing Darts around,
Had pierc'd Machaon with a distant Wound:
In his right Shoulder the broad Shaft appear'd,   630
And trembling Greece for her Physician fear'd.
To Nestor then Idomeneus begun;
Glory of Greece, old Neleus' valiant Son!
Ascend thy Chariot, haste with speed away,
And great Machaon to the Ships convey.
A wise Physician, skill'd our Wounds to heal,
Is more than Armies to the publick Weal.
    Old Nestor mounts the Seat: Beside him rode
The wounded Offspring of the healing God.
He lends the Lash; the Steeds with sounding Feet   640
Shake the dry Field, and thunder tow'rd the Fleet.
    But now Cebriones, from Hector's Car,
Survey'd the various Fortune of the War.
While here (he cry'd) the flying Greeks are slain;
Trojans on Trojans yonder load the Plain.
Before great Ajax, see the mingled Throng
Of Men and Chariots driv'n in heaps along!
I know him well, distinguish'd o'er the Field
By the broad glitt'ring of the sev'nfold Shield.

Thither, O Hector, thither urge thy Steeds;   650
There Danger calls, and there the Combat bleeds,
There Horse and Foot in mingled Deaths unite,
And Groans of Slaughter mix with Shouts of Fight.
  Thus having spoke, the Driver's Lash resounds;
Swift thro' the Ranks the rapid Chariot bounds;
Stung by the Stroke, the Coursers scour the Fields
O'er Heaps of Carcasses, and Hills of Shields.
The Horses Hoofs are bath'd in Heroes Gore,
And dashing purple all the Car before,
The groaning Axle sable Drops distills,   660
And mangled Carnage clogs the rapid Wheels.
Here Hector plunging thro' the thickest Fight
Broke the dark Phalanx, and let in the Light.
(By the long Lance, the Sword, or pondrous Stone,
The Ranks lie scatter'd, and the Troops o'erthrown)
Ajax he shuns, thro' all the dire Debate,
And fears that Arm whose Force he felt so late.
But partial Jove, espousing Hector's Part,
Shot heav'n-bred Horror thro' the Grecian's Heart;
Confus'd, unnerv'd in Hector's Presence grown,   670
Amaz'd he stood, with Terrors not his own.
O'er his broad Back his moony Shield he threw,
And glaring round, by tardy Steps withdrew.
Thus the grim Lion his Retreat maintains,
Beset with watchful Dogs, and shouting Swains,
Repuls'd by Numbers from the nightly Stalls,
Tho' Rage impells him, and tho' Hunger calls,
Long stands the show'ring Darts, and missile Fires;
Then sow'rly slow th' indignant Beast retires.
So turn'd stern Ajax, by whole Hosts repell'd,   680
While his swoln Heart at ev'ry Step rebell'd.
  As the slow Beast with heavy Strength indu'd,
In some wide Field by Troops of Boys pursu'd,
Tho' round his Sides a wooden Tempest rain,
Crops the tall Harvest, and lays waste the Plain;
Thick on his Hide the hollow Blows resound,
The patient Animal maintains his Ground,

Scarce from the Field with all their Efforts chas'd,
And stirs but slowly when he stirs at last.
On Ajax thus a Weight of Trojans hung,   690
The Strokes redoubled on his Buckler rung;
Confiding now in bulky Strength he stands,
Now turns, and backward bears the yielding Bands;
Now stiff recedes, yet hardly seems to fly,
And threats his Followers with retorted Eye.
Fix'd as the Bar between two warring Pow'rs,
While hissing Darts descend in Iron Show'rs:
In his broad Buckler many a Weapon stood;
Its Surface bristled with a quiv'ring Wood;
And many a Javelin, guiltless on the Plain,   700
Prints the dry Dust, and thirsts for Blood in vain.
But bold Eurypylus his Aid imparts,
And dauntless springs beneath a Cloud of Darts;
Whose eager Javelin launch'd against the Foe,
Great Apisaon felt the fatal Blow;
From his torn Liver the red Current flow'd,
And his slack Knees desert their dying Load.
The Victor rushing to despoil the Dead,
From Paris' Bow a vengeful Arrow fled.
Fix'd in his nervous Thigh the Weapon stood,   710
Fix'd was the Point, but broken was the Wood.
Back to the Lines the wounded Greek retir'd,
Yet thus, retreating, his Associates fir'd.

What God, O Grecians! has your Hearts dismay'd?
Oh, turn to Arms; 'tis Ajax claims your Aid.
This Hour he stands the Mark of hostile Rage,
And this the last brave Battel he shall wage:
Haste, join your Forces; from the gloomy Grave
The Warrior rescue, and your Country save.

Thus urg'd the Chief; a gen'rous Troop appears,   720
Who spread their Bucklers, and advance their Spears,
To guard their wounded Friend: While thus they stand
With pious Care, great Ajax joins the Band:
Each takes new Courage at the Hero's Sight;
The Hero rallies, and renews the Fight.

Thus rag'd both Armies like conflicting Fires,
While Nestor's Chariot far from Fight retires:
His Coursers steep'd in Sweat, and stain'd with Gore,
The Greeks Preserver, great Machaon bore.
That Hour, Achilles from the topmost Height   730
Of his proud Fleet, o'erlook'd the Fields of Fight;
His feasted Eyes beheld around the Plain
The Grecian Rout, the slaying, and the slain.
His Friend Machaon singled from the rest,
A transient Pity touch'd his vengeful Breast.
Strait to Mænetius' much-lov'd Son he sent;
Graceful as Mars, Patroclus quits his Tent,
(In evil Hour! Then Fate decreed his Doom;
And fix'd the Date of all his Woes to come!)
Why calls my Friend? thy lov'd Injunctions lay,   740
Whate'er thy Will, Patroclus shall obey.
O first of Friends! (Pelides thus reply'd)
Still at my Heart, and ever at my Side!
The Time is come, when yon' despairing Host
Shall learn the Value of the Man they lost:
Now at my Knees the Greeks shall pour their Moan,
And proud Atrides tremble on his Throne.
Go now to Nestor, and from him be taught
What wounded Warrior late his Chariot brought?
For seen at distance, and but seen behind,   750
His Form recall'd Machaon to my Mind;
Nor could I, thro' yon' Cloud, discern his Face,
The Coursers past me with so swift a Pace.
The Hero said. His Friend obey'd with haste,
Thro' intermingled Ships and Tents, he past;
The Chiefs descending from their Car he found;
The panting Steeds Eurymedon unbound.
The Warriors standing on the breezy Shore,
To dry their Sweat, and wash away the Gore,
Here paus'd a moment, while the gentle Gale   760
Convey'd that Freshness the cool Seas exhale;
Then to consult on Farther Methods went,
And took their Seats beneath the shady Tent.

The Draught prescrib'd, fair Hecamede Prepares,
Arsinous' Daughter, grac'd with golden Hairs:
(Whom to his aged Arms, a Royal Slave,
Greece, as the Prize of Nestor's Wisdom, gave)
A Table first with azure Feet she plac'd;
Whose ample Orb a brazen Charger grac'd:
Honey new-press'd, the sacred Flow'r of Wheat,   770
And wholsome Garlick crown'd the sav'ry Treat.
Next her white Hand an antique Goblet brings,
A Goblet sacred to the Pylian Kings,
From eldest Times: emboss'd with Studs of Gold,
Two Feet support it, and four Handles hold;
On each bright Handle, bending o'er the Brink,
In sculptur'd Gold two Turtles seem to drink:
A massy Weight; yet heav'd with ease by him,
When the brisk Nectar overlook'd the Brim.
Temper'd in this, the Nymph of Form divine   780
Pours a large Potion of the Pramnian Wine;
With Goat's-milk Cheese a flav'rous taste bestows,
And last with Flour the smiling Surface strows.
This for the wounded Prince the Dame prepares;
The cordial Bev'rage rev'rend Nestor shares:
Salubrious Draughts the Warrior's Thirst allay,
And pleasing Conference beguiles the Day.
    Mean time Patroclus, by Achilles sent,
Unheard approach'd, and stood before the Tent.
Old Nestor rising then, the Hero led   790
To his high Seat; the Chief refus'd, and said.
    'Tis now no Season for these kind Delays;
The great Achilles with Impatience stays.
To great Achilles this Respect I owe;
Who asks what Hero, wounded by the Foe,
Was born from combat by thy foaming Steeds?
With Grief I see the great Machaon bleeds.
This to report, my hasty Course I bend;
Thou know'st the fiery Temper of my Friend.
    Can then the Sons of Greece (the Sage rejoin'd)   800
Excite Compassion in Achilles' Mind?

Seeks he the Sorrows of our Host to know?
This is not half the Story of our Woe.
Tell him, not great Machaon bleeds alone,
Our bravest Heroes in the Navy groan,
Ulysses, Agamemnon, Diomed,
And stern Eurypylus, already bleed.
But ah! what flatt'ring Hopes I entertain?
Achilles heeds not, but derides our Pain;
Ev'n till the Flames consume our Fleet, he stays, 810
And waits the rising of the fatal Blaze.
Chief after Chief the raging Foe destroys;
Calm he looks on, and ev'ry Death enjoys.
Now the slow Course of all-impairing Time
Unstrings my Nerves, and ends my manly Prime;
Oh! had I still that Strength my Youth possess'd,
When this bold Arm th' Epeian[5] Pow'rs oppress'd,
The Bulls of Elis in glad Triumph led,
And stretch'd the great Itymonæus dead!
Then, from my Fury fled the trembling Swains, 820
And ours was all the Plunder of the Plains:
Fifty white Flocks, full fifty Herds of Swine,
As many Goats, as many lowing Kine;
And thrice the Number of unrival'd Steeds,
All teeming Females, and of gen'rous Breeds.
These, as my first Essay of Arms, I won;
Old Neleus glory'd in his conqu'ring Son.
Thus Elis forc'd, her long Arrears restor'd,
And Shares were parted to each Pylian Lord.
The State of Pyle was sunk to last Despair, 830
When the proud Elians first commenc'd the War.
For Neleus' Sons Alcides' Rage had slain;
Of twelve bold Brothers, I alone remain!
Oppress'd, we arm'd; and now, this Conquest gain'd,
My Sire three hundred chosen Sheep obtain'd.
(That large Reprizal he might justly claim,
For Prize defrauded, and insulted Fame,
When Elis' Monarch in the publick Course
Detain'd his Chariot and victorious Horse.)

[5] People of Elis, *Elians* (831), a city and region near Nestor's Pylos, *Pyle* (830)

The rest the People shar'd; my self survey'd   840
The just Partition, and due Victims pay'd.
Three Days were past, when Elis rose to War,
With many a Courser, and with many a Car;
The Sons of Actor at their Army's Head
(Young as they were) the vengeful Squadrons led.
High on a Rock fair Thryoëssa stands,
Our utmost Frontier on the Pylian Lands;
Not far the Streams of fam'd Alphæus flow;
The Stream they pass'd, and pitch'd their Tents below.
Pallas, descending in the Shades of Night,   850
Alarms the Pylians, and commands the Fight.
Each burns for Fame, and swells with martial Pride;
My self the foremost; but my Sire deny'd;
Fear'd for my Youth expos'd to stern Alarms;
And stopp'd my Chariot, and detain'd my Arms.
My Sire deny'd in vain: On foot I fled
Amidst our Chariots: For the Goddess led.
   Along fair Arene's delightful Plain,
Soft Minyas rolls his Waters to the Main.
There, Horse and Foot, the Pylian Troops unite,   860
And sheath'd in Arms, expect the dawning Light.
Thence, e'er the Sun advanc'd his noonday Flame,
To great Alphæus' sacred Source we came.
There first to Jove our solemn Rites were paid;
An untam'd Heifer pleas'd the blue-ey'd Maid,
A Bull Alphæus; and a Bull was slain
To the blue Monarch of the wat'ry Main.
In Arms we slept, beside the winding Flood,
While round the Town the fierce Epeians stood.
Soon as the Sun, with all-revealing Ray,   870
Flam'd in the Front of Heav'n, and gave the Day;
Bright Scenes of Arms, and Works of War appear;
The Nations meet; there Pylos, Elis here.
The first who fell, beneath my Javelin bled;
King Augias' Son, and Spouse of Agamede:
(She that all Simple's healing Virtues knew,
And ev'ry Herb that drinks the Morning Dew.)

I seiz'd his Car, the Van of Battel led;
Th' Epeians saw, they trembled, and they fled.
The Foe dispers'd, their bravest Warrior kill'd, 880
Fierce as a Whirlwind now I swept the Field:
Full fifty captive Chariots grac'd my Train;
Two Chiefs from each, fell breathless to the Plain.
Then Actor's Sons had dy'd, but Neptune shrouds
The youthful Heroes in a Veil of Clouds.
O'er heapy Shields, and o'er the postrate Throng,
Collecting Spoils, and slaught'ring all along,
Thro' wide Buprasian Fields we forc'd the Foes,
Where o'er the Vales th' Olenian Rocks arose;
Till Pallas stopp'd us where Alisium flows. 890
Ev'n there, the hindmost of their Rear I slay,
And the same Arm that led, concludes the Day;
Then back to Pyle triumphant take my way.
There to high Jove were publick Thanks assign'd
As first of Gods, to Nestor, of Mankind.
    Such then I was, impell'd by youthful Blood;
So prov'd my Valour for my Country's Good.
Achilles with unactive Fury glows,
And gives to Passion what to Greece he owes.
How shall he grieve, when to th' eternal Shade 900
Her Hosts shall sink, nor his the Pow'r to aid?
O Friend! my Memory recalls the Day,
When gath'ring Aids along the Grecian Sea,
I, and Ulysses, touch'd at Pthia's Port,
And enter'd Peleus' hospitable Court.
A Bull to Jove he slew in sacrifice,
And pour'd Libations on the flaming Thighs.
Thy self, Achilles, and thy rev'rend Sire
Menætius, turn'd the Fragments on the Fire.
Achilles sees us, to the Feast invites; 910
Social we sit, and share the genial Rites.
We then explain'd the Cause on which we came,
Urg'd you to Arms, and found you fierce for Fame.
Your ancient Fathers gen'rous Precepts gave;
Peleus said only this,—"My Son! be brave.

Menœtius thus; "Tho' great Achilles shine
"In Strength superior, and of Race divine,
"Yet cooler Thoughts thy elder Years attend;
"Let thy just Counsels aid, and rule thy Friend.
Thus spoke your Father at Thessalia's Court;   920
Words now forgot, tho' now of vast Import.
Ah! try the utmost that a Friend can fay,
Such gentle Force the fiercest Minds obey;
Some fav'ring God Achilles' Heart may move;
Tho' deaf to Glory, he may yield to Love.
If some dire Oracle his Breast alarm,
If ought from Heav'n with-hold his saving Arm;
Some Beam of Comfort yet on Greece may shine,
If thou but lead the Myrmidonian Line;
Clad in Achilles' Arms, if thou appear,   930
Proud Troy may tremble, and desist from War;
Press'd by fresh Forces her o'er-labour'd Train
Shall seek their Walls, and Greece respire again.
    This touch'd his gen'rous Heart, and from the Tent
Along the Shore with hasty Strides he went;
Soon as he came, where, on the crouded Strand,
The publick Mart and Courts of Justice stand,
Where the tall Fleet of great Ulysses lies,
And Altars to the guardian Gods arise:
There sad he met the brave Euæmon's Son,[6]   940
Large painful Drops from all his Members run,
An Arrow's Head yet rooted in his Wound,
The sable Blood in Circles mark'd the Ground.
As faintly reeling he confess'd the Smart;
Weak was his Pace, but dauntless was his Heart.
Divine Compassion touch'd Patroclus' Breast,
Who sighing, thus his bleeding Friend addrest.
    Ah hapless Leaders of the Grecian Host!
Thus must ye perish on a barb'rous Coast?
Is this your Fate, to glut the Dogs with Gore,   950
Far from your Friends, and from your native Shore!
Say, great Eurypylus! shall Greece yet stand?
Resists she yet the raging Hector's Hand!

[6] Eurypylus (952)

Or are her Heroes doom'd to die with Shame,
And this the Period of our Wars and Fame?
  Eurypylus replies: No more (my Friend)
Greece is no more! this Day her Glories end.
Ev'n to the Ships victorious Troy pursues,
Her Force encreasing, as her Toil renews.
Those Chiefs, that us'd her utmost Rage to meet,   960
Lie pierc'd with Wounds and bleeding in the Fleet.
But thou, Patroclus! act a friendly Part,
Lead to my Ships, and draw this deadly Dart;
With lukewarm Water wash the Gore away,
With healing Balms the raging Smart allay,
Such as sage Chiron, Sire of Pharmacy,
Once taught Achilles, and Achilles thee.
Of two fam'd Surgeons, Podalirius stands
This Hour surrounded by the Trojan Bands;
And great Machaon, wounded in his Tent,   970
Now wants that Succour which so oft' he lent.
  To him the Chief. What then remains to do?
Th' Event of Things the Gods alone can view.
Charg'd by Achilles' great Command I fly,
And bear with haste the Pylian King's Reply:
But thy Distress this Instant claims Relief.
He said, and in his Arms upheld the Chief.
The Slaves their Master's slow Approach survey'd,
And Hides of Oxen on the Floor display'd:
There stretch'd at length the wounded Hero lay,   980
Patroclus cut the forky Steel away.
Then in his Hands a bitter Root he bruis'd;
The Wound he wash'd, the Styptick Juice infus'd.
The closing Flesh that Instant ceas'd to glow,
The Wound to torture, and the Blood to flow.

ᴊᴊᴊᴊ

THE TWELFTH BOOK
OF THE ILIAD

THE ARGUMENT

The Battel at the Grecian Wall

THE GREEKS being retir'd into their Entrenchments, Hector attempts to
force them; but it proving impossible to pass the Ditch, Polydamas advises him to quit their Chariots, and manage the Attack on Foot. The
Trojans follow his Counsel, and having divided their Army into five
Bodies of Foot, begin the Assault. But upon the Signal of an Eagle with
a Serpent in his Talons, which appear'd on the left Hand of the Trojans,
Polydamas endeavours to withdraw them again. This Hector opposes, and
continues the Attack; in which, after many Actions, Sarpedon makes the
first Breach in the Wall: Hector also casting a Stone of a vast Size, forces
open one of the Gates, and enters at the Head of his Troops, who
victoriously pursue the Grecians even to their Ships.

While thus the Hero's pious Cares attend
The Cure and Safety of his wounded Friend,
Trojans and Greeks with clashing Shields engage,
And mutual Deaths are dealt with mutual Rage.
Nor long the Trench or lofty Walls oppose;
With Gods averse th' ill-fated Works arose;
Their Pow'rs neglected and no Victim slain,
The Walls were rais'd, the Trenches sunk in vain.
  Without the Gods, how short a Period stands
The proudest Monument of mortal Hands!   10

This stood, while Hector and Achilles rag'd,
While sacred Troy the warring Hosts engag'd;
But when her Sons were slain, her City burn'd,
And what surviv'd of Greece to Greece return'd;
Then Neptune and Apollo shook the Shore,
Then Ida's Summits pour'd their wat'ry Store;
Rhesus and Rhodius then unite their Rills,
Caresus roaring down the stony Hills,
Æsepus, Granicus, with mingled Force,
And Zanthus foaming from his fruitful Source;   20
And gulphy Simois, rolling to the Main
Helmets, and Shields, and God-like Heroes slain:
These, turn'd by Phœbus from their wonted ways,
Delug'd the Rampire nine continual Days;
The Weight of Waters saps the yielding Wall,
And to the Sea the floating Bulwarks fall.
Incessant Cataracts the Thund'rer pours,
And half the Skies descend in sluicy Show'rs.
The God of Ocean, marching stern before,
With his huge Trident wounds the trembling Shore,   30
Vast Stones and Piles from their Foundation heaves,
And whelms the smoaky Ruin in the Waves.
Now smooth'd with Sand, and levell'd by the Flood,
No Fragment tells where once the Wonder stood;
In their old Bounds the Rivers roll again,
Shine 'twixt the Hills, or wander o'er the Plain.
    But this the Gods in later Times perform;
As yet the Bulwark stood, and brav'd the Storm;
The Strokes yet echo'd of contending Pow'rs;
War thunder'd at the Gates, and Blood distain'd the Tow'rs.   40
Smote by the Arm of Jove, with dire Dismay,
Close by their hollow Ships the Grecians lay;
Hector's Approach in ev'ry Wind they hear,
And Hector's Fury ev'ry moment fear.
He, like a Whirlwind, toss'd the scatt'ring Throng,
Mingled the Troops, and drove the Field along.
So 'midst the Dogs and Hunter's daring Bands,
Fierce of his Might, a Boar or Lion stands;

Arm'd Foes around a dreadful Circle form,
And hissing Javelins rain an Iron Storm: 50
His Pow'rs untam'd their bold Assault defy,
And where he turns, the Rout disperse, or die:
He foams, he glares, he bounds against them all,
And if he falls, his Courage makes him fall.
With equal Rage encompass'd Hector glows;
Exhorts his Armies, and the Trenches shows.
The panting Steeds impatient Fury breathe,
But snort and tremble at the Gulph beneath;
Just on the Brink, they neigh, and paw the Ground,
And the Turf trembles, and the Skies resound.   60
Eager they view'd the Prospect dark and deep,
Vast was the Leap, and headlong hung the Steep;
The bottom bare, (a formidable Show!)
And bristled thick with sharpen'd Stakes below.
The Foot alone this strong Defence could force,
And try the Pass impervious to the Horse.
This saw Polydamas; who, wisely brave,
Restrain'd great Hector, and this Counsel gave.
    Oh thou! brave Leader of our Trojan Bands,
And you, confed'rate Chiefs from foreign Lands!   70
What Entrance here can cumb'rous Chariots find,
The Stakes beneath, the Grecian Walls behind?
No Pass thro' those, without a thousand Wounds,
No Space for Combat in yon' narrow Bounds.
Proud of the Favours mighty Jove has shown,
On certain Dangers we too rashly run:
If 'tis his Will our haughty Foes to tame,
Oh may this Instant end the Grecian Name!
Here, far from Argos, let their Heroes fall,
And one great Day destroy, and bury all!   80
But should they turn, and here oppress our Train,
What Hopes, what Methods of Retreat remain?
Wedg'd in the Trench, by our own Troops confus'd,
In one promiscuous Carnage crush'd and bruis'd,
All Troy must perish, if their Arms prevail,
Nor shall a Trojan live to tell the Tale.

Hear then ye Warriors! and obey with speed;
Back from the Trenches let your Steeds be led;
Then all alighting, wedg'd in firm Array,
Proceed on Foot, and Hector lead the way.   90
So Greece shall stoop before our conqu'ring Pow'r,
And this (if Jove consent) her fatal Hour.

   This Counsel pleas'd: the God-like Hector sprung
Swift from his Seat; his clanging Armour rung.
The Chief's Example follow'd by his Train,
Each quits his Car, and issues on the Plain.
By Orders strict the Charioteers enjoin'd,
Compell the Coursers to their Ranks behind.
The Forces part in five distinguish'd Bands,
And all obey their sev'ral Chief's Commands.   100
The best and bravest in the first conspire,
Pant for the Fight, and threat the Fleet with Fire:
Great Hector glories in the Van of these,
Polydamas, and brave Cebriones.
Before the next the graceful Paris shines,
And bold Alcathous, and Agenor joins.
The Sons of Priam with the third appear,
Deiphobus, and Helenus the Seer:
In Arms with these the mighty Asius stood,
Who drew from Hyrtacus his noble Blood,   110
And whom Arisba's yellow Coursers bore,
The Coursers fed on Selle's winding Shore.
Antenor's Sons the fourth Battalion guide,
And great Æneas, born on fount-full Ide.
Divine Sarpedon the last Band obey'd,
Whom Glaucus and Asteropæus aid,
Next him, the bravest at their Army's Head,
But he more brave than all the Hosts he led.

   Now with compacted Shields, in close Array,
The moving Legions speed their headlong way: 120
Already in their Hopes they fire the Fleet,
And see the Grecians gasping at their Feet.

   While ev'ry Trojan thus, and ev'ry Aid,
Th' Advice of wise Polydamas obey'd;

Asius alone, confiding in his Car,
His vaunted Coursers urg'd to meet the War.
Unhappy Hero! and advis'd in vain!
Those Wheels returning ne'er shall mark the Plain;
No more those Coursers with triumphant Joy
Restore their Master to the Gates of Troy!   130
Black Death attends behind the Grecian Wall,
And great Idomeneus shall boast thy Fall!
Fierce to the left he drives, where from the Plain
The flying Grecians strove their Ships to gain;
Swift thro' the Wall their Horse and Chariots past,
The Gates half-open'd to receive the last.
Thither, exulting in his Force, he flies;
His following Host with Clamours rend the Skies:
To plunge the Grecians headlong in the Main,
Such their proud Hopes, but all their Hopes were vain!   140
    To guard the Gates, two mighty Chiefs attend,
Who from the Lapiths warlike Race descend;
This Polypætes, great Perithous' Heir,
And that Leonteus, like the God of War.
As two tall Oaks, before the Wall they rise;
Their Roots in Earth, their Heads amidst the Skies,
Whose spreading Arms with leafy Honours crown'd,
Forbid the Tempest, and protect the Ground;
High on the Hills appears their stately Form,
And their deep Roots for ever brave the Storm.   150
So graceful these, and so the Shock they stand
Of raging Asius, and his furious Band.
Orestes, Acamas in Front appear,
And Oenomaus and Thoon close the Rear;
In vain their Clamours shake the ambient Fields,
In vain around them beat their hollow Shields;
The fearless Brothers[1] on the Grecians call,
To guard their Navies, and defend the Wall.
Ev'n when they saw Troy's sable Troops impend,
And Greece tumultuous from her Tow'rs descend,   160
Forth from the Portals rush'd th' intrepid Pair,
Oppos'd their Breasts, and stood themselves the War.

---

[1] The Lapiths, Polypaetes and Leonteus (142-44), not *Brothers* in Homer

So two wild Boars spring furious from their Den,
Rouz'd with the Cries of Dogs, and Voice of Men;
On ev'ry side the crackling Trees they tear,
And root the Shrubs, and lay the Forest bare;
They gnash their Tusks, with Fire their Eye-balls roll,
Till some wide Wound lets out their mighty Soul.
Around their Heads the whistling Javelins sung;
With sounding Strokes their brazen Targets rung: 170
Fierce was the Fight, while yet the Grecian Pow'rs
Maintain'd the Walls and mann'd the lofty Tow'rs:
To save their Fleet, the last Efforts they try,
And Stones and Darts in mingled Tempests fly.

As when sharp Boreas blows abroad, and brings
The dreary Winter on his frozen Wings;
Beneath the low-hung Clouds the Sheets of Snow
Descend, and whiten all the Fields below.
So fast the Darts on either Army pour,
So down the Rampires rolls the rocky Show'r;   180
Heavy, and thick, resound the batter'd Shields,
And the deaf Eccho rattles round the Fields.

With Shame repuls'd, with Grief and Fury driv'n,
The frantic Asius thus accuses Heav'n.
In Pow'rs immortal who shall now believe?
Can those too flatter, and can Jove deceive?
What Man could doubt but Troy's victorious Pow'r
Should humble Greece, and this her fatal Hour?
But look how Wasps from hollow Crannies drive,
To guard the Entrance of their common Hive,   190
Dark'ning the Rock, while with unweary'd Wings
They strike th' Assailants, and infix their Stings;
A Race determin'd, that to Death contend:
So fierce, these Greeks their last Retreats defend.
Gods! shall two Warriors only guard their Gates,
Repell an Army, and defraud the Fates?

These empty Accents mingled with the Wind,
Nor mov'd great Jove's unalterable Mind;
To God-like Hector and his matchless Might
Was ow'd the Glory of the destin'd Fight.   200

Like Deeds of Arms thro' all the Forts were try'd,
And all the Gates sustain'd an equal Tide;
Thro' the long Walls the Stony Show'rs were heard,
The Blaze of Flames, the Flash of Arms appear'd.
The Spirit of a God my Breast inspire,
To raise each Act to Life, and sing with Fire!
While Greece unconquer'd kept alive the War,
Secure of Death, confiding in Despair;
And all her guardian Gods in deep Dismay,
With unassisting Arms deplor'd the Day.   210
  Ev'n yet the dauntless Lapithæ maintain
The dreadful Pass, and round them heap the slain.
First Damasus, by Polypœtes' Steel,
Pierc'd thro' his Helmet's brazen Vizor, fell;
The Weapon drank the mingled Brains and Gore;
The Warrior sinks, tremendous now no more!
Next Ormenus and Pylon yield their Breath:
Nor less Leonteus strows the Field with Death;
First thro' the Belt Hippomachus he goar'd,
Then sudden wav'd his unresisted Sword;   220
Antiphates, as thro' the Ranks he broke,
The Faulchion strook, and Fate pursu'd the Stroke;
Iämenus, Orestes, Menon, bled;
And round him rose a Monument of Dead.
  Mean-time the bravest of the Trojan Crew
Bold Hector and Polydamas pursue;
Fierce with Impatience on the Works to fall,
And wrap in rowling Flames the Fleet and Wall.
These on the farther Bank now stood and gaz'd,
By Heav'n alarm'd, by Prodigies amaz'd: 230
A signal Omen stopp'd the passing Host,
Their martial Fury in their Wonder lost.
Jove's Bird on sounding Pinions beat the Skies;
A bleeding Serpent, of enormous Size,
His Talons truss'd; alive, and curling round,
He stung the Bird, whose Throat receiv'd the Wound:
Mad with the Smart, he drops the fatal Prey,
In airy Circles wings his painful way,

Floats on the Winds, and rends the Heav'ns with Cries:
Amidst the Host the fallen Serpent lies: 240
They, pale with Terror, mark its Spires unroll'd,
And Jove's Portent with beating Hearts behold.
Then first Polydamas the Silence broke,
Long weigh'd the Signal, and to Hector spoke.

How oft, my Brother, thy Reproach I bear,
For Words well meant, and Sentiments sincere?
True to those Counsels which I judge the best,
I tell the faithful Dictates of my Breast.
To speak his Thought, is ev'ry Freeman's Right,
In Peace and War, in Council, and in Fight;   250
And all I move, deferring to thy Sway,
But tends to raise that Pow'r which I obey.
Then hear my Words, nor may my Words be vain:
Seek not, this Day, the Grecian Ships to gain;
For sure to warn us Jove his Omen sent,
And thus my Mind explains its clear Event.
The Victor Eagle, whose sinister Flight
Retards our Host, and fills our Hearts with Fright,
Dismiss'd his Conquest in the middle Skies,
Allow'd to seize, but not possess the Prize;   260
Thus tho' we gird with Fires the Grecian Fleet,
Tho' these proud Bulwarks tumble at our Feet,
Toils unforeseen, and fiercer, are decreed;
More Woes shall follow, and more Heroes bleed.
So bodes my Soul, and bids me thus advise;
For thus a skilful Seer would read the Skies.

To him then Hector with Disdain return'd;
(Fierce as he spoke, his Eyes with Fury burn'd)
Are these the faithful Counsels of thy Tongue?
Thy Will is partial, not thy Reason wrong: 270
Or if the Purpose of thy Heart thou vent,
Sure Heav'n resumes the little Sense it lent.
What coward Counsels would thy Madness move,
Against the Word, the Will reveal'd of Jove?
The leading Sign, th' irrevocable Nod,
And happy Thunders of the fav'ring God,

These shall I slight? and guide my wav'ring Mind
By wand'ring Birds, that flit with ev'ry Wind?
Ye Vagrants of the Sky! your Wings extend,
Or where the Suns arise, or where descend;   280
To right, to left, unheeded take your way,
While I the Dictates of high Heav'n obey.
Without a Sign, his Sword the brave Man draws,
And asks no Omen but his Country's Cause.
But why should'st thou suspect the War's Success?
None fears it more, as none promotes it less:
Tho' all our Chiefs amid yon' Ships expire,
Trust thy own Cowardice to 'scape their Fire.
Troy and her Sons may find a gen'ral Grave,
But thou can'st live, for thou can'st be a Slave.   290
Yet should the Fears that wary Mind suggests
Spread their cold Poison thro' our Soldier's Breasts,
My Javelin can revenge so base a Part,
And free the Soul that quivers in thy Heart.

Furious he spoke, and rushing to the Wall,
Calls on his Host; his Host obey the Call;
With Ardour follow where their Leader flies:
Redoubling Clamours thunder in the Skies.
Jove breaths a Whirlwind from the Hills of Ide,
And Drifts of Dust the clouded Navy hide: 300
He fills the Greeks with Terror and Dismay,
And gives great Hector the predestin'd Day.
Strong in themselves, but stronger in his Aid,
Close to the Works their rigid Siege they laid.
In vain the Mounds and massy Beams defend,
While these they undermine, and those they rend;
Upheave the Piles that prop the solid Wall;
And Heaps on Heaps the smoaky Ruins fall.
Greece on her Ramparts stands the fierce Alarms;
The crowded Bulwarks blaze with waving Arms,   310
Shield touching Shield, a long-refulgent Row;
Whence hissing Darts, incessant, rain below.
The bold Ajaces fly from Tow'r to Tow'r,
And rouze, with Flame divine, the Grecian Pow'r.

The gen'rous Impulse ev'ry Greek obeys;
Threats urge the fearful, and the valiant, Praise.
 Fellows in Arms! whose Deeds are known to Fame,
And you whose Ardour hopes an equal Name!
Since not alike endu'd with Force or Art,
Behold a Day when each may act his Part!   320
A Day to fire the brave, and warm the cold,
To gain new Glories, or augment the old.
Urge those who stand, and those who faint excite;
Drown Hector's Vaunts in loud Exhorts of Fight;
Conquest, not Safety, fill the Thoughts of all;
Seek not your Fleet, but sally from the Wall;
So Jove once more may drive their routed Train,
And Troy lie trembling in her Walls again.
 Their Ardour kindles all the Grecian Pow'rs;
And now the Stones descend in heavier Show'rs.   330
As when high Jove his sharp Artill'ry forms,
And opes his cloudy Magazine of Storms;
In Winter's bleak, uncomfortable Reign,
A Snowy Inundation hides the Plain;
He stills the Winds, and bids the Skies to sleep;
Then pours the silent Tempest, thick, and deep:
And first the Mountain Tops are cover'd o'er,
Then the green Fields, and then the sandy Shore;
Bent with the Weight the nodding Woods are seen,
And one bright Waste hides all the Works of Men: 340
The circling Seas alone absorbing all,
Drink the dissolving Fleeces as they fall.
So from each side increas'd the stony Rain,
And the white Ruin rises o'er the Plain.
 Thus God-like Hector and his Troops contend
To force the Ramparts, and the Gates to rend;
Nor Troy could conquer, nor the Greeks would yield,
Till great Sarpedon tow'r'd amid the Field;
For mighty Jove inspir'd with martial Flame
His matchless Son, and urg'd him on to Fame.   350
In Arms he shines, conspicuous from afar,
And bears aloft his ample Shield in Air;

Within whose Orb the thick Bull-Hides were roll'd,
Pond'rous with Brass, and bound with ductile Gold:
And while two pointed Javelins arm his Hands,
Majestick moves along, and leads his Lycian Bands.
    So press'd with Hunger, from the Mountain's Brow
Descends a Lion on the Flocks below;
So stalks the lordly Savage o'er the Plain,
In sullen Majesty, and stern Disdain: 360
In vain loud Mastives bay him from afar,
And Shepherds gaul him with an Iron War;
Regardless, furious, he pursues his way;
He foams, he roars, he rends the panting Prey.
    Resolv'd alike, divine Sarpedon glows
With gen'rous Rage that drives him on the Foes.
He views the Tow'rs, and meditates their Fall,
To sure Destruction dooms th' aspiring Wall;
Then casting on his Friend an ardent Look,
Fir'd with the Thirst of Glory, thus he spoke.   370
    Why boast we, Glaucus! our extended Reign,
Where Xanthus' Streams enrich the Lycian Plain,
Our num'rous Herds that range the fruitful Field,
And Hills where Vines their purple Harvest yield,
Our foaming Bowls with purer Nectar crown'd,
Our Feasts enhanc'd with Music's sprightly Sound?
Why on those Shores are we with Joy survey'd,
Admir'd as Heroes, and as Gods obey'd?
Unless great Acts superior Merit prove,
And vindicate the bount'ous Pow'rs above.   380
'Tis ours, the Dignity they give, to grace;
The first in Valour, as the first in Place.
That when with wond'ring Eyes our martial Bands
Behold our Deeds transcending our Commands,
Such, they may cry, deserve the sov'reign State,
Whom those that envy, dare not imitate!
Could all our Care elude the gloomy Grave,
Which claims no less the fearful than the brave,
For Lust of Fame I should not vainly dare
In fighting Fields, nor urge thy Soul to War.   390

But since, alas! ignoble Age must come,
Disease, and Death's inexorable Doom;
The Life which others pay, let us bestow,
And give to Fame what we to Nature owe;
Brave tho' we fall, and honour'd if we live,
Or let us Glory gain, or Glory give!
  He said; his Words the list'ning Chief inspire
With equal Warmth, and rouze the Warrior's Fire;
The Troops pursue their Leaders with Delight,
Rush to the Foe, and claim the promis'd Fight.   400
Menestheus from on high the Storm beheld,
Threat'ning the Fort, and black'ning in the Field;
Around the Walls he gaz'd, to view from far
What Aid appear'd t' avert th' approaching War,
And saw where Teucer with th' Ajaces stood,
Of Fight insatiate, prodigal of Blood.
In vain he calls; the Din of Helms and Shields
Rings to the Skies, and ecchos thro' the Fields,
The brazen Hinges fly, the Walls resound,
Heav'n trembles, roar the Mountains, thunders all the Ground.   410
  Then thus to Thoos;—hence with speed, (he said)
And urge the bold Ajaces to our Aid;
Their Strength, united, best may help to bear
The bloody Labours of the doubtful War:
Hither the Lycian Princes bend their Course,
The best and bravest of the hostile Force.
But if too fiercely there the Foes contend;
Let Telamon, at least, our Tow'rs defend;
And Teucer haste with his unerring Bow,
To share the Danger, and repell the Foe.   420
  Swift as the Word, the Herald[2] speeds along
The lofty Ramparts, through the martial Throng;
And finds the Heroes, bath'd in Sweat and Gore,
Oppos'd in Combat on the dusty Shore.
Ye valiant Leaders of our warlike Bands!
Your Aid (said Thoos) Peteus' Son demands,
Your Strength, united, best may help to bear
The bloody Labours of the doubtful War:

[2] Thoos, properly Thoötes

Thither the Lycian Princes bend their Course,
The best and bravest of the hostile Force.   430
But if too fiercely, here, the Foes contend,
At least, let Telamon those Tow'rs defend,
And Teucer haste, with his unerring Bow,
To share the Danger, and repell the Foe.
  Strait to the Fort great Ajax turn'd his Care,
And thus bespoke his Brothers of the War.
Now valiant Lycomede! exert your Might,
And brave Oïleus, prove your Force in Fight:
To you I trust the Fortune of the Field,
Till by this Arm the Foe shall be repell'd;   440
That done, expect me to compleat the Day—
Then, with his sev'nfold Shield, he strode away.
With equal Steps bold Teucer press'd the Shore,
Whose fatal Bow the strong Pandion bore.
  High on the Walls appear'd the Lycian Pow'rs,
Like some black Tempest gath'ring round the Tow'rs;
The Greeks, oppress'd, their utmost Force unite,
Prepar'd to labour in th' unequal Fight;
The War renews, mix'd Shouts and Groans arise;
Tumultuous Clamour mounts, and thickens in the Skies.   450
Fierce Ajax first th' advancing Host invades,
And sends the brave Epicles to the Shades;
Sarpedon's Friend; A-cross the Warrior's way,
Rent from the Walls a rocky Fragment lay;
In modern Ages not the strongest Swain
Could heave th' unwieldy Burthen from the Plain.
He poiz'd, and swung it round; then toss'd on high,
It flew with Force, and labour'd up the Sky;
Full on the Lycian's Helmet thund'ring down,
The pond'rous Ruin crush'd his batter'd Crown.   460
As skilful Divers, from some airy Steep,
Headlong descend, and shoot into the Deep,
So falls Epicles; then in Groans expires,
And murm'ring to the Shades the Soul retires.
  While to the Ramparts daring Glaucus drew,
From Teucer's Hand a winged Arrow flew;

The bearded Shaft the destin'd Passage found,
And on his naked Arm inflicts a Wound.
The Chief, who fear'd some Foe's insulting Boast
Might stop the Progress of his warlike Host,   470
Conceal'd the Wound, and leaping from his Height,
Retir'd reluctant from th' unfinish'd Fight.
Divine Sarpedon with Regret beheld
Disabl'd Glaucus slowly quit the Field;
His beating Breast with gen'rous Ardour glows,
He springs to Fight, and flies upon the Foes.
Alcmäon first was doom'd his Force to feel;
Deep in his Breast he plung'd the pointed Steel;
Then, from the yawning Wound with Fury tore
The Spear, pursu'd by gushing Streams of Gore;   480
Down sinks the Warrior with a thund'ring Sound,
His brazen Armour rings against the Ground.
  Swift to the Battlement the Victor flies,
Tugs with full force, and ev'ry Nerve applies;
It shakes; the pond'rous Stones disjointed yield;
The rowling Ruins smoak along the Field.
A mighty Breach appears; the Walls lie bare;
And, like a Deluge, rushes in the War.
At once bold Teucer draws the twanging Bow,
And Ajax sends his Javelin at the Foe;   490
Fix'd in his Belt the feather'd Weapon stood,
And thro' his Buckler drove the trembling Wood;
But Jove was present in the dire Debate,
To shield his Off-spring, and avert his Fate.
The Prince gave back, not meditating Flight
But urging Vengeance, and severer Fight;
Then rais'd with Hopes, and fir'd with Glory's Charms,
His fainting Squadrons to new Fury warms.
O where, ye Lycians! is the Strength you boast?
Your former Fame, and ancient Virtue lost!   500
The Breach lies open, but your Chief in vain
Attempts alone the guarded Pass to gain:
Unite, and soon that hostile Fleet shall fall;
The Force of pow'rful Union conquers all.

This just Rebuke inflam'd the Lycian Crew,
They join, they thicken, and th' Assault renew;
Unmov'd th' embody'd Greeks their Fury dare,
And fix'd support the Weight of all the War:
Nor could the Greeks repell the Lycian Pow'rs,
Nor the bold Lycians force the Grecian Tow'rs.   510
As on the Confines of adjoining Grounds,
Two stubborn Swains with Blows dispute their Bounds;
They tugg, they sweat; but neither gain, nor yield,
One Foot, one Inch, of the contended Field:
Thus obstinate to Death, they fight, they fall;
Nor these can keep, nor those can win the Wall.
Their manly Breasts are pierc'd with many a Wound,
Loud Strokes are heard, and ratling Arms resound,
The copious Slaughter covers all the Shore,
And the high Ramparts drop with human Gore.   520
    As when two Scales are charg'd with doubtful Loads,
From side to side the trembling Balance nods,
(While some laborious Matron, just and poor,
With nice Exactness weighs her woolly Store)
Till pois'd aloft, the resting Beam suspends
Each equal Weight; nor this, nor that, descends.
So stood the War, till Hector's matchless Might
With Fates prevailing, turn'd the Scale of Fight.
Fierce as a Whirlwind up the Walls he flies,
And fires his Host with loud repeated Cries.   530
Advance ye Trojans! lend your valiant Hands,
Hast to the Fleet, and toss the blazing Brands!
They hear, they run, and gath'ring at his Call,
Raise scaling Engines, and ascend the Wall:
Around the Works a Wood of glitt'ring Spears
Shoots up, and all the rising Host appears.
A pond'rous Stone bold Hector heav'd to throw,
Pointed above, and rough and gross below:
Not two strong Men th' enormous Weight could raise,
Such Men as live in these degen'rate Days.   540
Yet this, as easy as a Swain could bear
The snowy Fleece, he toss'd, and shook in Air:

For Jove upheld, and lighten'd of its Load
Th' unwieldy Rock, the Labour of a God.
Thus arm'd, before the folded Gates he came,
Of massy Substance and stupendous Frame;
With Iron Bars and Brazen Hinges strong,
On lofty Beams of solid Timber hung.
Then thund'ring thro' the Planks, with forceful Sway,
Drives the sharp Rock; the solid Beams give way,550
The Folds are shatter'd; from the crackling Door
Leap the resounding Bars, the flying Hinges roar.
Now rushing in the furious Chief appears,
Gloomy as Night! and shakes two shining Spears:
A dreadful Gleam from his bright Armour came,
And from his Eye-balls flash'd the living Flame;
He moves a God, resistless in his Course,
And seems a Match for more than mortal Force.
Then pouring after thro' the gaping Space,
A Tyde of Trojans flows, and fills the Place;560
The Greeks behold, they tremble, and they fly;
The Shore is heap'd with Death, and Tumult rends the Sky.

THE THIRTEENTH BOOK
OF THE ILIAD

THE ARGUMENT

*The fourth Battel continued, in which Neptune
assists the Greeks: The Acts of Idomeneus*

NEPTUNE, CONCERN'D for the Loss of the Grecians, upon seeing the
Fortification forc'd by Hector, (who had enter'd the Gate near the Station of the Ajaxes) assumes the Shape of Calchas, and inspires those
Heroes to oppose him: Then in the Form of one of the Generals, encourages the other Greeks who had retir'd to their Vessels. The Ajaxes
form their Troops in a close Phalanx, and put a stop to Hector and the
Trojans. Several Deeds of Valour are perform'd; Meriones losing his Spear
in the Encounter, repairs to seek another at the Tent of Idomeneus. This
occasions a Conversation between those two Warriors, who return together to the Battel. Idomeneus signalizes his Courage above the rest; he
kills Othryoneus, Asius, and Alcathous. Deiphobus and Æneas march
against him, and at length Idomeneus retires. Menelaus wounds Helenus,
and kills Pisander. The Trojans are repuls'd in the Left Wing; Hector
still keeps his Ground against the Ajaxes, till being gaul'd by the Locrian
Slingers and Archers, Polydamas advises to call a Council of War: Hector
approves his Advice, but goes first to rally the Trojans; upbraids Paris,
rejoins Polydamas, meets Ajax again, and renews the Attack.

The eight and twentieth Day still continues. The Scene is between the
Grecian Wall and the Sea-shore.

When now the Thund'rer, on the Sea-beat Coast,
Had fix'd great Hector and his conqu'ring Host;

He left them to the Fates, in bloody Fray,
To toil and struggle thro' the well-fought Day.
Then turn'd to Thracia from the Field of Fight
Those Eyes, that shed insufferable Light,
To where the Mysians prove their martial Force,
And hardy Thracians tame the savage Horse;
And where the far-fam'd Hippemolgian strays,
Renown'd for Justice and for length of Days,   10
Thrice happy Race! that, innocent of Blood,
From Milk, innoxious, seek their simple Food:[1]
Jove sees delighted, and avoids the Scene
Of guilty Troy, of Arms, and dying Men:
No Aid, he deems, to either Host is giv'n,
While his high Law suspends the Pow'rs of Heav'n.
   Meantime the Monarch of the watry Main
Observ'd the Thund'rer, nor observ'd in vain.
In Samothracia, on a Mountain's Brow,
Whose waving Woods o'erhung the Deeps below,   20
He sate; and round him cast his azure Eyes,
Where Ida's misty Tops confus'dly rise;
Below, fair Ilion's glitt'ring Spires were seen,
The crowded Ships, and sable Seas between.
There, from the crystal Chambers of the Main
Emerg'd, he sate; and mourn'd his Argives slain.
At Jove incens'd, with Grief and Fury stung,
Prone down the rocky Steep, he rush'd along;
Fierce as he past, the lofty Mountains nod,
The Forests shake! Earth trembled as he trod,   30
And felt the Footsteps of th' immortal God.
From Realm to Realm three ample Strides he took,
And, at the fourth, the distant Ægæ shook.
   Far in the Bay his shining Palace stands,
Eternal Frame! not rais'd by mortal Hands:
This having reach'd, his brass-hoof'd Steeds he reins,
Fleet as the Winds, and deck'd with golden Manes.

---

[1] This "beautiful and moral Imagination," (P) that the virtues of the Hippe-
molgians are the result of a milk diet, depends on a now rejected reading of the
text.

Refulgent Arms his mighty Limbs infold,
Immortal Arms, of Adamant and Gold.
He mounts the Car, the golden Scourge applies;   40
He sits superior, and the Chariot flies.
His whirling Wheels the glassy Surface sweep;
Th' enormous Monsters, rolling o'er the Deep,
Gambol around him, on the watry way;
And heavy Whales in aukward Measures play:
The Sea subsiding spreads a level Plain,
Exults, and owns the Monarch of the Main;
The parting Waves before his Coursers fly;
The wond'ring Waters leave his Axle dry.

   Deep in the liquid Regions lies a Cave,   50
Between where Tenedos the Surges lave,
And rocky Imbrus breaks the rolling Wave:
There the great Ruler of the azure Round
Stop'd his swift Chariot, and his Steeds unbound,
Fed with ambrosial Herbage from his Hand,
And link'd their Fetlocks with a golden Band,
Infrangible, immortal: There they stay:
The Father of the Floods pursues his way;
Where, like a Tempest, dark'ning Heav'n around,
Or fiery Deluge that devours the Ground,   60
Th' impatient Trojans, in a gloomy Throng,
Embattel'd roll'd, as Hector rush'd along.
To the loud Tumult, and the barb'rous Cry,
The Heav'ns re-echo, and the Shores reply;
They vow Destruction to the Grecian Name,
And, in their Hopes, the Fleets already flame.

   But Neptune, rising from the Seas profound,
The God whose Earthquakes rock the solid Ground,
Now wears a mortal Form; like Calchas seen,
Such his loud Voice, and such his manly Mien;   70
His Shouts incessant ev'ry Greek inspire,
But most th' Ajaces, adding Fire to Fire.

   'Tis yours, O Warriors, all our Hopes to raise;
Oh recollect your ancient Worth and Praise!
'Tis yours to save us, if you cease to fear;
Flight, more than shameful, is destructive here.

On other Works tho' Troy with Fury fall,
And pour her Armies o'er our batter'd Wall;
There, Greece has strength: but this, this Part o'erthrown,
Her Strength were vain; I dread for you alone.   80
Here Hector rages like the Force of Fire,
Vaunts of his Gods, and calls high Jove his Sire.
If yet some heav'nly Pow'r your Breast excite,
Breathe in your Hearts, and string your Arms to Fight,
Greece yet may live, her threatned Fleet maintain,
And Hector's Force, and Jove's own Aid, be vain.

Then with his Sceptre that the Deep controuls,
He touch'd the Chiefs, and steel'd their manly Souls;
Strength, not their own, the Touch divine imparts,
Prompts their light limbs, and swells their daring hearts.   90
Then, as a Falcon from the rocky Height,
Her Quarry seen, impetuous at the Sight,
Forth-springing instant, darts her self from high,
Shoots on the Wing, and skims along the Sky:
Such, and so swift, the Pow'r of Ocean flew;
The wide Horizon shut him from their View.

Th' inspiring God, Oïleus' active Son
Perceiv'd the first, and thus to Telamon.

Some God, my Friend, some God in human form
Fav'ring descends, and wills to stand the Storm.   100
Not Calchas this, the venerable Seer;
Short as he turn'd, I saw the Pow'r appear:
I mark'd his parting, and the Steps he trod,
His own bright evidence reveals a God.
Ev'n now some Energy divine I share,
And seem to walk on Wings, and tread in Air.

With equal Ardour (Telamon returns)
My Soul is kindled, and my Bosom burns;
New rising Spirits all the Man alarm,
Lift each impatient Limb, and brace my Arm;   110
This ready Arm, unthinking, shakes the Dart;
The Blood pours back, and fortifies my Heart:
Singly methinks, yon' tow'ring Chief I meet,
And stretch the dreadful Hector at my Feet.

Full of the God that urg'd their burning Breast
The Heroes thus their mutual Warmth express'd.
Neptune meanwhile the routed Greeks inspir'd;
Who breathless, pale, with length of Labours tir'd,
Pant in the Ships; while Troy to Conquest calls,
And swarms victorious o'er their yielding Walls: 120
Trembling before th' impending Storm they lie,
While Tears of Rage stand burning in their Eye.
Greece sunk they thought, and this their fatal Hour;
But breathe new Courage as they feel the Pow'r:
Teucer and Leitus first his Words excite;
Then stern Peneleus rises to the Fight;
Thoas, Deïpyrus, in Arms renown'd,
And Merion next, th' impulsive Fury found;
Last Nestor's Son the same bold Ardour takes,
While thus the God the martial Fire awakes.   130
　　Oh lasting Infamy, oh dire Disgrace
To Chiefs of vig'rous Youth, and manly Race!
I trusted in the Gods and you, to see
Brave Greece victorious, and her Navy free:
Ah no—the glorious Combate you disclaim,
And one black Day clouds all her former Fame.
Heav'ns! what a prodigy these Eyes survey,
Unseen, unthought, till this amazing Day!
Fly we at length from Troy's oft-conquer'd Bands,
And falls our Fleet by such inglorious Hands?   140
A Rout undisciplin'd, a straggling Train,
Not born to Glories of the dusty Plain;
Like frighted Fawns from Hill to Hill pursu'd,
A Prey to every Savage of the Wood;
Shall these, so late who trembled at your Name,
Invade your Camps, involve your Ships in Flame?
A Change so shameful, say what Cause has wrought?
The Soldiers Baseness, or the Gen'ral's Fault?
Fools! will ye perish for your Leader's Vice?
The Purchase Infamy, and Life the Price!   150
'Tis not your Cause, Achilles' injur'd Fame:
Another's is the Crime, but yours the Shame.

Grant that our Chief offend thro' Rage or Lust,
Must you be Cowards, if your King's unjust?
Prevent this Evil, and your Country save:
Small Thought retrieves the Spirits of the Brave.
Think, and subdue! on Dastards dead to Fame
I waste no Anger, for they feel no Shame:
But you, the Pride, the Flow'r of all our Host,
My Heart weeps blood to see your Glory lost!   160
Nor deem this Day, this Battel, all you lose;
A Day more black, a Fate more vile, ensues.
Let each reflect, who prizes Fame or Breath,
On endless Infamy, on instant Death.
For lo! the fated Time, th' appointed Shore;
Hark! the Gates burst, the brazen Barriers roar!
Impetuous Hector thunders at the Wall;
The Hour, the Spot, to conquer, or to fall.
  These Words the Grecians fainting Hearts inspire,
And list'ning Armies catch the godlike Fire.   170
Fix'd at his Post was each bold Ajax found,
With well-rang'd Squadrons strongly circled round:
So close their Order, so dispos'd their Fight,
As Pallas' self might view with fixt Delight;
Or had the God of War inclin'd his Eyes,
The God of War had own'd a just Surprize.
A chosen Phalanx, firm, resolv'd as Fate,
Descending Hector and his Battel wait;
An Iron Scene gleams dreadful o'er the Fields,
Armour in Armour lock'd, and Shields in Shields,   180
Spears lean on Spears, on Targets Targets throng,
Helms stuck to Helms, and Man drove Man along.
The floating Plumes unnumber'd wave above,
As when an Earthquake stirs the nodding Grove;
And levell'd at the Skies with pointing Rays,
Their brandish'd Lances at each Motion blaze.
  Thus breathing Death, in terrible Array,
The close-compacted Legions urg'd their way:
Fierce they drove on, impatient to destroy;
Troy charg'd the first, and Hector first of Troy.   190

As from some Mountain's craggy Forehead torn,
A Rock's round Fragment flies, with Fury born,
(Which from the stubborn Stone a Torrent rends)
Precipitate the pond'rous Mass descends:
From Steep to Steep the rolling Ruin bounds;
At ev'ry Shock the crackling Wood resounds;
Still gath'ring Force, it smoaks; and, urg'd amain,
Whirls, leaps, and thunders down, impetuous to the Plain:
There stops—So Hector: Their whole Force he prov'd,
Resistless when he rag'd, and when he stop'd, unmov'd.   200
    On him the War is bent, the Darts are shed,
And all their Faulchions wave around his Head.
Repuls'd he stands; nor from his Stand retires;
But with repeated Shouts his Army fires.
Trojans, be firm; this Arm shall make your way
Thro' yon' square Body, and that black Array:
Stand, and my Spear shall rout their scatt'ring Pow'r,
Strong as they seem, embattel'd like a Tow'r.
For He that Juno's heav'nly Bosom warms,
The first of Gods, this Day inspires our Arms.   210
    He said, and rouz'd the Soul in ev'ry Breast;
Urg'd with Desire of Fame, beyond the rest,
Forth march'd Deïphobus; but marching held
Before his wary Steps, his ample Shield.
Bold Merion aim'd a Stroke (nor aim'd it wide)
The glitt'ring Javelin pierc'd the tough Bull-hide:
But pierc'd not thro: Unfaithful to his Hand,
The Point broke short, and sparkled in the Sand.
The Trojan Warrior, touch'd with timely Fear,
On the rais'd Orb to distance bore the Spear: 220
The Greek retreating mourn'd his frustrate Blow,
And curs'd the treach'rous Lance that spar'd a Foe;
Then to the Ships with surly Speed he went,
To seek a surer Javelin in his Tent.
    Meanwhile with rising Rage the Battel glows,
The Tumult thickens, and the Clamour grows.
By Teucer's Arm the warlike Imbrius bleeds,
The Son of Mentor, rich in gen'rous Steeds.

E're yet to Troy the Sons of Greece were led,
In fair Pedæus' verdant Pastures bred,   230
The Youth had dwelt; remote from War's alarms,
And bless'd in bright Medesicaste's Arms:
(This Nymph, the Fruit of Priam's ravish'd Joy,
Ally'd the Warrior to the House of Troy.)
To Troy, when Glory call'd his Arms, he came,
And match'd the bravest of her Chiefs in Fame:
With Priam's Sons, a Guardian of the Throne,
He liv'd, belov'd and honour'd as his own.
Him Teucer pierc'd between the Throat and Ear;
He groans beneath the Telamonian Spear.   240
As from some far-seen Mountain's airy Crown,
Subdu'd by Steel, a tall Ash tumbles down,
And soils its verdant Tresses on the Ground:
So falls the Youth; his Arms the Fall resound.
Then Teucer rushing to despoil the dead,
From Hector's Hand a shining Javelin fled:
He saw, and shun'd the Death; the forceful Dart
Sung on, and pierc'd Amphimachus his Heart,
Cteatus' Son, of Neptune's boasted Line;
Vain was his Courage, and his Race divine!   250
Prostrate he falls; his clanging Arms resound,
And his broad Buckler thunders on the Ground.
To seize his beamy Helm the Victor flies,
And just had fastned on the dazling Prize,
When Ajax' manly Arm a Javelin flung;
Full on the Shield's round Boss the Weapon rung;
He felt the Shock, nor more was doom'd to feel,
Secure in Mail, and sheath'd in shining Steel.
Repuls'd he yields; the Victor Greeks obtain
The Spoils contested, and bear off the slain.   260
Between the Leaders of th' Athenian Line,
(Stichius the brave, Menestheus the divine,)
Deplor'd Amphimachus, sad Object! lies;
Imbrius remains the fierce Ajaces' Prize.
As two grim Lyons bear across the Lawn
Snatch'd from devouring Hounds, a slaughter'd Fawn,

In their fell Jaws high-lifted thro' the Wood,
And sprinkling all the Shrubs with dropping Blood;
So these the Chief: Great Ajax from the dead
Strips his bright Arms, Oïleus lops his Head: 270
Toss'd like a Ball, and whirl'd in Air away,
At Hector's Feet the goary Visage lay.

　　The God of Ocean, fir'd with stern Disdain,
And pierc'd with Sorrow for his Grandson[2] slain,
Inspires the Grecian Hearts, confirms their Hands,
And breathes Destruction to the Trojan Bands.
Swift as a Whirlwind rushing to the Fleet,
He finds the Lance-fam'd Idomen of Crete;
His pensive Brow the gen'rous Care exprest
With which a wounded Soldier touch'd his Breast,   280
Whom in the Chance of War a Javelin tore,
And his sad Comrades from the Battel bore;
Him to the Surgeons of the Camp he sent;
That Office paid, he issu'd from his Tent,
Fierce for the Fight: To him the God begun,
In Thoas' Voice, Andræmon's valiant Son,
Who rul'd where Calydon's white Rocks arise,
And Pleuron's chalky Cliffs emblaze the Skies.

　　Where's now th' imperious Vaunt, the daring Boast
Of Greece victorious, and proud Ilion lost?   290

　　To whom the King. On Greece no blame be thrown,
Arms are her Trade, and War is all her own.
Her hardy Heroes from the well-fought Plains
Nor Fear with-holds, nor shameful Sloth detains.
'Tis Heav'n, alas! and Jove's all-pow'rful Doom,
That far, far distant from our native Home
Wills us to fall, inglorious! Oh my Friend!
Once foremost in the Fight, still prone to lend
Or Arms, or Counsels; now perform thy best,
And what thou canst not singly, urge the rest.   300

　　Thus he; and thus the God, whose Force can make
The solid Globe's eternal Basis shake.
Ah! never may he see his native Land,
But feed the Vulturs on this hateful Strand,

2 Amphimachus

Who seeks ignobly in his Ships to stay,
Nor dares to combate on this signal Day!
For this, behold! in horrid Arms I shine,
And urge thy Soul to rival Acts with mine:
Together let us battel on the Plain;
Two, not the worst; nor ev'n this Succour vain.   310
Not vain the weakest, if their Force unite;
But ours, the bravest have confess'd in Fight.

This said, he rushes where the Combate burns;
Swift to his Tent the Cretan King returns.
From thence, two Javelins glitt'ring in his Hand,
And clad in Arms that lighten'd all the Strand,
Fierce on the Foe th' impetuous Hero drove;
Like Light'ning bursting from the Arm of Jove,
Which to pale Man the Wrath of Heav'n declares,
Or terrifies th' offending World with Wars: 320
In streamy Sparkles, kindling all the Skies,
From Pole to Pole the Trail of Glory flies.
Thus his bright Armour o'er the dazled Throng
Gleam'd dreadful, as the Monarch flash'd along.

Him, near his Tent, Meriones attends;
Whom thus he questions: Ever best of Friends!
O say, in ev'ry Art of Battel skill'd,
What holds thy Courage from so brave a Field?
On some important Message art thou bound,
Or bleeds my Friend by some unhappy Wound?   330
Inglorious here, my Soul abhors to stay,
And glows with Prospects of th' approaching Day.

O Prince! (Meriones replies) whose Care
Leads forth th' embattel'd Sons of Crete to War;
This speaks my Grief; this headless Lance I wield;
The rest lies rooted in a Trojan Shield.

To whom the Cretan: Enter, and receive
The wanted Weapons; those my Tent can give.
Spears I have store, (and Trojan Lances all)
That shed a Lustre round th' illumin'd Wall.   340
Tho' I, disdainful of the distant War,
Nor trust the Dart, or aim th' uncertain Spear,

Yet hand to hand I fight, and spoil the slain;
And thence these Trophies and these Arms I gain.
Enter, and see on heaps the Helmets roll'd,
And high-hung spears, and shields that flame with Gold.
   Nor vain (said Merion) are our martial Toils;
We too can boast of no ignoble Spoils.
But those my Ship contains, whence distant far,
I fight conspicuous in the Van of War.   350
What need I more? If any Greek there be
Who knows not Merion, I appeal to thee.
   To this, Idomeneus. The Fields of Fight
Have prov'd thy Valour and unconquer'd Might;
And were some Ambush for the Foes design'd,
Ev'n there, thy Courage would not lag behind.
In that sharp Service, singled from the rest,
The Fear of each, or Valour, stands confest.
No Force, no Firmness, the pale Coward shows;
He shifts his Place, his Colour comes and goes;   360
A dropping Sweat creeps cold on ev'ry Part;
Against his Bosom beats his quiv'ring Heart;
Terror and Death in his wild Eye-balls stare;
With chatt'ring Teeth he stands, and stiff'ning Hair,
And looks a bloodless Image of Despair!
Not so the Brave—still dauntless, still the same,
Unchang'd his Colour, and unmov'd his Frame;
Compos'd his Thought, determin'd is his Eye,
And fix'd his Soul, to conquer or to die:
If ought disturb the Tenour of his Breast,   370
'Tis but the Wish to strike before the rest.
   In such Assays, thy blameless Worth is known,
And ev'ry Art of dang'rous War thy own.
By chance of Fight whatever Wounds you bore,
Those Wounds were glorious all, and all before;
Such as may teach, 'twas still thy brave Delight
T' oppose thy Bosom where the foremost fight.
But why, like Infants, cold to Honour's Charms,
Stand we to talk, when Glory calls to Arms?
Go—from my conquer'd Spears, the choicest take,   380
And to their Owners send them nobly back.

Swift as the Word bold Merion snatch'd a Spear,
And breathing Slaughter, follow'd to the War.
So Mars Armipotent invades the Plain,
(The wide Destroyer of the Race of Man)
Terror, his best lov'd Son, attends his Course,
Arm'd with stern Boldness, and enormous Force;
The Pride of haughty Warriors to confound,
And lay the Strength of Tyrants on the Ground:
From Thrace[3] they fly, call'd to the dire Alarms   390
Of warring Phlegyans, and Ephyrian Arms;
Invok'd by both, relentless they dispose
To these, glad Conquest, murd'rous Rout to those.
So march'd the Leaders of the Cretan Train,
And their bright Arms shot Horror o'er the Plain.

Then first spake Merion: Shall we join the Right,
Or combate in the Centre of the Fight?
Or to the Left our wanted Succour lend?
Hazard and Fame all Parts alike attend.

Not in the Centre, (Idomen reply'd)   400
Our ablest Chieftains the main Battel guide;
Each godlike Ajax makes that Post his Care,
And gallant Teucer deals Destruction there:
Skill'd, or with Shafts to gall the distant Field,
Or bear close Battel on the sounding Shield.
These can the Rage of haughty Hector tame;
Safe in their Arms, the Navy fears no Flame;
Till Jove himself descends, his Bolts to shed,
And hurl the blazing Ruin at our Head.
Great must he be, of more than human Birth,   410
Nor feed like Mortals on the Fruits of Earth,
Him neither Rocks can crush, nor Steel can wound,
Whom Ajax fells not on th' ensanguin'd Ground.
In standing Fight he mates Achilles' Force,
Excell'd alone in Swiftness in the Course.
Then to the Left our ready Arms apply,
And live with Glory, or with Glory die.

He said; and Merion to th' appointed Place,
Fierce as the God of Battels, urg'd his Pace.

[3] Home of Mars, and of a people "who liv'd in Perpetual Wars" (P)

Soon as the Foe the shining Chiefs beheld   420
Rush like a fiery Torrent o'er the Field,
Their Force embody'd, in a Tyde they pour;
The rising Combate sounds along the Shore.
As warring Winds, in Sirius' sultry Reign,
From diff'rent Quarters sweep the sandy Plain;
On ev'ry side the dusty Whirlwinds rise,
And the dry Fields are lifted to the Skies:
Thus by Despair, Hope, Rage, together driv'n,
Met the black Hosts, and meeting, darken'd Heav'n.
All dreadful glar'd the Iron Face of War,   430
Bristled with upright Spears, that flash'd afar;
Dire was the Gleam, of Breastplates, Helms and Shields,
And polish'd Arms emblaz'd the flaming Fields:
Tremendous Scene, that gen'ral Horror gave,
But touch'd with Joy the Bosoms of the Brave.
   Saturn's great Sons in fierce Contention vy'd,
And Crowds of Heroes in their Anger dy'd.
The Sire of Earth and Heav'n, by Thetis won
To crown with Glory Peleus' godlike Son,
Will'd not Destruction to the Grecian Pow'rs,   440
But spar'd a while the destin'd Trojan Tow'rs:
While Neptune rising from his azure Main,
Warr'd on the King of Heav'n with stern Disdain,
And breath'd Revenge, and fir'd the Grecian Train.
Gods of one Source, of one ethereal Race,
Alike divine, and Heav'n their native Place;
But Jove the greater, First-born of the Skies,
And more than Men, or Gods, supremely wise.
For this, of Jove's superior Might afraid,
Neptune in human Form conceal'd his Aid.
These Pow'rs inclose the Greek and Trojan Train   450
In War and Discord's adamantine Chain;
Indissolubly strong, the fatal Tye
Is stretch'd on both, and Heaps on Heaps they dye.
   Dreadful in Arms, and grown in Combats grey,
The bold Idomeneus controuls the Day.
First by his Hand Othryoneus was slain,
Swell'd with false Hopes, with mad Ambition vain!

Call'd by the Voice of War to martial Fame,
From high Cabesus' distant Walls he came; 460
Cassandra's Love he sought with Boasts of Pow'r,
And promis'd Conquest was the proffer'd Dow'r.
The King consented, by his Vaunts abus'd;
The King consented, but the Fates refus'd.
Proud of himself, and of th' imagin'd Bride,
The Field he measur'd with a larger Stride.
Him, as he stalk'd, the Cretan Javelin found;
Vain was his Breastplate to repel the Wound:
His Dream of Glory lost, he plung'd to Hell;
The Plains resounded as the Boaster fell. 470
 The great Idomeneus bestrides the dead:
And thus (he cries) behold thy Promise sped!
Such is the Help thy Arms to Ilion bring,
And such the Contract of the Phrygian King!
Our Offers now, illustrious Prince! receive;
For such an Aid what will not Argos give?
To conquer Troy, with ours thy Forces join,
And count Atrides' fairest Daughter thine.
Meantime, on farther Methods to advise,
Come, follow to the Fleet thy new Allies; 480
There hear what Greece has on her Part to say.
He spoke, and dragg'd the goary Corse away.
 This Asius view'd, unable to contain,
Before his Chariot warring on the Plain;
(His valu'd Coursers, to his Squire consign'd,
Impatient panted on his Neck behind)
To Vengeance rising with a sudden Spring,
He hop'd the Conquest of the Cretan King.
The wary Cretan, as his Foe drew near,
Full on his Throat discharg'd the forceful Spear: 490
Beneath the Chin the Point was seen to glide,
And glitter'd, extant at the farther side.
As when the Mountain Oak, or Poplar tall,
Or Pine, fit Mast for some great Admiral,
Groans to the oft-heav'd Axe, with many a Wound,
Then spreads a length of Ruin o'er the Ground.

So sunk proud Asius in that deathful Day,
And stretch'd before his much-lov'd Coursers lay.
He grinds the Dust distain'd with streaming Gore,
And, fierce in Death, lies foaming on the Shore.   500
Depriv'd of Motion, stiff with stupid Fear,
Stands all aghast his trembling Charoteer,
Nor shuns the Foe, nor turns the Steeds away,
But falls transfix'd, an unresisting Prey:
Pierc'd by Antilochus, he pants beneath
The stately Car, and labours out his Breath.
Thus Asius' Steeds (their mighty Master gone)
Remain the Prize of Nestor's youthful Son.

Stabb'd at the Sight, Deiphobus drew nigh,
And made, with force, the vengeful Weapon fly: 510
The Cretan saw; and stooping, caus'd to glance
From his slope Shield, the disappointed Lance.
Beneath the spacious Targe (a blazing Round,
Thick with Bull-hides, with brazen Orbits bound,
On his rais'd Arm by two strong Braces stay'd)
He lay collected, in defensive Shade.
O'er his safe Head the Javelin idly sung,
And on the tincling Verge more faintly rung.
Ev'n then, the Spear the vig'rous Arm confest,
And pierc'd, obliquely, King Hypsenor's Breast: 520
Warm'd in his Liver, to the Ground it bore
The Chief, his People's Guardian now no more!

Not unattended (the proud Trojan cries)
Nor unreveng'd, lamented Asius lies:
For thee, tho' Hell's black Portals stand display'd,
This Mate shall joy thy melancholy Shade.

Heart-piercing Anguish, at this haughty Boast,
Touch'd ev'ry Greek, but Nestor's Son the most.
Griev'd as he was, his pious Arms attend
And his broad Buckler shields his slaughter'd Friend;   530
Till sad Mecistheus and Alastor bore
His honour'd Body to the Tented Shore.

Nor yet from Fight Idomeneus withdraws;
Resolv'd to perish in his Country's Cause,

Or find some Foe whom Heav'n and he shall doom
To wail his Fate in Death's eternal Gloom.
He sees Alcathous in the Front aspire:
Great Æsyetes was the Hero's Sire;
His Spouse Hippodamè, divinely fair,
Anchises' eldest Hope, and darling Care;   540
Who charm'd her Parent's and her Husband's Heart,
With Beauty, Sense, and ev'ry Work of Art:
He once, of Ilion's Youth, the loveliest Boy,
The fairest she, of all the Fair of Troy.
By Neptune now the hapless Hero dies,
Who covers with a Cloud those beauteous Eyes,
And fetters ev'ry Limb: yet bent to meet
His Fate, he stands; nor shuns the Lance of Crete.
Fixt as some Column, or deep-rooted Oak,
(While the Winds sleep) his Breast receiv'd the Stroke.   550
Before the pond'rous Stroke his Corselet yields,
Long us'd to ward the Death in fighting Fields:
The riven Armour sends a jarring Sound:
His lab'ring Heart, heaves, with so strong a bound,
The long Lance shakes, and vibrates in the Wound:
Fast-flowing from its Source, as prone he lay,
Life's purple Tyde, impetuous, gush'd away.
    Then Idomen, insulting o'er the slain;
Behold, Deiphobus! nor vaunt in vain.
See! on one Greek three Trojan Ghosts attend,   560
This, my third Victim, to the Shades I send.
Approaching now, thy boasted Might approve,
And try the Prowess of the Seed of Jove.
From Jove, enamour'd on a mortal Dame,
Great Minos, Guardian of his Country, came:
Deucalion, blameless Prince! was Minos' Heir;
His First-born I, the third from Jupiter:
O'er spacious Crete, and her bold Sons I reign,
And thence my Ships transport me thro' the Main;
Lord of a Host, o'er all my Host I shine,   570
A Scourge to thee, thy Father, and thy Line.
    The Trojan heard; uncertain, or to meet
Alone, with vent'rous Arms, the King of Crete;

Or seek auxiliar Force; at length decreed
To call some Hero to partake the Deed.
Forthwith Æneas rises to his Thought;
For him, in Troy's remotest Lines, he sought,
Where he, incens'd at partial Priam, stands,
And sees superior Posts in meaner Hands.
To him, ambitious of so great an Aid,   580
The bold Deïphobus approach'd, and said.
    Now, Trojan Prince, employ thy pious Arms,
If e'er thy Bosom felt fair Honour's Charms.
Alcathous dies, thy Brother and thy Friend!
Come, and the Warrior's lov'd Remains defend.
Beneath his Cares thy early Youth was train'd,
One Table fed you, and one Roof contain'd.
This Deed to fierce Idomeneus we owe;
Haste, and revenge it on th' insulting Foe.
    Æneas heard, and for a Space resign'd   590
To tender Pity all his manly Mind;
Then rising in his Rage, he burns to fight:
The Greek awaits him, with collected Might.
As the fell Boar on some rough Mountain's Head,
Arm'd with wild Terrors, and to Slaughter bred,
When the loud Rusticks rise, and shout from far,
Attends the Tumult, and expects the War;
O'er his bent Back the bristly Horrors rise,
Fires stream in Light'ning from his sanguin Eyes,
His foaming Tusks both Dogs and Men engage,   600
But most his Hunters rouze his mighty Rage.
So stood Idomeneus, his Javelin shook,
And met the Trojan with a low'ring Look.
Antilochus, Deipyrus were near,
The youthful Offspring of the God of War,
Merion, and Aphareus, in Field renown'd:
To these the Warrior sent his Voice around.
Fellows in Arms! your timely Aid unite;
Lo, great Æneas rushes to the Fight:
Sprung from a God, and more than Mortal bold;   610
He fresh in Youth, and I in Arms grown old.

Else should this Hand, this Hour, decide the Strife,
The great Dispute, of Glory, or of Life.
 He spoke, and all as with one Soul obey'd;
Their lifted Bucklers cast a dreadful Shade
Around the Chief. Æneas too demands
Th' assisting Forces of his native Bands:
Paris, Deïphobus, Agenor join;
(Co-aids and Captains of the Trojan Line.)
In order follow all th' embody'd Train; 620
Like Ida's Flocks proceeding o'er the Plain;
Before his fleecy Care, erect and bold,
Stalks the proud Ram, the Father of the Fold:
With Joy the Swain surveys them, as he leads
To the cool Fountains, thro' the well-known Meads.
So joys Æneas, as his native Band
Moves on in Rank, and stretches o'er the Land.
 Round dead Alcathous now the Battel rose;
On ev'ry side the steely Circle grows;
Now batter'd Breastplates and hack'd Helmets ring, 630
And o'er their Heads unheeded Javelins sing.
Above the rest, two tow'ring Chiefs appear,
There great Idomeneus, Æneas here.
Like Gods of War, dispensing Fate, they stood,
And burn'd to drench the Ground with mutual Blood.
The Trojan Weapon whizz'd along in Air;
The Cretan saw, and shun'd the brazen Spear:
Sent from an Arm so strong, the missive Wood
Stuck deep in Earth, and quiver'd where it stood.
But Oenomas receiv'd the Cretan's stroke, 640
The forceful Spear his hollow Corselet broke,
It ripp'd his Belly with a ghastly Wound,
And roll'd the smoaking Entrails to the Ground.
Stretch'd on the Plain, he sobs away his Breath,
And furious, grasps the bloody Dust in Death.
The Victor from his Breast the Weapon tears;
His Spoils he could not, for the Show'r of Spears.
Tho' now unfit an active War to wage,
Heavy with cumb'rous Arms, stiff with cold Age,

His listless Limbs unable for the Course;   650
In standing Fight he yet maintains his Force:
Till faint with Labour, and by Foes repell'd,
His tir'd, slow Steps, he drags from off the Field.
    Deiphobus beheld him as he past,
And, fir'd with Hate, a parting Javelin cast:
The Javelin err'd, but held its Course along,
And pierc'd Ascalaphus, the brave and young:
The Son of Mars fell gasping on the Ground,
And gnash'd the Dust all bloody with his Wound.
    Nor knew the furious Father of his Fall;   660
High-thron'd amidst the great Olympian Hall,
On golden Clouds th' immortal Synod sate;
Detain'd from bloody War by Jove and Fate.
    Now, where in Dust the breathless Hero lay,
For slain Ascalaphus commenc'd the Fray.
Deiphobus to seize his Helmet flies,
And from his Temples rends the glitt'ring Prize;
Valiant as Mars, Meriones drew near,
And on his loaded Arm discharg'd his Spear:
He drops the Weight, disabled with the Pain,   670
The hollow Helmet rings against the Plain.
Swift as a Vultur leaping on his Prey,
From his torn Arm the Grecian rent away
The reeking Javelin, and rejoin'd his Friends.
His wounded Brother good Polites tends;
Around his Waste his pious Arms he threw,
And from the Rage of Combate gently drew:
Him his swift Coursers, on his splendid Car
Rapt from the less'ning Thunder of the War;
To Troy they drove him, groaning from the Shore,   680
And sprinkling, as he past, the Sands with Gore.
    Meanwhile fresh slaughter bathes the sanguin ground,
Heaps fall on Heaps, and Heav'n and Earth resound.
Bold Aphareus by great Æneas bled;
As tow'rd the Chief he turn'd his daring Head,
He pierc'd his Throat; the bending Head deprest
Beneath his Helmet, nods upon his Breast;

His Shield revers'd o'er the fall'n Warror lies;
And everlasting Slumber seals his Eyes.
Antilochus, as Thoon turn'd him round,   690
Transpierc'd his Back with a dishonest Wound:
The hollow Vein that to the Neck extends
Along the Chine, his eager Javelin rends:
Supine he falls, and to his social Train
Spreads his imploring Arms, but spreads in vain.
Th' exulting Victor leaping where he lay,
From his broad Shoulders tore the Spoils away;
His Time observ'd; for clos'd by Foes around,
On all sides thick, the Peals of Arms resound.
His Shield emboss'd the ringing Storm sustains,   700
But he impervious and untouch'd remains.
(Great Neptune's Care preserv'd from hostile Rage
This Youth, the Joy of Nestor's glorious Age)
In Arms intrepid, with the first he fought,
Fac'd ev'ry Foe, and ev'ry Danger sought;
His winged Lance, resistless as the Wind,
Obeys each Motion of the Master's Mind,
Restless it flies, impatient to be free,
And meditates the distant Enemy.
The Son of Asius, Adamas, drew near,   710
And struck his Target with the brazen Spear,
Fierce in his Front: but Neptune wards the Blow,
And blunts the Javelin of th' eluded Foe.
In the broad Buckler half the Weapon stood;
Splinter'd on Earth flew half the broken Wood.
Disarm'd, he mingled in the Trojan Crew;
But Merion's Spear o'ertook him as he flew,
Deep in the Belly's Rim an Entrance found,
Where sharp the Pang, and mortal is the Wound.
Bending he fell, and doubled to the Ground   720
Lay panting. Thus an Oxe, in Fetters ty'd,
While Death's strong Pangs distend his lab'ring Side,
His Bulk enormous on the Field displays;
His heaving Heart beats thick, as ebbing Life decays.
The Spear, the Conqu'ror from his Body drew,
And Death's dim Shadows swam before his View.

Next brave Deipyrus in Dust was lay'd;
King Helenus wav'd high the Thracian Blade,
And smote his Temples, with an Arm so strong
The Helm fell off, and roll'd amid the Throng: 730
There, for some luckier Greek it rests a Prize,
For dark in Death the godlike Owner lies!
With raging Grief great Menelaus burns,
And fraught with Vengeance, to the Victor turns;
That shook the pond'rous Lance, in Act to throw,
And this[4] stood adverse with the bended Bow:
Full on his Breast the Trojan Arrow fell,
But harmless bounded from the plated Steel.
As on some ample Barn's well-harden'd Floor,
(The Winds collected at each open Door)   740
While the broad Fan with Force is whirl'd around,
Light leaps the golden grain, resulting from the ground:
So from the Steel that guards Atrides' Heart,
Repell'd to distance flies the bounding Dart.
Atrides, watchful of th' unwary Foe,
Pierc'd with his Lance the Hand that grasp'd the Bow,
And nail'd it to the Eugh: The wounded Hand
Trail'd the long Lance that mark'd with Blood the Sand.
But good Agenor gently from the Wound   750
The Spear sollicites, and the Bandage bound;
A Slings soft Wool, snatch'd from a Soldier's side,
At once the Tent and Ligature supply'd.
   Behold! Pisander, urg'd by Fate's Decree,
Springs thro' the Ranks to fall, and fall by thee,
Great Menelaus! to enhance thy Fame,
High-tow'ring in the Front, the Warrior came.
First the sharp Lance was by Atrides thrown;
The Lance far distant by the Winds was blown.
Nor pierc'd Pisander thro' Atrides' Shield;
Pisander's Spear fell shiver'd on the Field.   760
Not so discourag'd, to the Future blind,
Vain Dreams of Conquest swell his haughty Mind;
Dauntless he rushes where the Spartan Lord
Like Light'ning brandish'd his far-beaming Sword.

[4] Helenus

His[5] left Arm high oppos'd the shining Shield;
His right, beneath, the cover'd Pole-Axe held;
(An Olive's cloudy Grain the Handle made,
Distinct with Studs; and brazen was the Blade)
This on the Helm discharg'd a noble Blow;
The Plume dropp'd nodding to the Plain below,   770
Shorn from the Crest. Atrides wav'd his Steel:
Deep thro' his Front the weighty Faulchion fell.
The crashing Bones before its Force gave way;
In Dust and Blood the groaning Hero lay;
Forc'd from their ghastly Orbs, and spouting Gore,
The clotted Eye-balls tumble on the Shore.
The fierce Atrides spurn'd him as he bled,
Tore off his Arms, and loud-exulting said.
    Thus, Trojans, thus, at length be taught to fear;
O Race perfidious, who delight in War!   780
Already noble Deeds ye have perform'd,
A Princess rap'd transcends a Navy storm'd:
In such bold Feats your impious Might approve,
Without th' Assistance, or the Fear of Jove.
The violated Rites, the ravish'd Dame,
Our Heroes slaughter'd, and our Ships on flame,
Crimes heap'd on Crimes, shall bend your Glory down,
And whelm in Ruins yon' flagitious Town.
O thou, great Father! Lord of Earth and Skies,
Above the Thought of Man, supremely wise!   790
If from thy Hand the Fates of Mortals flow,
From whence this favour to an impious Foe?
A godless Crew, abandon'd and unjust,
Still breathing Rapine, Violence, and Lust!
The best of Things beyond their Measure, cloy;
Sleeps balmy Blessing, Love's endearing Joy;
The Feast, the Dance; whate'er Mankind desire,
Ev'n the sweet Charms of sacred Numbers tire.
But Troy for ever reaps a dire Delight
In Thirst of Slaughter, and in Lust of Fight.   800
    This said, he seiz'd (while yet the Carcass heav'd)
The bloody Armour, which his Train receiv'd:

[5] Of Pisander, who strikes Menelaus' helmet (769)

Then sudden mix'd among the warring Crew,
And the bold Son of Pylæmenes slew.
Harpalion had thro' Asia travell'd far,
Following his martial Father to the War;
Thro' filial Love he left his native Shore,
Never, ah never, to behold it more!
His unsuccessful Spear he chanc'd to fling
Against the Target of the Spartan King; 810
Thus of his Lance disarm'd, from Death he flies,
And turns around his apprehensive Eyes.
Him, thro' the Hip transpiercing as he fled,
The Shaft of Merion mingled with the dead.
Beneath the Bone the glancing Point descends,
And driving down, the swelling Bladder rends:
Sunk in his sad Companion's Arms he lay,
And in short Pantings sobb'd his Soul away;
(Like some vile Worm extended on the Ground)
While Life's red Torrent gush'd from out the Wound. 820
   Him on his Car the Paphlagonian Train
In slow Procession bore from off the Plain.
The pensive Father, Father now no more!
Attends the mournful Pomp along the Shore,
And unavailing Tears profusely shed,
And unreveng'd, deplor'd his Offspring dead.
   Paris from far the moving Sight beheld,
With Pity soften'd, and with Fury swell'd:
His honour'd Host, a Youth of matchless Grace,
And lov'd of all the Paphlagonian Race! 830
With his full Strength he bent his angry Bow,
And wing'd the feather'd Vengeance at the Foe.
A Chief there was, the brave Euchenor nam'd,
For Riches much, and more for Virtue fam'd,
Who held his Seat in Corinth's stately Town;
Polydus' Son, a Seer of old Renown.
Oft' had the Father told his early Doom,
By Arms abroad, or slow Disease at home:
He climb'd his Vessel, prodigal of Breath,
And chose the certain, glorious Path to Death. 840

Beneath his Ear the pointed Arrow went;
The Soul came issuing at the narrow Vent:
His Limbs, unnerv'd, drop useless on the Ground,
And everlasting Darkness shades him round.

Nor knew great Hector how his Legions yield,
(Wrapt in the Cloud and Tumult of the Field)
Wide on the Left the Force of Greece commands,
And Conquest hovers o'er th' Achaian Bands:
With such a Tyde superior Virtue sway'd,
And he[6] that shakes the solid Earth, gave Aid.   850
But in the Centre Hector fix'd remain'd,
Where first the Gates were forc'd, and Bulwarks gain'd;
There, on the Margin of the hoary Deep,
(Their Naval Station where th' Ajaces keep,
And where low Walls confine the beating Tydes
Whose humble Barrier scarce the Foes divides,
Where late in Fight, both Foot and Horse engag'd,
And all the Thunder of the Battel rag'd)
There join'd, the whole Bœotian Strength remains,
The proud Ionians with their sweeping Trains,   860
Locrians and Pthians, and th' Epæan Force;
But join'd, repel not Hector's fiery Course.
The Flow'r of Athens, Stichius, Phidas led,
Bias, and great Menestheus at their Head.
Meges the strong th' Epeian Bands controul'd,
And Dracius prudent, and Amphion bold;
The Pthians Medon, fam'd for martial Might,
And brave Podarces, active in the Fight.
This[7] drew from Phylacus his noble Line;
Iphyclus' Son: and that (Oileus) thine: 870
(Young Ajax Brother, by a stol'n Embrace;
He dwelt far distant from his native Place,
By his fierce Stepdame from his Father's Reign
Expell'd and exil'd, for her Brother slain.)
These rule the Pthians, and their Arms employ
Mixt with Bœotians, on the Shores of Troy.

[6] Neptune
[7] This (869) refers to Podarces, son of Iphyclus, from the city of Phylaca (not Phylacus). That (870) refers to Medon, bastard son of Oïleus.

Now side by side, with like unweary'd Care,
Each Ajax labour'd thro' the Field of War.
So when two lordly Bulls, with equal Toil,
Force the bright Plowshare thro' the fallow Soil,   880
Join'd to one Yoke, the stubborn Earth they tear,
And trace large Furrows with the shining Share;
O'er their huge Limbs the Foam descends in Snow,
And Streams of Sweat down their sow'r Foreheads flow.
A Train of Heroes follow'd thro' the Field,
Who bore by turns great Ajax' sev'nfold Shield;
Whene'er he breath'd, remissive of his Might,
Tir'd with th' incessant Slaughters of the Fight.
His brave Associate had no following Band,
His Troops unpractis'd in the Fights of Stand: 890
For not the Spear the Locrian Squadrons wield,
Nor bear the Helm, nor lift the moony Shield;
But skill'd from far the flying Shaft to wing,
Or whirl the sounding Pebble from the Sling,
Dext'rous with these they aim a certain Wound,
Or fell the distant Warrior to the Ground.
Thus in the Van, the Telamonian Train
Throng'd in bright Arms, a pressing Fight maintain;
Far in the Rear the Locrian Archers lie,
Thick Stones and Arrows intercept the Sky,   900
The mingled Tempest on the Foes they pour;
Troy's scatt'ring Orders open to the Show'r.
    Now had the Greeks eternal Fame acquir'd,
And the gall'd Ilians to their Walls retir'd;
But sage Polydamas, discreetly brave,
Address'd great Hector, and this Counsel gave.
    Tho' great in all, thou seem'st averse to lend
Impartial Audience to a faithful Friend:
To Gods and Men thy matchless Worth is known,
And ev'ry Art of glorious War thy own;   910
But in cool Thought and Counsel to excel,
How widely differs this from warring well?
Content with what the bounteous Gods have giv'n,
Seek not alone t'engross the Gifts of Heav'n.

To some the Pow'rs of bloody War belong,
To some, sweet Music, and the Charm of Song;
To few, and wond'rous few, has Jove assign'd
A wise, extensive, all-consid'ring Mind;
Their Guardians these, the Nations round confess,
And Towns and Empires for their Safety bless.   920
If Heav'n have lodg'd this Virtue in my Breast,
Attend, O Hector, what I judge the best.
See, as thou mov'st, on Dangers Dangers spread,
And Wars whole Fury burns around thy Head.
Behold! distress'd within yon' hostile Wall,
How many Trojans yield, disperse, or fall?
What Troops, out-number'd, scarce the War maintain?
And what brave Heroes at the Ships lie slain?
Here cease thy Fury; and the Chiefs and Kings
Convok'd to Council, weigh the Sum of things.   930
Whether (the Gods succeeding our Desires)
To yon' tall Ships to bear the Trojan Fires;
Or quit the Fleet, and pass unhurt away,
Contented with the Conquest of the Day.
I fear, I fear, lest Greece (not yet undone)
Pay the large Debt of last revolving Sun;
Achilles, great Achilles, yet remains
On yonder Decks, and yet o'erlooks the Plains!
    The Counsel pleas'd; and Hector, with a Bound,
Leap'd from his Chariot on the trembling Ground;   940
Swift as he leap'd, his clanging Arms resound.
To guard this Post (he cry'd) thy Art employ,
And here detain the scatter'd Youth of Troy:
Where yonder Heroes faint, I bend my way,
And hasten back to end the doubtful Day.
    This said; the tow'ring Chief, prepar'd to go,
Shakes his white Plumes that to the Breezes flow,
And seems a moving Mountain topt with Snow.
Thro' all his Host, inspiring Force, he flies,
And bids anew the martial Thunder rise.   950
To Panthus' Son, at Hector's high Command,
Haste the bold Leaders of the Trojan Band:

But round the Battlements, and round the Plain,
For many a Chief he look'd, but look'd in vain;
Deiphobus, nor Helenus the Seer,
Nor Asius' Son, nor Asius' self appear.
For these were pierc'd with many a ghastly Wound,
Some cold in Death, some groaning on the Ground,
Some low in Dust (a mournful Object) lay,
High on the Wall some breath'd their Souls away.   960
 Far on the Left amid the Throng he found
(Cheering the Troops, and dealing Deaths around)
The graceful Paris; whom, with Fury mov'd,
Opprobrious, thus, th' impatient Chief reprov'd.
 Ill-fated Paris! Slave to Womankind,
As smooth of Face as fraudulent of Mind!
Where is Deiphobus, where Asius gone?
The godlike Father, and th' intrepid Son?
The Force of Helenus, dispensing Fate,
And great Othryoneus, so fear'd of late?   970
Black Fate hangs o'er thee from th' avenging Gods,
Imperial Troy from her Foundations nods;
Whelm'd in thy Country's Ruins shalt thou fall,
And one devouring Vengeance swallow all.
 When Paris thus: My Brother and my Friend,
Thy warm Impatience makes thy Tongue offend.
In other Battels I deserv'd thy Blame,
Tho' then not deedless, nor unknown to Fame:
But since yon' Rampart by thy Arms lay low,
I scatter'd Slaughter from my fatal Bow.   980
The Chiefs you seek on yonder Shore lie slain;
Of all those Heroes, two alone remain;
Deiphobus, and Helenus the Seer:
Each now disabled by a hostile Spear.
Go then, successful, where thy Soul inspires;
This Heart and Hand shall second all thy Fires:
What with this Arm I can, prepare to know,
Till Death for Death be paid, and Blow for Blow.
But 'tis not ours, with Forces not our own
To combate; Strength is of the Gods alone.   990

These Words the Hero's angry Mind asswage:
Then fierce they mingle where the thickest rage.
Around Polydamas, distain'd with Blood,
Cebrion, Phalces, stern Orthæus stood,
Palmus, with Polypætes the divine,
And two bold Brothers of Hippotion's Line:
(Who reach'd fair Ilion, from Ascania far,
The former Day; the next, engag'd in War.)
As when from gloomy Clouds a Whirlwind springs,
That bears Jove's Thunder on its dreadful Wings,   1000
Wide o'er the blasted Fields the Tempest sweeps,
Then, gather'd, settles on the hoary Deeps;
Th' afflicted Deeps, tumultuous, mix and roar;
The Waves behind impel the Waves before,
Wide-rolling, foaming high, and tumbling to the shore.
Thus Rank on Rank the thick Battalions throng,
Chief urg'd on Chief, and Man drove Man along:
Far o'er the Plains, in dreadful Order bright,
The brazen Arms reflect a beamy Light.
Full in the blazing Van great Hector shin'd,   1010
Like Mars commission'd to confound Mankind.
Before him flaming, his enormous Shield
Like the broad Sun, illumin'd all the Field:
His nodding Helm emits a streamy Ray;
His piercing Eyes thro' all the Battel stray,
And while beneath his Targe he flash'd along,
Shot Terrors round, that wither'd ev'n the Strong.
 Thus stalk'd he, dreadful; Death was in his Look;
Whole Nations fear'd: but not an Argive shook.
The tow'ring Ajax, with an ample Stride,   1020
Advanc'd the first; and thus the Chief defy'd.
 Hector! come on, thy empty Threats forbear:
'Tis not thy Arm, 'tis thund'ring Jove we fear:
The Skill of War to us not idly giv'n,
Lo! Greece is humbled not by Troy, but Heav'n.
Vain are the Hopes that haughty Mind imparts,
To force our Fleet: The Greeks have hands, and hearts.
Long e'er in Flames our lofty Navy fall,
Your boasted City and your god-built Wall

Shall sink beneath us, smoaking on the Ground;   1030
And spread a long, unmeasur'd Ruin round.
The time shall come, when chas'd along the Plain,
Ev'n thou shalt call on Jove, and call in vain;
Ev'n thou shalt wish, to aid thy desp'rate Course,
The Wings of Falcons for thy flying Horse;
Shalt run, forgetful of a Warrior's Fame,
While Clouds of friendly Dust conceal thy Shame.
    As thus he spoke, behold, in open View,
On sounding Wings a dexter Eagle flew.
To Jove's glad Omen all the Grecians rise,   1040
And hail, with Shouts, his Progress thro' the Skies:
Far-echoing Clamours bound from side to side;
They ceas'd; and thus the Chief of Troy reply'd.
    From whence this Menace, this insulting Strain,
Enormous Boaster! doom'd to vaunt in vain.
So may the Gods on Hector Life bestow,
(Not that short Life which Mortals lead below,
But such as those of Jove's high Lineage born,
The blue-ey'd Maid, or he that gilds the Morn.)
As this decisive Day shall end the Fame   1050
Of Greece, and Argos be no more a Name.
And thou, Imperious! if thy Madness wait
The Lance of Hector, thou shalt meet thy Fate:
That Giant-Corse, extended on the Shore,
Shall largely feast the Fowls with Fat and Gore.
    He said, and like a Lion stalk'd along:
With Shouts incessant Earth and Ocean rung,
Sent from his follo'wing Host: The Grecian Train
With answ'ring Thunders fill'd the echoing Plain;
A Shout, that tore Heav'ns Concave, and above   1060
Shook the fix'd Splendors the Throne of Jove.

ꝛꝛꝛꝛ

THE FOURTEENTH BOOK
OF THE ILIAD

THE ARGUMENT

Juno deceives Jupiter by the Girdle of Venus

NESTOR SITTING AT THE TABLE with Machaon, is alarm'd with the encreasing Clamour of the War, and hastens to Agamemnon: On his way
he meets that Prince with Diomed and Ulysses, whom he informs of the
Extremity of the Danger. Agamemnon proposes to make their Escape by
Night, which Ulysses withstands; to which Diomed adds his Advice, that,
wounded as they were, they should go forth and encourage the Army
with their Presence; which Advice is pursued. Juno seeing the Partiality
of Jupiter to the Trojans, forms a Design to over-reach him; she sets off
her Charms with the utmost Care, and (the more surely to enchant him)
obtains the Magick Girdle of Venus. She then applies herself to the God
of Sleep, and with some Difficulty, persuades him to seal the Eyes of
Jupiter; this done she goes to Mount Ida, where the God, at first sight,
is ravish'd with her Beauty, sinks in her Embraces, and is laid asleep.
Neptune takes advantage of his Slumber, and succours the Greeks:
Hector is struck to the Ground with a prodigious Stone by Ajax, and
carry'd off from the Battel: Several Actions succeed: till the Trojans
much distress'd, are obliged to give way: The lesser Ajax signalizes himself
in a particular manner.

But nor the genial Feast, nor flowing Bowl,
Could charm the Cares of Nestor's watchful Soul;
His startled Ears th' encreasing Cries attend;
Then thus, impatient, to his wounded Friend.

327

What new Alarm, divine Machaon say,
What mixt Events attend this mighty Day?
Hark! how the Shouts divide, and how they meet,
And now come full, and thicken to the Fleet!
Here, with the cordial Draught, dispel thy Care,
Let Hecamede the strength'ning Bath prepare,   10
Refresh thy Wound, and cleanse the clotted Gore;
While I th' Adventures of the Day explore.
    He said: and seizing Thrasimedes' Shield,
(His valiant Offspring) hasten'd to the Field;
(That Day, the Son his Father's Buckler bore)
Then snatch'd a Lance, and issu'd from the Door.
Soon as the Prospect open'd to his View,
His wounded Eyes the Scene of Sorrow knew;
Dire Disarray! the Tumult of the Fight,
The Wall in Ruins, and the Greeks in Flight.   20
As when old Ocean's silent Surface sleeps,
The Waves just heaving on the purple Deeps;
While yet th' expected Tempest hangs on high,
Weighs down the Cloud, and blackens in the Sky,
The Mass of Waters will no Wind obey;
Jove sends one Gust, and bids them roll away.
While wav'ring Counsels thus his Mind engage,
Fluctuates, in doubtful Thought, the Pylian Sage;
To join the Host, or to the Gen'ral haste,
Debating long, he fixes on the last: 30
Yet, as he moves, the Fight his Bosom warms;
The Field rings dreadful with the Clang of Arms;
The gleaming Faulchions flash, the Javelins fly;
Blows echo Blows, and all, or kill, or die.
    Him, in his March, the wounded Princes meet,
By tardy Steps ascending from the Fleet.
The King of Men, Ulysses the divine,
And who to Tydeus owes his noble Line.
(Their Ships at distance from the Battel stand,
In Lines advanc'd along the shelving Strand;   40
Whose Bay, the Fleet unable to contain
At length, beside the Margin of the Main,

Rank above Rank, the crowded Ships they moor;
Who landed first lay highest on the Shore.)
Supported on their Spears, they took their way,
Unfit to fight, but anxious for the Day.
Nestor's Approach alarm'd each Grecian Breast,
Whom thus the Gen'ral of the Host addrest.

O Grace and Glory of th' Achaian Name!
What drives thee, Nestor, from the Field of Fame?   50
Shall then proud Hector see his Boast fulfill'd,
Our Fleets in Ashes, and our Heroes kill'd?
Such was his Threat, ah now too soon made good,
On many a Grecian Bosom writ in Blood.
Is ev'ry Heart inflam'd with equal Rage
Against your King, nor will one Chief engage?
And have I liv'd to see with mournful Eyes
In ev'ry Greek a new Achilles rise?

Gerenian Nestor then. So Fate has will'd;
And all-confirming Time has Fate fulfill'd.   60
Not he that thunders from th' aerial Bow'r,
Not Jove himself, upon the Past has pow'r.
The Wall, our late inviolable Bound,
And best Defence, lies smoaking on the Ground:
Ev'n to the Ships their conqu'ring Arms extend,
And Groans of slaughter'd Greeks to Heav'n ascend.
On speedy Measures then employ your Thought;
In such Distress if Counsel profit ought;
Arms cannot much: Tho' Mars our Souls incite,
These gaping Wounds withhold us from the Fight.   70

To him the Monarch. That our Army bends,
That Troy triumphant our high Fleet ascends,
And that the Rampart, late our surest Trust,
And best Defence, lies smoaking in the Dust;
All this from Jove's afflictive Hand we bear:
Who, far from Argos, wills our Ruin here.
Past are the Days when happier Greece was blest,
And all his Favour, all his Aid confest;
Now Heav'n averse, our Hands from Battel ties,
And lifts the Trojan Glory to the Skies.   80

Cease we at length to waste our Blood in vain,
And launch what Ships lie nearest to the Main;
Leave these at Anchor till the coming Night:
Then if impetuous Troy forbear the Fight,
Bring all to Sea, and hoist each Sail for flight.
Better from Evils, well foreseen, to run,
Than perish in the Danger we may shun.
  Thus he. The sage Ulysses thus replies,
While Anger flash'd from his disdainful Eyes.
What shameful Words, (unkingly as thou art)   90
Fall from that trembling Tongue, and tim'rous Heart?
Oh were thy Sway the Curse of meaner Pow'rs,
And thou the Shame of any Host but ours!
A Host, by Jove endu'd with martial Might,
And taught to conquer, or to fall in Fight:
Advent'rous Combats and bold Wars to wage,
Employ'd our Youth, and yet employs our Age.
And wilt thou thus desert the Trojan Plain?
And have whole Streams of Blood been spilt in vain?
In such base Sentence if thou couch thy Fear,   100
Speak it in Whispers, lest a Greek should hear.
Lives there a Man so dead to Fame, who dares
To think such Meanness, or the Thought declares?
And comes it ev'n from him, whose sov'reign Sway
The banded Legions of all Greece obey?
Is this a Gen'ral's Voice, that calls to flight,
While War hangs doubtful, while his Soldiers fight?
What more could Troy? What yet their Fate denies
Thou giv'st the Foe: all Greece becomes their Prize.
No more the Troops, our hoisted Sails in view,   110
Themselves abandon'd, shall the Fight pursue,
Thy Ships first flying with Despair shall see,
And owe Destruction to a Prince like thee.
  Thy just Reproofs (Atrides calm replies)
Like Arrows pierce me, for thy words are wise.
Unwilling as I am to lose the Host,
I force not Greece to quit this hateful Coast.
Glad I submit, whoe'er, or young or old,
Ought, more conducive to our Weal, unfold.

Tydides cut him short, and thus began.   120
Such Counsel if you seek, behold the Man
Who boldly gives it, and what he shall say,
Young tho' he be, disdain not to obey:
A Youth, who from the mighty Tydeus springs,
May speak to Councils and assembled Kings.
Hear then in me the great Oenides' Son,
Whose honour'd Dust (his Race of Glory run)
Lies whelm'd in Ruins of the Theban Wall,
Brave in his Life, and glorious in his Fall.
With three bold Sons was gen'rous Prothous blest,   130
Who Pleuron's Walls and Calydon possest;
Melas and Agrius, but (who surpast
The rest in Courage) Oeneus was the last.
From him, my Sire: from Calydon expell'd,
He fled to Argos, and in Exile dwell'd;
The Monarch's Daughter there (so Jove ordain'd)
He won, and flourish'd where Adrastus reign'd:
There rich in Fortune's Gifts, his Acres till'd,
Beheld his Vines their liquid Harvest yield,
And num'rous Flocks, that whiten'd all the Field.   140
Such Tydeus was, the foremost once in Fame!
Nor lives in Greece a Stranger to his Name.
Then, what for common Good my Thoughts inspire,
Attend, and in the Son, respect the Sire.
Tho' sore of Battel, tho' with Wounds opprest,
Let each go forth, and animate the rest,
Advance the Glory which he cannot share,
Tho' not Partaker, Witness of the War.
But lest new Wounds on Wounds o'erpower us quite,
Beyond the missile Javelin's sounding Flight,   150
Safe let us stand; and from the Tumult far,
Inspire the Ranks, and rule the distant War.
    He added not: The list'ning Kings obey,
Slow moving on; Atrides leads the way.
The God of Ocean (to inflame their Rage)
Appears a Hero furrow'd o'er with Age;
Prest in his own, the Gen'ral's Hand he took,
And thus the venerable Warrior spoke.

Atrides, lo! with what disdainful Eye
Achilles sees his Country's Forces fly: 160
Blind impious Man! whose Anger is his Guide,
Who glories in inutterable Pride!
So may he perish, so may Jove disclaim
The Wretch relentless, and o'erwhelm with Shame!
But Heav'n forsakes not thee: O'er yonder Sands
Soon shalt thou view the scatter'd Trojan Bands
Fly diverse; while proud Kings, and Chiefs renown'd
Driv'n Heaps on Heaps, with Clouds involv'd around
Of rolling Dust, their winged Wheels employ,
To hide their ignominious Heads in Troy.   170
    He spoke, then rush'd amid the warring Crew;
And sent his Voice before him as he flew,
Loud, as the Shout encountring Armies yield,
When twice ten thousand shake the lab'ring Field;
Such was the Voice, and such the thund'ring Sound
Of him, whose Trident rends the solid Ground.
Each Argive Bosom beats to meet the Fight,
And grizly War appears a pleasing Sight.
    Meantime Saturnia from Olympus' Brow,
High-thron'd in Gold, beheld the Fields below;   180
With Joy the glorious Conflict she survey'd,
Where her great Brother gave the Grecians Aid.
But plac'd aloft, on Ida's shady Height
She sees her Jove, and trembles at the Sight.
Jove to deceive, what Methods shall she try,
What Arts, to blind his all-beholding Eye?
At length she trusts her Pow'r; resolv'd to prove
The old, yet still successful, Cheat of Love;
Against his Wisdom to oppose her Charms,
And lull the Lord of Thunders in her Arms.   190
    Swift to her bright Apartment she repairs,
Sacred to Dress, and Beauty's pleasing Cares:
With Skill divine had Vulcan form'd the Bow'r,
Safe from Access of each intruding Pow'r.
Touch'd with her secret Key, the Doors unfold;
Self-clos'd behind her shut the Valves of Gold.

Here first she bathes; and round her Body pours
Soft Oils of Fragrance, and ambrosial Show'rs:
The Winds perfum'd, the balmy Gale convey
Thro' Heav'n, thro' Earth, and all th' aerial Way;   200
Spirit divine! whose Exhalation greets
The Sense of Gods with more than mortal Sweets.
Thus while she breath'd of Heav'n, with decent Pride
Her artful Hands the radiant Tresses ty'd;
Part on her Head in shining Ringlets roll'd,
Part o'er her Shoulders wav'd like melted Gold.
Around her next a heav'nly Mantle flow'd,
That rich with Pallas' labour'd Colours glow'd;
Large Clasps of Gold the Foldings gather'd round,
A golden Zone her swelling Bosom bound.   210
Far-beaming Pendants tremble in her Ear,
Each Gemm illumin'd with a triple Star.
Then o'er her Head she casts a Veil more white
Than new fal'n Snow, and dazling as the Light.
Last her fair Feet celestial Sandals grace.
Thus issuing radiant, with majestic Pace,
Forth from the Dome th' Imperial Goddess moves,
And calls the Mother of the Smiles and Loves.
    How long (to Venus thus apart she cry'd)
Shall human Strifes celestial Minds divide?   220
Ah yet, will Venus aid Saturnia's Joy,
And set aside the Cause of Greece and Troy?
    Let Heav'n's dread Empress (Cytheræa said)
Speak her Request, and deem her Will obey'd.
Then grant me (said the Queen) those conqu'ring Charms,
That Pow'r, which Mortals and Immortals warms,
That Love, which melts Mankind in fierce Desires,
And burns the Sons of Heav'n with sacred Fires!
    For lo! I haste to those remote Abodes,
Where the great Parents (sacred Source of Gods!)   230
Ocean and Tethys their old Empire keep,
On the last Limits of the Land and Deep.
In their kind Arms my tender Years were past;
What-time old Saturn, from Olympus cast,

Of upper Heav'n to Jove resign'd the Reign,
Whelm'd under the huge Mass of Earth and Main.
For Strife, I hear, has made the Union cease,
Which held so long that ancient Pair in Peace.
What Honour, and what Love shall I obtain,
If I compose those Fatal Feuds again?   240
Once more their Minds in mutual Ties engage,
And what my Youth has ow'd, repay their Age.

  She said. With Awe divine the Queen of Love
Obey'd the Sister and the Wife of Jove:
And from her fragrant Breast the Zone unbrac'd,
With various Skill and high Embroid'ry grac'd.
In this was ev'ry Art, and ev'ry Charm,
To win the wisest, and the coldest warm:
Fond Love, the gentle Vow, the gay Desire,
The kind Deceit, the still-reviving Fire,   250
Persuasive Speech, and more persuasive Sighs,
Silence that spoke, and Eloquence of Eyes.
This on her Hand the Cyprian Goddess lay'd;
Take this, and with it all thy Wish, she said:
With Smiles she took the Charm; and smiling prest
The pow'rful Cestus to her snowy Breast.

  Then Venus to the Courts of Jove withdrew;
Whilst from Olympus pleas'd Saturnia flew.
O'er high Pieria thence her Course she bore,
O'er fair Emathia's ever pleasing Shore,   260
O'er Hæmus' Hills with Snows eternal crown'd;
Nor once her flying Foot approach'd the Ground.
Then taking wing from Athos' lofty Steep,
She speeds to Lemnos o'er the rowling Deep,
And seeks the Cave of Death's half-brother, Sleep.

  Sweet pleasing Sleep! (Saturnia thus began)
Who spread'st thy Empire o'er each God and Man;
If e'er obsequious to thy Juno's Will,
O Pow'r of Slumbers! hear, and favour still.
Shed thy soft Dews on Jove's immortal Eyes,   270
While sunk in Love's entrancing Joys he lies.
A splendid Footstool, and a Throne, that shine
With Gold unfading, Somnus, shall be thine;

The Work of Vulcan; to indulge thy Ease,
When Wine and Feasts thy golden Humours please.
   Imperial Dame (the balmy Pow'r replies)
Great Saturn's Heir, and Empress of the Skies!
O'er other Gods I spread my easy Chain;
The Sire of all, old Ocean, owns my Reign,
And his hush'd Waves lie silent on the Main.   280
But how, unbidden, shall I dare to steep
Jove's awful Temples in the Dew of Sleep?
Long since too vent'rous, at thy bold Command,
On those eternal Lids I laid my Hand;
What-time, deserting Ilion's wasted Plain,
His conqu'ring Son, Alcides, plow'd the Main:
When lo! the Deeps arise, the Tempests roar,
And drive the Hero to the Coan Shore:
Great Jove awaking, shook the blest Abodes,
With rising Wrath, and tumbled Gods on Gods;   290
Me chief he sought, and from the Realms on high
Had hurl'd indignant to the nether Sky,
But gentle Night, to whom I fled for Aid,
(The Friend of Earth and Heav'n) her Wings display'd;
Impow'r'd the Wrath of Gods and Men to tame,
Ev'n Jove rever'd the Venerable Dame.
   Vain are thy Fears (the Queen of Heav'n replies,
And speaking rolls her large, majestic Eyes)
Think'st thou that Troy has Jove's high Favour won,
Like great Alcides, his all-conqu'ring Son?   300
Hear, and obey the Mistress of the Skies,
Nor for the Deed expect a vulgar Prize;
For know, thy lov'd one shall be ever thine,
The youngest Grace, Pasithëa the divine.
   Swear then (he said) by those tremendous Floods
That roar thro' Hell, and bind th' invoking Gods:
Let the great Parent Earth one Hand sustain,
And stretch the other o'er the sacred Main.
Call the black Gods that round Saturnus dwell,
To hear, and witness from the Depths of Hell;   310
That, she, my lov'd one, shall be ever mine,
The youngest Grace, Pasithëa the divine.

The Queen assents, and from th' infernal Bow'rs
Invokes the sable Subtartarean Pow'rs,
And those who rule th' inviolable Floods,
Whom Mortals name the dread Titanian Gods.
    Then swift as Wind, o'er Lemnos smoaky Isle,
They wing their way, and Imbrus' Sea-beat Soil,
Thro' Air unseen involv'd in Darkness glide,
And light on Lectos, on the Point of Ide.   320
(Mother of Savages, whose echoing Hills
Are heard resounding with a hundred Rills)
Fair Ida trembles underneath the God;
Hush'd are her Mountains, and her Forests nod.
There on a Fir, whose spiry Branches rise
To join its Summit to the neighb'ring Skies,
Dark in embow'ring Shade, conceal'd from Sight,
Sate Sleep, in Likeness of the Bird of Night,
(Chalcis his Name with those of heav'nly Birth,
But call'd Cymindis by the Race of Earth.)   330
    To Ida's Top successful Juno flies:
Great Jove surveys her with desiring Eyes:
The God, whose Light'ning sets the Heav'ns on fire,
Thro' all his Bosom feels the fierce Desire;
Fierce as when first by stealth he seiz'd her Charms,
Mix'd with her Soul, and melted in her Arms.
Fix'd on her Eyes he fed his eager Look,
Then press'd her Hand, and thus with Transport spoke.
    Why comes my Goddess from th' æthereal Sky,
And not her Steeds and flaming Chariot nigh?   340
    Then she—I haste to those remote Abodes,
Where the great Parents of the deathless Gods,
The rev'rend Ocean and grey Tethys reign,
On the last Limits of the Land and Main.
I visit these, to whose indulgent Cares
I owe the nursing of my tender Years.
For Strife, I hear, has made that Union cease
Which held so long this ancient Pair in Peace.
The Steeds, prepar'd my Chariot to convey
O'er Earth and Seas, and thro' th' aërial way,   350

Wait under Ide: Of thy superior Pow'r
To ask Consent, I leave th' Olympian Bow'r;
Nor seek, unknown to thee, the sacred Cells
Deep under Seas, where hoary Ocean dwells.
  For that (said Jove) suffice another Day;
But eager Love denies the least Delay.
Let softer Cares the present Hour employ,
And be these Moments sacred all to Joy.
Ne'er did my Soul so strong a Passion prove,
Or for an earthly, or a heav'nly Love: 360
Not when I press'd Ixion's matchless Dame,
Whence rose Perithous like the Gods in Fame.
Not when fair Danaë felt the Show'r of Gold
Stream into Life, whence Perseus brave and bold.
Not thus I burn'd for either Theban Dame,
(Bacchus from this, from that Alcides came)
Not Phœnix' Daughter, beautiful and young,
Whence godlike Rhadamanth and Minos sprung.
Not thus I burn'd for fair Latona's Face,
Nor comelier Ceres' more majestic Grace.   370
Not thus ev'n for thy self I felt Desire,
As now my Veins receive the pleasing Fire.
  He spoke; the Goddess with the charming Eyes
Glows with celestial Red, and thus replies.
Is this a Scene for Love? On Ida's Height,
Expos'd to mortal, and immortal Sight;
Our Joys prophan'd by each familiar Eye;
The Sport of Heav'n, and Fable of the Sky!
How shall I e'er review the blest Abodes,
Or mix among the Senate of the Gods?   380
Shall I not think, that, with disorder'd Charms,
All Heav'n beholds me recent from thy Arms?
With Skill divine has Vulcan form'd thy Bow'r,
Sacred to Love and to the genial Hour;
If such thy Will, to that Recess retire,
And secret there indulge thy soft Desire.
  She ceas'd, and smiling with superior Love,
Thus answer'd mild the Cloud-compelling Jove.

Nor God, nor Mortal shall our Joys behold,
Shaded with Clouds, and circumfus'd in Gold,   390
Not ev'n the Sun, who darts thro' Heav'n his Rays,
And whose broad Eye th' extended Earth surveys.
    Gazing he spoke, and kindling at the view,
His eager Arms around the Goddess threw.
Glad Earth perceives, and from her Bosom pours
Unbidden Herbs, and voluntary Flow'rs;
Thick new-born Vi'lets a soft Carpet spread,
And clust'ring Lotos swell'd the rising Bed,
And sudden Hyacinths the Turf bestrow,
And flamy Crocus made the Mountain glow.   400
There golden Clouds conceal the heav'nly Pair,
Steep'd in soft Joys, and circumfus'd with Air;
Celestial Dews, descending o'er the Ground,
Perfume the Mount, and breathe Ambrosia round.
At length with Love and Sleep's soft Pow'r opprest,
The panting Thund'rer nods, and sinks to Rest.
    Now to the Navy born on silent Wings,
To Neptune's Ear soft Sleep his Message brings;
Beside him sudden, unperceiv'd he stood,
And thus with gentle Words address'd the God.   410
    Now, Neptune! now, th' important Hour employ,
To check a while the haughty Hopes of Troy:
While Jove yet rests, while yet my Vapours shed
The golden Vision round his sacred Head;
For Juno's Love, and Somnus' pleasing Ties,
Have clos'd those awful and eternal Eyes.
    Thus having said, the Pow'r of Slumber flew,
On human Lids to drop the balmy Dew.
Neptune, with Zeal encreas'd, renews his Care,
And tow'ring in the foremost Ranks of War,   420
Indignant thus—Oh once of martial Fame!
O Greeks! if yet ye can deserve the Name!
This half-recover'd Day shall Troy obtain?
Shall Hector thunder at your Ships again?
Lo still he vaunts, and threats the Fleet with Fires,
While stern Achilles in his Wrath retires.

One Hero's Loss too tamely you deplore,
Be still your selves, and we shall need no more.
Oh yet, if Glory any Bosom warms,
Brace on your firmest Helms, and stand to Arms: 430
His strongest Spear each valiant Grecian wield,
Each valiant Grecian seize his broadest Shield;
Let, to the weak, the lighter Arms belong,
The pond'rous Targe be wielded by the strong.
(Thus arm'd) not Hector shall our Presence stay;
My self, ye Greeks! my self will lead the way.

The Troops assent; their martial Arms they change,
The busy Chiefs their banded Legions range.
The Kings, tho' wounded, and oppress'd with Pain,
With helpful Hands themselves assist the Train. 440
The strong and cumb'rous Arms the valiant wield,
The weaker Warrior takes a lighter Shield.
Thus sheath'd in shining Brass, in bright Array,
The Legions march, and Neptune leads the way:
His brandish'd Faulchion flames before their Eyes,
Like Light'ning flashing thro' the frighted Skies.
Clad in his Might th' Earth-shaking Pow'r appears;
Pale Mortals tremble, and confess their Fears.

Troy's great Defender stands alone unaw'd,
Arms his proud Host, and dares oppose a God: 450
And lo! the God, and wond'rous Man appear;
The Sea's great Ruler there, and Hector here.
The roaring Main, at her great Master's Call,
Rose in huge Ranks, and form'd a watry Wall
Around the Ships: Seas hanging o'er the Shores,
Both Armies join: Earth thunders, Ocean roars.
Not half so loud the bellowing Deeps resound,
When stormy Winds disclose the dark Profound;
Less loud the Winds, that from th' Æolian Hall
Roar thro' the Woods, and make whole Forests fall; 460
Less loud the Woods, when Flames in Torrents pour,
Catch the dry Mountain, and its Shades devour.
With such a Rage the meeting Hosts are driv'n,
And such a Clamour shakes the sounding Heav'n.

The first bold Javelin urg'd by Hector's Force,
Direct at Ajax' Bosom wing'd its Course;
But there no Pass the crossing Belts afford,
(One brac'd his Shield, and one sustain'd his Sword.)
Then back the disappointed Trojan drew,
And curs'd the Lance that unavailing flew: 470
But 'scap'd not Ajax; his tempestuous Hand
A pond'rous Stone up-heaving from the Sand,
(Where Heaps lay'd loose beneath the Warrior's Feet,
Or serv'd to ballast, or to prop the Fleet)
Toss'd round and round, the missive Marble flings;
On the raz'd Shield the falling Ruin rings:
Full on his Breast and Throat with Force descends;
Nor deaden'd there its giddy Fury spends,
But whirling on, with many a fiery round,
Smoaks in the Dust, and ploughs into the Ground.   480
As when the Bolt, red-hissing from above,
Darts on the consecrated Plant of Jove,
The Mountain-Oak in flaming Ruin lies,
Black from the Blow, and Smoaks of Sulphur rise;
Stiff with Amaze the pale Beholders stand,
And own the Terrors of th' Almighty Hand!
So lies great Hector prostrate on the Shore;
His slacken'd Hand deserts the Lance it bore;
His following Shield the fallen Chief o'erspread;
Beneath his Helmet drop'd his fainting Head;   490
His Load of Armour, sinking to the Ground,
Clanks on the Field; a dead, and hollow Sound.
Loud Shouts of Triumph fill the crowded Plain;
Greece sees, in hope, Troy's great Defender slain:
All spring to seize him; Storms of Arrows fly;
And thicker Javelins intercept the Sky.
In vain an Iron Tempest hisses round;
He lies protected, and without a Wound.
Polydamas, Agenor the divine,
The pious Warrior[1] of Anchises' Line,   500
And each bold Leader of the Lycian Band;
With cov'ring Shields (a friendly Circle) stand.

[1] Aeneas

His mournful Followers with assistant Care,
The groaning Hero to his Chariot bear;
His foaming Coursers, swifter than the Wind,
Speed to the Town, and leave the War behind.
    When now they touch'd the Mead's enamel'd Side,
Where gentle Xanthus rolls his easy Tyde,
With watry Drops the Chief they sprinkle round,
Plac'd on the Margin of the flow'ry Ground.   510
Rais'd on his Knees, he now ejects the Gore;
Now faints anew, low-sinking on the Shore;
By fits he breathes, half views the fleeting Skies,
And seals again, by fits, his swimming Eyes.
    Soon as the Greeks the Chief's Retreat beheld,
With double Fury each invades the Field.
Oïlean Ajax first his Javelin sped,
Pierc'd by whose Point, the Son of Enops bled;
(Satnius the brave, whom beauteous Neis bore
Amidst her Flocks on Satnio's silver Shore)   520
Struck thro' the Belly's Rim, the Warrior lies
Supine, and Shades eternal veil his Eyes.
An arduous Battel rose around the dead;
By turns the Greeks, by turns the Trojans bled.
Fir'd with Revenge, Polydamas drew near,
And at Prothœnor shook the trembling Spear;
The driving Javelin thro' his Shoulder thrust,
He sinks to Earth, and grasps the bloody Dust.
Lo thus (the Victor cries) we rule the Field,
And thus their Arms the Race of Panthus wield: 530
From this unerring Hand there flies no Dart
But bathes its Point within a Grecian Heart.
Propt on that Spear to which thou ow'st thy Fall,
Go, guide thy darksome Steps, to Pluto's dreary Hall!
    He said, and Sorrow touch'd each Argive Breast:
The Soul of Ajax burn'd above the rest.
As by his side the groaning Warrior fell,
At the fierce Foe he launch'd his piercing Steel;
The Foe reclining, shunn'd the flying Death;
But Fate, Archelochus, demands thy Breath: 540

Thy lofty Birth no Succour could impart,
The Wings of Death o'ertook thee on the Dart,
Swift to perform Heav'n's fatal Will it fled,
Full on the Juncture of the Neck and Head,
And took the Joint, and cut the Nerves in twain:
The dropping Head first tumbled to the Plain.
So just the Stroke, that yet the Body stood
Erect, then roll'd along the Sands in Blood.
    Here, proud Polydamas, here turn thy Eyes!
(The tow'ring Ajax loud-insulting cries)   550
Say, is this Chief, extended on the Plain,
A worthy Vengeance for Prothœnor slain?
Mark well his Port! his Figure and his Face
Nor speak him vulgar, nor of vulgar Race;
Some Lines, methinks, may make his Lineage known,
Antenor's Brother, or perhaps his Son.
    He spake, and smil'd severe, for well he knew
The bleeding Youth: Troy sadden'd at the View.
But furious Acamas aveng'd his Cause;
As Promachus his slaughter'd Brother draws,   560
He pierc'd his Heart—Such Fate attends you all,
Proud Argives! destin'd by our Arms to fall.
Not Troy alone, but haughty Greece shall share
The Toils, the Sorrows, and the Wounds of War.
Behold your Promachus depriv'd of Breath,
A Victim ow'd to my brave Brother's Death.
Not unappeas'd, He enters Pluto's Gate,
Who leaves a Brother to revenge his Fate.
    Heart-piercing Anguish struck the Grecian Host,
But touch'd the Breast of bold Peneleus most: 570
At the proud Boaster he directs his Course;
The Boaster flies, and shuns superior Force.
But young Ilioneus receiv'd the Spear,
Ilioneus, his Father's only Care:
(Phorbas the rich, of all the Trojan Train
Whom Hermes lov'd, and taught the Arts of Gain)
Full in his Eye the Weapon chanc'd to fall,
And from the Fibres scoop'd the rooted Ball,

Drove thro' the Neck, and hurl'd him to the Plain;
He lifts his miserable Arms in vain!   580
Swift his broad Faulchion fierce Peneleus spread,
And from the spouting Shoulders struck his Head;
To Earth at once the Head and Helmet fly;
The Lance, yet sticking thro' the bleeding Eye,
The Victor seiz'd; and as aloft he shook
The goary Visage, thus insulting spoke.
   Trojans! your great Ilioneus behold!
Haste, to his Father let the Tale be told:
Let his high Roofs resound with frantic Woe,
Such, as the House of Promachus must know;   590
Let doleful Tidings greet his Mother's Ear,
Such, as to Promachus' sad Spouse we bear;
When we, victorious, shall to Greece return,
And the pale Matron in our Triumphs mourn.
   Dreadful he spoke, then toss'd the Head on high;
The Trojans hear, they tremble, and they fly:
Aghast they gaze, around the Fleet and Wall,
And dread the Ruin that impends on all.
   Daughters of Jove! that on Olympus shine,
Ye all-beholding, all-recording Nine!   600
O say, when Neptune made proud Ilion yield,
What Chief, what Hero first embru'd the Field?
Of all the Grecians, what immortal Name,
And whose blest Trophies, will ye raise to Fame?
   Thou first, great Ajax! on th' ensanguin'd Plain
Laid Hyrtius, Leader of the Mysian Train.
Phalces and Mermer, Nestor's Son o'erthrew.
Bold Merion, Morys and Hippotion slew.
Strong Periphætes and Prothoön bled,
By Teucer's Arrows mingled with the dead.   610
Pierc'd in the Flank by Menelaus' Steel,
His People's Pastor, Hyperenor fell;
Eternal Darkness wrapt the Warrior round,
And the fierce Soul came rushing thro' the Wound.
But stretch'd in heaps before Oïleus' Son,
Fall mighty Numbers; mighty Numbers run;
Ajax the less, of all the Grecian Race
Skill'd in Pursuit, and swiftest in the Chace.

THE FIFTEENTH BOOK
OF THE ILIAD

THE ARGUMENT

The fifth Battel, at the Ships; and the Acts of Ajax

JUPITER AWAKING, sees the Trojans repuls'd from the Trenches, Hector in a Swoon, and Neptune at the Head of the Greeks: He is highly incens'd at the Artifice of Juno, who appeases him by her Submissions; she is then sent to Iris and Apollo. Juno repairing to the Assembly of the Gods, attempts with extraordinary Address to incense them against Jupiter, in particular she touches Mars with a violent Resentment: He is ready to take Arms, but is prevented by Minerva. Iris and Apollo obey the Orders of Jupiter; Iris commands Neptune to leave the Battel, to which, after much Reluctance and Passion, he consents. Apollo re-inspires Hector with Vigour, brings him back to the Battel, marches before him with his Ægis, and turns the Fortune of the Fight. He breaks down great part of the Grecian Wall; the Trojans rush in and attempt to fire the first Line of the Fleet, but are, as yet, repell'd by the greater Ajax with a prodigious Slaughter.

Now in swift Flight they past the Trench profound,
And many a Chief lay gasping on the Ground:
Then stopp'd, and panted, where the Chariots lie;
Fear on their Cheek, and Horror in their Eye.
Meanwhile awaken'd from his Dream of Love,
On Ida's Summit sate imperial Jove:
Round the wide Fields he cast a careful view,
There saw the Trojans fly, the Greeks pursue,

These proud in Arms, those scatter'd o'er the Plain;
And, 'midst the War, the Monarch of the Main. 10
Not far, great Hector on the Dust he spies,
(His sad Associates round with weeping Eyes)
Ejecting Blood, and panting yet for Breath,
His Senses wandring to the Verge of Death.
The God beheld him with a pitying Look,
And thus, incens'd, to fraudful Juno spoke.
  O thou, still adverse to th' eternal Will,
For ever studious in promoting Ill!
Thy Arts have made the godlike Hector yield,
And driv'n his conqu'ring Squadrons from the Field. 20
Can'st thou, unhappy in thy Wiles! withstand
Our Pow'r immense, and brave th' Almighty Hand?
Hast thou forgot, when bound and fix'd on high,
From the vast Concave of the spangled Sky,
I hung thee trembling, in a golden Chain;
And all the raging Gods oppos'd in vain?
Headlong I hurl'd them from th' Olympian Hall,
Stunn'd in the Whirl, and breathless with the Fall.
For godlike Hercules these Deeds were done,
Nor seem'd the Vengeance worthy such a Son; 30
When by thy Wiles induc'd, fierce Boreas tost
The shipwrack'd Hero on the Coan Coast:
Him thro' a thousand Forms of Death I bore,
And sent to Argos, and his native Shore.
Hear this, remember, and our Fury dread,
Nor pull th' unwilling Vengeance on thy Head,
Lest Arts and Blandishments successless prove,
Thy soft Deceits, and well-dissembled Love.
    The Thund'rer spoke: Imperial Juno mourn'd,
And trembling, these submissive Words return'd. 40
    By ev'ry Oath that Pow'rs immortal ties,
The foodful Earth, and all-infolding Skies,
By thy black Waves, tremendous Styx! that flow
Thro' the drear Realms of gliding Ghosts below:
By the dread Honours of thy sacred Head,
And that unbroken Vow, our Virgin Bed!

Not by my Arts the Ruler of the Main
Steeps Troy in Blood, and rages round the Plain;
By his own Ardour, his own Pity sway'd
To help his Greeks; he fought, and disobey'd: 50
Else had thy Juno better Counsels giv'n,
And taught Submission to the Sire of Heav'n.
　Think'st thou with me? fair Empress of the Skies!
(Th' immortal Father with a Smile replies!)
Then soon the haughty Sea-God shall obey,
Nor dare to act, but when we point the way.
If Truth inspires thy Tongue, proclaim our Will
To yon' bright Synod on th' Olympian Hill;
Our high Decree let various Iris know,
And call the God that bears the silver Bow.   60
Let her descend, and from th' embattel'd Plain
Command the Sea-God to his watry Reign:
While Phœbus hastes, great Hector to prepare
To rise afresh, and once more wake the War,
His lab'ring Bosom re-inspires with Breath,
And calls his Senses from the Verge of Death.
Greece chas'd by Troy ev'n to Achilles' Fleet,
Shall fall by thousands at the Hero's Feet.
He, not untouch'd with Pity, to the Plain
Shall send Patroclus, but shall send in vain.   70
What Youth he slaughters under Ilion's Walls?
Ev'n my lov'd Son, divine Sarpedon falls!
Vanquish'd at last by Hector's Lance he lies.
Then, nor till then, shall great Achilles rise:
And lo! that Instant, godlike Hector dies.
From that great Hour the War's whole Fortune turns,
Pallas assists, and lofty Ilion burns.
Not till that Day shall Jove relax his Rage,
Nor one of all the heav'nly Host engage
In aid of Greece. The Promise of a God   80
I gave, and seal'd it with th' Almighty Nod,
Achilles' Glory to the Stars to raise;
Such was our Word, and Fate the Word obeys.
　The trembling Queen (th' Almighty Order giv'n)
Swift from th' Idæan Summit shot to Heav'n.

As some way-faring Man, who wanders o'er
In Thought, a Length of Lands he trod before,
Sends forth his active Mind from Place to Place,
Joins Hill to Dale, and measures Space with Space:
So swift flew Juno to the blest Abodes,   90
If Thought of Man can match the Speed of Gods.
There sate the Pow'rs in awful Synod plac'd;
They bow'd, and made Obeysance as she pass'd,
Thro' all the brazen Dome: With Goblets crown'd
They hail her Queen; the Nectar streams around.
Fair Themis first presents the golden Bowl,
And anxious asks, what Cares disturb her Soul?
   To whom the white-arm'd Goddess thus replies:
Enough thou know'st the Tyrant of the Skies,
Severely bent his Purpose to fulfill,   100
Unmov'd his Mind, and unrestrain'd his Will.
Go thou, the Feasts of Heav'n attend thy Call;
Bid the crown'd Nectar circle round the Hall;
But Jove shall thunder thro' the Ethereal Dome,
Such stern Decrees, such threatned Woes to come,
As soon shall freeze Mankind with dire Surprize,
And damp th' eternal Banquets of the Skies.
   The Goddess said, and sullen took her Place;
Blank Horror sadden'd each celestial Face.
To see the gath'ring Grudge in ev'ry Breast,   110
Smiles on her Lips a spleenful Joy exprest,
While on her wrinkled Front, and Eyebrow bent,
Sate stedfast Care, and low'ring Discontent.
Thus she proceeds—Attend ye Pow'rs above!
But know, 'tis Madness to contest with Jove:
Supreme he sits; and sees, in Pride of Sway,
Your Vassal Godheads grudgingly obey;
Fierce in the Majesty of Pow'r controuls,
Shakes all the Thrones of Heav'n, and bends the Poles.
Submiss, Immortals! all he wills, obey;   120
And thou great Mars, begin and shew the way.
Behold Ascalaphus! behold him die,
But dare not murmur, dare not vent a Sigh;

Thy own lov'd boasted Offspring lies o'erthrown,
If that lov'd boasted Offspring be thy own.

   Stern Mars, with Anguish for his slaughter'd Son,
Smote his rebelling Breast, and fierce begun.
Thus then, Immortals! thus shall Mars obey;
Forgive me Gods, and yield my Vengeance way:
Descending first to yon' forbidden Plain,   130
The God of Battels dares avenge the slain;
Dares, tho' the Thunder bursting o'er my Head
Should hurl me blazing on those heaps of dead.

   With that, he gives command to Fear and Flight
To join his rapid Coursers for the Fight:
Then grim in Arms, with hasty Vengeance flies;
Arms, that reflect a Radiance thro' the Skies.
And now had Jove, by bold Rebellion driv'n,
Discharg'd his Wrath on half the Host of Heav'n;
But Pallas springing thro' the bright Abode,   140
Starts from her azure Throne to calm the God.
Struck, for th' immortal Race with timely Fear,
From frantic Mars she snatch'd the Shield and Spear;
Then the huge Helmet lifting from his Head,
Thus, to th' impetuous Homicide she said.

   By what wild Passion, Furious! art thou tost?
Striv'st thou with Jove? Thou art already lost.
Shall not the Thund'rer's dread Command restrain,
And was Imperial Juno heard in vain?
Back to the Skies would'st thou with Shame be driv'n,   150
And in thy Guilt involve the Host of Heav'n?
Ilion and Greece no more should Jove engage;
The Skies would yield an ampler Scene of Rage,
Guilty and guiltless find an equal Fate,
And one vast Ruin whelm th' Olympian State.
Cease then thy Offspring's Death unjust to call;
Heroes as great have dy'd, and yet shall fall.
Why should Heav'n's Law with foolish Man comply,
Exempted from the Race ordain'd to die?

   This Menace fix'd the Warrior to his Throne;   160
Sullen he sate, and curb'd the rising Groan.

Then Juno call'd (Jove's Orders to obey)
The winged Iris, and the God of Day.
Go wait the Thund'rer's Will (Saturnia cry'd)
On yon' tall Summit of the fount-ful Ide:
There in the Father's awful Presence stand,
Receive, and execute his dread Command.
   She said, and sate: the God that gilds the Day,
And various Iris wing their airy way.
Swift as the Wind, to Ida's Hills they came,   170
(Fair Nurse of Fountains and of savage Game.)
There sate th' Eternal; He, whose Nod controuls
The trembling World, and shakes the steady Poles.
Veil'd in a Mist of Fragrance him they found,
With Clouds of Gold and Purple circled round.
Well-pleas'd the Thund'rer saw their earnest care,
And prompt Obedience to the Queen of Air;
Then (while a Smile serenes his awful Brow)
Commands the Goddess of the Show'ry Bow.
   Iris! descend, and what we here ordain   180
Report to yon' mad Tyrant of the Main.
Bid him from Fight to his own Deeps repair,
Or breathe from Slaughter in the Fields of Air.
If he refuse, then let him timely weigh
Our elder Birthright, and superior Sway.
How shall his Rashness stand the dire Alarms,
If Heav'ns Omnipotence descend in Arms?
Strives he with me, by whom his Pow'r was giv'n,
And is there Equal to the Lord of Heav'n?
   Th' Almighty spoke; the Goddess wing'd her Flight   190
To sacred Ilion from th' Idæan Height.
Swift as the rat'ling Hail, or fleecy Snows
Drive thro' the Skies, when Boreas fiercely blows;
So from the Clouds descending Iris falls;
And to blue Neptune thus the Goddess calls.
   Attend the Mandate of the Sire above,
In me behold the Messenger of Jove:
He bids thee from forbidden Wars repair
To thy own Deeps, or to the Fields of Air.

This if refus'd, he bids thee timely weigh   200
His elder Birthright, and superior Sway.
How shall thy Rashness stand the dire Alarms,
If Heav'ns Omnipotence descend in Arms?
Striv'st thou with him, by whom all Pow'r is giv'n?
And art thou Equal to the Lord of Heav'n?
   What means the haughty Sov'reign of the Skies,
(The King of Ocean thus, incens'd, replies)
Rule as he will his portion'd Realms on high;
No Vassal God, nor of his Train am I.
Three Brother Deities from Saturn came,   210
And ancient Rhea, Earth's immortal Dame:
Assign'd by Lot, our triple Rule we know;
Infernal Pluto sways the Shades below;
O'er the wide Clouds, and o'er the starry Plain,
Ethereal Jove extends his high Domain;
My Court beneath the hoary Waves I keep,
And hush the Roarings of the sacred Deep:
Olympus, and this Earth, in common lie;
What Claim has here the Tyrant of the Sky?
Far in the distant Clouds let him controul,   220
And awe the younger Brothers of the Pole;
There to his Children his Commands be giv'n,
The trembling, servile, second Race of Heav'n.
   And must I then (said she) O Sire of Floods!
Bear this fierce Answer to the King of Gods?
Correct it yet, and change thy rash Intent;
A noble Mind disdains not to repent.
To elder Brothers guardian Fiends are giv'n,
To scourge the Wretch insulting them and Heav'n.
   Great is the Profit (thus the God rejoin'd)   230
When Ministers are blest with prudent Mind:
Warn'd by thy Words, to pow'rful Jove I yield,
And quit, tho' angry, the contended Field.
Not but his Threats with Justice I disclaim,
The same our Honours, and our Birth the same.
If yet, forgetful of his Promise giv'n
To Hermes, Pallas, and the Queen of Heav'n;

To favour Ilion, that perfidious Place,
He breaks his Faith with half th' ethereal Race;
Give him to know, unless the Grecian Train   240
Lay yon' proud Structures level with the Plain,
Howe'er th' Offence by other Gods be past,
The Wrath of Neptune shall for ever last.
  Thus speaking, furious from the Field he strode,
And plung'd into the Bosom of the Flood.
The Lord of Thunders from his lofty Height
Beheld, and thus bespoke the Source of Light.
  Behold! the God whose liquid Arms are hurl'd
Around the Globe, whose Earthquakes rock the World;
Desists at length his Rebel-war to wage,   250
Seeks his own Seas, and trembles at our Rage!
Else had my Wrath, Heav'ns Thrones all shaking round,
Burn'd to the bottom of his Seas profound;
And all the Gods that round old Saturn dwell,
Had heard the Thunders to the Deeps of Hell.
Well was the crime, and well the Vengeance spar'd;
Ev'n Pow'r immense had found such Battel hard.
Go thou my Son! the trembling Greeks alarm,
Shake my broad Ægis[1] on thy active Arm,
Be godlike Hector thy peculiar Care,   260
Swell his bold Heart, and urge his Strength to War:
Let Ilion conquer, till th' Achaian Train
Fly to their Ships and Hellespont again:
Then Greece shall breathe from Toils—The Godhead said;
His Will divine the Son of Jove obey'd.
Not half so swift the sailing Falcon flies,
That drives a Turtle thro' the liquid Skies;
As Phœbus shooting from th' Idæan Brow,
Glides down the Mountain to the Plain below.
There Hector seated by the Stream he sees,   270
His Sense returning with the coming Breeze;
Again his Pulses beat, his Spirits rise;
Again his lov'd Companions meet his Eyes;

---

[1] Attribute of Jove and Athena, usually represented as a goat-skin, and exerting terrible power

Jove thinking of his Pains, they past away.
To whom the God who gives the golden Day.
   Why sits great Hector from the Field so far,
What grief, what wound, withholds him from the War?
   The fainting Hero, as the Vision bright
Stood shining o'er him, half unseal'd his Sight:
What blest Immortal, with commanding Breath,   280
Thus wakens Hector from the Sleep of Death?
Has Fame not told, how, while my trusty Sword
Bath'd Greece in Slaughter, and her Battel gor'd,
The mighty Ajax with a deadly Blow
Had almost sunk me to the Shades below?
Ev'n yet, methinks, the gliding Ghosts I spy,
And Hell's black Horrors swim before my Eye.
   To him Apollo. Be no more dismay'd;
See, and be strong! the Thund'rer sends thee Aid,
Behold! thy Phœbus shall his Arms employ,   290
Phœbus, propitious still to thee, and Troy.
Inspire thy Warriors then with manly Force,
And to the Ships impell thy rapid Horse:
Ev'n I will make thy fiery Coursers way,
And drive the Grecians headlong to the Sea.
   Thus to bold Hector spoke the Son of Jove,
And breath'd immortal Ardour from above.
As when the pamper'd Steed, with Reins unbound,
Breaks from his Stall, and pours along the Ground;
With ample Strokes he rushes to the Flood,   300
To bathe his Sides and cool his fiery Blood.
His Head now freed, he tosses to the Skies;
His Mane dishevel'd o'er his Shoulders flies;
He snuffs the Females in the well known Plain,
And springs, exulting, to his Fields again:
Urg'd by the Voice divine, thus Hector flew,
Full of the God; and all his Hosts pursue.
As when the Force of Men and Dogs combin'd
Invade the Mountain Goat, or branching Hind;
They gain th' impervious Rock, and safe retreat   310
(For Fate preserves them) from the Hunter's Threat.

When lo! a Lyon shoot across the way:
They fly; at once the Chasers and the Prey.
So Greece, that late in conq'ring Troops pursu'd,
And mark'd their Progress thro' the Ranks in Blood,
Soon as they see the furious Chief appear,
Forget to vanquish, and consent to fear.

Thoas with Grief observ'd his dreadful Course,
Thoas, the bravest of th' Ætolian Force:
Skill'd to direct the Javelin's distant Flight,   320
And bold to combate in the standing Fight;
Nor more in Councils fam'd for solid Sense,
Than winning Words and heav'nly Eloquence.
Gods! what Portent (he cry'd) these Eyes invades?
Lo! Hector rises from the Stygian Shades!
We saw him, late, by thund'ring Ajax kill'd;
What God restores him to the frighted Field;
And not content that half of Greece lie slain,
Pours new Destruction on her Sons again?
He comes not, Jove! without thy pow'rful Will;   330
Lo! still he lives, pursues, and conquers still!
Yet hear my Counsel, and his worst withstand;
The Greek's main Body to the Fleet command;
But let the few whom brisker Spirits warm,
Stand the first Onset, and provoke the Storm:
Thus point your Arms; and when such Foes appear,
Fierce as he is, let Hector learn to fear.

The Warrior spoke, the list'ning Greeks obey,
Thick'ning their Ranks, and form a deep Array.
Each Ajax, Teucer, Merion, gave command,   340
The valiant Leader of the Cretan Band,
And Mars-like Meges: These the Chiefs excite,
Approach the Foe, and meet the coming Fight.
Behind, unnumber'd Multitudes attend,
To flank the Navy, and the Shores defend.
Full on the Front the pressing Trojans bear,
And Hector first came tow'ring to the War.
Phœbus himself the rushing Battel led;
A Veil of Clouds involv'd his radiant Head:

High-held before him, Jove's enormous Shield 350
Portentous shone, and shaded all the Field,
Vulcan to Jove th' immortal Gift consign'd,
To scatter Hosts, and terrify Mankind.
The Greeks expect the Shock; the Clamours rise
From diff'rent parts, and mingle in the Skies.
Dire was the Hiss of Darts, by Heroes flung,
And Arrows leaping from the Bowstring sung;
These drink the Life of gen'rous Warriors slain;
Those guiltless fall, and thirst for Blood in vain.
As long as Phœbus bore unmov'd the Shield, 360
Sate doubtful Conquest hov'ring o'er the Field;
But when aloft he shakes it in the Skies,
Shouts in their Ears, and lightens in their Eyes,
Deep Horror seizes ev'ry Grecian Breast,
Their Force is humbled, and their Fear confest.
So flies a Herd of Oxen, scatter'd wide,
No Swain to guard 'em, and no Day to guide,
When two fell Lyons from the Mountain come,
And spread the Carnage thro' the shady Gloom.
Impending Phœbus pours around 'em Fear, 370
And Troy and Hector thunder in the Rear.
Heaps fall on Heaps: the Slaughter Hector leads;
First great Arcesilas, then Stichius bleeds;
One to the bold Bœotians ever dear,
And one Menestheus' Friend, and fam'd Compeer.
Medon and Iäsus, Æneas sped;
This sprung from Phelus, and th' Athenians led;
But hapless Medon from Oïleus came;
Him Ajax honour'd with a Brother's Name,
Tho' born of lawless Love: From home expell'd, 380
A banish'd Man, in Phylace he dwell'd,
Press'd by the Vengeance of an angry Wife;
Troy ends, at last, his Labours and his Life.
Mecistes next, Polydamas o'erthrew;
And thee, brave Clonius! great Agenor slew.
By Paris, Deiochus inglorious dies,
Pierc'd thro' the Shoulder as he basely flies.

Polites' Arm laid Echius on the Plain;
Stretch'd on one Heap, the Victors spoil the slain.
The Greeks dismay'd, confus'd, disperse or fall,   390
Some seek the Trench, some skulk behind the Wall,
While these fly trembling, others pant for Breath,
And o'er the Slaughter stalks gigantic Death.
On rush'd bold Hector, gloomy as the Night,
Forbids to plunder, animates the Fight,
Points to the Fleet: For by the Gods, who flies,
Who dares but linger, by this Hand he dies:
No weeping Sister his cold Eye shall close,
No friendly Hand his fun'ral Pyre compose.
Who stops to plunder, in this signal Hour,   400
The Birds shall tear him, and the Dogs devour.
    Furious he said; the smarting Scourge resounds;
The Coursers fly; the smoking Chariot bounds:
The Hosts rush on; loud Clamours shake the Shore;
The Horses thunder, Earth and Ocean roar!
Apollo, planted at the Trenche's Bound,
Push'd at the Bank: Down sunk th' enormous Mound:
Roll'd in the Ditch the heapy Ruin lay;
A sudden Road! a long and ample way.
O'er the dread Fosse (a late-impervious Space)   410
Now Steeds, and Men, and Cars, tumultuous pass.
The wond'ring Crowds the downward Level trod;
Before them flam'd the Shield, and march'd the God.
Then with his Hand he shook the mighty Wall;
And lo! the Turrets nod, the Bulwarks fall.
Easy, as when ashore an Infant stands,
And draws imagin'd Houses in the Sands;
The sportive Wanton, pleas'd with some new Play,
Sweeps the slight Works and fashion'd Domes away.
Thus vanish, at thy touch, the Tow'rs and Walls;   420
The Toil of thousands in a Moment falls.
    The Grecians gaze around with wild Despair,
Confus'd, and weary all the Pow'rs with Pray'r;
Exhort their Men, with Praises, Threats, Commands;
And urge the Gods, with Voices, Eyes, and Hands.

Experienc'd Nestor chief obtests the Skies,
And weeps his Country with a Father's Eyes.

O Jove! if ever, on his native Shore,
One Greek enrich'd thy Shrine with offer'd Gore;
If e'er, in hope our Country to behold,   430
We paid the fattest Firstlings of the Fold;
If e'er thou sign'st our Wishes with thy Nod;
Perform the Promise of a gracious God!
This Day, preserve our Navies from the Flame,
And save the Reliques of the Grecian Name.

Thus pray'd the Sage: Th' Eternal gave consent,
And Peals of Thunder shook the Firmament.
Presumptuous Troy mistook th' accepting Sign,
And catch'd new Fury at the Voice divine.
As, when black Tempests mix the Seas and Skies,   440
The roaring Deeps in watry Mountains rise,
Above the sides of some tall Ship ascend,
Its Womb they deluge, and its Ribs they rend:
Thus loudly roaring, and o'erpow'ring all,
Mount the thick Trojans up the Grecian Wall;
Legions on Legions from each side arise;
Thick sound the Keels; the Storm of Arrows flies.
Fierce on the Ships above, the Cars below,
These wield the Mace, and those the Javelin throw.

While thus the Thunder of the Battel rag'd,   450
And lab'ring Armies round the Works engag'd,
Still in the Tent Patroclus sate, to tend
The good Eurypylus, his wounded Friend.
He sprinkles healing Balmes, to Anguish kind,
And adds Discourse, the Med'cine of the Mind.
But when he saw, ascending up the Fleet,
Victorious Troy: Then, starting from his Seat,
With bitter Groans his Sorrows he exprest,
He wrings his Hands, he beats his manly Breast.
Tho' yet thy State require Redress (he cries)   460
Depart I must: What Horrors strike my Eyes?
Charg'd with Achilles' high Commands I go,
A mournful Witness of this Scene of Woe:

I haste to urge him by his Country's Care,
To rise in Arms, and shine again in War.
Perhaps some fav'ring God his Soul may bend;
The Voice is pow'rful of a faithful Friend.

He spoke; and speaking, swifter than the Wind
Sprung from the Tent, and left the War behind.
Th' embody'd Greeks the fierce Attack sustain,   470
But strive, tho' num'rous, to repulse in vain.
Nor could the Trojans, thro' that firm Array,
Force, to the Fleet and Tents, th' impervious way.
As when a Shipwright, with Palladian Art,
Smooths the rough Wood, and levels ev'ry Part;
With equal Hand he guides his whole Design,
By the just Rule, and the directing Line.
The martial Leaders, with like Skill and Care,
Preserv'd their Line, and equal kept the War.
Brave Deeds of Arms thro' all the Ranks were try'd,   480
And ev'ry Ship sustain'd an equal Tyde.
At one proud Bark, high-tow'ring o'er the Fleet
Ajax the Great, and Godlike Hector meet:
For one bright Prize the matchless Chiefs contend;
Nor this the Ships can fire, nor that defend;
One kept the Shore, and one the Vessel trod;
That fix'd as Fate, this acted[2] by a God.
The Son of Clytius, in his daring Hand,
The Deck approaching, shakes a flaming Brand;
But pierc'd by Telamon's huge Lance expires;   490
Thund'ring he falls, and drops th' extinguish'd Fires.
Great Hector view'd him with a sad Survey,
As stretch'd in Dust before the Stern he lay.
Oh! all of Trojan, all of Lycian Race!
Stand to your Arms, maintain this arduous Space!
Lo! where the Son of Royal Clytius lies,
Ah save his Arms, secure his Obsequies!
This said, his eager Javelin sought the Foe:
But Ajax shunn'd the meditated Blow.
Not vainly yet the forceful Lance was thrown;   500
It stretch'd in Dust unhappy Lycophron:

[2] Put in motion by, actuated

An Exile long, sustain'd at Ajax' Board,
A faithful Servant to a foreign Lord;
In Peace, in War, for ever at his side,
Near his lov'd Master, as he lived, he dy'd.
From the high Poop he tumbles on the Sand,
And lies, a lifeless Load, along the Land.
With Anguish Ajax views the piercing Sight,
And thus inflames his Brother to the Fight.

   Teucer, behold! extended on the Shore   510
Our Friend, our lov'd Companion! now no more!
Dear as a Parent, with a Parent's Care,
To fight our Wars, he left his native Air.
This Death deplor'd to Hector's Rage we owe;
Revenge, revenge it on the cruel Foe.
Where are those Darts on which the Fates attend?
And where the Bow, which Phœbus taught to bend?

   Impatient Teucer, hastening to his Aid,
Before the Chief his ample Bow display'd;
The well-stor'd Quiver on his Shoulders hung: 520
Then hiss'd his Arrow, and the Bowstring sung.
Clytus, Pisenor's Son, renown'd in Fame,
(To thee, Polydamas! an honour'd Name)
Drove thro' the thickest of th' embattel'd Plains
The startling Steeds, and shook his eager Reins.
As all on Glory ran his ardent Mind,
The pointed Death arrests him from behind:
Thro' his fair Neck the thrilling Arrow flies;
In Youth's first Bloom reluctantly he dies.
Hurl'd from the lofty Seat, at distance far,   530
The headlong Coursers spurn his empty Car;
Till sad Polydamas the Steeds restrain'd,
And gave, Astynous, to thy careful Hand;
Then, fir'd to Vengeance, rush'd amidst the Foe;
Rage edg'd his Sword, and strengthen'd ev'ry Blow.
   Once more bold Teucer, in his Country's Cause,
At Hector's Breast a chosen Arrow draws;
And had the Weapon found the destin'd way,
Thy Fall, great Trojan! had renown'd that Day.

But Hector was not doom'd to perish then: 540
Th' all-wise Disposer of the Fates of Men,
(Imperial Jove) his present Death withstands;
Nor was such Glory due to Teucer's Hands.
At his full Stretch, as the tough String he drew,
Struck by an Arm unseen, it burst in two;
Down drop'd the Bow: the Shaft with brazen Head
Fell innocent, and on the Dust, lay dead.
Th' astonish'd Archer to great Ajax cries;
Some God prevents our destin'd Enterprize:
Some God, propitious to the Trojan Foe,   550
Has, from my Arm unfailing, struck the Bow,
And broke the Nerve my Hands had twin'd with Art,
Strong to impell the Flight of many a Dart.
  Since Heav'n commands it (Ajax made reply)
Dismiss the Bow, and lay thy Arrows by;
Thy Arms no less suffice the Lance to wield,
And quit the Quiver for the pond'rous Shield.
In the first Ranks indulge thy Thirst of Fame,
Thy brave Example shall the rest enflame.
Fierce as they are, by long Successes vain;   560
To force our Fleet, or ev'n a Ship to gain,
Asks Toil, and Sweat, and Blood: Their utmost Might
Shall find its Match—No more: 'Tis ours to fight.
  Then Teucer laid his faithless Bow aside;
The fourfold Buckler o'er his Shoulder ty'd;
On his brave Head a crested Helm he plac'd,
With nodding Horsehair formidably grac'd;
A Dart, whose Point with Brass refulgent shines,
The Warrior wields; and his great Brother joins.
  This Hector saw, and thus express'd his Joy.   570
Ye Troops of Lycia, Dardanus, and Troy!
Be mindful of your selves, your ancient Fame,
And spread your Glory with the Navy's Flame.
Jove is with us; I saw his Hand, but now,
From the proud Archer strike his vaunted Bow.
Indulgent Jove! how plain thy Favours shine,
When happy Nations bear the Marks divine!

How easy then, to see the sinking State
Of Realms accurs'd, deserted, reprobate!
Such is the Fate of Greece, and such is ours: 580
Behold, ye Warriors, and exert your Pow'rs.
Death is the worst; a Fate which all must try;
And, for our Country, 'tis a Bliss to die.
The gallant Man, tho' slain in Fight he be,
Yet leaves his Nation safe, his Children free;
Entails a Debt on all the grateful State;
His own brave Friends shall glory in his Fate;
His Wife live honour'd, all his Race succeed;
And late Posterity enjoy the Deed!

    This rouz'd the Soul in ev'ry Trojan Breast: 590
The godlike Ajax next his Greeks addrest.
How long, ye Warriors of the Argive Race,
(To gen'rous Argos what a dire Disgrace!)
How long, on these curs'd Confines will ye lie,
Yet undertermin'd, or to live, or die!
What Hopes remain, what Methods to retire,
If once your Vessels catch the Trojan Fire?
Mark how the Flames approach, how near they fall,
How Hector calls, and Troy obeys his Call!
Not to the Dance that dreadful Voice invites,   600
It calls to Death, and all the Rage of Fights.
'Tis now no time for Wisdom or Debates;
To your own Hands are trusted all your Fates:
And better far, in one decisive Strife,
One Day should end our Labour, or our Life;
Than keep this hard-got Inch of barren Sands,
Still press'd, and press'd by such inglorious Hands.

    The list'ning Grecians feel their Leader's Flame,
And ev'ry kindling Bosom pants for Fame.
Then mutual Slaughters spread on either side;   610
By Hector here the Phocian Schedius dy'd;
There pierc'd by Ajax, sunk Laodamas,
Chief of the Foot, of old Antenor's Race.
Polydamas laid Otus on the Sand,
The fierce Commander of th' Epeian Band.

His Lance bold Meges at the Victor threw;
The Victor stooping, from the Death withdrew:
(That valu'd Life, O Phœbus! was thy Care)
But Crœsmus' Bosom took the flying Spear;
His Corps fell bleeding on the slipp'ry Shore;   620
His radiant Arms triumphant Meges bore.
Dolops, the Son of Lampus rushes on,
Sprung from the Race of old Laomedon,
And fam'd for Prowess in a well-fought Field;
He pierc'd the Centre of his sounding Shield:
But Meges, Phyleus' ample Breastplate wore,
(Well known in Fight on Selles' winding Shore,
For King Euphetes gave the golden Mail,
Compact, and firm with many a jointed Scale)
Which oft, in Cities storm'd, and Battels won,   630
Had sav'd the Father, and now saves the Son.
Full at the Trojan's Head he urg'd his Lance,
Where the high Plumes above the Helmet dance,
New-ting'd with Tyrian Dye: In Dust below,
Shorn from the Crest, the purple Honours glow.
Meantime their Fight the Spartan King survey'd,
And stood by Meges' side, a sudden Aid,
Thro' Dolops' Shoulder urg'd his forceful Dart,
Which held its Passage thro' the panting Heart,
And issu'd at his Breast. With thund'ring Sound   640
The Warrior falls, extended on the Ground.
In rush the conqu'ring Greeks to spoil the slain;
But Hector's Voice excites his kindred Train;
The Hero most, from Hicetaon sprung,
Fierce Melanippus, gallant, brave, and young.
He (e'er to Troy the Grecians cross'd the Main)
Fed his large Oxen on Percote's Plain;
But when oppress'd, his Country claim'd his Care,
Return'd to Ilion, and excell'd in War:
For this, in Priam's Court he held his Place,   650
Belov'd no less than Priam's Royal Race.
Him Hector singled, as his Troops he led,
And thus inflam'd him, pointing to the Dead.

Lo Melanippus! lo where Dolops lies;
And is it thus our Royal Kinsman dies?
O'ermatch'd he falls; to two at once a Prey,
And lo! they bear the bloody Arms away!
Come on—a distant War no longer wage,
But hand to hand thy Country's Foes engage:
Till Greece at once, and all her Glory end;   660
Or Ilion from her tow'ry Height descend,
Heav'd from the lowest Stone; and bury All,
In one sad Sepulchre, one common Fall.

Hector (this said) rush'd forward on the Foes:
With equal Ardour Melanippus glows:
Then Ajax thus—Oh Greeks! respect your Fame,
Respect your selves, and learn an honest Shame:
Let mutual Reverence mutual Warmth inspire,
And catch from Breast to Breast the noble Fire.
On Valour's side the odds of Combate lie,   670
The brave live glorious, or lamented die;
The Wretch that trembles in the Field of Fame,
Meets Death, and worse than Death, eternal Shame.

His gen'rous Sense he not in vain imparts;
It sunk, and rooted in the Grecian Hearts.
They join, they throng, they thicken at his Call,
And flank the Navy with a brazen Wall;
Shields touching Shields in order blaze above,
And stop the Trojans, tho' impell'd by Jove.
The fiery Spartan first, with loud Applause,   680
Warms the bold Son of Nestor in his Cause.
Is there (he said) in Arms a Youth like you,
So strong to fight, so active to pursue?
Why stand you distant, nor attempt a Deed?
Lift the bold Lance, and make some Trojan bleed.

He said, and backward to the Lines retir'd;
Forth rush'd the Youth, with martial Fury fir'd,
Beyond the foremost Ranks; his Lance he threw,
And round the black Battalions cast his View.
The Troops of Troy recede with sudden Fear,   690
While the swift Javelin hiss'd along in Air.

Advancing Melanippus met the Dart
With his bold Breast, and felt it in his Heart:
Thund'ring he falls; his falling Arms resound,
And his broad Buckler rings against the Ground.
The Victor leaps upon his prostrate Prize;
Thus on a Roe the well-breath'd Beagle flies,
And rends his side, fresh-bleeding with the Dart
The distant Hunter sent into his Heart.
Observing Hector to the Rescue flew;   700
Bold as he was, Antilochus withdrew:
So when a Savage, ranging o'er the Plain,
Has torn the Shepherd's Dog, or Shepherd Swain;
While conscious of the Deed, he glares around,
And hears the gath'ring Multitude resound,
Timely he flies the yet-untasted Food,
And gains the friendly Shelter of the Wood.
So fears the Youth; all Troy with Shouts pursue,
While Stones and Darts in mingled Tempest flew;
But enter'd in the Grecian Ranks, he turns   710
His manly Breast, and with new Fury burns.
   Now on the Fleet the Tydes of Trojans drove,
Fierce to fulfill the stern Decrees of Jove:
The Sire of Gods, confirming Thetis' Pray'r,
The Grecian Ardour quench'd in deep Despair;
But lifts to Glory Troy's prevailing Bands,
Swells all their Hearts, and strengthens all their Hands
On Ida's Top he waits with longing Eyes,
To view the Navy blazing to the Skies;
Then, nor till then, the Scale of War shall turn,   720
The Trojans fly, and conquer'd Ilion burn.
These Fates resolv'd in his almighty Mind,
He raises Hector to the Work design'd,
Bids him with more than mortal Fury glow,
And drives him, like a Light'ning, on the Foe.
So Mars, when human Crimes for Vengeance call,
Shakes his huge Javelin, and whole Armies fall.
Not with more Rage a Conflagration rolls,
Wraps the vast Mountains, and involves the Poles.

He foames with Wrath; beneath his gloomy Brow　　730
Like fiery Meteors his red Eyeballs glow:
The radiant Helmet on his Temples burns,
Waves when he nods, and lightens as he turns:
For Jove his Splendour round the Chief had thrown,
And cast the Blaze of both the Hosts on one.
Unhappy Glories! for his Fate was near,
Due to stern Pallas, and Pelides' Spear:
Yet Jove deferr'd the Death he was to pay,
And gave what Fate allow'd, the Honours of a Day!

Now all on fire for Fame; his Breast, his Eyes　　740
Burn at each Foe, and single ev'ry Prize;
Still at the closest Ranks, the thickest Fight,
He points his Ardour, and exerts his Might.
The Grecian Phalanx moveless as a Tow'r,
On all sides batter'd, yet resists his Pow'r:
So some tall Rock o'erhangs the hoary Main,
By Winds assail'd, by Billows beat in vain,
Unmov'd it hears, above, the Tempest blow,
And sees the watry Mountains break below.
Girt in surrounding Flames, he seems to fall　　750
Like Fire from Jove, and bursts upon them all:
Bursts as a Wave, that from the Clouds impends,
And swell'd with Tempests on the Ship descends;
White are the Decks with Foam; the Winds aloud
Howl o'er the Masts, and sing thro' ev'ry Shroud:
Pale, trembling, tir'd, the Sailors freeze with Fears;
And instant Death on ev'ry Wave appears.
So pale the Greeks the Eyes of Hector meet,
The Chief so thunders, and so shakes the Fleet.

As when a Lion, rushing from his Den,　　760
Amidst the Plain of some wide-water'd Fen,
(Where num'rous Oxen, as at ease they feed,
At large expatiate o'er the ranker Mead;)
Leaps on the Herds before the Herdman's Eyes;
The trembling Herdsman far to distance flies:
Some lordly Bull (the rest dispers'd and fled)
He singles out; arrests, and lays him dead.

Thus from the Rage of Jove-like Hector, flew
All Greece in Heaps; but one he seiz'd, and slew.
Mycenian Periphes, a mighty Name,   770
In Wisdom great, in Arms well known to Fame:
The Minister of stern Euristheus' Ire
Against Alcides, Copreus, was his Sire:
The Son redeem'd the Honours of the Race,
A Son as gen'rous as his Sire was base;
O'er all his Country's Youth conspicuous far,
In ev'ry Virtue, or of Peace or War:
But doom'd to Hector's stronger Force to yield!
Against the Margin of his ample Shield
He struck his hasty Foot: his Heels up-sprung;   780
Supine he fell; his brazen Helmet rung.
On the fall'n Chief th' invading Trojan prest,
And plung'd the pointed Javelin in his Breast.
His circling Friends, who strove to guard too late
Th' unhappy Hero; fled, or shar'd his Fate.

Chas'd from the foremost Line, the Grecian Train
Now man the next, receding tow'rd the Main:
Wedg'd in one Body at the Tents they stand,
Wall'd round with Sterns, a gloomy, desp'rate Band.
Now manly Shame forbids th' inglorious Flight;   790
Now Fear itself confines them to the Fight:
Man Courage Breathes in Man; but Nestor most
(The sage Preserver of the Grecian Host)
Exhorts, adjures, to guard these utmost Shores;
And by their Parents, by themselves, implores.

O Friends! be Men: your gen'rous Breasts inflame
With mutual Honour, and with mutual Shame!
Think of your Hopes, your Fortunes; all the Care
Your Wives, your Infants, and your Parents share:
Think of each living Father's rev'rend Head;   800
Think of each Ancestor with Glory dead;
Absent, by me they speak, by me they sue;
They ask their Safety and their Fame from you:
The Gods their Fates on this one Action lay,
And all are lost, if you desert the Day.

He spoke, and round him breath'd heroic Fires;
Minerva seconds what the Sage inspires.
The Mist of Darkness Jove around them threw,
She clear'd, restoring all the War to view;
A sudden Ray shot beaming o'er the Plain,   810
And shew'd the Shores, the Navy, and the Main:
Hector they saw, and all who fly, or fight,
The Scene wide-opening to the Blaze of Light.
First of the Field, great Ajax strikes their Eyes,
His Port majestick, and his ample Size:
A pond'rous Mace, with Studs of Iron crown'd,
Full twenty Cubits long, he swings around.
Nor fights like others, fix'd to certain Stands,
But looks a moving Tow'r above the Bands;
High on the Decks, with vast gigantic Stride,   820
The godlike Hero stalks from side to side.
So when a Horseman from the watry Mead
(Skill'd in the Manage of the bounding Steed)
Drives four fair Coursers, practis'd to obey,
To some great City thro' the publick way;
Safe in his Art, as side by side they run,
He shifts his Seat, and vaults from one to one;
And now to this, and now to that he flies;
Admiring Numbers follow with their Eyes.
From Ship to Ship thus Ajax swiftly flew,   830
No less the Wonder of the warring Crew.
As furious, Hector thunder'd Threats aloud,
And rush'd enrag'd before the Trojan Croud:
Then swift invades the Ships, whose beaky Prores
Lay rank'd contiguous on the bending Shores.
So the strong Eagle from his airy Height
Who marks the Swan's or Crane's embody'd Flight,
Stoops down impetuous, while they light for Food,
And stooping, darkens with his Wings the Flood.
Jove leads him on with his almighty Hand,   840
And breathes fierce Spirits in his following Band.
The warring Nations meet, the Battel roars,
Thick beats the Combate on the sounding Prores.

Thou wouldst have thought, so furious was their Fire,
No Force could tame them, and no Toil could tire;
As if new Vigour from new Fights they won,
And the long Battel was but then begun.
Greece yet unconquer'd, kept alive the War,
Secure of Death, confiding in Despair;
Troy in proud Hopes already view'd the Main   850
Bright with the Blaze, and red with Heroes slain:
Like Strength is felt, from Hope, and from Despair,
And each contends, as his were all the War.
    'Twas thou, bold Hector! whose resistless Hand
First seiz'd a Ship on that contested Strand;
The same which dead Protesilaus bore,
The first that touch'd th' unhappy Trojan Shore:
For this in Arms the warring Nations stood,
And bath'd their gen'rous Breasts with mutual Blood.
No room to poize the Lance, or bend the Bow;   860
But hand to hand, and Man to Man they grow.
Wounded, they wound; and seek each others Hearts
With Faulchions, Axes, Swords, and shorten'd Darts.
The Faulchions ring, Shields rattle, Axes sound,
Swords flash in Air, or glitter on the Ground;
With streaming Blood the slipp'ry Shores are dy'd,
And slaughter'd Heroes swell the dreadful Tyde.
    Still raging Hector with his ample Hand
Grasps the high Stern, and gives this loud Command.
    Haste, bring the Flames! the Toil of ten long Years   870
Is finish'd; and the Day desir'd appears!
This happy Day with Acclamations greet,
Bright with Destruction of yon' hostile Fleet.
The Coward-Counsels of a tim'rous Throng
Of rev'rend Dotards, check'd our Glory long:
Too long Jove lull'd us with lethargic Charms,
But now in Peals of Thunder calls to Arms;
In this great Day he crowns our full Desires,
Wakes all our Force, and seconds all our Fires.
    He spoke—the Warriors, at his fierce Command,   880
Pour a new Deluge on the Grecian Band.

Ev'n Ajax paus'd (so thick the Javelins fly)
Step'd back, and doubted or to live, or die.
Yet where the Oars are plac'd, he stands to wait
What Chief approaching dares attempt his Fate;
Ev'n to the last, his Naval Charge defends,
Now shakes his Spear, now lifts, and now protends,
Ev'n yet, the Greeks with piercing Shouts inspires,
Amidst Attacks, and Deaths, and Darts, and Fires.

   O Friends! O Heroes! Names for ever dear,   890
Once Sons of Mars, and Thunderbolts of War!
Ah yet be mindful of your old Renown,
Your great Forefathers Virtues, and your own.
What Aids expect you in this utmost Strait?
What Bulwarks rising between you and Fate?
No Aids, no Bulwarks your Retreat attend,
No Friends to help, no City to defend.
This Spot is all you have, to lose or keep;
There stand the Trojans, and here rolls the Deep.
'Tis hostile Ground you tread; your native Lands   900
Far, far from hence: your Fates are in your Hands.

   Raging he spoke; nor farther wastes his Breath,
But turns his Javelin to the Work of Death.
What'er bold Trojan arm'd his daring Hands
Against the sable Ships with flaming Brands,
So well the Chief his Naval Weapon sped,
The luckless Warrior at his Stern lay dead:
Full twelve, the boldest, in a Moment fell,
Sent by great Ajax to the Shades of Hell.

THE SIXTEENTH BOOK
OF THE ILIAD

THE ARGUMENT

The sixth Battel: The Acts and Death of Patroclus

PATROCLUS (in Pursuance of the Request of Nestor in the eleventh
Book) entreats Achilles to suffer him to go to the Assistance of the
Greeks with Achilles's Troops and Armour. He agrees to it, but at the
same time charges him to content himself with rescuing the Fleet, without farther Pursuit of the Enemy. The Armour, Horses, Soldiers, and
Officers of Achilles are described. Achilles offers a Libation for the Success of his Friend, after which Patroclus leads the Myrmidons to Battel.
The Trojans at the Sight of Patroclus in Achilles's Armour, taking him
for that Hero, are cast into the utmost Consternation: He beats them off
from the Vessels, Hector himself flies, Sarpedon is kill'd, tho' Jupiter was
averse to his Fate. Several other Particulars of the Battel are described;
in the Heat of which, Patroclus, neglecting the Orders of Achilles, pursues the Foe to the Walls of Troy; where Apollo repulses and disarms
him, Euphorbus wounds him, and Hector kills him, which concludes the
Book.

So warr'd both Armies on th' ensanguin'd Shore,
While the black Vessels smoak'd with human Gore.
Meantime Patroclus to Achilles flies;
The streaming Tears fall copious from his Eyes;
Not faster, trickling to the Plains below,
From the tall Rock the sable Waters flow.
Divine Pelides, with Compassion mov'd,
Thus spoke, indulgent to his best belov'd.

Patroclus, say, what Grief thy Bosom bears,
That flows so fast in these unmanly Tears?   10
No Girl, no Infant whom the Mother keeps
From her lov'd Breast, with fonder Passion weeps;
Not more the Mother's Soul that Infant warms,
Clung to her Knees, and reaching at her Arms,
Than thou hast mine! Oh tell me, to what end
Thy melting Sorrows thus pursue thy Friend?
    Griev'st thou for me, or for my martial Band?
Or come sad Tidings from our native Land?
Our Fathers live, (our first, most tender Care)
Thy good Menœtius breathes the vital Air,   20
And hoary Peleus yet extends his Days;
Pleas'd in their Age to hear their Children's Praise.
    Or may some meaner Cause thy Pity claim?
Perhaps yon' Reliques of the Grecian Name,
Doom'd in their Ships to sink by Fire and Sword,
And pay the Forfeit of their haughty Lord?
Whate'er the Cause, reveal thy secret Care,
And speak those Sorrows which a Friend would share.
    A Sigh, that instant, from his Bosom broke,
Another follow'd, and Patroclus spoke.   30
    Let Greece at length with Pity touch thy Breast,
Thy self a Greek; and, once, of Greeks the best!
Lo! ev'ry Chief that might her Fate prevent,
Lies pierc'd with Wounds, and bleeding in his Tent.
Eurypylus, Tydides, Atreus' Son,
And wise Ulysses, at the Navy groan
More for their Country's Wounds, than for their own.
Their Pain, soft Arts of Pharmacy can ease,
Thy Breast alone no Lenitives appease.
    May never Rage like thine my Soul enslave,   40
O great in vain! unprofitably brave!
Thy Country slighted in her last Distress,
What Friend, what Man, from thee shall hope redress?
No—Men unborn, and Ages yet behind,
Shall curse that fierce, that unforgiving Mind.
    O Man unpitying! if of Man thy Race;
But sure thou spring'st not from a soft Embrace,

Nor ever am'rous Hero caus'd thy Birth,
Nor ever tender Goddess brought thee forth.
Some rugged Rock's hard Entrails gave thee Form,   50
And raging Seas produc'd thee in a Storm,
A Soul well-suiting that tempestuous Kind,
So rough thy Manners, so untam'd thy Mind.
    If some dire Oracle thy Breast alarm,
If ought from Jove, or Thetis, stop thy Arm,
Some Beam of Comfort yet on Greece may shine,
If I but lead the Myrmidonian Line:
Clad in thy dreadful Arms if I appear,
Proud Troy shall tremble, and desert the War:
Without thy Person Greece shall win the Day,   60
And thy mere Image chase her Foes away.
Press'd by fresh Forces, her o'erlabour'd Train
Shall quit the Ships, and Greece respire again.
    Thus, blind to Fate! with supplicating Breath,
Thou beg'st his Arms, and in his Arms, thy Death.
Unfortunately Good! a boding Sigh
Thy Friend return'd; and with it, this Reply.
    Patroclus! thy Achilles knows no Fears;
Nor Words from Jove, nor Oracles he hears;
Nor ought a Mother's Caution can suggest;   70
The Tyrant's Pride lies rooted in my Breast.
My Wrongs, my Wrongs, my constant Thought engage,
Those, my sole Oracles, inspire my Rage:
I made him Tyrant; gave him Pow'r to wrong
Ev'n me: I felt it; and shall feel it long.
The Maid, my black-ey'd Maid, he forc'd away,
Due to the Toils of many a well-fought Day;
Due to my Conquest of her Father's Reign;
Due to the Votes of all the Grecian Train.
From me he forc'd her; me, the bold and brave;   80
Disgrac'd, dishonour'd, like the meanest Slave.
But bear we this—The Wrongs I grieve, are past;
'Tis time our Fury should relent at last:
I fix'd its Date; the Day I wish'd appears:
Now Hector to my Ships his Battel bears,
The Flames my Eyes, the Shouts invade my Ears.

Go then Patroclus! court fair Honour's Charms
In Troy's fam'd Fields, and in Achilles' Arms
Lead forth my martial Myrmidons to fight,
Go save the Fleets, and conquer in my right.   90
See the thin Reliques of their baffled Band,
At the last Edge of yon' deserted Land!
Behold all Ilion on their Ships descends;
How the Cloud blackens, how the Storm impends!
It was not thus, when, at my Sight amaz'd,
Troy saw and trembled, as this Helmet blaz'd:
Had not th' injurious King our Friendship lost,
Yon' ample Trench had bury'd half her Host.
No Camps, no Bulwarks now the Trojans fear,
Those are not dreadful, no Achilles there: 100
No longer flames the Lance of Tydeus' Son;
No more your Gen'ral calls his Heroes on;
Hector, alone, I hear; His dreadful Breath
Commands your Slaughter, or proclaims your Death.
Yet now, Patroclus, issue to the Plain;
Now save the Ships, the rising Fires restrain,
And give the Greeks to visit Greece again.
But heed my Words, and mark a Friend's Command
Who trusts his Fame and Honours in thy Hand,
And from thy Deeds expects, th' Achaian Host   110
Shall render back the beauteous Maid he lost:
Rage uncontroul'd thro' all the hostile Crew,
But touch not Hector, Hector is my due.
Tho' Jove in Thunder should command the War,
Be just, consult my Glory, and forbear.
The Fleet once sav'd, desist from farther chace,
Nor lead to Ilion's Walls the Grecian Race;
Some adverse God thy Rashness may destroy;
Some God, like Phœbus, ever kind to Troy.
Let Greece, redeem'd from this destructive Strait,   120
Do her own Work, and leave the rest to Fate.
Oh! would to all th' immortal Pow'rs above,
Apollo, Pallas, and almighty Jove!
That not one Trojan might be left alive,
And not a Greek of all the Race survive;

Might only we the vast Destruction shun,
And only we destroy th' accursed Town!

Such Conf'rence held the Chiefs: while on the Strand,
Great Jove with Conquest crown'd the Trojan Band.
Ajax no more the sounding Storm sustain'd,   130
So thick, the Darts an Iron Tempest rain'd:
On his tir'd Arm the weighty Buckler hung;
His hollow Helm with falling Javelins rung;
His Breath, in quick, short Pantings, comes, and goes;
And painful Sweat from all his Members flows.
Spent and o'erpow'r'd, he barely breathes at most;
Yet scarce an Army stirs him from his Post:
Dangers on Dangers all around him grow,
And Toil to Toil, and Woe succeeds to Woe.

Say, Muses, thron'd above the starry Frame,   140
How first the Navy blaz'd with Trojan Flame?

Stern Hector wav'd his Sword; and standing near
Where furious Ajax ply'd his Ashen Spear,
Full on the Lance a Stroke so justly sped,
That the broad Faulchion lopp'd its brazen Head:
His pointless Spear the Warrior shakes in vain;
The brazen Head falls sounding on the Plain.
Great Ajax saw, and own'd the Hand divine,
Confessing Jove, and trembling at the Sign;
Warn'd, he retreats. Then swift from all sides pour   150
The hissing Brands; thick streams the fiery Show'r;
O'er the high Stern the curling Volumes rise,
And Sheets of rolling Smoke involve the Skies.

Divine Achilles view'd the rising Flames,
And smote his Thigh, and thus aloud exclaims.
Arm, arm, Patroclus! Lo, the Blaze aspires!
The glowing Ocean reddens with the Fires.
Arm, e'er our Vessels catch the spreading Flame;
Arm, e'er the Grecians be no more a Name;
I haste to bring the Troops—The Hero said;   160
The Friend with Ardour and with Joy obey'd.

He cas'd his Limbs in Brass, and first around,
His manly Legs, with silver Buckles bound
The clasping Greaves; then to his Breast applies
The flamy Cuirass, of a thousand Dyes;

Emblaz'd with Studs of Gold, his Faulchion shone,
In the rich Belt, as in a starry Zone.
Achilles' Shield his ample Shoulders spread,
Achilles' Helmet nodded o'er his Head.
Adorn'd in all his terrible Array,   170
He flash'd around intolerable Day.
Alone, untouch'd, Pelides' Javelin stands,
Not to be pois'd but by Pelides' Hands:
From Pelion's shady Brow the Plant entire
Old Chiron rent, and shap'd it for his Sire;
Whose Son's great Arm alone the Weapon wields,
The Death of Heroes, and the dread of Fields.
   Then brave Automedon (an honour'd Name,
The second to his Lord in Love and Fame,
In Peace his Friend, and Part'ner of the War)   180
The winged Coursers harness'd to the Car.
Xanthus and Balius, of immortal Breed,
Sprung from the Wind, and like the Wind in speed;
Whom the wing'd Harpye, swift Podarge, bore,
By Zephyr pregnant on the breezy Shore.
Swift Pedasus was added to their side,
(Once great Aëtion's, now Achilles' Pride)
Who, like in Strength, in Swiftness, and in Grace,
A mortal Courser match'd th' immortal Race.
   Achilles speeds from Tent to Tent, and warms   190
His hardy Myrmidons to Blood and Arms.
All breathing Death, around their Chief they stand,
A grim, terrific, formidable Band:
Grim as voracious Wolves that seek the Springs
When scalding Thirst their burning Bowels wrings
(When some tall Stag fresh-slaughter'd in the Wood
Has drench'd their wide, insatiate Throats with Blood)
To the black Fount they rush a hideous Throng,
With Paunch distended, and with lolling Tongue,
Fire fills their Eyes, their black Jaws belch the Gore,   200
And gorg'd with Slaughter, still they thirst for more.
Like furious, rush'd the Myrmidonian Crew,
Such their dread Strength, and such their deathful View.
   High in the midst the great Achilles stands,
Directs their Order, and the War commands.

He, lov'd of Jove, had launch'd for Ilion's Shores
Full fifty Vessels, mann'd with fifty Oars:
Five chosen Leaders the fierce Bands obey,
Himself supreme in Valour, as in Sway.

First march'd Menestheus, of celestial Birth,   210
Deriv'd from thee whose Waters wash the Earth,
Divine Sperchius! Jove-descended Flood!
A mortal Mother mixing with a God.
Such was Menestheus, but mis-call'd by Fame
The Son of Borus, that espous'd the Dame.

Eudorus next; whom Polymele the gay,
Fam'd in the graceful Dance, produc'd to Day.
Her, sly Cyllenius lov'd; on her would gaze,
As with swift Step she form'd the running Maze:
To her high Chamber, from Diana's Quire,   220
The God pursu'd her, urg'd, and crown'd his Fire.
The Son confess'd his Father's heav'nly Race,
And heir'd his Mother's Swiftness, in the Chace.
Strong Echeclœus, blest in all those Charms
That pleas'd a God, succeeded to her Arms;
Not conscious of her Love, long hid from Fame,
With Gifts of Price he sought and won the Dame;
Her secret Offspring to her Sire she bare;
Her Sire caress'd him with a Parent's Care.

Pisander follow'd; matchless in his Art   230
To wing the Spear, or aim the distant Dart;
No Hand so sure of all th' Emathian Line,
Or if a surer, great Patroclus! thine.

The fourth by Phœnix' grave Command was grac'd;
Laerces' valiant Offspring led the last.

Soon as Achilles, with superior Care,
Had call'd the Chiefs, and order'd all the War,
This stern Remembrance to his Troops he gave:
Ye far-fam'd Myrmidons, ye fierce and brave!
Think with what Threats you dar'd the Trojan Throng,   240
Think what Reproach these Ears endur'd so long,
"Stern Son of Peleus (thus ye us'd to say,
While restless, raging, in your Ships you lay)
"Oh nurs'd with Gall, unknowing how to yield!
"Whose Rage defrauds us of so fam'd a Field.

"If that dire Fury must for ever burn,
"What make we here? Return, ye Chiefs, return!
Such were your words—Now Warriors grieve no more,
Lo there the Trojans! bath your Swords in Gore!
This Day shall give you all your Soul demands;   250
Glut all your Hearts! and weary all your Hands!

    Thus while he rowz'd the Fire in ev'ry Breast,
Close, and more close, the list'ning Cohorts prest;
Ranks wedg'd in Ranks; of Arms a steely Ring
Still grows, and spreads, and thickens round the King.
As when a circling Wall the Builder forms,
Of Strength defensive against Winds and Storms,
Compacted Stones the thick'ning Work compose,
And round him wide the rising Structure grows.
So Helm to Helm, and Crest to Crest they throng,   260
Shield urg'd on Shield, and Man drove Man along:
Thick, undistinguish'd Plumes, together join'd,
Float in one Sea, and wave before the Wind.

    Far o'er the rest, in glitt'ring Pomp appear,
There, bold Automedon; Patroclus here;
Brothers in Arms, with equal Fury fir'd;
Two Friends, two Bodies with one Soul inspir'd.

    But mindful of the Gods, Achilles went
To the rich Coffer, in his shady Tent:
There lay on Heaps his various Garments roll'd,   270
And costly Furs, and Carpets stiff with Gold.
(The Presents of the silver-footed Dame)
From thence he took a Bowl, of antique Frame,
Which never Man had stain'd with ruddy Wine,
Nor rais'd in Off'rings to the Pow'rs divine,
But Peleus' Son; and Peleus' Son to none
Had rais'd in Off'rings, but to Jove alone.
This ting'd with Sulphur, sacred first to Flame,
He purg'd; and wash'd it in the running Stream.
Then cleans'd his Hands; and fixing for a Space   280
His Eyes on Heaven, his Feet upon the Place
Of Sacrifice, the purple Draught he pour'd
Forth in the midst; and thus the God implor'd.

    Oh thou Supreme! high-thron'd, all Height above!
Oh Great! Pelasgic, Dodonæan Jove!

Who 'midst surrounding Frosts, and Vapours chill,
Preside on bleak Dodona's vocal Hill:
(Whose Groves, the Selli, Race austere! surround,
Their Feet unwash'd, their Slumbers on the Ground;
Who hear, from rustling Oaks, their dark Decrees;   290
And catch the Fates, low-whisper'd in the Breeze.)
Hear, as of old! Thou gav'st, at Thetis Pray'r,
Glory to me, and to the Greeks Despair:
Lo to the Dangers of the fighting Field
The best, the dearest of my Friends, I yield:
Tho' still determin'd, to my Ships confin'd,
Patroclus gone, I stay but half behind.
Oh! be his Guard thy providential Care,
Confirm his Heart, and string his Arm to War:
Press'd by his single Force, let Hector see,   300
His Fame in Arms, not owing all to me.
But when the Fleets are sav'd from Foes and Fire,
Let him with Conquest and Renown retire;
Preserve his Arms, preserve his social Train,
And safe return him to these Eyes again!
    Great Jove consents to half the Chief's Request,
But Heav'ns eternal Doom denies the rest;
To free the Fleet was granted to his Pray'r;
His safe Return, the Winds dispers'd in Air.
Back to his Tent the stern Achilles flies,   310
And waits the Combate with impatient Eyes.
    Meanwhile the Troops beneath Patroclus' Care,
Invade the Trojans, and commence the War.
As Wasps, provok'd by Children in their Play,
Pour from their Mansions by the broad High-way,
In Swarms the guiltless Traveller engage,
Whet all their Stings, and call forth all their Rage;
All rise in Arms, and with a gen'ral Cry
Assert their waxen Domes, and buzzing Progeny.
Thus from the Tents the fervent Legion swarms,   320
So loud their Clamours, and so keen their Arms.
Their rising Rage Patroclus' Breath inspires,
Who thus inflames them with heroick Fires.
    Oh Warriors, Part'ners of Achilles' Praise!
Be mindful of your Deeds in ancient Days:

Your godlike Master let your Acts proclaim,
And add new Glories to his mighty Name.
Think, your Achilles sees you fight: Be brave,
And humble the proud Monarch whom you save.
Joyful they heard, and kindling as he spoke   330
Flew to the Fleet, involv'd in Fire and Smoke.
From Shore to Shore the doubling Shouts resound,
The hollow Ships return a deeper Sound.
The War stood still, and all around them gaz'd,
When great Achilles' shining Armour blaz'd:
Troy saw, and thought the dread Achilles nigh,
At once they see, they tremble, and they fly.
  Then first thy Spear, divine Patroclus! flew,
Where the War rag'd, and where the Tumult grew.
Close to the Stern of that fam'd Ship, which bore   340
Unblest Protesilaus to Ilion's Shore,
The great Pæonian, bold Pyrechmes, stood;
(Who led his Bands from Axius' winding Flood)
His Shoulder-blade receives the fatal Wound;
The groaning Warrior pants upon the Ground.
His Troops, that see their Country's Glory slain,
Fly diverse, scatter'd o'er the distant Plain.
Patroclus' Arm forbids the spreading Fires,
And from the half-burn'd Ship proud Troy retires:
Clear'd from the Smoke the joyful Navy lies;   350
In Heaps on Heaps the Foe tumultuous flies,
Triumphant Greece her rescu'd Decks ascends,
And loud Acclaim the starry Region rends.
So when thick Clouds inwrap the Mountain's Head,
O'er Heav'ns Expanse like one black Cieling spread;
Sudden, the Thund'rer, with a flashing Ray,
Bursts thro' the Darkness, and lets down the Day:
The Hills shine out, the Rocks in Prospect rise,
And Streams, and Vales, and Forests strike the Eyes,
The smiling Scene wide opens to the Sight,   360
And all th' unmeasur'd Æther flames with Light.
  But Troy repuls'd, and scatter'd o'er the Plains,
Forc'd from the Navy, yet the Fight maintains.
Now ev'ry Greek some hostile Hero slew,
But still the foremost bold Patroclus flew:

As Areïlycus had turn'd him round,
Sharp in his Thigh he felt the piercing Wound;
The brazen-pointed Spear, with Vigour thrown,
The Thigh transfix'd, and broke the brittle Bone:
Headlong he fell. Next Thoas was thy Chance,   370
Thy Breast, unarm'd, receiv'd the Spartan Lance.
Phylides' Dart, (as Amphiclus drew nigh)
His Blow prevented, and transpierc'd his Thigh,
Tore all the Brawn, and rent the Nerves away:
In Darkness, and in Death, the Warrior lay.

In equal Arms two Sons of Nestor stand,
And two bold Brothers of the Lycian Band:
By great Antilochus, Atymnius dies,
Pierc'd in the Flank, lamented Youth! he lies.
Kind Maris, bleeding in his Brother's Wound,   380
Defends the breathless Carcase on the Ground;
Furious he flies, his Murd'rer to engage,
But godlike Thrasimed prevents his Rage,
Between his Arm and Shoulder aims a Blow,
His Arm falls spouting on the Dust below:
He sinks, with endless Darkness cover'd o'er,
And vents his Soul effus'd with gushing Gore.

Slain by two Brothers, thus two Brothers bleed,
Sarpedon's Friends, Amisodarus' Seed;
Amisodarus, who by Furies led,   390
The Bane of Men, abhorr'd Chimæra bred;
Skill'd in the Dart in vain, his Sons expire,
And pay the Forfeit of their guilty Sire.

Stopp'd in the Tumult Cleobulus lies,
Beneath Oïleus' Arm, a living Prize;
A living Prize not long the Trojan stood;
The thirsty Faulchion drank his reeking Blood:
Plung'd in his Throat the smoking Weapon lies;
Black Death, and Fate unpitying, seal his Eyes.

Amid the Ranks, with mutual Thirst of Fame,   400
Lycon the brave, and fierce Peneleus came;
In vain their Javelins at each other flew,
Now, met in Arms, their eager Swords they drew.
On the plum'd Crest of his Bœotian Foe,
The daring Lycon aim'd a noble Blow;

The Sword broke short; but his, Peneleus sped
Full on the Juncture of the Neck and Head:
The Head, divided by a Stroke so just,
Hung by the Skin: the Body sunk to Dust.
O'ertaken Neamas by Merion bleeds;   410
Pierc'd thro' the Shoulder as he mounts his Steeds;
Back from the Car he tumbles to the Ground;
His swimming Eyes eternal Shades surround.
Next Erymas was doom'd his Fate to feel,
His open'd Mouth receiv'd the Cretan Steel:
Beneath the Brain the Point a Passage tore,
Crash'd the thin Bones, and drown'd the Teeth in Gore:
His Mouth, his Eyes, his Nostrils pour a Flood;
He sobs his Soul out in the Gush of Blood.
As when the Flocks, neglected by the Swain   420
(Or Kids, or Lambs) lie scatter'd o'er the Plain,
A Troop of Wolves th' unguarded Charge survey,
And rend the trembling, unresisting Prey.
Thus on the Foe the Greeks impetuous came;
Troy fled, unmindful of her former Fame.
But still at Hector godlike Ajax aim'd,
Still, pointed at his Breast, his Javelin flam'd:
The Trojan Chief, experienc'd in the Field,
O'er his broad Shoulders spread the massy Shield;
Observ'd the Storm of Darts the Grecians pour,   430
And on his Buckler caught the ringing Show'r.
He sees for Greece the Scale of Conquest rise,
Yet stops, and turns, and saves his lov'd Allies.
As when the Hand of Jove a Tempest forms,
And rolls the Cloud to blacken Heav'n with Storms,
Dark o'er the Fields th' ascending Vapour flies,
And shades the Sun, and blots the golden Skies:
So from the Ships, along the dusky Plain,
Dire Flight and Terror drove the Trojan Train.
Ev'n Hector fled; thro' Heaps of Disarray   440
The fiery Coursers forc'd their Lord away:
While far behind, his Trojans fall confus'd,
Wedg'd in the Trench, in one vast Carnage bruis'd.
Chariots on Chariots rowl; the clashing Spokes
Shock; while the madding Steeds break short their Yokes:

In vain they labour up the steepy Mound;
Their Charioteers lie foaming on the Ground.
Fierce on the Rear, with Shouts, Patroclus flies;
Tumultuous Clamour fills the Fields and Skies;
Thick Drifts of Dust involve their rapid Flight,   450
Clouds rise on Clouds and Heav'n is snatch'd from sight.
Th' affrighted Steeds, their dying Lords cast down,
Scour o'er the Fields, and stretch to reach the Town.
Loud o'er the Rout was heard the Victor's Cry,
Where the War bleeds, and where the thickest die.
Where Horse and Arms, and Chariots lie o'erthrown,
And bleeding Heroes under Axles groan.
No Stop, no Check, the Steeds of Peleus knew;
From Bank to Bank th' immortal Coursers flew,
High-bounding o'er the Fosse: the whirling Car   460
Smoaks thro' the Ranks, o'ertakes the flying War,
And thunders after Hector; Hector flies,
Patroclus shakes his Lance; but Fate denies.
Not with less Noise, with less impetuous force,
The Tyde of Trojans urge their desp'rate Course,
Than when in Autumn Jove his Fury pours,
And Earth is loaden with incessant Show'rs,
(When guilty Mortals break th' eternal Laws,
And Judges brib'd, betray the righteous Cause)
From their deep Beds he bids the Rivers rise,   470
And opens all the Floodgates of the Skies:
Th' impetuous Torrents from their Hills obey,
Whole Fields are drown'd, and Mountains swept away;
Loud roars the Deluge till it meets the Main;
And trembling Man sees all his Labours vain!
   And now the Chief (the foremost Troops repell'd)
Back to the Ships his destin'd Progress held,
Bore down half Troy, in his resistless way,
And forc'd the routed Ranks to stand the Day.
Between the Space where silver Simois flows,   480
Where lay the Fleets, and where the Rampires rose,
All grim in Dust and Blood, Patroclus stands,
And turns the Slaughter on the conqu'ring Bands.
First Pronous dy'd beneath his fiery Dart,
Which pierc'd below the Shield his valiant Heart.

Thestor was next; who saw the Chief appear,
And fell the Victim of his coward Fear;
Shrunk up he sate, with wild and haggard Eye,
Nor stood to combate, nor had Force to fly:
Patroclus mark'd him as he shunn'd the War,   490
And with unmanly Tremblings shook the Car,
And dropp'd the flowing Reins. Him 'twixt the Jaws
The Javelin sticks, and from the Chariot draws:
As on a Rock that overhangs the Main,
An Angler, studious of the Line and Cane,
Some mighty Fish draws panting to the Shore;
Not with less ease the barbed Javelin bore
The gaping Dastard: As the Spear was shook;
He fell, and Life his heartless Breast forsook.
　　Next on Erylaus he flies; a Stone   500
Large as a Rock, was by his Fury thrown.
Full on his Crown the pond'rous Fragment flew,
And burst the Helm, and cleft the Head in two:
Prone to the Ground the breathless Warrior fell,
And Death involv'd him with the Shades of Hell.
Then low in Dust Epaltes, Echius, lie;
Ipheas, Evippus, Polymelus, die;
Amphoterus, and Erymas succeed,
And last, Tlepolemus and Pyres bleed.
Where'er he moves, the growing Slaughters spread   510
In Heaps on Heaps; a Monument of Dead.
　　When now Sarpedon his brave Friends beheld
Grov'ling in Dust, and gasping on the Field,
With this Reproach his flying Host he warms,
Oh Stain to Honour! oh Disgrace to Arms!
Forsake, inglorious, the contended Plain;
This Hand, unaided, shall the War sustain:
The Task be mine this Hero's Strength to try,
Who mows whole Troops, and makes an Army fly.
　　He spake; and speaking, leaps from off the Car;   520
Patroclus lights, and sternly waits the War.
As when two Vulturs on the Mountain's Height
Stoop with re-sounding Pinions to the Fight;
They cuff, they tear, they raise a screaming Cry;
The Desert echoes, and the Rocks reply:

The Warriors thus oppos'd in Arms, engage
With equal Clamours, and with equal Rage.
  Jove view'd the Combate, whose Event foreseen,
He thus bespoke his Sister and his Queen.
The Hour draws on; the Destinies ordain,   530
My godlike Son shall press the Phrygian Plain:
Already on the Verge of Death he stands,
His Life is ow'd to fierce Patroclus' Hands.
What Passions in a Parent's Breast debate!
Say, shall I snatch him from impending Fate,
And send him safe to Lycia, distant far
From all the Dangers and the Toils of War;
Or to his Doom my bravest Offspring yield,
And fatten, with celestial Blood, the Field?
  Then thus the Goddess with the radiant Eyes: 540
What Words are these, O Sov'reign of the Skies?
Short is the Date prescrib'd to mortal Man;
Shall Jove, for one, extend the narrow Span,
Whose Bounds were fix'd before his Race began?
How many Sons of Gods, foredoom'd to Death,
Before proud Ilion, must resign their Breath!
Were thine exempt, Debate would rise above,
And murm'ring Pow'rs condemn their partial Jove.
Give the bold Chief a glorious Fate in fight;
And when th' ascending Soul has wing'd her flight,   550
Let Sleep and Death convey, by thy Command,
The breathless Body to his native Land.
His Friends and People, to his future Praise,
A marble Tomb and Pyramid shall raise,
And lasting Honours to his Ashes give;
His Fame ('tis all the Dead can have!) shall live.
  She said; the Cloud-compeller overcome,
Assents to Fate, and ratifies the Doom.
Then, touch'd with Grief, the weeping Heav'ns distill'd
A Show'r of Blood o'er all the fatal Field.   560
The God, his Eyes averting from the Plain,
Laments his Son, predestin'd to be slain,
Far from the Lycian Shores, his happy native Reign.
  Now met in Arms, the Combatants appear,
Each heav'd the Shield, and pois'd the lifted Spear:

From strong Patroclus' Hand the Javelin fled,
And pass'd the Groin of valiant Thrasymed,
The Nerves unbrac'd no more his Bulk sustain,
He falls, and falling bites the bloody Plain.
Two sounding Darts the Lycian Leader threw;   570
The first aloof with erring Fury flew,
The next transpierc'd Achilles' mortal Steed,
The gen'rous Pedasus, of Theban Breed;
Fix'd in the Shoulders Joint, he reel'd around;
Rowl'd in the bloody dust, and paw'd the slip'ry ground.
His sudden Fall th' entangled Harness broke;
Each Axle crackled, and the Chariot shook:
When bold Automedon, to disengage
The starting Coursers, and restrain their Rage,
Divides the Traces with his Sword, and freed   580
Th' incumber'd Chariot from the dying Steed:
The rest move on, obedient to the Rein;
The Car rowls slowly o'er the dusty Plain.

The tow'ring Chiefs to fiercer Fight advance,
And first Sarpedon whirl'd his weighty Lance,
Which o'er the Warrior's Shoulder took its course,
And spent in empty Air its dying Force.
Not so Patroclus' never erring Dart;
Aim'd at his Breast, it pierc'd the mortal Part
Where the strong Fibres bind the solid Heart.   590
Then, as the Mountain Oak, or Poplar tall,
Or Pine (fit Mast for some great Admiral)
Nods to the Axe, till with a groaning Sound
It sinks, and spreads its Honours on the Ground;
Thus fell the King; and laid on Earth supine,
Before his Chariot stretch'd his Form divine:
He gasp'd the Dust distain'd with streaming Gore,
And pale in Death, lay groaning on the Shore.
So lies a Bull beneath the Lion's Paws,
While the grim Savage grinds with foamy Jaws   600
The trembling Limbs, and sucks the smoaking Blood;
Deep groans, and hollow roars, rebellow thro' the Wood.

Then to the Leader of the Lycian Band
The dying Chief address'd his last Command.

Glaucus, be bold; thy Task be first to dare
The glorious Dangers of destructive War,
To lead my Troops, to combate at their Head,
Incite the Living, and supply the Dead.
Tell 'em, I charg'd them with my latest Breath
Not unreveng'd to bear Sarpedon's Death.   610
What Grief, what Shame must Glaucus undergo,
If these spoil'd Arms adorn a Grecian Foe?
Then as a Friend, and as a Warrior, fight;
Defend my Corpse, and conquer in my Right;
That taught by great Examples, all may try
Like thee to vanquish, or like me to die.

He ceas'd; the Fates suppress'd his lab'ring Breath,
And his Eyes darken'd with the Shades of Death:
Th' insulting Victor with Disdain bestrode
The prostrate Prince, and on his Bosom trod;   620
Then drew the Weapon from his panting Heart,
The reeking Fibres clinging to the Dart;
From the wide Wound gush'd out a Stream of Blood,
And the Soul issu'd in the purple Flood.

His flying Steeds the Myrmidons detain,
Unguided now, their mighty Master slain.
All-impotent of Aid, transfix'd with Grief,
Unhappy Glaucus heard the dying Chief.
His painful Arm, yet useless with the Smart
Inflicted late by Teucer's deadly Dart,   630
Supported on his better Hand he stay'd;
To Phœbus then ('twas all he could) he pray'd.

All-seeing Monarch! whether Lycia's Coast
Or sacred Ilion, thy bright Presence boast,
Pow'rful alike to ease the Wretche's Smart;
Oh hear me! God of ev'ry healing Art!
Lo! stiff with clotted Blood, and pierc'd with Pain,
That thrills my Arm and shoots thro' ev'ry Vein,
I stand unable to sustain the Spear,
And sigh, at distance from the glorious War.   640
Low in the Dust is great Sarpedon laid,
Nor Jove vouchsaf'd his hapless Offspring Aid.
But thou, O God of Health! thy Succour lend,
To guard the Reliques of my slaughter'd Friend.

For thou, tho' distant, can'st restore my Might,
To head my Lycians, and support the Fight.

Apollo heard; and suppliant as he stood,
His heav'nly Hand restrain'd the Flux of Blood;
He drew the Dolours from the wounded Part,
And breath'd a Spirit in his rising Heart.   650
Renew'd by Art divine, the Hero stands,
And owns th' Assistance of immortal Hands.
First to the Fight his native Troops he warms,
Then loudly calls on Troy's vindictive Arms;
With ample Strides he stalks from Place to Place
Now fires Agenor, now Polydamas;
Æneas next, and Hector he accosts;
Inflaming thus the Rage of all their Hosts.

What Thoughts, regardless Chief! thy Breast employ?
Oh too forgetful of the Friends of Troy!   660
Those gen'rous Friends, who, from their Country far,
Breathe their brave Souls out, in another's War.
See! where in Dust the great Sarpedon lies,
In Action valiant, and in Council wise,
Who guarded Right, and kept his People free;
To all his Lycians lost, and lost to thee!
Stretch'd by Patroclus' Arm on yonder Plains,
Oh save from hostile Rage his lov'd Remains:
Ah let not Greece his conquer'd Trophies boast,
Nor on his Corpse revenge her Heroes lost.   670

He spoke; each Leader in his Grief partook,
Troy, at the Loss, thro' all her Legions shook.
Transfix'd with deep Regret, they view'd o'erthrown
At once his Country's Pillar, and their own;
A Chief, who led to Troy's beleaguer'd Wall
A Host of Heroes, and outshin'd them all.
Fir'd, they rush on; First Hector seeks the Foes,
And with superior Vengeance, greatly glows

But o'er the Dead the fierce Patroclus stands,
And rowzing Ajax, rowz'd the list'ning Bands.   680

Heroes, be Men! be what you were before;
Or weigh the great Occasion, and be more
The Chief who taught our lofty Walls to yield,
Lies pale in Death, extended on the Field.

To guard his Body Troy in Numbers flies;
'Tis half the Glory to maintain our Prize.
Haste, strip his Arms, the Slaughter round him spread,
And send the living Lycians to the Dead.

The Heroes kindle at his fierce Command;
The martial Squadrons close on either Hand: 690
Here Troy and Lycia charge with loud Alarms,
Thessalia there, and Greece, oppose their Arms.
With horrid Shouts they circle round the Slain;
The Clash of Armour rings o'er all the Plain.
Great Jove, to swell the Horrors of the Fight,
O'er the fierce Armies pours pernicious Night,
And round his Son confounds the warring Hosts,
His Fate ennobling with a Croud of Ghosts.

Now Greece gives way, and great Epigeus falls;
Agacleus' Son, from Budium's lofty Walls: 700
Who chas'd for Murder thence, a Suppliant came
To Peleus, and the silver-footed Dame;
Now sent to Troy, Achilles' Arms to aid,
He pays due Vengeance to his Kinsman's Shade.
Soon as his luckless Hand had touch'd the Dead,
A Rock's large Fragment thunder'd on his Head;
Hurl'd by Hectorean Force, it cleft in twain
His shatter'd Helm, and stretch'd him o'er the Slain.

Fierce to the Van of Fight Patroclus came;
And, like an Eagle darting at his Game,   710
Sprung on the Trojan and the Lycian Band;
What Grief thy Heart, what Fury urg'd thy Hand.
Oh gen'rous Greek! when with full Vigour thrown
At Stenelaus flew the weighty Stone,
Which sunk him to the dead: when Troy, too near
That Arm, drew back; and Hector learn'd to fear.
Far as an able Hand a Lance can throw,
Or at the Lists, or at the fighting Foe;
So far the Trojans from their Lines retir'd;
Till Glaucus' turning, all the rest inspir'd.   720
Then Bathyclæus fell beneath his Rage,
The only Hope of Chalcon's trembling Age:
Wide o'er the Land was stretch'd his large Domain,
With stately Seats, and Riches, blest in vain:

Him, bold with Youth, and eager to pursue
The flying Lycians, Glaucus met, and slew;
Pierc'd thro' the Bosom with a sudden Wound,
He fell, and falling, made the Fields resound.
Th' Achaians sorrow for their Hero slain;
With conqu'ring Shouts the Trojans shake the Plain,   730
And crowd to spoil the Dead: The Greeks oppose:
An Iron Circle round the Carcase grows.

Then brave Laogonus resign'd his Breath,
Dispatch'd by Merion to the Shades of Death:
On Ida's holy Hill he made abode,
The Priest of Jove, and honour'd like his God.
Between the Jaw and Ear the Javelin went;
The Soul, exhaling, issu'd at the vent.
His Spear Æneas at the Victor threw,
Who stooping forward from the Death withdrew;   740
The Lance hiss'd harmless o'er his cov'ring Shield,
And trembling strook, and rooted in the Field,
There yet scarce spent, it quivers on the Plain,
Sent by the great Æneas' Arm in vain.
Swift as thou art (the raging Hero cries)
And skill'd in Dancing to dispute the Prize,
My Spear, the destin'd Passage had it found,
Had fix'd thy active Vigour to the Ground.

Oh valiant Leader of the Dardan Host!
(Insulted Merion thus retorts the Boast)   750
Strong as you are, 'tis mortal Force you trust,
An Arm as strong may stretch thee in the Dust.
And if to this my Lance thy Fate be giv'n,
Vain are thy Vaunts, Success is still from Heav'n;
This Instant sends thee down to Pluto's Coast,
Mine is the Glory, his thy parting Ghost.

O Friend (Menœtius' Son this Answer gave)
With Words to combate, ill befits the Brave:
Not empty Boasts the Sons of Troy repell,
Your Swords must plunge them to the Shades of Hell.   760
To speak, beseems the Council; but to dare
In glorious Action, is the Task of War.

This said, Patroclus to the Battel flies;
Great Merion follows, and new Shouts arise:

Shields, Helmets rattle, as the Warriors close;
And thick and heavy sounds the Storm of Blows.
As thro' the shrilling Vale, or Mountain Ground,
The Labours of the Woodman's Axe resound;
Blows following Blows are heard re-echoing wide,
While crackling Forests fall on ev'ry side.   770
Thus echo'd all the Fields with loud Alarms,
So fell the Warriors, and so rung their Arms.

　　Now great Sarpedon, on the sandy Shore,
His heav'nly Form defac'd with Dust and Gore,
And stuck with Darts by warring Heroes shed;
Lies undistinguish'd from the vulgar dead.
His long-disputed Corpse the Chiefs inclose,
On ev'ry side the busy Combate grows;
Thick, as beneath some Shepherd's thatch'd Abode,
The Pails high-foaming with a milky Flood,   780
The buzzing Flies, a persevering Train,
Incessant swarm, and chas'd, return again.

　　Jove view'd the Combate with a stern Survey,
And Eyes that flash'd intolerable Day;
Fix'd on the Field his Sight, his Breast debates
The Vengeance due, and meditates the Fates;
Whether to urge their prompt Effect, and call
The Force of Hector to Patroclus' Fall,
This Instant see his short-liv'd Trophies won,
And stretch him breathless on his slaughter'd Son;   790
Or yet, with many a Soul's untimely flight,
Augment the Fame and Horror of the Fight?
To crown Achilles' valiant Friend with Praise
At length he dooms; and that his last of Days
Shall set in Glory; bids him drive the Foe;
Nor unattended, see the Shades below.
Then Hector's Mind he fills with dire Dismay;
He mounts his Car, and calls his Hosts away;
Sunk with Troy's heavy Fates, he sees decline
The Scales of Jove, and pants with Awe divine.   800

　　Then, nor before, the hardy Lycians fled,
And left their Monarch with the common dead:
Around, in heaps on heaps, a dreadful Wall
Of Carnage rises, as the Heroes fall.

(So Jove decreed!) At length the Greeks obtain
The Prize contested, and despoil the Slain.
The radiant Arms are by Patroclus born,
Patroclus' Ships the glorious Spoils adorn.
 Then thus to Phœbus, in the Realms above,
Spoke from his Throne the Cloud-compelling Jove.   810
Descend, my Phœbus! on the Phrygian Plain,
And from the Fight convey Sarpedon slain;
Then bathe his Body in the crystal Flood,
With Dust dishonour'd, and deform'd with Blood:
O'er all his Limbs Ambrosial Odours shed,
And with celestial Robes adorn the Dead.
Those Rites discharg'd, his sacred Corpse bequeath
To the soft Arms of silent Sleep and Death;
They to his Friends the mournful Charge shall bear,
His Friends a Tomb and Pyramid shall rear;   820
What Honours Mortals after Death receive,
Those unavailing Honours we may give!
 Apollo bows, and from Mount Ida's Height,
Swift to the Field precipitates his Flight;
Thence from the War the breathless Hero bore,
Veil'd in a Cloud, to silver Simois' Shore:
There bath'd his honourable Wounds, and drest
His manly Members in th' immortal Vest;
And with Perfumes of sweet Ambrosial Dews,
Restores his Freshness, and his Form renews.   830
Then Sleep and Death, two Twins of winged Race,
Of matchless Swiftness, but of silent Pace,
Receiv'd Sarpedon, at the God's Command,
And in a Moment reach'd the Lycian Land;
The Corpse amidst his weeping Friends they laid,
Where endless Honours wait the sacred Shade.
 Meanwhile Patroclus pours along the Plains,
With foaming Coursers, and with loosen'd Reins.
Fierce on the Trojan and the Lycian Crew,
Ah blind to Fate! thy headlong Fury flew: 840
Against what Fate and pow'rful Jove ordain,
Vain was thy Friend's Command, thy Courage vain.
For he, the God, whose Counsels uncontroll'd,
Dismay the mighty, and confound the bold:

The God who gives, resumes, and orders all,
He urg'd thee on, and urg'd thee on to fall.
　Who first, brave Hero! by that Arm was slain,
Who last, beneath thy Vengeance, press'd the Plain;
When Heav'n itself thy fatal Fury led,
And call'd to fill the Number of the Dead?　　　　　850
Adrestus first; Autonous then succeeds,
Echeclus follows; next young Megas bleeds;
Epistor, Menalippus, bite the Ground;
The Slaughter, Elasus and Mulius crown'd:
Then sunk Pylartes to eternal Night;
The rest dispersing, trust their Fates to Flight.
　Now Troy had stoop'd beneath his matchless Pow'r,
But flaming Phœbus kept the sacred Tow'r.
Thrice at the Battlement Patroclus strook,
His blazing Ægis thrice Apollo shook:　　　　　860
He try'd the fourth; when, bursting from the Cloud,
A more than mortal Voice was heard aloud.
　Patroclus! cease: This Heav'n-defended Wall
Defies thy Lance; not fated yet to fall;
Thy Friend, thy greater far, it shall withstand,
Troy shall not stoop ev'n to Achilles' Hand.
So spoke the God who darts celestial Fires:
The Greek obeys him, and with Awe retires.
While Hector checking at the Scæan Gates
His panting Coursers, in his Breast debates,　　　　870
Or in the Field his Forces to employ,
Or draw the Troops within the Walls of Troy.
Thus while he thought, beside him Phœbus stood,
In Asius' Shape, who reign'd by Sangar's Flood;
(Thy Brother, Hecuba! from Dymas sprung;
A valiant Warrior, haughty, bold, and young.)
Thus he accosts him. What a shameful Sight!
Gods! is it Hector that forbears the Fight?
Were thine my Vigour, this successful Spear
Should soon convince thee of so false a Fear.　　　　880
Turn then, ah turn thee to the Field of Fame;
And in Patroclus' Blood efface thy Shame.
Perhaps Apollo shall thy Arms succeed,
And Heav'n ordains him by thy Lance to bleed.

So spoke th' inspiring God; then took his flight,
And plung'd amidst the Tumult of the Fight.
He bids Cebrion drive the rapid Car;
The Lash resounds; the Coursers rush to War.
The God the Grecians sinking Souls deprest,
And pour'd swift Spirits thro' each Trojan Breast.   890
Patroclus lights, impatient for the Fight;
A Spear his Left, a Stone employs his Right:
With all his Nerves he drives it at the Foe;
Pointed above, and rough and gross below:
The falling Ruin crush'd Cebrion's Head,
(The lawless Offspring of King Priam's Bed,)
His Front, Brows, Eyes, one undistinguish'd Wound,
The bursting Balls drop sightless to the Ground.
The Charioteer, while yet he held the Rein,
Struck from the Car, falls headlong on the Plain.   900
To the dark Shades the Soul unwilling glides,
While the proud Victor thus his Fall derides,
    Good Heav'ns! what active Feats yon' Artist shows,
What skilful Divers are our Phrygian Foes!
Mark with what Ease they sink into the Sand!
Pity! that all their Practice is by Land.
    Then rushing sudden on his prostrate Prize,
To spoil the Carcase fierce Patroclus flies:
Swift as a Lion, terrible and bold,
That sweeps the Fields, depopulates the Fold;   910
Pierc'd thro' the dauntless Heart, then tumbles slain;
And from his fatal Courage finds his Bane.
At once bold Hector leaping from his Car,
Defends the Body, and provokes the War.
Thus for some slaughter'd Hind, with equal Rage,
Two lordly Rulers of the Wood engage;
Stung with fierce Hunger, each the Prey invades,
And echoing Roars rebellow thro' the Shades.
Stern Hector fastens on the Warrior's Head,
And by the Foot Patroclus drags the Dead.   920
While all around, Confusion, Rage, and Fright
Mix the contending Hosts in mortal Fight.
So pent by Hills, the wild Winds roar aloud
In the deep Bosom of some gloomy Wood;

Leaves, Arms, and Trees aloft in Air are blown,
The broad Oaks crackle, and the Sylvans groan;
This way and that, the ratt'ling Thicket bends,
And the whole Forest in one Crash descends.
Not with less Noise, with less tumultuous Rage,
In dreadful Shock the mingled Hosts engage.   930
Darts show'r'd on Darts, now round the Carcase ring;
Now Flights of Arrows bounding from the String:
Stones follow Stones; some clatter on the Fields,
Some, hard and heavy, shake the sounding Shields.
But where the rising Whirlwind clouds the Plains,
Sunk in soft Dust the mighty Chief remains,
And stretch'd in Death, forgets the guiding Reins!
   Now flaming from the Zenith, Sol had driv'n
His fervid Orb thro' half the Vault of Heav'n;
While on each Host with equal Tempest fell   940
The show'ring Darts, and Numbers sunk to Hell.
But when his Ev'ning Wheels o'erhung the Main,
Glad Conquest rested on the Grecian Train.
Then from amidst the Tumult and Alarms,
They draw the conquer'd Corpse, and radiant Arms.
Then rash Patroclus with new Fury glows,
And breathing Slaughter, pours amid the Foes.
Thrice on the Press like Mars himself he flew,
And thrice three Heroes at each Onset slew.
There ends thy Glory! there the Fates untwine   950
The last, black Remnant of so bright a Line.
Apollo dreadful stops thy middle way;
Death calls, and Heav'n allows no longer Day!
For lo! the God, in dusky Clouds enshrin'd,
Approaching dealt a stagg'ring Blow behind.
The weighty Shock his Neck and Shoulders feel;
His Eyes flash Sparkles, his stunn'd Senses reel
In giddy Darkness: Far to distance flung,
His bounding Helmet on the Champain rung.
Achilles' Plume is stain'd with Dust and Gore;   960
That Plume, which never stoop'd to Earth before,
Long us'd, untouch'd, in fighting Fields to shine,
And shade the Temples of the Man divine.

Jove dooms it now on Hector's Helm to nod;
Not long—For Fate pursues him, and the God.
   His Spear in Shivers falls: His ample Shield
Drops from his Arm: his Baldrick strows the Field:
The Corselet his astonish'd Breast forsakes:
Loose is each Joint; each Nerve with Horror shakes.
Stupid he stares, and all-assistless stands: 970
Such is the Force of more than mortal Hands!
   A Dardan Youth there was, well-known to Fame,
From Panthus sprung, Euphorbus was his Name;
Fam'd for the Manage of the foaming Horse,
Skill'd in the Dart, and matchless in the Course:
Full twenty Knights he tumbled from the Car,
While yet he learn'd his Rudiments of War.
His vent'rous Spear first drew the Hero's Gore;
He strook, he wounded, but he durst no more;
Nor tho' disarm'd, Patroclus' Fury stood: 980
But swift withdrew the long-protended Wood,
And turn'd him short, and herded in the Croud.
Thus, by an Arm divine, and mortal Spear,
Wounded at once, Patroclus yields to fear,
Retires for Succour to his social Train,
And flies the Fate, which Heav'n decreed, in vain.
Stern Hector, as the bleeding Chief he views,
Breaks thro' the Ranks, and his Retreat pursues:
The Lance arrests him with a mortal Wound;
He falls, Earth thunders, and his Arms resound.   990
With him all Greece was sunk; that Moment all
Her yet-surviving Heroes seem'd to fall.
So scorch'd with Heat along the desart Shore,
The roaming Lyon meets a bristly Boar,
Fast by the Spring; they both dispute the Flood,
With flaming Eyes, and Jaws besmear'd with Blood;
At length the sov'reign Savage wins the Strife,
And the torn Boar resigns his Thirst and Life.
Patroclus thus, so many Chiefs o'erthrown,
So many Lives effus'd, expires his own.   1000
As dying now at Hector's Feet he lies,
He sternly views him, and triumphing cries.

Lie there Patroclus! and with thee, the Joy
Thy Pride once promis'd, of subverting Troy;
The fancy'd Scenes, of Ilion wrapt in Flames,
And thy soft Pleasures serv'd with captive Dames!
Unthinking Man! I fought, those Tow'rs to free,
And guard that beauteous Race from Lords like thee:
But thou a Prey to Vulturs shalt be made!
The fierce Achilles cannot lend thee Aid;   1010
Tho much at parting that great Chief might say,
And much enjoin thee, this important Day.
"Return not, my brave Friend (perhaps he said)
"Without the bloody Arms of Hector dead:
He spoke, Patroclus march'd, and thus he sped.

 Supine, and wildly gazing on the Skies,
With faint, expiring Breath, the Chief replies.
Vain Boaster! cease, and know the Pow'rs divine;
Jove's and Apollo's is this Deed, not thine;
To Heav'n is ow'd whate'er your own you call,   1020
And Heav'n itself disarm'd me e'er my Fall.
Had twenty Mortals, each thy Match in Might,
Oppos'd me fairly, they had sunk in Fight:
By Fate and Phœbus was I first o'erthrown,
Euphorbus next; the third mean Part thy own.
But thou Imperious! hear my latest Breath;
The Gods inspire it, and it sounds thy Death.
Insulting Man! thou shalt be soon, as I;
Black Fate hangs o'er thee, and thy Hour draws nigh;
Ev'n now on Life's last Verge I see thee stand,   1030
I see thee fall, and by Achilles' Hand.

 He faints; the Soul unwilling wings her way,
(The beauteous Body left a Load of Clay)
Flits to the lone, uncomfortable Coast;
A naked, wand'ring, melancholy Ghost!

 Then Hector pausing, as his Eyes he fed
On the pale Carcase thus address'd the dead.
From whence this boding Speech, the stern Decree
Of Death denounc'd, or why denounc'd to me?
Why not as well Achilles' Fate be giv'n   1040
To Hector's Lance? Who knows the Will of Heav'n?

　　Pensive he said; then pressing as he lay
His breathless Bosom, tore the Lance away;
And upwards cast the Corps: The reeking Spear
He shakes, and charges the bold Charioteer.
But swift Automedon with loosned Reins
Rapt in the Chariot o'er the distant Plains,
Far from his Rage th' immortal Coursers drove;
Th' immortal Coursers were the Gift of Jove.

꒚꒚꒚

THE SEVENTEENTH BOOK
OF THE ILIAD

THE ARGUMENT

The seventh Battel, for the Body of Patroclus:
The Acts of Menelaus

MENELAUS, UPON THE DEATH of Patroclus, defends his Body from the
Enemy: Euphorbus who attempts it, is slain. Hector advancing, Menelaus
retires, but soon returns with Ajax, and drives him off. This Glaucus objects to Hector as a Flight, who thereupon puts on the Armour he had
won from Patroclus, and renews the Battel. The Greeks give way, till
Ajax rallies them: Æneas sustains the Trojans. Æneas and Hector at-
tempt the Chariot of Achilles, which is borne off by Automedon. The
Horses of Achilles deplore the Loss of Patroclus: Jupiter covers his Body
with a thick Darkness: The noble Prayer of Ajax on that Occasion.
Menelaus sends Antilochus to Achilles, with the News of Patroclus's
Death: Then returns to the Fight, where, tho' attack'd with the utmost
Fury, he, and Meriones assisted by the Ajaxes, bear off the Body to the
Ships.
The Time is the Evening of the eight and twentieth Day. The Scene
lies in the Fields before Troy.

On the cold Earth divine Patroclus spread,
Lies pierc'd with Wounds among the vulgar Dead.
Great Menelaus, touch'd with gen'rous Woe,
Springs to the Front, and guards him from the Foe:
Thus round her new fal'n Young, the Heifer moves,
Fruit of her Throes, and First-born of her Loves,

397

And anxious, (helpless as he lies, and bare)
Turns, and returns her, with a Mother's Care.
Oppos'd to each, that near the Carcase came,
His broad Shield glimmers, and his Lances flame.   10
　　The Son of Panthus, skill'd the Dart to send,
Eyes the dead Hero and insults the Friend.
This Hand, Atrides, laid Patroclus low;
Warrior! desist, nor tempt an equal Blow:
To me the Spoils my Prowess won, resign;
Depart with Life, and leave the Glory mine.
　　The Trojan thus: The Spartan Monarch burn'd
With generous Anguish, and in scorn return'd.
Laugh'st thou not, Jove! from thy superior Throne,
When Mortals boast of Prowess not their own?   20
Not thus the Lion glories in his Might,
Nor Panther braves his spotted Foe in Fight,
Nor thus the Boar (those Terrors of the Plain)
Man only vaunts his Force, and vaunts in vain.
But far the vainest of the Boastful Kind
These Sons of Panthus vent their haughty Mind.
Yet 'twas but late, beneath my conqu'ring Steel
This Boaster's Brother, Hyperenor fell,
Against our Arm which rashly he defy'd,
Vain was his Vigour, and as vain his Pride.   30
These Eyes beheld him on the Dust expire,
No more to chear his Spouse, or glad his Sire.
Presumptuous Youth! like his shall be thy Doom,
To wait thy Brother to the Stygian Gloom;
While yet thou may'st, avoid the threaten'd Fate;
Fools stay to feel it, and are wise too late.
　　Unmov'd, Euphorbus thus: That Action known,
Come, for my Brother's Blood repay thy own.
His weeping Father claims thy destin'd Head,
And spouse, a Widow in her bridal Bed.   40
On these thy conquer'd Spoils I shall bestow,
To sooth a Consort's and a Parent's Woe.
No longer then defer the glorious Strife,
Let Heav'n decide our Fortune, Fame, and Life.

Swift as the Word, the missile Lance he flings,
The well-aim'd Weapon on the Buckler rings,
But blunted by the Brass innoxious falls.
On Jove the Father, great Atrides calls,
Nor flies the Jav'lin from his Arm in vain,
It pierc'd his Throat, and bent him to the Plain;   50
Wide thro' the Neck appears the grizly Wound,
Prone sinks the Warrior, and his Arms resound.
The shining Circlets of his golden Hair,
Which ev'n the Graces might be proud to wear,
Instarr'd with Gems and Gold, bestrow the Shore,
With Dust dishonour'd, and deform'd with Gore.

As the young Olive, in some Sylvan Scene,
Crown'd by fresh Fountains with eternal Green,
Lifts the gay Head, in snowy Flourets fair,
And plays and dances to the gentle Air;   60
When lo! a Whirlwind from high Heav'n invades
The tender Plant, and withers all its Shades;
It lies uprooted from its genial Bed,
A lovely Ruin, now defac'd and dead.
Thus young, thus beautiful, Euphorbus lay,
While the fierce Spartan tore his Arms away.
Proud of his Deed, and glorious in the Prize,
Affrighted Troy the tow'ring Victor flies,
Flies, as before some Mountain Lion's Ire
The village Curs, and trembling Swains retire;   70
When o'er the slaughter'd Bull they hear him roar,
And see his Jaws distil with smoking Gore;
All pale with Fear, at distance scatter'd round,
They shout incessant, and the Vales resound.

Meanwhile Apollo view'd with envious Eyes,
And urg'd great Hector to dispute the Prize,
(In Mentes Shape, beneath whose martial Care
The rough Ciconians learn'd the Trade of War)
Forbear, he cry'd, with fruitless Speed to chace
Achilles' Coursers of æthereal Race;   80
They stoop not, these, to mortal man's Command,
Or stoop to none but great Achilles' Hand.

Too long amus'd with a Pursuit so vain,
Turn, and behold the brave Euphorbus slain!
By Sparta slain! for ever now supprest
The Fire which burn'd in that undaunted Breast!

Thus having spoke, Apollo wing'd his Flight
And mix'd with Mortals in the Toils of Fight:
His Words infix'd unutterable Care
Deep in great Hector's Soul: Thro' all the War   90
He darts his anxious Eye; and instant, view'd
The breathless Hero in his Blood imbru'd,
(Forth welling from the Wound, as prone he lay)
And in the Victor's Hands the shining Prey.
Sheath'd in bright Arms, thro' cleaving Ranks he flies,
And sends his Voice in Thunder to the Skies:
Fierce as a Flood of Flame by Vulcan sent,
It flew, and fir'd the Nations as it went.
Atrides from the Voice the Storm divin'd,
And thus explor'd his own unconquer'd Mind.   100

Then shall I quit Patroclus on the Plain,
Slain in my Cause, and for my Honour slain,
Desert the Arms, the Relicks of my Friend?
Or singly, Hector and his Troops attend?
Sure where such partial Favour Heav'n bestow'd,
To brave the Hero were to brave the God:
Forgive me, Greece, if once I quit the Field;
'Tis not to Hector, but to Heav'n I yield.
Yet, nor the God, nor Heav'n, shou'd give me Fear,
Did but the Voice of Ajax reach my Ear: 110
Still would we turn, still battle on the Plains,
And give Achilles all that yet remains
Of his and our Patroclus—This, no more,
The Time allow'd: Troy thicken'd on the Shore,
A sable Scene! The Terrors Hector led.
Slow he recedes, and sighing, quits the Dead.

So from the Fold th' unwilling Lion parts,
Forc'd by loud Clamours, and a Storm of Darts;
He flies indeed, but threatens as he flies,
With Heart indignant and retorted Eyes.   120

Now enter'd in the Spartan Ranks, he turn'd
His manly Breast, and with new Fury burn'd,
O'er all the black Battalions sent his View,
And thro' the Cloud the god-like Ajax knew;
Where lab'ring on the left the Warrior stood,
All grim in Arms, and cover'd o'er with Blood,
There breathing Courage, where the God of Day
Had sunk each Heart with Terror and Dismay.
To him the King. Oh Ajax, oh my Friend!
Haste, and Patroclus' lov'd Remains defend: 130
The Body to Achilles to restore,
Demands our Care; Alas! we can no more!
For naked now, despoil'd of Arms he lies;
And Hector glories in the dazling Prize.
He said, and touch'd his Heart. The raging Pair
Pierce the thick Battel, and provoke the War.
Already had stern Hector seiz'd his Head,
And doom'd to Trojan Dogs th' unhappy Dead;
But soon as Ajax rear'd his tow'rlike Shield,
Sprung to his Car, and measur'd back the Field.   140
His Train to Troy the radiant Armour bear,
To stand a Trophy of his Fame in War.
    Meanwhile great Ajax (his broad Shield display'd)
Guards the dead Hero with the dreadful Shade;
And now before, and now behind he stood:
Thus in the Center of some gloomy Wood,
With many a Step the Lioness surrounds
Her tawny Young, beset by Men and Hounds;
Elate her Heart, and rowzing all her Pow'rs,
Dark o'er the fiery Balls, each hanging Eye-brow lowrs.   150
Fast by his Side, the gen'rous Spartan glows
With great Revenge, and feeds his inward Woes.
    But Glaucus, Leader of the Lycian Aids,
On Hector frowning, thus his Flight upbraids.
Where now in Hector shall we Hector find?
A manly Form, without a manly Mind.
Is this, O Chief! a Hero's boasted Fame?
How vain, without the Merit is the Name?

Since Battel is renounc'd, thy Thoughts employ
What other Methods may preserve thy Troy?   160
'Tis time to try if Ilion's State can stand
By thee alone, nor ask a foreign Hand;
Mean, empty Boast! but shall the Lycians stake
Their Lives for you? those Lycians you forsake?
What from thy thankless Arms can we expect?
Thy Friend Sarpedon proves thy base Neglect:
Say, shall our slaughter'd Bodies guard your Walls
While unreveng'd the great Sarpedon falls?
Ev'n where he dy'd for Troy, you left him there,
A Feast for Dogs, and all the Fowls of Air.   170
On my Command if any Lycian wait,
Hence let him march, and give up Troy to Fate.
Did such a Spirit as the Gods impart
Impel one Trojan Hand, or Trojan Heart;
(Such, as shou'd burn in ev'ry Soul, that draws
The Sword for Glory, and his Country's Cause)
Ev'n yet our mutual Arms we might employ,
And drag yon' Carcass to the Walls of Troy.
Oh! were Patroclus ours, we might obtain
Sarpedon's Arms and honour'd Corse again!   180
Greece with Achilles' Friend shou'd be repaid,
And thus due Honours purchas'd to his Shade.
But Words are vain—Let Ajax once appear,
And Hector trembles and recedes with Fear;
Thou dar'st not meet the Terrors of his Eye;
And lo! already, thou prepar'st to fly.
   The Trojan Chief with fixt Resentment ey'd
The Lycian Leader, and sedate reply'd.
Say, is it just (my Friend) that Hector's Ear
From such a Warrior such a Speech shou'd hear?   190
I deem'd thee once the wisest of thy Kind,
But ill this Insult suits a prudent Mind.
I shun great Ajax? I desert my Train?
'Tis mine to prove the rash Assertion vain;
I joy to mingle where the Battel bleeds,
And hear the Thunder of the sounding Steeds.

But Jove's high Will is ever uncontroll'd,
The Strong he withers, and confounds the Bold,
Now crowns with Fame the mighty Man, and now
Strikes the fresh Garland from the Victor's Brow!   200
Come, thro' yon' Squadrons let us hew the Way,
And thou be Witness, if I fear to Day;
If yet a Greek the Sight of Hector dread,
Or yet their Hero dare defend the Dead.
    Then turning to the martial Hosts, he cries,
Ye Trojans, Dardans, Lycians, and Allies!
Be Men (my Friends) in Action as in Name,
And yet be mindful of your ancient Fame.
Hector in proud Achilles' Arms shall shine,
Torn from his Friend, by right of Conquest mine.   210
    He strode along the Field, as thus he said.
(The sable Plumage nodded o'er his Head)
Swift thro' the spacious Plain he sent a Look;
One Instant saw, one Instant overtook
The distant Band, that on the sandy Shore
The radiant Spoils to sacred Ilion bore.
There his own Mail unbrac'd, the Field bestrow'd;
His Train to Troy convey'd the massy Load.
Now blazing in th' immortal Arms he stands,
The Work and Present of celestial Hands;   220
By aged Peleus to Achilles given,
As first to Peleus by the Court of Heav'n:
His Father's Arms not long Achilles wears,
Forbid by Fate to reach his Father's Years.
    Him, proud in Triumph glitt'ring from afar,
The God, whose Thunder rends the troubled Air,
Beheld with Pity; as apart he sate,
And conscious, look'd thro' all the Scene of Fate.
He shook the sacred Honours of his Head;
Olympus trembled, and the Godhead said.   230
    Ah wretched Man! unmindful of thy End!
A Moment's Glory! and what Fates attend?
In heav'nly Panoply divinely bright
Thou stand'st, and Armies tremble at thy Sight

As at Achilles self! Beneath thy Dart
Lies slain the great Achilles' dearer Part:
Thou from the mighty Dead those Arms hast torn
Which once the greatest of Mankind had worn.
Yet live! I give thee one illustrious Day,
A Blaze of Glory, e'er thou fad'st away.   240
For ah! no more Andromache shall come,
With joyful Tears to welcome Hector home;
No more officious, with endearing Charms,
From thy tir'd Limbs unbrace Pelides' Arms!
   Then with his sable Brow he gave the Nod,
That seals his Word; the Sanction of the God.
The stubborn Arms (by Jove's Command dispos'd)
Conform'd spontaneous, and around him clos'd;
Fill'd with the God, enlarg'd his Members grew,
Thro' all his Veins a sudden Vigour flew,   250
The Blood in brisker Tides began to roll,
And Mars himself came rushing on his Soul.
Exhorting loud thro' all the Field he strode,
And look'd, and mov'd, Achilles, or a God.
Now Mesthles, Glaucus, Medon he inspires,
Now Phorcys, Chromius, and Hippothous fires;
The great Thersilochus like Fury found,
Asteropæus kindled at the Sound,
And Ennomus, in Augury renown'd.
Hear all ye Hosts, and hear, unnumber'd Bands   260
Of neighb'ring Nations, or of distant Lands!
'Twas not for State we summon'd you so far,
To boast our Numbers, and the Pomp of War;
Ye came to fight; a valiant Foe to chase,
To save our present, and our future Race.
For this, our Wealth, our Products you enjoy,
And glean the Relicks of exhausted Troy.
Now then to conquer or to die prepare,
To die, or conquer, are the Terms of War.
Whatever Hand shall win Patroclus slain,   270
Whoe'er shall drag him to the Trojan Train,
With Hector's self shall equal Honours claim;
With Hector part the Spoil, and share the Fame.

Fir'd by his Words, the Troops dismiss their Fears,
They join, they thicken, they protend their Spears;
Full on the Greeks they drive in firm Array,
And each from Ajax hopes the glorious Prey:
Vain hope! what Numbers shall the Field o'erspread,
What Victims perish round the mighty Dead?

Great Ajax mark'd the growing Storm from far,   280
And thus bespoke his Brother of the War.
Our fatal Day alas! is come (my Friend)
And all our Wars and Glories at an end!
'Tis not this Corpse alone we guard in vain,
Condemn'd to Vulturs on the Trojan Plain;
We too must yield: The same sad Fate must fall
On thee, on me, perhaps (my Friend) on all.
See what a Tempest direful Hector spreads,
And lo! it bursts, it thunders on our Heads!
Call on our Greeks, if any hear the Call,   290
The bravest Greeks: This Hour demands them all.

The Warrior rais'd his Voice, and wide around
The Field re-echo'd the distressful Sound.
Oh Chiefs! oh Princes! to whose Hand is giv'n
The Rule of Men; whose Glory is from Heav'n!
Whom with due Honours both Atrides grace;
Ye Guides and Guardians of our Argive Race!
All, whom this well-known Voice shall reach from far,
All, whom I see not thro' this Cloud of War,
Come all! Let gen'rous Rage your Arms employ,   300
And save Patroclus from the Dogs of Troy.

Oïlean Ajax first the Voice obey'd,
Swift was his Pace, and ready was his Aid;
Next him Idomeneus, more slow with Age,
And Merion, burning with a Hero's Rage.
The long-succeeding Numbers who can name?
But all were Greeks and eager all for Fame.
Fierce to the Charge great Hector led the Throng;
Whole Troy embodied, rush'd with Shouts along.
Thus, when a Mountain-Billow foams and raves,   310
Where some swoln River disembogues his Waves,

Full in the Mouth is stopp'd the rushing Tide,
The boiling Ocean works from Side to Side,
The River trembles to his utmost Shore,
And distant Rocks rebellow to the Roar.

   Nor less resolv'd, the firm Achaian Band
With brazen Shields in horrid Circle stand:
Jove, pouring Darkness o'er the mingled Fight,
Conceals the Warriors' shining Helms in Night:
To him, the Chief for whom the Hosts contend,   320
Had liv'd not hateful, for he liv'd a Friend:
Dead, he protects him with superior Care,
Nor dooms his Carcase to the Birds of Air.

   The first Attack the Grecians scarce sustain,
Repuls'd, they yield; the Trojans seize the slain:
Then fierce they rally, to Revenge led on
By the swift Rage of Ajax Telamon.
(Ajax, to Peleus' Son the second Name,
In graceful Stature next, and next in Fame.)
With headlong Force the foremost Ranks he tore;   330
So thro' the Thicket bursts the Mountain Boar,
And rudely scatters, far to distance round,
The frighted Hunter, and the baying Hound.
The Son of Lethus, brave Pelasgus' Heir,
Hippothous, dragg'd the Carcase thro' the War;
The sinewy Ancles bor'd, the Feet he bound
With Thongs, inserted thro' the double Wound:
Inevitable Fate o'ertakes the Deed;
Doom'd by great Ajax' vengeful Lance to bleed;
It cleft the Helmets brazen Cheeks in twain;   340
The shatter'd Crest, and Horse-hair, strow the Plain:
With Nerves relax'd he tumbles to the Ground:
The Brain comes gushing from the ghastly Wound;
He drops Patroclus' Foot, and o'er him spread
Now lies, a sad Companion of the Dead:
Far from Larissa lies, his native Air,
And ill requites his Parent's tender Care.
Lamented Youth! in Life's first Bloom he fell,
Sent by great Ajax to the Shades of Hell.

Once more at Ajax, Hector's Jav'lin flies; 350
The Grecian marking, as it cut the Skies,
Shun'd the descending Death; which hissing on,
Stretch'd in the Dust the great Iphytus' Son,
Schedius the brave, of all the Phocian Kind
The boldest Warrior, and the noblest Mind:
In little Panope for Strength renown'd,
He held his Seat, and rul'd the Realms around.
Plung'd in his Throat, the Weapon drank his Blood,
And deep transpiercing, thro' the Shoulder stood;
In clanging Arms the Hero fell, and all 360
The Fields resounded with his weighty Fall.

Phorcys, as slain Hippothous he defends,
The Telamonian Lance his Belly rends;
The hollow Armour burst before the Stroke,
And thro' the Wound the rushing Entrails broke.
In strong Convulsions panting on the Sands
He lies, and grasps the Dust with dying Hands.

Struck at the Sight, recede the Trojan Train:
The shouting Argives strip the Heroes slain.
And now had Troy, by Greece compell'd to yield, 370
Fled to her Ramparts, and resign'd the Field;
Greece, in her native Fortitude elate,
With Jove averse, had turn'd the Scale of Fate:
But Phoebus urg'd Æneas to the Fight;
He seem'd like aged Periphas to Sight.
(A Herald in Anchises' Love grown old,
Rever'd for Prudence, and with Prudence, bold.)
Thus He—what Methods yet, oh Chief! remain,
To save your Troy, tho' Heav'n its Fall ordain?
There have been Heroes, who by virtuous Care, 380
By Valour, Numbers, and by Arts of War,
Have forc'd the Pow'rs to spare a sinking State,
And gain'd at length the glorious Odds of Fate.
But you, when Fortune smiles, when Jove declares
His partial Favour, and assists your Wars,
Your shameful Efforts 'gainst your selves employ,
And force th' unwilling God to ruin Troy.

Æneas thro the Form assum'd descries
The Pow'r conceal'd, and thus to Hector cries.
Oh lasting Shame! to our own Fears a Prey,   390
We seek our Ramparts, and desert the Day.
A God (nor is he less) my Bosom warms,
And tells me, Jove asserts the Trojan Arms.

He spoke, and foremost to the Combat flew:
The bold Example all his Hosts pursue.
Then first, Leocritus beneath him bled,
In vain belov'd by valiant Lycomede;
Who view'd his Fall, and grieving at the Chance,
Swift to revenge it, sent his angry Lance;
The whirling Lance with vig'rous Force addrest,   400
Descends, and pants in Apisaon's Breast:
From rich Pæonias' Vales the Warrior came,
Next thee, Asteropeus! in Place and Fame.
Asteropeus with Grief beheld the Slain,
And rush'd to combate, but he rush'd in vain:
Indissolubly firm, around the Dead,
Rank within Rank, on Buckler Buckler spread,
And hemm'd with bristled Spears, the Grecians stood;
A brazen Bulwark, and an iron Wood.
Great Ajax eyes them with incessant Care,   410
And in an Orb, contracts the crowded War,
Close in their Ranks commands to fight or fall,
And stands the Center and the Soul of all:
Fixt on the Spot they war; and wounded, wound;
A sanguine Torrent steeps the reeking Ground;
On Heaps the Greeks, on Heaps the Trojans bled,
And thick'ning round 'em, rise the Hills of Dead.

Greece, in close Order and collected Might,
Yet suffers least, and sways the wav'ring Fight;
Fierce as conflicting Fires, the Combate burns,   420
And now it rises, now it sinks, by turns.
In one thick Darkness all the Fight was lost;
The Sun, the Moon, and all th' Etherial Host
Seem'd as extinct: Day ravish'd from their Eyes,
And all Heav'n's Splendors blotted from the Skies.

Such o'er Patroclus Body hung the Night,
The rest in Sunshine fought, and open Light:
Unclouded there, th' Aerial Azure spread,
No Vapour rested on the Mountain's Head,
The golden Sun pour'd forth a stronger Ray, 430
And all the broad Expansion flam'd with Day.
Dispers'd around the Plain, by fits they fight,
And here, and there, their scatter'd Arrows light:
But Death and Darkness o'er the Carcase spread,
There burn'd the War, and there the Mighty bled.

Meanwhile the Sons of Nestor, in the Rear,
Their Fellows routed, toss the distant Spear,
And skirmish wide: So Nestor gave Command,
When from the Ships he sent the Pylian Band.
The youthful Brothers thus for Fame contend, 440
Nor knew the Fortune of Achilles' Friend;
In thought they view'd him still, with martial Joy,
Glorious in Arms, and dealing Deaths to Troy.

But round the Corps, the Heroes pant for Breath,
And thick and heavy grows the Work of Death:
O'erlabour'd now, with Dust, and Sweat, and Gore,
Their Knees, their Legs, their Feet are cover'd o'er,
Drops follow Drops, the Clouds on Clouds arise,
And Carnage clogs their Hands, and Darkness fills their Eyes;
As when a slaughter'd Bull's yet reeking Hyde, 450
Strain'd with full Force, and tugg'd from Side to Side,
The brawny Curriers stretch; and labour o'er
Th' extended Surface, drunk with Fat and Gore;
So tugging round the Corps both Armies stood;
The mangled Body bath'd in Sweat and Blood:
While Greeks and Ilians equal Strength employ,
Now to the Ships to force it, now to Troy.
Not Pallas' self, her Breast when Fury warms,
Nor He, whose Anger sets the World in Arms,
Could blame this Scene; such Rage, such Horror reign'd, 460
Such, Jove to honour the great Dead ordain'd.

Achilles in his Ships at distance lay,
Nor knew the fatal Fortune of the Day;

He, yet unconscious of Patroclus' Fall,
In dust extended under Ilion's Wall,
Expects him glorious from the conquer'd Plain,
And for his wish'd Return prepares in vain;
Tho' well he knew, to make proud Ilion bend,
Was more than Heav'n had destin'd to his Friend,
Perhaps to Him: This Thetis had reveal'd;   470
The rest, in pity to her Son, conceal'd.

 Still rag'd the Conflict round the Hero dead,
And Heaps on Heaps by mutual Wounds they bled.
Curs'd be the Man (ev'n private Greeks would say)
Who dares desert this well-disputed Day!
First may the cleaving Earth before our Eyes
Gape wide, and drink our Blood for Sacrifice!
First perish all, e'er haughty Troy shall boast
We lost Patroclus, and our Glory lost.

 Thus they. While with one Voice the Trojans said,   480
Grant this Day, Jove! or heap us on the Dead!

 Then clash their sounding Arms; the Clangors rise,
And shake the brazen Concave of the Skies.

 Meantime, at distance from the Scene of Blood,
The pensive Steeds of great Achilles stood;
Their god-like Master slain before their Eyes,
They wept, and shar'd in human Miseries.
In vain Automedon now shakes the Rein,
Now plies the Lash, and sooths and threats in vain;
Nor to the Fight, nor Hellespont, they go;   490
Restive they stood, and obstinate in Woe:
Still as a Tomb-stone, never to be mov'd,
On some good Man, or Woman unreprov'd
Lays its eternal Weight; or fix'd as stands
A marble Courser by the Sculptor's Hands,
Plac'd on the Hero's Grave. Along their Face,
The big round Drops cours'd down with silent pace,
Conglobing on the Dust. Their Manes, that late
Circled their arching Necks, and wav'd in State,
Trail'd on the Dust beneath the Yoke were spread,   500
And prone to Earth was hung their languid Head:

Nor Jove disdain'd to cast a pitying Look,
While thus relenting to the Steeds he spoke.
  Unhappy Coursers of immortal Strain!
Exempt from Age, and deathless now in vain;
Did we your Race on mortal Man bestow,
Only alas! to share in mortal Woe?
For ah! what is there, of inferior Birth,
That breathes or creeps upon the Dust of Earth;
What wretched Creature of what wretched kind,   510
Than Man more weak, calamitous, and blind?
A miserable Race! But cease to mourn.
For not by you shall Priam's Son be born
High on the splendid Car: One glorious Prize
He rashly boasts; the rest our Will denies.
Ourself will Swiftness to your Nerves impart,
Ourself with rising Spirits swell your Heart.
Automedon your rapid Flight shall bear
Safe to the Navy thro' the Storm of War.
For yet 'tis giv'n to Troy, to ravage o'er   520
The Field, and spread her Slaughters to the Shore;
The Sun shall see her conquer, till his Fall
With sacred Darkness shades the Face of all.
  He said; and breathing in th' immortal Horse
Excessive Spirit, urg'd 'em to the Course;
From their high Manes they shake the Dust, and bear
The kindling Chariot thro' the parted War:
So flies a Vulture thro' the clam'rous Train
Of Geese, that scream, and scatter round the Plain.
From Danger now with swiftest Speed they flew,   530
And now to Conquest with like Speed pursue;
Sole in the Seat the Charioteer remains,
Now plies the Jav'lin, now directs the Reins:
Him brave Alcimedon beheld distrest,
Approach'd the Chariot, and the Chief addrest.
  What God provokes thee, rashly thus to dare,
Alone, unaided, in the thickest War?
Alas! thy Friend is slain, and Hector wields
Achilles' Arms triumphant in the Fields.

In happy time (the Charioteer replies)   540
The bold Alcimedon now greets my Eyes;
No Greek like him, the heav'nly Steeds restrains,
Or holds their Fury in suspended Reins:
Patroclus, while he liv'd, their Rage cou'd tame,
But now Patroclus is an empty Name!
To thee I yield the Seat, to thee resign
The ruling Charge: The Task of Fight be mine.
    He said. Alcimedon, with active Heat,
Snatches the Reins, and vaults into the Seat.
His Friend descends. The Chief of Troy descry'd,   550
And call'd Æneas fighting near his Side.
Lo, to my Sight beyond our Hope restor'd,
Achilles' Car, deserted of its Lord!
The glorious Steeds our ready Arms invite,
Scarce their weak Drivers guide them thro' the Fight:
Can such Opponents stand, when we assail?
Unite thy Force, my Friend, and we prevail.
    The Son of Venus to the Counsel yields;
Then o'er their Backs they spread their solid Shields;
With Brass refulgent the broad Surface shin'd,   560
And thick Bull-hides the Spacious Concave lin'd.
Them Chromius follows, Aretus succeeds,
Each hopes the Conquest of the lofty Steeds:
In vain, brave Youths, with glorious Hopes ye burn,
In vain advance! not fated to return.
    Unmov'd, Automedon attends the Fight,
Implores th' Eternal, and collects his Might.
Then turning to his Friend, with dauntless Mind:
Oh keep the foaming Coursers close behind!
Full on my Shoulders let their Nostrils blow,   570
For hard the Fight, determin'd is the Foe;
'Tis Hector comes; and when he seeks the Prize,
War knows no mean: he wins it, or he dies.
    Then thro' the Field he sends his Voice aloud,
And calls th' Ajaces from the warring Croud,
With great Atrides. Hither turn (he said)
Turn, where Distress demands immediate Aid;

The Dead, incircled by his Friends, forego,
And save the Living from a fiercer Foe.
Unhelp'd we stand, unequal to engage   580
The Force of Hector, and Æneas' Rage:
Yet mighty as they are, my Force to prove,
Is only mine: th' Event belongs to Jove.

   He spoke, and high the sounding Jav'lin flung,
Which pass'd the Shield of Aretus the young;
It pierc'd his Belt, emboss'd with curious Art;
Then in the lower Belly stuck the Dart.
As when the pond'rous Axe descending full,
Cleaves the broad Forehead of some brawny Bull;
Struck 'twixt the Horns, he springs with many a Bound,   590
Then tumbling rolls enormous on the Ground:
Thus fell the Youth; the Air his Soul receiv'd,
And the Spear trembled as his Entrails heav'd.

   Now at Automedon the Trojan Foe
Discharg'd his Lance; the meditated Blow
Stooping, he shun'd; the Jav'lin idly fled,
And hiss'd innoxious o'er the Hero's Head:
Deep rooted in the Ground, the forceful Spear
In long Vibrations spent its Fury there.
With clashing Falchions now the Chiefs had clos'd,   600
But each brave Ajax heard, and interpos'd;
Nor longer Hector with his Trojans stood,
But left their slain Companion in his Blood:
His Arms Automedon divests, and cries,
Accept, Patroclus! this mean Sacrifice.
Thus have I sooth'd my Griefs, and thus have paid
Poor as it is, some Off'ring to thy Shade.

   So looks the Lion o'er a mangled Boar,
All grim with Rage, and horrible with Gore:
High on the Chariot at one Bound he sprung,   610
And o'er his Seat the bloody Trophies hung.

   And now Minerva, from the Realms of Air
Descends impetuous, and renews the War;
For, pleas'd at length the Grecian Arms to aid,
The Lord of Thunders sent the blue-ey'd Maid.

As when high Jove, denouncing future Woe,
O'er the dark Clouds extends his Purple Bow,
(In sign of Tempests from the troubled Air,
Or from the Rage of Man, destructive War)
The drooping Cattel dread th' impending Skies,   620
And from his half-till'd Field the Lab'rer flies.
In such a Form the Goddess round her drew
A livid Cloud, and to the Battel flew.
Assuming Phœnix' Shape, on Earth she falls
And in his well-known Voice to Sparta calls.
    And lies Achilles' Friend, belov'd by all,
A Prey to Dogs beneath the Trojan Wall?
What Shame to Greece for future times to tell,
To thee the greatest, in whose Cause he fell!
O Chief, Oh Father! (Atreus' Son replies)   630
O full of Days! by long Experience wise!
What more desires my Soul, than here, unmov'd,
To guard the Body of the Man I lov'd?
Ah would Minerva send me Strength to rear
This weary'd Arm, and ward the Storm of War!
But Hector, like the Rage of Fire, we dread,
And Jove's own Glories blaze around his Head.
    Pleas'd to be first of all the Pow'rs addrest,
She breathes new Vigour in her Hero's Breast,
And fills with keen Revenge, with fell Despight,   640
Desire of Blood, and Rage, and Lust of Fight.
So burns the vengeful Hornet (Soul all o'er)
Repuls'd in vain, and thirsty still of Gore;
(Bold Son of Air and Heat) on angry Wings
Untam'd, untir'd, he turns, attacks, and stings:
Fir'd with like Ardour fierce Atrides flew,
And sent his Soul with ev'ry Lance he threw.
    There stood a Trojan not unknown to Fame,
Eëtion's Son, and Podes was his Name;
With Riches honour'd, and with Courage blest,   650
By Hector lov'd, his Comrade, and his Guest;
Thro' his broad Belt the Spear a Passage found,
And pond'rous as he falls, his Arms resound.

Sudden at Hector's Side Apollo stood,
Like Phænops, Asius' Son, appear'd the God;
(Asius the Great, who held his wealthy Reign
In fair Abydos by the rolling Main.)
Oh Prince (he cry'd) oh foremost once in Fame!
What Grecian now shall tremble at thy Name?
Dost thou at length to Menelaus yield?   660
A Chief, once thought no Terror of the Field;
Yet singly, now, the long disputed Prize
He bears victorious, while our Army flies.
By the same Arm illustrious Podes bled,
The Friend of Hector, unreveng'd, is dead:
This heard, o'er Hector spreads a Cloud of Woe,
Rage lifts his Lance, and drives him on the Foe.
    But now th' Eternal shook his sable Shield,
That shaded Ide, and all the subject Field
Beneath its ample Verge. A rolling Cloud   670
Involv'd the Mount; the Thunder roar'd aloud;
Th' affrighted Hills from their Foundations nod,
And blaze beneath the Lightnings of the God:
At one Regard of his all-seeing Eye,
The Vanquish'd triumph, and the Victors fly.
Then trembled Greece: The Flight Peneleus led;
For as the brave Bœotian turn'd his Head
To face the Foe, Polydamas drew near,
And raz'd his Shoulder with a shorten'd Spear:
By Hector wounded, Leitus quits the Plain,   680
Pierc'd thro' the Wrist; and raging with the Pain
Grasps his once Formidable Lance in vain.
As Hector follow'd, Idomen addrest
The flaming Jav'lin to his manly Breast;
The brittle Point before his Corselet yields;
Exulting Troy with Clamour fills the Fields:
High on his Chariot as the Cretan stood,
The Son of Priam whirl'd the missive Wood;
But erring from its Aim, th' impetuous Spear
Strook to the Dust the Squire, and Charioteer   690
Of martial Marion: Cœranus his Name,
Who left fair Lyctus for the Fields of Fame.

On foot bold Merion fought; and now laid low,
Had grac'd the Triumphs of his Trojan Foe;
But the brave Squire the ready Coursers brought,
And with his Life his Master's Safety bought.
Between his Cheek and Ear the Weapon went,
The Teeth it shatter'd, and the Tongue it rent.
Prone from the Seat he tumbles to the Plain;
His dying Hand forgets the falling Rein: 700
This Merion reaches, bending from the Car,
And urges to desert the hopeless War;
Idomeneus consents; the Lash applies;
And the swift Chariot to the Navy flies.

    Nor Ajax less the Will of Heav'n descry'd,
And Conquest shifting to the Trojan Side,
Turn'd by the Hand of Jove. Then thus begun,
To Atreus' Seed, the god-like Telamon.

    Alas! who sees not Jove's almighty Hand
Transfers the Glory to the Trojan Band;   710
Whether the Weak or Strong discharge the Dart,
He guides each Arrow to a Grecian Heart:
Not so our Spears: incessant tho' they rain,
He suffers ev'ry Lance to fall in vain.
Deserted of the God, yet let us try
What human Strength and Prudence can supply;
If yet this honour'd Corps, in Triumph born,
May glad the Fleets that hope not our return,
Who tremble yet, scarce rescu'd from their Fates,
And still hear Hector thund'ring at their Gates.   720
Some Hero too must be dispatch'd, to bear
The mournful Message to Pelides' Ear;
For sure he knows not, distant on the Shore,
His Friend, his lov'd Patroclus, is no more.
But such a Chief I spy not thro' the Host:
The Men, the Steeds, the Armies all are lost
In gen'ral Darkness—Lord of Earth and Air!
Oh King! oh Father! hear my humble Pray'r:
Dispel this Cloud, the Light of Heav'n restore;
Give me to see, and Ajax asks no more: 730

If Greece must perish, we thy Will obey,
But let us perish in the Face of Day!
    With Tears the Hero spoke, and at his Pray'r
The God relenting, clear'd the clouded Air;
Forth burst the Sun with all-enlight'ning Ray;
The Blaze of Armour flash'd against the Day.
Now, now, Atrides! cast around thy Sight,
If yet Antilochus survives the Fight,
Let him to great Achilles' Ear convey
The fatal News—Atrides hasts away.   740
    So turns the Lion from the nightly Fold,
Tho high in Courage, and with Hunger bold,
Long gall'd by Herdsmen, and long vext by Hounds,
Stiff with Fatigue, and fretted sore with Wounds;
The Darts fly round him from a hundred Hands,
And the red Terrors of the blazing Brands:
Till late, reluctant, at the Dawn of Day
Sow'r he departs, and quits th' untasted Prey.
So mov'd Atrides from his dang'rous Place
With weary'd Limbs, but with unwilling Pace: 750
The Foe, he fear'd, might yet Patroclus gain,
And much admonish'd, much adjur'd his Train.
    Oh guard these Relicks to your Charge consign'd,
And bear the Merits of the Dead in Mind;
How skill'd he was in each obliging Art;
The mildest Manners, and the gentlest Heart:
He was, alas! But Fate decreed his End;
In Death a Hero, as in Life a Friend!
    So parts the Chief; from Rank to Rank he flew,
And round on all sides sent his piercing View.   760
As the bold Bird, endu'd with sharpest Eye
Of all that wing the mid Aerial Sky,
The sacred Eagle, from his Walks above
Looks down, and sees the distant Thicket move;
Then stoops, and sowsing on the quiv'ring Hare,
Snatches his Life amid the Clouds of Air.
Not with less Quickness, his exerted Sight
Pass'd this, and that way, thro' the Ranks of Fight:

Till on the Left the Chief he sought, he found;
Chearing his Men, and spreading Deaths around.   770
  To him the King. Belov'd of Jove! draw near,
For sadder Tydings never touch'd thy Ear;
Thy Eyes have witness'd what a fatal Turn!
How Ilion triumphs, and th' Achaians mourn.
This is not all: Patroclus on the Shore,
Now pale and dead, shall succour Greece no more.
Fly to the Fleet, this Instant fly, and tell
The sad Achilles how his lov'd one fell:
He too may haste the naked Corps to gain;
The Arms are Hector's, who despoil'd the Slain.   780
  The youthful Warrior heard with silent Woe,
From his fair Eyes the Tears began to flow:
Big with the mighty Grief, he strove to say
What Sorrow dictates, but no Word found way.
To brave Laodocus his Arms he flung,
Who near him wheeling, drove his Steeds along;
Then ran, the mournful Message to impart,
With Tear-ful Eyes, and with dejected Heart.
  Swift fled the Youth; nor Menelaus stands,
(Tho' sore distrest) to aid the Pylian Bands;   790
But bids bold Thrasymede those Troops sustain;
Himself returns to his Patroclus slain.
Gone is Antilochus (the Hero said)
But hope not, Warriors! for Achilles' Aid:
Tho' fierce his Rage, unbounded be his Woe,
Unarm'd, he fights not with the Trojan Foe.
'Tis in our Hands alone our Hopes remain,
'Tis our own Vigour must the Dead regain;
And save our selves, while with impetuous Hate
Troy pours along, and this way rolls our Fate.   800
  'Tis well (said Ajax) be it then thy Care
With Merion's Aid, the weighty Corse to rear;
My self, and my bold Brother will sustain
The Shock of Hector and his charging Train:
Nor fear we Armies, fighting Side by Side;
What Troy can dare, we have already try'd,

Have try'd it, and have stood. The Hero said.
High from the Ground the Warriors heave the Dead;
A gen'ral Clamour rises at the Sight:
Loud shout the Trojans, and renew the Fight.   810
Not fiercer rush along the gloomy Wood,
With Rage insatiate and with Thirst of Blood,
Voracious Hounds, that many a Length before
Their furious Hunters, drive the wounded Boar;
But if the Savage turns his glaring Eye,
They howl aloof, and round the Forest fly.
Thus on retreating Greece the Trojans pour,
Wave their thick Falchions, and their Jav'lins show'r:
But Ajax turning, to their Fears they yield,
All pale they tremble, and forsake the Field.   820
   While thus aloft the Hero's Corse they bear,
Behind them rages all the Storm of War;
Confusion, Tumult, Horror, o'er the Throng
Of Men, Steeds, Chariots, urg'd the Rout along:
Less fierce the Winds with rising Flames conspire,
To whelm some City under Waves of Fire,
Now sink in gloomy Clouds the proud Abodes;
Now crack the blazing Temples of the Gods;
The rumbling Torrent thro' the Ruin rolls,
And Sheets of Smoak mount heavy to the Poles.   830
The Heroes sweat beneath their honour'd Load:
As when two Mules, along the rugged Road,
From the steep Mountain with exerted Strength
Drag some vast Beam, or Mast's unwieldly Length;
Inly they groan, big Drops of Sweat distill,
Th' enormous Timber lumbring down the Hill.
So these—Behind, the Bulk of Ajax stands,
And breaks the Torrent of the rushing Bands.
Thus when a River swell'd with sudden Rains
Spreads his broad Waters o'er the level Plains,   840
Some interposing Hill the Stream divides,
And breaks its Force, and turns the winding Tides.
Still close they follow, close the Rear engage;
Æneas storms, and Hector foams with Rage:

While Greece a heavy, thick Retreat maintains,
Wedg'd in one Body like a Flight of Cranes,
That shriek incessant, while the Faulcon hung
High on pois'd Pinions, threats their callow Young.
So from the Trojan Chiefs the Grecians fly,
Such the wild Terror, and the mingled Cry.   850
Within, without the Trench, and all the way,
Strow'd in bright Heaps, their Arms and Armour lay;
Such Horror Jove imprest! Yet still proceeds
The Work of Death, and still the Battel bleeds.

ᒏᒏᒏᒏ

THE EIGHTEENTH BOOK
OF THE ILIAD

THE ARGUMENT

The Grief of Achilles, and new Armour made him by Vulcan

THE NEWS OF THE DEATH OF PATROCLUS, is brought to Achilles by
Antilochus. Thetis hearing his Lamentations comes with all her Sea-
Nymphs to comfort him. The Speeches of the Mother and Son on this
Occasion. Iris appears to Achilles by the Command of Juno, and orders
him to shew himself at the Head of the Intrenchments. The Sight of him
turns the Fortune of the Day, and the Body of Patroclus is carried off by
the Greeks. The Trojans call a Council, where Hector and Polydamas
disagree in their Opinions; but the Advice of the former prevails, to
remain encamp'd in the Field: The Grief of Achilles over the Body of
Patroclus.

Thetis goes to the Palace of Vulcan to obtain new Arms for her Son.
The Description of the wonderful Works of Vulcan, and lastly, that
noble one of the Shield of Achilles.

The latter part of the nine and twentieth Day, and the Night ensuing,
take up this Book. The Scene is at Achilles's Tent on the Sea-shore, from
whence it changes to the Palace of Vulcan.

Thus like the Rage of Fire the Combat burns,
And now it rises, now it sinks by turns.
Meanwhile, where Hellespont's broad Waters **flow**
Stood Nestor's Son, the Messenger of Woe:
There sate Achilles, shaded by his Sails,
On hoisted Yards extended to the Gales;

Pensive he sate; for all that Fate design'd,
Rose in sad Prospect to his boding Mind.
Thus to his Soul he said. Ah! what constrains
The Greeks, late Victors, now to quit the Plains?   10
Is this the Day, which Heav'n so long ago
Ordain'd, to sink me with the Weight of Woe?
(So Thetis warn'd) when by a Trojan Hand,
The bravest of the Myrmidonian Band
Should lose the Light? Fulfill'd is that Decree;
Fal'n is the Warrior, and Patroclus he!
In vain I charg'd him soon to quit the Plain,
And warn'd to shun Hectorean Force in vain!
    Thus while he thinks, Antilochus appears,
And tells the melancholy Tale with Tears.   20
Sad Tydings, Son of Peleus! thou must hear;
And wretched I, th' unwilling Messenger!
Dead is Patroclus! For his Corps they fight;
His naked Corps: His Arm's are Hector's Right.
    A sudden Horror shot thro' all the Chief,
And wrapt his Senses in the Cloud of Grief;
Cast on the Ground, with furious Hands he spread
The scorching Ashes o'er his graceful Head;
His purple Garments, and his golden Hairs,
Those he deforms with Dust, and these he tears: 30
On the hard Soil his groaning Breast he threw,
And roll'd and grovel'd, as to Earth he grew.
The Virgin Captives, with disorder'd Charms,
(Won by his own, or by Patroclus' Arms)
Rush'd from the Tents with Cries; and gath'ring round
Beat their white Breasts, and fainted on the Ground:
While Nestor's Son sustains a manlier Part,
And mourns the Warrior with a Warrior's Heart;
Hangs on his Arms, amidst his frantic Woe,
And oft prevents the meditated Blow.   40
    Far in the deep Abysses of the Main,
With hoary Nereus, and the watry Train,
The Mother Goddess from her crystal Throne
Heard his loud Cries, and answer'd Groan for Groan.

The circling Nereids with their Mistress weep,
And all the Sea-green Sisters of the Deep.
Thalia, Glauce, (ev'ry wat'ry Name)
Nesæa mild, and Silver Spio came.
Cymothoe and Cymodoce were nigh,
And the blue Languish of soft Alia's Eye.   50
Their Locks Actæa and Limnoria rear,
Then Proto, Doris, Panope appear;
Thoa, Pherusa, Doto, Melita;
Agave gentle, and Amphithoe gay:
Next Callianira, Callianassa show
Their Sister Looks; Dexamene the slow,
And swift Dynamene, now cut the Tydes:
Iæra now the verdant Wave divides;
Nemertes with Apseudes lifts the Head:
Bright Galatea quits her pearly Bed: 60
These Orythia, Clymene, attend,
Mæra, Amphinome, the Train extend,
And black Janira, and Janassa fair,
And Amatheia with her amber Hair.
All these, and all that deep in Ocean held
Their sacred Seats, the glimm'ring Grotto fill'd;
Each beat her Iv'ry Breast with silent Woe,
Till Thetis' Sorrows thus began to flow.
    Hear me, and judge, ye Sisters of the Main!
How just a Cause has Thetis to complain?   70
How wretched, were I mortal, were my Fate!
How more than wretched in th' immortal State!
Sprung from my Bed a god-like Hero came,
The bravest far that ever bore the Name;
Like some fair Olive, by my careful Hand
He grew, he flourish'd, and adorn'd the Land:
To Troy I sent him; but the Fates ordain
He never, never must return again.
So short a space the Light of Heav'n to view,
So short alas! and fill'd with Anguish too?   80
Hear how his Sorrows echo thro' the Shore!
I cannot ease them, but I must deplore;

I go at least to bear a tender part,
And mourn my lov'd one with a Mother's Heart.
   She said, and left the Caverns of the Main.
All bath'd in Tears, the melancholy Train
Attend her Way. Wide-opening part the Tides,
While the long Pomp the silver Wave divides.
Approaching now, they touch'd the Trojan Land;
Then, two by two, ascended up the Strand. 90
Th' immortal Mother, standing close beside
Her mournful Offspring, to his Sighs reply'd;
Along the Coast their mingled Clamours ran,
And thus the silver-footed Dame began.
   Why mourns my Son? thy late-preferr'd Request
The God has granted, and the Greeks distrest:
Why mourns my Son? thy Anguish let me share,
Reveal the Cause, and trust a Parent's Care.
   He, deeply groaning—To this cureless Grief
Not ev'n the Thund'rers Favour brings Relief. 100
Patroclus—Ah!—Say Goddess can I boast
A Pleasure now? Revenge itself is lost:
Patroclus, lov'd of all my martial Train,
Beyond Mankind, beyond my self, is slain!
Lost are those Arms the Gods themselves bestow'd
On Peleus; Hector bears the glorious Load.
Curs'd be that Day, when all the Pow'rs above
Thy Charms submitted to a mortal Love:
Oh had'st thou still, a Sister of the Main,
Pursu'd the Pleasures of the wat'ry Reign; 110
And happier Peleus, less ambitious, led
A mortal Beauty to his equal Bed!
E'er the sad Fruit of thy unhappy Womb
Had caus'd such Sorrows past, and Woes to come.
For soon alas! that wretched Offspring slain,
New Woes, new Sorrows shall create again:
'Tis not in Fate th' Alternate now to give;
Patroclus dead, Achilles hates to live.
Let me revenge it on proud Hector's Heart,
Let his last Spirit smoak upon my Dart; 120

On these Conditions will I breathe: Till then,
I blush to walk among the Race of Men.
  A Flood of Tears, at this, the Goddess shed;
Ah then, I see thee dying, see thee dead!
When Hector falls, thou dy'st.—Let Hector die,
And let me fall! (Achilles made reply)
Far lyes Patroclus from his native plain!
He fell, and falling wish'd my Aid in vain.
Ah then, since from this miserable Day
I cast all hope of my Return away,   130
Since unreveng'd, a hundred Ghosts demand
The Fate of Hector from Achilles' hand;
Since here, for brutal Courage far renown'd,
I live an idle Burden to the Ground,
(Others in Council fam'd for nobler Skill,
More useful to preserve, than I to kill)
Let me—But oh! ye gracious Pow'rs above!
Wrath and Revenge from Men and Gods remove:
Far, far too dear to ev'ry mortal Breast,
Sweet to the Soul, as Hony to the Taste;   140
Gath'ring like Vapours of a noxious kind
From fiery Blood, and dark'ning all the Mind.
Me Agamemnon urg'd to deadly Hate;
'Tis past—I quell it; I resign to Fate.
Yes—I will meet the Murd'rer of my Friend,
Or (if the Gods ordain it) meet my End.
The Stroke of Fate the bravest cannot shun:
The great Alcides, Jove's unequal'd Son,
To Juno's Hate at length resign'd his Breath,
And sunk the Victim of all-conqu'ring Death.   150
So shall Achilles fall! stretch'd pale and dead,
No more the Grecian Hope, or Trojan Dread!
Let me, this instant, rush into the Fields,
And reap what Glory Life's short Harvest yields.
Shall I not force some widow'd Dame to tear
With frantic Hands, her long dishevell'd Hair?
Shall I not force her Breast to heave with Sighs,
And the soft Tears to trickle from her Eyes?

Yes, I shall give the Fair those mournful Charms—
In vain you hold me—Hence! my Arms, my Arms!   160
Soon shall the sanguine Torrent spread so wide,
That all shall know, Achilles swells the Tide.
  My Son (Cœrulean Thetis made reply,
To Fate submitting with a secret Sigh)
The Host to succour, and thy Friends to save,
Is worthy thee; the Duty of the Brave.
But can'st thou, naked, issue to the Plains?
Thy radiant Arms the Trojan Foe detains,
Insulting Hector bears the Spoils on high,
But vainly glories, for his Fate is nigh.   170
Yet, yet awhile, thy gen'rous Ardor stay;
Assur'd, I meet thee at the dawn of Day,
Charg'd with refulgent Arms (a glorious Load)
Vulcanian Arms, the Labour of a God.
  Then turning to the Daughters of the Main,
The Goddess thus dismiss'd her azure Train.
  Ye Sister Nereids! to your Deeps descend,
Haste, and our Fathers sacred Seat attend,
I go to find the Architect divine,
Where vast Olympus starry Summits shine: 180
So tell our hoary Sire—This Charge she gave:
The Sea-green Sisters plunge beneath the Wave:
Thetis once more ascends the blest Abodes,
And treads the brazen Threshold of the Gods.
  And now the Greeks, from furious Hector's Force,
Urge to broad Hellespont their headlong Course:
Nor yet their Chiefs Patroclus' Body bore
Safe thro' the Tempest, to the Tented Shore.
The Horse, the Foot, with equal Fury join'd,
Pour'd on the Rear, and thunder'd close behind;   190
And like a Flame thro' Fields of ripen'd Corn,
The Rage of Hector o'er the Ranks was born:
Thrice the slain Hero by the Foot he drew;
Thrice to the Skies the Trojan Clamours flew.
As oft' th' Ajaces his Assault sustain;
But check'd, he turns; repuls'd, attacks again.

With fiercer Shouts his ling'ring Troops he fires,
Nor yields a Step, nor from his Post retires:
So watchful Sheperds strive to force, in vain,
The hungry Lion from a Carcase slain.   200
Ev'n yet, Patroclus had he born away,
And all the Glories of th' extended Day;
Had not high Juno, from the Realms of Air,
Secret, dispatch'd her trusty Messenger.
The various Goddess of the painted Bow,
Shot in a Whirlwind to the Shore below;
To great Achilles at his Ships she came,
And thus began the many-colour'd Dame.

　Rise, Son of Peleus! rise divinely brave!
Assist the Combate, and Patroclus save: 210
For him the Slaughter to the Fleet they spread,
And fall by mutual Wounds around the Dead.
To drag him back to Troy the Foe contends;
Nor with his Death the Rage of Hector ends:
A Prey to Dogs he dooms the Corse to lye,
And marks the Place to fix his Head on high.
Rise, and prevent (if yet thou think of Fame)
Thy Friend's Disgrace, thy own eternal Shame!

　Who sends thee, Goddess! from th' Etherial Skies?
Achilles thus. And Iris thus replies.   220
I come, Pelides! from the Queen of Jove,
Th' immortal Empress of the Realms above;
Unknown to him who sits remote on high,
Unknown to all the Synod of the Sky.
Thou com'st in vain, he cries (with Fury warm'd)
Arms I have none, and can I fight unarm'd?
Unwilling as I am, of force I stay,
Till Thetis bring me at the dawn of Day
Vulcanian Arms: What other should I wield?
Except the mighty Telamonian Shield?   230
That, in my Friends Defence, has Ajax spread,
While his strong Lance around him heaps the Dead:
The gallant Chief defends Menœtius' Son,
And does, what his Achilles should have done.

Thy want of Arms (said Iris) well we know,
But tho unarm'd, yet clad in Terrors, go!
Let but Achilles o'er yon' Trench appear,
Proud Troy shall tremble, and consent to fear;
Greece from one Glance of that tremendous Eye
Shall take new Courage, and disdain to fly.   240
  She spoke, and past in Air. The Hero rose;
Her Ægis, Pallas o'er his Shoulders throws;
Around his Brows a golden Cloud she spread;
A Stream of Glory flam'd above his Head.
As when from some beleaguer'd Town arise
The Smokes high-curling to the shaded Skies;
(Seen from some Island, o'er the Main afar,
When Men distrest hang out the Sign of War)
Soon as the Sun in Ocean hides his Rays,
Thick on the Hills the flaming Beacons blaze;   250
With long-projected Beams the Seas are bright,
And Heav'ns high Arch reflects the ruddy Light;
So from Achilles' Head the Splendours rise,
Reflecting Blaze on Blaze, against the Skies.
Forth march'd the Chief, and distant from the Croud,
High on the Rampart rais'd his Voice aloud;
With her own Shout Minerva swells the Sound;
Troy starts astonish'd, and the Shores rebound.
As the loud Trumpet's brazen Mouth from far
With shrilling Clangor sounds th' Alarm of War;   260
Struck from the Walls, the Echoes float on high,
And the round Bulwarks, and thick Tow'rs reply:
So high his brazen Voice the Hero rear'd:
Hosts dropp'd their Arms, and trembled as they heard;
And back the Chariots roll, and Coursers bound,
And Steeds and Men lye mingled on the Ground.
Aghast they see the living Light'nings play,
And turn their Eye-balls from the flashing Ray.
Thrice from the Trench his dreadful Voice he rais'd;
And thrice they fled, confounded and amaz'd.   270
Twelve in the Tumult wedg'd, untimely rush'd
On their own Spears, by their own Chariots crush'd:

While shielded from the Darts, the Greeks obtain
The long-contended Carcase of the Slain.
  A lofty Bier the breathless Warrior bears;
Around, his sad Companions melt in Tears:
But chief Achilles, bending down his Head,
Pours unavailing Sorrows o'er the Dead.
Whom late, triumphant with his Steeds and Car,
He sent refulgent to the Field of War,   280
(Unhappy Change!) now senseless, pale, he found,
Stretch'd forth, and gash'd with many a gaping Wound.
  Meantime, unweary'd with his heavenly Way,
In Ocean's Waves th' unwilling Light of Day
Quench'd his red Orb, at Juno's high Command,
And from their Labours eas'd th' Achaian Band.
The frighted Trojans (panting from the War,
Their Steeds unharness'd from the weary Car)
A sudden Council call'd: Each Chief appear'd
In haste, and standing; for to sit they fear'd.   290
'Twas now no Season for prolong'd Debate;
They saw Achilles, and in him their Fate.
Silent they stood: Polydamas at last,
Skill'd to discern the Future by the past,
The Son of Panthus, thus exprest his Fears;
(The Friend of Hector, and of equal Years:
The self same Night to both a Being gave,
One wise in Council, one in Action brave.)
   In free Debate, my Friends, your Sentence speak:
For me, I move, before the Morning break   300
To raise our Camp: Too dang'rous here our Post,
Far from Troy Walls, and on a naked Coast.
I deem'd not Greece so dreadful, while engag'd
In mutual Feuds, her King and Hero rag'd;
Then, while we hop'd our Armies might prevail,
We boldly camp'd beside a thousand Sail.
I dread Pelides now: his Rage of Mind
Not long continues to the Shores confin'd,
Nor to the Fields, where long in equal Fray
Contending Nations won and lost the Day;   310

For Troy, for Troy, shall henceforth be the Strife,
And the hard Contest not for Fame, but Life.
Haste then to Ilion, while the fav'ring Night
Detains those Terrors, keeps that Arm from Fight;
If but the Morrow's Sun behold us here,
That Arm, those Terrors, we shall feel, not fear;
And Hearts that now disdain, shall leap with Joy,
If Heav'n permits them then to enter Troy.
Let not my fatal Prophecy be true,
Nor what I tremble but to think, ensue.   320
Whatever be our Fate, yet let us try
What Force of Thought and Reason can supply;
Let us on Counsel for our Guard depend;
The Town, her Gates and Bulwarks shall defend:
When Morning dawns, our well-appointed Pow'rs
Array'd in Arms, shall line the lofty Tow'rs.
Let the fierce Hero then, when Fury calls,
Vent his mad Vengeance on our rocky Walls,
Or fetch a thousand Circles round the Plain,
Till his spent Coursers seek the Fleet again: 330
So may his Rage be tir'd, and labour'd down;
And Dogs shall tear him, e'er he sack the Town.

    Return? (said Hector, fir'd with stern Disdain)
What, coop whole Armies in our Walls again?
Was't not enough, ye valiant Warriors say,
Nine Years imprison'd in those Tow'rs ye lay?
Wide o'er the World was Ilion fam'd of old
For Brass exhaustless, and for Mines of Gold:
But while inglorious in her Walls we stay'd,
Sunk were her Treasures, and her Stores decay'd;   340
The Phrygians now her scatter'd spoils enjoy,
And proud Mæonia wasts the Fruits of Troy.
Great Jove at length my Arms to Conquest calls,
And shuts the Grecians in their wooden Walls:
Dar'st thou dispirit whom the Gods incite?
Flies any Trojan? I shall stop his Flight.
To better Counsel then Attention lend,
Take due Refreshment, and the Watch attend.

If there be one whose Riches cost him Care,
Forth let him bring them, for the Troops to share;   350
'Tis better gen'rously bestow'd on those,
Than left the Plunder of our Country's Foes.
Soon as the Morn the rosie Orient warms
Fierce on yon' Navy will we pour our Arms.
If great Achilles rise in all his Might,
His be the Danger: I shall stand the Fight.
Honor, ye Gods! or let me gain, or give;
And live he glorious, whosoe'er shall live!
Mars is our common Lord, alike to all;
And oft' the Victor triumphs, but to fall.   360
  The shouting Host in loud Applauses join'd;
So Pallas robb'd the Many[1] of their Mind,
To their own Sense condemn'd! and left to chuse
The worse Advice, the better to refuse.
  While the long Night extends her sable Reign,
Around Patroclus mourn'd the Grecian Train.
Stern in superior Grief Pelides stood;
Those slaught'ring Arms, so us'd to bathe in Blood,
Now clasp his clay-cold Limbs: Then gushing start
The Tears, and Sighs burst from his swelling Heart.   370
The Lion thus, with dreadful Anguish stung,
Roars thro' the Desart, and demands his Young;
When the grim Savage to his rifled Den
Too late returning, snuffs the Track of Men,
And o'er the Vales, and o'er the Forrest bounds;
His clam'rous Grief the bellowing Wood resounds.
So grieves Achilles; and impetuous, vents
To all his Myrmidons, his loud Laments.
  In what vain Promise, Gods! did I engage?
When to console Menætius' feeble Age,   380
I vow'd his much-lov'd Offspring to restore,
Charg'd with rich Spoils, to fair Opuntia's Shore!
But mighty Jove cuts short, with just Disdain,
The long, long Views of poor, designing Man!
One Fate the Warrior and the Friend shall strike,
And Troy's black Sands must drink our Blood alike:

[1] Pope's anti-popular translation of *them* in the original

Me too, a wretched Mother shall deplore,
An aged Father never see me more!
Yet, my Patroclus! yet a space I stay,
Then swift pursue thee on the darksome way.   390
E'er thy dear Relicks in the Grave are laid,
Shall Hector's Head be offer'd to thy Shade;
That, with his Arms, shall hang before thy Shrine,
And twelve, the noblest of the Trojan Line,
Slain by this Hand, sad Sacrifice! expire;
Their Lives effus'd around thy flaming Pyre.
Thus let me lie till then! thus, closely prest,
Bathe thy cold Face, and sob upon thy Breast!
While Trojan Captives here thy Mourners stay,
Weep all the Night, and murmur all the Day: 400
Spoils of my Arms, and thine; when, wasting wide,
Our Swords kept time, and conquer'd side by side.
    He spoke, and bid the sad Attendants round
Cleanse the pale Corse, and wash each honour'd Wound.
A massy Caldron of stupendous Frame
They brought, and plac'd it o'er the rising Flame:
Then heap the lighted Wood; the Flame divides
Beneath the Vase, and climbs around the Sides:
In its wide Womb they pour the rushing Stream;
The boiling Water bubbles to the Brim: 410
The Body then they bathe with pious Toil,
Embalm the Wounds, anoint the Limbs with Oyl;
High on a Bed of State extended laid,
And decent cover'd with a linen Shade;
Last o'er the Dead the milkwhite Mantle threw;
That done, their Sorrows and their Sighs renew.
    Meanwhile to Juno, in the Realms above,
(His Wife and Sister) spoke almighty Jove.
At last thy Will prevails: Great Peleus' Son
Rises in Arms: Such Grace thy Greeks have won.   420
Say (for I know not) is their Race divine,
And thou the Mother of that martial Line?
    What Words are these (th' Imperial Dame replies,
While Anger flash'd from her majestick Eyes)

Succour like this a mortal Arm might lend,
And such Success mere human Wit attend:
And shall not I, the second Pow'r above,
Heav'ns Queen, and Consort of the thund'ring Jove,
Say, shall not I one Nation's Fate command,
Not wreak my Vengeance on one guilty Land?   430
  So they. Meanwhile the silver-footed Dame
Reach'd the Vulcanian Dome, Eternal Frame!
High eminent amid the Works divine,
Where Heav'ns far-beaming, brazen Mansions shine.
There the lame Architect the Goddess found,
Obscure in Smoak, his Forges flaming round,
While bath'd in Sweat from Fire to Fire he flew,
And puffing loud, the roaring Bellows blew.
That Day, no common Task his Labour claim'd;
Full twenty Tripods for his Hall he fram'd,   440
That plac'd on living Wheels of massy Gold,
(Wond'rous to tell) instinct with Spirit roll'd
From Place to Place, around the blest Abodes,
Self-mov'd, obedient to the Beck of Gods:
For their fair Handles now, o'erwrought with Flow'rs,
In Molds prepar'd, the glowing Ore he pours.
Just as responsive to his Thought, the Frame
Stood prompt to move, the Azure Goddess came:
Charis, his Spouse, a Grace divinely fair,
(With purple Fillets round her braided Hair)   450
Observ'd her ent'ring; her soft Hand she press'd,
And smiling, thus the wat'ry Queen address'd.
  What, Goddess! this unusual Favour draws?
All hail, and welcome! whatsoe'er the Cause:
Till now a Stranger, in a happy Hour
Approach, and taste the Dainties of the Bow'r.
  High on a Throne, with Stars of silver grac'd
And various Artifice, the Queen she plac'd;
A Footstool at her Feet: then calling, said,
Vulcan draw near, 'tis Thetis asks your Aid.   460
  Thetis (reply'd the God) our Pow'rs may claim,
An ever dear, and ever honour'd Name!

When my proud Mother hurl'd me from the Sky,
(My aukward Form, it seems, displeas'd her Eye)
She, and Eurynome, my Griefs redrest,
And soft receiv'd me on their silver Breast.
Ev'n then, these Arts employ'd my infant Thought;
Chains, Bracelets, Pendants, all their Toys I wrought.
Nine Years kept secret in the dark Abode,
Secure I lay, conceal'd from Man and God: 470
Deep in a cavern'd Rock my Days were led;
The rushing Ocean murmur'd o'er my Head.
Now since her Presence glads our Mansion, say,
For such Desert what Service can I pay?
Vouchsafe, O Thetis! at our Board to share
The genial Rites, and hospitable Fare;
While I my Labours of the Forge forego,
And bid the roaring Bellows cease to blow.
    Then from his Anvil the lame Artist rose;
Wide with distorted Legs, oblique he goes,   480
And stills the Bellows, and (in order laid)
Locks in their Chest his Instruments of Trade.
Then with a Sponge the sooty Workman drest
His brawny Arms imbrown'd, and hairy Breast.
With his huge Scepter grac'd, and red Attire,
Came halting forth the Sov'reign of the Fire:
The Monarch's Steps two Female Forms uphold,
That mov'd, and breath'd, in animated Gold;
To whom was Voice, and Sense, and Science given
Of Works divine (such Wonders are in Heav'n!)   490
On these supported, with unequal Gait,
He reach'd the Throne where pensive Thetis sate;
There plac'd beside her on the shining Frame,
He thus address'd the silver-footed Dame.
    Thee, welcome Goddess! what Occasion calls,
(So long a Stranger) to these honour'd Walls?
'Tis thine, fair Thetis, the Command to lay,
And Vulcan's Joy, and Duty, to obey.
    To whom the mournful Mother thus replies,
(The crystal Drops stood trembling in her Eyes)   500

Oh Vulcan! say, was ever Breast divine
So pierc'd with Sorrows, so o'erwhelm'd as mine?
Of all the Goddesses, did Jove prepare
For Thetis only such a Weight of Care?
I, only I, of all the wat'ry Race,
By Force subjected to a Man's Embrace,
Who, sinking now with Age, and Sorrow, pays
The mighty Fine impos'd on length of Days.
Sprung from my Bed a god-like Hero came,
The bravest sure that ever bore the Name;   510
Like some fair Plant beneath my careful Hand
He grew, he flourish'd, and he grac'd the Land:
To Troy I sent him! but his native Shore
Never, ah never, shall receive him more;
(Ev'n while he lives, he wastes with secret Woe)
Nor I, a Goddess, can retard the Blow!
Robb'd of the Prize the Grecian Suffrage gave,
The King of Nations forc'd his royal Slave:
For this he griev'd; and till the Greeks opprest
Requir'd his Arm, he sorrow'd unredrest.   520
Large Gifts they promise, and their Elders send;
In vain—He arms not, but permits his Friend
His Arms, his Steeds, his Forces to employ;
He marches, combates, almost conquers Troy:
Then slain by Phœbus (Hector had the Name)
At once resigns his Armour, Life, and Fame.
But thou, in Pity, by my Pray'r be won;
Grace with immortal Arms this short-liv'd Son,
And to the Field in martial Pomp restore,
To shine with Glory, till he shines no more!   530
     To her the Artist-God. Thy Griefs resign,
Secure, what Vulcan can, is ever thine.
O could I hide him from the Fates as well,
Or with these Hands the cruel Stroke repell,
As I shall forge most envy'd Arms, the Gaze
Of wond'ring Ages, and the World's Amaze!
     Thus having said, the Father of the Fires
To the black Labours of his Forge retires.

Soon as he bade them blow, the Bellows turn'd
Their iron Mouths; and where the Furnace burn'd,   540
Resounding breath'd: At once the Blast expires,
And twenty Forges catch at once the Fires;
Just as the God directs, now loud, now low,
They raise a Tempest, or they gently blow.
In hissing Flames huge silver Bars are roll'd,
And stubborn Brass, and Tin, and solid Gold:
Before, deep fix'd, th' eternal Anvils stand;
The pond'rous Hammer loads his better Hand,
His left with Tongs turns the vex'd Metal round;
And thick, strong Strokes, the doubling Vaults rebound.   550
  Then first he form'd th' immense and solid Shield;
Rich, various Artifice emblaz'd the Field;
Its utmost Verge a threefold Circle bound;
A silver Chain suspends the massy Round;
Five ample Plates the broad Expanse compose,
And god-like Labours on the Surface rose.
There shone the Image of the Master Mind:
There Earth, there Heav'n, there Ocean he design'd;
Th' unweary'd Sun, the Moon compleatly round;
The starry Lights that Heav'ns high Convex crown'd;   560
The Pleiads, Hyads, with the Northern Team;
And great Orion's more refulgent Beam;
To which, around the Axle of the Sky,
The Bear revolving, points his golden Eye,
Still shines exalted on th' ætherial Plain,
Nor bends his blazing Forehead to the Main
  Two Cities radiant on the Shield appear,
The Image one of Peace, and one of War.
Here sacred Pomp, and genial Feast delight,
And solemn Dance, and Hymenæal Rite;   570
Along the Street the new-made Brides are led,
With Torches flaming, to the nuptial Bed;
The youthful Dancers in a Circle bound
To the soft Flute, and Cittern's silver Sound:
Thro' the fair Streets, the Matrons in a Row,
Stand in their Porches, and enjoy the Show.

There, in the Forum swarm a num'rous Train;
The Subject of Debate, a Townsman slain:
One pleads the Fine discharg'd, which one deny'd,
And bade the Publick and the Laws decide: 580
The Witness is produc'd on either Hand;
For this, or that, the partial People stand:
Th' appointed Heralds still the noisy Bands,
And form a Ring, with Scepters in their Hands;
On Seats of Stone, within the sacred Place,
The rev'rend Elders nodded o'er the Case;
Alternate, each th' attesting Scepter took,
And rising solemn, each his Sentence spoke.
Two golden Talents lay amidst, in sight,
The Prize of him who best adjudg'd the Right.   590
    Another Part (a Prospect diff'ring far)
Glow'd with refulgent Arms, and horrid War.
Two mighty Hosts a leaguer'd Town embrace,
And one would pillage, one wou'd burn the Place.
Meantime the Townsmen, arm'd with silent Care,
A secret Ambush on the Foe prepare:
Their Wives, their Children, and the watchful Band,
Of trembling Parents on the Turrets stand.
They march; by Pallas and by Mars made bold;
Gold were the Gods, their radiant Garments Gold,   600
And Gold their Armour: These the Squadron led,
August, Divine, Superior² by the Head!
A Place for Ambush fit, they found, and stood
Cover'd with Shields, beside a silver Flood.
Two Spies at distance lurk, and watchful seem
If Sheep or Oxen seek the winding Stream.
Soon the white Flocks proceeded o'er the Plains,
And Steers slow-moving, and two Shepherd Swains;
Behind them, piping on their Reeds, they go,
Nor fear an Ambush, nor suspect a Foe.   610
In Arms the glitt'ring Squadron rising round
Rush sudden; Hills of Slaughter heap the Ground,
Whole Flocks and Herds lye bleeding on the Plains,
And, all amidst them, dead, the Shepherd Swains!

² Taller, larger in scale than *the Squadron*

The bellowing Oxen the Besiegers hear;
They rise, take Horse, approach, and meet the War;
They fight, they fall, beside the silver Flood;
The waving Silver seem'd to blush with Blood.
There Tumult, there Contention stood confest;
One rear'd a Dagger at a Captive's Breast,   620
One held a living Foe, that freshly bled
With new-made Wounds; another dragg'd a dead;
Now here, now there, the Carcasses they tore:
Fate stalk'd amidst them, grim with human Gore.
And the whole War came out, and met the Eye;
And each bold Figure seem'd to live, or die.
   A Field deep-furrow'd, next the God design'd,
The third time labour'd by the sweating Hind;
The shining Shares full many Plowmen guide,
And turn their crooked Yokes on ev'ry side.   630
Still as at either End they wheel around,
The Master meets 'em with his Goblet crown'd;
The hearty Draught rewards, renews their Toil;
Then back the turning Plow-shares cleave the Soil:
The new-ear'd Earth in blacker Ridges roll'd;
Sable it look'd, tho form'd of molten Gold.
   Another Field rose high with waving Grain;
With bended Sickles stand the Reaper-Train:
Here stretch'd in Ranks the level'd Swarths are found,
Sheaves heap'd on Sheaves, here thicken up the Ground.   640
With sweeping Stroke the Mowers strow the Lands;
The Gath'rers follow, and collect in Bands;
And last the Children, in whose Arms are born
(Too short to gripe them) the brown Sheaves of Corn.
The rustic Monarch of the Field descries
With silent Glee, the Heaps around him rise.
A ready Banquet on the Turf is laid,
Beneath an ample Oak's expanded Shade.
The Victim-Ox the sturdy Youth prepare;
The Reaper's due Repast, the Women's Care.   650
   Next, ripe in yellow Gold, a Vineyard shines,
Bent with the pond'rous Harvest of its Vines;

A deaper Dye the dangling Clusters show,
And curl'd on silver Props, in order glow:
A darker Metal mixt, intrench'd the Place;
And Pales of glitt'ring Tin th' Enclosure grace.
To this, one Pathway gently winding leads,
Where march a Train with Baskets on their Heads,
(Fair Maids, and blooming Youths) that smiling bear
The purple Product of th' Autumnal Year.   660
To these a Youth awakes the warbling Strings,
Whose tender Lay the Fate of Linus sings;
In measur'd Dance behind him move the Train,
Tune soft the Voice, and answer to the Strain.

Here, Herds of Oxen march, erect and bold,
Rear high their Horns, and seem to lowe in Gold,
And speed to Meadows on whose sounding Shores
A rapid Torrent thro' the Rushes roars:
Four golden Herdsmen as their Guardians stand,
And nine sour Dogs compleat the rustic Band.   670
Two Lions rushing from the Wood appear'd;
And seiz'd a Bull, the Master of the Herd:
He roar'd: in vain the Dogs, the Men withstood,
They tore his Flesh, and drank the sable Blood.
The Dogs (oft' chear'd in vain) desert the Prey,
Dread the grim Terrors, and at distance bay.

Next this, the Eye the Art of Vulcan leads
Deep thro' fair Forests, and a Length of Meads;
And Stalls, and Folds, and scatter'd Cotts between;
And fleecy Flocks, that whiten all the Scene.   680
A figur'd Dance succeeds: Such once was seen
In lofty Gnossus, for the Cretan Queen,
Form'd by Dædalean Art. A comely Band
Of Youths and Maidens, bounding Hand in Hand:
The Maids in soft Cymarrs[3] of Linen drest;
The Youths all graceful in the glossy Vest;
Of those the Locks with flow'ry Wreaths inroll'd,
Of these the Sides adorn'd with Swords of Gold,
That glitt'ring gay, from silver Belts depend.
Now all at once they rise, at once descend,   690

[3] A loose, light garment

With well-taught Feet: Now shape, in oblique ways,
Confus'dly regular, the moving Maze:
Now forth at once, too swift for sight, they spring,
And undistinguish'd blend the flying Ring:
So whirls a Wheel, in giddy Circle tost,
And rapid as it runs, the single Spokes are lost.
The gazing Multitudes admire around;
Two active Tumblers in the Center bound;
Now high, now low, their pliant Limbs they bend,
And gen'ral Songs the sprightly Revel end.   700
   Thus the broad Shield complete the Artist crown'd
With his last Hand, and pour'd the Ocean round:
In living Silver seem'd the Waves to roll,
And beat the Buckler's Verge, and bound the whole.
   This done, whate'er a Warrior's Use requires
He forg'd; the Cuirass that outshone the Fires;
The Greaves of ductile Tin, the Helm imprest
With various Sculpture, and the golden Crest.
At Thetis' Feet the finish'd Labour lay;
She, as a Falcon cuts th' Aerial way,   710
Swift from Olympus' snowy Summit flies,
And bears the blazing Present through the Skies.

THE NINETEENTH BOOK
OF THE ILIAD

THE ARGUMENT

The Reconciliation of Achilles and Agamemnon

THETIS BRINGS TO HER SON the Armour made by Vulcan. She preserves
the Body of his Friend from Corruption, and commands him to assemble
the Army, to declare his Resentment at an end. Agamemnon and Achilles
are solemnly reconcil'd: The Speeches, Presents, and Ceremonies on that
Occasion. Achilles is with great Difficulty persuaded to refrain from the
Battel till the Troops have refresh'd themselves, by the Advice of Ulysses.
The Presents are convey'd to the Tent of Achilles; where Briseis laments
over the Body of Patroclus. The Hero obstinately refuses all repast, and
gives himself up to Lamentations for his Friend. Minerva descends to
strengthen him, by the Order of Jupiter. He arms for the Fight; his
Appearance described. He addresses himself to his Horses, and reproaches
them with the Death of Patroclus. One of them is miraculously endued
with Voice, and inspir'd to prophecy his Fate; but the Hero, not astonish'd by that Prodigy, rushes with Fury to the Combate.

The thirtieth Day. The Scene is on the Sea-shore.

Soon as Aurora heav'd her orient Head
Above the Waves that blush'd with early Red,
(With new-born Day to gladden mortal Sight,
And gild the Courts of Heav'n with sacred Light.)
Th' immortal Arms the Goddess-Mother bears
Swift to her Son: Her Son she finds in Tears,
Stretch'd o'er Patroclus Corse; while all the rest
Their Sov'reign's Sorrows in their own exprest.

A Ray divine her heav'nly Presence shed,
And thus, his Hand soft-touching, Thetis said.   10
  Suppress (my Son) this Rage of Grief, and know
It was not Man, but Heav'n that gave the Blow;
Behold what Arms by Vulcan are bestow'd,
Arms worthy thee, or fit to grace a God.
  Then drops the radiant Burden on the Ground;
Clang the strong Arms, and ring the Shores around:
Back shrink the Myrmidons with dread Surprize,
And from the broad Effulgence turn their Eyes.
Unmov'd, the Hero kindles at the Show,
And feels with Rage divine his Bosom glow: 20
From his fierce Eye-balls living Flames expire,
And flash incessant like a Stream of Fire:
He turns the radiant Gift; and feeds his Mind
On all th' immortal Artist had design'd.
  Goddess (he cry'd) these glorious Arms that shine
With matchless Art, confess the Hand divine.
Now to the bloody Battel let me bend:
But ah! the Relicks of my slaughter'd Friend!
In those wide Wounds thro' which his Spirit fled,
Shall Flies and Worms obscene, pollute the Dead?   30
  That unavailing Care be laid aside,
(The Azure Goddess to her Son reply'd)
Whole Years untouch'd, uninjur'd shall remain
Fresh as in Life, the Carcase of the Slain.
But go, Achilles, (as Affairs require)
Before the Grecian Peers renounce thine Ire:
Then uncontroll'd in boundless War engage,
And Heav'n with Strength supply the mighty Rage!
  Then in the Nostrils of the Slain she pour'd
Nectareous Drops, and rich Ambrosia showr'd   40
O'er all the Corse: The Flies forbid their Prey,
Untouch'd it rests, and sacred from Decay.
Achilles to the Strand obedient went;
The Shores resounded with the Voice he sent.
The Heroes heard, and all the Naval Train
That tend the Ships, or guide them o'er the Main,
Alarm'd, transported, at the well-known Sound,
Frequent and full, the great Assembly crown'd;

Studious to see that Terror of the Plain,
Long lost to Battel, shine in Arms again. 50
　Tydides and Ulysses first appear,
Lame with their Wounds, and leaning on the Spear;
These on the sacred Seats of Council plac'd,
The King of Men, Atrides, came the last:
He too sore wounded by Agenor's[1] Son.
Achilles (rising in the midst) begun.
　Oh Monarch! better far had been the Fate
Of thee, of me, of all the Grecian State,
If, (e'er the Day when by mad Passion sway'd,
Rash we contended for the black-ey'd Maid) 60
Preventing Dian had dispatch'd her Dart,
And shot the shining Mischief to the Heart!
Then many a Hero had not press'd the Shore,
Nor Troy's glad Fields been fatten'd with our Gore:
Long, long shall Greece the Woes we caus'd, bewail,
And sad Posterity repeat the Tale.
But this, no more the Subject of Debate,
Is past, forgotten, and resign'd to Fate:
Why should (alas) a mortal Man, as I,
Burn with a Fury that can never die? 70
Here then my Anger ends: Let War succeed,
And ev'n as Greece has bled, let Ilion bleed.
Now call the Hosts, and try, if in our Sight,
Troy yet shall dare to camp a second Night?
I deem, their Mightiest, when this Arm he knows,
Shall 'scape with Transport, and with Joy repose.
　He said: His finish'd Wrath with loud Acclaim
The Greeks accept, and shout Pelides' Name.
When thus, not rising from his lofty Throne,
In State unmov'd, the King of Men begun. 80
　Hear me ye Sons of Greece! with Silence hear!
And grant your Monarch an impartial Ear;
Awhile your loud, untimely Joy suspend,
And let your rash, injurious Clamours end:
Unruly Murmurs, or ill-tim'd Applause,
Wrong the best Speaker, and the justest Cause.

---

[1] Rightly, Antenor's son, Coön

Nor charge on me, ye Greeks, the dire Debate;
Know, angry Jove, and all-compelling Fate,
With fell Erynnis, urg'd my Wrath that Day
When from Achilles' Arms I forc'd the Prey. 90
What then cou'd I, against the Will of Heaven?
Not by my self, but vengeful Ate[2] driv'n;
She, Jove's dread Daughter, fated to infest
The Race of Mortals, enter'd in my Breast.
Not on the Ground that haughty Fury treads,
But prints her lofty Footsteps on the Heads
Of mighty Men; inflicting as she goes
Long-fest'ring Wounds, inextricable Woes!
Of old, she stalk'd amid the bright Abodes;
And Jove himself, the Sire of Men and Gods, 100
The World's great Ruler, felt her venom'd Dart;
Deceiv'd by Juno's Wiles, and female Art.
For when Alcmena's nine long Months were run,
And Jove expected his immortal Son;
To Gods and Goddesses th' unruly Joy
He show'd, and vaunted of his matchless Boy:
From us (he said) this Day an Infant springs,
Fated to rule, and born a King of Kings.
Saturnia ask'd an Oath, to vouch the Truth,
And fix Dominion on the favour'd Youth. 110
The Thund'rer, unsuspicious of the Fraud,
Pronounc'd those solemn Words that bind a God.
The joyful Goddess, from Olympus' Height,
Swift to Achaian Argos bent her Flight;
Scarce sev'n Moons gone, lay Sthenelus his Wife;
She push'd her ling'ring Infant into Life:
Her Charms Alcmena's coming Labours stay,
And stop the Babe, just issuing to the Day.
Then bids Saturnius bear his Oath in mind;
A Youth (said she) of Jove's immortal Kind 120
Is this Day born: From Sthenelus he[3] springs,
And claims thy Promise to be King of Kings.
Grief seiz'd the Thund'rer, by his Oath engag'd;
Stung to the Soul, he sorrow'd, and he rag'd.

[2] IX, 627 n.
[3] Eurystheus, for whom Hercules performed his labors

From his Ambrosial Head, where perch'd she sate,
He snatch'd the Fury-Goddess of Debate,
The dread, th' irrevocable Oath he swore,
Th' immortal Seats should ne'er behold her more;
And whirl'd her headlong down, for ever driv'n
From bright Olympus and the starry Heav'n: 130
Thence on the nether World the Fury fell;
Ordain'd with Man's contentious Race to dwell.
Full oft' the God his Son's hard Toils bemoan'd,
Curs'd the dire Fury, and in secret groan'd.
Ev'n thus, like Jove himself, was I misled,
While raging Hector heap'd our Camps with Dead.
What can the Errors of my Rage attone?
My martial Troops, my Treasures, are thy own:
This Instant from the Navy shall be sent
Whate'er Ulysses promis'd at thy Tent: 140
But thou! appeas'd, propitious to our Pray'r,
Resume thy Arms, and shine again in War.

O King of Nations! whose superiour Sway
(Returns Achilles) all our Hosts obey!
To keep, or send the Presents, be thy Care;
To us, 'tis equal: All we ask is War.
While yet we talk, or but an instant shun
The Fight, our glorious Work remains undone.
Let ev'ry Greek who sees my Spear confound
The Trojan Ranks, and deal Destruction round, 150
With Emulation, what I act, survey,
And learn from thence the Business of the Day.

The Son of Peleus thus: And thus replies
The great in Councils, Ithacus the Wise.
Tho' god-like Thou art by no Toils opprest,
At least our Armies claim Repast and Rest:
Long and laborious must the Combate be,
When by the Gods inspir'd, and led by thee.
Strength is deriv'd from Spirits and from Blood,
And those augment by gen'rous Wine and Food; 160
What boastful Son of War, without that Stay,
Can last a Hero thro' a single Day?
Courage may prompt; but, ebbing out his Strength,
Mere unsupported Man must yield at length;

Shrunk with dry Famine, and with Toils declin'd,
The dropping Body will desert the Mind:
But built anew with Strength-conferring Fare,
With Limbs and Soul untam'd, he tires a War.
Dismiss the People then, and give command,
With strong Repast to hearten ev'ry Band;   170
But let the Presents, to Achilles made,
In full Assembly of all Greece be laid.
The King of Men shall rise in publick Sight,
And solemn swear, (observant of the Rite)
That spotless as she came, the Maid removes,
Pure from his Arms, and guiltless of his Loves.
That done, a sumptuous Banquet shall be made,
And the full Price of injur'd Honour paid.
Stretch not henceforth, O Prince! thy sov'reign Might,
Beyond the Bounds of Reason and of Right;   180
'Tis the chief Praise that e'er to Kings belong'd,
To right with Justice, whom with Pow'r they wrong'd.
    To him the Monarch. Just is thy Decree,
Thy Words give Joy, and Wisdom breathes in thee.
Each due Atonement gladly I prepare;
And Heav'n regard me as I justly swear!
Here then awhile let Greece assembled stay,
Nor great Achilles grudge this short Delay;
Till from the Fleet our Presents be convey'd,
And, Jove attesting, the firm Compact made.   190
A Train of noble Youth the Charge shall bear;
These to select, Ulysses, be thy Care:
In order rank'd let all our Gifts appear,
And the fair Train of Captives close the Rear:
Talthybius shall the Victim Boar convey,
Sacred to Jove, and yon' bright Orb of Day.
    For this (the stern Æacides replies)
Some less important Season may suffice,
When the stern Fury of the War is o'er,
And Wrath extinguish'd burns my Breast no more.   200
By Hector slain, their Faces to the Sky,
All grim with gaping Wounds, our Heroes lye:
Those call to War! and might my Voice incite,
Now, now, this Instant, shou'd commence the Fight.

Then, when the Day's complete, let gen'rous Bowls
And copious Banquets, glad your weary Souls.
Let not my Palate know the Taste of Food,
Till my insatiate Rage be cloy'd with Blood:
Pale lyes my Friend, with Wounds disfigur'd o'er,
And his cold Feet are pointed to the Door.   210
Revenge is all my Soul! no meaner Care,
Int'rest, or Thought, has room to harbour there;
Destruction be my Feast, and mortal Wounds,
And Scenes of Blood, and agonizing Sounds.
   O first of Greeks (Ulysses thus rejoin'd)
The best and bravest of the Warrior-Kind!
Thy Praise it is in dreadful Camps to shine,
But old Experience and calm Wisdom, mine.
Then hear my Counsel, and to Reason yield,
The bravest soon are satiate of the Field;   220
Tho' vast the Heaps that strow the crimson Plain,
The bloody Harvest brings but little Gain:
The Scale of Conquest ever wav'ring lies,
Great Jove but turns it, and the Victor dies!
The Great, the Bold, by Thousands daily fall,
And endless were the Grief, to weep for all.
Eternal Sorrows what avails to shed?
Greece honours not with solemn Fasts the Dead:
Enough, when Death demands the Brave, to pay
The Tribute of a melancholy Day.   230
One Chief with Patience to the Grave resign'd,
Our Care devolves on others left behind.
Let gen'rous Food Supplies of Strength produce,
Let rising Spirits flow from sprightly Juice,
Let their warm Heads with Scenes of Battel glow,
And pour new Furies on the feebler Foe.
Yet a short Interval, and none shall dare
Expect a second Summons to the War;
Who waits for that, the dire Effect shall find,
If trembling in the Ships he lags behind.   240
Embodied, to the Battel let us bend,
And all at once on haughty Troy descend.
   And now the Delegates Ulysses sent,
To bear the Presents from the royal Tent.

The Sons of Nestor, Phyleus' valiant Heir,
Thias and Merion, Thunderbolts of War,
With Lycomedes of Creiontian Strain,
And Melanippus; form'd the chosen Train.
Swift as the Word was giv'n, the Youths obey'd;
Twice ten bright Vases in the midst they laid;   250
A Rowe of six fair Tripods then succeeds;
And twice the Number of high-bounding Steeds:
Sev'n Captives next a lovely Line compose;
The eighth Briseis, like the blooming Rose,
Clos'd the bright Band: Great Ithacus, before,
First of the Train, the golden Talents bore:
The rest in publick View the Chiefs dispose,
A splendid Scene! Then Agamemnon rose:
The Boar Talthybius held: The Grecian Lord
Drew the broad Cutlace sheath'd beside his Sword;   260
The stubborn Bristles from the Victim's Brow
He crops, and off'ring meditates his Vow.
His Hands uplifted to th' attesting Skies,
On Heav'ns broad marble Roof were fix'd his Eyes,
The solemn Words a deep Attention draw,
And Greece around sate thrill'd with sacred Awe.

   Witness thou First! thou greatest Pow'r above!
All good, all-wise, and all-surveying Jove!
And Mother Earth, and Heav'ns revolving Light,
And ye, fell Furies of the Realms of Night,   270
Who rule the Dead, and horrid Woes prepare
For perjur'd Kings, and all who falsely swear!
The black-ey'd Maid inviolate removes,
Pure and unconscious of my manly Loves.
If this be false, Heav'n all its Vengeance shed,
And level'd Thunder strike my guilty Head!

   With that, his Weapon deep inflicts the Wound;
The bleeding Savage tumbles to the Ground:
The sacred Herald rolls the Victim slain
(A Feast for Fish) into the foaming Main.   280

   Then thus Achilles. Hear, ye Greeks! and know
Whate'er we feel, 'tis Jove inflicts the Woe:
Not else Atrides could our Rage inflame,
Nor from my Arms, unwilling, force the Dame.

'Twas Jove's high Will alone, o'erruling all,
That doom'd our Strife, and doom'd the Greeks to fall.
Go then ye Chiefs! indulge the genial Rite;
Achilles waits ye, and expects the Fight.

The speedy Council at his Word adjourn'd;
To their black Vessels all the Greeks return'd.   290
Achilles sought his Tent. His Train before
March'd onward, bending with the Gifts they bore.
Those in the Tents the Squires industrious spread;
The foaming Coursers to the Stalls they led.
To their new Seats the Female Captives move;
Briseis, radiant as the Queen of Love,
Slow as she past, beheld with sad survey
Where gash'd with cruel Wounds, Patroclus lay.
Prone on the Body fell the heav'nly Fair,
Beat her sad Breast, and tore her golden Hair;   300
All-beautiful in Grief, her humid Eyes
Shining with Tears, she lifts, and thus she cries.

Ah Youth! for ever dear, for ever kind,
Once tender Friend of my distracted Mind!
I left thee fresh in Life, in Beauty gay;
Now find thee cold, inanimated Clay!
What Woes my wretched Race of Life attend?
Sorrows on Sorrows, never doom'd to end!
The first lov'd Consort of my virgin Bed
Before these Eyes in fatal Battel bled: 310
My three brave Brothers in one mournful Day
All trod the dark, irremeable Way:
Thy friendly Hand uprear'd me from the Plain,
And dry'd my Sorrows for a Husband slain;
Achilles' Care you promis'd I shou'd prove,
The first, the dearest Partner of his Love,
That Rites divine should ratify the Band,
And make me Empress in his native Land.
Accept these grateful Tears! For thee they flow,
For thee, that ever felt another's Woe!   320

Her Sister Captives echo'd Groan for Groan,
Nor mourn'd Patroclus' Fortunes, but their own.
The Leaders press'd the Chief on ev'ry side;
Unmov'd, he heard them, and with Sighs deny'd.

If yet Achilles have a Friend, whose Care
Is bent to please him; this Request forbear:
Till yonder Sun descend, ah let me pay
To Grief and Anguish one abstemious Day.

He spoke, and from the Warriors turn'd his Face:
Yet still the Brother-Kings of Atreus' Race: 330
Nestor, Idomeneus, Ulysses sage,
And Phœnix; strive to calm his Grief and Rage.
His Rage they calm not, nor his Grief controul;
He groans, he raves, he sorrows from his Soul.

Thou too, Patroclus! (thus his Heart he vents)
Hast spread th' inviting Banquet in our Tents;
Thy sweet Society, thy winning Care,
Oft' stay'd Achilles, rushing to the War.
But now alas! to Death's cold Arms resign'd,
What Banquet but Revenge can glad my Mind?   340
What greater Sorrow could afflict my Breast,
What more, if hoary Peleus were deceast?
(Who now, perhaps, in Pthia dreads to hear
His Son's sad Fate, and drops a tender Tear.)
What more, should Neoptolemus the brave,
(My only Offspring) sink into the Grave?
If yet that Offspring lives, (I distant far,
Of all neglectful, wage a hateful War.)
I cou'd not this, this cruel Stroke attend;
Fate claim'd Achilles, but might spare his Friend.   350
I hop'd Patroclus might survive, to rear
My tender Orphan with a Parent's Care,
From Scyros Isle conduct him o'er the Main,
And glad his Eyes with his paternal Reign,
The lofty Palace, and the large Domain.
For Peleus breaths no more the vital Air;
Or drags a wretched Life of Age and Care,
But till the News of my sad Fate invades
His hastening Soul, and sinks him to the Shades.

Sighing he said: His Grief the Heroes join'd,   360
Each stole a Tear for what he left behind.
Their mingled Grief the Sire of Heav'n survey'd,
And thus, with Pity, to his blue-ey'd Maid.

Is then Achilles now no more thy Care,
And dost thou thus desert the Great in War?
Lo, where yon' Sails their canvas Wings extend,
All comfortless he sits, and wails his Friend:
E'er Thirst and Want his Forces have opprest
Haste and infuse Ambrosia in his Breast.
He spoke, and sudden as the Word of Jove   370
Shot the descending Goddess from above.
So swift thro' Æther the shrill Harpye springs,
The wide Air floating to her ample Wings.
To great Achilles she her Flight addrest,
And pour'd divine Ambrosia in his Breast,
With Nectar sweet, (Refection of the God's!)
Then, swift ascending, sought the bright Abodes.
Now, issued from the Ships the warrior Train,
And like a Deluge pour'd upon the Plain.
As when the piercing Blasts of Boreas blow,   380
And scatter o'er the Fields the driving Snow;
From dusky Clouds the fleecy Winter flies,
Whose dazling Lustre whitens all the Skies:
So Helms succeeding Helms, so Shields from Shields
Catch the quick Beams, and brighten all the Fields;
Broad-glitt'ring Breastplates, Spears with pointed Rays
Mix in one Stream, reflecting Blaze on Blaze:
Thick beats the Center as the Coursers bound,
With Splendor flame the Skies, and laugh the Fields around.
Full in the midst, high tow'ring o'er the rest,   390
His Limbs in Arms divine Achilles drest;
Arms which the Father of the Fire bestow'd,
Forg'd on th' Eternal Anvils of the God.
Grief and Revenge his furious Heart inspire,
His glowing Eye-balls roll with living Fire,
He grinds his Teeth, and furious with Delay
O'erlooks th' embattled Host, and hopes the bloody Day.
The silver Cuishes first his Thighs infold;
Then o'er his Breast was brac'd the hollow Gold:
The brazen Sword a various Baldrick ty'd,   400
That, starr'd with Gems, hung glitt'ring at his side;
And like the Moon, the broad refulgent Shield
Blaz'd with long Rays, and gleam'd athwart the Field.

So to Night-wand'ring Sailors, pale with Fears,
Wide o'er the wat'ry Waste, a Light appears,
Which on the far-seen Mountain blazing high,
Streams from some lonely Watch-tow'r to the Sky:
With mournful Eyes they gaze, and gaze again;
Loud howls the Storm, and drives them o'er the Main.

Next, his high Head the Helmet grac'd; behind   410
The sweepy Crest hung floating in the Wind:
Like the red Star, that from his flaming Hair
Shakes down Diseases, Pestilence and War;
So stream'd the golden Honours from his Head,
Trembled the sparkling Plumes, and the loose Glories shed.

The Chief beholds himself with wond'ring eyes;
His Arms he poises, and his Motions tries;
Buoy'd by some inward Force, he seems to swim,
And feels a Pinion lifting ev'ry Limb.

And now he shakes his great paternal Spear,   420
Pond'rous and huge! which not a Greek could rear.
From Pelion's cloudy Top an Ash entire
Old Chiron fell'd, and shap'd it for his Sire;
A Spear which stern Achilles only wields,
The Death of Heroes, and the Dread of Fields.

Automedon and Alcimus prepare
Th' immortal Coursers, and the radiant Car,
(The silver Traces sweeping at their side)
Their fiery Mouths resplendent Bridles ty'd,
The Iv'ry studded Reins, return'd behind,   430
Wav'd o'er their Backs, and to the Chariot join'd.
The Charioteer then whirl'd the Lash around,
And swift ascended at one active Bound.
All bright in heav'nly Arms, above his Squire
Achilles mounts, and sets the Field on Fire;
Not brighter, Phœbus in th' Æthereal Way,
Flames from his Chariot, and restores the Day.
High o'er the Host, all terrible he stands,
And thunders to his Steeds these dread Commands.

Xanthus and Balius! of Podarges' Strain,   440
(Unless ye boast that heav'nly Race in vain)
Be swift, be mindful of the Load ye bear,
And learn to make your Master more your Care:

Thro' falling Squadrons bear my slaught'ring Sword,
Nor, as ye left Patroclus, leave your Lord.
  The gen'rous Xanthus, as the Words he said,
Seem'd sensible of Woe, and droop'd his Head:
Trembling he stood before the golden Wain,
And bow'd to Dust the Honours of his Mane,
When strange to tell! (So Juno will'd) he broke   450
Eternal Silence, and portentous spoke.
  Achilles! yes! this Day at least we bear
Thy rage in safety thro' the Files of War:
But come it will, the fatal Time must come,
Nor ours the Fault, but God decrees thy Doom.
Not thro' our Crime, or Slowness in the Course;
Fell thy Patroclus, but by heav'nly Force.
The bright far-shooting God who gilds the Day,
(Confest we saw him) tore his Arms away.
No—could our Swiftness o'er the Winds prevail,   460
Or beat the Pinions of the Western Gale,
All were in vain—The Fates thy Death demand,
Due to a mortal and immortal Hand.
  Then ceas'd for ever, by the Furies ty'd,
His fate-ful Voice. Th' intrepid Chief reply'd
With unabated Rage—So let it be!
Portents and Prodigies are lost on me.
I know my Fates: To die, to see no more
My much lov'd Parents, and my native Shore—
Enough—When Heav'n ordains, I sink in Night,   470
Now perish Troy! He said, and rush'd to Fight.

THE TWENTIETH BOOK
OF THE ILIAD

THE ARGUMENT

The Battel of the Gods, and the Acts of Achilles

JUPITER UPON ACHILLES'S RETURNING to the Battel, calls a Council of the
Gods, and permits them to assist either Party. The Terrors of the Combate describ'd, when the Deities are engag'd. Apollo encourages Æneas
to meet Achilles. After a long Conversation, these two Heroes encounter;
but Æneas is preserv'd by the Assistance of Neptune. Achilles falls upon
the rest of the Trojans, and is upon the point of killing Hector, but
Apollo conveys him away in a Cloud. Achilles pursues the Trojans with
great Slaughter.

The same Day continues. The Scene is in the Field before Troy.

Thus round Pelides breathing War and Blood,
Greece sheath'd in Arms, beside her Vessels stood;
While near impending from a neighb'ring Height,
Troy's black Battalions wait the Shock of Fight.
Then Jove to Themis gives Command, to call
The Gods to Council in the starry Hall:
Swift o'er Olympus hundred Hills she flies,
And summons all the Senate of the Skies.
These shining on, in long Procession come
To Jove's eternal Adamantine Dome.   10
Not one was absent; not a Rural Pow'r
That haunts the verdant Gloom, or rosy Bow'r,
Each fair-hair'd Dryad of the shady Wood,
Each azure Sister of the silver Flood;

454

All but old Ocean, hoary Sire! who keeps
His ancient Seat beneath the sacred Deeps.
On Marble Thrones with lucid Columns crown'd,
(The Work of Vulcan) sate the Gods around.
Ev'n He whose Trident sways the watry Reign,
Heard the loud Summons, and forsook the Main,   20
Assum'd his Throne amid the bright Abodes,
And question'd thus the Sire of Men and Gods.

What moves the God who Heav'n and Earth commands,
And grasps the Thunder in his awful Hands,
Thus to convene the whole ætherial State?
Is Greece and Troy the Subject in debate?
Already met, the low'ring Hosts appear,
And Death stands ardent on the Edge of War.

'Tis true (the Cloud-compelling Pow'r replies)
This Day, we call the Council of the Skies   30
In Care of human Race; ev'n Jove's own Eye
Sees with Regret unhappy Mortals die.
Far on Olympus' Top in secret State
Ourself will sit, and see the Hand of Fate
Work out our Will. Celestial Pow'rs! descend,
And as your Minds direct, your Succour lend
To either Host. Troy soon must lye o'erthrown,
If uncontroll'd Achilles fights alone:
Their Troops but lately durst not meet his Eyes;
What can they now, if in his Rage he rise?   40
Assist them Gods! or Ilion's sacred Wall
May fall this Day, tho' Fate forbids the Fall.

He said, and fir'd their heav'nly Breasts with Rage:
On adverse Parts the warring Gods engage.
Heav'ns awful Queen; and He whose azure Round
Girds the vast Globe; the Maid in Arms renown'd;
Hermes, of profitable Arts the Sire,
And Vulcan, the black Sov'reign of the Fire:
These to the Fleet repair with instant Flight,
The Vessels tremble as the Gods alight.   50
In aid of Troy, Latona, Phœbus came,
Mars fiery-helm'd, the Laughter-loving Dame,
Xanthus whose Streams in golden Currents flow,
And the chast Huntress of the silver Bow.

E'er yet the Gods their various Aid employ,
Each Argive Bosom swell'd with manly Joy,
While great Achilles, (Terror of the Plain)
Long lost to Battel, shone in Arms again.
Dreadful he stood in Front of all his Host;
Pale Troy beheld, and seem'd already lost; 60
Her bravest Heroes pant with inward Fear,
And trembling see another God of War.
    But when the Pow'rs descending swell'd the Fight,
Then Tumult rose; fierce Rage and pale Affright
Vary'd each Face; then Discord sounds Alarms,
Earth echoes, and the Nations rush to Arms.
Now thro' the trembling Shores Minerva calls,
And now she thunders from the Grecian Walls.
Mars hov'ring o'er his Troy, his Terror shrouds
In gloomy Tempests, and a Night of Clouds: 70
Now thro' each Trojan Heart he Fury pours
With Voice divine from Ilion's topmost Tow'rs,
Now shouts to Simois, from her beauteous Hill;[1]
The Mountain shook, the rapid Stream stood still.
Above, the Sire of Gods his Thunder rolls,
And Peals on Peals redoubled rend the Poles.
Beneath, stern Neptune shakes the solid Ground,
The Forests wave, the Mountains nod around;
Thro' all their Summits tremble Ida's Woods,
And from their Sources boil her hundred Floods. 80
Troy's Turrets totter on the rocking Plain;
And the toss'd Navies beat the heaving Main.
Deep in the dismal Regions of the Dead,
Th' infernal Monarch rear'd his horrid Head,
Leap'd from his Throne, lest Neptunes Arm should lay
His dark Dominions open to the Day,
And pour in Light on Pluto's drear Abodes,
Abhorr'd by Men, and dreadful ev'n to Gods.
    Such War th' Immortals wage: Such Horrors rend
The World's vast Concave, when the Gods contend. 90
First silver-shafted Phœbus took the Plain
Against blue Neptune, Monarch of the Main:

---

[1] Callicolone, hill near Troy

The God of Arms his Giant Bulk display'd,
Oppos'd to Pallas, War's triumphant Maid.
Against Latona march'd the Son[2] of May;
The quiver'd Dian, Sister of the Day,
(Her golden Arrows sounding at her side)
Saturnia, Majesty of Heav'n, defy'd.
With fiery Vulcan last in Battel stands
The sacred Flood that rolls on golden Sands;   100
Xanthus his Name with those of heavenly Birth,
But call'd Scamander by the Sons of Earth.
    While thus the Gods in various League engage,
Achilles glow'd with more than mortal Rage:
Hector he sought; in search of Hector turn'd
His Eyes around, for Hector only burn'd;
And burst like Light'ning thro' the Ranks, and vow'd
To glut the God of Battels with his Blood.
    Æneas was the first who dar'd to stay;
Apollo wedg'd him in the Warrior's Way,   110
But swell'd his Bosom with undaunted Might,
Half-forc'd, and half-persuaded to the Fight.
Like young Lycaon, of the Royal Line,
In Voice and Aspect, seem'd the Pow'r divine;
And bade the Chief reflect, how late with Scorn
In distant Threats he brav'd the Goddess-born.
    Then thus the Hero of Anchises' Strain.
To meet Pelides you persuade in vain:
Already have I met, nor void of Fear
Observ'd the Fury of his flying Spear;   120
From Ida's Woods he chas'd us to the Field,
Our Force he scatter'd, and our Herds he kill'd;
Lyrnessus, Pedasus in Ashes lay;
But (Jove assisting) I surviv'd the Day.
Else had I sunk opprest in fatal Fight,
By fierce Achilles and Minerva's Might.
Where'ere he mov'd, the Goddess shone before,
And bath'd his brazen Lance in hostile Gore.
What mortal Man Achilles can sustain?
Th' Immortals guard him thro' the dreadful Plain,   130
And suffer not his Dart to fall in vain.

[2] Hermes, son of Maia

Were God my Aid, this Arm should check his Pow'r,
Tho' strong in Battel as a brazen Tow'r.
  To whom the Son of Jove, That God implore,
And be, what great Achilles was before.
From heav'nly Venus thou deriv'st thy Strain,
And he, but from a Sister of the Main;
An aged Sea-God, Father of his Line,
But Jove himself the sacred Source of thine.
Then lift thy Weapon for a noble Blow,   140
Nor fear the vaunting of a mortal Foe.
This said, and Spirit breath'd into his Breast,
Thro' the thick Troops th' embolden'd Hero prest:
His vent'rous Act the white-arm'd Queen survey'd,
And thus, assembling all the Pow'rs, she said.
  Behold an Action, Gods! that claims your Care,
Lo great Æneas rushing to the War;
Against Pelides he directs his Course,
Phœbus impells, and Phœbus gives him Force.
Restrain his bold Career; at least, t' attend   150
Our Favour'd Hero, let some Pow'r descend.
To guard his Life, and add to his Renown,
We, the great Armament of Heav'n came down.
Hereafter let him fall, as Fates design,
That spun so short his Life's illustrious Line:
But lest some adverse God now cross his Way,
Give him to know, what Pow'rs assist this Day:
For how shall Mortal stand the dire Alarms,
When Heav'ns refulgent Host appear in Arms?
  Thus she, and thus the God whose Force can make 160
The solid Globe's eternal Basis shake.
Against the Might of Man, so feeble known,
Why should cœlestial Pow'rs exert their own?
Suffice, from yonder Mount to view the Scene;
And leave to War the Fates of mortal Men.
But if th' Armipotent, or God of Light,
Obstruct Achilles, or commence the Fight,
Thence on the Gods of Troy we swift descend:
Full soon, I doubt not, shall the Conflict end,
And these, in Ruin and Confusion hurl'd,   170
Yield to our conqu'ring Arms the lower World.

Thus having said, the Tyrant of the Sea
Cœrulean Neptune, rose, and led the Way.
Advanc'd upon the Field there stood a Mound
Of Earth congested, wall'd, and trench'd around;
In elder Times to guard Alcides made,
(The Work of Trojans, with Minerva's Aid)
What-time, a vengeful Monster of the Main
Swept the wide Shore, and drove him to the Plain.

Here Neptune, and the Gods of Greece repair, 180
With Clouds encompass'd, and a Veil of Air:
The adverse Pow'rs, around Apollo laid,
Crown the fair Hills that silver Simois shade.
In Circle close each heav'nly Party sate,
Intent to form the future Scheme of Fate;
But mix not yet in Fight, tho' Jove on high
Gives the loud signal, and the Heav'ns reply.

Meanwhile the rushing Armies hide the Ground;
The trampled Center yields a hollow Sound:
Steeds cas'd in Mail, and Chiefs in Armour bright, 190
The gleamy Champain glows with brazen Light.
Amid both Hosts (a dreadful Space) appear
There, great Achilles, bold Æneas here.
With tow'ring Strides Æneas first advanc'd;
The nodding Plumage on his Helmet danc'd,
Spread o'er his Breast the fencing Shield he bore,
And, as he mov'd, his Jav'lin flam'd before.
Not so Pelides; furious to engage,
He rush'd impetuous. Such the Lion's Rage,
Who viewing first his Foes with scornful Eyes, 200
Tho' all in Arms the peopled City rise,
Stalks careless on, with unregarding Pride;
Till at the length, by some brave Youth defy'd,
To His bold Spear the Savage turns alone,
He murmurs Fury with an hollow Groan;
He grins, he foams, he rolls his Eyes around;
Lash'd by his Tail his heaving sides resound;
He calls up all his Rage; he grinds his Teeth,
Resolv'd on Vengeance, or resolv'd on Death.
So fierce Achilles on Æneas flies; 210
So stands Æneas, and his Force defies.

E'er yet the stern Encounter join'd, begun
The Seed of Thetis thus to Venus' Son.
  Why comes Æneas thro' the Ranks so far?
Seeks he to meet Achilles' Arm in War,
In hope the Realms of Priam to enjoy,
And prove his Merits to the Throne of Troy?
Grant that beneath thy Lance Achilles dies,
The partial Monarch may refuse the Prize;
Sons he has many, those thy Pride may quell;   220
And 'tis his Fault to love those Sons too well.
Or, in reward of thy victorious Hand,
Has Troy propos'd some spacious Tract of Land?
An ample Forest, or a fair Domain,
Of Hills for Vines, and Arable for Grain?
Ev'n this, perhaps, will hardly prove thy Lot:
But can Achilles be so soon forgot?
Once (as I think) you saw this brandish'd Spear
And then the great Æneas seem'd to fear.
With hearty Haste from Ida's Mount he fled,   230
Nor, till he reach'd Lyrnessus, turn'd his Head.
Her lofty Walls not long our Progress stay'd;
Those, Pallas, Jove, and We, in Ruins laid:
In Grecian Chains her captive Race were cast;
'Tis true, the great Æneas fled too fast.
Defrauded of my Conquest once before,
What then I lost, the Gods this Day restore.
Go; while thou may'st, avoid the threaten'd Fate;
Fools stay to feel it, and are wise too late.
  To this Anchises' Son. Such Words employ   240
To one that fears thee, some unwarlike Boy:
Such we disdain; the best may be defy'd
With mean Reproaches, and unmanly Pride:
Unworthy the high Race from which we came,
Proclaim'd so loudly by the Voice of Fame,
Each from illustrious Fathers draws his Line;
Each Goddess-born; half human, half divine.
Thetis' this Day, or Venus' Offspring dies,
And Tears shall trickle from cœlestial Eyes:
For when two Heroes, thus deriv'd, contend,   250
'Tis not in Words the glorious strife can end.

If yet thou farther seek to learn my Birth
(A Tale resounded thro' the spacious Earth)
Hear how the glorious Origine we prove
From ancient Dardanus, the first from Jove:
Dardania's Walls he rais'd; for Ilion, then,
(The City since of many-languag'd Men)
Was not. The Natives were content to till
The shady Foot of Ida's Fount-ful Hill.
From Dardanus, great Erichthonius springs,   260
The richest, once, of Asia's wealthy Kings;
Three thousand Mares his spacious Pastures bred,
Three thousand Foals beside their Mothers fed.
Boreas, enamour'd of the sprightly Train,
Conceal'd his Godhead in a flowing Mane,
With Voice dissembled to his Loves he neigh'd,
And cours'd the dappled Beauties o'er the Mead:
Hence sprung twelve others of unrival'd Kind,
Swift as their Mother Mares, and Father Wind.
These lightly skimming, when they swept the Plain,   270
Nor ply'd the Grass, nor bent the tender Grain;
And when along the level Seas they flew,
Scarce on the Surface curl'd the briny Dew.
Such Erichthonius was: From him there came
The sacred Tros, of whom the Trojan Name.
Three Sons renown'd adorn'd his nuptial Bed,
Ilus, Assaracus, and Ganymed:
The matchless Ganymed, divinely fair,
Whom Heaven enamour'd snatch'd to upper Air,
To bear the Cup of Jove (Ætherial Guest)   280
The Grace and Glory of th' Ambrosial Feast.
The two remaining Sons the Line divide:
First rose Laomedon from Ilus' Side;
From him Tithonus, now in Cares grown old,
And Priam, (blest with Hector, brave and bold:)
Clytius and Lampus, ever-honour'd Pair;
And Hicetaon, Thunderbolt of War.
From great Assaracus sprung Capys, He
Begat Anchises, and Anchises me.
Such is our Race: 'Tis Fortune gives us Birth,   290
But Jove alone endues the Soul with Worth:

He, Source of Pow'r and Might! with boundless Sway,
All human Courage, gives, or takes away.
Long in the Field of Words we may contend,
Reproach is infinite, and knows no end,
Arm'd or with Truth or Falshood, Right or Wrong,
So voluble a Weapon is the Tongue;
Wounded, we wound; and neither side can fail,
For ev'ry Man has equal Strength to rail:
Women alone, when in the Streets they jar,   300
Perhaps excel us in this wordy War;
Like us they stand, encompass'd with the Crowd,
And vent their Anger, impotent and loud.
Cease then—Our Business in the Field of Fight
Is not to question, but to prove our Might.
To all those Insults thou hast offer'd here,
Receive this Answer: 'Tis my flying Spear.
    He spoke. With all his Force the Jav'lin flung,
Fix'd deep, and loudly in the Buckler rung.
Far on his out-stretch'd Arm, Pelides held   310
(To meet the thund'ring Lance) his dreadful Shield,
That trembled as it stuck; nor void of Fear
Saw, e'er it fell, th' immeasurable Spear.
His Fears were vain; impenetrable Charms
Secur'd the Temper of th' Ætherial Arms.
Thro' two strong Plates the Point its Passage held,
But stopp'd, and rested, by the third repell'd;
Five Plates of various Metal, various Mold,
Compos'd the Shield; of Brass each outward Fold,
Of Tin each inward, and the middle Gold: 320
There stuck the Lance. Then rising e'er he threw,
The forceful Spear of great Achilles flew,
And pierc'd the Dardan Shield's extremest Bound,
Where the shrill Brass return'd a sharper Sound:
Thro' the thin Verge the Pelian Weapon glides,
And the slight Cov'ring of expanded Hydes.
Æneas his contracted Body bends,
And o'er him high the riven Targe extends,
Sees, thro' its parting Plates, the upper Air,
And at his Back perceives the quiv'ring Spear: 330

A Fate so near him, chills his Soul with Fright,
And swims before his Eyes the many-colour'd Light.
Achilles, rushing in with dreadful Cries,
Draws his broad Blade, and at Æneas flies:
Æneas rouzing as the Foe came on,
(With Force collected) heaves a mighty Stone:
A Mass enormous! which in modern Days
No two of Earth's degen'rate Sons could raise
But Ocean's God, whose Earthquakes rock the Ground,
Saw the Distress, and mov'd the Pow'rs around.   340
   Lo! on the Brink of Fate Æneas stands,
An instant Victim to Achilles Hands:
By Phœbus urg'd; but Phœbus has bestow'd
His Aid in vain: The Man o'erpow'rs the God.
And can ye see this righteous Chief attone
With guiltless Blood, for Vices not his own?
To all the Gods his constant Vows were paid;
Sure, tho' he wars for Troy, he claims our Aid.
Fate wills not this; nor thus can Jove resign
The future Father of the Dardan Line: 350
The first great Ancestor obtain'd his Grace,
And still his Love descends on all the Race.
For Priam now, and Priam's faithless Kind,
At length are odious to th' all-seeing Mind;
On great Æneas shall devolve the Reign,
And Sons succeeding Sons, the lasting Line sustain.
   The great Earth-shaker thus: To whom replies
Th' Imperial Goddess with the radiant Eyes.
Good as he is, to immolate or spare
The Dardan Prince, O Neptune, be thy Care;   360
Pallas and I, by all that Gods can bind,
Have sworn Destruction to the Trojan Kind;
Not ev'n an Instant to protract their Fate,
Or save one Member of the sinking State;
Till her last Flame be quench'd with her last Gore,
And ev'n her crumbling Ruins are no more.
   The King of Ocean to the Fight descends,
Thro' all the whistling Darts his Course he bends,
Swift interpos'd between the Warriors flies,
And casts thick Darkness o'er Achilles' Eyes.   370

From great Æneas' Shield the Spear he drew,
And at its Master's Feet the Weapon threw.
That done, with Force divine, he snatch'd on high
The Dardan Prince, and bore him thro' the Sky,
Smooth-gliding without Step, above the Heads,
Of warring Heroes, and of bounding Steeds.
Till at the Battel's utmost Verge they light,
Where the slow Caucons close the Rear of Fight.
The Godhead there (his heav'nly Form confess'd)
With Words like these the panting Chief address'd.   380

What Pow'r, O Prince, with Force inferior far,
Urg'd thee to meet Achilles' Arm in War?
Henceforth beware, nor antedate thy Doom,
Defrauding Fate of all thy Fame to come.
But when the Day decreed (for come it must)
Shall lay this dreadful Hero in the Dust,
Let then the Furies of that Arm be known,
Secure, no Grecian Force transcends thy own.

With that, he left him wond'ring as he lay,
Then from Achilles chas'd the Mist away: 390
Sudden, returning with the Stream of Light,
The Scene of War came rushing on his Sight.
Then thus, amaz'd: What Wonders strike my Mind!
My Spear, that parted on the Wings of Wind,
Laid here before me! and the Dardan Lord
That fell this instant, vanish'd from my Sword!
I thought alone with Mortals to contend,
But Pow'rs cœlestial sure this Foe defend.
Great as he is, our Arm he scarce will try,
Content for once, with all his Gods, to fly.   400
Now then let others bleed—This said, aloud
He vents his Fury, and inflames the Crowd.
O Greeks (he cries, and every Rank alarms)
Join Battel, Man to Man, and Arms to Arms!
'Tis not in me, tho' favour'd by the Sky,
To mow whole Troops, and make whole Armies fly:
No God can singly such a Host engage,
Not Mars himself, nor great Minerva's Rage.
But whatsoe'er Achilles can inspire,
Whate'er of active Force, or acting Fire,   410

Whate'er this Heart can prompt, or Hand obey;
All, all Achilles, Greeks! is yours to Day.
Thro' yon wide Host this Arm shall scatter Fear,
And thin the Squadrons with my single Spear.

He said: Nor less elate with martial Joy,
The god-like Hector warm'd the Troops of Troy.
Trojans to War! Think Hector leads you on;
Nor dread the Vaunts of Peleus' haughty Son;
Deeds must decide our Fate. Ev'n those with Words
Insult the Brave, who tremble at their Swords: 420
The weakest Atheist-Wretch all Heav'n defies,
But shrinks and shudders, when the Thunder flies.
Nor from yon' Boaster shall your Chief retire,
Not tho' his Heart were Steel, his Hands were Fire;
That Fire, that Steel, your Hector shou'd withstand,
And brave that vengeful Heart, that dreadful Hand.

Thus, breathing Rage thro' all, the Hero said;
A Wood of Lances rises round his Head,
Clamors on Clamors tempest all the Air,
They join, they throng, they thicken to the War.   430
But Phœbus warns him from high Heav'n, to shun
The single Fight with Thetis' god-like Son;
More safe to combate in the mingled Band,
Nor tempt too near the Terrors of his Hand.
He hears, obedient to the God of Light,
And plung'd within the Ranks, awaits the Fight.

Then fierce Achilles, shouting to the Skies,
On Troy's whole Force with boundless Fury flies.
First falls Iphytion, at his Army's Head;
Brave was the Chief, and brave the Host he led;   440
From great Otrynteus he deriv'd his Blood,
His Mother was a Naïs of the Flood;
Beneath the Shades of Tmolus, crown'd with Snow,
From Hyde's Walls, he rul'd the Lands below.
Fierce as he springs, the Sword his Head divides;
The parted Visage falls on equal Sides:
With loud-resounding Arms he strikes the Plain;
While thus Achilles glories o'er the Slain.

Lye there Otryntides! the Trojan Earth
Receives thee dead, tho' Gygæ boast thy Birth;   450

Those beauteous Fields where Hyllus' Waves are roll'd,
And plenteous Hermus swells with Tides of Gold,
Are thine no more—Th' insulting Hero said,
And left him sleeping in Eternal Shade.
The rolling Wheels of Greece the Body tore,
And dash'd their Axles with no vulgar Gore.
   Demoleon next, Antenor's Offspring, laid
Breathless in Dust, the Price of Rashness paid.
Th' impatient Steel with full-descending Sway
Forc'd thro' his brazen Helm its furious Way,   460
Resistless drove the batter'd Skull before,
And dash'd and mingled all the Brains with Gore.
This sees Hippodamas, and seiz'd with Fright,
Deserts his Chariot for a swifter Flight:
The Lance arrests him: an ignoble Wound
The panting Trojan rivets to the Ground.
He groans away his Soul: Not louder roars
At Neptunes Shrine on Helice's high Shores
The Victim Bull; the Rocks rebellow round,
And Ocean listens to the grateful Sound.   470
   Then fell on Polydore his vengeful Rage,
The youngest Hope of Priam's stooping Age:
(Whose Feet for Swiftness in the Race surpast)
Of all his Sons, the dearest, and the last.
To the forbidden Field he takes his Flight
In the first Folly of a youthful Knight,
To vaunt his Swiftness, wheels around the Plain,
But vaunts not long, with all his Swiftness slain.
Struck where the crossing Belts unite behind,
And golden Rings the double Back-plate join'd: 480
Forth thro' the Navel burst the thrilling Steel;
And on his Knees with piercing Shrieks he fell;
The rushing Entrails pour'd upon the Ground
His Hands collect; and Darkness wraps him round.
When Hector view'd, all ghastly in his Gore
Thus sadly slain, th' unhappy Polydore;
A Cloud of Sorrow overcast his Sight,
His Soul no longer brook'd the distant Fight,
Full in Achilles' dreadful Front he came,
And shook his Jav'lin like a waving Flame.   490

The Son of Peleus sees, with Joy possest,
His Heart high-bounding in his rising Breast:
And, lo! the Man, on whom black Fates attend;
The Man, that slew Achilles, in his Friend!
No more shall Hector's and Pelides' Spear
Turn from each other in the Walks of War—
Then with revengeful Eyes he scan'd him o'er:
Come, and receive thy Fate! He spake no more.

   Hector, undaunted, thus. Such Words employ
To one that dreads thee, some unwarlike Boy: 500
Such we could give, defying and defy'd,
Mean Intercourse of Obloquy and Pride!
I know thy Force to mine superior far;
But Heav'n alone confers Success in War:
Mean as I am, the Gods may guide my Dart,
And give it Entrance in a braver Heart.

   Then parts the Lance: But Pallas' heav'nly Breath,
Far from Achilles wafts the winged Death:
The bidden Dart again to Hector flies,
And at the Feet of its great Master lies.   510
Achilles closes with his hated Foe,
His Heart and Eyes with flaming Fury glow:
But present to his Aid, Apollo shrouds
The favour'd Hero in a Veil of Clouds.
Thrice struck Pelides with indignant Heart,
Thrice in impassive Air he plung'd the Dart:
The Spear a fourth time bury'd in the Cloud,
He foams with Fury, and exclaims aloud.

   Wretch! Thou hast scap'd again. Once more thy Flight
Has sav'd thee, and the partial God of Light.   520
But long thou shalt not thy just Fate withstand,
If any Pow'r assist Achilles' Hand.
Fly then inglorious! But thy Flight this Day
Whole Hecatombs of Trojan Ghosts shall pay.

   With that, he gluts his Rage on Numbers slain:
Then Dryops tumbled to th' ensanguin'd Plain,
Pierc'd thro' the Neck: He left him panting there,
And stopp'd Demuchus, great Philetor's Heir,
Gigantic Chief! Deep gash'd th' enormous Blade,
And for the Soul an ample Passage made.   530

Laogonus and Dardanus expire,
The valiant Sons of an unhappy Sire;
Both in one Instant from the Chariot hurl'd,
Sunk in one Instant to the nether World;
This Diff'rence only their sad Fates afford,
That one the Spear destroy'd, and one the Sword.
  Nor less unpity'd young Alastor bleeds;
In vain his Youth, in vain his Beauty pleads:
In vain he begs thee with a Suppliant's Moan,
To spare a Form, and Age so like thy own!   540
Unhappy Boy! no Pray'r, no moving Art
E'er bent that fierce, inexorable Heart!
While yet he trembled at his Knees, and cry'd,
The ruthless Falchion op'd his tender Side;
The panting Liver pours a Flood of Gore,
That drowns his Bosom, till he pants no more.
  Thro' Mulius' Head then drove th' impetuous Spear,
The Warrior falls, transfix'd from Ear to Ear.
Thy Life Echeclus! next the Sword bereaves,
Deep thro' his Front the pond'rous Falchion cleaves;   550
Warm'd in the Brain the smoaking Weapon lies,
The purple Death comes floating o'er his Eyes,
Then brave Deucalion dy'd: The Dart was flung
Where the knit Nerves the pliant Elbow strung;
He dropp'd his Arm, an unassisting Weight,
And stood all impotent, expecting Fate:
Full on his Neck the falling Falchion sped,
From his broad Shoulders hew'd his crested Head:
Forth from the Bone the spinal Marrow flies,
And sunk in Dust, the Corps extended lies.   560
Rhigmus, whose Race from fruitful Thracia came,
(The Son of Pireus, an illustrious Name,)
Succeeds to Fate: The Spear his Belly rends;
Prone from his Car the thund'ring Chief descends,
The Squire who saw expiring on the Ground
His prostrate Master, rein'd the Steeds around;
His Back scarce turn'd, the Pelian Jav'lin gor'd;
And stretch'd the Servant o'er his dying Lord.
As when a Flame the winding Valley fills,
And runs on crackling Shrubs between the Hills;   570

Then o'er the Stubble up the Mountain flies,
Fires the high Woods, and blazes to the Skies,
This way and that, the spreading Torrent roars;
So sweeps the Hero thro' the wasted Shores;
Around him wide, immense Destruction pours,
And Earth is delug'd with the sanguine Show'rs.
As with Autumnal Harvests cover'd o'er,
And thick bestrown, lies Ceres' sacred Floor,
When round and round with never-weary'd Pain,
The trampling Steers beat out th' unnumber'd Grain.   580
So the fierce Coursers, as the Chariot rolls,
Tread down whole Ranks, and crush out Hero's Souls.
Dash'd from their Hoofs while o'er the Dead they fly,
Black bloody Drops the smoaking Chariot die:
The spiky Wheels thro' Heaps of Carnage tore;
And thick the groaning Axles dropp'd with Gore.
High o'er the Scene of Death Achilles stood,
All grim with Dust, all horrible in Blood:
Yet still insatiate, still with Rage on flame;
Such is the Lust of never-dying Fame!   590

THE TWENTY-FIRST BOOK
OF THE ILIAD

THE ARGUMENT

The Battel in the River Scamander

THE TROJANS FLY BEFORE ACHILLES, some towards the Town, others to the River Scamander. He falls upon the latter with great slaughter, takes twelve captives alive, to sacrifice to the Manes of Patroclus; and kills Lycaon and Asteropæus. Scamander attacks him with all his waves; Neptune and Pallas assist the Hero; Simois joins Scamander; at length Vulcan, by the instigation of Juno, almost dries up the River. This Combate ended, the other Gods engage each other. Meanwhile Achilles continues the slaughter, drives the rest into Troy; Agenor only makes a stand, and is convey'd away in a cloud by Apollo; who (to delude Achilles) takes upon him Agenor's shape, and while he pursues him in that disguise, gives the Trojans an opportunity of retiring into their City.

The same Day continues. The Scene is on the Banks, and in the Stream, of Scamander.

And now to Xanthus' gliding Stream they drove,
Xanthus, Immortal Progeny of Jove.
The River here divides the scatt'ring Train.
Part to the Town fly diverse o'er the Plain,
Where late their Troops triumphant bore the Fight,
Now chac'd, and trembling in ignoble flight:
(These with a gather'd Mist Saturnia shrouds,
And rolls behind the Rout a Heap of Clouds)
Part plunge into the Stream: Old Xanthus roars,
The flashing Billows beat the whiten'd Shores: 10

With Cries promiscuous all the Banks resound,
And here, and there, in Eddies whirling round,
The flouncing Steeds and shrieking Warriors drown'd.
As the scorch'd Locusts from their Fields retire,
While fast behind them runs the Blaze of Fire;
Driv'n from the Land before the smoky Cloud,
The clust'ring Legions rush into the Flood:
So plung'd in Xanthus by Achilles' Force,
Roars the resounding Surge with Men and Horse.
His bloody Lance the Hero casts aside,   20
(Which spreading Tam'risks on the Margin hide)
Then like a God, the rapid Billows braves,
Arm'd with his Sword, high-brandish'd o'er the Waves;
Now down he plunges, now he whirls it round,
Deep groan the Waters with the dying Sound;
Repeated Wounds the red'ning River dy'd,
And the warm Purple circled on the Tyde.
Swift thro' the foamy Flood the Trojans fly,
And close in Rocks or winding Caverns lye.
So the huge Dolphin tempesting the Main,   30
In Shoals before him fly the scaly Train,
Confus'dly heap'd, they seek their inmost Caves,
Or pant and heave beneath the floating Waves.
Now tir'd with Slaughter, from the Trojan Band
Twelve chosen Youths he drags alive to Land;
With their rich Belts their Captive Arms constrains,
(Late their proud Ornaments, but now their Chains.)
These his Attendants to the Ships convey'd,
Sad Victims! destin'd to Patroclus' Shade.

Then, as once more he plung'd amid the Flood,   40
The young Lycaon in his Passage stood;
The Son of Priam, whom the Hero's Hand
But late made captive in his Father's Land,
(As on a Fig-tree Top, his sounding Steel
Lopp'd the green Arms to spoke a Chariot Wheel)
To Lemnos' Isle he sold the Royal Slave,
Where Jason's Son the Price demanded gave;
But kind Eëtion touching on the Shore,
The ransom'd Prince to fair Arisbe bore.

Ten Days were past, since in his Father's Reign   50
He felt the Sweets of Liberty again;
The next, that God whom Men in vain withstand,
Gives the same Youth to the same conqu'ring Hand;
Now never to return! and doom'd to go
A sadder Journey to the Shades below.
His well-known Face when great Achilles ey'd,
(The Helm and Vizor he had cast aside
With wild Affright, and dropt upon the Field
His useless Lance and unavailing Shield.)
As trembling, panting, from the Stream he fled,   60
And knock'd his fault'ring Knees, the Hero said.
   Ye mighty Gods! what Wonders strike my View:
Is it in vain our conqu'ring Arms subdue?
Sure I shall see yon' Heaps of Trojans kill'd
Rise from the Shades, and brave me on the Field:
As now the Captive, whom so late I bound
And sold to Lemnos, stalks on Trojan Ground!
Not him the Seas unmeasur'd Deeps detain,
That barr such numbers from their native Plain:
Lo! he returns! Try then, my flying spear!   70
Try, if the Grave can hold the Wanderer;
If Earth at length this active Prince can seize,
Earth, whose strong Grasp has held down Hercules.
   Thus while he spake, the Trojan pale with Fears
Approach'd, and sought his Knees with suppliant Tears;
Loth as he was to yield his youthful Breath,
And his Soul shiv'ring at th' Approach of Death.
Achilles rais'd the Spear, prepar'd to wound;
He kiss'd his Feet, extended on the Ground:
And while above the Spear suspended stood,   80
Longing to dip its thirsty Point in Blood;
One Hand embrac'd them close, one stopt the Dart;
While thus these melting Words attempt his Heart.
   Thy well-known Captive, great Achilles! see,
Once more Lycaon trembling at thy Knee;
Some Pity to a Suppliant's Name afford,
Who shar'd the Gifts of Ceres at thy Board,

Whom late thy conqu'ring Arm to Lemnos bore,
Far from his Father, Friends, and native Shore;
A hundred Oxen were his Price that Day,   90
Now Sums immense thy Mercy shall repay.
Scarce respited from Woes I yet appear,
And scarce twelve morning Suns have seen me here;
Lo! Jove again submits me to thy Hands,
Again, her Victim cruel Fate demands!
I sprung from Priam, and Laothöe fair,
(Old Alte's Daughter, and Lelegia's Heir;
Who held in Pedasus his fam'd Abode,
And rul'd the Fields where silver Satnio flow'd)
Two Sons (alas, unhappy Sons) she bore,   100
For ah! one Spear shall drink each Brother's Gore,
And I succeed to slaughter'd Polydore.
How from that Arm of Terror shall I fly?
Some Dæmon urges! 'tis my Doom to die!
If ever yet soft Pity touch'd thy mind,
Ah! think not me too much of Hector's Kind:
Not the same Mother gave thy Suppliant Breath,
With his, who wrought thy lov'd Patroclus' Death.
    These Words, attended with a Show'r of Tears,
The Youth addrest to unrelenting Ears: 110
Talk not of Life, or Ransom, (he replies)
Patroclus dead, whoever meets me, dies:
In vain a single Trojan sues for Grace;
But least, the Sons of Priam's hateful Race.
Die then, my Friend! what boots it to deplore?
The great, the good Patroclus is no more!
He, far thy Better, was fore-doom'd to die,
And thou, dost thou, bewail Mortality?
See'st thou not me, whom Nature's Gifts adorn,
Sprung from a Hero, from a Goddess born;   120
The Day shall come (which nothing can avert)
When by the Spear, the Arrow, or the Dart,
By Night, or Day, by Force or by Design,
Impending Death and certain Fate are mine.
Die then—He said; and as the Word he spoke
The fainting Stripling sunk, before the Stroke;

His Hand forgot its Grasp, and left the Spear;
While all his trembling Frame confest his Fear.
Sudden, Achilles his broad Sword display'd,
And buried in his Neck the reeking Blade.   130
Prone fell the Youth; and panting on the Land,
The gushing Purple dy'd the thirsty Sand:
The Victor to the Stream the Carcass gave,
And thus insults him, floating on the Wave.

  Lie there, Lycaon! let the Fish surround
Thy bloated Corse, and suck thy goary Wound:
There no sad Mother shall thy Fun'rals weep,
But swift Scamander roll thee to the Deep,
Whose ev'ry Wave some wat'ry Monster brings,
To feast unpunish'd on the Fat of Kings.   140
So perish Troy, and all the Trojan Line!
Such Ruin theirs, and such Compassion mine.
What boots ye now Scamander's worship'd Stream,
His earthly Honours, and immortal Name;
In vain your immolated Bulls are slain,
Your living Coursers glut his Gulphs in vain:
Thus he rewards you, with this bitter Fate;
Thus, till the Grecian Vengeance is compleat;
Thus is aton'd Patroclus honour'd Shade,
And the short Absence of Achilles paid.   150

  These boastful Words provoke the raging God;
With Fury swells the violated Flood.
What Means divine may yet the Pow'r employ,
To check Achilles, and to rescue Troy?
Meanwhile the Hero springs in Arms, to dare
The great Asteropeus to mortal War;
The Son of Pelagon, whose lofty Line
Flows from the Source of Axius, Stream divine!
(Fair Peribæa's Love the God had crown'd,
With all his refluent Waters circled round)   160
On him Achilles rush'd: He fearless stood,
And shook two Spears, advancing from the Flood;
The Flood impell'd him, on Pelides' Head
T'avenge his Waters choak'd with Heaps of Dead.

Near as they drew, Achilles thus began.
What art thou, boldest of the Race of Man?
Who, or from whence? Unhappy is the Sire,
Whose Son encounters our resistless Ire.
  O Son of Peleus! what avails to trace
(Reply'd the Warrior) our illustrious Race?   170
From rich Pæonia's Vallies I command
Arm'd with protended Spears, my native Band;
Now shines the tenth bright Morning since I came
In aid of Ilion to the Fields of Fame:
Axius, who swells with all the neighb'ring Rills,
And wide around the floated Region fills,
Begot my Sire, whose Spear such Glory won:
Now lift thy Arm, and try that Hero's Son!
  Threat'ning he said: The hostile Chiefs advance;
At once Asteropeus discharg'd each Lance,   180
(For both his dext'rous Hands the Lance cou'd wield)
One struck, but pierc'd not the Vulcanian Shield;
One raz'd Achilles Hand; the spouting Blood
Spun forth, in Earth the fasten'd Weapon stood.
Like Lightning next the Pelian Jav'lin flies;
Its erring Fury hiss'd along the Skies;
Deep in the swelling Bank was driv'n the Spear,
Ev'n to the middle earth'd; and quiver'd there.
Then from his side the Sword Pelides drew,
And on his Foe with doubled Fury flew.   190
The Foe thrice tugg'd, and shook the rooted Wood;
Repulsive of his Might the Weapon stood:
The fourth, he tries to break the Spear in vain;
Bent as he stands, he tumbles to the Plain;
His Belly open'd with a ghastly Wound,
The reeking Entrails pour upon the Ground.
Beneath the Hero's Feet he panting lies,
And his Eye darkens, and his Spirit flies:
While the proud Victor thus triumphing said,
His radiant Armour tearing from the Dead: 200
  So ends thy Glory! Such the Fate they prove
Who strive presumptuous with the Sons of Jove.

Sprung from a River didst thou boast thy Line,
But great Saturnius is the Source of mine.
How durst thou vaunt thy wat'ry Progeny?
Of Peleus, Æacus, and Jove, am I;
The Race of these superior far to those,
As he that thunders to the Stream that flows.
What Rivers can, Scamander might have shown;
But Jove he dreads, nor wars against his Son.   210
Ev'n Achelöus might contend in vain,
And all the roaring Billows of the Main.
Th' Eternal Ocean, from whose Fountains flow
The Seas, the Rivers, and the Springs below,
The thund'ring Voice of Jove abhors to hear,
And in his deep Abysses shakes with Fear.
  He said; then from the Bank his Jav'lin tore,
And left the breathless Warrior in his Gore.
The floating Tydes the bloody Carcass lave,
And beat against it, Wave succeeding Wave;   220
Till roll'd between the Banks, it lies the Food
Of curling Eels, and Fishes of the Flood.
All scatter'd round the Stream (their Mightiest slain)
Th' amaz'd Pæonians scour along the Plain:
He vents his Fury on the flying Crew,
Thrasius, Astypylus, and Mnesus slew;
Mydon, Thersilochus, with Ænius fell;
And Numbers more his Lance had plung'd to Hell;
But from the Bottom of his Gulphs profound,
Scamander spoke; the Shores return'd the Sound.   230
  O first of Mortals! (for the Gods are thine)
In Valour matchless, and in Force divine!
If Jove have giv'n thee every Trojan Head,
'Tis not on me thy Rage should heap the Dead.
See! my choak'd Streams no more their Course can keep,
Nor roll their wonted Tribute to the Deep.
Turn then, Impetuous! from our injur'd Flood;
Content, thy Slaughters could amaze a God.
  In human Form confess'd before his Eyes
The River thus; and thus the Chief replies.   240

O sacred Stream! thy Word we shall obey;
But not till Troy the destin'd Vengeance pay,
Not till within her Tow'rs the perjur'd Train
Shall pant, and tremble at our Arms again;
Not till proud Hector, Guardian of her Wall,
Or stain this Lance, or see Achilles fall.
  He said; and drove with Fury on the Foe.
Then to the Godhead of the silver Bow
The yellow Flood began: O Son of Jove!
Was not the Mandate of the Sire above   250
Full and express? that Phœbus should employ
His sacred Arrows in defence of Troy,
And make her conquer, till Hyperion's Fall
In awful Darkness hide the Face of all?
  He spoke in vain—The Chief without Dismay
Ploughs thro' the boiling Surge his desp'rate Way.
Then rising in his Rage above the Shores,
From all his Deeps the bellowing River roars,
Huge Heaps of Slain disgorges on the Coast,
And round the Banks the ghastly Dead are tost.   260
While all before, the Billows rang'd on high
(A wat'ry Bulwark) screen the Bands who fly.
Now bursting on his Head with thund'ring Sound,
The falling Deluge whelms the Hero round:
His loaded Shield bends to the rushing Tide;
His Feet, upborn, scarce the strong Flood divide,
Slidd'ring, and stagg'ring. On the Border stood
A spreading Elm, that overhung the Flood;
He seiz'd a bending Bough, his Steps to stay;
The Plant uprooted to his Weight gave way,   270
Heaving the Bank, and undermining all;
Loud flash the Waters to the rushing Fall
Of the thick Foliage. The large Trunk display'd
Bridg'd the rough Flood across: The Hero stay'd
On this his Weight, and rais'd upon his Hand,
Leap'd from the Chanel, and regain'd the Land.
Then blacken'd the wild Waves; the Murmur rose;
The God pursues, a huger Billow throws,

And bursts the Bank, ambitious to destroy
The Man whose Fury is the Fate of Troy.   280
He, like the warlike Eagle speeds his Pace,
(Swiftest and strongest of th' aerial Race)
Far as a Spear can fly, Achilles springs
At every Bound; His clanging Armour rings:
Now here, now there, he turns on ev'ry side,
And winds his Course before the following Tide;
The Waves flow after, wheresoe'er he wheels,
And gather fast, and murmur at his Heels.
So when a Peasant to his Garden brings
Soft Rills of Water from the bubbling Springs,   290
And calls the Floods from high, to bless his Bow'rs
And feed with pregnant Streams the Plants and Flow'rs;
Soon as he clears whate'er their passage staid,
And marks their future Current with his Spade,
Swift o'er the rolling Pebbles, down the Hills
Louder and louder purl the falling Rills,
Before him scatt'ring, they prevent his pains,
And shine in mazy Wand'rings o'er the Plains.
     Still flies Achilles, but before his eyes
Still swift Scamander rolls where'er he flies: 300
Not all his Speed escapes the rapid Floods;
The first of Men, but not a Match for Gods.
Oft' as he turn'd the Torrent to oppose,
And bravely try if all the Pow'rs were Foes;
So oft' the Surge, in wat'ry Mountains spread,
Beats on his Back, or bursts upon his Head.
Yet dauntless still the adverse Flood he braves,
And still indignant bounds above the Waves.
Tir'd by the Tides, his Knees relax with Toil;
Wash'd from beneath him, slides the slimy Soil;   310
When thus (his Eyes on Heav'ns Expansion thrown)
Forth bursts the Hero with an angry Groan.
     Is there no God Achilles to befriend,
No Pow'r t'avert his miserable End?
Prevent, oh Jove! this ignominious Date,
And make my future Life the Sport of Fate.

Of all Heav'ns Oracles believ'd in vain,
But most of Thetis, must her Son complain;
By Phœbus' Darts she prophesy'd my Fall,
In glorious Arms before the Trojan Wall.   320
Oh! had I dy'd in Fields of Battel warm,
Stretch'd like a Hero, by a Hero's Arm!
Might Hector's Spear this dauntless Bosom rend,
And my swift Soul o'ertake my slaughter'd Friend!
Ah no! Achilles meets a shameful Fate,
Oh how unworthy of the Brave and Great!
Like some vile Swain, whom, on a rainy Day,
Crossing a Ford, the Torrent sweeps away,
An unregarded Carcase to the Sea.

　　Neptune and Pallas haste to his Relief,   330
And thus in human Form address the Chief:
The Pow'r of Ocean first. Forbear thy Fear,
O Son of Peleus! Lo thy Gods appear!
Behold! from Jove descending to thy Aid,
Propitious Neptune, and the blue-ey'd Maid.
Stay, and the furious Flood shall cease to rave;
'Tis not thy Fate to glut his angry Wave.
But thou, the Counsel Heav'n suggests, attend!
Nor breathe from Combate, nor thy Sword suspend,
Till Troy receive her flying Sons, till all   340
Her routed Squadrons pant behind their Wall:
Hector alone shall stand his fatal Chance,
And Hector's Blood shall smoke upon thy Lance.
Thine is the Glory doom'd. Thus spake the Gods;
Then swift ascended to the bright Abodes.

　　Stung with new Ardor, thus by Heav'n impell'd,
He springs impetuous, and invades the Field:
O'er all th' expanded Plain the Waters spread;
Heav'd on the bounding Billows, danc'd the Dead,
Floating midst scatter'd Arms; while Casques of Gold   350
And turn'd up Bucklers glitter'd as they roll'd.
High o'er the surging Tide, by Leaps and Bounds,
He wades, and mounts; the parted Wave resounds.
Not a whole River stops the Hero's Course,
While Pallas fills him with immortal Force.

With equal Rage, indignant Xanthus roars,
And lifts his Billows, and o'erwhelms his Shores.
　　Then thus to Simois: Haste, my Brother Flood!
And check this Mortal that controuls a God:
Our bravest Heroes else shall quit the Fight,　　　　　360
And Ilion tumble from her tow'ry Height.
Call then thy subject Streams, and bid them roar,
From all thy Fountains swell thy wat'ry Store,
With broken Rocks, and with a Load of Dead,
Charge the black Surge, and pour it on his Head.
Mark how resistless thro' the Floods he goes,
And boldly bids the warring Gods be Foes!
But nor that Force, nor Form divine to Sight
Shall ought avail him, if our Rage unite:
Whelm'd under our dark Gulphs those Arms shall lie　370
That blaze so dreadful in each Trojan Eye;
And deep beneath a sandy Mountain hurl'd
Immers'd remain this Terror of the World.
Such pond'rous Ruin shall confound the Place,
No Greek shall e'er his perish'd Relicks grace,
No Hand his Bones shall gather, or inhume;
These his cold Rites, and this his wat'ry Tomb.
　　He said; and on the Chief descends amain,
Increas'd with Gore, and swelling with the Slain.
Then murm'ring from his Beds, he boils, he raves,　　380
And a Foam whitens on the purple Waves
At ev'ry Step, before Achilles stood
The crimson Surge, and delug'd him with Blood.
Fear touch'd the Queen of Heav'n: She saw dismay'd,
She call'd aloud, and summon'd Vulcan's Aid.
　　Rise to the War! th' insulting Flood requires
Thy wasteful Arm: Assemble all thy Fires!
While to their aid, by our Command enjoin'd,
Rush the swift Eastern and the Western Wind:
These from old Ocean at my Word shall blow,　　　　390
Pour the red Torrent on the wat'ry Foe,
Corses and Arms to one bright Ruin turn,
And hissing Rivers to their bottoms burn.

Go, mighty in thy Rage! display thy Pow'r,
Drink the whole Flood, the crackling Trees devour,
Scorch all the Banks! and (till our Voice reclaim)
Exert th' unweary'd Furies of the Flame!
  The Pow'r Ignipotent her Word obeys:
Wide o'er the Plain he pours the boundless Blaze;
At once consumes the Dead, and dries the Soil;   400
And the shrunk Waters in their Chanel boil:
As when Autumnal Boreas sweeps the Sky,
And instant, blows the water'd Garden dry:
So look'd the Field, so whiten'd was the Ground,
While Vulcan breath'd the fiery Blast around.
Swift on the sedgy Reeds the Ruin preys;
Along the Margin winds the running Blaze:
The Trees in flaming rows to Ashes turn,
The flow'ry Lotos, and the Tam'risk burn,
Broad Elm, and Cypress rising in a Spire;   410
The wat'ry Willows hiss before the Fire.
Now glow the Waves, the Fishes pant for Breath,
The Eels lie twisting in the Pangs of Death:
Now flounce aloft, now dive the scaly Fry,
Or gasping, turn their Bellies to the Sky.
At length the River rear'd his languid Head,
And thus short-panting, to the God he said.
  O Vulcan, oh! what Pow'r resists thy Might?
I faint, I sink, unequal to the Fight—
I yield—Let Ilion fall; if Fate decree—   420
Ah—bend no more thy fiery Arms on me!
  He ceas'd; wide Conflagration blazing round;
The bubbling Waters yield a hissing Sound.
As when the Flames beneath a Caldron rise,
To melt the Fat of some rich Sacrifice,
Amid the fierce Embrace of circling Fires
The Waters foam, the heavy Smoak aspires:
So boils th' imprison'd Flood, forbid to flow,
And choak'd with Vapours, feels his Bottom glow.
To Juno then, Imperial Queen of Air,   430
The burning River sends his earnest Pray'r.

Ah why, Saturnia! must thy Son engage
Me, only me, with all his wastfull Rage?
On other Gods his dreadful Arm employ,
For mightier Gods assert the Cause of Troy.
Submissive I desist, if thou command,
But ah! withdraw this all-destroying Hand.
Hear then my solemn Oath, to yield to Fate
Unaided Ilion, and her destin'd State,
Till Greece shall gird her with destructive Flame,   440
And in one Ruin sink the Trojan Name.

His warm Intreaty touch'd Saturnia's Ear;
She bade th' Ignipotent his Rage forbear,
Recall the Flame, nor in a mortal cause
Infest[1] a God: Th' obedient Flame withdraws:
Again, the branching Streams begin to spread,
And soft re-murmur in their wonted Bed.

While these by Juno's Will the Strife resign,
The warring Gods in fierce Contention join:
Re-kindling Rage each heavenly Breast alarms;   450
With horrid Clangor shock th' ætherial Arms:
Heav'n in loud Thunder bids the Trumpet sound;
And wide beneath them groans the rending Ground.
Jove, as his Sport, the dreadful Scene descries,
And views contending Gods with careless Eyes.
The Pow'r of Battels[2] lifts his brazen Spear,
And first assaults the radiant Queen of War,

What mov'd thy Madness, thus to disunite
Æthereal Minds, and mix all Heav'n in Fight?
What wonder this, when in thy frantick Mood   460
Thou drov'st a Mortal to insult a God;
Thy impious Hand Tydides' Jav'lin bore,
And madly bath'd it in celestial Gore.

He spoke, and smote the loud-resounding Shield,
Which bears Jove's Thunder on its dreadful Field;
The Adamantine Ægis of her Sire,
That turns the glancing Bolt, and forked Fire.

[1] Attack
[2] Mars, who attacks Minerva, *Queen of War*

Then heav'd the Goddess in her mighty Hand
A Stone, the Limit of the neighb'ring Land;
There fix'd from eldest times; black, craggy, vast: 470
This, at the heav'nly Homicide she cast.
Thund'ring he falls; a Mass of monstrous Size,
And sev'n broad Acres covers as he lies.
The stunning Stroke his stubborn Nerves unbound;
Loud o'er the Fields his ringing Arms resound:
The scornful Dame her Conquest views with Smiles,
And glorying thus, the prostrate God reviles.
   Hast thou not yet, insatiate Fury! known,
How far Minerva's Force transcends thy own?
Juno, whom thou rebellious dar'st withstand,   480
Corrects thy Folly thus by Pallas' Hand;
Thus meets thy broken Faith with just Disgrace,
And partial Aid to Troy's perfidious Race.
   The Goddess spoke, and turn'd her Eyes away
That beaming round, diffus'd celestial Day.
Jove's Cyprian Daughter stooping on the Land,
Lent to the wounded God her tender Hand:
Slowly he rises, scarcely breathes with Pain,
And propt on her fair Arm, forsakes the Plain.
This the bright Empress of the Heav'ns survey'd,   490
And scoffing, thus, to War's victorious Maid.
   Lo, what an Aid on Mars's Side is seen!
The Smiles' and Love's unconquerable Queen!
Mark with what Insolence, in open view,
She moves: Let Pallas, if she dares, pursue.
   Minerva smiling heard, the Pair o'ertook,
And slightly on her Breast the Wanton strook:
She, unresisting, fell; (her Spirits fled)
On Earth together lay the Lovers spread.
And like these Hero's, be the Fate of all   500
(Minerva cries) who guard the Trojan Wall!
To Grecian Gods such let the Phrygian be,
So dread, so fierce, as Venus is to me;
Then from the lowest Stone shall Troy be mov'd—
Thus she, and Juno with a Smile approv'd.

Meantime, to mix in more than mortal Fight,
The God of Ocean dares the God of Light.
What Sloath has seiz'd us, when the Fields around
Ring with conflicting Pow'rs, and Heav'n returns the Sound?
Shall ignominious We with shame retire,   510
No Deed perform'd, to our Olympian Sire?
Come, prove thy Arm! for first the War to wage,
Suits not my Greatness, or superior Age.
Rash as thou art to prop the Trojan Throne,
(Forgetful of my Wrongs, and of thy own)
And guard the Race of proud Laomedon![3]
Hast thou forgot, how at the Monarch's Pray'r,
We shar'd the lengthen'd Labours of a Year?
Troy Walls I rais'd (for such were Jove's Commands)
And yon' proud Bulwarks grew beneath my Hands: 520
Thy Task it was, to feed the bellowing Droves
Along fair Ida's Vales, and pendent Groves.
But when the circling Seasons in their Train
Brought back the grateful Day that crown'd our Pain;
With Menace stern the fraudful King defy'd
Our latent Godhead, and the Prize deny'd:
Mad as he was, he threaten'd servile Bands,
And doom'd us Exiles far in barb'rous Lands.
Incens'd, we heav'nward fled with swiftest wing,
And destin'd Vengeance on the perjur'd King.   530
Dost thou, for this, afford proud Ilion Grace,
And not like us, infest the faithless Race?
Like us, their present, future Sons destroy,
And from its deep Foundations heave their Troy?
    Apollo thus: To combat for Mankind
Ill suits the Wisdom of celestial Mind:
For what is Man? Calamitous by Birth,
They owe their Life and Nourishment to Earth;
Like yearly Leaves, that now, with Beauty crown'd,
Smile on the Sun; now, wither on the Ground: 540
To their own Hands commit the frantick Scene,
Nor mix Immortals in a Cause so mean.

g VII, 539 n.

Then turns his Face, far-beaming heav'nly Fires,
And from the Senior Pow'r, submiss retires;
Him, thus retreating, Artemis upbraids,
The quiver'd Huntress of the Sylvan Shades.
And is it thus the youthful Phœbus flies,
And yields to Ocean's hoary Sire, the Prize?
How vain that martial Pomp, and dreadful Show,
Of pointed Arrows, and the silver Bow!   550
Now boast no more in yon' celestial Bow'r,
Thy Force can match the great Earth-shaking Pow'r.
Silent, he heard the Queen of Woods upbraid:
Not so Saturnia bore the vaunting Maid;
But furious thus. What Insolence has driv'n
Thy Pride to face the Majesty of Heav'n?
What tho' by Jove the female Plague design'd,
Fierce to the feeble Race of Womankind,
The wretched Matron feels thy piercing Dart;
Thy Sexe's Tyrant, with a Tyger's Heart?   560
What tho' tremendous in the woodland Chase,
Thy certain Arrows pierce the savage Race?
How dares thy Rashness on the Pow'rs divine
Employ those Arms, or match thy Force with mine?
Learn hence, no more unequal War to wage—
She said, and seiz'd her Wrists with eager Rage;
These in her Left-Hand lock'd, her Right unty'd
The Bow, the Quiver, and its plumy Pride.
About her Temples flies the busy Bow;
Now here, now there, she winds her from the Blow;   570
The scatt'ring Arrows rattling from the Case,
Drop round, and idly mark the dusty Place.
Swift from the Field the baffled Huntress flies,
And scarce restrains the Torrent in her Eyes:
So, when the Falcon wings her way above,
To the cleft Cavern speeds the gentle Dove,
(Not fated yet to die) There safe retreats,
Yet still her Heart against the Marble beats.
To her, Latona hasts with tender Care;
Whom Hermes viewing, thus declines the War.   580

How shall I face the Dame, who gives Delight[4]
To him whose Thunders blacken Heav'n with Night?
Go matchless Goddess! triumph in the Skies,
And boast my Conquest, while I yield the Prize.

    He spoke; and past: Latona, stooping low,
Collects the scatter'd Shafts, and fallen Bow,
That glitt'ring on the Dust, lay here and there;
Dishonour'd Relicks of Diana's War.
Then swift pursu'd her to the blest Abode,
Where, all confus'd, she sought the Sov'reign God;   590
Weeping she grasp'd his Knees: Th' Ambrosial Vest
Shook with her Sighs, and panted on her Breast.

    The Sire, superior smil'd; and bade her show,
What heav'nly Hand had caus'd his Daughter's Woe?
Abash'd, she names his own Imperial Spouse;
And the pale Crescent fades upon her Brows.

    Thus they above: While swiftly gliding down,
Apollo enters Ilion's sacred Town:
The Guardian God now trembled for her Wall,
And fear'd the Greeks, tho' Fate forbade her Fall.   600
Back to Olympus, from the War's Alarms,
Return the shining Bands of Gods in Arms;
Some proud in Triumph, some with Rage on fire;
And take their Thrones around th' Æthereal Sire.

    Thro' Blood, thro' Death, Achilles still proceeds,
O'er slaughter'd Heroes, and o'er rolling Steeds
As when avenging Flames with Fury driv'n,
On guilty Towns exert the Wrath of Heav'n;
The Pale Inhabitants, some fall, some fly;
And the red Vapours purple all the Sky.   610
So rag'd Achilles: Death, and dire Dismay,
And Toils, and Terrors, fill'd the dreadful Day.

    High on a Turret hoary Priam stands,
And marks the Waste of his destructive Hands;
Views, from his Arm, the Trojans scatter'd Flight,
And the near Hero rising on his Sight!
No Stop, no Check, no Aid! With feeble pace,
And settled Sorrow on his aged Face,

---

[4] Latona was one of Jove's many wives.

Fast as he could, he sighing quits the Walls;
And thus, descending, on the Guards he calls. 620
   You to whose care our City Gates belong,
Set wide your Portals to the flying Throng.
For lo! he comes, with unresisted Sway;
He comes, and Desolation marks his way!
But when within the Walls our Troops take Breath,
Lock fast the brazen Bars, and shut out Death.
Thus charg'd the rev'rend Monarch: Wide were flung
The opening Folds; the sounding Hinges rung.
Phœbus rush'd forth, the flying Bands to meet,
Strook Slaughter back, and cover'd the Retreat. 630
On Heaps the Trojans crowd to gain the Gate,
And gladsome see their last Escape from Fate:
Thither, all parch'd with Thirst, a heartless Train,
Hoary with Dust, they beat the hollow Plain;
And gasping, panting, fainting, labour on
With heavier Strides, that lengthen tow'rd the Town.
Enrag'd Achilles follows with his Spear;
Wild with Revenge, insatiable of War.
   Then had the Greeks Eternal Praise acquir'd,
And Troy inglorious to her Walls retir'd; 640
But he,[5] the God who darts æthereal Flame,
Shot down to save her, and redeem her Fame.
To young Agenor Force divine he gave,
(Antenor's Offspring, haughty, bold and brave)
In aid of him, beside the Beech he sate,
And wrapt in Clouds, restrain'd the Hand of Fate.
When now the gen'rous Youth Achilles spies,
Thick beats his Heart, the troubled Motions rise,
(So, e're a Storm, the Waters heave and roll)
He stops, and questions thus his mighty Soul. 650
   What, shall I fly this Terror of the Plain?
Like others fly, and be like others slain?
Vain hope! to shun him by the self-same Road
Yon' Line of slaughter'd Trojans lately trod.
No: with the common Heap I scorn to fall—
What if they pass'd me to the Trojan Wall,

[5] Apollo

While I decline to yonder Path, that leads
To Ida's Forests and surrounding Shades?
So may I reach, conceal'd, the cooling Flood,
From my tir'd Body wash the Dust and Blood,   660
As soon as Night her dusky Veil extends,
Return in safety to my Trojan Friends.
What if?— But wherefore all this vain Debate?
Stand I to doubt, within the reach of Fate?
Ev'n now perhaps, e'er yet I turn the Wall,
The fierce Achilles sees me, and I fall:
Such is his Swiftness, 'tis in vain to fly,
And such his Valour, that who stands must die.
Howe'er, 'tis better, fighting for the State,
Here, and in publick view, to meet my Fate.   670
Yet sure He too is mortal; He may feel
(Like all the Sons of Earth) the Force of Steel;
One only Soul informs that dreadful Frame;
And Jove's sole Favour gives him all his Fame.
    He said, and stood; collected in his Might;
And all his beating Bosom claim'd the Fight.
So from some deep grown Wood a Panther starts,
Rouz'd from his Thicket by a Storm of Darts;
Untaught to fear or fly, he hears the Sounds
Of shouting Hunters, and of clam'rous Hounds,   680
Tho' strook, tho' wounded, scarce perceives the Pain,
And the barb'd Jav'lin stings his Breast in vain:
On their whole War, untam'd the Savage flies;
And tears his Hunter, or beneath him dies.
Not less resolv'd, Antenor's valiant Heir
Confronts Achilles, and awaits the War,
Disdainful of Retreat: High-held before,
His Shield (a broad Circumference) he bore;
Then graceful as he stood, in act to throw
The lifted Jav'lin, thus bespoke the Foe.   690
    How proud Achilles glories in his Fame!
And hopes this day to sink the Trojan Name
Beneath her Ruins! Know, that Hope is vain;
A thousand Woes, a thousand Toils remain.

Parents and Children our just Arms employ,
And strong, and many, are the Sons of Troy.
Great as thou art, ev'n thou may'st stain with Gore
These Phrygian Fields, and press a foreign Shore.
  He said: With matchless Force the Jav'lin flung
Smote on his Knee; the hollow Cuishes rung   700
Beneath the pointed Steel; but safe from Harms
He stands impassive in th' Æthereal Arms.
Then fiercely rushing on the daring Foe,
His lifted Arm prepares the fatal Blow;
But jealous of his Fame, Apollo shrouds
The god-like Trojan in a Veil of Clouds;
Safe from Pursuit, and shut from mortal View,
Dismiss'd with Fame, the favour'd Youth withdrew.
Meanwhile the God, to cover their Escape,
Assumes Agenor's Habit, Voice, and Shape,   710
Flies from the furious Chief in this Disguise,
The furious Chief still follows where he flies.
Now o'er the Fields they stretch with lengthen'd Strides,
Now urge the Course where swift Scamander glides:
The God now distant scarce a Stride before,
Tempts his Pursuit, and wheels about the Shore.
While all the flying Troops their Speed employ,
And pour on Heaps into the Walls of Troy.
No stop, no stay; no thought to ask, or tell,
Who scap'd by Flight, or who by Battel fell.   720
'Twas Tumult all, and Violence of Flight;
And sudden Joy confus'd, and mix'd Affright:
Pale Troy against Achilles shuts her Gate;
And Nations breathe, deliver'd from their Fate.

꜊꜊꜊

THE TWENTY-SECOND BOOK
OF THE ILIAD

THE ARGUMENT

The Death of Hector

THE TROJANS BEING SAFE within the Walls, Hector only stays to oppose Achilles. Priam is struck at his approach, and tries to persuade his Son to re-enter the Town. Hecuba joins her Entreaties, but in vain. Hector consults within himself what Measures to take; but at the advance of Achilles, his Resolution fails him, and he flies; Achilles pursues him thrice round the Walls of Troy. The Gods debate concerning the Fate of Hector, at length Minerva descends to the aid of Achilles. She deludes Hector in the Shape of Deiphobus, he stands the Combate, and is slain. Achilles drags the dead Body at his Chariot, in the sight of Priam and Hecuba. Their Lamentations, Tears, and Despair. Their Cries reach the Ears of Andromache, who, ignorant of this, was retired into the inner part of the Palace: She mounts up to the Walls, and beholds her dead Husband. She swoons at the Spectacle. Her Excess of Grief, and Lamentation.

The thirtieth Day still continues. The Scene lies under the Walls, and on the Battlements of Troy.

Thus to their Bulwarks, smit with Panick Fear,
The herded Ilians rush like driven Deer;
There safe, they wipe the briny Drops away,
And drown in Bowls the Labours of the Day.
Close to the Walls advancing o'er the Fields,
Beneath one Roof of well-compacted Shields
March, bending on, the Greeks embodied Pow'rs,
Far-stretching in the Shade of Trojan Tow'rs.

Great Hector singly stay'd; chain'd down by Fate,
There fixt he stood before the Scæan Gate;   10
Still his bold Arms determin'd to employ,
The Guardian still of long-defended Troy.
   Apollo now to tir'd Achilles turns;
(The Pow'r confest in all his Glory burns)
And what (he cries) has Peleus' Son in view,
With mortal Speed a Godhead to pursue?
For not to thee to know the Gods is giv'n,
Unskill'd to trace the latent Marks of Heav'n.
What boots thee now, that Troy forsook the Plain?
Vain thy past Labour, and thy present vain: 20
Safe in their Walls are now her Troops bestow'd,
While here thy Frantick Rage attacks a God.
   The Chief incens'd—Too partial God of Day!
To check my Conquests in the middle way:
How few in Ilion else had Refuge found?
What gasping Numbers now had bit the Ground?
Thou robb'st me of a Glory justly mine,
Pow'rful of Godhead, and of Fraud Divine:
Mean Fame, alas! for one of heav'nly Strain,
To cheat a Mortal, who repines in vain.   30
   Then to the City, terrible and strong,
With high and haughty steps he towr'd along.
So the proud Courser, victor of the prize,
To the near Goal with doubled Ardor flies.
Him, as he blazing shot across the Field,
The careful Eyes of Priam first beheld.
Not half so dreadful rises to the Sight
Thro' the thick Gloom of some tempestuous Night
Orion's Dog (the Year when Autumn weighs)
And o'er the feebler Stars exerts his Rays;   40
Terrific Glory! for his burning Breath
Taints the red Air with Fevers, Plagues, and Death.
So flam'd his fiery Mail. Then wept the Sage;
He strikes his rev'rend Head now white with Age:
He lifts his wither'd Arms; obtests the Skies;
He calls his much lov'd Son with feeble Cries;
The Son, resolv'd Achilles' Force to dare,
Full at the Scæan Gates expects the War;

While the sad Father on the Rampart stands,
And thus adjures him, with extended Hands.   50
  Ah stay not, stay not! guardless and alone;
Hector! my lov'd, my dearest, bravest Son!
Methinks already I behold thee slain,
And stretch'd beneath that Fury of the Plain.
Implacable Achilles! might'st thou be
To all th' Immortals hateful as to me!
Thee, Vultures wild should scatter round the Shore,
And bloody Dogs grow fiercer from thy Gore.
How many valiant Sons I late enjoy'd,
Valiant in vain! by thy curst Arm destroy'd: 60
Or, worse than slaughter'd, sold in distant Isles
To shameful Bondage and unworthy Toils.
Two, while I speak, my Eyes in vain explore,
Two from one Mother sprung, my Polydore,
And lov'd Lycaon; now perhaps no more!
Oh if in yonder hostile Camp they live,
What Heaps of Gold, what Treasures would I give?
(Their Grandsire's[1] Wealth, by right of Birth their own,
Consign'd his Daughter with Lelegia's Throne)
But if (which Heav'n forbid) already lost,   70
All pale they wander on the Stygian Coast;
What Sorrows then must their sad Mother know,
What Anguish I? Unutterable Woe!
Yet less that Anguish, less to her, to me,
Less to all Troy, if not depriv'd of thee,
Yet shun Achilles! enter yet the Wall;
And spare thy self, thy Father, spare us all!
Save thy dear Life; or if a Soul so brave
Neglect that Thought, thy dearer Glory save.
Pity, while yet I live, these silver Hairs;   80
While yet thy Father feels the Woes he bears,
Yet curst with Sense! a Wretch, whom in his Rage
(All trembling on the Verge of helpless Age)
Great Jove has plac'd, sad Spectacle of Pain!
The bitter Dregs of Fortune's Cup to drain:
To fill with Scenes of Death his closing Eyes,
And number all his Days by Miseries!

[1] Their grandfather, Altes, was King of the Leleges, a people of the Troad.

My Heroes slain, my Bridal Bed o'erturn'd,
My Daughters ravish'd, and my City burn'd,
My bleeding Infants dash'd against the Floor;   90
These I have yet to see, perhaps yet more!
Perhaps ev'n I, reserv'd by angry Fate
The last sad Relick of my ruin'd State,
(Dire Pomp of sov'reign Wretchedness!) must fall,
And stain the Pavement of my regal Hall;
Where famish'd Dogs, late Guardians of my Door,
Shall lick their mangled Master's spatter'd Gore.
Yet for my Sons I thank ye Gods! 'twas well:
Well have they perish'd, for in Fight they fell.
Who dies in Youth, and Vigor, dies the best,   100
Struck thro' with Wounds, all honest on the Breast.
But when the Fates, in Fulness of their Rage,
Spurn[2] the hoar Head of unresisting Age,
In Dust the rev'rend Lineaments deform,
And pour to Dogs the Life-blood scarcely warm;
This, this is Misery! the last, the worst,
That Man can feel; Man, fated to be curst!
    He said, and acting what no Words could say,
Rent from his Head the silver Locks away.
With him the mournful Mother bears a Part;   110
Yet all their Sorrows turn not Hector's Heart:
The Zone unbrac'd, her Bosom she display'd;
And thus, fast-falling the salt Tears, she said.
    Have mercy on me, O my Son! Revere
The Words of Age; attend a Parent's Pray'r!
If ever thee in these fond Arms I prest,
Or still'd thy infant Clamours at this Breast;
Ah do not thus our helpless Years foregoe,
But by our Walls secur'd, repel the Foe.
Against his Rage if singly thou proceed,   120
Should'st thou (but Heav'n avert it!) should'st thou bleed,
Nor must thy Corps lye honour'd on the Bier,
Nor Spouse nor Mother grace thee with a Tear;
Far from our pious Rites, those dear Remains
Must feast the Vultures on the naked Plains.

[2] Trample

So they, while down their Cheeks the Torrents roll;
But fix'd remains the Purpose of his Soul:
Resolv'd he stands, and with a fiery Glance
Expects the Hero's terrible Advance.
So roll'd up in his Den, the swelling Snake   130
Beholds the Traveller approach the Brake;
When fed with noxious Herbs his turgid Veins
Have gather'd half the Poisons of the Plains;
He burns, he stiffens with collected Ire,
And his red Eye-balls glare with living Fire.
Beneath a Turret, on his Shield reclin'd,
He stood, and question'd thus his mighty Mind.
    Where lyes my Way? To enter in the Wall?
Honour and Shame th' ungen'rous Thought recall:
Shall proud Polydamas before the Gate   140
Proclaim, his Counsels are obey'd too late,
Which, timely follow'd but the former Night,
What Numbers had been sav'd by Hector's Flight?
That wise Advice rejected with Disdain,
I feel my Folly in my People slain.
Methinks my suff'ring Country's Voice I hear,
But most, her worthless Sons insult my Ear,
On my rash Courage charge the Chance of War,
And blame those Virtues which they cannot share.
No—If I e'er return, return I must   150
Glorious, my Country's Terror laid in Dust:
Or if I perish, let her see me fall
In Field at least, and fighting for her Wall.
And yet suppose these Measures I forego,
Approach unarm'd, and parly with the Foe,
The Warrior-Shield, the Helm, and Lance lay down,
And treat on Terms of Peace to save the Town:
The Wife with-held, the Treasure ill detain'd,
(Cause of the War, and Grievance of the Land)
With honourable Justice to restore;   160
And add half Ilion's yet remaining Store,
Which Troy shall, sworn, produce; that injur'd Greece
May share our Wealth, and leave our Walls in Peace.

But why this Thought? Unarm'd if I should go,
What hope of Mercy from this vengeful Foe?
But Woman-like to fall, and fall without a Blow.
We greet not here, as Man conversing Man
Met at an Oak, or journeying o'er a Plain;
No Season now for calm familiar Talk,
Like Youths and Maidens in an Evening Walk: 170
War is our Business; but to whom is giv'n
To die or triumph, that, determine Heav'n!
    Thus pond'ring, like a God the Greek drew nigh;
His dreadful Plumage nodded from on high;
The Pelian Jav'lin, in his better Hand,
Shot trembling Rays that glitter'd o'er the Land;
And on his Breast the beamy Splendors shone
Like Jove's own Lightning, or the rising Sun.
As Hector sees, unusual Terrors rise,
Struck by some God, he fears, recedes, and flies.   180
He leaves the Gates, he leaves the Walls behind;
Achilles follows like the winged Wind.
Thus at the panting Dove a Falcon flies,
(The swiftest Racer of the liquid Skies)
Just when he holds or thinks he holds his Prey,
Obliquely wheeling thro' th' aerial Way;
With open Beak and shrilling Cries he springs,
And aims his Claws, and shoots upon his Wings:
No less fore-right the rapid Chace they held,
One urg'd by Fury, one by Fear impell'd;   190
Now circling round the Walls their Course maintain,
Where the high Watch-tow'r overlooks the Plain;
Now where the Fig-trees spread their Umbrage broad,
(A wider Compass) smoak along the Road.
Next by Scamander's double Source they bound,
Where two fam'd Fountains burst the parted Ground;
This hot thro' scorching Clefts is seen to rise,
With Exhalations steaming to the Skies;
That the green Banks in Summer's Heat o'erflows,
Like Crystal clear, and cold as Winter-Snows.   200
Each gushing Fount a marble Cistern fills,
Whose polish'd Bed receives the falling Rills;

Where Trojan Dames, (e'er yet alarm'd by Greece)
Wash'd their fair Garments in the Days of Peace.
By these they past, one chasing, one in Flight,
(The Mighty fled, pursu'd by stronger Might)
Swift was the Course; No vulgar Prize they play,
No vulgar Victim must reward the Day,
(Such as in Races crown the speedy Strife)
The Prize contended was great Hector's Life.   210
As when some Hero's Fun'rals are decreed
In grateful Honour of the mighty Dead;
Where High Rewards the vig'rous Youth inflame,
(Some golden Tripod, or some lovely Dame)
The panting Coursers swiftly turn the Goal,
And with them turns the rais'd Spectator's Soul.
Thus three times round the Trojan Wall they fly;
The gazing Gods lean forward from the Sky:
To whom, while eager on the Chace they look,
The Sire of Mortals and Immortals spoke.   220
    Unworthy Sight! The Man, belov'd of Heav'n,
Behold, inglorious round yon' City driv'n!
My Heart partakes the gen'rous Hector's Pain;
Hector, whose Zeal whole Hecatombs has slain,
Whose grateful Fumes the Gods receiv'd with Joy,
From Ida's Summits, and the Tow'rs of Troy:
Now see him flying! to his Fears resign'd,
And Fate, and fierce Achilles, close behind.
Consult, ye Pow'rs! ('tis worthy your Debate)
Whether to snatch him from impending Fate,   230
Or let him bear, by stern Pelides slain,
(Good as he is) the Lot impos'd on Man?
    Then Pallas thus: Shall he whose Vengeance forms
The forky Bolt, and blackens Heav'n with Storms,
Shall he prolong one Trojan's forfeit Breath!
A Man, a Mortal, pre-ordain'd to Death!
And will no Murmurs fill the Courts above,
No Gods indignant blame their partial Jove?
    Go then (return'd the Sire) without delay,
Exert thy Will: I give the Fates their Way.   240

Swift at the Mandate pleas'd Tritonia[3] flies,
And stoops impetuous from the cleaving Skies.

As thro' the Forest, o'er the Vale and Lawn,
The well-breath'd Beagle drives the flying Fawn;
In vain he tries the Covert of the Brakes,
Or deep beneath the trembling Thicket shakes;
Sure of the Vapour in the tainted Dews,
The certain Hound his various Maze pursues.
Thus step by step, where'er the Trojan wheel'd,
There swift Achilles compass'd round the Field.   250
Oft' as to reach the Dardan Gates he bends,
And hopes th' Assistance of his pitying Friends,
(Whose show'ring Arrows, as he cours'd below,
From the high Turrets might oppress the Foe.)
So oft' Achilles turns him to the Plain:
He eyes the City, but he eyes in vain.
As Men in Slumbers seem with speedy pace,
One to pursue, and one to lead the Chace,
Their sinking Limbs the fancy'd Course forsake,
Nor this can fly, nor that can overtake.   260
No less the lab'ring Heroes pant and strain;
While that but flies, and this pursues, in vain.

What God, O Muse! assisted Hector's Force,
With Fate itself so long to hold the Course?
Phœbus it was; who, in his latest Hour,
Endu'd his Knees with strength, his Nerves with Pow'r:
And great Achilles, lest some Greek's Advance
Should snatch the Glory from his lifted Lance,
Sign'd to the Troops, to yield his Foe the Way,
And leave untouch'd the Honours of the Day.   270
Jove lifts the golden Balances, that show
The Fates of mortal Men, and things below:
Here each contending Hero's Lot he tries,
And weighs, with equal Hand, their Destinies.
Low sinks the Scale surcharg'd with Hector's Fate;
Heavy with Death it sinks, and Hell receives the Weight.

Then Phœbus left him. Fierce Minerva flies
To stern Pelides, and triumphing, cries.

[3] Pallas; *Tritonia* for the Greek *Tritogeneia*, an epithet of uncertain meaning

Oh lov'd of Jove! this Day our Labours cease,
And Conquest blazes with full Beams on Greece.   280
Great Hector falls; that Hector fam'd so far,
Drunk with Renown, insatiable of War,
Falls by thy Hand, and mine! Nor Force, nor Flight
Shall more avail him, nor his God of Light.
See, where in vain he supplicates above,
Roll'd at the Feet of unrelenting Jove!
Rest here: My self will lead the Trojan on,
And urge to meet the Fate he cannot shun.

　　Her Voice divine the Chief with joyful Mind
Obey'd; and rested, on his Lance reclin'd.   290
While like Deïphobus the martial Dame
(Her Face, her Gesture, and her Arms the same)
In show an Aid, by hapless Hector's Side
Approach'd, and greets him thus with Voice bely'd.

　　Too long, O Hector! have I born the Sight
Of this Distress, and sorrow'd in thy Flight:
It fits us now a noble Stand to make,
And here, as Brothers, equal Fates partake.

　　Then he. O Prince! ally'd in Blood and Fame,
Dearer than all that own a Brother's Name;   300
Of all that Hecuba to Priam bore,
Long try'd, long lov'd; much lov'd, but honour'd more!
Since You of all our num'rous Race, alone
Defend my Life regardless of your own.

　　Again the Goddess. Much my Father's Pray'r,
And much my Mother's, prest me to forbear:
My Friends embrac'd my Knees, adjur'd my stay,
But stronger Love impell'd, and I obey.
Come then, the glorious Conflict let us try,
Let the Steel sparkle, and the Jav'lin fly: 310
Or let us stretch Achilles on the Field,
Or to his Arm our bloody Trophies yield.

　　Fraudful she said; then swiftly march'd before;
The Dardan Hero shuns his Foe no more.
Sternly they met. The Silence Hector broke;
His dreadful Plumage nodded as he spoke.

　　Enough, O Son of Peleus! Troy has view'd
Her Walls thrice circled, and her Chief pursu'd.

But now some God within me bids me try
Thine, or my Fate: I kill thee, or I die.   320
Yet on the Verge of Battel let us stay,
And for a Moment's space, suspend the Day:
Let Heav'ns high Pow'rs be call'd to arbitrate
The just Conditions of this stern Debate.
(Eternal Witnesses of all below,
And faithful Guardians of the treasur'd Vow!)
To them I swear; if Victor in the Strife
Jove by these Hands shall shed thy noble Life;
No vile Dishonour shall thy Corse pursue;
Stript of its Arms alone (the Conqu'rors Due)   330
The rest to Greece uninjur'd I'll restore:
Now plight thy mutual Oath, I ask no more.
   Talk not of Oaths (the dreadful Chief replies,
While Anger flash'd from his disdainful Eyes)
Detested as thou art, and ought to be,
Nor Oath nor Pact Achilles plights with thee:
Such Pacts, as Lambs and rabid Wolves combine,
Such Leagues, as Men and furious Lions join,
To such I call the Gods! One constant state
Of lashing Rancour and eternal Hate: 340
No Thought but Rage, and never-ceasing Strife,
Till Death extinguish Rage, and Thought, and Life.
Rouze then thy Forces this important Hour;
Collect thy Soul, and call forth all thy Pow'r.
No Farther Subterfuge, no farther Chance;
'Tis Pallas, Pallas gives thee to my Lance.
Each Grecian Ghost by thee depriv'd of Breath,
Now hovers round, and calls thee to thy Death.
   He spoke, and lanch'd his Jav'lin at the Foe;
But Hector shun'd the meditated Blow: 350
He stoop'd, while o'er his Head the flying Spear
Sung innocent, and spent its Force in Air.
Minerva watch'd it falling on the Land,
Then drew, and gave to great Achilles' Hand,
Unseen of Hector, who, elate with Joy,
Now shakes his Lance, and braves the Dread of Troy.
   The Life you boasted to that Jav'lin giv'n,
Prince! you have mist. My Fate depends on Heav'n.

To thee (presumptuous as thou art) unknown,
Or what must prove my Fortune or thy own.   360
Boasting is but an Art, our Fears to blind,
And with false Terrors sink another's Mind.
But know, whatever Fate I am to try,
By no dishonest Wound shall Hector die;
I shall not fall a Fugitive at least,
My Soul shall bravely issue from my Breast.
But first, try thou my Arm; and may this Dart
End all my Country's Woes, deep buried in thy Heart!
   The Weapon flew, its Course unerring held,
Unerring, but the heav'nly Shield repell'd   370
The mortal Dart; resulting with a Bound
From off the ringing Orb, it struck the Ground.
Hector beheld his Jav'lin fall in vain,
Nor other Lance, nor other Hope remain;
He calls Deïphobus, demands a Spear,
In vain, for no Deïphobus was there.
All comfortless he stands: Then, with a Sigh,
'Tis so—Heav'n wills it, and my Hour is nigh!
I deem'd Deïphobus had heard my Call,
But he secure lyes guarded in the Wall.   380
A God deceiv'd me; Pallas, 'twas thy Deed.
Death, and black Fate approach! 'Tis I must bleed.
No Refuge now, no Succour from above;
Great Jove deserts me, and the Son of Jove,
Propitious once, and kind! Then welcome Fate!
'Tis true I perish, yet I perish great:
Yet in a mighty Deed I shall expire,
Let future Ages hear it, and admire!
   Fierce, at the Word, his weighty Sword he drew,
And, all collected, on Achilles flew.   390
So Jove's bold Bird, high-balanc'd in the Air,
Stoops from the Clouds to truss the quiv'ring Hare.
Nor less Achilles his fierce Soul prepares;
Before his Breast his flaming Shield he bears,
Refulgent Orb! Above his four-fold Cone
The gilded Horsehair sparkled in the Sun,
Nodding at ev'ry Step: (Vulcanian Frame!)
And as he mov'd, his Figure seem'd on flame.

As radiant Hesper shines with keener Light,
Far-beaming o'er the silver Host of Night,   400
When all the starry Train emblaze the Sphere:
So shone the Point of great Achilles' Spear.
In his right Hand he waves the Weapon round,
Eyes the whole Man, and meditates the Wound;
But the rich Mail Patroclus lately wore,
Securely cas'd the Warrior's Body o'er.
One place at length he spies, to let in Fate,
Where 'twixt the Neck and Throat the jointed Plate
Gave entrance: Thro' that penetrable Part
Furious he drove the well-directed Dart: 410
Nor pierc'd the Windpipe yet, nor took the Pow'r
Of Speech, Unhappy! from thy dying Hour.
Prone on the Field the bleeding Warrior lies,
While thus triumphing, stern Achilles cries.

At last is Hector stretch'd upon the Plain,
Who fear'd no Vengeance for Patroclus slain:
Then Prince! you should have fear'd, what now you feel;
Achilles absent, was Achilles still.
Yet a short space the great Avenger stay'd,
Then low in Dust thy Strength and Glory lay'd.   420
Peaceful He sleeps, with all our Rites adorn'd,
For ever honour'd, and for ever mourn'd:
While cast to all the Rage of hostile Pow'r,
Thee, Birds shall mangle, and the Dogs devour.

Then Hector, fainting at th' approach of Death.
By thy own Soul! by those who gave thee Breath!
By all the sacred Prevalence of Pray'r;
Ah, leave me not for Grecian Dogs to tear!
The common Rites of Sepulture bestow,
To sooth a Father's and a Mother's Woe;   430
Let their large Gifts procure an Urn at least,
And Hector's Ashes in his Country rest.

No, Wretch accurst! Relentless he replies,
(Flames, as he spoke, shot flashing from his Eyes)
Not those who gave me Breath shou'd bid me spare,
Nor all the sacred Prevalence of Pray'r.
Could I my self the bloody Banquet join!
No—to the Dogs that Carcase I resign.

Shou'd Troy, to bribe me, bring forth all her Store,
And giving thousands, offer thousands more;   440
Should Dardan Priam, and the weeping Dame
Drain their whole Realm to buy one fun'ral Flame;
Their Hector on the Pile they should not see,
Nor rob the Vultures of one Limb of thee.
   Then thus the Chief his dying Accents drew;
Thy Rage, Implacable! too well I knew:
The Furies that relentless Breast have steel'd,
And curs'd thee with a Heart that cannot yield.
Yet think, a Day will come, when Fate's Decree
And angry Gods, shall wreak this Wrong on thee;   450
Phœbus and Paris shall avenge my Fate,
And stretch thee here, before this Scæan Gate.
   He ceas'd. The Fates supprest his lab'ring Breath,
And his Eyes stiffen'd at the Hand of Death;
To the dark Realm the Spirit wings its Way,
(The manly Body left a Load of Clay)
And plaintive glides along the dreary Coast,
A naked, wandring, melancholy Ghost!
   Achilles, musing as he roll'd his eyes
O'er the dead Hero, thus (unheard) replies.   460
Die thou the first! When Jove and Heav'n ordain,
I follow thee—He said, and stripp'd the Slain.
Then forcing backward from the gaping Wound
The reeking Jav'lin, cast it on the Ground.
The thronging Greeks behold with wond'ring Eyes
His manly Beauty, and superiour Size:
While some ignobler, the great Dead deface
With Wounds ungen'rous, or with Taunts disgrace.
"How chang'd that Hector! who like Jove of late,
"Sent Lightning on our Fleets, and scatter'd Fate?   470
   High o'er the Slain the great Achilles stands,
Begirt with Heroes, and surrounding Bands;
And thus aloud, while all the Host attends.
Princes and Leaders; Countrymen and Friends!
Since now at length the pow'rful Will of Heav'n
The dire Destroyer to our Arm has giv'n,
Is not Troy fall'n already? Haste, ye Pow'rs!
See, if already their deserted Tow'rs

Are left unman'd; or if they yet retain
The Souls of Heroes, their great Hector slain?   480
But what is Troy, or Glory what to me?
Or why reflects my Mind on ought but thee
Divine Patroclus! Death has seal'd his Eyes;
Unwept, unhonour'd, uninterr'd he lies!
Can his dear Image from my Soul depart,
Long as the vital Spirit moves my Heart?
If, in the silent Shades of Hell below,
The Flames of Friends and Lovers cease to glow,
Yet mine shall sacred last; mine, undecay'd,
Burn on thro' Death, and animate my Shade.   490
Meanwhile ye Sons of Greece! in Triumph bring
The Corps of Hector, and your Pæans sing.
Be this the Song, slow-moving tow'rd the Shore,
"Hector is dead, and Ilion is no more.
     Then his fell Soul a Thought of Vengeance bred,
(Unworthy of himself, and of the Dead)
The nervous Ancles bor'd, his Feet he bound
With Thongs inserted thro' the double Wound;
These fix'd up high behind the rolling Wain,
His graceful Head was trail'd along the Plain.   500
Proud on his Car th' insulting Victor stood,
And bore aloft his Arms, distilling Blood.
He smites the Steeds; the rapid Chariot flies;
The sudden Clouds of circling Dust arise.
Now lost is all that formidable Air;
The Face divine, and long-descending Hair
Purple the Ground, and streak the sable Sand;
Deform'd, dishonour'd, in his native Land!
Giv'n to the Rage of an insulting Throng!
And, in his Parent's Sight, now dragg'd along!   510
     The Mother first beheld with sad survey;
She rent her Tresses, venerably grey,
And cast, far off, the regal Veils away.
With piercing Shrieks his bitter Fate she moans,
While the sad Father answers Groans with Groans,
Tears after Tears his mournful Cheeks o'erflow,
And the whole City wears one Face of Woe.
No less, than if the Rage of hostile Fires

From her Foundations curling to her Spires,
O'er the proud Citadel at length should rise,   520
And the last Blaze send Ilion to the Skies.
The wretched Monarch of the falling State
Distracted, presses to the Dardan Gate.
Scarce the whole People stop his desp'rate Course,
While strong Affliction gives the Feeble Force:
Grief tears his Heart, and drives him to and fro,
In all the raging Impotence of Woe.
At length he roll'd in Dust, and thus begun:
Imploring all, and naming one by one.
Ah! let me, let me go where Sorrow calls;   530
I, only I, will issue from your Walls,
(Guide or Companion, Friends! I ask ye none)
And bow before the Murd'rer of my Son.
My Griefs perhaps his Pity may engage;
Perhaps at least he may respect my Age.
He has a Father too; a Man like me,
One, not exempt from Age and Misery,
(Vig'rous no more, as when his young Embrace
Begot this Pest of me, and all my Race.)
How many valiant Sons, in early Bloom,   540
Has that curst Hand sent headlong to the Tomb?
Thee, Hector! last: Thy Loss (divinely brave)
Sinks my sad Soul with Sorrow to the Grave.
Oh had thy gentle Spirit past in Peace,
The Son expiring in the Sire's Embrace;
While both thy Parents wept thy fatal Hour,
And bending o'er thee, mix'd the tender Show'r!
Some Comfort that had been, some sad Relief,
To melt in full Satiety of Grief!
    Thus wail'd the Father, grov'ling on the Ground,   550
And all the Eyes of Ilion stream'd around.
    Amidst her Matrons Hecuba appears,
(A Mourning Princess, and a Train in Tears)
Ah why has Heav'n prolong'd this hated Breath,
Patient of Horrors, to behold thy Death?
O Hector, late thy Parents Pride and Joy,
The Boast of Nations! the Defence of Troy!

To whom her Safety and her Fame she ow'd,
Her Chief, her Hero, and almost her God!
O fatal Change! become in one sad Day   560
A senseless Corps! inanimated Clay!
   But not as yet the fatal News had spread
To fair Andromache, of Hector dead;
As yet no Messenger had told his Fate,
Nor ev'n his Stay without the Scæan Gate.
Far in the close Recesses of the Dome,
Pensive she ply'd the melancholy Loom;
A growing Work employ'd her secret Hours,
Confus'dly gay with intermingled Flow'rs.
Her fair-hair'd Handmaids heat the brazen Urn,   570
The Bath preparing for her Lord's Return:
In vain: Alas! her Lord returns no more!
Unbath'd he lies, and bleeds along the Shore!
Now from the Walls the Clamours reach her Ear,
And all her Members shake with sudden Fear;
Forth from her Iv'ry Hand the Shuttle falls,
As thus, astonish'd, to her Maids she calls.
   Ah follow me! (she cry'd) what plaintive Noise
Invades my Ear? 'Tis sure my Mother's Voice.
My falt'ring Knees their trembling Frame desert,   580
A Pulse unusual flutters at my Heart.
Some strange Disaster, some reverse of Fate
(Ye Gods avert it) threats the Trojan State.
Far be the Omen which my Thoughts suggest!
But much I fear my Hector's dauntless Breast
Confronts Achilles; chas'd along the Plain,
Shut from our Walls! I fear, I fear him slain!
Safe in the Crowd he ever scorn'd to wait,
And sought for Glory in the Jaws of Fate:
Perhaps that noble Heat has cost his Breath,   590
Now quench'd for ever in the Arms of Death.
   She spoke; and furious, with distracted Pace,
Fears in her Heart, and Anguish in her Face,
Flies thro' the Dome, (the Maids her Steps pursue)
And mounts the Walls, and sends around her View.

Too soon her Eyes the killing Object found,
The god-like Hector dragg'd along the Ground.
A sudden Darkness shades her swimming Eyes:
She faints, she falls; her Breath, her Colour flies.
Her Hair's fair Ornaments, the Braids that bound,   600
The Net that held them, and the Wreath that crown'd,
The Veil and Diadem, flew far away;
(The Gift of Venus on her bridal Day)
Around, a Train of weeping Sisters stands,
To raise her sinking with assistant Hands.
Scarce from the Verge of Death recall'd, again
She faints, or but recovers to complain.
    O wretched Husband of a wretched Wife!
Born with one Fate, to one unhappy Life!
For sure one Star its baneful Beam display'd   610
On Priam's Roof, and Hippoplacia's Shade.
From diff'rent Parents, diff'rent Climes we came,
At diff'rent Periods, yet our Fate the same!
Why was my Birth to great Aëtion ow'd,
And why was all that tender Care bestow'd?
Would I had never been!—O thou, the Ghost
Of my dead Husband! miserably lost!
Thou to the dismal Realms for ever gone!
And I abandon'd, desolate, alone!
An only Child, once Comfort of my Pains,   620
Sad Product now of hapless Love, remains!
No more to smile upon his Sire! no Friend
To help him now! No Father to defend!
For should he 'scape the Sword, the common Doom,
What Wrongs attend him, and what Griefs to come?
Ev'n from his own paternal Roof expell'd,
Some Stranger plows his patrimonial Field.
The Day, that to the Shades the Father sends,
Robs the sad Orphan of his Father's Friends:
He, wretched Outcast of Mankind! appears   630
For ever sad, for ever bath'd in Tears;
Amongst the Happy, unregarded he,
Hangs on the Robe, or trembles at the Knee,

While those his Father's former bounty fed,
Nor reach the Goblet, nor divide the Bread:
The Kindest but his present Wants allay,
To leave him wretched the succeeding Day.
Frugal Compassion! Heedless they who boast
Both Parents still, nor feel what he has lost,
Shall cry, "Begone! Thy Father feasts not here: 640
The Wretch obeys, retiring with a Tear.
Thus wretched, thus retiring all in Tears,
To my sad Soul Astyanax appears!
Forc'd by repeated Insults to return,
And to his widow'd Mother vainly mourn.
He, who with tender Delicacy bred,
With Princes sported, and on Dainties fed,
And when still Ev'ning gave him up to Rest,
Sunk soft in Down upon the Nurse's Breast,
Must—ah what must he not? Whom Ilion calls 650
Astyanax, from her well-guarded Walls,
Is now that Name no more, unhappy Boy!
Since now no more the Father guards his Troy.
But thou my Hector ly'st expos'd in Air,
Far from thy Parent's and thy Consort's Care,
Whose Hand in vain, directed by her Love,
The martial Scarf and Robe of Triumph wove.
Now to devouring Flames be these a Prey,
Useless to thee, from this accursed Day!
Yet let the Sacrifice at least be paid, 660
An Honour to the Living, not the Dead!
    So spake the mournful Dame: Her Matrons hear,
Sigh back her Sighs, and answer Tear with Tear.

THE TWENTY-THIRD BOOK
OF THE ILIAD

THE ARGUMENT

The Funeral of Patroclus

ACHILLES AND THE MYRMIDONS do Honours to the Body of Patroclus.
After the funeral Feast he retires to the Sea-Shore, where falling asleep,
the Ghost of his Friend appears to him, and demands the Rites of Burial;
the next Morning the Soldiers are sent with Mules and Waggons to fetch
Wood for the Pyre. The funeral Procession, and the offering of their
Hair to the Dead. Achilles sacrifices several Animals, and lastly, twelve
Trojan Captives at the Pile, then sets fire to it. He pays Libations to the
Winds, which (at the instance of Iris) rise, and raise the Flames. When
the Pile has burn'd all Night, they gather the Bones, place 'em in an Urn
of Gold, and raise the Tomb. Achilles institutes the funeral Games: The
Chariot Race, the Fight of the Cæstus, the Wrestling, the Foot-Race, the
single Combate, the Discus, the shooting with Arrows, the darting the
Javelin: The various Descriptions of which, and the various Success of the
several Antagonists, make the greatest part of the Book.

    In this Book ends the thirtieth Day: The Night following, the Ghost
of Patroclus appears to Achilles: The one and thirtieth Day is employ'd
in felling the Timber for the Pile; the two and thirtieth in burning it;
and the three and thirtieth in the Games. The Scene is generally on the
Sea-Shore.

Thus humbled in the Dust, the pensive Train
Thro' the sad City mourn'd her Hero slain.
The Body soil'd with Dust, and black with Gore,
Lyes on broad Hellespont's resounding Shore:

The Grecians seek their Ships, and clear the Strand,
All, but the martial Myrmidonian Band:
These yet assembled great Achilles holds,
And the stern purpose of his Mind unfolds.

   Not yet (my brave Companions of the War)
Release your smoaking Coursers from the Car;   10
But, with his Chariot each in order led,
Perform due Honours to Patroclus dead.
E'er yet from Rest or Food we seek Relief,
Some Rites remain, to glut our Rage of Grief.

   The Troops obey'd; and thrice in order led
(Achilles first) their Coursers round the Dead;
And thrice their Sorrows and Laments renew;
Tears drop the Sands, and Tears their Arms bedew.
For such a Warrior Thetis aids their Woe,
Melts their strong Hearts, and bids their Eyes to flow.   20
But chief, Pelides: thick succeeding Sighs
Burst from his Heart, and Torrents from his Eyes:
His slaught'ring Hands, yet red with Blood, he laid
On his dead Friend's cold Breast, and thus he said.

   All hail Patroclus! let thy honour'd Ghost
Hear, and rejoice on Pluto's dreary Coast;
Behold! Achilles' Promise is compleat;
The bloody Hector stretch'd before thy Feet.
Lo! to the Dogs his Carcass I resign;
And twelve sad Victims of the Trojan Line   30
Sacred to Vengeance, instant shall expire,
Their Lives effus'd around thy fun'ral Pyre.

   Gloomy he said, and (horrible to view)
Before the Bier the bleeding Hector threw,
Prone on the Dust. The Myrmidons around
Unbrac'd their Armour, and the Steeds unbound.
All to Achilles' sable Ship repair,
Frequent and full, the genial Feast to share.
Now from the well-fed Swine black Smokes aspire,
The bristly Victims hissing o'er the Fire;   40
The huge Ox bellowing falls; with feebler cries
Expires the Goat; the Sheep in Silence dies:

Around the Hero's prostrate Body flow'd
In one promiscuous Stream, the reeking Blood.
And now a Band of Argive Monarchs brings
The glorious Victor to the King of Kings.
From his dead Friend the pensive Warrior went,
With Steps unwilling, to the regal Tent.
Th'attending Heralds, as by Office bound,
With kindled Flames the Tripod-Vase surround; 50
To cleanse his conqu'ring Hands from hostile Gore,
They urg'd in vain; the Chief refus'd, and swore.
 No Drop shall touch me, by almighty Jove!
The first and greatest of the Gods above!
Till on the Pyre I place thee; till I rear
The grassy Mound, and clip thy sacred Hair.
Some Ease at least those pious Rites may give,
And sooth my Sorrows, while I bear to live.
Howe'er, reluctant as I am, I stay,
And share your Feast; but, with the Dawn of Day, 60
(O King of Men!) it claims thy royal Care,
That Greece the Warrior's fun'ral Pile prepare,
And bid the Forests fall: (Such Rites are paid
To Heroes slumb'ring in Eternal Shade)
Then, when his earthly Part shall mount in Fire,
Let the leagu'd Squadrons to their Posts retire.
 He spoke; they hear him, and the Word obey;
The Rage of Hunger and of Thirst allay,
Then ease in Sleep the Labours of the Day.
But great Pelides, stretch'd along the Shore 70
Where dash'd on Rocks the broken Billows roar,
Lies inly groaning; while on either Hand
The martial Myrmidons confus'dly stand:
Along the Grass his languid Members fall,
Tir'd with his Chase around the Trojan Wall;
Hush'd by the Murmurs of the rolling Deep
At length he sinks in the soft Arms of Sleep.
When lo! the Shade before his closing Eyes
Of sad Patroclus rose, or seem'd to rise;
In the same Robe the Living wore, he came, 80
In Stature, Voice, and pleasing Look, the same.

The Form familiar hover'd o'er his Head,
And sleeps Achilles, (thus the Phantom said)
Sleeps my Achilles, his Patroclus dead?
Living, I seem'd his dearest, tend'rest Care,
But now forgot, I wander in the Air:
Let my pale Corse the Rites of Burial know,
And give me Entrance in the Realms below:
Till then, the Spirit finds no resting place,
But here and there th' unbody'd Spectres chace   90
The vagrant Dead around the dark Abode,
Forbid to cross th' irremeable Flood.
Now give thy Hand; for to the farther Shore
When once we pass, the Soul returns no more.
When once the last Funereal Flames ascend,
No more shall meet, Achilles and his Friend,
No more our Thoughts to those we lov'd make known,
Or quit the dearest, to converse alone.
Me Fate has sever'd from the Sons of Earth,
The Fate fore-doom'd that waited from my Birth: 100
Thee too it waits; before the Trojan Wall
Ev'n great and god-like Thou art doom'd to fall.
Hear then; and as in Fate and Love we joyn,
Ah suffer that my Bones may rest with thine!
Together have we liv'd, together bred,
One House receiv'd us, and one Table fed;
That golden Urn thy Goddess Mother gave
May mix our Ashes in one common Grave.
    And is it thou (he answers) to my Sight
Once more return'st thou from the Realms of Night?   110
Oh more than Brother! Think each Office paid,
Whate'er can rest a discontented Shade;
But grant one last Embrace, unhappy Boy!
Afford at least that melancholy joy.
    He said, and with his longing Arms essay'd
In vain to grasp the visionary Shade;
Like a thin Smoke he sees the Spirit fly,
And hears a feeble, lamentable Cry.

Confus'd he wakes; Amazement breaks the Bands
Of golden Sleep, and starting from the Sands,   120
Pensive he muses with uplifted Hands.
　'Tis true, 'tis certain; Man, tho' dead, retains
Part of himself; th' immortal Mind remains:
The Form subsists, without the Body's Aid,
Aerial Semblance, and an empty Shade!
This Night my Friend, so late in Battel lost,
Stood at my side, a pensive, plaintive Ghost;
Ev'n now familiar, as in Life, he came,
Alas how diff'rent! yet how like the same!
　Thus while he spoke, each Eye grew big with Tears: 130
And now the rosy-finger'd Morn appears,
Shews every mournful Face with Tears o'erspread,
And glares on the pale Visage of the Dead.
But Agamemnon, as the Rites demand,
With Mules and Waggons sends a chosen Band;
To load the Timber and the Pile to rear,
A Charge consign'd to Merion's faithful Care.
With proper Instruments they take the Road,
Axes to cut, and Ropes to sling the Load.
First march the heavy Mules, securely slow,   140
O'er Hills, o'er Dales, o'er Crags, o'er Rocks, they go:
Jumping high o'er the Shrubs of the rough Ground,
Rattle the clatt'ring Cars, and the shockt Axles bound.
But when arriv'd at Ida's spreading Woods,
(Fair Ida, water'd with descending Floods)
Loud sounds the Axe, rebounding Strokes on Strokes;
On all sides round the Forest hurles her Oaks
Headlong. Deep-echoing groan the Thickets brown;
Then rustling, crackling, crashing, thunder down.
The Wood the Grecians cleave, prepar'd to burn;   150
And the slow Mules the same rough Road return.
The sturdy Woodmen equal Burthens bore
(Such charge was giv'n 'em) to the sandy Shore;
There on the Spot which great Achilles show'd,
They eas'd their Shoulders, and dispos'd the Load;
Circling around the Place, where Times to come
Shall view Patroclus' and Achilles' Tomb.

The Hero bids his martial Troops appear
High on their Cars, in all the Pomp of War;
Each in refulgent Arms his Limbs attires,   160
All mount their Chariots, Combatants and Squires.
The Chariots first proceed, a shining Train;
Then Clouds of Foot that smoak along the Plain;
Next these a melancholy Band appear,
Amidst, lay dead Patroclus on the Bier:
O'er all the Corse their scatter'd Locks they throw.
Achilles next, opprest with mighty Woe,
Supporting with his Hands the Hero's Head,
Bends o'er th' extended Body of the Dead.
The Body decent, on th' appointed Ground   170
They place, and heap the Sylvan Pile around.
But great Achilles stands apart in Pray'r,
And from his Head divides the yellow Hair;
The curling Locks which from his Youth he vow'd,
And sacred grew to Sperchius honour'd Flood:
Then sighing, to the Deep his Looks he cast,
And roll'd his Eyes around the wat'ry Waste.
    Sperchius! whose Waves in mazy Errors lost
Delightful roll along my native Coast!
To whom we vainly vow'd, at our return,   180
These Locks to fall, and Hecatombs to burn;
Full fifty Rams to bleed in Sacrifice,
Where to the Day thy silver Fountains rise,
And where in Shade of consecrated Bow'rs
Thy Altars stand, perfum'd with native Flow'rs!
So vow'd my Father, but he vow'd in vain;
No more Achilles sees his native Plain;
In that vain Hope these Hairs no longer grow,
Patroclus bears them to the Shades below.
    Thus o'er Patroclus while the Hero pray'd,   190
On his cold Hand the sacred Lock he laid.
Once more afresh the Grecian Sorrows flow:
And now the Sun had set upon their Woe;
But to the King of Men thus spoke the Chief.
Enough, Atrides! give the Troops Relief:

Permit the mourning Legions to retire,
And let the Chiefs alone attend the Pyre;
The pious Care be ours, the Dead to burn—
He said: The People to their Ships return:
While those deputed to inter the Slain   200
Heap with a rising Pyramid the Plain.
A hundred Foot in length, a hundred wide,
The growing Structure spreads on ev'ry Side;
High on the Top the manly Corse they lay,
And well-fed Sheep, and sable Oxen slay:
Achilles cover'd with their Fat the Dead,
And the pil'd Victims round the Body spread.
Then Jars of Honey, and of fragrant Oil
Suspends around, low-bending o'er the Pile.
Four sprightly Coursers, with a deadly Groan   210
Pour forth their Lives, and on the Pyre are thrown.
Of nine large Dogs, domestick at his Board,
Fall two, selected to attend their Lord.
Then last of all, and horrible to tell,
Sad Sacrifice! twelve Trojan Captives fell.
On these the Rage of Fire victorious preys,
Involves, and joins them in one common Blaze.
Smear'd with the bloody Rites, he stands on high,
And calls the Spirit with a dreadful Cry.
    All hail, Patroclus! let thy vengeful Ghost   220
Hear, and exult on Pluto's dreary Coast
Behold, Achilles' Promise fully paid,
Twelve Trojan Heroes offer'd to thy Shade;
But heavier Fates on Hector's Corse attend,
Sav'd from the Flames, for hungry Dogs to rend.
    So spake he, threat'ning: But the Gods made vain
His Threat, and guard inviolate the Slain:
Celestial Venus hover'd o'er his Head,
And roseate Unguents, heav'nly Fragrance! shed:
She watch'd him all the Night, and all the Day,   230
And drove the Bloodhounds from their destin'd Prey.
Nor sacred Phœbus less employ'd his Care;
He pour'd around a Veil of gather'd Air,

And kept the Nerves undry'd, the Flesh entire,
Against the Solar Beam and Sirian Fire.
    Nor yet the Pile where dead Patroclus lies,
Smokes, nor as yet the sullen Flames arise;
But fast beside Achilles stood in Pray'r,
Invok'd the Gods whose Spirit moves the Air,
And Victims promis'd, and Libations cast,   240
To gentle Zephyr and the Boreal Blast:
He call'd th' Aerial Pow'rs, along the Skies
To breathe, and whisper to the Fires to rise.
The winged Iris heard the Hero's Call,
And instant hasten'd to their airy Hall,
Where, in old Zephyr's open Courts on high,
Sate all the blustring Brethren of the Sky.
She shone amidst them, on her painted Bow;
The rocky Pavement glitter'd with the Show.
All from the Banquet rise, and each invites   250
The Various Goddess to partake the Rites.
    Not so, (the Dame reply'd) I haste to go
To sacred Ocean, and the Floods below:
Ev'n now our solemn Hecatombs attend,
And Heav'n is feasting on the World's green End,
With righteous Æthiops (uncorrupted Train!)
Far on th' extreamest Limits of the Main.
But Peleus' Son intreats, with Sacrifice,
The Western Spirit, and the North to rise;
Let on Patroclus' Pile your Blast be driv'n,   260
And bear the blazing Honours high to Heav'n.
Swift as the Word, she vanish'd from their View;
Swift as the Word, the Winds tumultuous flew;
Forth burst the stormy Band with thundring Roar,
And Heaps on Heaps the Clouds are tost before.
To the wide Main then stooping from the Skies,
The heaving Deeps in wat'ry Mountains rise:
Troy feels the Blast along her shaking Walls,
Till on the Pyle the gather'd Tempest falls.
The Structure crackles in the roaring Fires,   270
And all the Night the plenteous Flame aspires.

All Night, Achilles hails Patroclus Soul,
With large Libation from the golden Bowl.
As a poor Father helpless and undone,
Mourns o'er the Ashes of an only Son,
Takes a sad Pleasure the last Bones to burn,
And pour in Tears, e'er yet they close the Urn.
So stay'd Achilles, circling round the Shore,
So watch'd the Flames, till now they flam'd no more.
'Twas when, emerging thro' the Shades of Night,   280
The Morning Planet told th' approach of Light;
And fast behind, Aurora's warmer Ray
O'er the broad Ocean pour'd the golden Day:
Then sunk the Blaze, the Pyle no longer burn'd,
And to their Caves the whistling Winds return'd:
Across the Thracian Seas their Course they bore;
The ruffled Seas beneath their Passage roar.
Then parting from the Pyle he ceas'd to weep,
And sunk to Quiet in th' Embrace of Sleep,
Exhausted with his Grief: Meanwhile the Crowd   290
Of thronging Grecians round Achilles stood;
The Tumult wak'd him: From his Eyes he shook
Unwilling Slumber, and the Chiefs bespoke.
    Ye Kings and Princes of th' Achaian Name!
First let us quench the yet-remaining Flame
With sable Wine; then, (as the Rites direct,)
The Hero's Bones with careful view select:
(Apart, and easy to be known they lye,
Amidst the Heap, and obvious to the Eye;
The rest around the Margins will be seen,   300
Promiscuous, Steeds, and immolated Men)
These wrapt in double Cauls of Fat, prepare;
And in the golden Vase dispose with Care;
There let them rest, with decent Honour laid,
Till I shall follow to th' Infernal Shade.
Meantime erect the Tomb with pious Hands,
A common Structure on the humble Sands;
Hereafter Greece some nobler Work may raise,
And late Posterity record our Praise.

The Greeks obey; where yet the Embers glow,   310
Wide o'er the Pyle the sable Wine they throw,
And deep subsides the ashy Heap below.
Next the white Bones his sad Companions place
With Tears collected, in the golden Vase.
The sacred Relicks to the Tent they bore;
The Urn a Veil of Linen cover'd o'er.
That done, they bid the Sepulchre aspire,
And cast the deep Foundations round the Pyre;
High in the midst they heap the swelling Bed
Of rising Earth, Memorial of the Dead.   320
    The swarming Populace the Chief detains,
And leads amidst a wide Extent of Plains;
There plac'd 'em round: Then from the Ships proceeds
A Train of Oxen, Mules, and stately Steeds,
Vases and Tripods, for the Fun'ral Games,
Resplendent Brass, and more resplendent Dames.
First stood the Prizes to reward the Force
Of rapid Racers in the dusty Course.
A Woman for the first, in Beauty's Bloom,
Skill'd in the Needle, and the lab'ring Loom;   330
And a large Vase, where two bright Handles rise,
Of twenty Measures its capacious Size.
The second Victor claims a Mare unbroke,
Big with a Mule, unknowing of the Yoke:
The third, a Charger yet untouch'd by Flame;
Four ample Measures held the shining Frame:
Two golden Talents for the fourth were plac'd;
An ample double Bowl contents the last.
These in fair Order rang'd upon the Plain,
The Hero, rising, thus addrest the Train.   340
    Behold the Prizes, valiant Greeks! decreed
To the brave Rulers of the racing Steed;
Prizes which none beside our self could gain,
Should our immortal Coursers take the Plain;
(A Race unrival'd, which from Ocean's God
Peleus receiv'd, and on his Son bestow'd.)
But this no time our Vigour to display,
Nor suit, with them, the Games of this sad Day:

Lost is Patroclus now, that wont to deck
Their flowing Manes, and sleek their glossy Neck. 350
Sad, as they shar'd in human Grief, they stand,
And trail those graceful Honours on the Sand!
Let others for the noble Task prepare,
Who trust the Courser, and the flying Car.

   Fir'd at his Word, the Rival Racers rise;
But far the first, Eumelus hopes the Prize,
Fam'd thro' Pieria for the fleetest Breed,
And skill'd to manage the high-bounding Steed.
With equal Ardor bold Tydides swell'd
The Steeds of Tros beneath his Yoke compell'd, 360
(Which late obey'd the Dardan Chief's Command,
When scarce a God redeem'd him from his Hand)
Then Menelaus his Podargus brings,
And the fam'd Courser of the King of Kings:
Whom rich Echepolus, (more rich than brave)
To 'scape the Wars, to Agamemnon gave,
(Æthe her Name) at home to end his Days,
Base Wealth preferring to eternal Praise.
Next him Antilochus demands the Course,
With beating Heart, and chears his Pylian Horse. 370
Experienc'd Nestor gives the Son the Reins,
Directs his Judgment, and his Heat restrains;
Nor idly warns the hoary Sire, nor hears
The prudent Son with unattending Ears.

   My Son! tho' youthful Ardor fire thy Breast,
The Gods have lov'd thee, and with Arts have blest.
Neptune and Jove on thee conferr'd the Skill,
Swift round the Goal to turn the flying Wheel.
To guide thy Conduct, little Precept needs;
But slow, and past their Vigour, are my Steeds. 380
Fear not thy Rivals, tho' for Swiftness known,
Compare those Rivals Judgment, and thy own:
It is not Strength, but Art, obtains the Prize,
And to be swift is less than to be wise:
'Tis more by Art, than Force of num'rous Strokes,
The dext'rous Woodman shapes the stubborn Oaks;

By Art, the Pilot thro' the boiling Deep
And howling Tempest, stears the fearless Ship;
And 'tis the Artist wins the glorious Course,
Not those, who trust in Chariots and in Horse.   390
In vain unskilfull to the Goal they strive,
And short, or wide, th' ungovern'd Courser drive:
While with sure Skill, tho' with inferior Steeds,
The knowing Racer to his End proceeds;
Fix'd on the Goal his Eye fore-runs the Course,
His Hand unerring steers the steady Horse,
And now contracts, or now extends the Rein,
Observing still the foremost on the Plain.
Mark then the Goal, 'tis easy to be found;
Yon' aged Trunk, a Cubit from the Ground;   400
Of some once-stately Oak the last Remains,
Or hardy Fir, unperish'd with the Rains.
Inclos'd with Stones conspicuous from afar,
And round, a Circle for the wheeling Car.
(Some Tomb perhaps of old, the Dead to grace;
Or then, as now, the Limit of a Race)
Bear close to this, and warily proceed,
A little bending to the left-hand Steed;
But urge the Right, and give him all the Reins;
While thy strict Hand his Fellows Head restrains,   410
And turns him short; till, doubling as they roll,
The Wheel's round Naves appear to brush the Goal.
Yet (not to break the Car, or lame the Horse)
Clear of the stony Heap direct the Course;
Lest thro' Incaution failing, thou may'st be
A Joy to others, a Reproach to me.
So shalt thou pass the Goal, secure of Mind,
And leave unskilful Swiftness far behind.
Tho' thy fierce Rival drove the matchless Steed
Which bore Adrastus,[1] of celestial Breed;   420
Or the fam'd Race thro' all the Regions known,
That whirl'd the Car of proud Laomedon.

---

[1] King of Sicyon, leader of the Seven Against Thebes, who survived thanks to his wonderful horse, Arion

Thus, (nought unsaid) the much-advising Sage
Concludes; then sate, stiff with unwieldly Age.
Next bold Meriones was seen to rise,
The last, but not least ardent for the Prize.
They mount their Seats; the Lots their Place dispose;
(Roll'd in his Helmet, these Achilles throws.)
Young Nestor leads the Race: Eumelus then;
And next, the Brother of the King of Men: 430
Thy Lot, Meriones, the fourth was cast;
And, far the bravest, Diomed, was last.
They stand in order, an impatient Train;
Pelides points the Barrier on the Plain,
And sends before old Phœnix to the Place,
To mark the Racers, and to judge the Race.
At once the Coursers from the Barrier bound;
The lifted Scourges all at once resound;
Their Heart, their Eyes, their Voice, they send before;
And up the Champain thunder from the Shore: 440
Thick, where they drive, the dusty Clouds arise,
And the lost Courser in the Whirlwind flies;
Loose on their Shoulders the long Manes reclin'd,
Float in their Speed, and dance upon the Wind:
The smoking Chariots, rapid as they bound,
Now seem to touch the Sky, and now the Ground.
While hot for Fame, and Conquest all their Care,
(Each o'er his flying Courser hung in Air)
Erect with Ardour, pois'd upon the Rein,
They pant, they stretch, they shout along the Plain.   450
Now, (the last Compass fetch'd around the Goal)
At the near Prize each gathers all his Soul,
Each burns with double Hope, with double Pain,
Tears up the Shore, and thunders tow'rd the Main.
First flew Eumelus on Pheretian Steeds;
With those of Tros, bold Diomed succeeds:
Close on Eumelus' Back they puff the Wind,
And seem just mounting on his Car behind;
Full on his Neck he feels the sultry Breeze,
And hov'ring o'er, their stretching Shadows sees.   460

Then had he lost, or left a doubtful Prize;
But angry Phœbus to Tydides flies,
Strikes from his Hand the Scourge, and renders vain
His matchless Horses labour on the Plain.
Rage fills his Eye with Anguish, to survey
Snatch'd from his Hope, the Glories of the Day.
The Fraud celestial Pallas sees with Pain,
Springs to her Knight, and gives the Scourge again,
And fills his Steeds with Vigour. At a Stroke,
She breaks his Rivals Chariot from the Yoke;   470
No more their Way the startled Horses held;
The Car revers'd came rat'ling on the Field;
Shot headlong from his Seat, beside the Wheel,
Prone on the Dust th' unhappy Master fell;
His batter'd Face and Elbows strike the Ground;
Nose, Mouth and Front, one undistinguish'd Wound:
Grief stops his Voice, a Torrent drowns his Eyes;
Before him far the glad Tydides flies;
Minerva's Spirit drives his matchless Pace,
And crowns him Victor of the labour'd Race.   480
    The next, tho' distant, Menelaus succeeds;
While thus young Nestor animates his Steeds.
Now, now, my gen'rous Pair, exert your Force;
Not that we hope to match Tydides' Horse,
Since great Minerva wings their rapid Way,
And gives their Lord the Honours of the Day.
But reach Atrides! Shall his Mare out-go
Your Swiftness? Vanquish'd by a female Foe?
Thro' your neglect if lagging on the Plain
The last ignoble Gift be all we gain;   490
No more shall Nestor's Hand your Food supply,
The old Man's Fury rises, and ye die.
Haste then; yon' narrow Road before our Sight
Presents th' occasion, could we use it right.
    Thus He. The Coursers at their Master's Threat
With quicker Steps the sounding Champain beat.
And now Antilochus, with nice survey,
Observes the Compass of the hollow way.

'Twas where by Force of wintry Torrents torn,
Fast by the Road a Precipice was worn: 500
Here, where but one could pass, to shun the Throng
The Spartan Hero's Chariot smoak'd along.
Close up the vent'rous Youth resolves to keep,
Still edging near, and bears him tow'rd the Steep.
Atrides, trembling casts his Eye below,
And wonders at the Rashness of his Foe.
Hold, stay your Steeds—What Madness thus to ride?
This narrow way? Take larger Field (he cry'd)
Or both must fall—Atrides cry'd in vain;
He flies more fast, and throws up all the Rein.   510
Far as an able Arm the Disk can send,
When youthful Rivals their full Force extend,
So far Antilochus! thy Chariot flew
Before the King: He, cautious, backward drew
His Horse compell'd; foreboding in his Fears
The rattling Ruin of the clashing Cars,
The flound'ring Coursers rolling on the Plain,
And Conquest lost thro' frantick Haste to gain.
But thus upbraids his Rival as he flies;
Go, furious Youth! ungen'rous and unwise!   520
Go, but expect not I'll the Prize resign;
Add Perjury to Fraud, and make it thine.—
Then to his Steeds with all his Force he cries;
Be swift, be vig'rous, and regain the Prize!
Your Rivals, destitute of youthful Force,
With fainting Knees shall labour in the Course,
And yield the Glory yours—The Steeds obey;
Already at their Heels they wing their Way,
And seem already to retrieve the Day.
   Meantime the Grecians in a Ring beheld   530
The Coursers bounding o'er the dusty Field.
The first who markd them was the Cretan King;
High on a rising Ground, above the Ring,
The Monarch sate; from whence with sure survey
He well observ'd the Chief who led the way,
And heard from far his animating Cries,
And saw the foremost Steed with sharpen'd Eyes;

On whose broad Front a Blaze of shining white,
Like the full Moon, stood obvious to the Sight.
He saw; and rising, to the Greeks begun.   540
Are yonder Horse discern'd by me alone?
Or can ye, all, another Chief survey,
And other Steeds, than lately led the Way?
Those, tho' the swiftest, by some God with-held,
Lie sure disabled in the middle Field:
For since the Goal they doubled, round the Plain
I search to find them, but I search in vain.
Perchance the Reins forsook the Driver's Hand,
And, turn'd too short, he tumbled on the Strand,
Shot from the Chariot; while his Coursers stray   550
With frantick Fury from the destin'd Way.
Rise then some other, and inform my Sight,
(For these dim Eyes, perhaps, discern not right)
Yet sure he seems, (to judge by Shape and Air,)
The great Ætolian Chief,[2] renown'd in War.
　　Old Man! (Oïleus rashly thus replies)
Thy Tongue too hastily confers the Prize.
Of those who view the Course, not sharpest ey'd,
Nor youngest, yet the readiest to decide.
Eumelus' Steeds high-bounding in the Chace,   560
Still, as at first, unrivall'd lead the Race,
I well discern him, as he shakes the Rein,
And hear his Shouts victorious o'er the Plain.
　　Thus he. Idomeneus incens'd rejoin'd:
Barb'rous of Words! and arrogant of Mind!
Contentious Prince! of all the Greeks beside
The last in Merit, as the first in Pride.
To vile Reproach what Answer can we make?
A Goblet or a Tripod let us stake,
And be the King the Judge. The most unwise   570
Will learn their Rashness, when they pay the Price.
　　He said: and Ajax by mad Passion born,
Stern had reply'd; fierce Scorn inhancing Scorn
To fell extreams. But Thetis' god-like Son,
Awful, amidst them rose; and thus begun.

[2] Diomedes

Forbear ye Chiefs! reproachful to contend;
Much would ye blame, should others thus offend:
And lo! th' approaching Steeds your Contest end.
No sooner had he spoke, but thund'ring near
Drives, thro' a Stream of Dust, the Charioteer;   580
High o'er his Head the circling Lash he wields;
His bounding Horses scarcely touch the Fields:
His Car amidst the dusty Whirlwind roll'd,
Bright with the mingled Blaze of Tin and Gold,
Refulgent thro' the Cloud, no Eye could find
The Track his flying Wheels had left behind:
And the fierce Coursers urg'd their rapid Pace
So swift, it seem'd a Flight, and not a Race.
Now Victor at the Goal Tydides stands,
Quits his bright Car, and springs upon the Sands;   590
From the hot Steeds the sweaty Torrents stream;
The well-ply'd Whip is hung athwart the Beam;
With Joy brave Sthenelus receives the Prize,
The Tripod-Vase, and Dame with radiant Eyes:
These to the Ships his Train triumphant leads,
The Chief himself unyokes the panting Steeds.
    Young Nestor[3] follows (who by Art, not Force,
O'er-past Atrides) second in the Course.
Behind, Atrides urg'd the Race, more near
Than to the Courser in his swift Career   600
The following Car, just touching with his Heel
And brushing with his Tail the whirling Wheel.
Such, and so narrow now the Space between
The Rivals, late so distant on the Green.
So soon swift Æthe her lost Ground regain'd,
One Length, one Moment had the Race obtain'd.
    Merion pursu'd, at greater Distance still,
With tardier Coursers, and inferior Skill.
Last came, Admetus! thy unhappy Son;
Slow dragg'd the Steeds his batter'd Chariot on: 610
Achilles saw, and pitying thus begun.
    Behold! the Man whose matchless Art surpast
The Sons of Greece! the ablest, yet the last!

[3] Antilochus

Fortune denies, but Justice bids us pay
(Since great Tydides bears the first away)
To him the second Honours of the Day.
   The Greeks consent with loud applauding Cries,
And then Eumelus had receiv'd the Prize,
But youthful Nestor, jealous of his Fame,
Th' Award opposes, and asserts his Claim.   620
Think not (he cries) I tamely will resign
O Peleus Son! the Mare so justly mine.
What if the Gods, the Skilful to confound,
Have thrown the Horse and Horseman to the Ground?
Perhaps he sought not Heav'n by Sacrifice,
And Vows omitted forfeited the Prize.
If yet (Distinction to thy Friend to show,
And please a Soul, desirous to bestow,)
Some Gift must grace Eumelus; view thy Store
Of beauteous Handmaids, Steeds, and shining Ore,   630
An ample Present let him thence receive,
And Greece shall praise thy gen'rous Thirst to give.
But this, my Prize, I never shall forego;
This, who but touches, Warriors! is my Foe.
   Thus spake the Youth, nor did his Words offend;
Pleas'd with the well-turn'd Flattery of a Friend,
Achilles smil'd: The Gift propos'd (he cry'd)
Antilochus! we shall our self provide.
With Plates of Brass the Corselet cover'd o'er,
(The same renown'd Asteropæus wore)   640
Whose glitt'ring Margins rais'd with Silver shine;
(No vulgar Gift) Eumelus, shall be thine.
   He said: Automedon at his Command
The Corselet brought, and gave it to his Hand.
Distinguish'd by his Friend, his Bosom glows
With gen'rous Joy: Then Menelaus rose;
The Herald plac'd the Sceptre in his Hands,
And still'd the Clamour of the shouting Bands.
Not without Cause incens'd at Nestor's Son,
And inly grieving, thus the King begun: 650
   The Praise of Wisdom, in thy Youth obtain'd,
An Act so rash (Antilochus) has stain'd.

Robb'd of my Glory and my just Reward,
To you O Grecians! be my Wrong declar'd:
So not a Leader shall our Conduct blame,
Or judge me envious of a Rival's Fame.
But shall not we, ourselves, the Truth maintain?
What needs appealing in a Fact so plain?
What Greek shall blame me, if I bid thee rise,
And vindicate by Oath th' ill-gotten Prize.   660
Rise if thou dar'st, before thy Chariot stand,
The driving Scourge high-lifted in thy Hand,
And touch thy Steeds, and swear, thy whole Intent
Was but to conquer, not to circumvent.
Swear by that God whose liquid Arms surround
The Globe, and whose dread Earthquakes heave the Ground.
  The prudent Chief with calm Attention heard;
Then mildly thus: Excuse, if Youth have err'd;
Superior as thou art, forgive th' Offence,
Nor I thy Equal, or in Years, or Sense.   670
Thou know'st the Errors of unripen'd Age,
Weak are its Counsels, headlong is its Rage.
The Prize I quit, if thou thy Wrath resign;
The Mare, or ought thou ask'st, be freely thine,
E'er I become (from thy dear Friendship torn)
Hateful to thee, and to the Gods forsworn.
  So spoke Antilochus; and at the Word
The Mare contested to the King restor'd.
Joy swells his Soul, as when the vernal Grain
Lifts the green Ear above the springing Plain,   680
The Fields their Vegetable Life renew,
And laugh and glitter with the Morning Dew:
Such Joy the Spartan's shining Face o'erspread,
And lifted his gay Heart, while thus he said.
  Still may our Souls, O gen'rous Youth! agree,
'Tis now Atrides' turn to yield to thee.
Rash Heat perhaps a Moment might controul,
Not break, the settled Temper of thy Soul.
Not but (my Friend) 'tis still the wiser way
To wave Contention with superior Sway;   690

For ah! how few, who should like thee offend,
Like thee, have Talents to regain the Friend?
To plead Indulgence and thy Fault attone,
Suffice thy Father's Merits, and thy own:
Gen'rous alike, for me, the Sire and Son
Have greatly suffer'd, and have greatly done.
I yield; that all may know, my Soul can bend,
Nor is my Pride preferr'd before my Friend.

He said; and pleas'd his Passion to command,
Resign'd the Courser to Noëmon's Hand,   700
Friend of the youthful Chief: Himself content,
The shining Charger to his Vessel sent.
The golden Talents Merion next obtain'd;
The fifth Reward, the double Bowl, remain'd.
Achilles this to rev'rend Nestor bears,
And thus the purpose of his Gift declares.

Accept thou this, O sacred Sire! (he said)
In dear Memorial of Patroclus dead;
Dead, and for ever lost Patroclus lies,
For ever snatch'd from our desiring Eyes!   710
Take thou this Token of a grateful Heart,
Tho' 'tis not thine to hurl the distant Dart,
The Quoit to toss, the pond'rous Mace to wield,
Or urge the Race, or wrestle on the Field.
Thy present Vigour Age has overthrown,
But left the Glory of the past thy own.

He said, and plac'd the Goblet at his side;
With Joy, the venerable King reply'd.

Wisely and well, my Son, thy Words have prov'd
A Senior honour'd, and a Friend belov'd!   720
Too true it is, deserted of my Strength,
These wither'd Arms and Limbs have fail'd at length.
Oh! had I now that Force I felt of yore,
Known thro' Buprasium and the Pylian Shore!
Victorious then in ev'ry solemn Game
Ordain'd to Amaryncas' mighty Name;
The brave Epeians gave my Glory way,
Ætolians, Pylians, all resign'd the Day.

I quell'd Clytomedes in Fights of Hand,
And backward hurl'd Ancæus on the Sand,   730
Surpast Iphyclus in the Swift Career,
Phyleus and Polydorus, with the Spear.
The Sons of Actor won the Prize of Horse,
But won by Numbers, not by Art or Force:
For the fam'd Twins, impatient to survey
Prize after Prize by Nestor born away,
Sprung to their Car; and with united Pains
One lash'd the Coursers, while one rul'd the Reins.
Such once I was! Now to these Tasks succeeds
A younger Race, that emulate our Deeds: 740
I yield alas! (to Age who must not yield?)
Tho' once the foremost Hero of the Field.
Go thou, my Son! by gen'rous Friendship led,
With martial Honours decorate the Dead;
While pleas'd I take the Gift thy Hands present,
(Pledge of Benevolence, and kind Intent)
Rejoic'd, of all the num'rous Greeks, to see
Not one but honours sacred Age and me:
Those due distinctions thou so well can'st pay,
May the just Gods return another Day.   750
    Proud of the Gift, thus spake the Full of Days:
Achilles heard him, prouder of the Praise.
    The Prizes next are order'd to the Field
For the bold Champions who the Cæstus[4] wield.
A stately Mule, as yet by Toils unbroke,
Of six years Age, unconscious of the Yoke,
Is to the Circus led, and firmly bound;
Next stands a Goblet, massy, large and round.
Achilles rising, thus: Let Greece excite
Two Heroes equal to this hardy Fight;   760
Who dares his Foe with lifted Arms provoke,
And rush beneath the long-descending Stroke?
On whom Apollo shall the Palm bestow,
And whom the Greeks supreme by Conquest know,

---

[4] Greek boxers wore protective strips of leather, a sort of light boxing glove, *not* the Roman *Cæstus* with its iron points.

This Mule his dauntless Labours shall repay;
The Vanquish'd bear the massy Bowl away.
    This dreadful Combate great Epæus chose,
High o'er the Crowd, enormous Bulk! he rose,
And seiz'd the Beast, and thus began to say:
Stand forth some Man, to bear the Bowl away!   770
(Price of his Ruin:) For who dares deny
This Mule my right? th' undoubted Victor I.
Others 'tis own'd, in Fields of Battel shine,
But the first Honours of this Fight are mine;
For who excells in all? Then let my Foe
Draw near, but first his certain Fortune know,
Secure, this Hand shall his whole Frame confound,
Mash all his Bones, and all his Body pound:
So let his Friends be nigh, a needful Train
To heave the batter'd Carcase off the Plain.   780
    The Giant spoke; and in a stupid Gaze
The Host beheld him, silent with Amaze!
'Twas thou, Euryalus! who durst aspire
To meet his Might, and emulate thy Sire,
The great Mecistheus; who in Days of yore
In Theban Games the noblest Trophy bore,
(The Games ordain'd dead Oedipus to grace)
And singly vanquish'd the Cadmæan Race.
Him great Tydides urges to contend,
Warm with the Hopes of Conquest for his Friend,   790
Officious with the Cincture girds him round;
And to his Wrists the Gloves of Death are bound.
Amid the Circle now each Champion stands,
And poises high in Air his Iron Hands;
With clashing Gantlets now they fiercely close,
Their crackling Jaws re-echoe to the Blows,
And painful Sweat from all their Members flows.
At length Epæus dealt a weighty Blow
Full on the Cheek of his unwary Foe;
Beneath that pond'rous Arm's resistless Sway   800
Down dropt he, nerveless, and extended lay.
As a large Fish, when Winds and Waters roar,
By some huge Billow dash'd against the Shore,

Lies panting: Not less batter'd with his Wound,
The bleeding Hero pants upon the Ground.
To rear his fallen Foe, the Victor lends
Scornful, his Hand; and gives him to his Friends;
Whose Arms support him, reeling thro' the Throng,
And dragging his disabled Legs along;
Nodding, his Head hangs down his Shoulder o'er;   810
His Mouth and Nostrils pour the clotted Gore;
Wrapt round in Mists he lies, and lost to Thought:
His Friends receive the Bowl, too dearly bought.
  The third bold Game Achilles next demands,
And calls the Wrestlers to the level Sands:
A massy Tripod for the Victor lies,
Of twice six Oxen its reputed Price;
And next, the Losers Spirits to restore,
A female Captive, valu'd but at four.
Scarce did the Chief the vig'rous Strife propose,   820
When tow'r-like Ajax and Ulysses rose.
Amid the Ring each Nervous Rival stands,
Embracing rigid with implicit Hands:
Close lock'd above, their Heads and Arms are mixt;
Below, their planted Feet at distance fixt:
Like two strong Rafters which the Builder forms
Proof to the wintry Winds and howling Storms,
Their Tops connected, but at wider space
Fixt on the Center stands their solid Base.
Now to the Grasp each manly Body bends;   830
The humid Sweat from ev'ry Pore descends;
Their Bones resound with Blows: Sides, Shoulders, Thighs
Swell to each Gripe, and bloody Tumours rise.
Nor could Ulysses, for his Art renown'd,
O'erturn the Strength of Ajax on the Ground;
Nor could the Strength of Ajax overthrow
The watchful Caution of his artful Foe.
While the long Strife ev'n tir'd the Lookers-on,
Thus to Ulysses spoke great Telamon.
Or let me lift thee, Chief, or lift thou me: 840
Prove we our Force, and Jove the rest decree.

He said; and straining, heav'd him off the Ground
With matchless Strength; that time Ulysses found
The Strength t' evade, and where the Nerves combine,
His Ankle strook: The Giant fell supine:
Ulysses following, on his Bosom lies;
Shouts of Applause run rattling thro the Skies.
Ajax to lift, Ulysses next essays,
He barely stirr'd him, but he could not raise:
His Knee lock'd fast the Foe's Attempt deny'd;   850
And grappling close, they tumble side by side.
Defil'd with honourable Dust, they roll,
Still breathing Strife, and unsubdu'd of Soul:
Again they rage, again to Combat rise;
When great Achilles thus divides the Prize.

Your noble Vigour, oh my friends restrain;
Nor weary out your gen'rous Strength in vain.
Ye both have won: Let others who excell
Now prove that Prowess you have prov'd so well.

The Hero's Words the willing Chiefs obey,   860
From their tir'd Bodies wipe the Dust away,
And, cloth'd anew, the following Games survey.
And now succeed the Gifts, ordain'd to grace
The Youths contending in the rapid Race.
A silver Urn; that full six Measures held,
By none in Weight or Workmanship excell'd:
Sidonian Artists taught the Frame to shine,
Elaborate, with Artifice divine;
Whence Tyrian Sailors did the Prize transport,
And gave to Thoas at the Lemnian Port: 870
From him descended good Eunæus heir'd
The glorious Gift; and, for Lycaon spar'd,
To brave Patroclus gave the rich Reward.
Now, the same Hero's Funeral Rites to grace,
It stands the Prize of Swiftness in the Race.
A well-fed Ox was for the second plac'd;
And half a Talent must content the last.
Achilles rising then bespoke the Train:
Who hopes the Palm of Swiftness to obtain,
Stand forth, and bear these Prizes from the Plain.   880

The Hero said, and starting from his Place
Oïlean Ajax rises to the Race;
Ulysses next; and he whose Speed surpast
His youthful Equals, Nestor's Son the last.
Rang'd in a Line the ready Racers stand;
Pelides points the Barrier with his Hand;
All start at once; Oïleus led the Race;
The next Ulysses, meas'ring Pace with Pace;
Behind him, diligently close, he sped,
As closely following as the running Thread   890
The Spindle follows, and displays the Charms
Of the fair Spinster's Breast, and moving Arms:
Graceful in Motion thus, his Foe he plies,
And treads each Footstep e'er the Dust can rise:
His glowing Breath upon his Shoulders plays;
Th' admiring Greeks loud Acclamations raise,
To him they give their Wishes, Hearts, and Eyes,
And send their Souls before him as he flies.
Now three times turn'd in prospect of the Goal,
The panting Chief to Pallas lifts his Soul: 900
Assist O Goddess! (thus in Thought he pray'd)
And present at his Thought, descends the Maid.
Buoy'd by her heav'nly Force, he seems to swim,
And feels a Pinion lifting ev'ry Limb.
All fierce, and ready now the Prize to gain,
Unhappy Ajax stumbles on the Plain;
(O'erturn'd by Pallas) where the slipp'ry Shore
Was clogg'd with slimy Dung, and mingled Gore.
(The self-same Place beside Patroclus' Pyre,
Where late the slaughter'd Victims fed the Fire)   910
Besmear'd with Filth, and blotted o'er with Clay,
Obscene to sight, the ruefull Racer lay;
The well-fed Bull (the second Prize) he shar'd,
And left the Urn Ulysses' rich Reward.
Then, grasping by the Horn the mighty Beast,
The baffled Hero thus the Greeks addrest.
Accursed Fate! the Conquest I forego;
A Mortal I, a Goddess was my Foe:

She urg'd her Fav'rite on the rapid Way,
And Pallas, not Ulysses won the Day.   920
Thus sow'rly wail'd he, sputt'ring Dirt and Gore;
A burst of Laughter echo'd thro' the Shore.
Antilochus, more hum'rous than the rest,
Takes the last Prize, and takes it with a Jest.
   Why with our wiser Elders should we strive?
The Gods still love them, and they always thrive.
Ye see, to Ajax I must yield the Prize;
He to Ulysses, still more ag'd and wise;
(A green old Age unconscious of Decays,
That proves the Hero born in better Days!)   930
Behold his Vigor in this active Race!
Achilles only boasts a swifter Pace:
For who can match Achilles? He who can,
Must yet be more than Hero, or than Man.
   Th' Effect succeeds the Speech. Pelides cries,
Thy artful Praise deserves a better Prize.
Nor Greece in vain shall hear thy Friend extoll'd;
Receive a Talent of the Purest Gold.
The Youth departs content. The Hosts admire
The Son of Nestor, worthy of his Sire.   940
   Next these a Buckler, Spear and Helm, he brings,
Cast on the Plain the brazen Burthen rings:
Arms, which of late divine Sarpedon wore,
And great Patroclus in short Triumph bore.
Stand forth the bravest of our Host! (he cries)
Whoever dares deserve so rich a Prize!
Now grace the Lists before our Army's Sight,
And sheath'd in Steel, provoke his Foe to fight.
Who first the jointed Armour shall explore,
And stain his Rival's Mail with issuing Gore;   950
The Sword, Asteropeus possest of old,
(A Thracian Blade, distinct with Studs of Gold)
Shall pay the Stroke, and grace the Striker's Side:
These Arms in common let the Chief divide:
For each brave Champion, when the Combat ends,
A sumptuous Banquet at our Tent attends.

Fierce, at the Word, uprose great Tydeus' Son,
And the huge Bulk of Ajax Telamon.
Clad in refulgent Steel on either hand,
The dreadful Chiefs amid the Circle stand: 960
Low'ring they meet, tremendous to the Sight;
Each Argive Bosom beats with fierce Delight.
Oppos'd in Arms not long they idly stood,
But thrice they clos'd, and thrice the Charge renew'd.
A furious Pass the Spear of Ajax made
Thro' the broad Shield, but at the Corselet stay'd:
Not thus the Foe: His Jav'lin aim'd above
The Buckler's Margin, at the Neck he drove.
But Greece now trembling for her Hero's Life,
Bade share the Honours, and surcease the Strife. 970
Yet still the Victor's Due Tydides gains,
With him the Sword and studded Belt remains.
   Then hurl'd the Hero, thund'ring on the Ground
A Mass of Iron, (an enormous Round)
Whose Weight and Size the circling Greeks admire,
Rude from the Furnace, and but shap'd by Fire.
This mighty Quoit Aëtion wont to rear,
And from his whirling Arm dismiss in Air:
The Giant by Achilles slain, he stow'd
Among his Spoils this memorable Load. 980
For this, he bids those nervous Artists vie,
That teach the Disk to sound along the Sky.
Let him whose Might can hurl this Bowl, arise,
Who farthest hurls it, take it as his Prize:
If he be one, enrich'd with large Domain
Of Downs for Flocks, and Arable for Grain,
Small Stock of Iron needs that Man provide:
His Hinds and Swains whole years shall be supply'd
From hence: Nor ask the neighb'ring City's Aid,
For Plowshares, Wheels, and all the rural Trade. 990
   Stern Polypætes stept before the Throng,
And great Leonteus, more than mortal strong;
Whose Force with rival Forces to oppose,
Uprose great Ajax; up Epæus rose.

Each stood in order: First Epæus threw;
High o'er the wond'ring Crowds the whirling Circle flew.
Leonteus next a little space surpast,
And third, the Strength of god-like Ajax cast.
O'er both their Marks it flew; till fiercely flung
From Polypætes Arm, the Discus sung: 1000
Far, as a Swain his whirling Sheephook throws,
That distant falls among the grazing Cows,
So past them all the rapid Circle flies:
His Friends (while loud Applauses shake the Skies)
With Force conjoin'd heave off the weighty Prize.
    Those, who in skilful Archery contend
He next invites the twanging Bow to bend:
And twice ten Axes casts amidst the Round,
(Ten double-edg'd, and ten that singly wound.)
The Mast, which late a first-rate Galley bore,   1010
The Hero fixes in the sandy Shore:
To the tall Top a milk-white Dove they tye,
The trembling Mark at which their Arrows fly.
Whose Weapon strikes yon' flutt'ring Bird, shall bear
These two-edg'd Axes, terrible in War;
The single, he, whose Shaft divides the Cord.
He said: Experienc'd Merion took the Word;
And skilful Teucer: In the Helm they threw
Their Lots inscrib'd, and forth the latter flew.
Swift from the String the sounding Arrow flies;   1020
But flies unblest! No grateful Sacrifice,
No firstling Lambs, unheedful! didst thou vow,
To Phœbus, Patron of the Shaft and Bow.
For this, thy well-aim'd Arrow, turn'd aside,
Err'd from the Dove, yet cut the Cord that ty'd:
A-down the Main-mast fell the parted String,
And the free Bird to Heav'n displays her Wing:
Seas, Shores, and Skies with loud Applause resound,
And Merion eager meditates the Wound;
He takes the Bow, directs the Shaft above,   1030
And following with his Eye the soaring Dove,
Implores the God to speed it thro' the Skies,
With Vows of firstling Lambs, and grateful Sacrifice.

The Dove, in airy Circles as she wheels,
Amid the Clouds the piercing Arrow feels;
Quite thro' and thro' the Point its Passage found,
And at his Feet fell bloody to the Ground.
The wounded Bird, e'er yet she breath'd her last,
With flagging Wings alighted on the Mast,
A Moment hung, and spread her Pinions there,   1040
Then sudden dropt, and left her Life in Air.
From the pleas'd Crowd new Peals of Thunder rise,
And to the Ships brave Merion bears the Prize.

 To close the Fun'ral Games, Achilles last
A massy Spear amid the Circle plac'd,
And ample Charger of unsullyed Frame,
With Flow'rs high-wrought, not blacken'd yet by Flame.
For these he bids the Heroes prove their Art
Whose dext'rous Skill directs the flying Dart.
Here too great Merion hopes the noble Prize;   1050
Nor here disdain'd the King of Men to rise.
With Joy Pelides saw the Honour paid,
Rose to the Monarch and respectful said.

 Thee first in Virtue, as in Pow'r supreme,
O King of Nations! all thy Greeks proclaim;
In ev'ry martial Game thy Worth attest,
And know thee both their Greatest, and their Best.
Take then the Prize, but let brave Merion bear
This beamy Jav'lin in thy Brother's war.

 Pleas'd from the Hero's Lips his Praise to hear,   1060
The King to Merion gives the brazen Spear:
But, set apart for sacred Use, commands
The glitt'ring Charger to Talthybius' Hands.

꜀꜀꜀

THE TWENTY-FOURTH BOOK
OF THE ILIAD

THE ARGUMENT

The Redemption of the Body of Hector

THE GODS DELIBERATE about the Redemption of Hector. Jupiter sends Thetis to Achilles to dispose him for the restoring it, and Iris to Priam, to encourage him to go in Person, and treat for it. The old King, notwithstanding the Remonstrances of his Queen, makes ready for the Journey, to which he is encourag'd by an Omen from Jupiter. He sets forth in his Chariot, with a Waggon loaded with Presents under the Charge of Idæus the Herald. Mercury descends in the Shape of a young Man, and conducts him to the Pavilion of Achilles. Their Conversation on the way. Priam finds Achilles at his Table, casts himself at his Feet, and begs for the Body of his Son; Achilles, mov'd with Compassion, grants his Request, detains him one Night in his Tent, and the next Morning sends him home with the Body: The Trojans run out to meet him. The Lamentations of Andromache, Hecuba, and Helen, with the Solemnities of the Funeral.

The Time of twelve Days is employ'd in this Book, while the Body of Hector lies in the Tent of Achilles. And as many more are spent in the Truce allow'd for his Interment. The Scene is partly in Achilles's Camp, and partly in Troy.

Now from the finish'd Games the Grecian Band
Sought their black Ships, and clear'd the crowded Strand;
All stretch'd at ease the genial Banquet share,
And pleasing Slumbers quiet all their Care.

Not so Achilles: He, to Grief resign'd,
His Friend's dear Image present to his Mind,
Takes his sad Couch, more unobserv'd to weep,
Nor tastes the Gifts of all-composing Sleep.
Restless he roll'd around his weary Bed,
And all his Soul on his Patroclus fed: 10
The Form so pleasing, and the Heart so kind,
That youthful Vigour, and that manly Mind,
What Toils they shar'd, what martial Works they wrought,
What Seas they measur'd, and what Fields they fought;
All past before him in Remembrance dear,
Thought follows Thought, and Tear succeeds to Tear.
And now supine, now prone, the Hero lay,
Now shifts his Side, impatient for the Day:
Then starting up, disconsolate he goes
Wide on the lonely Beach to vent his Woes.   20
There as the solitary Mourner raves,
The ruddy Morning rises o'er the Waves;
Soon as it rose, his furious Steeds he join'd;
The Chariot flies, and Hector trails behind.
And thrice Patroclus! round thy Monument
Was Hector dragg'd, then hurry'd to the Tent.
There Sleep at last o'ercomes the Hero's Eyes;
While foul in Dust th' unhonour'd Carcase lies,
But not deserted by the pitying Skies.
For Phœbus watch'd it with superior Care,   30
Preserv'd from gaping Wounds, and tainting Air;
And ignominious as it swept the Field,
Spread o'er the sacred Corse his golden Shield.
All Heav'n was mov'd, and Hermes will'd to go
By Stealth to snatch him from th' insulting Foe:
But Neptune this, and Pallas this denies,
And th' unrelenting Empress of the Skies:
E'er since that Day implacable to Troy,
What time young Paris, simple Shepherd Boy,
Won by destructive Lust (Reward obscene)   40
Their Charms rejected for the Cyprian Queen.
But when the tenth cœlestial Morning broke;
To Heav'n assembled, thus Apollo spoke.

Unpitying Pow'rs! how oft each holy Fane
Has Hector ting'd with Blood of Victims slain?
And can ye still his cold Remains pursue?
Still grudge his Body to the Trojans View?
Deny to Consort, Mother, Son, and Sire,
The last sad Honours of the fun'ral Fire?
Is then the dire Achilles all your Care?   50
That Iron Heart, inflexibly severe;
A Lion, not a Man, who slaughters wide
In Strength of Rage and Impotence of Pride,
Who hastes to murder with a savage Joy,
Invades around, and breathes but to destroy.
Shame is not of his Soul; nor understood,
The greatest Evil and the greatest Good.
Still for one Loss he rages unresign'd,
Repugnant to the Lot of all Mankind;
To lose a Friend, a Brother, or a Son,   60
Heav'n dooms each Mortal, and its Will is done:
A while they sorrow, then dismiss their Care;
Fate gives the Wound, and Man is born to bear.
But this Insatiate the Commission giv'n
By Fate, exceeds; and tempts the Wrath of Heav'n:
Lo how his Rage dishonest drags along
Hector's dead Earth insensible of Wrong!
Brave tho' he be, yet by no Reason aw'd,
He violates the Laws of Man and God.

If equal Honours by the partial Skies   70
Are doom'd both Heroes, (Juno thus replies)
If Thetis' Son must no Distinction know,
Then hear, ye Gods! the Patron of the Bow.
But Hector only boasts a mortal Claim,
His Birth deriving from a mortal Dame:
Achilles of your own Ætherial Race
Springs from a Goddess, by a Man's Embrace;
(A Goddess by our self to Peleus giv'n,
A Man divine, and chosen Friend of Heav'n.)
To grace those Nuptials, from the bright Abode   80
Your selves were present; where this Minstrel-God

(Well-pleas'd to share the Feast,) amid the Quire
Stood proud to Hymn, and tune his youthful Lyre.
   Then thus the Thund'rer checks th' imperial Dame:
Let not thy Wrath the Court of Heav'n inflame;
Their Merits, nor their Honours, are the same.
But mine, and ev'ry God's peculiar Grace
Hector deserves, of all the Trojan Race:
Still on our Shrines his grateful Off'rings lay,
(The only Honours Men to Gods can pay)   90
Nor ever from our smoking Altar ceast
The pure Libation, and the holy Feast.
Howe'er by Stealth to snatch the Corse away,
We will not: Thetis guards it Night and Day.
But haste, and summon to our Courts above
The Azure Queen; let her Persuasion move
Her furious Son from Priam to receive
The proffer'd Ransom, and the Corps to leave.
   He added not: And Iris from the Skies
Swift as a Whirlwind, on the Message flies,   100
Meteorous[1] the Face of Ocean sweeps,
Refulgent gliding o'er the sable Deeps.
Between where Samos wide his Forests spreads,
And rocky Imbrus lifts its pointed Heads,
Down plung'd the Maid; (the parted Waves resound)
She plung'd, and instant shot the dark Profound.
As bearing Death in the fallacious Bait
From the bent Angle sinks the loaden Weight;
So past the Goddess thro' the closing Wave,
Where Thetis sorrow'd in her secret Cave: 110
There plac'd amidst her melancholy Train
(The blue-hair'd Sisters of the sacred Main)
Pensive she sate, revolving Fates to come,
And wept her god-like Son's approaching Doom:
   Then thus the Goddess of the painted Bow.
Arise! O Thetis, from thy Seats below.
'Tis Jove that calls. And why (the Dame replies)
Calls Jove his Thetis to the hated Skies?

---

[1] Adjective, meaning *through the mid-air*

Sad Object as I am for heav'nly Sight!
Ah! may my Sorrows ever shun the Light! 120
Howe'er be Heav'ns almighty Sire obey'd—
She spake, and veil'd her Head in sable Shade,
Which, flowing long, her graceful Person clad;
And forth she pac'd, majestically sad.
 Then thro' the World of Waters, they repair
(The Way fair Iris led) to upper Air.
The Deeps dividing, o'er the Coast they rise,
And touch with momentary Flight the Skies.
There in the Light'nings Blaze the Sire they found,
And all the Gods in shining Synod round. 130
Thetis approach'd with Anguish in her Face,
(Minerva rising, gave the Mourner place)
Ev'n Juno sought her Sorrows to console,
And offer'd from her Hand the Nectar Bowl:
She tasted, and resign'd it: Then began
The sacred Sire of Gods and mortal Man:
 Thou com'st fair Thetis, but with Grief o'ercast,
Maternal Sorrows, long, ah long to last!
Suffice, we know and we partake thy Cares:
But yield to Fate, and hear what Jove declares. 140
Nine Days are past, since all the Court above
In Hector's Cause have mov'd the Ear of Jove;
'Twas voted, Hermes from his god-like Foe
By Stealth should bear him, but we will'd not so:
We will, thy Son himself the Corse restore,
And to his Conquest add this Glory more.
Then hye thee to him, and our Mandate bear;
Tell him he tempts the Wrath of Heav'n too far:
Nor let him more (our Anger if he dread)
Vent his mad Vengeance on the sacred Dead: 150
But yield to Ransom and the Father's Pray'r.
The mournful Father Iris shall prepare,
With Gifts to sue; and offer to his Hands
Whate'er his Honour asks, or Heart demands.
 His Word the silver-footed Queen attends,
And from Olympus' snowy Tops descends.

Arriv'd, she heard the Voice of loud Lament,
And echoing Groans that shook the lofty Tent.
His Friends prepare the Victim, and dispose
Repast unheeded, while he vents his Woes.   160
The Goddess seats her by her pensive Son,
She prest his Hand, and tender thus begun.

 How long, unhappy! shall thy Sorrows flow,
And thy Heart waste with life-consuming Woe?
Mindless of Food, or Love whose pleasing Reign
Sooths weary Life, and softens human Pain.
O snatch the Moments yet within thy Pow'r,
Nor long to live, indulge the am'rous Hour!
Lo! Jove himself (for Jove's Command I bear)
Forbids to tempt the Wrath of Heav'n too far,   170
No longer then (his Fury if thou dread)
Detain the Relicks of great Hector dead;
Nor vent on senseless Earth thy Vengeance vain,
But yield to Ransom, and restore the Slain.
 To whom Achilles: Be the Ransom giv'n,
And we submit, since such the Will of Heav'n.
 While thus they commun'd, from th' Olympian Bow'rs
Jove orders Iris to the Trojan Tow'rs.
Haste, winged Goddess! to the sacred Town,
And urge her Monarch to redeem his Son;   180
Alone, the Ilian Ramparts let him leave,
And bear what stern Achilles may receive:
Alone, for so we will: No Trojan near;
Except, to place the Dead with decent Care,
Some aged Herald, who with gentle Hand,
May the slow Mules and fun'ral Car command.
Nor let him Death, nor let him Danger dread,
Safe thro' the Foe by our Protection led:
Him Hermes to Achilles shall convey,
Guard of his Life, and Partner of his Way.   190
Fierce as he is, Achilles self shall spare
His Age, nor touch one venerable Hair,
Some Thought there must be, in a Soul so brave,
Some Sense of Duty, some Desire to save.

Then down her Bow the winged Iris drives,
And swift at Priam's mournful Court arrives;
Where the sad Sons beside their Father's Throne
Sate bath'd in Tears, and answer'd Groan with Groan.
And all amidst them lay the hoary Sire,
(Sad Scene of Woe!) His Face his wrapt Attire   200
Conceal'd from Sight; With frantick Hands he spread
A Show'r of Ashes o'er his Neck and Head.
From Room to Room his pensive Daughters roam;
Whose Shrieks and Clamours fill the vaulted Dome;
Mindful of those, who, late their Pride and Joy,
Lye pale and breathless round the Fields of Troy!
Before the King Jove's Messenger appears,
And thus in Whispers greets his trembling Ears.
    Fear not, oh Father! no ill News I bear;
From Jove I come, Jove makes thee still his Care: 210
For Hector's sake these Walls he bids thee leave,
And bear what stern Achilles may receive:
Alone, for so he wills: No Trojan near,
Except to place the Dead with decent Care,
Some aged Herald, who with gentle Hand
May the slow Mules and fun'ral Car command.
Nor shalt thou Death, nor shalt thou Danger dread;
Safe thro' the Foe by his Protection led:
Thee Hermes to Pelides shall convey,
Guard of thy Life, and Partner of thy Way.   220
Fierce as he is, Achilles' self shall spare
Thy Age, nor touch one venerable Hair,
Some Thought there must be, in a Soul so brave,
Some Sense of Duty, some Desire to save.
    She spoke, and vanish'd. Priam bids prepare
His gentle Mules, and harness to the Car,
There, for the Gifts, a polish'd Casket lay:
His pious Sons the King's Command obey.
Then past the Monarch to his Bridal-Room,
Where Cedar-Beams the lofty Roofs perfume,   230
And where the Treasures of his Empire lay;
Then call'd his Queen, and thus began to say.

Unhappy Consort of a King distrest!
Partake the Troubles of thy Husband's Breast:
I saw descend the Messenger of Jove,
Who bids me try Achilles' Mind to move,
Forsake these Ramparts, and with Gifts obtain
The Corps of Hector, at yon' Navy slain.
Tell me thy Thought: My Heart impells to go
Thro' hostile Camps, and bears me to the Foe.   240
  The hoary Monarch thus. Her piercing Cries
Sad Hecuba renews, and then replies.
Ah! whither wanders thy distemper'd Mind,
And where the Prudence now that aw'd Mankind,
Thro' Phrygia once, and foreign Regions known,
Now all confus'd, distracted, overthrown!
Singly to pass thro' Hosts of Foes! to face
(Oh Heart of Steel!) the Murd'rer of thy Race!
To view that deathful Eye, and wander o'er
Those Hands, yet red with Hector's noble Gore!   250
Alas! my Lord! he knows not how to spare,
And what his Mercy, thy slain Sons declare;
So brave! so many fall'n! To calm his Rage
Vain were thy Dignity, and vain thy Age.
No—pent in this sad Palace let us give
To Grief the wretched Days we have to live.
Still, still for Hector let our Sorrows flow,
Born to his own, and to his Parents Woe!
Doom'd from the Hour his luckless Life begun,
To Dogs, to Vultures, and to Peleus' Son!   260
Oh! in his dearest Blood might I allay
My Rage, and these Barbarities repay!
For ah! could Hector merit thus? whose Breath
Expir'd not meanly, in unactive Death:
He pour'd his latest Blood in manly Fight,
And fell a Hero in his Country's Right.
  Seek not to stay me, nor my Soul affright
With Words of Omen like a Bird of Night.
(Reply'd unmov'd the venerable Man)
'Tis Heav'n commands me, and you urge in vain.   270

Had any mortal Voice th' Injunction laid,
Nor Augur, Priest, or Seer had been obey'd.
A present Goddess brought the high command,
I saw, I heard her, and the Word shall stand.
I go, ye Gods! obedient to your Call:
If in yon' Camp your Pow'rs have doom'd my Fall,
Content—By the same Hand let me expire!
Add to the slaughter'd Son the wretched Sire!
One cold Embrace at least may be allow'd,
And my last Tears flow mingled with his Blood!   280
    From forth his open'd Stores, this said, he drew
Twelve costly Carpets of refulgent Hue,
As many Vests, as many Mantles told,
And twelve fair Veils, and Garments stiff with Gold.
Two Tripods next and twice two Chargers shine,
With ten pure Talents from the richest Mine;
And last a large well-labour'd Bowl had place,
(The Pledge of Treaties once with friendly Thrace)
Seem'd all too mean the Stores he could employ,
For one last Look to buy him back to Troy!   290
    Lo! the sad Father, frantick with his Pain,
Around him furious drives his menial Train:
In vain each Slave with duteous Care attends,
Each Office hurts him, and each Face offends.
What make ye here? Officious Crowds? (he cries)
Hence! Nor obtrude your Anguish on my Eyes.
Have ye no Griefs at Home, to fix ye there?
Am I the only Object of Despair?
Am I become my People's common Show,
Set up by Jove your Spectacle of Woe?   300
No, you must feel him too; your selves must fall;
The same stern God to Ruin gives you all.
Nor is great Hector lost by me alone;
Your sole Defence, your guardian Pow'r is gone!
I see your Blood the Fields of Phrygia drown,
I see the Ruins of your smoking Town!
Oh send me, Gods! e'er that sad Day shall come,
A willing Ghost to Pluto's dreary Dome!

He said, and feebly drives his Friends away;
The sorrowing Friends his frantick Rage obey.   310
Next on his Sons his erring Fury falls,
Polites, Paris, Agathon, he calls,
His Threats Deïphobus and Dius hear,
Hippothous, Pammon, Helenus the Seer,
And gen'rous Antiphon: For yet these nine
Surviv'd, sad Relicks of his num'rous Line.
     Inglorious Sons of an unhappy Sire!
Why did not all in Hector's Cause expire?
Wretch that I am! my bravest Offspring slain,
You, the Disgrace of Priam's House, remain!   320
Mestor the brave, renown'd in Ranks of War,
With Troilus, dreadful on his rushing Car,
And last great Hector, more than Man divine,
For sure he seem'd not of terrestrial Line!
All those relentless Mars untimely slew,
And left me these, a soft and servile Crew,
Whose Days the Feast and wanton Dance employ,
Gluttons and Flatt'rers, the Contempt of Troy!
Why teach ye not my rapid Wheels to run,
And speed my Journey to redeem my Son?   330
     The Sons their Father's wretched Age revere,
Forgive his Anger, and produce the Car.
High on the Seat the Cabinet they bind:
The new-made Car with solid Beauty shin'd;
Box was the Yoke, embost with costly Pains,
And hung with Ringlets to receive the Reins;
Nine Cubits long the Traces swept the Ground;
These to the Chariots polish'd Pole they bound,
Then fix'd a Ring the running Reins to guide,
And close beneath the gather'd Ends were ty'd.   340
Next with the Gifts (the Price of Hector slain)
The sad Attendants load the groaning Wain:
Last to the Yoke the well-match'd Mules they bring,
(The Gift of Mysia to the Trojan King.)
But the fair Horses, long his darling Care,
Himself receiv'd and harness'd to his Car:

Griev'd as he was, he not this Task deny'd;
The hoary Herald help'd him at his Side.
While careful these the gentle Coursers join'd,
Sad Hecuba approach'd with anxious Mind; 350
A golden Bowl that foam'd with fragrant Wine,
(Libation destin'd to the Pow'r divine)
Held in her right, before the Steeds she stands,
And thus consigns it to the Monarch's Hands.

Take this, and pour to Jove: that safe from Harms,
His Grace restore thee to our Roof, and Arms;
Since Victor of thy Fears, and slighting mine,
Heav'n, or thy Soul, inspire this bold Design:
Pray to that God, who high on Ida's Brow
Surveys thy desolated Realms below, 360
His winged Messenger to send from high,
And lead thy way with heav'nly Augury:
Let the strong Sov'reign of the plumy Race
Tow'r on the right of yon' æthereal Space.
That Sign beheld, and strengthen'd from above,
Boldly pursue the Journey mark'd by Jove;
But if the God his Augury denies,
Suppress thy Impulse, nor reject Advice.

'Tis just (said Priam) to the Sire above
To raise our Hands, for who so good as Jove? 370
He spoke, and bad th' attendant Handmaid bring
The purest Water of the living Spring;
(Her ready Hands the Ew'er and Bason held)
Then took the golden Cup his Queen had fill'd,
On the mid Pavement pours the rosy Wine,
Uplifts his Eyes, and calls the Pow'r divine.

Oh First, and Greatest! Heav'ns Imperial Lord!
On lofty Ida's holy Hill ador'd!
To stern Achilles now direct my ways,
And teach him Mercy when a Father prays. 380
If such thy Will, dispatch from yonder Sky
Thy sacred Bird, cœlestial Augury!
Let the strong Sov'reign of the plumy Race
Tow'r on the right of yon' æthereal Space.

So shall thy Suppliant, strengthen'd from above,
Fearless pursue the Journey mark'd by Jove.

Jove heard his Pray'r, and from the Throne on high
Dispatch'd his Bird, cœlestial Augury!
The swift-wing'd Chaser of the feather'd Game,
And known to Gods by Percnos' lofty Name. 390
Wide as appears some Palace Gate display'd,
So broad, his Pinions stretch their ample Shade,
As stooping dexter with resounding Wings
Th' imperial Bird descends in airy Rings.
A Dawn of Joy in ev'ry Face appears;
The mourning Matron dries her tim'rous Tears.
Swift on his Car th' impatient Monarch sprung;
The brazen Portal in his Passage rung.
The Mules preceding draw the loaded Wain,
Charg'd with the Gifts; Idæus holds the Rein, 400
The King himself his gentle Steeds controuls,
And thro surrounding Friends the Chariot rolls.
On his slow Wheels the following People wait,
Mourn at each Step, and give him up to Fate,
With Hands uplifted, eye him as he past,
And gaze upon him as they gaz'd their last.
Now forward fares the Father on his way,
Thro' the lone Fields, and back to Ilion they.
Great Jove beheld him as he crost the Plain,
And felt the Woes of miserable Man. 410
Then thus to Hermes. Thou whose constant Cares
Still succour Mortals, and attend their Pray'rs;
Behold an Object to thy Charge consign'd,
If ever Pity touch'd thee for Mankind.
Go, guard the Sire; th' observing Foe prevent,
And safe conduct him to Achilles' Tent.

The God obeys, his golden Pinions binds,
And mounts incumbent on the Wings of Winds,
That high thro' Fields of Air his Flight sustain,
O'er the wide Earth, and o'er the boundless Main: 420
Then grasps the Wand that causes Sleep to fly,
Or in soft Slumbers seals the wakeful Eye;

Thus arm'd, swift Hermes steers his airy way,
And stoops on Hellespont's resounding Sea.
A beauteous Youth, majestick and divine,
He seem'd, fair Offspring of some princely Line!
Now Twilight veil'd the glaring Face of Day,
And clad the dusky Fields in sober Gray;
What time the Herald and the hoary King
Their Chariots stopping, at the silver Spring   430
That circling Ilus' ancient Marble flows,
Allow'd their Mules and Steeds a short Repose.
Thro' the dim Shade the Herald first espies
A Man's approach, and thus to Priam cries.
I mark some Foes Advance: O King! beware;
This hard Adventure claims thy utmost Care:
For much I fear, Destruction hovers nigh:
Our State asks Counsel; is it best to fly?
Or, old and helpless, at his Feet to fall,
(Two wretched Suppliants) and for Mercy call?   440
    Th' afflicted Monarch shiver'd with Despair;
Pale grew his Face, and upright stood his Hair;
Sunk was his Heart; his Colour went and came;
A sudden Trembling shook his aged Frame:
When Hermes greeting, touch'd his royal Hand,
And gentle, thus accosts with kind Demand.
    Say whither, Father! when each mortal Sight
Is seal'd in Sleep, thou wander'st thro' the Night?
Why roam thy Mules and Steeds the Plains along,
Thro' Grecian Foes, so num'rous and so strong?   450
What couldst thou hope, should these thy Treasures view,
These, who with endless Hate thy Race pursue?
For what Defence alas! couldst thou provide?
Thy self not young, a weak old Man thy Guide.
Yet suffer not thy Soul to sink with Dread;
From me, no Harm shall touch thy rev'rend Head;
From Greece I'll guard thee too; for in those Lines
The living Image of my Father shines.
    Thy Words, that speak Benevolence of Mind
Are true, my Son! (the godlike Sire rejoin'd)   460

Great are my Hazards; but the Gods survey
My Steps, and send thee, Guardian of my way.
Hail, and be blest! For scarce of mortal Kind
Appears thy Form, thy Feature, and thy Mind.

   Nor true are all thy Words, nor erring wide;
(The sacred Messenger of Heav'n reply'd)
But say, convey'st thou thro' the lonely Plains
What yet most precious of thy Store remains,
To lodge in safety with some friendly Hand?
Prepar'd perchance to leave thy native Land.   470
Or fly'st thou now? What Hopes can Troy retain?
Thy matchless Son, her Guard and Glory, slain!

   The King, alarm'd. Say what, and whence thou art,
Who search the Sorrows of a Parent's Heart,
And know so well how god-like Hector dy'd?
Thus Priam spoke, and Hermes thus reply'd.

   You tempt me, Father, and with Pity touch:
On this sad Subject you enquire too much.
Oft have these Eyes that godlike Hector view'd
In glorious Fight with Grecian Blood embru'd: 480
I saw him, when like Jove, his Flames he tost
On thousand Ships, and wither'd half an Host:
I saw, but help'd not: Stern Achilles' Ire
Forbad Assistance, and enjoy'd the Fire.
For him I serve, of Myrmidonian Race;
One Ship convey'd us from our native Place;
Polyctor is my Sire, an honour'd Name,
Old like thy self, and not unknown to Fame;
Of sev'n his Sons, by whom the Lot was cast
To serve our Prince, it fell on me, the last.   490
To watch this Quarter my Adventure falls,
For with the Morn the Greeks attack your Walls;
Sleepless they sit, impatient to engage,
And scarce their Rulers check the martial Rage.

   If then thou art of stern Pelides' Train,
(The mournful Monarch thus rejoin'd again)
Ah tell me truly, where, oh where are laid
My Son's dear Relicks? what befalls him dead?

Have Dogs dismember'd on the naked Plains,
Or yet unmangled rest his cold Remains?   500
  O favor'd of the Skies! (Thus answer'd then
The Pow'r that mediates between Gods and Men)
Nor Dogs nor Vultures have thy Hector rent,
But whole he lies, neglected in the Tent:
This the twelfth Evening since he rested there,
Untouch'd by Worms, untainted by the Air.
Still as Aurora's ruddy Beam is spread,
Round his Friend's Tomb Achilles drags the Dead;
Yet undisfigur'd, or in Limb, or Face,
All fresh he lies, with ev'ry living Grace,   510
Majestical in Death! No Stains are found
O'er all the Corse, and clos'd is ev'ry Wound,
(Tho' many a Wound they gave) Some heav'nly Care,
Some Hand divine, preserves him ever fair:
Or all the Host of Heav'n, to whom he led
A Life so grateful, still regard him dead.
  Thus spoke to Priam the cœlestial Guide,
And joyful thus the royal Sire reply'd.
Blest is the Man who pays the Gods above
The constant Tribute of Respect and Love: 520
Those who inhabit the Olympian Bow'r
My Son forgot not, in exalted Pow'r;
And Heav'n, that ev'ry Virtue bears in mind,
Ev'n to the Ashes of the Just, is kind.
But thou, oh gen'rous Youth! this Goblet take,
A Pledge of Gratitude for Hector's sake;
And while the fav'ring Gods our Steps survey,
Safe to Pelides' Tent conduct my way.
  To whom the latent God. O King forbear
To tempt my Youth, for apt is Youth to err: 530
But can I, absent from my Prince's Sight,
Take Gifts in secret, that must shun the Light?
What from our Master's Int'rest thus we draw,
Is but a licens'd Theft that 'scapes the Law.
Respecting him, my Soul abjures th' Offence;
And as the Crime I dread the Consequence.

Thee, far as Argos, pleas'd I could convey;
Guard of thy Life, and Partner of thy Way.
On thee attend, thy Safety to maintain,
O'er pathless Forests, or the roaring Main.   540
    He said, then took the Chariot at a Bound,
And snatch'd the Reins, and whirl'd the Lash around:
Before th' inspiring God that urg'd them on,
The Coursers fly with Spirit not their own.
And now they reach'd the naval Walls, and found
The Guards repasting, while the Bowls go round;
On these the Virtue of his Wand he tries,
And pours deep Slumber on their watchful Eyes:
Then heav'd the massy Gates, remov'd the Bars,
And o'er the Trenches led the rolling Cars.   550
Unseen, thro' all the hostile Camp they went,
And now approach'd Pelides' lofty Tent
Of Fir the Roof was rais'd, and cover'd o'er
With Reeds collected from the marshy Shore;
And, fenc'd with Palisades, a Hall of State,
(The Work of Soldiers) where the Hero sate.
Large was the Door, whose well-compacted Strength
A solid Pine-tree barr'd of wond'rous Length;
Scarce three strong Greeks could lift its mighty Weight,
But great Achilles singly clos'd the Gate.   560
This Hermes (such the Pow'r of Gods) set wide;
Then swift alighted the cœlestial Guide,
And thus, reveal'd—Hear Prince! and understand
Thou ow'st thy Guidance to no mortal Hand:
Hermes I am, descended from above,
The King of Arts, the Messenger of Jove.
Farewell: To shun Achilles' Sight I fly;
Uncommon are such Favours of the Sky,
Nor stand confest to frail Mortality.
Now fearless enter, and prefer thy Pray'rs;   570
Adjure him by his Father's silver Hairs,
His Son, his Mother! urge him to bestow
Whatever Pity that stern Heart can know.
    Thus having said, he vanish'd from his Eyes,
And in a moment shot into the Skies:

The King, confirm'd from Heav'n, alighted there,
And left his aged Herald on the Car.
With solemn Pace thro' various Rooms he went,
And found Achilles in his inner Tent:
There sate the Hero; Alcimus the brave, 580
And great Automedon, Attendance gave:
These serv'd his Person at the royal Feast,
Around, at awful distance, stood the rest.

Unseen by these, the King his Entry made;
And prostrate now before Achilles laid,
Sudden, (a venerable Sight!) appears;
Embrac'd his Knees, and bath'd his Hands in Tears;
Those direful Hands his Kisses press'd, embru'd
Ev'n with the best, the dearest of his Blood!

As when a Wretch, (who conscious of his Crime 590
Pursu'd for Murder, flies his native Clime)
Just gains some Frontier, breathless, pale! amaz'd!
All gaze, all wonder: Thus Achilles gaz'd:
Thus stood th' Attendants stupid with Surprize;
All mute, yet seem'd to question with their Eyes:
Each look'd on other, none the Silence broke,
Till thus at last the Kingly Suppliant spoke.

Ah think, thou favour'd of the Pow'rs Divine!
Think of thy Father's Age, and pity mine!
In me, that Father's rev'rend Image trace, 600
Those silver Hairs, that venerable Face;
His trembling Limbs, his helpless Person, see!
In all my Equal, but in Misery!
Yet now perhaps, some Turn of human Fate
Expells him helpless from his peaceful State;
Think from some pow'rful Foe thou see'st him fly,
And beg Protection with a feeble Cry,
Yet still one Comfort in his Soul may rise;
He hears his Son still lives to glad his Eyes;
And hearing still may hope, a better Day 610
May send him thee to chase that Foe away.
No Comfort to my Griefs, no Hopes remain,
The best, the bravest of my Sons are slain!

Yet what a Race? e'er Greece to Ilion came,
The Pledge of many a lov'd, and loving Dame;
Nineteen one Mother bore—Dead, all are dead!
How oft, alas! has wretched Priam bled?
Still One was left, their Loss to recompense;
His Father's Hope, his Country's last Defence.
Him too thy Rage has slain! beneath thy Steel   620
Unhappy, in his Country's Cause he fell!
    For him, thro' hostile Camps I bent my way,
For him thus prostrate at thy Feet I lay;
Large Gifts, proportion'd to thy Wrath, I bear;
Oh hear the Wretched, and the Gods revere!
    Think of thy Father, and this Face behold!
See him in me, as helpless and as old!
Tho' not so wretched: There he yields to me,
The First of Men in sov'reign Misery.
Thus forc'd to kneel, thus grov'ling to embrace   630
The Scourge and Ruin of my Realm and Race;
Suppliant my Childrens Murd'rer to implore,
And kiss those Hands yet reeking with their Gore!
    These Words soft Pity in the Chief inspire,
Touch'd with the dear Remembrance of his Sire.
Then with his Hand (as prostrate still he lay)
The Old Man's Cheek he gently turn'd away.
Now each by turns indulg'd the Gush of Woe,
And now the mingled Tides together flow:
This low on Earth, that gently bending o'er,   640
A Father one, and one a Son, deplore:
But great Achilles diff'rent Passions rend,
And now his Sire he mourns, and now his Friend.
Th' infectious Softness thro' the Heroes ran;
One universal, solemn Show'r began;
They bore as Heroes, but they felt as Man.
    Satiate at length with unavailing Woes,
From the high Throne divine Achilles rose;
The rev'rend Monarch by the Hand he rais'd;
On his white Beard and Form majestick gaz'd,   650
Not unrelenting: Then serene began
With Words to sooth the miserable Man.

Alas! what Weight of Anguish hast thou known?
Unhappy Prince! thus guardless and alone
To pass thro' Foes, and thus undaunted face
The Man whose Fury has destroy'd thy Race?
Heav'n sure has arm'd thee with a Heart of Steel,
A Strength proportion'd to the Woes you feel.
Rise then: Let Reason mitigate our Care:
To mourn, avails not: Man is born to bear.   660
Such is, alas! the Gods severe Decree;
They, only they are blest, and only free.
Two Urns by Jove's high Throne have ever stood,
The Source of Evil one, and one of Good;
From thence the Cup of mortal Man he fills,
Blessings to these, to those distributes Ills;
To most, he mingles both: The Wretch decreed
To taste the bad, unmix'd, is curst indeed;
Pursu'd by Wrongs, by meagre Famine driv'n,
He wanders, Outcast both of Earth and Heav'n.   670
The Happiest taste not Happiness sincere,
But find the cordial Draught is dash'd with Care.
Who more than Peleus shone in Wealth and Pow'r?
What Stars concurring blest his natal Hour?
A Realm, a Goddess, to his Wishes giv'n,
Grac'd by the Gods with all the Gifts of Heav'n!
One Evil yet o'ertakes his latest Day,
No Race succeeding to imperial Sway:
One only Son! and he (alas!) ordain'd
To fall untimely in a foreign Land!   680
See him, in Troy, the pious Care decline
Of his weak Age, to live the Curse of thine!
Thou too, Old Man, hast happier Days beheld;
In Riches once, in Children once excell'd;
Extended Phrygia own'd thy ample Reign,
And all fair Lesbos' blissful Seats contain,
And all wide Hellespont's unmeasur'd Main.
But since the God his Hand has pleas'd to turn,
And fill thy Measure from his bitter Urn,
What sees the Sun, but hapless Heroes Falls?   690
War, and the Blood of Men, surround thy Walls!

What must be, must be. Bear thy Lot, nor shed
These unavailing Sorrows o'er the Dead;
Thou can'st not call him from the Stygian Shore,
But thou alas! may'st live, to suffer more!
　　To whom the King. Oh favour'd of the Skies!
Here let me grow to Earth! since Hector lies
On the bare Beach, depriv'd of Obsequies.
Oh give me Hector! to my Eyes restore
His Corse, and take the Gifts: I ask no more.   700
Thou, as thou may'st, these boundless Stores enjoy;
Safe may'st thou sail, and turn thy Wrath from Troy;
So shall thy Pity and Forbearance give
A weak old Man to see the Light and live!
　　Move me no more (Achilles thus replies
While kindling Anger sparkled in his Eyes)
Nor seek by Tears my steady Soul to bend;
To yield thy Hector I my self intend:
For know, from Jove my Goddess-Mother came,
(Old Ocean's Daughter, silver-footed Dame)   710
Nor com'st thou but by Heav'n; nor com'st alone,
Some God impells with Courage not thy own:
No human Hand the weighty Gates unbarr'd,
Nor could the boldest of our Youth have dar'd
To pass our Outworks, or elude the Guard.
Cease; lest neglectful of high Jove's Command
I show thee, King! thou tread'st on hostile Land;
Release my Knees, thy suppliant Arts give o'er,
And shake the Purpose of my Soul no more.
　　The Sire obey'd him, trembling and o'er-aw'd.   720
Achilles, like a Lion, rush'd abroad:
Automedon and Alcimus attend,
Whom most he honour'd, since he lost his Friend;
These to unyoke the Mules and Horses went,
And led the hoary Herald to the Tent;
Next heap'd on high the num'rous Presents bear
(Great Hector's Ransome) from the polish'd Car.
Two splendid Mantles, and a Carpet spread,
They leave; to cover, and inwrap the Dead.

Then call the Handmaids with assistant Toil 730
To wash the Body, and anoint with Oil;
Apart from Priam, lest th' unhappy Sire
Provok'd to Passion, once more rouze to Ire
The stern Pelides; and nor sacred Age
Nor Jove's Command, should check the rising Rage.
This done, the Garments o'er the Corse they spread;
Achilles lifts it to the fun'ral Bed:
Then, while the Body on the Car they laid,
He groans, and calls on lov'd Patroclus' Shade.

If, in that Gloom which never Light must know, 740
The Deeds of Mortals touch the Ghosts below;
O Friend! forgive me, that I thus fulfill
(Restoring Hector) Heav'ns unquestion'd Will.
The Gifts the Father gave, be ever thine,
To grace thy Manes, and adorn thy Shrine.

He said, and entring, took his Seat of State,
Where full before him rev'rend Priam sate:
To whom, compos'd, the god-like Chief begun.
Lo! to thy Pray'r restor'd, thy breathless Son:
Extended on the Fun'ral Couch he lies; 750
And soon as Morning paints the Eastern Skies,
The Sight is granted to thy longing Eyes.
But now the peaceful Hours of sacred Night
Demand Refection, and to Rest invite:
Nor thou O Father! thus consum'd with Woe,
The common Cares that nourish Life, foregoe.
Not thus did Niobe, of Form divine,
A Parent once, whose Sorrows equal'd thine:
Six youthful Sons, as many blooming Maids
In one sad Day beheld the Stygian Shades; 760
These by Apollo's silver Bow were slain,
Those, Cynthia's Arrows stretch'd upon the Plain.
So was her Pride chastiz'd by Wrath divine,
Who match'd her own with bright Latona's Line;
But two the Goddess, twelve the Queen enjoy'd;
Those boasted twelve th' avenging two destroy'd.
Steep'd in their Blood, and in the Dust outspread,
Nine Days neglected lay expos'd the Dead;

None by to weep them, to inhume them none;
(For Jove had turn'd the Nation all to Stone:)   770
The Gods themselves at length relenting, gave
Th' unhappy Race the Honours of a Grave.
Her self a Rock, (for such was Heav'ns high Will)
Thro' Desarts wild now pours a weeping Rill;
Where round the Bed whence Acheloüs springs
The wat'ry Fairies dance in mazy Rings,
There high on Sipylus his shaggy Brow,
She stands her own sad Monument of Woe;
The Rock for ever lasts, the Tears for ever flow!

    Such Griefs, O King! have other Parents known;   780
Remember theirs, and mitigate thy own.
The Care of Heav'n thy Hector has appear'd,
Nor shall he lye unwept, and uninterr'd;
Soon may thy aged Cheeks in Tears be drown'd,
And all the Eyes of Ilion stream around.

    He said, and rising, chose the Victim Ewe
With silver Fleece, which his Attendants slew.
The Limbs they sever from the reeking Hyde,
With Skill prepare them, and in Parts divide:
Each on the Coals the sep'rate Morsels lays,   790
And hasty, snatches from the rising Blaze.
With Bread the glitt'ring Canisters they load,
Which round the Board Automedon bestow'd:
The Chief himself to each his Portion plac'd,
And each indulging shar'd in sweet Repast.
When now the Rage of Hunger was represt,
The wond'ring Hero eyes his royal Guest;
No less the royal Guest the Hero eyes,
His god-like Aspect and majestick Size;
Here, youthful Grace and noble Fire engage,   800
And there, the mild Benevolence of Age.
Thus gazing long, the Silence neither broke,
(A solemn Scene!) at length the Father spoke.

    Permit me now, belov'd of Jove! to steep
My careful Temples in the Dew of Sleep:
For since the Day that numbred with the Dead
My hapless Son, the Dust has been my Bed,

Soft Sleep a Stranger to my weeping Eyes,
My only Food my Sorrows and my Sighs!
Till now, encourag'd by the Grace you give, 810
I share thy Banquet, and consent to live.
    With that, Achilles bad prepare the Bed,
With Purple soft, and shaggy Carpets spread;
Forth, by the flaming Lights, they bend their way,
And place the Couches, and the Cov'rings lay.
Then he: Now Father sleep, but sleep not here,
Consult thy Safety, and forgive my Fear,
Lest any Argive, (at this Hour awake,
To ask our Counsel or our Orders take,)
Approaching sudden to our open'd Tent, 820
Perchance behold thee, and our Grace prevent.
Should such report thy honour'd Person here,
The King of Men the Ransom might defer.
But say with speed, if ought of thy Desire
Remains unask'd; what Time the Rites require
T' inter thy Hector? For, so long we stay
Our slaught'ring Arm, and bid the Hosts obey.
    If then thy Will permit (the Monarch said)
To finish all due Honours to the Dead,
This, of thy Grace, accord: To thee are known 830
The Fears of Ilion, clos'd within her Town,
And at what distance from our Walls aspire
The Hills of Ide, and Forests for the Fire.
Nine Days to vent our Sorrows I request,
The tenth shall see the Fun'ral and the Feast;
The next, to raise his Monument be giv'n;
The twelfth we war, if War be doom'd by Heav'n!
    This thy Request (reply'd the Chief) enjoy:
Till then, our Arms suspend the Fall of Troy.
    Then gave his Hand at parting, to prevent 840
The Old Man's Fears, and turn'd within the Tent;
Where fair Briseïs bright in blooming Charms
Expects her Hero with desiring Arms.
But in the Porch the King and Herald rest,
Sad Dreams of Care yet wand'ring in their Breast.

Now Gods and Men the Gifts of Sleep partake;
Industrious Hermes only was awake,
The King's Return revolving in his Mind,
To pass the Ramparts, and the Watch to blind.
The Pow'r descending hover'd o'er his Head: 850
And sleep'st thou Father! (thus the Vision said)
Now dost thou sleep, when Hector is restor'd?
Nor fear the Grecian Foes, nor Grecian Lord?
Thy Presence here shou'd stern Atrides see,
Thy still-surviving Sons may sue for thee,
May offer all thy Treasures yet contain,
To spare thy Age; and offer all in vain!
    Wak'd with the Word, the trembling Sire arose,
And rais'd his Friend: The God before him goes,
He joins the Mules, directs them with his Hand,   860
And moves in Silence thro' the hostile Land.
When now to Xanthus' yellow Stream they drove,
(Xanthus, immortal Progeny of Jove)
The winged Deity forsook their View,
And in a Moment to Olympus flew.
Now shed Aurora round her Saffron Ray,
Sprung thro' the Gates of Light, and gave the Day:
Charg'd with their mournful Load, to Ilion goe
The Sage and King, majestically slow.
Cassandra first beholds, from Ilion's Spire,   870
The sad Procession of her hoary Sire,
Then, as the pensive Pomp advanc'd more near,
Her breathless Brother stretch'd upon the Bier:
A Show'r of Tears o'erflows her beauteous Eyes,
Alarming thus all Ilion with her Cries.
    Turn here your steps, and here your eyes employ,
Ye wretched Daughters, and ye Sons of Troy!
If e'er ye rush'd in Crowds, with vast Delight
To hail your Hero glorious from the Fight;
Now meet him dead, and let your Sorrows flow!   880
Your common Triumph, and your common Woe.
    In thronging Crowds they issue to the Plains,
Nor Man, nor Woman, in the Walls remains.

In ev'ry Face the self-same Grief is shown,
And Troy sends forth one universal Groan.
At Scæa's Gates they meet the mourning Wain,
Hang on the Wheels, and grovel round the Slain.
The Wife and Mother, frantic with Despair,
Kiss his pale Cheek, and rend their scatter'd Hair:
Thus wildly wailing, at the Gates they lay;   890
And there had sigh'd and sorrow'd out the Day;
But god-like Priam from the Chariot rose:
Forbear (he cry'd) this Violence of Woes,
First to the Palace let the Car proceed,
Then pour your boundless Sorrows o'er the Dead.

The Waves of People at his Word divide,
Slow rolls the Chariot thro' the following Tide;
Ev'n to the Palace the sad Pomp they wait:
They weep, and place him on the Bed of State.
A melancholy Choir attend around,   900
With plaintive Sighs, and Musick's solemn Sound:
Alternately they sing, alternate flow
Th' obedient Tears, melodious in their Woe.
While deeper Sorrows groan from each full Heart,
And Nature speaks at ev'ry Pause of Art.

First to the Corse the weeping Consort flew;
Around his Neck her milk-white Arms she threw,
And oh my Hector! oh my Lord! she cries,
Snatch'd in thy Bloom from these desiring Eyes!
Thou to the dismal Realms for ever gone!   910
And I abandon'd, desolate, alone!
An only Son, once Comfort of our Pains,
Sad Product now of hapless Love, remains!
Never to manly Age that Son shall rise,
Or with increasing Graces glad my Eyes:
For Ilion now (her great Defender slain)
Shall sink, a smoaking Ruin on the Plain.
Who now protects her Wives with guardian Care?
Who saves her Infants from the Rage of War?
Now hostile Fleets must waft those Infants o'er,   920
(Those Wives must wait 'em) to a foreign Shore!

Thou too my Son! to barb'rous Climes shalt goe,
The sad Companion of thy Mother's Woe;
Driv'n hence a Slave before the Victor's Sword;
Condemn'd to toil for some inhuman Lord.
Or else some Greek whose Father prest the Plain,
Or Son, or Brother, by great Hector slain;
In Hector's Blood his Vengeance shall enjoy,
And hurl thee headlong from the Tow'rs of Troy.
For thy stern Father never spar'd a Foe: 930
Thence all these Tears, and all this Scene of Woe!
Thence, many Evils his sad Parents bore,
His Parents many, but his Consort more.
Why gav'st thou not to me thy dying Hand?
And why receiv'd not I thy last Command?
Some Word thou would'st have spoke, which sadly dear,
My Soul might keep, or utter with a Tear;
Which never, never could be lost in Air,
Fix'd in my Heart, and oft repeated there!
   Thus to her weeping Maids she makes her Moan;   940
Her weeping Handmaids echo Groan for Groan.
   The mournful Mother next sustains her Part.
Oh thou, the best, the dearest to my Heart!
Of all my Race thou most by Heav'n approv'd,
And by th' Immortals ev'n in Death belov'd!
While all my other Sons in barb'rous Bands
Achilles bound, and sold to foreign Lands,
This felt no Chains, but went a glorious Ghost
Free, and a Hero, to the Stygian Coast.
Sentenc'd, 'tis true, by his inhuman Doom,   950
Thy noble Corse was dragg'd around the Tomb,
(The Tomb of him thy warlike Arm had slain)
Ungen'rous Insult, impotent and vain!
Yet glow'st thou fresh with ev'ry living Grace,
No mark of Pain, or Violence of Face;
Rosy and fair! as Phœbus' silver Bow
Dismiss'd thee gently to the Shades below.
   Thus spoke the Dame, and melted into Tears.
Sad Helen next in Pomp of Grief appears:

Fast from the shining Sluices of her Eyes   960
Fall the round crystal Drops, while thus she cries.
    Ah dearest Friend! in whom the Gods had join'd
The mildest Manners with the bravest Mind!
Now twice ten Years (unhappy Years) are o'er
Since Paris brought me to the Trojan Shore;
(Oh had I perish'd, e'er that Form divine
Seduc'd this soft, this easy Heart of mine!)
Yet was it ne'er my Fate, from thee to find
A Deed ungentle, or a Word unkind:
When others curst the Auth'ress of their Woe,   970
Thy Pity check'd my Sorrows in their Flow:
If some proud Brother ey'd me with Disdain,
Or scornful Sister with her sweeping Train,
Thy gentle Accents soften'd all my Pain.
For thee I mourn; and mourn my self in thee,
The wretched Source of all this Misery!
The Fate I caus'd, for ever I bemoan;
Sad Helen has no Friend now thou art gone!
Thro' Troy's wide Streets abandon'd shall I roam,
In Troy deserted, as abhorr'd at Home!   980
    So spoke the Fair, with Sorrow-streaming Eye:
Distressful Beauty melts each Stander-by;
On all around th' infectious Sorrow grows;
But Priam check'd the Torrent as it rose.
Perform, ye Trojans! what the Rites require,
And fell the Forests for a fun'ral Pyre;
Twelve Days, nor Foes, nor secret Ambush dread;
Achilles grants these Honours to the Dead.
    He spoke; and at his Word, the Trojan Train
Their Mules and Oxen harness to the Wain,   990
Pour thro' the Gates, and, fell'd from Ida's Crown,
Roll back the gather'd Forests to the Town.
These Toils continue nine succeeding Days,
And high in Air a Sylvan Structure raise.
But when the tenth fair Morn began to shine,
Forth to the Pile was born the Man divine,
And plac'd aloft: while all, with streaming Eyes,
Beheld the Flames and rolling Smokes arise.

Soon as Aurora, Daughter of the Dawn,
With rosy Lustre streak'd the dewy Lawn;　　　　1000
Again the mournful Crowds surround the Pyre,
And quench with Wine the yet remaining Fire.
The snowy Bones his Friends and Brothers place
(With Tears collected) in a golden Vase;
The golden Vase in purple Palls they roll'd,
Of softest Texture, and inwrought with Gold;
Last o'er the Urn the sacred Earth they spread,
And rais'd the Tomb, Memorial of the Dead.
(Strong Guards and Spies, till all the Rites were done,
Watch'd from the rising to the setting Sun)　　　1010
All Troy then moves to Priam's Court again,
A solemn, silent, melancholy Train.
Assembled there, from pious Toil they rest,
And sadly shar'd the last Sepulcral Feast.
Such Honours Ilion to her Hero paid,
And peaceful slept the mighty Hector's Shade.

The End of the I L I A D.

ERRORS CORRECTED IN THIS EDITION

Errata listed in the first edition

I.517	The undaunted] Th'un-daunted	VIII.480	to stand] they stand
		VIII.688	sheds] spreads
II.77	Ill suits] Ill fits	X.116	agrees] agree
II.666	martial] marshal	XI.701	drinks] prints
III.43	high Chariot] proud Chariot	XIV.304 and 312	Pasithaë] Pasithëa
		XVI.199	rolling] lolling
III.444	his Death . . . the Foe] the Death . . . his Foe	XVI.1010	great Achilles] fierce Achilles
III.575	just] loud	XVIII.353	Welkin] Orient
V.647	kroken] broken	XVIII.415	Linen] Mantle
V.930	to stand] they stand	XIX.372	sings] springs
VI.451	insert commas after Bands and prest	XXI.3	flying] scatt'ring
		XXIII.509	mull] must
VIII.264	Bands] Brands	XXIII.599	delete or

Errata noted and corrected by the editors

I.348	Name.] Name;	XVII.623	Battle] Battel
I.402	Way.] Way,	XVIII.262	Towr's] Tow'rs
II.171	Grecians fly] Grecians, fly	XVIII.285	Quench] Quench'd
IV.139	peirc'd] pierc'd	XVIII.498	obey,] obey.
IV.179	aud] and	XIX.188	Achiles] Achilles
V.60	Tarne] Tarnè	XIX.235	Battle] Battel
VI.27	bold beautiful] bold, beautiful	XIX.285	o'eruling] o'erruling
		XIX.332	Rage] Rage.
VI.426	to Day] to-Day	XX.10	Joves] Jove's
VIII.2	Lawn.] Lawn;	XXI.81	thristy] thirsty
X.64	Creet] Crete	XXI.118	delete inverted commas
XI.249	shull] shall	XXI.493	Smiles and] Smiles' and
XII.225	delete redundant the	XXI.584	yeild] yield
XII.361	delete redundant from	XXII.569	Flowr's] Flow'rs
XII.544	unweildy] unwieldy	XXII.583	open parenthesis before Ye, not after
XIV.188	Delete inverted comma		
XV.692	Menalippus] Melanippus	XXIII.481	Menelas] Menelaus
XVI.500	Eryalus] Erylaus	XXIII.642	No] (No
XVI.642	Off'ring] Offspring	XXIII.991	Polyphætes] Polypætes
XVII, heading	Battle] Battel	XXIV.324	terrestial] terrestrial
XVII.398	veiw'd] view'd	XXIV.423	hie] his
XVII.446	sweat and] sweat, and	XXIV.606	tho] thou

GLOSSARY OF NAMES AND PLACES

Achaia Greece
Achaians the Greeks
Achelous river of Greece and a god
Achilles Pelides, Aeacides, son of Peleus and Thetis, grandson of Aeacus
Aeacides Achilles
Aeneas son of Anchises and Venus
Aëtion Eëtion, King of Thebè near Troy, father of Andromache
Agamemnon son of Atreus, King of Mycenae, commander of the Greek forces
Agenor son of Antenor, killed by Achilles, XXI, 643-712
Ajax (1) son of Telamon, the mighty hero from Salamis; (2) son of Oïleus, of Locris, "Ajax the Less," referred to by Pope as "Oïleus."
Alcides Hercules
Alcmena mother of Hercules by Jove, XIX, 103-18
Alexander Paris
Anchises father of Aeneas by Venus, II, 993
Andromache wife of Hector, VI, 462-647
Antenor counselor of the Trojans
Antilochus son of Nestor
Aphrodite Venus
Apollo Phoebus, Smintheus, son of Jove and Latona, ally of the Trojans
Archeptolemus Hector's charioteer
Ares Mars
Argos (1) Diomedes' city; (2) region in Peloponnese; (3) Greece; (4) Pelasgic Argos, in Achilles' domain
Asius a Trojan ally, killed by Idomeneus, XIII, 483-508
Asteropeus leader of Paeonians, killed by Achilles, XXI, 155-98
Astyanax son of Hector and Andromache, VI, 467-619
Athene Minerva
Atreus father of Agamemnon and Menelaus
Aulis port in Greece from which the Greeks sailed for Troy, II, 366-85
Automedon charioteer of Achilles and Patroclus
Axius a river

Bellerophon grandfather of Glaucus, the friend of Sarpedon, VI, 194-260
Briseïs captive girl from Lyrnessus, Achilles' prize of war

Cassandra most beautiful of Priam's daughters, XXIV, 870-75

Cebriones brother and charioteer of Hector

Chiron centaur, teacher of Achilles

Chryseïs Chruseïs, daughter of Chryses, captive prize of Agamemnon

Chryses priest of Apollo, father of Chryseïs

Clytemnestra Agamemnon's queen, who remained in Mycenae

Cronus Saturn

Dardanus legendary ancestor of the Trojan kings; hence, "Dardanians" for Trojans

Deiphobus son of Priam, prominent warrior on the Trojan side, XIII, 211-20; 509-89

Diomedes Diomed, son of Tydeus, a ruler of Argos; his genealogy, XIV, 125-144

Diana Phoebe

Dione mother of Venus, V, 461-506

Discord Eris, IV, 501-507

Dolon a Trojan spy, X, 370-531

Eumelus son of Admetus, who races his chariot in the games of Book XXIII, 429-622

Euphorbus son of Panthus, Trojan warrior who wounds Patroclus, XVI, 972-86

Eurybates herald of Agamemnon

Eurymedon (1) charioteer of Agamemnon; (2) charioteer of Nestor

Eurypylus son of Euaemon, warrior from Thessaly, wounded by Paris and cared for by Patroclus, XI, 702-13; 940-85

Glaucus leader of Lycians and friend of Sarpedon, who exchanged weapons with Diomedes, VI, 147-295; XII, 365-472

Gnossus Knossos, city in Crete

Hades Pluto

Hebè daughter of Jove and Juno, cupbearer of the gods

Hector son of Priam, chief defender of Troy

Hecuba Priam's wife

Helen wife of Menelaus and mistress of Paris, III, 165-314, 473-558

Helenus son of Priam, warrior and prophet

Hephaestus Vulcan

Hera Juno

Hermes Mercury

Ida Ide, mountain in Troad

Idaeus herald of Priam

Idomeneus Idomen, leader of Cretans at Troy

Ilion Troy
Ilus son of Tros and founder of Troy
Iphidamas son of Antenor, "his Death finely describ'd" (P), XI, 283-320
Iris messenger of the gods
Ithacus Ulysses, whose home was in the island of Ithaca

Jove chief of the Olympian gods
Juno queen of the gods, wife and sister of Jove

Laomedon father of Priam, XXI, 516-30
Latona mother of Apollo and Diana
Lemnos island near Troy
Lycaon (1) father of Pandarus; (2) son of Priam, killed by Achilles, XXI, 41-150
Lycia country in Asia Minor from which Sarpedon came
Lyrnessus city near Troy

Machaon Greek physician, whose wounding is noted by Achilles, XI, 728-39
Mars god of war, ally of the Trojans
Melanippus son of Hicetaon, Trojan warrior, XV, 644-95
Meleager killer of the Calydonian boar, IX, 653-708
Menelaus son of Atreus and brother of Agamemnon, King of Sparta
Menestheus leader of the Athenians, II, 655-70
Mercury Hermes, messenger and guide sent by the gods, XXIV, 411-575
Meriones Merion, Cretan hero, companion of Idomeneus
Minerva Pallas, daughter of Jove; in the *Iliad* a fierce goddess of war, "Martial courage with wisdom" (P)
Mycenae Agamemnon's city
Myrmidons followers of Achilles

Nereus sea god, father of Thetis and the other Nereids, XVIII, 41-68
Nestor son of Neleus, aged ruler of Pylos, sometimes called "Gerenian" (from the city Gerenia in the Peloponnese)
Niobe whose children were killed by Apollo and Diana (Cynthia), XXIV, 757-79

Odysseus Ulysses
Oïleus of Locris, father of "Locrian" Ajax
Olympus mountain in Thessaly, home of the gods

Pallas Minerva, Tritonia
Pandarus son of Lycaon (1), from Zeleia; also called "Leader of the Lycian Band"; IV, 119-81, V, 212-368
Paris son of Priam, lover of Helen, III, 315-574

Patroclus son of Menoetius, Achilles' friend
Peleus son of Aeacus and father of Achilles; hence "Pelides" for Achilles
Philoctetes bowman, II, 874-81
Phoebe Diana, sister of Phoebus
Phoebus Apollo
Phoenix Achilles' tutor, IX, 558-712
Phrygia region near Troy; hence "Phrygian" for "Trojan"
Phthia Pthia, Achilles' homeland
Pluto Hades (a person), god of the underworld
Poeon Paean, god of healing
Polydamas a Trojan, "wisely brave" counselor of Hector, XII, 67-92, 225-66
Polydore Priam's youngest son, killed by Achilles, XX, 471-84
Poseidon Neptune
Priam King of Troy
Protesilaüs Protesilas, first Greek killed at Troy, II, 853-63
Pylos Pyle, Nestor's city, in the Peloponnese

Rhesus a Thracian ally of Priam, famed for his horses, X, 505-11; 540-617

Sarpedon son of Jove, leader of the Lycians, XII, 365-504, XVI, 512-836
Saturn father of Jove and other Olympians
Saturnia Saturn's daughter, Juno
Saturnius Saturn's son, Jove
Scamander Xanthus, river on the plain of Troy
Simoïs river near Troy
Socus killed by Ulysses, whom he wounded, XI, 538-77
Sthenelus son of Capaneus, like Diomedes, a ruler of Argos

Talthybius herald of Agamemnon
Tartarus the "Tartarean Gulf," deeper than the realm of Pluto (Hades), where the enemies of Jove are imprisoned, VIII, 15-20, 599-603
Tenedos island near Troy
Tethys wife of Ocean
Teucer half-brother of Telamonian Ajax, a great bowman
Thamyris bard struck blind by the Muses, II, 721-30
Thebè Thebes, three cities: (1) in Boeotia, scene of the Theban Wars; (2) in Egypt; (3) of King Aëtion, near Troy
Themis goddess of custom or law
Thersites malicious critic of the Greek heroes, II, 255-331
Thetis sea-goddess, mother of Achilles
Thoas leader of the Aetolians (Greeks), XV, 318-337
Thrasimed Thrasymed, son of Nestor
Tlepolemus son of Hercules, leader of the men of Rhodes, V, 776-831

Troas Troad, district of which Troy was the chief city
Tros early Trojan king, ancestor of Priam
Tydeus father of Diomedes, hence "Tydides" for "Diomedes"
Tyrinthè Tiryns, city in the Argive plain, near Mycenae

Ulysses Ithacus, ruler of Ithaca

Venus Paphian Queen, goddess of love, protector of Paris, and ally of Troy
Vulcan artisan god, I, 738-71; XVIII, 431-709

Xanthus (1) the river Scamander; (2) a river in Lycia; (3) one of Hector's horses; (4) one of Achilles' horses, who foretells his death, XIX, 446-65

Zeus Jove

R. A. B.

SELECT BIBLIOGRAPHY

1. The *Iliad* and the Heroic Tradition.

   Erich Auerbach: *Mimesis*, Chap. 1 (Princeton, 1953)

   C. M. Bowra: *Heroic Poetry* (London, 1961)

   G. S. Kirk: *The Songs of Homer* (Cambridge, England, 1962)

   Albert B. Lord: *The Singer of Tales* (Cambridge, Massachusetts, 1960)

   Milman Parry: "Studies in the Epic Technique of Oral Verse-Making," I and II, *Harvard Studies in Classical Philology*, xli. 73-147 and xliii. 1-50

   George Steiner and Robert Fagles, ed.: *Homer*, (*Twentieth Century Views*, Englewood Cliffs, N.J., 1962)

   Simone Weil: *The Iliad, or The Poem of Force*, translated by Mary McCarthy, (Pendle Hill, Wallingford, Pa., 1956)

   Cedric H. Whitman: *Homer and the Heroic Tradition* (Cambridge, Massachusetts, 1958)

2. The Renaissance Tradition of Heroic Poetry.

   C. M. Bowra: *From Virgil to Milton* (London, 1957)

   John Dryden: "The Dedication of the *Aeneis*," in *The Poems and Fables of John Dryden*, ed. James Kinsley (Oxford, 1958), iii. 1003-64

   Georg Finsler: *Homer in der Neuzeit* (Leipzig and Berlin, 1912)

   H. T. Swedenberg, Jr.: *The Theory of the Epic in England 1650-1800* (Berkeley and Los Angeles, 1944)

   E. M. W. Tillyard: *The English Epic and Its Background* (London, 1954)

3. Alexander Pope.

   The Twickenham Edition of the Poems of Alexander Pope, General Editor, John Butt, vols. i-vi (London, 1939-61); text of this edition is reprinted in one volume (London, 1963)

   Reuben A. Brower: *Alexander Pope, The Poetry of Allusion* (Oxford, 1959)

   Douglas Knight: *Pope and the Heroic Tradition* (New Haven, 1951)

F. R. Leavis: *Revaluation*, chap. 3 (London, 1949)

George Sherburn: *The Early Career of Alexander Pope* (Oxford, 1934); reprinted (New York, 1963)

Geoffrey Tillotson: *On the Poetry of Pope*, 2nd ed. (Oxford, 1950)

4. Bibliography of Early Editions of Pope.

R. H. Griffith: *Alexander Pope, a Bibliography* (Austin, Texas, 1922-27)

R. H. Griffith: "A Piracy of Pope's *Iliad*," *Studies in Philology*, XXVIII (1931), pp. 737-41